The Tragedie of Macbeth

The Tragedie of Macbeth

A Frankly Annotated First Folio Edition

WILLIAM SHAKESPEARE

Annotated and with an
Introduction by Demitra Papadinis

McFarland & Company, Inc., Publishers
Jefferson, North Carolina, and London

LIBRARY OF CONGRESS CATALOGUING-IN-PUBLICATION DATA

Shakespeare, William, 1564–1616.
   [Macbeth]
   The tragedie of Macbeth : a frankly annotated first folio edition /
William Shakespeare ; annotated and with an introduction by Demitra
Papadinis.
      p.   cm.
   Includes bibliographical references.

   ISBN 978-0-7864-6479-1
   softcover : acid free paper ∞

   1. Macbeth, King of Scotland, 11th cent.— Drama.   2. Scotland —
History — To 1057 — Drama.   3. Scotland — Kings and rulers —
Drama.   4. Regicides — Drama.   I. Papadinis, Demitra.   II. Title.
PR2823.A2P24 2012
822.3'3 — dc23
                                                   2012029654

BRITISH LIBRARY CATALOGUING DATA ARE AVAILABLE

On the cover: an element of a poster for a c. 1884 American production
of *Macbeth*, starring Thomas W. Keene. W.J. Morgan & Co. Lith.
(Library of Congress); background text from Act I of *Macbeth;* ribbon
© 2012 Shutterstock

Manufactured in the United States of America

*McFarland & Company, Inc., Publishers
   Box 611, Jefferson, North Carolina 28640
   www.mcfarlandpub.com*

For John Tsiakos, Jr.

Acknowledgments

This work would not have been possible without those who have shared a long and perilous journey through the uncharted waters of performing Shakespeare's early texts in the early manner, including Evan Alboum, Brian Allard, Collin Biddle, Amanda Bruton, Jim Butterfield, Jennifer Brown, Kacey Camp, Kim Carrell, Craig Colfelt, Lawrence Cranor, Jarel Davidow, Natasha Giardina, Bill Green, Christine Kahler, Bill Kincaid, Andrew Kirtland, John and Kate Kissingford, Michelle Kovacs, Jenifer Kudulis, Natalie Lebert, Christopher LeCrenn, Alan Milner, Alexander Richard, Dave Robinson, Elizabeth Ruelas, Karen Sternberg, Melinda Stewart, Justin Tyler, Jean Ann Wertz, Alan White, Jonathan Wolfe, Michael Yahn, and many, many others.

Contents

Preface

As a director and producer, I long ago stopped using edited, modernized versions of Shakespeare's plays because: (1) they obliterate essential meaning and reduce performability by altering spelling, punctuation, and lineation; and (2) the annotation provided is either inadequate, inaccurate, or both. For these reasons, among others too numerous to list, I began to prepare my own scripts exclusively from the First Folio of 1623, and, in the process, launched my own investigation into the signification of the dialogue. The resulting scripts are not only faithful to the original but also fully elucidated and practical for use in performance. I hope the reader finds them entertaining, enlightening, and useful.

D.P.
New Hampshire 2012

"When *I* use a word," Humpty Dumpty said, in rather a scornful tone, "it means just what I choose it to mean — neither more nor less."

"The question is," said Alice, "whether you *can* make words mean so many different things."

"The question is," said Humpty Dumpty, "which is to be master — that's all."

— Lewis Carroll, *Through the Looking-Glass*

Introduction

*Of Forthright Footnotes (or, putting the "count"
  back in "country")*

The purpose of this book is simple: to make obvious that which should be obvious in Shakespeare but which has been muddled through centuries of editorial interference, the standardization of spelling and grammar, and repressive social mores.

Take, for example, the word "count." In both modern English and modern American speech, the "cou" in "count" rhymes with "'cow." By contrast, "count" was formerly pronounced identically to the first syllable in "country" (as is evident from early spelling variants of "count" as "cunte"; and of "country" as "cuntry" and "cuntrie"). So when, in Act I, scene iii of *The Tragedie of Romeo and Juliet, Lady Capulet* says to her daughter, "By my count / I was your Mother, much upon these yeares / That you are now a Maide," it should be clear that "count" does not simply mean "reckoning."[1]

Such linguistic details are not inconsequential verbal flourishes; they are vital to the life of the characters both on the page and in performance. Sadly, such details are continually overlooked or omitted. Most Shakespearean annotators would never dream of expounding on such lewd, deplorable, filthy language — probably for fear of getting the venerable Mr. Shakespeare kicked out of school. After all, if the "N-word" is enough to banish Mark Twain from respectable classrooms, how can William Shakespeare hope to survive when he drops the "C-bomb"?

Shakespearean editors abide eternally in the Never-Never-Land of the seventh-grade classroom. The trouble is, of course, that the rest of us grow up — and read, research, produce, direct, and perform Shakespeare's plays in the grown-up world. Nevertheless, most grown-ups still use the same jejune scripts and footnotes prepared for twelve-year-olds and thus remain unwittingly trapped in a pre-pubescent Shakespearean universe. Quite simply, it's way past time for the Bard's hormones to kick in. It's time to put the "count" back in "country."

If we seek to fully understand Shakespeare, we must accept that neither his world nor his works are PG-rated. Whereas denizens of the 21st century consider theatre an elevated and refined art form, to the Elizabethans it was common entertainment no more elite than sports are today. The theatres, banished from the city limits of London by the prim city fathers, set up shop in the suburbs across the Thames. Here they competed in close proximity with other "low" entertainments: brothels, bull and bear baiting rings, cockfighting, taverns, gaming houses, and bowling alleys. Sex and violence were as prevalent in Shakespeare's time as today, and the theatres had to serve up healthy doses of both in order to keep their doors open.[2]

The abundant nearby "naughty-houses" operated openly (if not strictly legally) under the protection of some powerful patron and featured a smorgasbord of services rivaling anything that can be found nowadays. Whether in the market for male or female companionship, one need not have looked far. Equally accessible were the bull and bear baiting pits, where spectators could enjoy a bloody life-and-death battle between the chained, tormented animals and savage dogs and perhaps even win some money by betting on the outcome.[3]

Public executions provided an afternoon's entertainment free of charge. Hangings were most common, but occasionally one might be treated to a burning, beheading, or drawing and quartering.[4] These spectacles also boasted the added attraction of real human blood; for use in their mock murders and duels, players were limited to whatever animal entrails could be found that day at the local butcher shop.

Given such competition, it is small wonder that Elizabethan plays are filled with perverse gore and carnal glee. However, from the blandness of most footnotes, one would think Shakespeare's plays about as boisterous as a game of Parcheesi, as is the case in the following exchange between the *Clowne* and *Maria* in Act I, scene v of *Twelfe Night, or what you will*:

> *Ma.* ...my Lady will hang thee for thy absence.
> *Clo.* Let her hange me: hee that is well hang'de in this
> world, needs to feare no colours.

In typical sterile fashion, most footnotes tersely proclaim that "fear no colors" is proverbial for "fear nothing" with a further pun on "collar" meaning noose. Such prim and proper definitions completely ignore that fact that a man who is "well hung" is genitally well endowed, and that "'colours'" is a pun on "culls," common slang for the testicles. Therefore the submerged witticism of the line is that a well-endowed man need never fear rivals in (physical) love. The *Clowne* shortly revisits this theme with the quip that "Many a good hanging, prevents a bad marriage."

Some passages that seem like pointless jabber take on new weight if bawdiness is factored into the equation, as in Act IV, scene iv of *The Taming of the Shrew*:

> *Biond.* I cannot tarry: I knew a wench maried in an
> afternoone as shee went to the Garden for Parseley to
> stuffe a Rabit, and so may you sir: and so adew sir, my
> master hath appointed me to goe to Saint *Lukes* to bid the
> priest be readie to come against you come with your
> appendix.

True to form, on the subject of stuffing rabbits with parsley, most footnotes either maintain an obstinate silence or expound in a copious non-sequitur describing in minute detail the ingredients of Elizabethan cookery.

Instead of red herrings, red flags should immediately be raised by the words "Rabit" (which bears the same connotation as the modern "beaver") and "stuffe" (identical in sense to "fuck," as in "Get stuffed!"). No word is ever arbitrary in Shakespeare, so the next logical question is why the girl is looking for "Parseley" as opposed to any other herb. Parsley has a long folkloric association with both pregnancy and its prevention. Inserted vaginally (or, in the vulgar, "stuffed into a rabbit") it was thought to induce abortion.[5] The young lady in question was apparently "in trouble" and about to take matters into her own hands when the groom showed up to make an "honest woman" of her. In light of the fact that *Biondello* is arranging an elopement, his innuendo is far from innocuous.

As early as 1947, logophile Eric Partridge attempted to rid Shakespeare of his undeserved reputation for decency with his watershed work, *Shakespeare's Bawdy*. Ever since then, many fearless explorers have plunged themselves into the jungle of Shakespeare's language in an attempt to map his metaphors. The problem is that they have chosen to publish their discoveries solely in the form of scholarly lexicon, essay, or thesis. As a result, the only people who ever read their work are other scholars working on yet another scholarly lexicon, essay, or thesis. The information just never seems to trickle down into the footnotes that are so conveniently at hand and to which most readers solely refer.

The footnotes accompanying this text do not claim to excavate every nuance of a word or to find *the* interpretation of a passage, but they do provide possible explanations not commonly found elsewhere. Hopefully this annotation will serve as a starting point for the reader to launch his own investigation, which is in no way difficult: all that is required is patience, a good dictionary, and an open mind.

Yes, Shakespeare's poetry is beautiful, but his works boast a salacious genius, shameless audacity, and crude vitality that is all-too-often expunged. Instead of condemning Shakespeare's language as archaic and difficult, we should just take off our blinders and accept that *Pistol* says exactly what he means when he states that his "cocke is up." And no, *Romeo* is not describing a shoe rosette when he refers to his "well-flowered pump." The prudish and faint of heart should probably just steer clear of Shakespeare altogether, but the rest of us have a choice: continue to look at Shakespeare only from the neck up, or take down our pants and hang on for the ride.

"Filthy Plaies and Enterluds"

Shortly before a young William Shakespeare set out to pursue a theatrical career, God-fearing Puritan (and all around fun-loving guy) Philip Stubbes attacked "filthy plaies and enterluds" for luring people in with the irresistible bait of "bawdry, wanton shewes, & uncomely gestures" (*Anatomie of Abuses,* 1583). Stubbes was certainly not alone in his view that playhouses were an express elevator that would take players, playwrights, and playgoers directly to Hell: the venerable City of London had already kicked playhouses out of its precincts, banishing them to the Bank-side[6] in 1576.

Such was Shakespeare's success in this thoroughly disreputable line of work that by 1633 he was posthumously singled out for attack by William Prynne (also a God-fearing Puritan and all around fun-loving guy). In *Histriomastix,* Prynne expressed disgust that such vile, corruptive matter as plays "are grown from Quarto to Folio" and that "Shackspeers Plaies are printed in the best Crown paper, far better than most… Bibles." Prynne's buddies in Parliament agreed that plays were worthless at best and dangerous at worst. The "Ordinance of the Lords and Commons concerning Stage-plays" issued on September 2, 1642, forbade the public performance of plays for "too commonly expressing lascivious Mirth and Levity."

Evidence indicates that Shakespeare was anything but a goody-two-shoes. His wife, Anne Hathaway, was three months pregnant when they married. His *Sonnets* suggest that he simultaneously carried on extramarital affairs with both a married woman and a younger man. In 1596, a certain William Wayte took out the equivalent of a restraining order against him because he feared "he stood in danger of death, or bodily hurt," from "William Shakspere." A telling illustration of Shakespeare's personality, although apocryphal, involves his rivalry with fellow actor Richard Burbadge over the sexual favors of a female fan. On March 13, 1602, barrister John Manningham records the following anecdote:

> Upon a tyme when Burbidge played Rich. 3. there was a citizen greue soe farr in liking with him, that before shee went from the play shee appointed him to come that night unto hir by the name of Ri: the 3. Shakespeare overhearing their conclusion went before, was intertained, and at his game ere Burbidge came. Then

message being brought that Rich. the 3.d was at the dore, Shakespeare caused returne to be made that William the Conquerour was before Rich. the 3.

So just how did this bad boy from the Bank-side become such a bastion of respectability? Certainly it was through no fault of his own. John Hemminge and Henry Condell, two of Shakespeare's colleagues, preserved the Bard's "filthy plaies and enterluds" in all their down-and-dirty glory in the First Folio of 1623. Things soon changed. By the time the Second Folio came to press in 1632, everyone who had played a major part in the publication of the First Folio was dead. This minor point did not, however, prevent printer Thomas Cotes and publisher Robert Alcott from independently making thousands of "corrections," thus launching the time-honored editorial tradition of making "improvements" to Shakespeare's plays based on absolutely nothing but sheer opinion and personal whim.

By the early eighteenth century, the integrity of Shakespeare's text was already in the coffin, but that didn't keep publisher Jacob Tonson, Jr. from driving in a few more nails. In 1721 Tonson hired Alexander Pope for the purposes of "correcting and Writing a Preface and making Notes and Explaining the obscure passages in the Works of Mr William Shakespear." Pope possessed the excellent qualification of being in no way connected with the theatre, so he seemed an ideal choice.

The esteemed Mr. Pope understood that Shakespeare was a mere player and playwright and thus could not be expected to write plays properly. In his preface, Pope denounced the plays' "great defects" of "mean buffoonery, vile ribaldry, and unmannerly jests of fools and clowns." However, Pope magnanimously forgave Shakespeare, because he understood "that Stage-Poetry of all other is more particularly levell'd to please the *Populace*" and that Shakespeare was therefore "obliged to please the lowest of people." As any self-respecting elitist knows, obliging the lowest of people is a great impediment to making highly cultured and inaccessible Art. Obviously the Bard needed a facelift, and Pope had the scalpel ready. He got right to work making the plays... well, less like *plays*. His endeavors were certainly successful; he removed much of the tiresomely entertaining "ribaldry" and made the scripts much more "mannerly."

Shakespearean editing reached an all-time low in 1807 when siblings Thomas and Harriet Bowdler published their "Family Edition" that removed "those words and expressions which cannot with propriety be read aloud in a family."[7] The verbal carnage was so ruthless that the Bowdlers have the dubious honor of adding a new word to the English language: "bowdlerize," which means "to expurgate (a book or writing), by omitting or modifying words or passages considered indelicate or offensive; to castrate" (*Oxford English Dictionary*, 2nd Edition).

Unfortunately, Shakespeare's manhood has yet to be restored. Modern

Shakespearean editors fall right into step with the snobbish Mr. Pope and the pious Thomas and Harriet. They both (a) "correct" the text based on nothing but speculation; and (b) change, remove or ignore any passage that would make the volume unacceptable in a seventh-grade classroom. These so-called improvements certainly do clean things up; it is of seemingly no consequence that they also render the plays nonsensical and deadly dull.

The First Folio, by its own report, is intended for the enjoyment of the "Great Variety of Readers, From the most able, to him that can but spell." Despite the allegations of Mr. Pope *et al.*, the truth is that we, the lowest of people, simply have no need for a middleman to interpret what Shakespeare *meant* to write. We can go directly to the source to see for ourselves what he actually *wrote*. No matter what one's previous exposure to Shakespeare, no one should be afraid to consult Shakespeare's early texts. Far from being sealed, sacred works whose mysteries unfold themselves to only the initiated few, the original versions are coherent, comprehensible, and above all entertaining — much more so than watered-down modernized versions.

Why the First Folio?

In 1623, printer Isaac Jaggard and publisher Edward Blount produced a collected volume of Shakespeare's plays entitled "Mr. William Shakespeare's Comedies, Histories, & Tragedies" (now referred to as the "First Folio"). This publication was a risky venture, since plays were generally considered to hold about as much literary merit as comic books do now.[8] Prior to the Folio's publication, only about half of Shakespeare's plays had been printed in cheap quarto format.

The terms "quarto" and "folio" simply describe a book's printed size and structure. Books printed *in folio* are comprised of sheets of paper folded only once to form two leaves of equal size, or four printed pages (from L. *folium*: "leaf"). Works printed *in quarto* are comprised of sheets of paper folded twice to form four leaves of equal size, resulting in eight printed pages (from L. *quartus*: "fourth").

Shakespearean quartos exist in two forms: good and bad. A quarto is termed "good" (fairly accurate) if its printing was authorized by the acting company that owned the script (playwrights would sell their works outright to theatres). A quarto is termed "bad" (inaccurate or incomplete) if it is what is traditionally considered to be a pirated version.

In Shakespeare's time, acting companies guarded their scripts closely and were in no rush to publish a play so long as it could still turn a profit at the box office.[9] The concept of intellectual property was non-extant, so once a play was printed there wasn't much to prevent a rival theatre from staging it. Consequently, acting companies would seek to publish a play only if (a) it was old and no longer commercially viable in performance; or (b) there was pressing financial need to do so.[10]

The players' reluctance to publish their plays did not prevent opportunistic printers from doing so anyway: hence, the bad quartos. An unscrupulous publisher who wanted to capitalize on a play's success could obtain the script in a variety of ways. A simple avenue was to pay the price of admission, attend the play with paper and pencil in hand, and scribble down as much as could be caught by ear while the play was in progress.

Yet another way a printer could illicitly obtain a script was to enlist the aid of an actor or actors who had performed in the play. These actors would then attempt to reconstruct the whole from their own individual part-scripts and memory — quite a feat, since the part-scripts or cue-scripts employed by Elizabethan actors contained only the lines and cues for a single character. Here is the entire cue-script for the character of the *Captaine* in *The Tragedie of Hamlet, Prince of Denmarke*:

> _____ were ne're begun.
> *Enter Fortinbras with an Armie.*
> _____ And let him know so.
> I will doo't, my Lord.
> _____ Go safely on.
> *Exit.*[11]

Cue-scripts had a twofold purpose: (1) to save time and expense, as paper was costly and copying-out had to be done by hand; and (2) to minimize the number of full copies and thus reduce the risk of a play's falling into undesirable hands. A greedy or disgruntled player with a complete script could sell it to either a printer or a rival playhouse; a player who had only a cue-script could do far less damage if he ever broke away from the fold.[12]

Whereas the quartos were quickly and cheaply produced, the Folio was an expensive volume intended to accurately preserve the plays. The cost of a play printed in quarto was sixpence; the original price of the First Folio was twenty shillings.[13] A book with such a price could not be shoddily produced, and great care was given to its printing and proofreading. Although the Folio appeared seven years after Shakespeare's death, two of his long-time colleagues and business partners, John Hemminge and Henry Condell, played a substantial role in its publication.[14] Printed by the reputable Isaac Jaggard, the Folio contains 36 of the 39 extant plays ascribed in full or in part to Shakespeare.[15]

The Folio's title page claims that it was "Published according to the True Originall Copies," and all evidence supports this. Of the 36 plays in the Folio, sixteen were previously printed as quartos (both good and bad). However, in only three cases does the Folio extensively follow earlier quartos.[16] This suggests that the majority of the Folio was compiled from original playhouse manuscripts supplied by Hemminge and Condell.

These handwritten manuscripts are termed either "Foul Papers" or "Fair Papers." "Foul Papers" are the author's original handwritten manuscripts; they are labeled "foul" because they include revisions and corrections and are therefore somewhat difficult to read.[17] "Fair Papers" were the official prompt-books copied out neatly, accurately, and legibly by the playhouse scribe (who would also have been tasked with making up cue-scripts).

The First Folio's source material, whether foul or fair, holds an impressive pedigree. The Foul Papers (albeit somewhat rough around the edges) are traceable directly to Shakespeare himself; the Fair Papers were actual prompt-books used in performance.[18] Hemminge and Condell's careful oversight of the Folio's printing must also be taken into account in assessing the First Folio's authority. In their introduction addressed "To the great Variety of Readers," Hemminge and Condell write that

> It had bene a thing, we confesse, worthie to have bene wished, that the Author himselfe had liv'd to have set forth, and overseen his owne writings; But since it hath bin ordain'd otherwise, and he by death departed from that right, we pray you do not envie his Friends, the office of their care, and paine, to have collected & publish'd them; and so to have publish'd them, as where (before) you were abus'd with diverse stolne, and surreptitious copies, maimed, and deformed by the frauds and stealthes of injurious impostors, that expos'd them : even those, are now offer'd to your view cur'd, and perfect of their limbes; and all the rest, absolute in their numbers, as he conceived them.

There is absolutely no reason to doubt that this is true.[19]

What's Wrong with Editing?

In addition to modernizing punctuation and spelling, the Shakespearean editor spends much time and effort "rectifying" the text. In an effort to produce *the* definitive version of any given play, he compares and amalgamates variant quarto and Folio readings and selects which individual passages, lines, and words he considers to be ultimately "correct."

There is a fundamental error in reasoning inherent in such comparative editing (if reason can truly be said to come into play at all). Unlike a novel, which is forever unchanging once printed, a play script continually evolves in performance. Lines, characters, and entire scenes that seemed flawless when the playwright committed them to paper may prove to have substantial defects when actually performed. It is certainly no secret that the modern playwright will continue to re-write a script while a play is in rehearsal, preview, or even after opening. Should a show close and several years lapse before a play's revival, considerable changes may be made to the script.

Take as an example the works of twentieth-century American playwright Tennessee Williams. Williams considered his plays to be ongoing works in progress and subjected them to constant revision. He did not consider a play finished or forever set simply because it had been produced on the stage or had appeared in print. Therefore, the hapless English or Drama student told to pick up a copy of a Williams play for class may find that he has a text that differs extensively from that of his teacher or classmates.

Which of these differing versions of Williams' plays is ultimately "correct"? The answer, of course, is that they *all* are. An earlier version is "correct" in that it is a perfect reflection of the playwright's intent at the point in time it was produced. A variant later version is equally "correct" — in that it is a perfect reflection of the playwright's intent at the point in time when *it* was produced.[20]

In regards to which differing third act of *Cat on a Hot Tin Roof* is superior, Williams himself said that "the reader can, if he wishes, make up his own mind about it."[21] Good advice it is, too. The reader can compare both versions and simply decide which he likes best. (This advice, however, is not so practical for the producer who must ultimately pick only one version to stage.)

Now imagine if, some 400 years in the future, an editor attempted to "rectify" the variant third acts of *Cat on a Hot Tin Roof* in order to make multiple discrete texts into one "übertext." The editor would take a line from one and a line from the other; re-insert lines from the first version deleted in the second version; and freely intersperse dialogue from both while at the same time deleting lines of which he can make no sense in his new mongrel rendition.

Undeniably, such an attempt would be preposterous. Any self-respecting Williams scholar would balk at the mere suggestion, because the text would be adulterated to the point of being both unreadable and unperformable. Simply put, the resulting playscript would be mush.

Yet, incredibly, this is exactly what the modern Shakespearean editor does. He draws a line from a third quarto and follows it with a line from a second quarto. He re-inserts a dozen or so lines from a first quarto that don't appear in the Folio. He sets a line of verse using the third word from a second quarto and the fifth word from the Folio. To make matters worse, editors will frequently consult and incorporate material from the *bad* quartos. The result is that when the unsuspecting reader, student, teacher, actor, or director picks up an edited script of Shakespeare, he is served up page upon page of mixed-up, watered-down mush.

Shakespeare's good quartos are not "wrong" any more than the First Folio is "right"; but to attempt to marry quartos in an uneasy alliance with the Folio is unnecessary at best and ludicrous at worst. The quarto scripts may be considered valid in and of themselves but lose any such integrity when combined with each other and with the Folio. It is painfully ironic that, through the very act of editing, most editors who purport to clarify the intent of the deceased writer do exactly the reverse.[22]

Just as with the works of Tennessee Williams, everyone has the option of reading and examining all variant versions of Shakespeare's plays and deciding which he likes best. The quarto texts are readily available to those who wish to read, study, or stage productions from them. Common sense dictates, however, that the most recent version of a play reflects its highest point of evolution. These are the versions that were refined in the fire of performance before a living audience. These are the versions that the playwright himself, through benefit of experience and hindsight, considered to be the best, for otherwise no changes would have been made to earlier scripts. This in itself is reason enough to choose the Folio over the quartos.

The Importance of Spelling

In a quest for *the* definitive text, editors spend countless hours picking apart and putting back together the Folio and variant quartos. Similarly, they also standardize spelling in an attempt to find *the* definitive word. There is a fundamental flaw in this practice, because Shakespeare, the undisputed master of the English language, rarely uses a word in just one way or to mean just one thing.

Unfortunately for the editor who prefers his text clean, pat, and shallow, Shakespeare employs not only double but treble, quadruple, and quintuple entendre as well. Layer upon layer of meaning can be found in a single passage, a single word, or even a single syllable, and oftentimes the original spelling provides a vital clue to these multiple strata.

A somewhat straightforward example can be found in the first four lines of *The Life and Death of Richard III*. As printed in the First Folio, these lines appear as:

1. NOw is the Winter of our Discontent,
2. Made glorious Summer by this Son of Yorke:
3. And all the clouds that lowr'd upon our house
4. In the deepe bosome of the Ocean buried.

And in a text whose spelling has been "modernized":

1. Now is the winter of our discontent
2. Made glorious summer by this son of York,
3. And all the clouds that loured upon our house
4. In the deep bosom of the ocean buried.

The word "Son" (male child) in line two obviously carries the additional connotation of "sun" (heavenly body) on the evidence of the contextual words "Winter," "Summer," and "clouds." In this case, the editor has left the spelling of "son" intact (although the word has been robbed of its initial capital).

In the case of the word "lowr'd" in line three, the spelling has been changed to "loured" (probably because, unlike "lowr'd," "loured" will pass computerized spell-check). "Lour" is a verb meaning "to frown or scowl, to lurk, to look dark and angry" (OED), and this sense certainly is present. The word "lowr'd" is in all likelihood assonant and should be pronounced to rhyme with "clouds," "our," and "house"; but to remove the "w" erases the additional sense of "lower": "to descend or sink; to lessen the elevation of; to bring down in rank; to degrade or dishonor" (OED). A vital portion of this word's significance has disappeared by standardizing its spelling. Moreover, in removing the apostrophe from "lowr'd" and spelling it out as "loured," the editor has also erased Shakespeare's unmistakable intention that this word occupy one beat, not two, in the poetic meter.

A somewhat more extreme example of spelling change can be found in Act I, scene iv of *The Tragedie of Romeo and Juliet*, wherein *Mercutio* describes *Queene Mab*, "the Fairies Midwife," and how she travels nightly bringing dreams to men. Here is an excerpt as printed in the First Folio:

> ... her coullers of the
> Moonshines watry Beames, her Whip of Crickets bone,
> the Lash of Philome, her Waggoner, a small gray-coated
> Gnat...

And in the second (good) quarto of 1599:

> ... her collors
> of the moonshines watry beams, her whip of Crickets bone, the
> lash of Philome, her waggoner, a small grey coated Gnat...

In the First Folio and second quarto (the two primary authoritative texts), these lines, which are clearly written in prose, read "the Lash of Philome" and "the lash of Philome" respectively. Philome (a.k.a. Philomel or Philomela) is a character from Greek mythology. Her story is as follows:

> Philomel's sister, Procne, was the wife of King Tereus of Thrace. Procne bore Tereus a son, Itys, who over time developed an unhealthy sexual attraction for his aunt Philomel. Itys subsequently kidnapped Philomel, raped her, cut out her tongue so that she should not reveal what he had done, and then hid her among his slaves. Luckily Philomel was able to communicate with her sister Procne by weaving a tapestry that told the whole sordid story. Procne then killed Itys, and for additional revenge cooked his remains and fed them to his father, King Tereus. When Tereus discovered what had happened, he tried to kill Procne and Philomel. At this point, the gods of Olympus came to the women's aid, and Philomel, Procne, and Tereus were all turned into birds.

In some versions Philomel became a swallow; in others, a nightingale. The nightingale eventually won out, and in English, "Philomel" is a poetic term for a nightingale. Considering the imagery of the speech, in which *Mab* rides in a tiny hazelnut-shell coach driven by a gnat, it makes perfect sense that the fantastic little contraption should be pulled by a nightingale.

Even so, without exception, currently all commercially available edited versions emend these lines as follows[23]:

> Her collars of the moonshine's watt'ry beams:
> Her whip of cricket's bone, the lash of film:
> Her wagoner a small grey-coated gnat,

This transmutation both (a) obliterates the brutal tale of Philome and the imagery of her avian incarnation; and (b) reduces beautiful prose to mediocre verse. Incredibly, these changes are made on the spurious evidence of a single counterfeit quarto. The only possible source for the verse arrangement and the substitution of "film" for "Philome" is the first (bad) quarto of 1597[24]:

> The traces are the Moone-shine watrie beames,
> The collers crickets bones, the lash of filmes,
> Her waggoner is a small gray coated flie,

Although the first quarto is indisputably corrupt, for some reason editors always feel compelled to consult it when piecing together a textual hodgepodge.

Using material from the bad quartos to justify textual changes is damaging enough, but sometimes editors pluck words out of thin air with no textual justification at all. In these cases, the "corrections" cannot be supported by the Folio or any extant quarto, good or bad. This practice is usually rationalized with the done-to-death assertion that the Folio's compositors were inexperienced, incompetent, and/or negligent.

Such is the case in *The Tragedie of Macbeth*, the only source for which is the Folio. Consider this passage from Act V, scene iii, where *Macbeth* pointedly asks the *Doctor*:

> What Rubarb, Cyme, or what Purgative drugge
> Would scowre these English hence: hear'st thou of them?

And as printed in a modern edited version:

> What rhubarb, senna, or what purgative drug
> Would scour these English hence? Hear'st thou of them?

Editors collectively allege that "Cyme" is a typesetter's misreading of "Cynne" and therefore means "senna"—despite the fact that there is no evidence that "senna" was ever spelled with a "c" (OED gives only two spelling variants of the word as "senna" and "sena"). Moreover, changing the monosyllabic "Cyme" to the disyllabic "senna" completely upsets the line's poetic meter.

Since *Macbeth* considers the English to be just so much "shit" plugging up his kingdom, he seeks a "Purgative drugge" (a drug to cleanse the bowels) that will "scowre" ("evacuate the stomach or bowels," OED) them out. One such "Purgative" would be "Rubarb," defined in John Bullokar's 1616 dictionary as "A costly roote much used in Phisicke to purge choler." Another such "Purgative" would be "Cyme."

The OED's headword "cyme" is cross-referrenced to "cyma": "the young Sprout of Coleworts," and Thomas Thomas' 1587 Latin / English dictionary defines "Cyma" as "A young colewort."[25] "Colewort" is an old name for cabbage, known since ancient times as a highly effective "Purgative."

It is beyond belief that "Cyme" should be changed to "senna," especially as all that is required to accurately define this word is to look it up in the dictionary. With the understanding that such emendation is both unnecessary and misguided, original spelling is herein preserved intact.

The Importance of Punctuation

It can be argued that punctuation *is* meaning, as in the following well-known example:

> A woman without her man is nothing.
> A woman: without her, man is nothing.

In spite of this, Shakespearean editors freely alter punctuation and, in the process, also drastically alter meaning.

Since the living presence of the playwright is lacking, all editorial views as to Shakespearean punctuation must remain purely conjectural. However, evidence suggests that Shakespeare set great store by his punctuation and had great disdain for those players who did not follow it in speaking. Consider the prologue of "the most lamentable comedy, and most cruell death of *Pyramus* and *Thisbie*," the play-within-a-play in Act V, scene i of *A Midsommer Nights Dreame*. This prologue (supposedly written by the character *Peter Quince*) is delivered as follows:

> *Pro.* If we offend, it is with our good will.
>   That you should thinke, we come not to offend,
>   But with good will. To shew our simple skill,
>   That is the true beginning of our end.
>   Consider then, we come but in despight.
>   We do not come, as minding to content you,
>   Our true intent is. All for your delight,
>   We are not heere. That you should here repent you,
>   The Actors are at hand; and by their show,
>   You shall know all, that you are like to know.

This speech might initially seem nonsensical, but it makes perfect sense when punctuated differently:

> *Pro.* If we offend: it is with our good will
> That you should thinke we come not to offend;
> But with good will, to shew our simple skill,
> That is the true beginning of our end.
> Consider then: we come, but in despight
> We do not come. As minding to content you,
> Our true intent is all for your delight.
> We are not heere that you should here repent you.
> The Actors are at hand, and (by their show)
> You shall know all that you are like to know.

This coherent (albeit not brilliant) speech is reduced to gibberish simply because the *Prologue* does not obey his punctuation in speaking. This is further made clear from the commentary quips of *Theseus* and *Lysander*, two of the play-within-a-play's spectators:

> *Thes.* This fellow doth not stand upon points.
> *Lys.* He hath rid his Prologue, like a rough Colt: he
> knowes not the stop. A good morall my Lord. It is not
> enough to speake, but to speake true.

This dialogue establishes that Shakespeare thought "points" (punctuation marks) and the "stop" (both a "mark or point of punctuation" and a "pause or breaking-off made by one speaking," OED) to be crucial to performance. It is therefore interesting to conjecture what Shakespeare would truly think of the armies of editors who, for the last four hundred years, have changed literally millions of commas, periods, colons, semi-colons, parentheses, periods, and dashes in an effort to "fix" his punctuation for him.

In Shakespeare's day, there was no "correct" way to punctuate, just as there was no "correct" way to spell. Moreover, it is very important to remember that Shakespeare was not an author but a playwright. He wrote plays intended to be spoken and acted before an audience, not books intended to be read quietly to oneself. This distinction is vital. Shakespeare employed not grammatical but elocutionary punctuation (punctuation as a tool for speaking). Grammatical correctness on the page might be paramount to an editor, but to Shakespeare it was completely inconsequential.[26]

In his preface to *The Tragedie of Anthonie and Cleopatra* (New Variorum edition, 1907), Dr. Horace Howard Furness states that in making changes to the Folio "the omission of punctuation, which at times makes the difference between sense and nonsense, may be censured as ill-advised." Nevertheless, over a century later, Shakespearean editors routinely damage both punctuation and meaning. Such disruption is evident in a speech by *Lady Percy* in *The*

Second Part of Henry the Fourth, Act II, scene iii. This speech appears in the First Folio of 1623 as follows:

> He was the Marke, and Glasse, Coppy, and Booke,
> That fashion'd others. And him, O wondrous! him,
> O Miracle of Men! Him did you leave
> (Second to none) un-seconded by you,
> To looke upon the hideous God of Warre,
> In dis-advantage, to abide a field,
> Where nothing but the sound of *Hotspurs* Name
> Did seeme defensible: so you left him.

And as commonly printed in edited versions:

> He was the mark and glass, copy and book,
> That fashion'd others. And him — O wondrous him!
> O miracle of men! — him did you leave —
> Second to none, unseconded by you —
> To look upon the hideous god of war
> In disadvantage, to abide a field
> Where nothing but the sound of Hotspur's name
> Did seem defensible. So you left him.

In this example, no less than eleven punctuation changes have been made to eight lines of text. These eight lines do not occur in the quartos (all of which are bad anyway), so the editor's only guide for this passage is the Folio. In the Folio's "O wondrous!," *Lady Percy* sarcastically expresses her exasperated disbelief at her father-in-law's behavior. Moving the exclamation point from behind the word "wondrous" to behind the word "him" completely alters the sense of the line.

Dramatic characters reveal themselves through speech, and their essential nature is found not only in what they say but also in how they say it. Punctuation indicates the manner in which a character speaks and is thus as important as the words themselves. Consider these lines spoken by the bumbling constable *Dogberry* in Act III, scene v of *Much adoe about Nothing* as they appear in the First Folio:

> *Con.Dog.* A good old man sir, hee will be talking as
> they say, when the age is in the wit is out, God helpe us,
> it is a world to see: well said yfaith neighbour *Verges*,
> well, God's a good man, and two men ride of a horse, one
> must ride behinde, an honest soule yfaith sir, by my
> troth he is, as ever broke bread, but God is to bee wor-
> shipt, all men are not alike, alas good neighbour.

And as printed in a modern edited version:

> *Dogberry.* A good old man, sir, he will be talking. As they
> say, "When the age is in, the wit is out." God help us, it

is a world to see! Well said, I'faith, neighbour Verges.
Well, God's a good man. An two men ride of a horse,
one must ride behind. An honest soul, I'faith, sir,
by my troth, he is, as ever broke bread. But, God is
to be worshipped, all men are not alike. Alas, good
neighbour.

As evidenced by the Folio's seemingly interminable run-on sentence, the
good constable has a very high opinion of himself and loves the sound of his
own voice. When the grammar is "corrected" and the speech chopped up into
nine separate sentences, the garrulous *Dogberry* becomes as measured and
thoughtful as a schoolmaster. Punctuation, especially as manifested in speech,
is essential to both meaning and character, and those who seek to get to the
heart of Shakespeare's plays would do best to leave it alone.

NOTES

1. Like most profane words, the "c-word" has an ancient pedigree. Its earliest recorded
use is on a map of London from 1230 that shows a "Gropecunte Lane." Not surprisingly,
this street was in a district where many brothels were in operation. The oh-so-proper OED
omits to cite a single quotation of the word from the works of Shakespeare. However, on
close examination it will often turn up, as in *Hamlet*, III.ii.:

    Ham. Ladie, shall I lye in your Lap?
    Ophe. No my Lord.
    Ham. I meane, my Head upon your Lap?
    Ophe. I my Lord.
    Ham. Do you thinke I meant Country matters?

2. Many theatre owners — including Philip Henslowe of *The Rose*, Ned Alleyn of *The
Fortune*, Francis Langley of *The Swan*, and Aaron Holland of *The Red Bull* — also owned
brothels; some invested in bear-baiting as well. To place "entertainment" prices in perspec-
tive: basic admission to the Globe Theatre cost one penny and the exlusive seats (on the
stage) cost sixpence. The cheapest (and most squalid) prostitutes charged tuppence, although
sixpence was the average rate.

3. The structural resemblance between the bear-baiting ring and the Elizabethan playhouse is no coincidence. Entrepreneur James Burbadge took considerable financial risk
when he built the first permanent, dedicated theatre in London in 1576 (suitably named
simply "The Theatre"). Burbadge, fearful of losing his investment, deliberately built in the
design of a bear-baiting ring. If the theatrical venture failed, the building could easily be
converted. Burbadge need not have feared: such was the theatre's widespread success that
blood sport arenas such as *The Beare Garden* began to offer plays, and *The Cocke-pit* was
later converted for exclusive use as a playhouse. It is interesting to note that today's pop-
ulist sports arenas follow the same basic design as the bear-baiting ring while elitist theatre
architecture has altered radically. The revolutionary Puritan Parliament shut down all the
public playhouses in 1642; anyone caught performing was judged a criminal, and anyone
caught attending a play could be fined. The abandoned playhouses were torn down by order
of Parliament in 1647. When the exiled King Charles II returned from France in 1660, theatre reappeared in England much transformed in style, content, and architecture.

4. A draconian form of execution not fully abolished in Great Britain until 1870. The
punishment is described in the sentence passed on Thomas Howard, Fourth Duke of Nor-

folk, for the crime of High Treason: "this Bench judgeth thee be led backe from hence to the Tower, then to be layd uppon an Hurdle, and drawne through the middest of the City to the Gallowes, there to be hanged, and being halfe dead to bee taken downe, Bowelled, and after thy Head is cut off, to be quartered into foure parts, thy Head and Body to be done with according to the Queenes pleasure. And God have mercy on thy soule." Luckily for the Duke, his sentence was reduced to simple beheading. Not so lucky was a certain *Doctour Story,* whose execution is described in John Foxe's 1563 *Book of Martyrs*: "he being layde upon an hurdle, and drawne from the tower along the streetes to Tiborn, where he being hanged till he was halfe dead, was cut downe and stripped, & (which is not to be forgot) when the executioner had cut off his privy members, he rushing up upon a sodeine gave him a blow upon the eare, to the great wonder of all that stood by."

5. "Take Parsly, bruise it, and press out the Juice, and dip a Linnen-cloth in it, and put it up so dipped into the Mouth of the Womb, it will presently cause the Child to come away, tho' it be dead; and will bring away the After-burthen also" (Anonymous, *Aristotle's Compleat and Experience'd Midwife,* 1700).

6. The "red light" district outside the London city limits where the theatres were located. William Shakespeare both worked and resided there.

7. The volume appeared under Thomas' name alone in order to protect Harriet's reputation. The Bowdlers removed the more obvious vulgarities, but, alas, if they had truly known Shakespeare's depths of depravity they would never have undertaken the venture. If every single indecency were removed, nary a single line would be left.

8. Sir Thomas Bodley, founder of the famous library at Oxford University that bears his name, wrote to librarian Thomas James in 1612 that he should not collect "suche bookes, as almanackes, plaies & an infinit number, that are daily printed, of very unworthy maters & handling... some plaies may be worthy the keeping: but hardly one in fortie." The Bodleian unenthusiastically accepted a First Folio when Jaggard donated a copy in 1624. The volume was not granted the honor of listing in the catalogues and was sold as part of a lot for an unknown amount sometime around 1660–70. In 1905, when the Bodleian decided that a First Folio was perhaps "worthy the keeping" after all, it paid £10,000 (approx. $1,500,000 in modern currency) to Henry C. Folger to buy back its original copy.

9. In his preface to *The English Traveller,* author and playwright Thomas Heywood (ca. 1575–1650) complained that his plays were "not exposed unto the world in Volumes" partly because they were "still retained in the hands of some Actors, who thinke it against their peculiar profit to have them come in Print."

10. Such need arose when the London theatres were closed due to plague from June to December, 1592 and from April to December, 1593. As a result, roughly three times as many plays appeared in print in 1593–94 than in the previous eight years. A similar glut of plays flooded the market in 1600 when, due to pressure from conservative Puritans, the Lords of the Privy Council briefly threatened to permanently close all but two of the London theatres. Unable to earn an income from performing, the players had no option but to release their precious plays for sale in print.

11. In Act III, scene i of *A Midsommer Nights Dreame,* impresario *Peter Quince* scolds player *Francis Flute* for his inability to decipher a cue-script: "you speake all your part at once, cues and all." For more on the use of cue-scripts in the Elizabethan theatre, see Patrick Tucker's *Secrets of Acting Shakespeare: The Original Approach* (Oberon, 2002).

12. The infamous 1603 bad quarto of *Hamlet* was possibly assembled from memory by a supporting actor. It prints the play's most famous line, "To be, or not to be, that is the Question," as "To be, or not to be, I there's the point," but the minor part of *Marcellus* (one of the palace guards) is remarkably intact.

13. To place this sum in context: artisans earned about seven shillings per week. Incidentally, this wage was comparable to that of a hired actor, who earned between six and ten shillings per week.

14. Some theatres and acting companies were owned and managed outright by individuals, but both the Globe and Blackfriars theatres and their resident company, the Lord Chamberlain's (later King's) Men, were owned jointly by shareholders. Hemminge, Condell and Shakespeare were all Actor-Sharers, and all three are listed in the First Folio's "Names of the Principall Actors in all these Playes." Shakespeare and Hemminge were original founders of the Globe, and all three men were founders of the Blackfriars. In addition, Hemminge served as business manager and continued with the company right up until his death in 1630.

15. Those not included are *Pericles*, *Sir Thomas More*, and *The Two Noble Kinsmen*, all of which are collaborations of only partial Shakespearean authorship.

16. These are the "corrected and augmented" 1598 quarto of *Loves Labours Lost*, the 1600 quarto of *Merchant of Venice*, and the 1609 "corrected, augmented and amended" reprint of the 1599 quarto of *Romeo and Juliet*. The words "corrected" and "amended" usually appeared on a (good) quarto title page only when an inferior (bad) copy was already in circulation.

17. Edward Knight, a book-keeper (a.k.a. prompter) for the King's Men, may have originated the term when he apologized for the inferiority of his transcription of John Fletcher's play *Bonduca*: "the occasion. why these are wanting here. the booke where by it was first Acted from is lost: and this hath beene transcrib'd from the fowle papers of the Authors wch were found."

18. Some who question the integrity of the First Folio argue that the fair papers are suspect because they are not written out in the author's own hand; therefore, they are marred by copying errors made by the playhouse scribe. This argument is specious, since Shakespeare himself obviously thought the scribe's copies sufficiently accurate for use in staging his plays at the theatre in which he was part owner.

19. For the orthodox view of the publication and provenance of extant quartos and Folios, see Alfred W. Pollard's *Shakespeare Folios and Quartos* (Cooper Square Publishers, 1909).

20. E.g., the first quarto of *Richard III*, which differs significantly from later versions, probably reflects a practical adaptation for performance by a reduced cast while on tour.

21. "A Note of Explanation" to *Cat on a Hot Tin Roof* (Signet, 1958).

22. As Don Weingust observes in *Acting from Shakespeare's First Folio: Theory, Text, and Performance* (Routledge, 2006), "As any tinkerer knows, once something complex has been taken apart, it is nearly impossible to put it back together again just as it was."

23. All modern editions are so alike in both textual changes and annotation that one suspects them to be not original arrangements but rather mindless imitations of their forebears.

24. The source of this unauthorized quarto may have been a literary pirate who attended a performance and jotted down dialogue while the play was in progress.

25. The *Macbeth* quotation is inexplicably excluded from both the OED's entries for "cyma" n. and "cyme" n.l., which are dated as 1706 and 1877 respectively. Instead, it is offered as the first and only quotation under the completely separate headword "cyme" n.2., along with the somewhat feeble "definition" that the word is "supposed to be an error for cynne, SENNA." For more on the chronological unreliability of lexicons, see *Notes on the Annotation*, p. 21 below.

26. For in-depth exploration of Shakespeare's use of elocutionary punctuation, see Percy Simpson's *Shakespearian Punctuation* (Oxford, 1911); Richard Flatter's *Shakespeare's Producing Hand* (Norton, 1948); Doug Moston's Introduction to *The First Folio of Shakespeare 1623* (Applause, 1995); Patrick Tucker's *Secrets of Acting Shakespeare: The Original Approach* (Oberon, 2002); and Don Weingust's *Acting from Shakespeare's First Folio: Theory, Text, and Performance* (Routledge, 2006).

Notes on the Annotation

1 Traditionally, any lexicographical entry that post-dates Shakespeare is discarded in annotation. However, in *Explorations in Shakespeare's Language* (Longmans, Green and Co., 1962), Hilda Hulme ably demonstrates that even the most trustworthy lexicons misdate word usage by as much as four centuries.

Consider the word "pilcher" in the following line from Act III, scene i of *The Tragedie of Romeo and Juliet*:

> *Mer.* ...Will you
> pluck your Sword out of his Pilcher by the eares?

Because "pilcher" meaning "scabbard" has appeared nowhere else in the English language before or since, its usage here has proven highly puzzling to both lexicographers and annotators. The clearly perplexed editors of the OED offer only the following obtuse explanation for the above quotation:

> With use in quot. 1599 at sense 1 perh. cf. forms at PILCHARD n. (this use may perh. pun on this word), or perh. cf. PILCHER n.2

OED defines "pilchard" as "A small sea fish, Clupea pilchardus, closely allied to the herring, but smaller," and "pilcher" (n.2) as "A term of abuse for: a person considered worthless, contemptible, or insignificant."

A pun most certainly is in play, and the wordplay is indeed on "pilchard" (the fish), not "pilcher" (the term of abuse). The pilchard (pronounced with silent "d") is a small fish of the salmon family. The basic quibble is easily decipherable:

"pilcher" = "case" = "scabbard"

The OED dates "case" or "case-char" meaning "A fish of the family Salmonidæ" from 1751 but significantly can give no account of its etymology. The first supporting quotation under "case" (of only two total) reads: "There is a fish very much like it [the char] (but of another species supposed to be the case)." The OED's entry at "char" reads: "A small fish (*Salmo salvelinus*) of the trout kind, found in the lakes of mountainous districts in the north and in

Wales, and esteemed a delicacy." "Char" is dated from 1662, but the OED's etymological note states that the word is "Known in books only since 17th c.; but may have been in local use long before."

Shakespeare's punning use of "pilcher" is in and of itself suggestive that "case" meant "fish" far before 1751. Further evidence is arguably found in George Wilkins' *The Painfull Adventures of Pericles Prince of Tyre* (1608):

> the Fishermen... beganne to lewre and hallow to their Maister for more helpe, crying that there was a fish hung in their net, like a poore mans case in the Lawe...

And a further case for "case" can be made by Robert Herrick's poem entitled "Upon Case" (1648):

> *Case* is a Lawyer, that near pleads alone,
> But when he hears the like confusion,
> As when the disagreeing Commons throw
> About their House, their clamorous I, or No:
> Then *Case*, as loud as any *Serjant* there,
> Cries out, (my lord, my Lord) the Case is clear:
> But when all's hush't, *Case* then a fish more mute,
> Bestirs his Hand, but starves in hand the Suite.

The purpose of the present work is to provide practical and sensible annotation to Shakespeare's Folio text, not to make comprehensive argument for each and every chronologically suspect lexicographic entry. Suffice to say that so-called "anachronistic" definitions are included "if the shoe fits." If "case" meaning "fish" were to be automatically discarded due to an 18th c. lexical date, then not much in terms of sense could be offered. All definitions herein are intended to posit, not prove, usage and content.

2   Period dictionaries commonly define a headword by a list of words and phrases with identical or overlapping shades of meaning. For example, John Florio's entry for "Porcile di venere" in his 1598 Italian / English dictionary is as follows:

> Porcile di venere, the hogs-stye of Venus, a womans privities or geare.

It can therefore safely be assumed that to Shakespeare's contemporaries "geare" meant "a womans privities." Consequently, "geare" is herein defined as "a woman's privities," with Florio's entry for "Porcile di venere" cited as the source. (N.B. that in this instance the OED's dating is off by at least 77 years, giving the first usage of "gear" meaning "organs of generation" as 1675.)

3   Words are sometimes herein defined by their synonyms. For example, the OED gives "luxury" as a definition for "deliciousness." The two can

therefore be considered synonyms, and "deliciousness" is herein defined as follows:

deliciousnesse ("luxury": "lasciviousness, lust," OED)

4   Play text is based on the 1876 J.O. Halliwell-Phillipps facsimile of the First Folio of 1623. Unless otherwise noted, quotations from other Shakespeare plays are from the same volume.

5   Quotations from Shakespeare's Sonnets are from the 1609 quarto.

6   Unless otherwise noted, biblical quotations are from the King James Bible, 1611 edition.

7   Greek words have been transcribed using the western alphabet.

Abbreviations of
Key Reference Works

DPF . . . . . E. Cobham Brewer, *Dictionary of Phrase and Fable.*

EC . . . . . . E.A.M. Colman, *The dramatic use of Bawdy in Shakespeare.*

EC2 . . . . . Elisha Coles, *An English Dictionary.*

EP. . . . . . . Eric Partridge, *Shakespeare's Bawdy.*

F&H . . . . John S. Farmer and William E. Henley, *Slang and its Analogues.*

FG . . . . . . Frances Grose, *Lexicon Balatronicum.*

FR . . . . . . Frankie Rubinstein, *A Dictionary of Shakespeare's Sexual Puns and Their Significance.*

GW . . . . . Gordon Williams, *A Glossary of Shakespeare's Sexual Language.*

GW2 . . . . Gordon Williams, *A Dictionary of Sexual Language and Imagery in Shakespearean and Stuart Literature.*

HC . . . . . . Henry Cockeram, *The English Dictionarie.*

HH. . . . . . Hilda M. Hulme, *Explorations in Shakespeare's Language.*

HK . . . . . . Helge Kökeritz, *Shakespeare's Pronunciation.*

JA . . . . J.N. Adams, *The Latin Sexual Vocabulary.*

JB . . . . John Bullokar, *An English Expositor.*

JC. . . . . . . Juan Eduardo Cirlot, *A Dictionary of Symbols.*

JF . . . . John Florio, *A worlde of wordes.*

JH. . . . . . . James T. Henke, *Courtesans and Cuckolds.*

JJ . . . . John Jamieson, *An Etymological Dictionary of the Scottish Language.*

JM . . . . . . John Minsheu, *A dictionarie in Spanish and English.*

JP . . . . John Palsgrave, *Leclarcissement de la langue francoyse.*

JT . . . . Jack Tresidder, *The Complete Dictionary of Symbols.*

LD . . . . . . "Latin Dictionary and Grammar Aid."

ND. . . . . . *A New Dictionary of the Terms Ancient and Modern of the Canting Crew.*

OED . . . . *Oxford English Dictionary.*

RC . . . . . . Randle Cotgrave, *A dictionarie of the French and English tongues.*

RC2 . . . . . Robert Cawdrey, *A table alphabeticall.*

RH . . . . . . Raphael Holinshed, *Chronicles of England, Scotland and Ireland.*

RS . . . . . . Reginald Scot, *The Discovery of Witchcraft.*

TB . . . . . . Thomas Blount, *Glossographia.*

TDL . . . . . Thomas De Laune, *Tropologia.*

TE . . . . . . Thomas Elyot, *The Dictionary of syr Thomas Eliot knyght.*

TR . . . . . . Thomas W. Ross, *Chaucer's Bawdy.*

TT . . . . . . Thomas Thomas, *Dictionarium Linguae Latinae et Anglicanae.*

TW . . . . . . Thomas Wilson, *A Christian Dictionarie.*

The Tragedie of Macbeth.
First Folio Play-script
with Accompanying Annotation

Act I, scene i

Actus Primus. Scæna Prima.   [1]

Thunder and Lightning. Enter three Witches.   [I.i.1]

{*Witch 1.*}   When shall we three meet againe?

Notes I.i.

2. Thunder and Lightning... three Witches. *Witches* supposedly possessed the power to "raise and suppress Lightning and Thunder, Rain and Hail, Clouds and Winds, Tempests and Earthquakes" (RS). *Witches* were especially powerful during storms, because for the working of "Magical feats, the fittest time is the brightest Moonlight, or when storms of lightning, winde, or thunder, are raging through the air; because at such times the infernal Spirits are nearer unto the earth, and can more easily hear the Invocations" (RS). The *Thunder and Lightning* also suggests that these *three*

Witches are something more than mortal women. See note: *we three*, line 3, below; and *Thunder, Lightning, or in Raine*, line 4, below.

2. ***three Witches.*** An entry in the account records kept by Edmund Tilney, Master of the Revels to King James I of England, records the following payment to the business manager of Shakespeare's company: "To John Hemynges one of his M^{ts} players upon Warrant dated 18th October 1606 for three playes before his Matie and the kinge of Denmarke two of them at Grenewich and one at Hampton Courte xxx^{li}." Although Tilney's records do not name which three plays the King's Men performed at court during the King of Denmark's visit, there is good reason to believe that *Macbeth* was among them.

Shakespeare's source for *Macbeth* was Raphael Holinshed's *Chronicles of England, Scotland and Ireland*, a work in which the *Witches* occupy barely two paragraphs (see note: *Macbeth doth come*, I.iii.35). In order to cater to the supernatural interests of his patron, King James I, Shakespeare places "Witchcraft" ("The Blacke Art, divellish Magicke," RC, s.v. "Goëtie") at the nucleus of the story and greatly expands the *Witches'* roles. James fancied himself an expert on *Witches* and had written his own tract on the subject, *Dæmonologie*, which was first published in 1597. As a young man, James had even gone so far as to personally examine the so-called *Witches* who were accused of cursing his ships with adverse winds (see notes: *in a Syve*, I.iii.11; and *Ship-mans Card*, I.iii.20).

3. ***When.*** *When* is a fitting first word for a play that deals with the playing out of destiny as planted in *the Seedes of Time* (I.iii.64). The next two scenes begin with the words *What* (I.ii.5) and *Where* (I.iii.3).

3. ***When shall we three meet againe.*** *Three* is one of "the most 'potent' numbers in magic" (Vincent Foster Hopper, *Medieval Number Symbolism*, p. 122), for "3 is all: beginning, middle, and end... In the human cycle, to go no further in search of analogies, birth, life, and death represent the triple division which is common to all mundane affairs. This conception of life is recognized in the Greek fates (Klotho is the spinner, Lachesis assigns the lot, Atropos cuts the thread), and in the Norns (Urd, past; Verdandi, present; Skuld, future)" (ibid., p. 6).

Holinshed himself suggests that the *three Witches* may in fact be "the weird sisters, that is (as ye would say) the Goddesses of destinie" (RH), the "three Parcae or Fates, who arbitrarily controlled the birth, events, and death of every man. They are called cruel because they pay no regard to the wishes and requirements of anyone" (DPF, s.v. "Fates"; also see note: *weyward Sisters*, I.iii.36). On the other hand, Shakespeare's *First Witch* asks the other two when the *three* of them shall *meet againe*, which clearly indicates that they have the power to separate — something that the indivisible *three* Fates could never do.

Renaissance Christians believed that pagan deities such as the *three* Fates were truly demons who had tricked the ancients into believing that they were divine (cf. "Lucifer... retaining that pride wherewith he arrogantlie affected the majestie of God, hath still his ministring Angels about him, whome he emploies in severall charges, to seduce and deceive as him seemeth best: as those spirites which the Latines call Jovios and Antemeridianos, to speake out of Oracles, and make the people worship them as gods, when they are nothing but deluding Divels," Thomas Nashe, *Pierce Penilesse his Supplication to the Divell*; also see note: *Heccats*, II.i.67). It is therefore likely that original audiences perceived these *three Witches* as diabolical beings, particularly as elemental spirits; see note: line 4, below.

In Thunder, Lightning, or in Raine?

{*Witch 2.*}   When the Hurley-burley's done,   [5]

           When the Battaile's lost, and wonne.

{*Witch 3.*}   That will be ere the set of Sunne.

{*Witch 1.*}   Where the place?

{*Witch 2.*}   Upon the Heath.

{*Witch 3.*}   There to meet with *Macbeth*.   [10]

---

4. **Thunder, Lightning, or in Raine.** As vehicles of elemental spirits, *Thunder, Lightning,* and *Raine* provided a particularly auspicious environment for *Witches'* convocations (see note: *Thunder and Lightning,* line 2, above). These elemental spirits supposedly arose after Satan "was cast out into the earth, and his angels were cast out with him" (Revelation 12:9), for "at the fall of Lucifer, some Spirites fell in the aire, some in the fire, some in the water, some in the lande: In which Elementes they still remaine" (James I, *Dæmonologie*). In *Pierce Penilesse his Supplication to the Divell,* Thomas Nashe describes the formation of the "spirits of the air," who originally were God's angels

> whose bodies are compact of the purest airie Element... those *Apostata* spirits that rebelled with Belzebub: whose bodies, before their fall, were bright and pure all like to the former: but, after their transgression, they were obscured with a thick ayrie matter & ever after assigned to darknes... *Lucifer* (before his fall) an Archangel, was a cleer bodie compact of the purest, and brightest of the aire; but after his fall, he was vailed with a grosser substance, and tooke a new forme of darke and thick ayre, which he still reteineth. Neither did he onlie fall, when he strove with *Michael,* but drew a number of Aungels to his faction; who joint partakers of his proud revolt, were likewise partakers of his punishmente, and all thrust out of heaven togither by one judgement: who ever since do nothing but wander about the Earth, and tempt and inforce fraile men to enterprise all wickednesse that maie be, and commit most horrible and abhominable things against God.

Through conversation with their familiars, *Witches* presumably had power over these types of demons. However, these *Witches* may themselves be elementals, for "The spirits of the aire will mixe themselves with thunder & lightening, and so infect the Clyme where they raise any tempest, that sodainly great mortalitie shal ensue to the inhabitants, from the infectious vapors which arise from their motions" (Thomas Nashe, *Pierce Penilesse his Supplication to the Divell*). Cf. and see notes: lines 5–7 and 13, below; I.iii.87–89; and IV.i.173.

5. **Hurley-burley's.** The nearby *Hurley-burley* ("a braule, a quarrell, a fray," JF, s.v. "Mescolanza"; "a rout, overthrow, discomfiture, as of an armie," RC, s.v. "Desarroy") both (a) arose from a *Hurley-burley* ("sedition, insurrection," TT, s.v. "Tŭmultus"; cf. *Revolt*, I.ii.6); and (b) occurs during a *Hurley-burley* ("a storme," JF, s.v. "Stormo").

The *three Witches* probably had a hand in bringing about this *Hurley-burley*, for it was believed that one of Satan's principal aims was to overthrow God's divinely ordered human society: "This gallant Devill mooving at the first (before his Incarnation) a mutiny in heaven among the Angels, hath now assumed a body to raise tumults on the earth, and breake *sacrum societatis vinculum*, the sacred bond of society" (Thomas Lodge, *Wits Miserie*). Also see note: *The Earth hath bubbles*, I.iii.87.

5–10. **done... meet with Macbeth.** The *Witches* knows that *the Battaile* will be *done* ("dispatched, ended, brought to passe," TT, s.v. "Effectus") *ere* (before) *the set of Sunne*. They also know that thereafter they will *meet with Macbeth Upon the Heath* ("a desert, a waste, a wildernes," JF, s.v. "Desérto"; cf. *blasted Heath*, I.iii.83). For early audiences, this foretelling of future events would instantly mark the *Witches* as agents of evil (see notes: *why doe you start*, I.iii.57; and *prediction*, I.iii.61).

9–10. **Heath... Macbeth.** The sound that most closely approximates contemporary pronunciation of the "ea" in *Heath* is a slightly elongated "e" as in the modern "get" (HK, p. 199). *Heath* would have made a close (if not exact) rhyme with the "-eth" of *Macbeth*, which was pronounced with a short "i" as in the modern "it" (HK, p. 266).

Londoners pronounced the "ee" in *meet* as either a short "i" (as in the modern "it") or as "e" in the modern "get" (HK, p. 191). However, in order to maintain the septenary meter, *meet* must here be pronounced as two syllables with the first syllable stressed ("MEH-ut" or "MIH-ut"; cf. OED's spelling variants "meit" and "miet"). This pronunciation of *meet* is one of many verbal clues that the characters in this play speak in Scottish dialect.

Shakespeare initially wrote *Macbeth* to be performed at court before King James I of England, a native Scotsman who was also King James VI of Scotland. To please this king of Scottish heritage, Shakespeare and his fellow actors dramatically reenacted a story drawn from Scottish legend, which they performed in Scottish dress (see note: *My Countryman*, IV.iii.184). In such circumstances, the actors would have been negligent indeed to portray Scotsmen without also attempting to speak like Scotsmen. (For a sampling of other orthographic and verbal indicators of Scottish dialect in this play, cf. and see notes: *weyward*, I.iii.36; *ha's*, I.iii.87; *Deed*, I.vii.18; and *cold*, IV.i.8.)

10. **meet with.** The *Witches* plan to (a) *meet with* ("incounter," "come to, or light on, casually," RC, s.v. "Rencontrer") *Macbeth*; (b) *meet* ("come together in conflict," OED) *with Macbeth*; and/or (c) "mete" *with* ("estimate or judge the greatness or value of," OED) *Macbeth*.

If *meet* puns "mate" (which OED gives as a pre-seventeenth century Scottish spelling of *meet*), then the *Witches* also plan to "mate" *with Macbeth* in order to "mate" him ("render [him] powerless, deprive [him] of strength," "bring [him] to nothing, overthrow [him]," OED). Cf. and see notes: I.iii.152–155; *Loves*, III.v.16; *strange & self-abuse*, III.iv.178; and *mated*, V.i.80.

{*Witch 1.*}   I come, *Gray-Malkin.*

All {*Witches*}.   *Padock* calls anon: faire is foule, and foule is faire,

Hover through the fogge and filthie ayre.

Exeunt.

11–12. *Gray-Malkin... Padock calls anon.* The *Witches* may answer the call of their familiars, who appear to them in the shapes of a "Grimalkin" ("A cat," FG) and a *Padock* ("a Toad," TB). RS notes that *Witches* commonly "keep Devils and Spirits in the likeness of Todes and Cats," and that the *Witches'* "first and principal King (which is of the power of the East) is called Baell; who when he is conjured up, appeareth with three heads; the first like a Toad; the second like a Man; the third like a Cat."

Alternatively, the *Witches* might not answer an immediate summons but foresee that *Padock* will call them *anon* ("forthwith, by and by, shortly, or a little after," TT, s.v. "Mox"). It is also possible that the *First Witch* speaks not to her familiar but addresses the *Third Witch* as *Gray-Malkin*, which can mean (a) "an old she-cat; contemptuously applied to a jealous or imperious old woman" (OED); and/or (b) an old *Malkin* ("slattern," F&H) with a *Malkin* ("female pudendum: i.e., 'pussie,'" F&H) that is *Gray*.

12. *faire is foule, and foule is faire.* By making that which is *faire* (good) seem *foule* (evil) and that which is *foule* ("Contrary, unfavourable," OED) seem *faire* ("promising, advantageous, suitable," OED), the *Witches* hope to lure *Macbeth* to damnation, for many people "consent to their owne perditions... deceived by the craft of Satan... He perswaded them, that good was evill, and evill was good" (John Craig, *A Short Summe of the whole Catechisme*). Cf. Isaiah 5:20: "Woe unto them that call evill good, and good evill, that put darkenes for light, and light for darkenesse." Also cf. I.iii.43 and 57–58; and I.vii.96–97.

13. *Hover through the... filthie ayre.* The *Witches* will (a) *Hover* ("flye," JF, s.v. "stravolare") *through the ayre*; (b) *Hover* ("linger about a thing as a kite doth about his pray," JF, s.v. "Aiare") about their intended victims; and (c) *Hover* ("watch, and seeke occasion or opportunity," TT, s.v. "Immĭnĕo") to create mischief.

The *Witches* probably here make their exit by flying *through the ayre* (see note: *Come away*, III.v.40), and this *ayre* is (a) *filthie* ("duskie, gloomie, sable, obscure," JF, s.v. "Adro"); and/or (b) *filthie* ("poysonous," TT, s.v. "Foedus"). Supposedly, *Witches* could "by the power of their Master, cure or cast on disseases" (James I, *Dæmonologie*), and in popular tradition "a Witch is such a one as killeth people by Poysons, and can infect the Air, and bring many mortal Diseases by Witchcraft, and by the same craft can kill any particular Man or Beast with looks, by poysoning the Air in a direct line" (Thomas Ady, *A Perfect Discovery of Witches*).

Witches would purportedly engender and transmit infection by means of a *fogge* ("a cloude, an overcasting of the skie, a miste," JF, s.v. "Nebbia"), for "The aire full of fogges and vapours... dispose the ayre to sicknesses and putrifaction" (Thomas Lodge, *A Treatise of the Plague*). Also see note: *Thunder, Lightning, or in Raine*, line 4, above; and cf. IV.i.173.

In spiritual terms, the *filthie ayre* represents divine displeasure, for "Almightie God doeth use Satan for to worke his signes and judgements... he can infect and poyson the ayer and water with pestiferous exhalations when God sendes him, as in the plagues of Egypt" (Henry Holland, *A Treatise Against Witchcraft*). Thus, humanity is afflicted with *fogge* ("adversitie or trouble or any thing wherewith the knowledge of man is hidde and overcast," JF, s.v. "Nebbia") due to its own *filthie* ("bad, wicked, sinful," RC, s.v. "Vicieux") *ayre* (character, manner).

Act I, scene ii

Scena Secunda.   [1]

Alarum within. Enter King{,} Malcome, Donal-

baine, Lenox, with attendants, meeting

a bleeding Captaine.   [I.ii.1]

King.   What bloody man is that? he can report,   [5]

               As seemeth by his plight, of the Revolt

               The newest state.

Mal.   This is the Serjeant,

               Who like a good and hardie Souldier fought

               'Gainst my Captivitie: Haile brave friend;   [10]

               Say to the King, the knowledge of the Broyle,

               As thou didst leave it.

Notes I.ii.

2. **Alarum within.** An *Alarum* is (a) "a calling together to Arms, as is usually done in a Garrison, upon the approach of an enemy" (TB, q.v.); (b) "a kinde of march sounded upon the drum and trumpet" (JF, s.v. "Dar al'arma"); and (c) "A sudden or unexpected attack; necessitating a rush to arms; a surprise; an assault" (OED). Therefore, the *Alarum* heard *within* (off-stage, or *within* the tiring-house that formed the facade at the back wall of the stage) encompasses the sounds of an entire battle.

2–3. **King, Malcome, Donalbaine.** The *King* is *Duncane* I (a.k.a. "Donnchad mac Crínáin," ca. 1001–1040), who, like *Macbeth* (a.k.a. "Mac Bethad mac Findláich," 1005–1057), was in his thirties at the time of the 1040 Makdowald uprising (cf. *The* *mercilesse Macdonwald*, line 15, below). *King Duncane's* two sons, *Malcome* (a.k.a. "Máel Coluim mac Donnchada," 1031–1093) and *Donalbaine* (a.k.a. "Domnall Bán," ca. 1033–1098) were respectively nine and seven years old at the time that this scene supposedly takes place. However, Shakespeare portrays *Duncane* as considerably older (cf. II.ii.17–18, II.iii.146–147, and V.i.41–42), and Shakespeare likewise ages *Duncane's* sons so that they are old enough to accompany their father on a military campaign.

3. **Lenox.** This character is apparently the "Thane" (see note: *Thane*, line 56, below) of "Lennox" (a "County in South-Scotland," EC2).

4–8. ***bleeding Captaine... Serjeant.*** The titles *Captaine* and *Serjeant* formerly had a wide range of application. *Serjeant* was used to describe any "tenant by military service under the rank of a knight" (OED), so a *Serjeant* could very well be a *Captaine* (a generic term for "A military leader of skill and experience" as well as "A subordinate officer holding command under a sovereign, a general, or the like," OED). There is therefore no disparity between *Malcome's* description of this character as a *Serjeant* and the stage direction and speech prefixes which describe this same man as a *Captaine*.

Moreover, it must be remembered that original audiences did not read the play beforehand, nor did they receive a printed program listing the characters' names. Because this *bleeding* man is described in the dialogue as a *Serjeant* (line 8), to Shakespeare's audience a *Serjeant* he would be.

5. ***bloody.*** *Bloody* can mean (a) "bleeding, imbrued, full of bloud" (RC, s.v. "Sanglant"); and/or (b) "fierce, eager," "bold, stout, confident, couragious" (RC, s.v. "Fier").

5–7. ***he can report... The newest state.*** The *King* fears that his forces may have been put to *Revolt* ("put to flight," JF, s.v. "Revoltare"); cf. lines 15–21, below. The *Captaine's* bleeding reveals that he has recently been on the battlefield, so *As seemeth* (*As* it appears) *by his plight* ("Bodily or physical condition; state of health," OED) *he can report The newest* (most recent) *state* ("report of the numbers of a corps, regiment, etc. in the field, with details of casualties," OED) in this *Revolt* ("rebellion," RC, s.v. "Revolte").

The *Revolt* is that described by Holinshed as the "trayterous enterpryse" of "Makdowald," who sought the *Revolt* ("overthrow," JF, s.v. "Revolta") of *Duncane*. Shakespeare combines Makdowald's *Revolt* with Holinshed's accounts of three other "warres that Duncane had with forrayne enimies in the seventh yeare of his reygne." These are (1) "the incursions of the Danes" under *Sweno* and their victory over *Duncane's* forces; (2) *Sweno's* failed besieging of *Duncane* in "the castell of Bertha"; and (3) Canute's invasion of Scotland. See notes: lines 61–62 and 68, below.

9. ***good.*** *Good* means "gallant; valiant" (RC, s.v. "Gaillard").

9. ***hardie.*** "Strong, puissant, valiant, manlie, stout," "of good courage: fierce and warlike, constant" (TT, s.v. "Fortis").

10. ***my Captivitie.*** Shakespeare drew inspiration for Prince *Malcome's Captivitie* ("the taking and destruction of: an assaulting and besieging round about," TT, s.v. "Hǎlōsis") from an episode in Holinshed: "Makdowald thus having a mightie puyssaunce about him... by fine force tooke theyr captaine Malcolme, and after the end of the batayle smoote of his head." (Obviously, Holinshed's "captaine Malcolme" is not the *King's* son of the same name.)

11. ***Broyle.*** A *Broyle* is a civil uprising, a "hurly burly, that riseth of a sodaine great feare: sedition, insurrection, commotion of people," "uprore or mutinie" (TT, s.v. "Tǔmultus"). Cf. and see note: *Hurley-burley's*, I.i.5.

Cap.   Doubtfull it stood,

As two spent Swimmers, that doe cling together,

And choake their Art: The mercilesse *Macdonwald*   [15]

(Worthie to be a Rebell, for to that

The multiplying Villanies of Nature

Doe swarme upon him) from the Westerne Isles

Of Kernes and Gallowgrosses is supply'd,

And Fortune on his damned Quarry smiling,   [20]

Shew'd like a Rebells Whore: but all's too weake:

13–15. *Doubtfull it stood... choake their Art.* The metaphor of this passage centers on "swimming" meaning "doubting, wavering, uncertainetie, inconstancie" (RC, s.v. "Fluctuation"). The outcome of the battle is *Doubtfull* ("uncertaine," TT, s.v. "Ambĭgŭus") because, even though both armies are *spent* ("out of heart, or faint-hearted, cleane done," RC, s.v. "Recreant"), neither will retreat. The combatants' weapons *cling* ("By-form of clink," OED: "strike together so that they emit a sharp ringing sound," OED) as they *choake together* (i.e., lock in battle; to "chokk togeder" is "to thrust or ram together," OED, s.v. "chok"; "chock" and "choak" are variant spellings of "shock," OED; cf. "to but, to chock, to frunt, to jussle violently," JF, s.v. "Dar di cozzo").

The exhausted yet determined opponents are *As Doubtfull* ("intangled, twisted togither," JF, s.v. "Perplesso") *As two spent* ("weakened, feeble and wearied," TT, s.v. "Fractus") *Swimmers that doe cling* ("embrace," "cleave or sticke," JF, s.v. "Ghermire") *together*. The opposing sides *choake* ("stifle, smother," RC, s.v. "Estouffer") one another's *Art* (homophone of "heart": courage) *As Swimmers* who *choake* ("kill," JF, s.v. "Soffocare") one another's *Art* (skill, ability). One swimmer will ultimately *choake* ("drowne," JF, s.v. "Affogare") the other, and ultimately one army will *choake* ("shock": "damage or weaken by impact or collision," "destroy the stability of," OED) the other. As with the *Swimmers*, each army's chances are *Doubtfull* ("indifferent," TB, s.v. "Mĕdius"). It is therefore impossible to say which will ultimately gain mastery. In the encounter between these *two* forces, victory "swimme[s] under the water" ("stand[s] on doubtfull, indifferent, or uncertaine tearmes," RC, s.v. "Nager entre deux eaux").

15–18. *The mercilesse Macdonwald... upon him.* The *mercilesse* ("bloudie, cruell, fell," "bloudthirstie," JF, s.v. "Sanguinoso") *Macdonwald* is *Worthie* ("mightie, strong," "of great force," JF, s.v. "Valénte") *to be a Rebell, for to that* (i.e., "when"; *for to* is equivalent to "Sc[ottish] *till*," OED, which means "While, during the time that,"

JJ) The multiplying ("breeding, proliferating," OED) *Villanies* ("person[s] or thing[s] that [are] the source of discredit or disgrace," OED) *of Nature Doe swarme* ("come or goe together," "assemble," "waxe thick," TT, s.v. "Cŏĕ") *upon him.*

Macdonwald is indeed *Worthie to be* (with play on *be* / "bee") *a Rebell* when a *swarme* ("a rabble or rout, the many-headed-monster multitude," JF, s.v. "Turba") *of Villanies Doe swarme upon him* like a *swarme* of bees — or like a *swarme* of flies *upon Nature* ("excrement," OED).

The *Captaine* also suggests that *Macdonwald* is a "ribald" ("a knave, a varlet, a lout," JF, s.v. "Ribaldo"; *Rebell* and "ribald" were interchangeably spelled, OED) who is *Worthie* (suitable, fit) to lead a *Rebell* (variant of "rabble," OED). *Macdonwald* is also a "Ribauld" ("fornicator, whoremunger, bawdie-house haunter," RC, q.v.) who will "screw" anybody, so he readily invites *Villanies* (i.e., sexual acts; "villainy" is used for fornication, GW, s.v. "ribald") *of Nature* (the "generative organs," F&H).

18. **the Westerne Isles.** The "Iles aunciently called Ebonides, afterwards Hebrides, but now by the Scottes, the western Iles, bycause they lie on the west halfe of Scotlande" (RH).

19. **Of.** "With" (OED).

19. **Kernes and Gallowgrosses.** A "Kern" is "in Ireland... a kind of Foot Souldier, lightly armed with a Dart or Skeyn... We take a Kern most commonly for a Farmer or Country Bumpkin" (TB, q.v.). A "gallowglass" is "An armed servitor (or foot-soldier) of an ancient Irish chief" (DPF). Holinshed relates that the mutinous Makdowald

> had got togither a mightie power of men: for out of the westerne Isles, there came unto him a great multitude of people, offering themselves to assist him in that rebellious quarell, and out of Ireland in hope of the spoyle came no small number of Kernes & Galloglasses offering gladly to serve under him, whither it shoulde please him to lead them.

The "gall" in "gallowglass" derives from Irish and Gaelic "gall" meaning "foreigner, stranger" (OED) and is etymologically unconnected with "Gauls" or "Gallogrecians" (the Greek-speaking Gauls who inhabited "Gallogrois" or "Gallogrecia," a region in Asia Minor). However, it is possible that the "r" spelling (*Gallowgrosses*) arises from confusion of the "Gaelic," the "Gallic," and the "Gaulic." Then again, *Gallowgrosses* may be a straightforward variant of "galloglasses" (for the dialectal substitution of "r" for "l," see note: *Aroynt*, I.iii.9).

19. **supply'd.** To "supply" can mean (a) "to aide, to defende" (JF, s.v. "Sussidiare"); and (b) to reinforce (a "supply" is a "filling up of a defective companie of souldiers," RC, s.v. "Recreuë").

20–21. **Fortune... Shew'd like a Rebells Whore.** Initially, the goddess *Fortune Shew'd* ("employed or bestowed," TT, s.v. "Exprōmor") her favors on *Macdonwald, smiling on his damned* ("accursed, damnable, execrable," OED) *Quarry* (i.e., assault; literally "The swooping attack made by a hawk; an instance of a hawk's seizing its prey," OED). In fawning on *Macdonwald, Fortune Shew'd* (sexually displayed, GW) herself *like a Rebells Whore,* seemingly *smiling on* (i.e., giving her sexual favors to) *Macdonwald* and permitting him to "dam[n]" ("fuck," FR; to "dam" is literally to "stop up," EC2) her *Quarry* ("female pudendum; Cunt," F&H, s.v. "monosyllable").

However, the goddess *Fortune* (also known as the *Whore Fortune* because she was so extremely inconstant in her favors) has no true allegiance to any man. She merely presented a "show" ("An unreal or illusory appearance," OED) of partiality towards *Macdonwald* before abandoning him and allowing the *King's* forces to gain the upper hand.

For brave *Macbeth* (well hee deserves that Name)

Disdayning Fortune, with his brandisht Steele,

Which smoak'd with bloody execution

(Like Valours Minion) carv'd out his passage,   [25]

Till hee fac'd the Slave:

Which nev'r shooke hands, nor bad farwell to him,

Till he unseam'd him from the Nave toth' Chops,

And fix'd his Head upon our Battlements.

21–25. *all's too weake… carv'd out his passage.* *All* of *Macdonwald's* efforts were *too weake* to win the victory, for *Macbeth* "disdained" ("wearied, troubled, molested," JM, s.v. "Enfastidiádo") *Macdonwald's* protectress, *Fortune*. *Macbeth carv'd* (hacked, cut) *out his passage* ("way, path, pace, course"; also a "safe-conduct, or licence given for the free passage, travell, or transportation," RC, q.v.). *Macbeth's Steele* (sword) *smoak'd* ("move[d] like smoke," "dr[o]ve at a rapid pace or great speed," OED) *with bloody* ("merciless," TB, s.v. "Sanguinolent") *execution* ("destructive effect, infliction of damage or slaughter," OED).

Ultimately, *Macdonwald's* "awl" (penis, JH; an "awl" is literally a "sharp-pointed blade, with which holes may be pierced," OED) was *too weake* ("impotent," JM, s.v. "Féble"; "effeminate," RC, s.v. "Enervé") to master *Fortune*. By contrast, *Macbeth* easily "distained" (sexually defiled, EC) *Fortune* with his *Steele* ("Penis. Lit[erally] an instrument or weapon," FR), which he *brandisht* (to "brandish" literally means "to shake a sword," HC, q.v., and is used "in contexts describing lascivious movements," JA, p. 137). *Macbeth's Steele* (penis) *carv'd out* (with "Innuendo of to copulate," JH, s.v. "carve") *his passage* (sexual entry) into *Fortune's passage* ("vagina," GW2). *Macbeth smoak'd* ("copulate[d]," F&H) *with bloody* (i.e., virile or passionate; "blood" is "sexual appetite, lust," OED) *execution* ("copulation," GW2). In ravishing *Fortune*, *Macbeth* also "buggered" *Macdonwald* in the *passage* (anus, JA, pp. 89 and 113). Cf. and see note: *fac'd the Slave*, line 26, below.

22. *brave Macbeth… that Name.* *Macbeth well deserves* the *Name* (title) of *brave* due to his *Name* (reputation) for bravery. His "title" (variant of "tittle": "prick," FR) is also *brave* (synonymous with "courageous": capable of "corage," or phallic erection, TR).

25. *Valours Minion.* *Macdonwald* was aided by his *Whore*, the goddess *Fortune* (lines 20–21, above), but *Macbeth* was a *Minion* ("a darling, a favorite," JF, s.v. "Aio") of Arete, the goddess of *Valour*. *Macbeth's Valour* (synonymous with "virtue": "potency,

virility," FR) easily overpowered *Fortune* and made her his *Minion* ("lover or paramour," EC); cf. and see note: *weake*, line 21, above.

Macbeth's "potency," and his subsequent loss of it, is a major theme of the play. Cf. and see notes: I.iii.21 and 152–153; I.iv.60–62; I.v.26–27; I.vii.49–51, 63–64 and 67; II.ii.57–58; III.i.75–78, 81–83, and 131–132; III.ii.22–25; IV.i.141; V.ii.20–21; V.iii.29–30; and V.vii.69.

26. **fac'd the Slave.** Shakespeare's *Macdonwald* dies facing *Macbeth* in battle, but Holinshed's Makdowald

> gave batayle unto Makbeth, with the residue whiche remained with him, but being overcome and fleing for refuge into a castell (within the whiche hys wyfe and chyldren were enclosed,) at length when he saw how he coulde neyther defend the hold any longer against his enimies, nor yet upon surrender be suffered to depart with lyfe saved, he first slew his wife & children, and lastly himselfe, least if he had yeelded simply, he shoulde have bene executed in most cruell wise for an example to other[s].

Macbeth fac'd the Slave (rascal, knave) *Macdonwald*, meaning that he (a) met him in battle; (b) forced him to retreat (*fac'd* is used "Of a body of soldiers: that has turned or faced about," OED); (c) killed him ("face" is used for "deface": "To destroy, demolish," "To blot out of existence," OED); and/or (d) "buggered" *Macdonwald* ("face" alludes to the posteriors, FR, who links the semantics to Fr. "fesse": "buttock") and used him like a *Slave* (catamite or pathic, FR).

27. **Which.** Who (OED).

27. **shooke hands.** I.e., waved goodbye (to "shake" is to "wave," RC, s.v. "Vaciller"). Cf. "Nothing more ordinary in the occurrences of common life then this gesture... to shake our hand as farre as ever we can see, to bid our friends farewell and adieu" (John Bulwer, *Chirologia*).

28. **unseam'd him... toth' Chops.** Macbeth unseam'd ("und[id] the seam or seams of," OED) *Macdonwald*, or flayed him alive (the skin was regarded as "an unseamed garment covering the whole bodie," Helkiah Crooke, *Mikrokosmographia*). *Macbeth* also "enseam[ed]" him ("cleanse[d him] of superfluous fat," OED) *from the Nave* ("navel," OED) *toth' Chops* ("mouth," FG). Moreover, *Macbeth unseam'd Macdonwald* (emasculated him, or deprived him of "seem": "semen," FR) by splitting open his *Chops* ("shop[s]": "codpiece region, housing and advertising the genitals," GW; "chop" is a spelling variant of "shop," OED; for dialectal interchangeability of "sh" and "ch," see HH, p. 317, and cf. *choake*, line 15, above).

29. **fix'd his Head upon our Battlements.** In Holinshed, *Macbeth* forces Makdowald to retreat into his castle where Makdowald later kills himself (see note: *fac'd the Slave*, line 26, above). Holinshed reports that

> Makbeth entring into the castel by the gates, as then set open, founde the carkase of Makdowald lying dead there amongst the residue of the slaine bodies, whiche when he behelde, remitting no peece of his cruell nature with that pitifull sight, he caused the head to be cut off, and set upon a pooles ende, & so sent it as a present to the king.

The severed heads of traitors were by no means an unusual sight in Shakespeare's London, for they were routinely displayed upon the gates of London Bridge and in other prominent places around the city.

King.	O valiant Cousin, worthy Gentleman.	[30]
Cap.	As whence the Sunne 'gins his reflection,	
	Shipwracking Stormes, and direfull Thunders:	
	So from that Spring, whence comfort seem'd to come,	
	Discomfort swells: Marke King of Scotland, marke,	
	No sooner Justice had, with Valour arm'd,	[35]
	Compell'd these skipping Kernes to trust their heeles,	
	But the Norweyan Lord, surveying vantage,	
	With furbusht Armes, and new supplyes of men,	
	Began a fresh assault.	
King.	Dismay'd not this our Captaines, *Macbeth* and	[40]
	Banquoh?	

---

30. **valiant Cousin.** Holinshed figures *Macbeth* as *Duncane's* first *Cousin*: Malcolme [*Duncane's* grandfather, Malcolm II, a.k.a. "Máel Coluim mac Cináeda," ca. 954–1034] had two daughters, the one which was… Beatrice, being given in mariage unto one Abbanath Crinen, a man of great nobilitie, and Thane of the Isles and west partes of Scotlande, [who] bare of that mariage the foresayd Duncan: The other called Doada, was maried unto Synell the Thane of Glammis, by whom she had issue one Makbeth a valiant gentleman.

30. **worthy.** *Worthy* can mean (a) "deserving" (JF, s.v. "Digno"); (b) "noble, and excellent" (JF, s.v. "Massimo"); and/or (c) "couragious, hardie, full of prowesse" (JF, s.v. "Prò"). *Macbeth* is also *worthy* (i.e., subject to "werth": "Fate, destiny," JJ).

31–34. **As whence the Sunne… Discomfort swells.** *Macbeth's* efforts gave *comfort* ("aid, succour, support," OED) to *Duncane's* troops, and his victory over *Macdonwald* apparently heralded the *Spring* (i.e., the dawn or "daie spring," "That is a litle before day light," TT, s.v. "Sublūcānus"). Unfortunately, *As whence* ("From the place in which, from where," OED) *the Sunne 'gins* (begins) *his reflection* (used in the general sense of "shining"; cf. "May never glorious Sunne reflex his beames Upon the Countrey where you make abode," *1 Henry VI*, V.iii), there instead arose a *Spring* ("spring tide": "a deluge," JF, s.v. "Inondatione") of *Shipwracking Stormes, and direfull Thunders.* The resulting "swell" ("The rising or heaving of the sea or other body of water in a succession of long rolling waves, as after a storm," OED) came in the form of *swells* (increases, rising amounts) of troops from the *Norweyan Lord, Sweno* (lines 37 and 73, below). Consequently, the *King's* forces unexpectedly suffered *Discomfort* ("Undoing or loss of courage; discouragement, disheartening," OED, which also notes that *Discomfort* was formerly confused with "discomfit": "defeat, rout").

35. **Justice... Valour.** In addition to being *Valours Minion* (line 25, above) and a darling of *Fortune* (line 20, above), *Macbeth* is also an instrument of the goddess *Justice*.

36. **skipping Kernes.** The *Kernes* might be (a) *skipping* ("foolish," JF, s.v. "Sbazzigante"); (b) *skipping* ("trembling," TT, s.v. "Sěliens") with fear; (c) *skipping* ("running away," JF, s.v. "Rimbalzo"); (d) "Leaping and skipping for joy" (TT, s.v. "Gestiens") to celebrate their presumed victory; and/or (e) *skipping* (hopping about) like a plague of "skip[s]" ("grasshopper[s]," F&H, q.v.). Cf. *swarme*, line 18, above.

37. **Norweyan Lord.** The *Norweyan Lord* is *Sweno, the Norwayes King* (line 73, below). Holinshed's "Sueno" (Shakespeare's *Sweno*) is apparently King Sven II (reigned 1047–1074), but Holinshed's version of "history" often has little or no relation to actual facts. Given *Sweno's* year of ascension, he could not possibly have invaded Scotland in 1040, the year of the *Macdonwald* uprising (cf. lines 15–19, above).

37. **surveying.** *Surveying* means "recognising" (JF, s.v. "Riconoscénte").

37. **vantage.** *Sweno* had a *vantage* ("Advantage," "opportunity," "chance," OED) due to a *vantage* ("A surplusage, over-measure," RC, s.v. "Surcroist") of fresh troops.

38. **furbusht.** In a simple sense, *furbusht* means "Burnished," "pollished" (RC, s.v. "Bruni"). The word also carries the implication of renewal or repair: to "furbish" means (a) to "get out rust, fetch off rustinesse" (RC, s.v. "Desrouiller"); and (b) "To dresse, mend, scowre," "trimme or tricke up, an old thing for sale" (RC, s.v. "Regrater"; this sense survives in the modern "refurbished").

40–43. **Dismay'd... the Lyon.** *Macbeth* and *Banquoh* were not *Dismay'd* at all, for *the Hare* traditionally symbolizes cowardice and *the Lyon* courage. Moreover, "the Eagle with his bloody clawes / Doth massacre the house-frequenting Sparrow" (Francis Sabie, *Adams Complaint*).

40–41. **our Captaines, Macbeth and Banquoh.** A medieval king would usually lead his forces himself (as does the invading *Sweno* in lines 64–66, below). However, according to Holinshed, *Duncane* was "softe and gentle of nature" and possessed "small skill in warlyke affayres," "a dull cowarde, and slouthfull person" whom the rebel Makdowald calls a "faynt harted milkesop, more meete to governe a sort of idle monkes in some cloyster, than to have the rule of suche valiant and hardy men of warre as the Scottes" (RH). Unable or unwilling to lead his own army against Makdowald, *Duncane* instead appointed *Macbeth and Banquoh* to be his *Captaines* (i.e., field commanders; see note: *Captaine*, line 4, above).

Duncane's weak governance was at fault for the rebellions in his kingdom, for "after it was perceyved how negligent he was in punishing offenders, many misruled persons tooke occasion thereof to trouble the peace and quiet state of the common wealth, by seditious commotions" (RH). Although *Macbeth* spoke "muche against the kings softnesse, & over muche slacknesse in punishing offenders, whereby they had such time to assemble togither," he "promised notwithstanding, if the charge were committed unto him and to Banquho, so to order the mater, that the rebelles should be shortly vanquished and quite put downe, and that not so much as one of them shoulde be founde to make resistance within the countrey" (RH).

For the identity of *Banquoh*, see note: *Your Children shall be Kings*, I.iii.95.

Cap.	Yes, as Sparrowes, Eagles;	
	Or the Hare, the Lyon:	
	If I say sooth, I must report they were	
	As Cannons over-charg'd with double Cracks,	[45]
	So they doubly redoubled stroakes upon the Foe:	
	Except they meant to bathe in reeking Wounds,	
	Or memorize another *Golgotha*,	
	I cannot tell: but I am faint,	
	My Gashes cry for helpe.	[50]
King.	So well thy words become thee, as thy wounds,	
	They smack of Honor both: Goe get him Surgeons.	

{*Exit Attendants with Captaine.*}

Enter Rosse and Angus.   [I.ii.2]

Who comes here?   [55]

Mal.	The worthy *Thane* of Rosse.	

---

44. **say sooth… report.** To *say sooth* can mean (a) to speak the truth; and/or (b) to "soothsay" or prognosticate (OED, s.v. "sooth"). The *Captaine's* reassuring report also provides the *King* with "sooth" ("Associated with senses of the verb soothe," OED; to "soothe" is to "encourage" or "render calm," OED).

Given the ordnance imagery of line 45, below, *report* meaning "to relate, recount, tell" (OED) probably plays on *report* meaning "To fire a gun" (OED). Likewise, *sooth* possibly puns "shoot," for these two words would have been pronounced very much alike. The terminal "th" of *sooth* was pronounced as a "t" (HK, p. 320), and the "h" in "shoot" was dropped, so "shoot and suit were pronounced alike" (HK, p. 145). Although these words were "not true homophones in Elizabethan pronunciation, the similarity in sound would have permitted the forced pun" (JH, s.v. "Forsooth").

45–46. **As Cannons over-charg'd… the Foe.** *Macbeth* and *Banquoh* were *over-charg'd* ("overpower[ed] by superior force," OED). However, each was a *double* ("A counterpart; an image, or exact copy," OED) of the other, for both fought with *double* their own strength. Both laid *Cracks* ("sharp, heavy, sounding blow[s]," OED) on the enemy *As* (like) *Cannons* loaded with *double* the customary amount of "charge" (gunpowder), as well as *double* the amount of "crack" ("cannon-shot," OED). With supernatural strength, *Macbeth* and *Banquoh doubly redoubled* ("repeat[ed] a thrust or stroke," OED) *stroakes upon the Foe.*

With their *Cannons* (i.e., genitals; "In the modern world the gun has replaced the sword as a sexual symbol," JA, p. 169), *Banquoh* and *Macbeth* display incredible "potency" (both "strength" and the "Ability to achieve erection or ejaculation in sexual intercourse," OED). Their *double* "Cannon-Balls" ("testicles," F&H) carry a surplus "charge" ("load of semen," JH) which allows them to *double* (copulate, GW2) and "redouble" their *stroakes* ("thrust[s] of the penis," JH) *upon Cracks* ("whore[s]," FG; also the female genitalia, F&H). Cf. the dialogue between *Falstaff* and *Pistol* (pronounced "pizzle") in Act II, scene iv of *2 Henry IV*: "*Falst.* Welcome Ancient *Pistol.* Here (*Pistol*) I charge you with a Cup of Sacke: doe you discharge upon mine Hostesse. *Pist.* I will discharge upon her (Sir *John*) with two Bullets." Also cf. F&H's "double fight": to copulate; and F&H's "double-barrelled gun": a harlot.

Despite the skillfully crafted imagery, *Cannons* are nevertheless an anachronism in medieval Scotland.

47–48. ***Except they meant... another Golgotha.*** *Macbeth* and *Banquoh* were so greatly outnumbered that their attack was inexplicable, *Except* ("unless," OED) *they meant to bathe in reeking* ("smoking or piping-hot, as Pies out of the Oven, Iron out of the Forge, or Blood from a warm Wound," ND, s.v. "Reaking") *Wounds.* Perhaps they meant to martyr themselves and thus *memorize* ("perpetuate the memory of," "keep alive the memory or recollection of," OED) *another Golgotha* ("A Syrian word, signifying, a place of dead mens sculles. It was a place at Hierusalem on the North side of Mount Sion, so called because there lay the sculles of offenders put to death," JB, q.v.). *Golgotha* is indeed memorable, for, according to Matthew 27:33, Mark 15:22, and John 19:17, it was the place of Christ's execution.

50. ***helpe.*** "Relief, cure, remedy" (OED).

52. ***smack.*** To "taste, to savour" (JF, s.v. "Saporire").

54–56. ***Enter Rosse and Angus... The worthy Thane of Rosse.*** *Rosse* and *Angus* are these characters' titles, not their names. Both hold the rank of *Thane*, "A title of honour, used among the ancient Scots... He, who enjoyed this title, seems to have presided in a county, and sometimes in a province... It may also be supposed, that he had a partial command in the army, at least of the forces in his own district" (JJ, q.v.). Shakespeare is little concerned with the historical *Rosse* and *Angus*, drawing these titles directly from a generic list in Holinshed (see note: *Henceforth be Earles*, V.vii.129).

As *Thane*, *Angus* governs *Angus*, a district in northeastern Scotland (according to RH, "The countrey aunciently called Horestia, was given unto twoo bretherne; Angusian and Mernan, by reason whereof the one parte of the same countrey was called Angus, and the other the Mernes"). The *Thane of Rosse* governs *Rosse*, a highland county in northwestern Scotland which borders the Minch channel (*Rosse* presumably derives from Gaelic "ros": "headland").

Malcome's response (line 56) to the *King's* question (line 55) makes it clear that *Angus* is expected but *Rosse* is not. *The worthy Rosse* has come from the battlefield (see note: *worthy*, line 30, above), but *Angus* is a member of *Duncane's* retinue who ushers *Rosse* into the *King's* presence. Cf. I.iii.112–115, where *Angus* and *Rosse* together summon *Macbeth* to attend on *Duncane*.

Lenox.   What a haste lookes through his eyes?

So should he looke, that seemes to speake things strange.

Rosse.   God save the King.

King.   Whence cam'st thou, worthy *Thane*?   [60]

Rosse.   From Fiffe, great King,

Where the Norweyan Banners flowt the Skie,

And fanne our people cold.

Norway himselfe, with terrible numbers,

Assisted by that most disloyall Traytor,   [65]

The *Thane* of Cawdor, began a dismall Conflict,

Till that *Bellona's* Bridegroome, lapt in proofe,

57–58. **haste... seemes to speake things strange.** In *haste, Rosse seemes* ("appeere[s] or come[s] in sight," JF, s.v. "Apparire") *to speake things strange* (i.e., to deliver the most recent news). OED gives *strange* meaning "News" only in the plural, but cf. "Nuovo, new, of late. Also a new report, a tidings, newes, simple, strange" (JF, q.v.); and "A novell, newes; tidings; an (unexpected) message; a strange report" (RC, s.v. "Nouvelle").

61–62. **From Fiffe... Norweyan Banners flowt the Skie.** Holinshed states that "Sueno king of Norway" landed in *Fiffe* (see note: *Norway himselfe*, line 64, below) with a number of Danish troops (see notes: *selfe-comparisons*, line 68, below; and *Sweno, the Norwayes King*, line 73, below). *Fiffe* lies on a peninsula in the North Sea which separates Scotland from Norway, so it was a logical place for *Sweno* to land.

Shakespeare presumably changed the nationality of the invading army from Danish to *Norweyan* because King James I's brother-in-law, Christian IV of Denmark, was present at *Macbeth's* initial court performance (see note: *three Witches*, I.i.2). This attempt at tact was probably futile, however, because (a) as a Danish king himself, Christian would inevitably know (as Holinshed and Shakespeare did not) that *Sweno* was actually King of Denmark, not Norway (see note: *the Norwayes King*, line 73, below); and (b) by all accounts Christian did not speak English.

The *Norweyan Banners* ("Flag[s] or Streamer[s] for the War," TB, s.v. "Labarum") displayed on Scottish soil in *Fiffe* are abominable *Banners* ("railer[s]," "curser[s]," "detracter[s]," JF, s.v. "Straparlatore") that "ban" ("address with angry and maledictory language," OED) and *flowt* ("scoffe, deride, ride, mocke, gibe at," RC, s.v. "Copier") *the Skie* ("heaven; the heavenly power, the deity," OED). They thus offer an insult worthy to draw down God's avenging "ban" ("curse," OED).

There is possible additional play on *Fiffe* as "a pipe of a reed, a flute" (JM, s.v. "Fláuta") and on "flowte" as a variant of "flute" (OED); the *Fiffe* and the *flowt* are both traditional military instruments.

63–64. *fanne our people... Norway himselfe.* *Norway himselfe* is *Sweno, the Norwayes King* (line 73, below), who immediately after *Macdonwald's* rebellion "arrived in Fyfe with a puysant army to subdue the whole realme of Scotland" (RH). It was not *Sweno's* banners but his actions that "fanned" fear into *Duncane's people* and made them *cold* (gloomy or dispirited; also adverse or hostile), for the "crueltie of this Sueno was such, that he neither spared man, woman, nor child, of what age, condition, or degree soever they were" (RH).

65–66. *Assisted by... The Thane of Cawdor.* Shakespeare's *Thane of Cawdor* did not openly support *Sweno* or *Macdonwald* but *Assisted* them in a covert way (cf. I.iii.120–129). In Holinshed, Makdowald's rebellion and the *Thane of Cawdor's* treason are unconnected to each other or to *Sweno's* invasion. Holinshed relates that "the pretence of his [Sueno's] comming was to revenge the slaughter of his uncle Camus and other of the Danishe nation slayne at Barre, Crowdane, and Gemmer," not to lend support to Makdowald's domestic uprising.

66. *dismall.* *Dismall* means (a) "bloudie, deadlie" (RC, s.v. "Tragique"); (b) "unfortunate, unluckie" (JF, s.v. "Infausto"); and/or (c) "Disasterous" (HC, s.v. "Unfortunate").

67. *Bellona's Bridegroome, lapt in proofe.* *Bellona* ("The Goddess of War," TB, q.v.) figuratively represents "blood slaughter, murder, and destruction" (Abraham Fraunce, *The Third part of the Countesse of Pembrokes Yuychurch*). If *Bellona's Bridegroome* carries a similar sense to the modern "Bride of Christ," then *Rosse* compares *Macbeth* to one of *Bellona's* priests who "Sacrificed not with any other mans blood, but with their own; their shoulders being lanced, and with both hands brandishing naked swords, they run and leaped up and down like mad men" (Thomas Godwin, *Moses and Aaron*).

Bellona was variously depicted as the "Sister or Wife to Mars" (William Burton, *A Commentary on Antoninus*). If *Bellona* is understood to be the wife of Mars, god of war, then *Rosse* compares *Macbeth* to Mars himself.

If *Bellona* is understood as a virgin goddess, then as *Bellona's Bridegroome Macbeth* is a man worthy not only to serve but to rule her. In the standard metaphor, *Bellona* is figured as "The souldiers warlike mistresse" (Francis Kinnaston, *Leoline and Sydanis*), and her embrace combines eroticism and destruction, for "Sex being in some measure bound up with aggression, it has been represented from ancient times by the martial figure" (GW2, s.v. "war"). Cf. Canto 2 of Samuel Rowlands' *The Famous History, of Guy Earle of Warwicke*:

> Come my Bellona doe thou gird my Sword,
> Imbrace my Armour in thy Yvory armes,
> And such kinde kisses as thou canst afford,
> Bestow upon me in the stead of Charmes.

Either way, as *Bellona's Bridegroome Macbeth* (a) is *lapt* (wrapped, clothed, enclosed) *in proofe* (strong armor); and (b) has his *proofe* (erect penis, FR; to *proofe* dough is to cause it to rise) *lapt* ("clasp[ed], embrace[d]," OED) by *Bellona's* "lap" ("female pudendum," TR).

Confronted him with selfe-comparisons,

Point against Point, rebellious Arme 'gainst Arme,

Curbing his lavish spirit: and to conclude,   [70]

The Victorie fell on us.

King.   Great happinesse.

Rosse.   That now *Sweno*, the Norwayes King,

Craves composition:

---

68. **Confronted him with selfe-comparisons.** Early in the conflict, "after a sore and cruell foughten batayle, Sueno remayned victorious" (RH). *Sweno* held the advantage until *Macbeth Confronted him with selfe-comparisons*—i.e., *with* a "comparison" ("Rivalry, contention," OED) which stood in "comparison" (an "equaling," JF, s.v. "Equiperantia") to *Sweno's* own.

In Holinshed, *Sweno* is defeated through a combination of force and trickery. Holinshed reports that the besieged *Duncane*

> fell in fayned communication with Sueno as though he would have yeelded up the Castell into his handes under certaine conditions, and this did he to drive time, and to put his enimies out of all suspition of any enterpryse ment against them... At length when they were fallen at a poynt for rendring up the holde, Duncane offered to sende foorth of the castell into the campe greate provision of vitayles to refresh the army, whiche offer was gladly accepted of the Danes for that they had bene in great penurie of sustenaunce many dayes before.

However, the provisions sent to the enemy were poisoned with "the juyce of Mekilwort beries" ("Mekilwort" is "Deadly nightshade," JJ), which

> spred in suche sorte through all the partes of their bodies, that they were in the ende brought into a fast dead sleepe, that in maner it was unpossible to awake them. Then foorthwith Duncane sent unto Makbeth, commaunding him with

all diligence to come and set upon the enimies, being in easie pointe to be overcome. Makbeth making no delay came with his people to the place, where his
enimies were lodged, & first killing the watche, afterwards entred the campe,
and made suche slaughter on all sides without any resistance, that it was a wonderfull mater to behold, for the Danes were so heavy of sleepe, that the most
parte of them were slayne & never styrred: other that were awakened eyther by
the noyse or otherwayes foorth, were so amazed and dyzzie headed upon their
wakening, that they were not able to make any defence.

Shakespeare bypasses this episode because he wishes to introduce *Macbeth* as a soldier
who openly confronts his opponents in a fair fight, not as a sneaking assassin who cuts
men's throats as they sleep. Shakespeare therefore conflates *Sweno's* invasion with
Canute's. Holinshed reports that after *Sweno's* defeat

woorde was brought that a newe fleete of Danes was arrived at Kingcorne, sent
thyther by Canute king of England in revenge of his brothers Suenoes overthrow.
To resist these enimies, whiche were already landed, and busie in spoiling the
countrey, Makbeth and Banquho were sente with the kings authoritie, who having with them a convenient power, encountred the enimies, slewe parte of them,
and chased the other to their shippes.

(Holinshed is incorrect in stating that Sven II was the brother of Canute the Great,
who reigned from 1018–1036: *Sweno* was in fact Canute's nephew.)

69–70. ***Point against Point... lavish spirit.*** *Macbeth's Point* ("point of the sword,"
OED) was a match for *Sweno's Arme* ("Deeds or feats of arms," OED). At every *Point*
(moment), in every *Point* ("a deed of valour, an exploit," OED), *Macbeth* met *Sweno*
"point after point" ("directly, exactly, throughly," RC, s.v. "Ponctuellement"). *Macbeth's* valiant efforts "curbed" ("Restrained, stopped, repressed," RC, s.v. "Cohibé")
Sweno's lavish ("riotous, raging, unlawfull, contentious," JF, s.v. "Riottóso") *spirit*
("Courage," "hart, stomacke; valour, stoutnesse, bouldnesse, hardinesse, forwardnesse;
also, confidence, assurance," RC, s.v. "Courage").

Macbeth's "potency" is so great that his *Arme* ("Penis," FR) and *Point* ("penis...
with a hint at erection," GW) easily "curb" ("bend, bow," OED) *Sweno's* lavish ("Huge,
unmeasurable, immense, infinite, exceeding great; enormous," RC, s.v. "Desmesuré")
spirit ("penis erectus," FR). *Macbeth* easily puts down *Sweno's* "rebellion" ("phallic erection," GW, s.v. "rebel"; a "rebellion" is literally an "uprising").

73. ***Sweno, the Norwayes King.*** Norway and Denmark were united for a brief
period after Canute the Great conquered Norway in 1027. The two kingdoms remained
under the rule of a single sovereign until 1041, but properly *Sweno* (a.k.a. Sven II),
who became King of Denmark in 1047, was never *the Norwayes King* (see note: *Norweyan Lord*, line 37, above).

Holinshed was misinformed about the dates of *Sweno's* kingship, but he was correct in assuming Denmark and Norway to have been united in 1040, the year of the
Makdowald uprising (which explains why in Holinshed *the Norwayes King Sweno* leads
Danish troops). Shakespeare incorrectly labels *Sweno* as *the Norwayes King* because he
follows Holinshed, but Shakespeare deliberately changes the nationality of *Sweno's*
troops to prevent creating awkwardness between James I and his brother-in-law, the
visiting King Christian IV of Denmark (see notes: *three Witches*, I.i.2; and *Norweyan
Banners*, line 62, above).

74. ***composition.*** An "agreement, reconciliation, league, peace, made betweene
friends fallen out" (RC, s.v. "Appoinctement").

Nor would we deigne him buriall of his men,   [75]

Till he disbursed, at Saint *Colmes* ynch,

Ten thousand Dollars, to our generall use.

King.   No more that *Thane* of Cawdor shall deceive

Our Bosome interest: Goe pronounce his present death,

And with his former Title greet *Macbeth*.   [80]

Rosse.   Ile see it done.

King.   What he hath lost, Noble *Macbeth* hath wonne.

Exeunt.

75–76. ***buriall of his men... at Saint Colmes ynch.*** An *ynch* is "An island, generally one of a small size" (JJ, s.v. "Inch"). *Saint Colmes ynch* is "Inchcolm," a small island off the coast of *Fiffe* (see note: line 61, above). Like *Colmekill* (II.iv.46), one of the *Westerne Isles* (line 18, above), *Saint Colmes ynch* is named for the Irish missionary *Saint Colme* (a.k.a. "Saint Calum" or "Saint Columba," A.D. 521–597). According to Holinshed, after Canute's defeat the Danes

> that escaped and got once to theyr shippes, obtayned of Makbeth for a great summe of golde, that suche of theyr freendes as were slaine at this last bickering might be buried in Saint Colmes Inche. In memorie whereof, many olde Sepultures are yet in the sayde Inche, there to be seene graven with the armes of the Danes, as the maner of burying noble men still is, and heretofore hath bene used.

77. ***Ten thousand Dollars.*** "Dollar" was used for the "rigsdaler of Denmark" (OED), a form of currency also used in Norway. The dollar was unknown in *Sweno's* time, but it was in use when *Macbeth* was written. A contemporary account of Christian IV's 1606 visit to James I records that "The King of Denmark in his gifts... hath given in court 30,000 dollars" (Robert Folkestone Williams, *The Court and Times of James the First*, p. 67).

77. ***our generall use.*** I.e., for the use of the commonwealth (*generall* means "common, belonging to all," JF, s.v. "Universale").

78–79. ***No more that Thane... Our Bosome interest.*** The deceitful *Thane of Cawdor* managed to "Insinuate" ("to put in his bosom, to put in ones mind covertly, to wind, steal, or convey himself into, to creep by little into ones favor," RC, q.v.) himself into *Duncane's Bosome* ("inward mind, or thought; the height, or depth of the heart, or affection," RC, s.v. "Sein"). *Duncane* is wiser now, and he vows that *that Thane of Cawdor shall No more* deceive his *Bosome* ("Intimate, confidential," OED) *interest* ("feeling of concern," OED). (Nevertheless, *Duncane* will allow himself to be deceived by the next *Thane of Cawdor*, *Macbeth*; see note: *An absolute Trust*, I.iv.19.)

79. ***pronounce.*** To *pronounce* is (a) to "declare, to proclaime" (TT, s.v. "Ostendo"); and (b) "to judge or give sentence" (TT, s.v. "Prōnuncio").

79. ***present.*** Immediate.

80. ***with his former Title greet Macbeth.*** "There is good evidence, in Shakespeare's time and later, that 'great' in one type of speech had the pronunciation normally given to 'greet'" (HH, p. 232). *Duncane* commands *Rosse* to both *greet* (salute) and "great" ("make great," "aggrandize," OED) *Macbeth* with the *Title Thane of Cawdor*.

81. ***Ile see it done.*** *Rosse* will not personally witness the *Thane of Cawdor's* execution, but he will "see to it" ("ensure by supervision or vigilance that something shall be done," OED, s.v. "see"). Cf. I.iii.123–124.

82. ***What he hath lost... wonne.*** Cf. I.i.6.

Act I, scene iii

Scena Tertia.   [1]

Thunder. Enter the three Witches.   [I.iii.1]

{*Witch 1.*}   Where hast thou beene, Sister?

{*Witch 2.*}   Killing Swine.

{*Witch 3.*}   Sister, where thou?   [5]

{*Witch 1.*}   A Saylors Wife had Chestnuts in her Lappe,

And mouncht, & mouncht, and mouncht:

Give me, quoth I.

Aroynt thee, Witch, the rumpe-fed Ronyon cryes.

Notes I.iii.

3. **Where hast thou beene.** In Ben Jonson's witchcraft-themed work, *The Masque of Queenes*, Jonson explains that "Amongst our vulgar witches, the honor of Dame... is given with a kinde of preeminence to some speciall one at their meetings." Jonson further explains that witches are customarily "examined, either by the Divell, or their Dame, at their meetings, of what mischiefe they have done; and what they can conferre to a future hurt." Jonson's own "dame" commands her coven to "relate me, what you have sought, / Where you have beene, and what you have brought."

As the text of *Macbeth* stands, the *Witches'* "dame" is the goddess *Hecat* (III.v.3). However, it is possible that Shakespeare originally conceived the *three Witches* not as mortal women but as the Three Fates or as demons in that form (see notes: *we three*, I.i.3; and *Pale Heccats*, II.i.67). The *Witches* therefore relate their misdeeds not to their "dame" but to each other.

4. **Killing Swine.** *Killing Swine* and other livestock was a charge frequently leveled against (so-called) *Witches*. In *Select Cases of Conscience Touching Witches and Witchcrafts*, John Gaule asks

What Conscience then can here bee in common people that are carryed away not onely with suspition but superstition? Every poore and peevish olde Creature (such is their Ignorance and Uncharitablenesse) cannot but fall under their suspition, nay their infamous exprobation; every Accident, (more then ordinary) every disease whereof they neither understand the Cause, nor are acquainted with the Symptomes must bee suspected for witch-craft. His Cow or his Hog, cannot be strangely taken, but straight it must bee reckoned and rumored for bewitcht.

Witches also supposedly possessed a lust for murder, so the *Swine* here spoken of may not be porcine but human. Cf. and see notes: *sticking place*, I.vii.72; and *Swinish*, I.vii.79.

6. ***A Saylors Wife had Chestnuts in her Lappe.*** The *Saylors Wife* ate the *Chestnuts* (a reputed aphrodisiac, GW2, s.v. "nut") *in her Lappe* in hopes of having *Chestnuts* ("testicles," GW2, s.v. "nut") *in her Lappe* (vagina; see note: *lapt*, I.ii.67). Cf. and see note: *rumpe-fed Ronyon*, line 9, below.

7. ***mouncht.*** To "munch" is "to eat greedily in a corner" (RC, s.v. "Lopiner"); to "munchion alone in a corner" is "to conceale, obscure, or spend privately his goods, good things, or parts, that others may have no part of them with them" (RC, s.v. "Manger son pain en son sac"). Cf. *rumpe-fed*, line 9, below.

9. ***Aroynt thee.*** *Aroynt* means "apparently: Avaunt! Begone!" (OED). OED gives the etymology as unknown, but so "rynt" is "To make way, give place, stand aside" (OED). John Ray's 1674 *Collection of English Words not Generally Used* has "Rynt ye: By your leave, stand handsomly. As Rynt you witch, quoth Besse Locket to her Mother, Proverb, Chesh[ire]," and Ray's *Correspondence* further makes clear that the word was used as a command to both *Witches* and livestock: "*to Ray, Ryndta*, used to cows to make them give way" (q.v.).

The "interchange of *l, n, r* is found in several English dialects" (HH, p. 214), so *Aroynt* possibly derives from Old French "aloigner" or Anglo-French "aloyner," which means "to remove far off" (HH, pp. 216–217). Given the fluidity of the letters l, n, and r, it is also possible that *Aroynt* derives from "anoint," especially considering that *Witches* "When they are to be transported from place to place, they use to anoynt themselves, and sometimes, the things they ride on" (Ben Jonson, *The Masque of Queenes*). Cf. the spelling of "are ointed" in Richard Stanyhurst's 1582 translation of Virgil's *Aeneid*: "his temples with black swart poyson ar oyncted."

It should also be noted that the spelling *Aroynt* might represent a dialectal pronunciation and/or variant spelling of the verb "errant," which means "To travel abroad" (OED). Cf. the spelling of "baily errants" as "bayly arauntes" in William Tyndale's *The Christen rule.*

9. ***rumpe-fed Ronyon.*** The *Saylors Wife* is a *rumpe-fed Ronyon* ("A term of contempt to a woman," DPF) in that she is (a) decrepit (*Ronyon* "is the French *rogneux* [scabby, mangy]," DPF); (b) well fed (cf. John Florio's definition of "Gropponeg-giáreto" in *Queen Anna's New World of Words*: "to pick for good morsels, to feede on rumps"); (c) so well *fed* that she is "well buttockt, broad arst, bumbasted about the bumme" (JF, s.v. "Naticuta"); (d) *fed* (sexually gratified, GW, s.v. "feed") by a *Ronyon* ("male organ," OED) in her *rumpe* ("vagina," GW); and/or (e) sexually *fed* in her *rumpe* ("Posteriors," EC) and *Ronyon* ("the bottom, the fundament," TR). Cf. the Earl of Rochester's "[Satyr]": "the Rump-fed-Runts shall mourn, / Till slimey Cunt, to grimey A-se hole turn."

Her Husband's to Aleppo gone, Master o'th' *Tiger*.   [10]

But in a Syve Ile thither sayle,

And like a Rat without a tayle,

Ile doe, Ile doe, and Ile doe.

{*Witch 2.*}   Ile give thee a Winde.

{*Witch 1.*}   Th'art kinde.   [15]

{*Witch 3.*}   And I another.

{*Witch 1.*}   I my selfe have all the other,

---

10. ***Her Husband's to Aleppo gone... th' Tiger.*** *Aleppo* (a major trading center in Syria located about seventy miles inland of the Mediterranean Sea) was a common destination for many English merchants. *Th' Tiger* was a fairly common ship's name, but Shakespeare may have chosen the appellation because *th' Tiger* is "a striped/stripped (castrated) animal; symbol for the... eunuch" (FR). Cf. and sea note: *Ile dreyne him drie as Hay,* line 21, below.

10. ***Master.*** Captain.

11. ***in a Syve Ile thither sayle.*** The *Syve* (in modern spelling, "sieve"), like the broom, is a traditional means of transportation for *Witches.* These lines were probably inspired by James Carmichael's 1592 *Newes from Scotland,* which Shakespeare doubt-less read as "research" while writing *Macbeth.* Carmichael's tract describes alleged witches' attacks on Shakespeare's patron, King James, including a failed attempt "to bewitch and drowne his Majestie in the sea comming from Denmarke." Carmichael states that one of the accused witches, Agnis Tompson, confessed under torture that

at the time when his Majestie was in Denmarke, she… tooke a Cat and chris-
tened it, and afterward bound to each parte of that Cat, the cheefest partes of
a dead man, and severall joynts of his bodie, and that in the night following the
saide Cat was conveied into the midst of the sea by all these witches sayling in
their riddles or Cives as is aforesaide, and so left the saide Cat right before the
Towne of Lieth in Scotland: this doone, there did arise such a tempest in the
Sea, as a greater hath not beene seene: which tempest was the cause of the per-
rishing of a Boate or vessell comming over from the towne of Brunt Iland to the
towne of Lieth, wherein was sundrye Jewelles and riche giftes, which should
have been presented to the now Queen of Scotland, at her Majesties comming
to Lieth.

Also see note: *Ship-mans Card*, line 20, below.

    12–13. *like a Rat without a tayle… Ile doe.* In order to wreak havoc on *th' Tiger*,
the *First Witch* plans to transform herself into *a Rat without a tayle* (i.e., "a cunning
old rat that hath before been catch'd by the taile in a trap," Richard Watson, *Akolouthos*).
In *The Observations of Sir Richard Hawkins, Kt., in his Voyage into the South Sea*, A.D.
1593, Hawkins makes clear the extreme menace that *a Rat* poses to a seafaring
vessel:

> When I came to the sea, it was not suspected that I had a ratt in my shippe; but
> with the bread in caske, which we transported out of the Hawke, and the going
> to and againe of our boates unto our prise, though we had diverse catts and used
> other preventions, in a small time they multiplyed in such a maner as is incred-
> ible. It is one of the generall calamities of all long voyages, and would bee care-
> fully prevented as much as may bee. For besides that which they consume of the
> best victuals, they eate the sayles; and neither packe nor chest is free from their
> surprises. I have knowne them to make a hole in a pipe water, and saying the
> pumpe, have put all in feare, doubting least some leake had beene sprung upon
> the ship. Moreover, I have heard credible persons report, that shippes have beene
> put in danger by them to be sunke, by a hole made in the bulge. All which is
> easily remedied at the first, but if once they be somewhat increased, with difficulty
> they are to be destroyed.

    As *a Rat without a tayle* (i.e., a female rat, one *without a tayle*: "Penis," EP), the
First Witch will *doe* ("copulate," EP), and *doe*, and *doe*, thus reproducing many more
rats to inflict destruction on the ship. The *First Witch* and her *Rat* offspring will imperil
both the *Master's* physical and financial well being, for "when Coffers, Packs, or Pipes,
and other marked Commodities or Goods are delivered close packed or sealed, and
afterwards shall be received open and loose, the Master is to be charged for it… he
must also answer for the harm which Rats do in a Ship to any Merchandise for want
of a Cat" (Gerard Malines, *Consuetudo, vel, Lex Mercatoria*).

    14–17. *Ile give thee a Winde… the other.* Because *Witches* possess the power to
raise winds (see note: *Thunder and Lightning*, I.i.2), "Witches for gold will sell a man
a wind" (Thomas Nashe, *Summers last will and Testament*). The *Second Witch* gener-
ously gives the *First Witch a Winde*, and the *Third Witch another*, probably in the form
of a *Winde* ("a flatus," FR) from the *other* ("arse," FR; "anus," JH, s.v. "other places").
Cf. and see notes: *Ports*, *blow*, and *Quarters*, lines 18–19 below; and Ben Jonson's
Bartholomew Fayre: "The Wind-mill blowne downe by the witches fart."

    14–15. *Winde… kinde.* *Winde* rhymed with *kinde* in Shakespeare's time (HK,
p. 493), although neither word was pronounced exactly as it is today.

And the very Ports they blow,

All the Quarters that they know,

I'th' Ship-mans Card.   [20]

Ile dreyne him drie as Hay:

Sleepe shall neyther Night nor Day

Hang upon his Pent-house Lid:

He shall live a man forbid:

Wearie Sev'nights, nine times nine,   [25]

Shall he dwindle, peake, and pine:

17–20. *I my selfe have all the other… Ship-mans Card.* The *First Witch* receives two winds from her sister *Witches* (lines 14–16, above). She herself has *all the other* winds that she needs to raise a storm, including *the Quarters* (i.e., "quarter wind[s]": "side wind[s]; as North-west, Southeast, &c.," RC, s.v. "Vent collateral"). The *First Witch* will cause these winds to *blow* (buffet) *the very* (suitable or requisite) *Ports* (harbors, save-havens) from *All the Quarters* ("the four cardinal points of the compass; each of these four points," OED) *that they know I'th Ship-man's Card* (i.e., "A sea-card, wherein all the quarter winds, or travers boords, are delineated," RC, s.v. "Carte arrumée"). Thus, she will effectively keep the *Tiger* out at sea. Cf. the proverb "No one can blow him to good whom destinie will not harbour" (RC, s.v. "Nul vent ne fait pour celuy qui n'a point de port destiné").

A "port" is also "an aperture in the side of a ship for a cannon; a porthole" (OED). The *Witches* will apparently *blow* ("cast a savour or smell," TT, s.v. "Spīro") "winds" (farts; see note: *Winde*, line 14, above) from their *Ports* ("port-hole[s]": "fundament[s]," F&H) and *Quarters* ("hindquarters," OED).

In crafting *The Tragedie of Macbeth*, Shakespeare primarily drew on two episodes in Holinshed: (1) the murder of King *Duncane* I by *Macbeth*; and (2) the murder of King Duff of Alba (930–966) by his retainer Donwalde. In neither story do *Witches* curse a ship, so Shakespeare probably drew inspiration from James I's personal experiences as reported in James Carmichael's *Newes from Scotland*. Carmichael relates the confession of Geillis Duncane, one of the *Witches* whose curse was supposedly the

> cause that the Kinges Majesties Ship at his comming foorth of Denmarke, had a contrary winde to the rest of his Ships, then being in his companye, which thing was most strange and true, as the Kings Majestie acknowledgeth, for when the rest of the Shippes had a faire and good winde, then was the winde contrarye and altogither against his Majestie: and further the saide witche declared,

that his Majestie had never come safelye from the Sea, if his faith had not prevailed above their ententions.

(Such spells seem ridiculous today, but witchcraft was once a serious crime. Of the witches accused of cursing James' ships, Carmichael reports that "some are alreadye executed, the rest remaine in prison, to receive the doome of Judgement at the Kings majesties will and pleasure.")

21. *Ile dreyne him drie as Hay.* The tormenting of the sea-captain is adapted from Holinshed's account of the bewitching of King Duff, in which King Duff's body was "brought into such a decay & consumption (so as there remayned unneth [i.e., "scarcely"] any thing upon him save skin & bone:)… yet could he not sleepe in the night time by any provocations that could be devised, but still fell into exceeding sweates, which by no meanes might be restreyned."

The first curse that the *First Witch* inflicts on the *Master* is to *dreyne* ("exhaust, empty," "wast, consume, or sucke up the moisture of," RC, s.v. "Espuiser") *him* until he is *drie* ("withered, which hath loste his naturall humour," TT, s.v. "Arĭdus"). This will make him "drayned of (naturall) moisture" ("Languishing, drooping, pining, faint, failing in strength," "deprived of vigor," RC, s.v. "Langoureux").

As the *First Witch's* real object is to punish the *Master's* wife, she will also *dreyne* ("empty of semen," GW) the *Master* and make him *drie* ("barren, sterile, unfruitful," OED). *Witches* were commonly accused of inflicting impotence: "We know for certain that magicians, witches, and conjurers, have by charmes so bound some, that they could not have to do with their wives; and have made others so impotent, as if they had bin gelt or made eunuches" (Ambroise Paré, *The Workes of that famous Chirurgion Ambrose Parey*). Also see note: *Beards*, line 51, below.

22–23. *Sleepe… his Pent-house Lid.* The second punishment inflicted on the *Master* is sleep deprivation. The *First Witch* vows that *Sleepe shall neyther Night nor Day Hang upon* (attach, cling to) *his Pent-house Lid* ("a heavy or overhanging eyelid," OED; the sense derives from *Pent-house* meaning "The extending or jutting of a thing out, or over," TT, s.v. "Prominentia"; "a downe-hanging," JF, s.v. "Pendice").

24. *a man forbid.* The *First Witch* "forbode[s]" ("soothsay[s]," "foretell[s]," "foreshew[s]," "divine[s]," JF, s.v. "Augurare") that the *Master* will be *a man forbid* (i.e., "a forbodin fellow, an unhappy fellow… one lying under an interdict," JJ, s.v. "forbodin"). The *First Witch* will *forbid* ("barre or keepe away," JB, s.v. "Interdict") the *Master* from landing in port. As *a man forbid* ("la[id] under a ban, curse, interdict," OED), the *Master* will be banished from the land like *a man* under an "interdiction" ("banishment, or outlawrie, of a man, proclaimed," RC, s.v. "Bannie").

25. *Sev'nights, nine times nine.* Sev'nights, nine times nine equates to eighty-one weeks, or one year, four months, and seven days. As the product of three times three, *nine* is an especially potent magical number (see note: *we three*, I.i.3). *Nine* was also considered an inherently evil number: it symbolized failure and defect because it fell short of ten, the Pythagorean "perfect" number (Christopher Butler, *Number Symbolism*, p. 35).

26. *dwindle.* To "shrink, waste away, decline"; also "To shrink with fear" (OED).

26. *peake.* The *Saylors Wife* has "piqued" ("wound[ed] the pride of, irritate[d], or offend[ed]," OED) the *First Witch*, so the *Master* will *peake* ("flag or fail in health and spirits," "languish, waste away," "become sickly or emaciated," OED).

26. *pine.* To "suffer," "to tyre, to linger, to languish, to carke and care, to toyle and moyle both with bodie and minde" (JF, s.v. "Stentare").

Though his Barke cannot be lost,

Yet it shall be Tempest-tost.

Looke what I have.

{*Witch 2.*}   Shew me, shew me.   [30]

{*Witch 1.*}   Here I have a Pilots Thumbe,

Wrackt, as homeward he did come.

Drum within.

{*Witch 3.*}   A Drumme, a Drumme:

Macbeth doth come.   [35]

----

27. **his Barke cannot be lost.** Despite her malediction, the *First Witch* knows that the *Master's Barke* ("a swyfte lyttelle shyppe," TE, s.v. "Lembus") *cannot be lost*, which suggests that the *three Witches* are (or impersonate) the Three Fates or Destinies. The *First Witch* cannot kill the *Master* at sea because he has been pre-ordained another death, and "whatsoever dependeth of destenie or the divine ordinance, cannot be avoided, albeit it be foretold" (Matthieu Coignet, *Politique Discourses upon Trueth and Lying*). Also see notes: *we three*, I.i.3; and *weyward Sisters*, line 36, below.

If she could, the *First Witch* would also cause the *Master's Barke* (foreskin, JA, p. 74) to *be lost*, but, alas, she cannot effect this either (see notes: *a Pilots Thumbe*, line 31, below; and *the frame of things dis-joynt*, III.ii.22).

31–32. **a Pilots Thumbe… homeward he did come.** *Witches* supposedly dismembered corpses for use in their spells (see notes: *in a Syve Ile thither sayle*, line 11, above; and *Grewell*, IV.i.34), so the *First Witch* probably plans to use the *Pilots Thumbe* in her charm against the *Master*. The *Thumbe*, which has many ancient magical associations, signifes "Power — a meaning derived from the thumb's key role in manual skill and gripping strength, and from its phallic symbolism" (JT). Charms to fend off *Witches*, ghosts, and demons were made by grasping the *Thumbe*, and supposedly a *Witch's* pact with the Devil was "written with the bloud of the left thumbe" (Thomas Heywood, *The Hierarchie of the blessed Angells*).

Perhaps the *First Witch* has acquired not the *Pilots Thumbe* (finger) but his *Thumbe* (penis, GW2). This was *Wrackt* ("separate[d] by force," OED, s.v. "rack") *as he* "racked" (copulated, GW2) and *did come* (with play on *come* as orgasm) *homeward* (where "home" means the "Vulva," FR, and/or "to compel the sexual spasm," F&H). Such a charm would be especially useful in inflicting impotence (cf. and see note: *dreyne him drie as Hay*, line 21, above).

34. *A Drumme.* *Macbeth* and *Banquoh* are traveling alone (see note: *Macbeth doth come*, line 35, below), so the *Drumme* cannot belong to their army. Perhaps the witches themselves play the *Drumme* as part of their invocation. In *Pandaemonium*, Richard Bovet describes the *Drumme's* magical use by witches of "Lappland":

> Amongst the many ways they have to call the Spirits to their Attendance, none is more in use then that of a Magical Drum they have, and in great esteem amongst them... When one of these Drums is beaten (with the addition of some Diabolical Ceremonies, and Incantations,) the Spirit presently attends, and either answers to what is demanded, out of the Drum, or else appears in some form in a place assigned him.

It is also possible that the noise of the *Drumme* is diabolical, for devils were sometimes the cause "that Drums and Trumpets have been heard when neither Drummer nor Trumpeter was near" (R.T., *The Opinion of Witchcraft Vindicated*). That the sound of the *Drumme* is supernatural is evidenced by the fact that it provides the beat to which the *Witches* dance (lines 38–40, below). Also cf. and see note: *Peace*, line 41, below.

35. *Macbeth doth come.* The subsequent events of this scene are drawn directly from Holinshed, who relates that

> It fortuned as Makbeth & Banquho journeyed towarde Fores, where the king as then lay, they went sporting by the way togither without other companie, save only themselves, passing through the woodes and fieldes, when sodenly in the middes of a launde [i.e., "clearing"], there met them .iii. women in straunge & ferly [i.e., "astonishing"] apparell, resembling creatures of an elder worlde, whom when they attentively behelde, wondering much at the sight. The first of them spake & sayde: All hayle Makbeth Thane of Glammis (for he had lately entred into that dignitie and office by the death of his father Synel.) The .ii. of them said: Hayle Makbeth Thane of Cawder: but the third sayde: All Hayle Makbeth that hereafter shall be king of Scotland.
>
> Then Banquho, what maner of women (saith he) are you, that seeme so litle favourable unto me, where as to my fellow here, besides highe offices, yee assigne also the kingdome, appointyng foorth nothing for me at all? Yes sayth the firste of them, wee promise greater benefites unto thee, than unto him, for he shall reygne in deede, but with an unluckie ende: neyther shall he leave any issue behinde him to succeede in his place, where contrarily thou in deede shalt not reygne at all, but of thee those shall be borne whiche shall governe the Scottishe kingdome by long order of continuall discent. Herewith the foresayde women vanished immediatly out of theyr sight. This was reputed at the first but some vayne fantasticall illusion by Makbeth and Banquho, in so muche that Banquho woulde call Makbeth in jeste kyng of Scotland, and Makbeth againe would call him in sporte likewise, the father of many kings. But afterwards the common opinion was, that these women were eyther the weird sisters, that is (as ye would say) the Goddesses of destinie, or els some Nimphes or Feiries, endewed with knowledge of prophesie by their Nicromanticall science, bicause every thing came to passe as they had spoken. For shortly after, the Thane of Cawder being condemned at Fores of treason against the king committed, his landes, livings and offices were given of the kings liberalitie unto Makbeth.

All {Witches}.   The weyward Sisters, hand in hand,

               Posters of the Sea and Land,

               Thus doe goe, about, about,

               Thrice to thine, and thrice to mine,

               And thrice againe, to make up nine.   [40]

               Peace, the Charme's wound up.

Enter Macbeth and Banquo.   [I.iii.2]

Macb.   So foule and faire a day I have not seene.

Banquo.   How farre is't call'd to Soris? What are these,

               So wither'd, and so wilde in their attyre,   [45]

               That looke not like th' Inhabitants o'th' Earth,

               And yet are on't? Live you, or are you aught

               That man may question? you seeme to understand me,

               By each at once her choppie finger laying

               Upon her skinnie Lips: you should be Women,   [50]

36–37. **The weyward Sisters... Sea and Land.** *Weyward* is a variant spelling of "weird" ("Fate, destiny," JJ) which reflects the word's pronunciation in Scotland and the North of England (cf. "you look like one o'the Scottish wayward sisters," Richard Brome, *The late Lancashire Witches*). Although these three women exhibit stereotypical characteristics of mortal *Witches*, they are the "Weird Sisters" ("the Fates," JJ) or demons in that form (cf. and see notes: *we three*, I.i.3; and *Pale Heccats*, II.i.67). The *Sisters* ("the fatal or three sisters, the Fates or Parcæ," OED) are known to be both *weyward* ("Perverse," "unjust," OED) and *weyward* ("Unruly, Masterless," ND, s.v. "Resty";

see note: *his Barke cannot be lost,* line 27, above). The *Sisters* are also *weyward* ("weird": "of the eye: Perverted," OED) in that they can exert malignant influence by means of the "evil eye" (HH, p. 236; cf. Matthew 6:23: "But if thine eye be evil," given in the 1382 Wycliffe Bible as "but if thin iye be weiward"; also see note: *filthie ayre,* I.i.13). As *Posters* (swift travelers) *of the Sea and Land,* the *Sisters* are also "wayward" (an apheutic form of "awayward" meaning "Of motion: Away," OED).

36–38. **hand in hand... Thus doe goe, about.** The *Witches* join *hand in hand* and dance *about,* which means (a) "in a circular course" (OED); and (b) "So as to face in the opposite way; from front to back or back to front" (OED). In Ben Jonson's *Masque of Queenes,* the witches dance "ABout, about, and about, / Till the Mist arise, and the Lights flie out." Jonson's marginal note explains that witches "at their meetings, do all things contrary to the custom of Men, dancing back to back, and hip to hip, their hands joined, and making their circles backward, to the left hand, with strange phantastick motions of their heads, and bodies."

41. **Peace, the Charme's wound up.** During their dance, the *Witches* "winde up" ("wheele or turne round," JF, s.v. "Rótolare") until their *Charme's wound up,* which means (a) "set in readiness for action" (OED); and (b) "close[d], conclude[d], terminate[d]" (OED).

All the *Witches* know that *the Charme's wound up,* so they have no need to call *Peace* to silence one another. Rather, *Peace* is their command to silence the sound of the supernatural *Drumme* that began to beat in line 33, above.

43. **So foule and faire a day.** Holinshed states that "The Scottes having wonne so notable a victory... caused... thankes to be given to almightie God, that had sent them so fayre a day over their enimies." Although the weather has been *foule* ("wet and stormy," OED), the *day* ("day of military conflict," OED) has been *faire* (successful, propitious). Cf. I.i.2–4 and 12; and I.ii.31–34.

44. **call'd.** Reckoned.

44. **Soris.** A probable typographical error for *Foris,* a town that lies about thirty miles east of Inverness. In Holinshed, *Macbeth* and *Banquo* are on their way to "Fores" when they meet the *Witches* (see note: *Macbeth doth come,* line 35, above).

45. **wither'd.** Wither'd means "growne full of wrinkles, wrinkled, shronken up" (JF, s.v. "Raggrinzato").

45. **wilde in their attyre.** See note: *Macbeth doth come,* line 35, above.

46. **th' Inhabitants o'th' Earth.** Th' Inhabitants o'th' Earth is a phrase which denotes "Not such as doe dwell and abide here on earth, for so the faithfull doe, but such as minde earthly thinges, beeing reprobate and unregenerate" (TW).

48. **question.** Talk to; converse with.

49–50. **each at once her choppie finger... Lips.** Skinnie Lips traditionally denote a treacherous disposition: "The lippes formed thinne, if the upper be turned and folding outwarde, and the same lose hanging: doe denote such a creature, to be a deceyver, subtile, and a theefe for the more part" (Thomas Hill, *The Contemplation of Mankinde*).

Possibly, *each* of the *Witches at once* (at the same time) lays *her choppie* (i.e., "chappy": "Full of chaps or clefts," OED) *finger Upon her skinnie Lips* to enjoin silence, but the gesture was also used to "intimate we know somewhat, which neverthelesse we will not utter" (John Bulwer, *Chirologia*). Laying the *finger Upon* the *Lips* also warns against over-inquisitiveness: "the old Philosophers and wise men, very politickly caused to mould and pourtrait their gods with their *Fingers* upon their lips, to teach men (their adorers) not to be too curious enquirers after their nature" (ibid.).

And yet your Beards forbid me to interpret

That you are so.

Mac.   Speake if you can: what are you?

{*Witch 1.*}   All haile *Macbeth*, haile to thee *Thane* of Glamis.

{*Witch 2.*}   All haile *Macbeth*, haile to thee *Thane* of Cawdor.   [55]

{*Witch 3.*}   All haile *Macbeth*, that shalt be King hereafter.

Banq.   Good Sir, why doe you start, and seeme to feare

Things that doe sound so faire? i'th' name of truth

Are ye fantasticall, or that indeed

Which outwardly ye shew? My Noble Partner   [60]

You greet with present Grace, and great prediction

Of Noble having, and of Royall hope,

---

51. **Beards.** A woman with a beard was highly unlucky: "If thou meete a red man, and a bearded woman, greet them three myle of" (John Florio, *Florio His Firste fruites*). *Beards* were also a stereotypical feature of *Witches*, who were regarded as "hermaphrodites, ambisexuals, masculine women; castrators" (FR, s.v. "witch").

53. **Speake if you can.** The *Witches* do not *Speake* when questioned by *Banquo* (lines 47–48, above), but they immediately respond to *Macbeth's* command. The *Witches* can *looke into the Seedes of Time* (line 64, below), so they already know that *Banquo* will not succumb to temptation as will *Macbeth*. Cf. and see notes: *why doe you start*, line 57, below; *prediction*, line 61, below; and *He will not be commanded*, IV.i.90.

54. **All haile.** To *All haile* is "to greete, to salute, to recommind," "to bid good morrow or god speede, to do reverence, to sende commendations" (JF, s.v. "Salutare").

57. **why doe you start.** It was believed that "Prophecie proceedeth onelie of GOD: and the Devill hath no knowledge of things to come" (James I, *Dæmonologie*), so the *Witches'* prediction arises not from certain knowledge of pre-ordained events but from

Satan's ability to assess and nurture each man's aptitude for sin (see notes: *prediction*, line 61, below; *strange Intelligence*, line 82, below; *insane Root*, line 93, below; and *He knowes thy thought*, IV.i.82).

The *Witches'* words cause *Macbeth* to *start* ("To tremble, shrud, shrug, shiver, quake, extreamly, or upon an extreame feare," RC, s.v. "Tremousser") because they give voice to that which he himself has already considered: the murder of *Duncane* as a means of achieving sovereignty. *Macbeth's* guilty reaction reveals that his own sinful thoughts have already caused him to *start* ("desert or revolt from," OED) God, a lapse which allows Satan entrance into his heart, mind, and soul (see note: *fantasticall*, line 157, below). Early audiences would have viewed *Macbeth* as complicit in his own damnation, not as a victim of the Devil, "since it is most certaine, that God will not permit him so to deceive his own: but only such, as first wilfully deceives themselves, by running unto him, whome God then suffers to fall in their owne snares, and justlie permittes them to be illuded with great efficacy of deceit" (James I, *Dæmonologie*). As Thomas Nashe explains in *Pierce Penilesse his Supplication to the Divell*:

> although that divells be most mightie spirits, yet can they not hurt but permis-
> sively, or by some special dispensation: as when a man is falne into the state of
> an out-law, the lawe dispenseth with them that kils him, & the prince excludes
> him from the protection of a subject, so, when a man is a relaps from God and
> his lawes, God withdrawes his providence from watching over him, & autho-
> rizeth the devil, as his instrument, to assault him and torment him.

Tellingly, the innocent-minded *Banquo* exhibits a completely different reaction upon hearing the *Witches'* predictions. Cf. and see note: *cursed thoughts*, II.i.14.

57–58. feare... faire. *Feare* and *faire* "were often pronounced alike" (HK, p. 106).

58. Things that doe sound so faire. See note: *faire is foule*, I.i.12.

59. fantasticall. *Fantasticall* means "imaginary," "that never was, nor ever will be" (TB, s.v. "Chimerical").

60. shew. Appear.

60. Partner. A "companion" (TT, s.v. "Complex").

61. Grace. *Macbeth* will enjoy *Grace* ("a priviledge conferred," RC, s.v. "Octroy") and *Grace* (the "good opinion of men," RC, s.v. "air"), but *Banquo* will achieve *Grace* ("The free and eternall favour and good will of God," TW). Unlike *Macbeth*, *Banquo* will also achieve *Grace* (an "erect penis," FR). Cf. I.vii.29–30; II.iii.126–127; III.i.75–84; IV.i.126–153; IV.iii.255; and V.iii.29–30.

61. prediction. It was thought that the Devil had no power of *prediction* ("fore-telling, presaging," RC, q.v.; see note: *why do you start*, line 57, above), but he could trick men into believing that he did. As James I explains in *Dæmonologie*,

> as to the divelles foretelling of things to come, it is true that he knowes not all
> thinges future, but yet that he knowes parte... not that he hath any prescience,
> which is only proper to God: or yet knows anie thing by loking upon God, as
> in a mirrour (as the good Angels doe) he being for ever debarred from the favor-
> able presence & countenance of his creator, but only by one of these two meanes,
> either as being worldlie wise, and taught by an continuall experience, ever since
> the creation, judges by likelie-hood of things to come, according to the like
> that hath passed before, and the naturall causes, in respect of the vicissitude of
> all things worldly: Or else by Gods employing of him in a turne, and so fore-
> seene thereof.

That he seemes wrapt withall: to me you speake not.

If you can looke into the Seedes of Time,

And say, which Graine will grow, and which will not,   [65]

Speake then to me, who neyther begge, nor feare

Your favors, nor your hate.

{*Witch 1.*}   Hayle.

    {*Witch 2.*}   {*Witch 3.*}

    Hayle.   Hayle.   [70]

{*Witch 1.*}   Lesser than *Macbeth*, and greater.

{*Witch 2.*}   Not so happy, yet much happyer.

{*Witch 3.*}   Thou shalt get Kings, though thou be none:

    So all haile *Macbeth*, and *Banquo*.

{*Witch 1.*}   *Banquo*, and *Macbeth*, all haile.   [75]

Macb.   Stay you imperfect Speakers, tell me more:

    By *Sinells* death, I know I am *Thane* of Glamis,

    But how, of Cawdor? the *Thane* of Cawdor lives

    A prosperous Gentleman: And to be King,

    Stands not within the prospect of beleefe,   [80]

63. ***wrapt.*** *Macbeth* is *wrapt* (beside himself; deeply buried in thought), for the *Witches'* suggestion is a "rap" ("a hard Knocking at a Door," ND; cf. lines 154–155, below) that prompts *Macbeth* to "rap" ("exchange or barter," FG) with the powers of darkness (cf. *Trade, and Trafficke,* III.v.7; and *palter,* V.vii.71). Consequently, *Macbeth* will be "rapped" ("curse[d]," FG, s.v. "rap") and "rapped" ("ruined"; also "knocked out of time," FG; cf. and see note: *What is the night,* III.iv.161).

63. ***withall.*** *Withall* was formerly substituted for "with" in "postposition, esp. at the end of a relative clause" (OED).

64–65. ***the Seedes of Time... which will not.*** As in the biblical parable of the sower (Matthew 13:3–8), *Seedes* are "Symbolic of latent, non-manifest forces, or of the mysterious potentialities the presence of which, sometimes unsuspected, is the justification for hope. These potentialities also symbolize the mystic Centre — the non-apparent point which is the irradiating origin of every branch and shoot of the great Tree of the World" (JC). *Banquo* hopes that the *Witches can looke into the Seedes* (undeveloped potentialities) *of Time* yet to come *And say, which Graine will grow, and which will not.*

The *Witches* predict (lines 68–75, below) that the *Seedes* ("semen," OED) of *Banquo* planted in the *Graine* ("vagina," GW2; literally "The fork of the body," OED) will in *Time* ("The period of gestation," OED) *grow* ("In pregnancy," EC), thus producing royal *Seedes* ("Offspring, progeny," OED) who will claim the "sede" ("seat": "The throne of a particular kingdom," OED).

71. ***Lesser than... and greater.*** Of both lower and higher rank. Cf. *more and lesse,* V.iv.20.

72. ***happy.*** Both "content" and "fortunate."

73. ***get.*** Beget, engender.

76. ***imperfect.*** *Imperfect* means (a) "uncompleat," "unfinished, insufficient" (RC, s.v. "Imperfaict"); (b) unknown or unknowable (cf. and see note: *perfect,* III.i.160); and/or (c) "evil" (OED). The *Witches'* speech also predicts that *Macbeth* will be "an unperfect man" ("halfe a man, a womanish fellow," "an eunuch, one that is guelded," JF, s.v. "Semiviro") and thus *im-* (a prefix meaning "not") *perfect* (i.e., without "perfection": the ability to "achieve orgasm and ejaculate," JA, pp. 143–144).

77. ***Sinells death.*** Holinshed says that *Macbeth's* father was named *Sinell* (see notes: *Cousin,* I.ii.30; and *Macbeth doth come,* line 35, above), but his name was actually "Findlaech" (see note: *Macbeths Wife,* I.v.2).

80. ***prospect.*** A *prospect* is (a) "A place from whence one may see farre" (HC); (b) "a (limitted) view, or survey" (RC, s.v. "Prospective"); (c) "A mental picture or vista, esp. of something future or expected" (OED); and (d) "Forethought; consideration or knowledge of something in the future" (OED).

No more then to be Cawdor. Say from whence

You owe this strange Intelligence, or why

Upon this blasted Heath you stop our way

With such Prophetique greeting?

Speake, I charge you.   [85]

Witches vanish.   [I.iii.3]

Banq.   The Earth hath bubbles, as the Water ha's,

And these are of them: whither are they vanish'd?

Macb.   Into the Ayre: and what seem'd corporall,

Melted, as breath into the Winde.   [90]

Would they had stay'd.

Banq.   Were such things here, as we doe speake about?

Or have we eaten on the insane Root,

That takes the Reason Prisoner?

81–82. *from whence You owe this strange Intelligence.* Early audiences would
have assumed that the *Witches owe* their *strange* ("woonderfull, marvellous," JF, s.v. "Mira-
bile"; also "Harsh to the taste, bitter," JJ) *Intelligence* ("Understanding"; also "private
notice of occurrences given," RC, q.v.) to Satan. Cf. TB's definition of "Divination":

a presage or foretelling of things to come… which hath in former times been prac-
tised by wicked spirits in Oracles and Answers given by them in Idols, is at this
day sometime seen in possessed persons, who by suggestion of the Devil may fore-
tel things to come, and this is but a Natural Divination: For though to us it seem
miraculous, because of our ignorance in the causes and courses of things, yet in
those spirits it is but natural, who by their long experience and great observation,
besides the knowledge of secrets in nature, and their quick intelligence from all
places, are able to fore-see much more, then we by nature can.

Also see notes: *why doe you start,* line 57, above; *prediction,* line 61 above; and line 120,
below.

84. **Prophetique.** "Propheticall; prophecying; of a Prophet; belonging to a prophecie" (RC, q.v.).

87–88. **The Earth hath bubbles... these are of them.** In pronouncing the *Witches* to be *of The bubbles of The Earth*, *Banquo* hints at their wicked nature. Cf. Thomas Adams' *The Forest of Thorns*:

> As if good works were brought forth like children, not without pain and travail: evil works [are] but cast out like froth or scum; as easily vented as invented. Therefore the earth is said *ebullire*, to bubble or boil out such things as mere excretions. Our proverb says, An evil weed grows apace... The basest things are ever most plentiful.

Shakespeare's contemporaries believed that all material things in the universe, including sentient beings, were comprised of "The Fire, Ayre, Water, Earth, called Elements, because they be the beginning whereof other visible Creatures are compounded" (TW). Air was considered the proper element of *Witches* and demons because the Devil is "the prince and the power of the aire, the spirit that now worketh in the children of disobedience" (Ephesians 2:2). Thus, the *Witches* appropriately vanish into a "bubble" (literally "a quantity of air or gas occluded within a liquid," OED). Cf. I.i.13; and cf. and see notes: *Thunder, Lightning, or in Raine*, I.i.4; lines 88–90, below; and IV.i.173.

87. **ha's.** The spelling of "has" as *ha's* occurs in the Folio text of *Macbeth* sixteen times, while "has" occurs only twice (I.vii.35 and III.iv.100). The spelling *ha's* might be an indicator of dialect, here specifically Scots, for it also occurs in the speech of the Welsh *Evans* in *The Merry Wives of Windsor*; the Welsh *Fluellen* in *Henry V*; and the Gloucestershire native *Justice Silence* in *2 Henry IV*.

88–90. **vanish'd... Into the Ayre... the Winde.** Although the *Witches* seem *corporall* ("that hath a bodie," TT, s.v. "Corpŏrālis"), their manner of departure suggests that they may not be mortal *Witches* who travel by "flying in the air" (RS). They may instead be elemental spirits "of air... because they vanish away so suddenly" (RS). Elemental spirits were thought to be "meerly composed of the most spiritual part of the Elements: And when they are worn out, they return into their proper essence or primary quality again; as Ice when it is resolved into Water... They... have power sometimes to make great commotions in the Air, and in the Clowds, and also to cloath themselves with visible bodies, out of the four Elements" (RS). Also see note: *Thunder, Lightning, or in Raine*, I.i.4.

93. **eaten of the insane Root.** If *eaten*, many a *Root* (including Hemlock, Nightshade, Mandrake, and Henbane, which was also termed "herba insana") was known to make a person *insane* ("unsound in body or mind," EC2). However, *Banquo* ponders the ingestion not of a physical *Root* but of sin, the *Root* (cause) of insanity: "all wickednesse is madness... 'tis the cause of madness, which is a judgement attending upon sin, as the effect follows the cause" (Thomas Hall, *A Practical and Polemical Commentary*). In "Of sinne, and of the kindes thereof," Heinrich Bullinger explains that

> sinne doth not spring from else where, but of our selves, that is to saye, of our corrupt judgement, depraved will, and the suggestion of the divell. For the roote of evil is yet remaining in our flesh by reason of that first corruption: which roote bringeth foorth a corrupt braunche in nature like unto it selfe: which braunch Satan even nowe, as hee hath done alwayes, doeth by his sleightes, subtilties, and lyes, cherish, tende, and tender as an impe of his owne planting.

Cf. and see notes: *can the Devill speake true*, line 120, below; *fantasticall*, line 157, below; *He knowes thy thought*, IV.i.82; and IV.iii.61–63.

Macb.	Your Children shall be Kings.	[95]
Banq.	You shall be King.	
Macb.	And *Thane* of Cawdor too: went it not so?	
Banq.	Toth' selfe-same tune and words: who's here?	

    Enter Rosse and Angus.   [I.iii.4]

Rosse.	The King hath happily receiv'd, *Macbeth*,	[100]
	The newes of thy successe: and when he reades	
	Thy personall Venture in the Rebels fight,	
	His Wonders and his Prayses doe contend,	
	Which should be thine, or his: silenc'd with that,	
	In viewing o're the rest o'th' selfe-same day,	[105]
	He findes thee in the stout Norweyan Rankes,	
	Nothing afeard of what thy selfe didst make	
	Strange Images of death, as thick as Tale	
	Can post with post, and every one did beare	
	Thy prayses in his Kingdomes great defence,	[110]
	And powr'd them downe before him.	

95–96. ***Your Children shall be Kings... King.*** When *Macbeth* was written, it was commonly believed that the Stuart kings (including Shakespeare's patron, James I of England and VI of Scotland) were part of "the originall line of those kings, whiche have discended from the foresayde Banquho... whiche have enjoyed the kingdome by so long continuaunce of discent, from one to an other, & that even unto these our dayes may be knowen from whence they had theyr first beginning" (RH). In reality, however, *Banquo's Children* ("Descendants," OED) were never *Kings* because *Banquo* never existed.

Banquo and his son *Fleance* make their first appearance in "history" in Hector Boece's 1526 *Scotorum Historiæ*, a work on which Holinshed drew heavily in compiling his chronicles. Boece, in an attempt to please his patron, King James V of Scotland, invented *Banquo* to lengthen and strengthen the pedigree of the Stuart line (through *Banquo's* fictitious grandson Walter, the supposed son of *Fleance* and the Welsh Princess Nesta, the Stuarts could claim descent from the legendary King Arthur). Also see notes: *Fleans, flye,* III.iii.29; and *A shew of eight Kings,* IV.i.138.

Both here and in lines 134–138, below, *Macbeth* and *Banquo* probably make light of the prophecy (see note: *Macbeth doth come,* line 35, above).

98. **Toth' selfe-same tune and words.** In Shakespeare's time, it was customary to set many different sets of lyrics to the *same tune*. Therefore, to speak *Toth' selfe-same tune and words* is to quote verbatim. Cf. "If you expect such elegant-seeming Paraphrases... I shall deceave your expectation: For, I have purposely avoyded those Descants, & confined by self to the grave, & simple Language of the Text" (George Wither, *The Psalms of David*).

100–104. **The King... silenc'd with that.** The King "contends" (struggles) with his feelings *when he reades* (considers or discovers) *Macbeth's personall* ("Corporall, bodilie," RC, s.v. "Corporel") *Venture* (hazard, risk) *in the Rebels fight* ("a battell, a skirmish, a conflict, a combat, a foughten field," JF, s.v. "Prelio"). *Prayses should be Macbeth's,* but *The King's Wonders* (feelings of wonder or astonishment) have *silenc'd* him ("stun[ned] him," FG).

106. **stout.** *Stout* can mean (a) "strong, mightie, sturdie, powrefull, puissant" (JF, s.v. "Poderoso"); (b) "audacious, daring, saucie, malapert, presumptuous; rash" (RC, s.v. "Audacieux"); and/or (c) "full of confidence, full of assurance, full of assurednesse" (RC, s.v. "Courageux").

107–108. **Nothing afeard... Strange Images of death.** *Strange death* is a term for sudden, violent or gruesome *death*. Cf. Sirach 19:5: "And that thy people might passe a wonderfull way: but they might find a strange death"; and OED's "strong death": "a violent or cruel death" (*Strange* is a variant spelling of "strong," OED). On the battlefield, *Macbeth* has created *Images* (visible manifestations, OED) *of Strange death,* but he is *Nothing afeard* (not at all afraid) of suffering such a *death* himself.

108–110. **as thick as Tale... Thy prayses.** *Macbeth's prayses* arrived *as thick* ("Occurring in quick succession," OED) *as Tale* ("a discourse, a newes, a message," JF, s.v. "Novella") could *post* ("runne," "gallop; make speed, hye apace, goe verie hastily; passe verie swiftly; runne on; proceed fast," RC, s.v. "Courir") *with post* ("a running poste or currier, or messenger," JF, s.v. "Posta"). Cf. "Some have the agility to ride Post, some the facility to run Post; some the dexterity to write Post, and some the ability to speak Post" (John Taylor, *The Great Eater of Kent*). Also cf. JF's entries for "Affoltare": "to presse, to thrust, to crowd, to heape, to thicken, to speake very thicke or fast" (q.v.); and JF's "Affoltata": "a hudling speech, a faste, thicke tolde tale" (q.v.).

111. **powr'd.** *Powr'd* is a variant spelling of "poured," which means (a) "To send (words, etc.) forth or out as in a stream" (OED); and (b) "to come or go in great numbers, continuously, or in rapid succession" (OED). Cf. *thick as Tale,* line 108, above.

Ang. Wee are sent,

To give thee from our Royall Master thanks,

Onely to harrold thee into his sight,

Not pay thee.   [115]

Rosse. And for an earnest of a greater Honor,

He bad me, from him, call thee *Thane* of Cawdor:

In which addition, haile most worthy *Thane*,

For it is thine.

Banq. What, can the Devill speake true?   [120]

Macb. The *Thane* of Cawdor lives:

Why doe you dresse me in borrowed Robes?

Ang. Who was the *Thane*, lives yet,

But under heavie Judgement beares that Life,

Which he deserves to loose.   [125]

Whether he was combin'd with those of Norway,

Or did lyne the Rebell with hidden helpe,

And vantage; or that with both he labour'd

In his Countreyes wracke, I know not:

But Treasons Capitall, confess'd, and prov'd,   [130]

Have overthrowne him.

114. ***harrold.*** A variant spelling of "herald," which means "to usher in" (OED).

116–118. ***for an earnest... addition.*** *For an earnest* ("A deposit in part of payment, to bind a bargain," FG) *of a greater Honor*, the *King* ordered *Rosse* (I.ii.78–80) to greet *Macbeth* with the *addition* ("any title given to a man beside his name which title sheweth his estate, trade, course of life, and also dwelling place," JB, q.v.) *Thane of Cawdor. Rosse's* calling *Macbeth* by the *addition* (title) of *Thane of Cawdor* is merely an *earnest* (down payment) for the *greater Honor* of *Macbeth's* actually becoming *Thane of Cawdor*. However, *Macbeth* probably misinterprets *Rosse's* words to mean that the *King* intends to name *Macbeth* his successor. Cf. and see notes: *Two Truths are told*, line 145, below; and *The Prince of Cumberland*, I.iv.50.

120. ***can the Devill speake true.*** The *Devill* dangles scraps of truth like bait, and *Macbeth* falls right into *the Devill's* trap. In *Of Ghosts and Spirits Walking By Night*, Ludwig Lavater warns that

> the Dyvell is a lyer, and is called by Christe, the father of lyes... That whiche he dothe he, doth it to this ende, that he may purchase credite unto his words, and that he might the better thrust other things upon men, and bring and drive them into sundry erroures, whereby they forsaking the worde of God might give eare unto Spirits... He speaketh some good things, that he may intermedle evil things therwith, he speaketh truth, that he may scatter abroade lyes, and roote them in mens hearts...
>
> Sathan dothe imitate craftie gamsters, who suffer a plaine and simple yong man to winne a while of them, that afterwards being greedy to play, they may lurche him of all his golde and silver... Sith we know these things, let us in no wise beleeve the divell, nay rather if he say any thyng that is truth, let us flie from him and shunne him.

Cf. lines 140–143, below; IV.i.174; and V.v.52–54.

122. ***dresse me in borrowed Robes.*** When *Rosse* "dresses" ("address[es]": "direct[s] spoken words or a written message to," OED) *Macbeth* as *Thane of Cawdor* (line 117, above), *Macbeth* feels "dressed" (clothed) *in borrowed* ("not one's own; assumed, counterfeit," OED) *Robes* (used figuratively for "People of high rank or office," OED). Cf. the proverb, "A borrowed gowne does well on no mans shoulders; apparell graces none but them that owe it" (RC, s.v. "Robbe d'autruy ne fait honneur à nulluy").

124. ***Judgement.*** The "counsell spoken or written concerning the life of a man: the sentence of a Judge" (TT, s.v. "Sententia").

126–128. ***combin'd with those of Norway... vantage.*** The former *Thane of Cawdor* was either *combin'd* ("allied with," "Leagued, in league with; confederate," RC, s.v. "Ligué") *with those of Norway, Or* he *did lyne* ("reinforce, fortify," OED) *the Rebell* (either "Rebellion" or "Rebels collectively," OED) *with hidden helpe, And vantage* (i.e., advance information; *vantage* is both "vantage-ground; a vantage-point," OED, and also "The position, state, or circumstance of being in advance or ahead of another," OED, s.v. "advantage").

128–129. ***labour'd In his Countreyes wracke.*** The *Thane of Cawdor* attempted to effect *his Countreyes wracke* ("wast, havocke, spoile; subversion, desolation, overthrow, undoing, destruction," RC, s.v. "Ruine"). In attempting to "screw" his country (with probable play on "country" / "cunt"), he *labour'd* (copulated, TR) *In his Countreyes wracke* ("Ruin of honour or maidenhead," EC).

130. ***Capitall.*** *Capitall* is "most hainous, deadly, death-meriting; worthie of disgrace, or of great punishment" (RC, q.v.).

Macb.	Glamys, and *Thane* of Cawdor:
	The greatest is behinde. Thankes for your paines.
	Doe you not hope your Children shall be Kings,
	When those that gave the *Thane* of Cawdor to me, [135]
	Promis'd no lesse to them.
Banq.	That trusted home,
	Might yet enkindle you unto the Crowne,
	Besides the *Thane* of Cawdor. But 'tis strange:
	And oftentimes, to winne us to our harme, [140]
	The Instruments of Darknesse tell us Truths,
	Winne us with honest Trifles, to betray's
	In deepest consequence.
	Cousins, a word, I pray you.
Macb.	Two Truths are told, [145]
	As happy Prologues to the swelling Act
	Of the Imperiall Theame. I thanke you Gentlemen:

---

133. **The greatest is behinde.** *Behinde* means (a) "After, afterward, after that" (TT, s.v. "Pōst"); and (b) "the backe-side" (RC, s.v. "Derriere"). *Macbeth* thinks that *The greatest* honor *is behinde* (yet to come), but he will instead be made a *behinde* (an ass). Cf. and see notes: lines 154–155, below; and *Oracles,* III.i.11.

135. **gave.** Both (a) bestowed, handed over; and (b) "put forth in words," "pronounce[d]" (OED).

136. **no lesse.** With possible play on *lesse* meaning "lies" (JJ).

137. **trusted home.** If *Macbeth* trusts the prophecy *home* ("as far as it will go," "thoroughly," OED), then the *King* must go *home* ("To the place of final rest, to the 'long home'; to the grave," OED).

138. **enkindle you.** *Enkindle you* can mean (a) make you eager for; (b) raise you; and/or (c) incite or encourage you.

141–143. **The Instruments of Darknesse... consequence.** Cf. and see note: *can the Devill speake true*, line 120, above.

142. **Trifles.** *Trifles* are (a) "things of small estimation"; and (b) "Vaine words, and meere lies" (TT, s.v. "Affăniæ").

142. **betray's.** This unique contraction of "betray us" occurs in the First Folio only here. See note: *ha's*, line 87, above.

143. **deepest.** Both (a) most profound; and (b) "of hell, hellish, infernall" (TT, s.v. "Infernus").

143. **consequence.** *Consequence* means both (a) result; and (b) "weight, importance" (JM, s.v. "Consequéncia").

144. **Cousins.** "Cousin" can indicate kinship but is also used "As a term of intimacy, friendship, or familiarity" (OED).

145–147. **Two Truths... the Imperiall Theame.** The *Witches* have *told* (discerned, revealed, or predicted) *Two Truths*: (1) that *Macbeth* is *Thane of Glamis* (line 54, above); and (2) that *Macbeth* is *Thane of Cawdor* (line 55, above). These *Two Truths* serve as a "prologue" (a "fore-speech; a preamble to a Play," RC, q.v.) *to the swelling* ("Grand, magnificent, stately, majestic," OED) *Act* ("part of a play," "One of the main divisions of a dramatic work," OED) which is yet to come. The subsequent *Act* promises an *Imperiall* ("royall, majesticall," JF, s.v. "Imperiale") *Theame* ("subject or grounde to speake or write of," JF, s.v. "Theme"), but *Macbeth* contemplates whether he can "swell" (rise in rank, become greater) without his own *Act* (i.e., the murder of *Duncane*; *Act* means "Activity, action, as opposed to passivity," OED). Cf. lines 162–164, below.

The first *Two* (with allusion to *Two* as "The two testicles," FR) *Truths* serve as *Prologues* (i.e., foreplay; a "prologue" is literally a "preliminary act," OED; cf. "After we had kissed and imbraced, and as it were even amid the prologue of our incounter, who should come, but the jealous knave her husband," *A Most pleasaunt and excellent conceited Comedie, of Syr John Falstaffe, and the merrie Wives of Windsor*, Q1). Only *Macbeth's swelling* ("sexual erection," JH, s.v. "swell") can bring about the third and final *swelling* (pregnancy, EP, with play on "pregnant" meaning "full of significance, momentous," OED) *Act* ("The act of procreation; sexual intercourse," OED).

By rights, *Theame* ("Offspring, progeny, issue, family, line of descendants; race, stock," OED) should result from *Macbeth's Imperiall* (i.e., "erect"; literally "lofty" or "elevated," OED, s.v. "empyreal") *Theame* (testicles and genitals, FR, s.v. "team" and "theme"; *Theame* could be dialectally pronounced "team"; cf. the OED spelling variants of "team" as "theam," "theme," and "teem"). However, *Macbeth* recognizes that the third prophecy at once renders him both "potent" (powerful, mighty) and "impotent" (cf. and see note: *unfixe my Heire*, line 153, below).

146. **happy.** Both (a) "Coming or happening by chance" (OED); and (b) "boding good fortune, constituting a good omen" (JJ).

This supernaturall solliciting

Cannot be ill; cannot be good.

If ill? why hath it given me earnest of successe,   [150]

Commencing in a Truth? I am *Thane* of Cawdor.

If good? why doe I yeeld to that suggestion,

Whose horrid Image doth unfixe my Heire,

And make my seated Heart knock at my Ribbes,

Against the use of Nature? Present Feares   [155]

Are lesse then horrible Imaginings:

---

148. **solliciting.** *Solliciting* can mean (a) "entising, or mooving to doe a thing" (TT, s.v. "Sŏllĭcĭtātĭo"); (b) "disturb[ing], disquiet[ing], troubl[ing]," "mak[ing] anxious, fill[ing] with concern" (OED, s.v. "solicit"); (c) "induc[ing] or persuad[ing], to some act of lawlessness or insubordination" (OED, s.v. "solicit"); and/or (d) "mak[ing] a sexual proposition" (GW). Cf. and see note: *Trade, and Trafficke*, III.v.7.

149. **ill.** Attributable to "The *evil*, or fatal effects ascribed to the influence of witchcraft. *He's gotten ill*, he has been fascinated" (JJ). *Macbeth* has already rejected *Banquo's* notion that the *Witches* are illusionary (lines 93–94, above), and he finds it

equally difficult to believe *Banquo's* suggestion that they are agents of the Devil (lines 140–143, above).

150. *earnest.* See note: *earnest*, line 116, above.

150. *successe.* With play on *successe* meaning (a) "Prosperitie, happinesse, good lucke" (RC, s.v. "Prosperité"); and (b) "posteritie, issue" (JM, s.v. "Sucésso").

152–153. *why doe I yeeld… unfixe my Heire.* *Macbeth* does not want to *yeeld* (surrender, give way) to the *suggestion* ("Prompting or incitement to evil," "a tempta- tion of the evil one," OED) occasioned by the *suggestion* ("prompting or putting of a thing into ones minde," JB) that he will be king. When *Macbeth* imagines himself as a regicide, the *horrid* (hideous, dreadful) *Image* (idea) *doth unfixe* ("loose out," JF, s.v. "Difiggere"; "unsettle," RC, s.v. "Desficher") his *Heire* (i.e., makes his "hair" stand on end).

The prophecy predicts that *Macbeth* will be king, but he will be *yeeld* (variant spelling of "yeld": "Barren," OED). He will leave behind no *Image* (i.e., child; liter- ally a "person in which the aspect, form, or character of another is reproduced; an exact likeness; a counterpart, copy," OED). Thus, his *Heire* ("offspring," OED) is "unfixed" (i.e., unengendered; to "fix" is to "Fornicate," FR), so both *Macbeth* and his unborn progeny are *horrid* (i.e., "whored" or "fucked"). Cf. and see notes: III.i.79; and *haire*, IV.i.141.

The connection between *Macbeth's* sin and his impotence is not trivial or ran- dom, for it was believed "that the power of the devil lies in the privy parts of men" (Heinrich Institoris and Jakob Sprenger, *Malleus Maleficarum*, p. 26). Consequently, "God allows the devil greater power against men's venereal acts than against their other actions… since the first corruption of sin by which man became the slave of the devil came to us through the act of generation, therefore greater power is allowed by God to the devil in this act than in all others" (ibid., p. 48).

154–155. *my seated Heart… Against the use of Nature.* *Macbeth's Heart* ("emo- tional nature"; also "moral sense, conscience," OED) is usually *seated* (firm, steadfast). However, the "things comming against nature" ("foretokens or prodigies," JF, s.v. "Ostenti") which predict that *Macbeth* will be *seated* (enthroned; to "seat" is "to enthrone a king," OED) *make* his *Heart seated* ("besieged," JM, s.v. "Sitiádo"). His *Heart's* "knocking" ("beating, pounding," RC, s.v. "Contusion"; also "jurring, joulting, vio- lently meeting," "Shocking, pushing," RC, s.v. "Heurtant") *at* his *Ribbes* is *Against* (con- trary to) *the use* (habitual practice, custom) *of* his *Nature* (constitution, disposition). This "knocking" of *Macbeth's Heart* is due not solely to fear but also to the stirrings of his conscience: see note: *Knocke*, II.ii.73.

Normally, *Macbeth's Heart* ("courage": "Sexual vigour," OED; also phallic erec- tion; see note: *brave*, I.ii.22) is *Heart* (i.e., "hard"; *Heart* "may have been pronounced so as to echo 'hard,'" JH) and *seated* (i.e., "seeded," or endowed with semen). Now, the prophecy tempts *Macbeth* "to commit sinne against Nature" ("to bugger," JF, s.v. "Moncerare") and "bugger" (ruin, destroy) *Duncane*, but *Macbeth* suspects that if he succumbs to this *use* ("sexual urge; sexual desire," OED), he will also "bugger" him- self. *Macbeth's* own *Heart* (i.e., "arse"; "hart" was pronounced "art" which plays on L. "ars": "art," FR) might be *seated* (i.e., having "seed" in the "seat": "posteriors," OED), and his attempts to *knock* (copulate, F&H, s.v. "Ride") will result only in *Ribbes* (i.e., failed sexual attempts; a "rib" is a "Ribroasting, a Dry-basting," ND; a "dry bob" is "copulation without emission," FG). Cf. and see note: *Unmannerly breech'd with gore*, II.iii.151. Also cf. II.iv.14–15 and 39; and V.i.73–74.

My Thought, whose Murther yet is but fantasticall,

Shakes so my single state of Man,

That Function is smother'd in surmise,

And nothing is, but what is not.   [160]

Banq.   Looke how our Partner's rapt.

157–160. ***My Thought... nothing is, but what is not.*** Man was considered a "microcosm" (small world) which mirrored the "macrocosm" (large world). Each man's *single* (individual) *state* ("bodily form"; also "Physical condition as regards internal make or constitution," OED) was regarded as a *single* ("Undivided, unbroken, absolute," OED) *state* (country, realm, government) ruled by *Thought*: "Reason and Rulers beynge lyke in offyce, (for the one ruleth the body of man, the other ruleth the bodye of the common wealthe)" (Roger Ascham, *Toxophilus*). *Macbeth's* homicidal *Thought Shakes* ("disturb[s], upset[s]," OED) his inner realm of *Thought* to the point that his entire body *Shakes* (quakes, trembles). Cf. lines 153–155, above, and *Julius Cæsar*, II.i.:

> Betweene the acting of a dreadfull thing,
> And the first motion, all the Interim is
> Like a Phantasma, or a hideous Dreame:
> The Genius, and the mortall Instruments
> Are then in councell; and the state of a man,
> Like to a little Kingdome, suffers then
> The nature of an Insurrection.

Although *Macbeth's Murther yet is but fantasticall* (imaginary), his contemplation of a murderous *Thought* (idea) makes him susceptible to the powers of evil. Supposedly, "the Devill entreth in, beginning with the fantasie, by which he doth more easily betray the other faculties of the soule: for the fantasie is most apt to bee abused by vaine apprehensions" (Walter Raleigh, *The History of the World*). In *The Second Part of the French Academie*, Pierre La Primaudaye cautions that

> fantasie is a very dangerous thing. For if it bee not guided and brideled by reason, it troubleth and mooveth all the sense and understanding, as a tempest doeth the sea. For it is easily stirred up not onely by the externall senses, but also by the complexion and disposition of the body. Heereof it proceedeth that even the spirites both good and bad have great accesse unto it, to stirre it either to good or evill... Wherefore as the Angelles have meanes to represent to our mindes the images of good, heavenly, and divine things, both waking and sleeping: so can evill spirites greatly trouble them by divers illusions: the proofe whereof wee have in many, whome badde spirites find apt and disposed thereunto... the divell, having once power over them, doeth in such sort print in their fantasie the images of those things hee representeth unto them, and which he woulde have them beleeve to be true, that they can not thinke otherwise but that it is so... wee use commonly to say, that fancie breedes the fact which it imagineth.... Therefore we ought to eschew all occasions of evill, that may be presented to our senses, to stirre up our imagination and fantasie to wicked and dishonest things.

Because *Macbeth's* reason has been overthrown (see note: *Function*, line 159, below), his "fantasy" (imagination) runs amok and makes him believe in *nothing* except *what is not* (i.e., the as *yet* unreal murder of *Duncane* and *Macbeth's* subsequent ascent to the throne).

Macbeth also fears that he will end up *single* ("withered," JM, s.v. "Cençeño," with possible play on "ingle" meaning "a buggering boy," JF, s.v. "Bardascia") and with *nothing* ("no thing," or "lacking a thing, penis," GW). In *Macbeth's horrible Imaginings* (line 156, above), his *what* ("penis," F&H) is *not* ("nought": nothing), and he is afraid that his *single* ("singular": "standing alone," OED) *state* ("suggestive of the erected penis," JH, s.v. "Stately") will "shake" ("lose firmness," OED). *Macbeth's* fears also "shake" (i.e., "fuck"; "shake" is "the ancient form of shag," F&H) his *single* (i.e., gluteal; *single* literally means "The taile of a Stagge or other Deere," JB) *state* ("a man's seat or arse. Lit[erally] a throne," FR). Cf. and see notes: *behinde*, line 133, above; and *Oracles*, III.i.11.

158. **Man.** With play on *Man* as (a) mankind, mortal human existence; (b) "Wickedness" (OED); and/or (c) the male sexual parts (GW2).

159. **Function is smother'd in surmise.** *Macbeth's* (a) *Function* (intellectual and moral power, OED) *is smother'd* ("Stifled, suffocated," RC, s.v. "Estouffé") *in surmise* (conjecture, supposition); (b) *Function* ("dutie," JF, s.v. "Parte") as *Duncane's* subject *is smother'd in surmise* (i.e., the prophecy; to *surmise* is "To tell by divination what shall happen: to divine," TT, s.v. "Auguro"); (c) destined *Function* ("magistracie, dignitie," RC, s.v. "Office"; "Vocation," HC, s.v. "Calling or trade of life") as king *is smother'd in* the *surmise* ("false or craftie accusation, a forged crime," "cavill or detraction to slander or trouble one," JF, s.v. "Calunnia") of *Duncane's* imagined murder; and/or (d) *Function* ("virility or potency," EP) *is smother'd in surmise* (i.e., emasculation; *surmise* is "Supputation," RC, q.v.; "Supputation" is "a pruyning, or cutting Trees," TB, q.v.; "pruning" is "A gelding, or cutting awaie of the stones," TT, s.v. "Castrātĭo").

161. **Partner's.** See note: *Partner*, line 60, above.

161. **rapt.** See note: *wrapt*, line 63, above.

Macb.   If Chance will have me King,

Why Chance may Crowne me,

Without my stirre.

Banq.   New Honors come upon him   [165]

Like our strange Garments, cleave not to their mould,

But with the aid of use.

Macb.   Come what come may,

Time, and the Houre, runs through the roughest Day.

Banq.   Worthy *Macbeth*, wee stay upon your ley-   [170]

sure.

Macb.   Give me your favour:

My dull Braine was wrought with things forgotten.

Kinde Gentlemen, your paines are registred,

Where every day I turne the Leafe,   [175]

To reade them.

163–164. ***Chance my Crowne me... stirre.*** *Macbeth* reflects that he might become king by *Chance* ("fate, fortune, lot, destinie," JF, s.v. "Sórte") *Without* his *stirre* (action, provocation). *Chance* ("a hap, or an accident," JF, s.v. "Occorénza") might *Crowne* him *Without* his *stirre* ("sedition," "insurrection," RC, s.v. "Tumulte"). Holinshed states that "Makbeth revolving the thing in his minde, began even then to devise howe he mighte attayne to the kingdome: but yet hee thought with himselfe that he must tary a time, whiche shoulde advaunce him thereto (by the divine providence) as it had come to passe in his former preferment."

Unfortunately, the *Witches'* prophecy is not divine but diabolical, and its sole purpose is to prompt *Macbeth* to sin. See notes: *why doe you start*, line 57, above; *prediction*, line 61, above; *from whence You owe this strange Intelligence*, lines 81–82, above; and cf. lines 140–143, above.

166–167. **strange Garments... the aid of use.** *Strange* (new, unfamiliar) *Garments* will *not cleave* (cling, adhere) *to their mould* ("the human body or its substance," OED) without *the aid of use* (wear). Cf. *borrowed Robes*, line 122, above.

In Holinshed, *Banquo* supports *Macbeth* in *Duncane's* murder, but Shakespeare downplays *Banquo's* involvement in the crime as much as possible (cf. and see note: *cursed thoughts*, II.i.14). Even so, *Banquo* seems tacitly complicit in *Macbeth's* plot, for he here conceals the prophecy from *Rosse* and *Angus*. Moreover, if *Banquo* suspects *Macbeth's* murderous thoughts, he does not reveal them when he has the chance to speak to *Duncane* without *Macbeth* present (I.iv.67–69). On the other hand, *Banquo* might be uncharacteristically guarded about the matter simply because he hopes to protect his friend *Macbeth* from undue suspicion.

168–169. **Come what come may... the roughest Day.** *Macbeth*, who is *rapt* (line 161, above), continues his train of thought from lines 162–164, above. *Macbeth* comforts himself with the idea that events are out of his hands: *Come what come may, Time, and the Houre* (i.e., the ordained events or course of life) will "run through" ("be or continue present in," "pervade," OED) *the roughest Day* (i.e., the most adverse circumstances). Cf. "But what estate stands free from fortunes powre? / The Fates have guidance of our time and howre" (Michael Drayton, "The second Booke of the Barrons warres").

170–171. **wee stay upon your leysure.** To "attend the leasure of" is "To waite on" (RC, s.v. "Brider la mule à").

172. **favour.** Pardon.

173. **My dull Braine... things forgotten.** *Macbeth's Braine* is *dull*, which can mean (a) "slow," "heavie," "numme or benummed" (TT, s.v. "Torpeo"); (b) "giddie, dizie, madde, foolish, frantike, raving in the head" (JF, s.v. "Stordito"); (c) "pensive, agreeved, in a melancholie mood, all in dumpes" (RC, s.v. "Morne"); and/or (d) "Hard of hearing" (JJ).

Macbeth's dull Braine (mind) *was wrought* ("intangled, inwrapped," RC, s.v. "Ennicroché"), but it was not *with things forgotten* (i.e., trivial *things* not worth remembering). In truth, he is greatly troubled by the threat of a *dull* (impotent, JH; literally "Slacke," "loose," TT, s.v. "Rĕmissus") *Braine* (penis, scrotum, FR; also semen, GW; it was formerly believed that semen originated in the *Braine* and descended through the spine to the testicles: cf. "For hire with what foolishe and vaine reasons they dispute of Sperme... Alcmeon affirmeth it to be a parte of ye braine, because the eies of them that fulfill the fleashly lustes, doo ake, whiche are partes of the braine," Heinrich Cornelius Agrippa von Nettesheim, *Of the Vanitie and uncertaintie of Artes and Sciences*).

174–176. **your paines are registred... reade them.** Proverbially, "The mind is a smooth white table [i.e., "table-book"], on which memorie writeth the occurrents of mans lyfe" (John Bodenham and Nicholas Ling, *Politeuphuia*). *Macbeth* has *registred* (noted or remembered; also "set in a booke," JM, s.v. "Empadronádo") the *paines* (efforts) which *Rosse* and *Angus* have taken on his behalf. No matter what *Macbeth's reade* ("reid": "weird, fate, lot," JJ), he promises *To reade* these grateful memories *every day* in which he turns *the Leafe* (page)—i.e., to remember them *every day* of his life.

Let us toward the King: thinke upon

What hath chanc'd: and at more time,

The *Interim* having weigh'd it, let us speake

Our free Hearts each to other.   [180]

Banq.   Very gladly.

Macb.   Till then enough:

Come friends.

Exeunt.

178–180. ***at more time… each to other.*** By the time *Macbeth* and *Banquo speake* of the prophecy again, they will have *weigh'd* ("considered, pondered, examined," TT, s.v. "Pensĭtātus") *it* in *The Interim* ("the mean space or time," TE; *Interim* is italicized because it was considered a foreign word at the time of the Folio's publication). *Macbeth* promises *Banquo* that *at* a *more* ("better," OED) *time*, or "with more time and leasure" (JF, s.v. "A più tempo"), they will *speake to each other* their *free* (unrestrained; also conscientious or guiltless) *Hearts* ("inmost thoughts and secret feelings," OED). By the time the two of them speak of the prophecy again, however, *Macbeth's* trust in *Banquo* will have evaporated; cf. II.i.29–43.

Act I, scene iv

Scena Quarta.   [1]

Flourish. Enter King, Lenox, Malcolme,

Donalbaine, and Attendants.   [I.iv.1]

King.   Is execution done on *Cawdor*?

               Or not those in Commission yet return'd?   [5]

Mal.   My Liege, they are not yet come back.

               But I have spoke with one that saw him die:

               Who did report, that very frankly hee

               Confess'd his Treasons, implor'd your Highnesse Pardon,

               And set forth a deepe Repentance: [10]

               Nothing in his Life became him,

               Like the leaving it. Hee dy'de,

               As one that had beene studied in his death,

               To throw away the dearest thing he ow'd,

               As 'twere a carelesse Trifle.   [15]

King.   There's no Art,

               To finde the Mindes construction in the Face.

               He was a Gentleman, on whom I built

               An absolute Trust.

Enter Macbeth, Banquo, Rosse, and Angus.   [I.iv.2] [20]

Notes I.iv.

2. **Flourish.** A *Flourish* is a musical fanfare. The "principal use of the Flourish… was to signify the presence of Royal persons" (Edward Woodall Naylor, *Shakespeare and Music*, p. 168).

5. **those in Commission.** *Those* who hold *Commission* ("Authority," HC, q.v.) through a *Commission* ("A writing testifying that one or many have some authoritie in a matter of trust, committed to their charge," JB).

6. **My Liege.** *Liege* "is a word borrowed from the Feudists, and hath two several significations in our Common Law; sometimes being used for Leige Lord… sometime for Leigeman… Leige-Lord, is he that acknowledges no Superior… Liege-man, is he that owes ligeancy to his Liege Lord" (TB, q.v.).

10. **set forth.** "Exhibited; presented, offered," "publickly shewed" (RC, s.v. "Exhibé").

10. **deepe.** "Intense, profound"; also "humble" (OED).

13. **studied.** "That hath mused or bethought himselfe, that hath provided & considered sufficiently what to saie or doe: prepared before hand, or one that hath his answere readie" (TT, s.v. "Mĕdĭtātus").

14. **dearest.** Most valuable.

14. **ow'd.** Owned.

15. **As 'twere.** The still-current "as it were" means "even as," "as though" (TT, s.v. "Atque").

15. **carelesse.** *Carelesse* means "emptie, idle and vaine" (JF, s.v. "Vacuo"). Also, one who is "carelesse of himselfe" is "wearie of his life" (RC, s.v. "Assode").

16–19. **There's no Art… An absolute Trust.** The *King* muses that *There's no Art* (science or skill) that will allow him *To finde* (discover, ascertain) *the Mindes construction* (composition, disposition) *in the Face*. He placed *An absolute* ("whole, total," JF, s.v. "Plenaria") *Trust* in the former *Thane of Cawdor*, who merely "set a good face on a bad mind" ("play[ed] the hypocrite," "dissemble[d], or counterfeit[ed] goodnesse," RC, s.v. "Hypocriser"). Cf. I.v.74–78 and 84–85; I.vii.97; II.iii.180–181; and III.ii.36–44.

Despite this realization, the *King* is about to make the same mistake again and place the same *absolute Trust* in the new *Thane of Cawdor* as he did in the old. Thus, the *King* (a) makes himself *An absolute* ("an ass/arse… from OFr *assolu*," FR); and (b) allows himself to be "buggered" in the *absolute* (synonym of "whole," with play on "hole": "arse-hole," F&H). Where the former *Thane of Cawdor* failed, *Macbeth* will succeed in putting his *construction* ("erection," OED) in *Duncane's* "mind" ("Buttocks," FR; also see note: *Braine*, I.iii.173) and *Face* (i.e., ass; see note: *fac'd*, I.ii.26). Cf. and see note: *Unmannerly breech'd with gore*, II.iii.151.

18. **I.** *Duncane* here uses the first person singular, which indicates that he speaks informally or intimately. *Duncane* switches to the first person plural when he proclaims *Malcolme* his heir (lines 48–50, below), which indicates that he speaks in his official capacity as sovereign.

O worthyest Cousin,

The sinne of my Ingratitude even now

Was heavie on me. Thou art so farre before,

That swiftest Wing of Recompence is slow,

To overtake thee. Would thou hadst lesse deserv'd,   [25]

That the proportion both of thanks, and payment,

Might have beene mine: onely I have left to say,

More is thy due, then more then all can pay.

Macb.   The service, and the loyaltie I owe,

In doing it, payes it selfe.   [30]

Your Highnesse part, is to receive our Duties:

And our Duties are to your Throne, and State,

Children, and Servants; which doe but what they should,

By doing every thing safe toward your Love

And Honor.   [35]

King.   Welcome hither:

I have begun to plant thee, and will labour

To make thee full of growing. Noble *Banquo,*

---

21. **Cousin.** *Duncane* does not suspect that his *Cousin Macbeth* (see note: *Cousin,* I.ii.30) is a "cozener" ("a deceiver, an affronter," JF, s.v. "Cantoniére"). Cf. "Our neer-est friends oft makes us the worst accounts; so may a cosen safely be tearmed a cousener" (RC, s.v. "Entre deux comperes se perdit le fossoir").

22. **sinne of my Ingratitude.** According to Holinshed, *Duncane* was a deeply religious man. See note: *our Captaines,* I.ii.40.

23. ***before.*** *Macbeth* (a) has "gone *before*" ("hath overrunne another," RC, s.v. "Devancier"); and (b) is *before* ("best, more esteemed," "more excellent, chiefe, principall, highest," "above others," JF, s.v. "Primo").

24–25. ***swiftwest Wing... overtake thee.*** *Macbeth* is so "swift" (speedy, quick) that even the *Wing* ("flight," OED) of a "swift" ("Martinet, Martlet," EC2, q.v.) *is slow To overtake* him. Cf. *Barlet*, I.vi.9.

The *King* speaks a truth he does not realize: *Macbeth* is much "swifter" (i.e., quick-witted) than he. Because the *King* is "slow of apprehension" (RC, s.v. "Dur"), *Macbeth* can easily *overtake* ("deceive," OED) him.

26–27. ***the proportion... Might have beene mine.*** *Duncane* wishes he could give *Macbeth thanks, and payment* in *proportion* ("equalnes," JF, s.v. "Proportionalità") to *Macbeth's* great deserving.

27. ***onely I have.*** I.e., *I onely have*.

29–30. ***The service... payes it selfe.*** This sentiment was commonplace: cf. "The onely fruite of service, is love, and the plesure thereof, humility and obedience" (John Bodenham and Nicholas Ling, *Politeuphuia*). Renaissance society was based on the idea of a *scala naturae* (L. for "stair-way of nature," otherwise known as the "ladder of life" or "Great Chain of Being"), a divinely-ordained hierarchy in which every person and thing occupied a prescribed place. Members of each social strata owed obedience to those situated above, and all were expected to "doe their duties to their Masters, not for feare, or reward, but for Conscience sake, because God hath bound them to his subjection" (Nicholas Byfield, *A Commentary: Or, Sermons Upon the Second Chapter of the First Epistle of Saint Peter*).

Ostensibly, *Macbeth* says that *The service* ("discharge of any office or dutie, doing of worke," JM, s.v. "Ministério") *and the loyaltie* ("Fealtie; fidelitie, faithfulnesse," RC, s.v. "Feaulté") that he "owes" (is obligated to give) to *Duncane* (a monarch who rules by divine right) *payes it selfe*. However, *Macbeth's* words might be equivocal: *The service and the loyaltie* that he "owes" (owns, acknowledges) are to himself only. If *Macbeth* now considers himself a divinely-ordained king, *In doing it* (i.e., in murdering *Duncane*) *Macbeth* will claim his own reward (i.e., the crown).

32–35. ***Duties... your Love And Honor.*** Another proverbial sentiment: cf. "In doing that we ought, deserves no praise, because it is duty" (John Bodenham and Nicholas Ling, *Politeuphuia*).

Children, and Servants is not here the subject (i.e., *Macbeth* does not say that *Children, and Servants doe but what they should*). The semicolon after *Servants* (line 33) indicates that *which* refers to *Duties* (line 32). *Macbeth* says that *By doing every thing safe* ("with due respect," OED) *toward* ("in attendance upon," OED) *Duncane's Love And Honor*, *Macbeth's Duties*, which he owes not only to *Duncane* but also to his *Children, and Servants, doe but* (only) *what they* (i.e., his *Duties*) *should*.

Additionally, OED notes that "The phrase *to ward* was sometimes written as one word" (s.v. "toward"). Therefore, *Macbeth* might say that his *Duties* do *every thing safe* ("Conducive to safety," OED) *"to ward"* (to protect or defend) *Duncane's Love And Honor*.

37–38. ***begun to plant thee... growing.*** *Duncane* has *begun to plant* (i.e., promote; to *plant* is "To establish or set up in a particular position or situation," OED) *Macbeth*, and *Duncane* trusts that hereafter *Macbeth* will be *full of growing* ("ris[ing] by degrees to a position of eminence," OED). Cf. Psalms 92:13: "Those that be planted in the house of the LORD, shall flourish in the courts of our God."

That hast no lesse deserv'd, nor must be knowne

No lesse to have done so: Let me enfold thee,   [40]

And hold thee to my Heart.

Banq.   There if I grow,

The Harvest is your owne.

King.   My plenteous Joyes,

Wanton in fulnesse, seeke to hide themselves   [45]

In drops of sorrow. Sonnes, Kinsmen, *Thanes*,

And you whose places are the nearest, know,

We will establish our Estate upon

Our eldest, *Malcolme*, whom we name hereafter,

The Prince of Cumberland: which Honor must   [50]

Not unaccompanied, invest him onely,

But signes of Noblenesse, like Starres, shall shine

On all deservers. From hence to Envernes,

And binde us further to you.

Macb.   The Rest is Labor, which is not us'd for you: [55]

39–40. **nor must be knowne No lesse to have done so.** I.e., "You *must No lesse be knowne to have done so.*"

41–43. **my Heart... your owne.** If *Banquo* grows in *Duncane's Heart*, then *The Harvest* ("The product or 'fruit' of any action or effort," OED) will be *Duncane's owne.* Cf. lines 37–38, above.

44–46. **My plenteous Joyes... drops of sorrow.** *Duncane's Joyes* are so *plenteous* ("very full, exceeding much," RC, s.v. "Abondant") as to be *Wanton* ("prodigall," TT, s.v. "Asōtus") *in fulnesse* ("plentie, excesse," RC, s.v. "Saturité"). His *Joyes* are also *Wanton* ("Capricious," OED) *in fulnesse* ("Of the 'heart': The state of being overcharged with emotion," OED), so his *Joyes hide* (disguise) *themselves In drops of sorrow* (tears). The fact that *Duncane's* emotions are so *Wanton* ("Undisciplined, ungoverned," OED) suggests that he is *Wanton* ("effeminate, weake, a milkesop," JF, s.v. "Delicato"); also see note: *our Captaines,* I.ii.40.

47. **places.** With play on "place" meaning (a) status, rank; and (b) "The position of a celestial object on the celestial sphere" (OED). Cf. lines 52–53 and 62–63, below.

47. **nearest.** Both (a) most closely related by blood; and (b) "close, intimate, familiar" (OED).

48. **We.** See note: *I,* line 18, above.

48–50. **establish our Estate... Prince of Cumberland.** In naming *Malcolme The Prince of Cumberland, Duncane* officially announces his intention to *establish* ("appoint, or assigne unto; also, to settle," RC, s.v. "Constituer") his *Estate* ("seat of estate, where a king sitteth: a throne, a seat royall," TT, s.v. "Sŏlĭum") upon his first-born son.

In medieval Scotland, the right of primogeniture was not universally observed. Very often, the most eligible (i.e., puissant) member of the royal family took over when the reigning king died (e.g., when *Malcolme* himself died in 1093, it was not *Malcolme's* son Edgar but *Malcolme's* younger brother *Donalbaine* who assumed the throne). Therefore, *Macbeth* probably feels that *Duncane's* naming *Malcolme* as his successor is a personal slight. Holinshed reports that

> Duncane having two sonnes by his wife which was the daughter of Sywarde Earle of Northumberland, he made the elder of them cleped [i.e., "called"] Malcolme prince of Cumberlande, as it were thereby to appoint him his successor in the kingdome, immediatly after his deceasse.
>
> Makbeth sore troubled herewith, for that he sawe by this meanes his hope sore hindered, (where by the olde lawes of the realme, the ordinance was, that if he that shoulde succeede were not of able age to take the charge upon himselfe; he that was nexte of bloud unto him, shoulde be admitted) he beganne to take counsell howe he might usurpe the kingdome by force, having a juste quarell so to do (as he tooke the mater,) for that Duncane did what in him lay to defraude him of all maner of title and clayme, whiche hee mighte in tyme to come, pretende unto the crowne.

50. **Honor.** An "honourable estate, inheritance, or title, bestowed by a Prince, or great Lord" (RC, s.v. "Honneur").

51. **invest.** To "adorne, or decke, or grace" (RC2, q.v.).

52. **signes.** *Signes* are (a) "tokens of honour, whereby everie estate or great authoritie is knowne" (TT, s.v. "Insignĭa"); and (b) "signe[s] in the Zodiake," "celestiall signe[s]" (RC, s.v. "Un signe au ciel").

53. **Envernes.** *Macbeth's* castle was located in *Envernes* (or "Inverness"), which derives from Scots Gaelic "inbhir Nis": "mouth of the River Ness."

54. **binde.** To "make bounden, or beholden unto" (RC, s.v. "Obliger").

55. **The Rest is Labor... us'd for you.** "Love makes labor light" is a proverb that still survives in the modern phrase "a labor of love." *Macbeth* takes the adage a step further in saying that even *Rest* (repose, recreation) is burdensome when *not us'd* (employed) *for Duncane.*

Macbeth's blandishments conceal his intent to "screw" the *King,* for *Macbeth* will use his *Rest* (phallic erection; the metaphor is drawn from the joust, wherein a "lance

Ile be my selfe the Herbenger, and make joyfull

The hearing of my Wife, with your approach:

So humbly take my leave.

King.   My worthy *Cawdor*.

Macb.   The Prince of Cumberland: that is a step,   [60]

On which I must fall downe, or else o're-leape,

For in my way it lyes. Starres hide your fires,

Let not Light see my black and deepe desires:

The Eye winke at the Hand: yet let that bee,

Which the Eye feares, when it is done to see.   [65]

Exit {Macbeth}.   [I.iv.3]

King.   True worthy *Banquo*: he is full so valiant,

And in his commendations, I am fed:

It is a Banquet to me. Let's after him,

Whose care is gone before, to bid us welcome: [70]

It is a peerelesse Kinsman.

Flourish. Exeunt.

in rest" was held upright; a "lance in rest" is "An erection of the penis," F&H) and *Labor* (sexual efforts; see note: *labour'd*, I.iii.128) to "use" (i.e., sexually use or abuse) *Duncane*. Cf. and see note: lines 16–19, above.

56. **Herbenger.** "Herbenger (from the Fr. Herberger... to harbour or lodge) signifies with us an Officer of the Princes Court, that alots the Noble men, and those of the Household their lodgings" (TB, q.v.). Despite *Macbeth's* stated intention to be his own *Herbenger* (one "sent before to prepare," RC2, q.v.), he sends at least one other messenger besides himself (cf. I.v.32–41).

60–62. **a step... in my way it lyes.** As *Duncane's* son, *Malcolme* holds *a step* ("a degree in consanguinitie," TE, s.v. "Gradus") closer than *Macbeth's* own. Moreover, *Duncane* has granted *Malcolme* the *step* ("degree, ranke, or place of honour," RC, s.v. "Degré") *Prince of Cumberland* (see note: line 50, above). *Malcolme* therefore represents *a step* ("a staire, a round in a ladder," JM, s.v. "Gráda") which *Macbeth must o're-leape* ("leap or jump over," TB, s.v. "Transult") in his ascent to sovereignty, *or else he must fall downe* ("be frustrate or disapointed," TT, s.v. "Dēcĭdo"; also "fall downe prostrate, flat, and groveling," TT, s.v. "Procĭdo").

To become king, *Macbeth* must *leape* (i.e., fuck; literally "mount, coitally," EC) *Malcolme* as though he were an *o're* (pronounced identically to "whore," HK, pp. 117–118). Should *Macbeth fall downe* (i.e., become impotent; literally "slacken," "hang flagging downeward," RC, s.v. "Alachir"), he must himself *fall downe* ("assume the supine position of copulation," JH). Cf. and see notes: I.vii.29–32; and *Unmannerly breech'd with gore*, II.iii.151.

62. **Starres hide your fires.** *Macbeth* wishes to *hide* his "fire" ("ardent courage or zeal; fervour, enthusiasm," OED) for his *Starres* (i.e., his destiny as king; "According to astrology, those leading stars which are above the horizon at a person's birth influence his life and fortune," DPF). He also hopes that his own "fire" ("Luminosity or glowing appearance," OED) will eclipse the fortunes of the other *Starres* (i.e., courtiers; cf. *Starres*, line 52, above). Cf. and see note: V.vii.120.

63. **deepe.** *Deepe* can mean (a) "Grave, heinous"; (b) "Deep-rooted in the breast"; and (c) "Profound in craft or subtlety" (OED; a "deep-one" is "A thorough-paced rogue, a sly designing fellow," FG).

64–65. **The Eye winke at the Hand... done to see.** Proverbial: "What the Eye ne'er sees the Heart ne'er rues: Or out of Sight, out of Mind" (ND, s.v. "Eye-sore"). *Macbeth* desires his *Eye* to *winke at* ("suffer, tollerate, beare with; to see and not to see; to make as though he neither saw, nor knew ought of," RC, s.v. "Conniver") the actions of his *Hand*. By feigning blindness, *Macbeth's Eye* will *let* (permit, allow) *that Which the Eye feares* (the action of the *Hand*, or the murder of *Duncane*) to *bee* (exist, happen) *when it is done to see* (performed and exhibited to view). Cf. "He that winketh with the eies worketh evil" (Sirach 27:22); and "a man may be content to hide his eies, where he may feele his profit" (Anonymous, *The Life of Sir John Old-castle*). Also cf. and see note: II.ii.76.

67. **full so valiant.** I.e., "so fully valiant."

70. **care.** *Care* is both (a) "heed, respect regard" (RC, s.v. "Cure"); and (b) "diligence, industrie" (JF, s.v. "Stúdio").

71. **It is.** "He is." *It* formerly "occurs where *he*, *she*, or *that* would now be preferred" (OED).

71. **Kinsman.** See note: *Cousin*, I.ii.30.

Act I, scene v

Enter Macbeths Wife alone with a Letter.   [I.v.1]

{*Lady.*}   *They met me in the day of successe: and I have*

learn'd by the perfect'st report, they have more in them, then

mortall knowledge. When I burnt in desire to question them   [5]

further, they made themselves Ayre, into which they vanish'd.

Whiles I stood rapt in the wonder of it, came Missives from

the King, who all-hail'd me Thane *of Cawdor, by which Title*

before, these weyward Sisters saluted me, and referr'd me to

the comming on of time, with haile King that shalt be. This   [10]

have I thought good to deliver thee (my dearest Partner of

Greatnesse) that thou might'st not loose the dues of rejoycing

by being ignorant of what Greatnesse is promis'd thee. Lay

it to thy heart, and farewell.

Notes I.v.

2. **Macbeths Wife.** Only one mention of *Macbeths Wife* (a.k.a. "Lady Macbeth")
exists in historical record: she is named along with her husband in a land grant to a
church made by "Macbeth son of Findlaech… and Gruoch daughter of Bodhe [Boite],
King and Queen of Scotland" (Olga L. Valbuena, *Subjects to the King's Divorce*, p. 102).
Macbeths Wife occupies only one sentence in Holinshed's fabricated version of history,
which states that *Macbeths* "wife lay sore upon him to attempt the thing [i.e., the murder of *Duncan*], as she that was very ambitious brenning [i.e., "burning"] in unquenchable desire to beare the name of a Queene." Shakespeare also drew inspiration for her
character from Holinshed's account of the assassination of King Duff, in which the

murderous *Donwalde* was "kindled in wrath by the woordes of his wife, [and] deter-mined to follow hyr advise in the execution of so haynous an acte."

3. ***They met me in the day of successe.*** *Macbeth's* letter, which states that the *Witches* met him *in the day of successe* (victory; see note: *So foule and faire a day*, I.iii.43), is a chronological inconsistency. There would be no time for the delivery of such a let-ter in Shakespeare's condensed timeline, in which the battle with *Macdonwald*, the *Wiches'* prophecy, and the arrival of *Duncan* at *Macbeth's* castle happen in the course of a single day (cf. I.i.3–10; I.iii.43; I.iv.53–57; and lines 69 and 80, below). Incon-gruously, *Macbeth* has time to write not just one but multiple letters to his *Wife* (cf. line 65, below), to which she may even have had time to reply (cf. V.i.9–10). These letters, along with *Banquo's* statement in II.i.29 that he *dreamt last Night* of the *Witches'* prophecy, irreconcilably place at least one day between *Macbeth's* hasty departure in I.iv.66 and his breathless arrival in line 62, below.

4. ***perfect'st.*** *Perfect'st* can mean (a) most "Accurate, correct," "exactly correspon-ding to the facts" (OED); and/or (b) most "righteous, holy; immaculate; spiritually pure or blameless" (OED). If *Macbeth* means the latter, then he is woefully deceived (see notes: *why doe you start*, I.iii.57; *prediction*, I.iii.61; *strange Intelligence*, I.iii.82; and *can the Devill speake true*, I.iii.120).

6. ***they made themselves Ayre… vanish'd.*** Cf. and see note: *Into the Ayre*, I.iii.89.

7. ***rapt.*** See note: *wrapt*, I.iii.63.

7–8. ***Missives from the King, who.*** A "missive" is "a sending" (JB, q.v.); a "send-ing" is "A message" (RC, s.v. "Envoy"). Therefore, *Missives from the King* means "mes-sages from the king." *Who* refers to *the King*, not to his *Missives* (messages). (OED also defines *Missives* as "messenger[s]," but this definition is suspect. OED gives Shake-speare's usage here as the first example of the word in this sense, and OED's two addi-tional supporting quotations which purport to illustrate this signification are equally doubtful.)

A "missive" is also a "missile": "Gifts, such as sweets and perfumes, thrown by Roman emperors to crowds as largesse" (OED). *Macbeth* equates the title of *Thane of Cawdor* as a mere "missive" (i.e., token gift) when compared to the promise of sover-eignty.

8. ***all-hail'd.*** See note: *All haile*, I.iii.54.

9. ***weyward Sisters.*** See note: *weyward Sisters*, I.iii.36.

10. ***comming on of time.*** *Comming on* ("sexual orgasm," JH) is a necessary step in bringing anything to birth, and *Macbeth* expects his promised sovereignty to "come" ("as progeny, offspring, descendants from a parent or ancestor," OED) from *time* (the term of pregnancy; see note: *Time*, I.iii.64). For additional childbirth imagery in this speech, cf. and see notes: *deliver*, line 11, below; *Greatnesse*, line 12, below; *dues*, line 12, below; *Milke*, line 17, below; *cryes*, line 23, below; and *Golden Round*, line 29, below.

11. ***deliver.*** *Deliver* can mean (a) to "give, to yeeld: to put in writing"; "to put or commit in trust to one" (TT, s.v. "Trādo"); and (b) "to bring to childbirth" (OED).

12. ***Greatnesse.*** "Great" means both (a) "majesticall, soveraigne," "royall, lord-like" (JF, s.v. "Maestale"); and (b) "Big with child" (EP). "Great" (or a derivative thereof) is repeated in lines 13, 18, 23, 63, 64, and 80, below.

12. ***the dues of rejoycing.*** *The dues* (rightful share) of *rejoycing* (happiness), with possible play on "due" as the time of childbirth.

13–14. ***Lay it to thy heart.*** To *Lay to heart* is "To take into one's serious consid-eration, as a thing to be kept carefully in mind; to think seriously about" (OED).

Glamys thou art, and Cawdor, and shalt be   [15]

What thou art promis'd: yet doe I feare thy Nature,

It is too full o'th' Milke of humane kindnesse,

To catch the neerest way. Thou would'st be great,

Art not without Ambition, but without

The illnesse should attend it. What thou would'st highly,   [20]

That would'st thou holily: would'st not play false,

And yet would'st wrongly winne.

Thould'st have, great Glamys, that which cryes,

Thus thou must doe, if thou have it;

And that which rather thou do'st feare to doe,   [25]

Then wishest should be undone. High thee hither,

16–18. *I feare thy Nature… Thou would'st be great.* A person's *Nature* (mental disposition and physical constitution) was thought to be formed by the nurse's *Milke*: "truely the condicion of the Noursse, and nature of the milke, disposeth almost the greater part of the childes condition, whiche (notwithstanding the fathers seede, and creation of the bodie and mynde, within the mothers wombe) doth now in the beginning of his nouriture, configurate and frame a newe disposition in him" (William Painter, *The Palace of Pleasure*).

Macbeths Wife "fears" (doubts or distrusts; feels uneasy about) her husband's *Nature* because as an infant he suckled too much *Milke* imbued with *humane* ("belonging to man: gentle, courteous, tractable, mercifull, friendlie," TT, s.v. "Hūmănus") *kindnesse* ("humanitie, courtesie; indulgencie, mercie, clemencie," RC, s.v. "Douceur"). This turned *Macbeth* into a "milk-sop" ("a cowarde," "a hartlesse fellow," JM, s.v. "Cobárde"; "a tender sot that lookes to be alwayes fed with pap," RC, s.v. "Poupart"), so his *Nature* is too "milky" (soft, weak) *To catch* ("apprehend," "conceive," JM, s.v. "Aprehendér") that *the neerest way* ("readiest course," RC, s.v. "Plaindre") to greatness is to murder *Duncan*. (*Macbeths Wife* is wrong in this assumption: cf. and see note: *why doe you start*, I.iii.57).

Even though *Macbeth* "would" ("Desire[s]," "ha[s] a mind to," OED, s.v. "will") *be great* (with play on *great* as phallic erection; *great* literally means "High, tall; hautie, loftie," RC, s.v. "Haut"), *Lady Macbeth* fears that "greatness" will escape him. If *Macbeth* were a "man's man," his *kindnesse* ("sex, gender," FR) would be full of *Milke* ("Semen," F&H). Unfortunately, *Macbeth* is marred by his "milky" ("soft, gentle"; "timorous, weak, compliant; effeminate," OED) *Nature* (genitals; see note: *Nature*, I.ii.17). *Macbeth's catch* ("Male prick," FR; Fr. "Caiche" is the "membre viril," RC, q.v.) is simply too weak *To catch* ("Fornicate [with]; impregnate," FR) *the neerest* (i.e., sexually apt; see note: *neer'st*, III.i.145) *way* ("vagina," GW).

19–20. ***Ambition... The illnesse should attend it.*** *Ambition* (which was often described as "the sin of *Ambition*") was by no means a commendable quality in Renaissance England. The entire universe, including human society, was believed to conform to a divinely ordained hierarchy (see note: I.iv.29–30). Consequently, *Ambition* (which means both "arogance," JP, q.v., and "excessive desire of honor, preferment, or promotion," RC, q.v.) was seen as an affront to God. *The illnesse* ("Bad moral quality," OED) most commonly understood to *attend* ("to waite upon, to do service unto," JF, s.v. "Servire") *Ambition* was "Treacherie, treason, unfaithfulnesse, disloyaltie" (RC, s.v. "Foy de Granes"), for "Treachery ever attendes upon Ambition" (Robert Wilson, *The Three Lords and Three Ladies of London*).

20–21. ***What thou would'st highly... holily.*** What Macbeth "would" (desires, wishes for) *highly* ("earnestly," OED; "Profoundly, deeply," RC, s.v. "Profondement"), he "would" (desires) *holily* ("sincerely, justly, purely, uprightly," "blameleslie, honestlie," TT, s.v. "Intĕgrē").

23–24. ***that which cryes... if thou have it.*** To "cry" is (a) "to proclaim; to appoint or ordain by proclamation" (OED); (b) "To call, to bidde, to will and invite" (TT, s.v. "voco"); (c) to "demand loudly" (OED); and (d) "To be in labour, to be in a state of parturition" (JJ; "crying" is "Childbirth, labour," JJ). *That which cryes* (i.e., *Macbeth's* incipient sovereignty, *that which* has been supernaturally proclaimed) *cryes* (invites) him by "crying" (demanding), "*Thus thou must do, if thou have it*" (i.e., "You *must* kill the king *if* you are to *have* the crown").

25–26. ***And that which... should be undone.*** *Macbeths Wife* continues her thought from line 23, above. If *Macbeth* is to attain the crown, the situation *cryes* (demands, requires) *rather that Macbeth feare to doe* the murder *Then* to wish it *should be undone* ("Not done; unaccomplished, uneffected," OED). *Lady Macbeth* feels it will be far easier to dispel her husband's fears than to overcome his unwillingness.

26. ***High.*** *High* is a variant spelling of "hie" meaning "To hasten, make haste" (OED). There is possible additional play on *High* as (a) "Of exalted rank" (OED); and (b) an "innuendo of the sexual erection" (JH). Cf. *Spirits*, line 27, below; and I.vii.72–73.

That I may powre my Spirits in thine Eare,

And chastise with the valour of my Tongue

All that impeides thee from the Golden Round,

Which Fate and Metaphysicall ayde doth seeme   [30]

To have thee crown'd withall.

Enter Messenger.   [I.v.2]

What is your tidings?

Mess.   The King comes here to Night.

---

27. **powre my Spirits in thine Eare.** *Lady Macbeth's* words evoke Proverbs 1:23: "Turne you at my reproofe: behold, I will powre out my spirit unto you, I will make knowen my wordes unto you." *Macbeths Wife* fears that her husband lacks "spirit" ("Courage; mettall," "hart, stomacke; valour, stoutnesse, bouldnesse, hardinesse, forwardnesse; also, confidence, assurance," RC, s.v. "Courage"). She will therefore *powre* (variant spelling of "pour"; see note: *powr'd*, I.iii.111) her own *Spirits* (bodily and mental qualities; vital force) into his *Eare*.

Lady Macbeth also fears that her husband lacks "spirit" ("semen," EP) and "spirit" (sexual potency; "the Elizabethans thought that 'wind' in the body was one cause of tumescence and that this 'wind' was described, in contemporary writings, as 'spirits' or 'vaporous spirits.' Hence 'spirit' = erection-causing wind," JH); cf. lines 16–17, above. *Macbeths Wife* will *powre* her own "manly" *Spirits* ("Vital power or energy," OED) into her husband's *Eare* ("Testicles," FR; literally "the part of a cereal plant which contains its flowers or seeds," OED). She will thus infuse him with her own *powre* ("power": "sexual capacity," JH). Cf. *the valour of my Tongue*, line 28, below; and lines 48–50, below.

28–29. **chastise... All that impeides thee from the Golden Round.** *Lady Macbeth* intends to *chastise* ("correct, reprove," TB, s.v. "Castigate") *All* in her husband's character that *impeides* him *from the Golden Round* (ostensibly, "*the Golden* crown"; *Round* can mean any "spherical object," OED). *Golden Round* also calls to mind Ecclesiastes 12:6 ("Whiles the silver corde is not lengthened, nor the golden round broken, nor the pitcher broken at the well, nor the wheele broken at the Cisterne, & dust returne to earth as it was, and the Spirit to God that gave it," James Melville, *Ane Fruit-*

ful and Comfortable Exhortatioun anent Death). *Golden Round* is variously worded in different editions of the Bible as "golden bowl" (King James Bible), "golden headband" (1610 Douay Bible), and "golden well" (1568 Bishops' Bible). The marginal note to the parallel verse in the Bishops' Bible (Ecclesiastes 12:7) explains that the "golden well" is "The yelowe skinne that co[uereth the brayne," but in a wider sense *the Golden Round* symbolizes consciousness and the life-force.

A *Round* is also a "step, of a ladder" (RC, s.v. "Eschellon d'eschelle"). Biblically, *the Golden Round* is associated with Jacob's vision of "a ladder set up on the earth, and the top of it reached to heaven" (Genesis 28:12), "a golden ladder, (embleme of prayer, by whose steppes wee climbe to Heaven)" (Thomas Dekker, *Brittannia's Honor*). In Medieval and Renaissance philosophy, Jacob's ladder was linked with the *scala naturae*, "And this is that Homers golden chaine, which reacheth downe from heaven to earth, by which every creature is anexed and depends of his Creator" (Robert Burton, *Anatomy of Melancholy*). *Macbeths Wife*, however, has no regard for the "ladder of pure golde, so artificially wrought, that who so listeth to goe there on: shall be sure to come safely up into the presence chamber of Gods ever lasting glory" (Saint Augustine, *The Ladder of Paradise*). Worldly ascent is her sole concern, for "The wicked in this world doe easily run up... all the golden steps of honours and preferments; but upon the highest staire they find the most slipperie standing, and the top of their earthly felicitie is the most immediate and certaine descent unto their greatest downefall" (Robert Bolton, *A Discourse About the State of True Happinesse*). Cf. and see notes: I.iv.29–30 and 60–62.

Macbeth has the opportunity to ascend each *Golden Round* (rung) to the summit of the "ladder of life," and *All that impeedes* him *from* wearing *the Golden Round* (crown) is *the Golden Round* (life, vital spirit) that flows within *Duncan's Golden Round* (braincase, pia mater). *Lady Macbeth* intends to *chastise* ("free from faults, purify," OED; also "strike, or beate," TT, s.v. "Plecto") *from Macbeth's* overly-compassionate *Golden Round* ("pia mater": L. for "tender mother," OED) *All that impeedes* him *from* seizing the crown. Cf. and see notes: *Milke of humane kindnesse*, line 17, above; I.vii.10–11; and II.iii.89–91 and 147.

28. **the valour of my Tongue.** *Valour* is (a) "fortitude, power, strength, force" (JF, s.v. "Fortezza"); and (b) sexual potency (see note: *Valours*, I.ii.25). *Tongue* means both (a) "voice, speech; words; language" (OED); and (b) the genitals (see note: *Trumpet-tongu'd*, I.vii.23).

30. **Metaphysicall.** In a simple sense, *Metaphysicall* refers to "Things supernaturall" (TT, s.v. "Mĕtăphysĭca"). "Metaphysikes" also means "Arts which lifting themselves above the changeable nature of things, doe consider of such as doe subsist in their owne essence, not subject to any alteration; so that the Metaphysickes dealeth only with incorporall, and everlasting things; and in this sense schoole Divinitie is the highest part of the Metaphysickes, being chiefly occupied in contemplatory knowledge of God, angels, and soules of men" (JB, q.v.).

30. **seeme.** *Seeme* can mean (a) "vouchsafe, deign"; (b) "ratify, confirm"; and/or (c) "think fit" (OED).

32–33. **Enter Messenger... tidings.** The messenger whom *Macbeth* sent delivered his *tidings* (which is singular, just like "news") to the *Messenger* who enters in line 32. This second *Messenger* in turn delivers *Macbeth's tidings* to *Lady Macbeth*, because the *Messenger* who originally received the message is too worn out from his journey to deliver it himself (cf. lines 39–41, below).

Lady.	Thou'rt mad to say it.	[35]
	Is not thy Master with him? who, wer't so,	
	Would have inform'd for preparation.	
Mess.	So please you, it is true: our *Thane* is comming:	
	One of my fellowes had the speed of him;	
	Who almost dead for breath, had scarcely more	[40]
	Then would make up his Message.	
Lady.	Give him tending,	
	He brings great newes,	

Exit Messenger.   [I.v.3]

The Raven himselfe is hoarse,   [45]

That croakes the fatall entrance of *Duncan*

Under my Battlements. Come you Spirits,

That tend on mortall thoughts, unsex me here,

And fill me from the Crowne to the Toe, top-full

36. **him.** The king.

37. **inform'd.** To "inform" is (a) to "give notice" (RC2, q.v.); and (b) "to deliver instructions" (JM, s.v. "Informár").

39. **One of my fellowes.** I.e., "*One of my* fellow servants."

39. **had the speed of.** Outdistanced; got ahead of.

40. **for breath.** I.e., "*for* want of *breath.*"

42. **him.** The original messenger, who is exhausted from his journey.

45–47. **The Raven... my Battlements.** *The Raven* is "A bird of ill omen. They are said to forebode death" (DPF). *The Raven That croakes* ("speake[s] hoarsely, or with a broken voice"; "sing[s] harshly, untuneably," RC, s.v. "Grailler") at *the fatall* (both "Pertaining to destinie" and "mortall, deadly," JF, s.v. "Fātālis") *entrance of Duncan Under Lady Macbeth's Battlements is hoarse* ("hath lost his voice," RC, s.v. "Il a veu le loup") from giving warning that *Duncan* will soon "croak" ("die," F&H).

Duncan's entrance will in fact be heralded not by a *Raven* but a martin, and *Duncan* will find the castle not dangerous but seductive (cf. and see notes: I.vi.5–15). *Duncan* does not suspect that he is about to be "ravened" ("carr[ied] off as prey," OED) and "ravened" (i.e., "fucked"; to "raven" is to engage in rough or brutal sex, EP) like *hoarse* (homonym of "whores," HK, pp. 115–116).

47–48. **Come you Spirits... mortall thoughts.** *Macbeths Wife* wishes to fortify her *Spirits* ("Mettle; vigour of mind; ardour; courage; disposition or readiness to assert oneself or to hold one's own," OED). She therefore summons the *Spirits That tend* ("looke unto; to deale in, or meddle with," "also, to covenant, or contract," RC, s.v. "Traicter") *on mortall* ("cruell, deadlie, abhominable," TT, s.v. "Fūnestus") *thoughts.* Whereas *Macbeth* is duped by the Devil into moral transgression (see notes: *why doe you start*, I.iii.57; *can the Devill speake true*, I.iii.120; and I.iii.157–160), *Macbeths Wife* knowingly strikes a deal with the powers of darkness. Any spirit that answers her murderous call must be an "uncleane spirit" ("A wicked Angell or a Devill, uncleane in himselfe, and authour of uncleannesse in others," TW; also see note: *sightlesse substances*, line 56, below).

49. **Crowne to the Toe.** "From the crown to the toes" means "head to foot, all over" (OED), with additional play on *Crowne* as (a) the regal diadem; and (b) the "Genitals" (FR); see notes through line 55, below.

49. **top-full.** "Full to the top; brim-full" (OED).

Of direst Crueltie: make thick my blood,   [50]

Stop up th' accesse, and passage to Remorse,

That no compunctious visitings of Nature

Shake my fell purpose, nor keepe peace betweene

Th' effect, and hit. Come to my Womans Brests,

50–52. **make thick my blood… visitings of Nature.** *Macbeths Wife* wishes for *thick blood* because "They that have the thickest and fattest bloude, are the strongest" (Pliny the Elder, *A Summarie of the Antiquities, and wonders of the worlde*). In *The Touchstone of Complexions*, Levinus Lemnius notes that those

of grosse bloud and thicke Spyrites, are seene to be bolde and full of venturous courage, rude, unmanerlye, terrible, cruell, fierce, and such as wyth very threatening countenaunce and manacinge wordes, make others to stande in feare of them. As concerning any daungerous exploite, they are not a whitte afrayde to hazarde theyr bodyes in the adventure of anye perillous extremitie… For whatsoever they be that have thick grosse bloude, have consequently corpulent and stronge spirites, and hereuppon it groweth that they wil beare a grudge in memorye a longe time, and not easelye forgette those motions and heddines that they once take: & hereuppon also it happeneth that many of them being wounded or hurt in fight, uppon the sight of their owne bloude, do runne upon their enemy more fiercely and egrely, and bestow theyr blowes more vehemently, then afore.

Macbeths Wife wishes for no more *compunctious* (remorseful) *visitings* (used "Of influences affecting the mind," OED) *of Nature* ("Natural feeling or affection," OED).

She wishes for *blood* so *thick* that it will *Stop up* (close, shut, block off) *th' accesse* (admittance; also increase) *and passage* (transmission, access) *to Remorse* ("Doubtful-nesse in conscience, to doe a thing," JB, q.v.; the "pricke of conscience; that part of the soule which opposeth it selfe unto sinne," RC, s.v. "Synderese").

She also wills her *blood* to become so *thick* that it will *Stop up* ("obstruct a canal, duct, passage or pipe in the animal body," OED) her *passage* (vagina; see note: *passage*, I.ii.25). Thus, she will no longer be troubled with the "visiting" ("onset of men-struation," GW2) *of Nature* ("Menstrual discharge," OED). Such *thick blood* might ensure a fierce and ruthless disposition, but unfortunately it also puts a woman at risk for mental and physical ailments: "Sanguis menstrualis… if it be holden beyond due time, is cause and occasion of full great griefes and sickenesse" (Stephen Bateman, *Bat-man uppon Bartholome*); also see note: *purge*, V.iii.67.

Nevertheless, *Macbeths Wife* wishes to be "unsexed" (line 48, above), so she must forego any *visitings of Nature* ("sexual urge; sexual desire," OED). From now on, she will prevent *accesse* ("sexual entry," FR) and *Remorse* (i.e., sexual penetration; *Remorse* is literally "a pricking," JF, s.v. "Pungimento"). She will allow *no visitings of Nature* ("semen," F&H), and bids farewell forever to "compunction" ("Sexual pricking or cop-ulation," FR; "Compunction" is literally "a pricking or stitch, remorse of conscience," TB).

Macbeth's letter to his *Wife* (lines 3–14, above) relates the prediction that he will be king but omits the prediction that he will have no heir. It is uncertain if *Macbeths Wife* ever learns this part of the prophecy (cf. and see note: III.ii.48), but she seems quite willing to exchange fertility for worldly power. By contrast, *Macbeth* is horrified by (and fights tirelessly against) the threat of impotence and sterility (cf. and see notes: I.iii.152–155 and 159; II.iii.126–127; III.i.75–84; III.iv.177–180; IV.i.140–143 and 148–152; and V.iii.29–30).

53. Shake my fell purpose. *Macbeths Wife's fell* ("unmercifull; bloudie, bloud-thirstie, bloudie minded," RC, s.v. "Cruel") *purpose* ("Resolution, determination, inten-tion," OED) is to *fell* ("To kill," JJ) *Duncan*. In order that nothing *Shake* ("weaken, or abate," TT, s.v. "Convello") her resolve, she must make her heart as stony and impenetrable as a *fell* ("A precipitous rock, a rocky hill," JJ).

Macbeths Wife renounces her femininity with the vow that her *fell* ("eager": "Sex-ually eager, passionate," JH) *purpose* ("Buttocks, genitals; fornication," FR; a *purpose* is literally an "end," RC, s.v. "But"; "end" is "allusive of the genital area," GW, and also means "the anus," JH) will not *Shake* (copulate or masturbate, F&H; also see note: *Shakes*, I.iii.158).

53–54. keepe peace betweene Th' effect, and hit. *Macbeths Wife* does not wish any *compunctious visitings of Nature* (line 52, above) to *keepe peace* (prevent hostile action) *betweene* ("In the interval following one event or point of time and preceding another," OED) her *effect* ("purpose," JM, s.v. "Efécto") and its *hit* ("the issue, or suc-cesse of a thing; a working, bringing to passe, making to be," RC, q.v.). She must fol-low through so that *Duncan* sustains a *hit* ("a hurt, a wound, or stroke," JF, s.v. "Feríta").

Despite her usual *effect* (variant of "affect": "amorous desire," EP; "lust," GW), *Macbeths Wife* renounces the *hit* ("copulation," JH). She abandons her *Nature* (sexu-ality and fertility; see note: lines 50–52, above), so she will not *keepe peace* (i.e., a "piece": penis, FR) *betweene* her "affect" (synonymous with "affection": "The seat of the affections and the affections themselves were the 'reins' … the loins," FR) *and hit* (pronounced "it": "The female pudendum," F&H).

And take my Milke for Gall, you murth'ring Ministers,   [55]

Where-ever, in your sightlesse substances,

You wait on Natures Mischiefe. Come thick Night,

And pall thee in the dunnest smoake of Hell,

That my keene Knife see not the Wound it makes,

54–55. **Come to my Womans Brests... Gall.** Properly, *Gall* is "The gall-blad-der and its contents" (OED). "Choler," or "flowing of the gall" (JF, s.v. "Cólera"), was thought to engender "choler" ("anger, ire, wrath," "disdaine, desire of revenge, vexa-tion, rage," JF, s.v. "Ira"). *Gall* therefore came to mean (a) "Bitterness of spirit, asper-ity, rancour" (OED); (b) "Poison, venom" (OED); and (c) "The evill workes of wicked men, whereby they grieve God and man" (TW).

According to ancient physiological wisdom, "every member receiveth nourishment from the stomacke, and doth convert it, according to the nature of the member, as that which the liver receiveth, becomes bloud, that which the gall receiveth, becomes choler, that which the lungs receive, becomes phlegme, and that which passeth into the paps becomes milke" (Francis Meres, *Wits Common Wealth: The Second Part*). *Mac-beths Wife* desires the stoppage of *Milke* and blood (line 50, above) so that only *Gall* (bile, wickedness, poison) will flow in her body. Perhaps (a) she invites the Devil's min-ions to *take* (remove) *Milke* from her *Womans Brests for* ("in exchange for," OED) *Gall*; or (b) her fierce resolve is such that *Milke* (mercy or compassion) no longer flows in her *Womans Brests*, and she invites the demons to suckle *And take* ("receive into one's body," "drink," OED) her *Milke for* ("as," OED) *Gall*. Cf. and see note: *Milke of humane kindnesse*, line 17, above.

55. **murth'ring Ministers.** The *murth'ring Ministers* are Satan's *Ministers* ("ser-vant[s]," "furtherer[s] of," "that serveth or helpeth one in, &c.," TT, s.v. "Mĭnister"), the demons that inspire mankind to murder.

Ministers also contains an "innuendo of copulation" (JH; to "minister" is literally "to be of help, comfort, or service to," OED). If *Macbeths Wife* is "unsexed" (line 48, above), she will lose the ability to conceive when she "mird-ers" ("sport[s] amorously,"

HH, p. 259). Her self-imposed barrenness could in itself be considered an act of homicide, for "the Church decreed as early as the ninth century that any form of contraception other than abstinence was an act of murder" (Meg Lota Brown and Kari Boyd McBride, *Women's Roles in the Renaissance*, p. 95).

56. *sightlesse substances.* Spiritual beings (including angels, devils, and disembodied human souls) may be *sightlesse* (invisible), but they were nevertheless thought to have "substance" ("Substantial existence," "mass," OED). Like the rest of God's creation, incorporeal beings were supposedly composed "of a matter without form or shape. And as St. Jerom interpreteth it, *Ex materia invisa, Of an unseen or invisible thing*" (Robert Fludd, *Mosaicall Philosophy*). In *Dialogicall Discourses Of Spirits and Divels*, John Deacon and John Walker explain that

> the Angels of God (whether good or evill) are truely essentiall and substantiall spirits... Aristotle, he prooves this world to be perfect, for that it consistes of all those things which can be desired therein, or which may in any wise appertain to the perfection thereof. Howbeit, to the perfection of the whole, there is required therein, three severall sorts of substances: the first invisible, the second visible, and the third partly invisible & partly visible. The second sort, namely the visible substances, are the heavens, the elements, and all things made of the elements. The third sort, namely the substances, partly invisible, and partly visible, are men who consist of a soule and body togither, the soule invisible, and the bodie visible. Now then, if Angels, who are of themselves invisible, should not be substances, then should there be wanting to the world, invisible substances: and so, the worlde should be unperfect. But the world, it is perfect, as all, both Philosophers and Divines do affirme. And therefore Angels they be substances invisible and spirituall.

Cf. and see notes: *Thunder, Lightning, or in Raine*, I.i.4; *what seem'd corporall*, I.iii.89; and *the sightlesse Curriors of the Ayre*, I.vii.27.

57. *wait on.* To "serve, attend," "also, to helpe, stead, availe, assist, fit ones turne" (RC, s.v. "Servir").

57. *Mischiefe.* *Mischiefe* is (a) "a shameful & naughtie act: an ill, or villanous deede" (TT, s.v. "Făcĭnus"); (b) "Ill chance, misfortune, mishap, misadventure" (TT, s.v. "Infortūnĭum"); and (c) "Death, great domage, hurt, daunger," "destruction, corruption, undoing" (TT, s.v. "Pernĭcĭes").

57–58. *thick Night... dunnest smoake of Hell.* To *pall* (cover, drape) the *Macbeths'* deadly activities, *Night* must wear the *smoake* (variant spelling of both "smoke" and "smock," OED) *of Hell* as a "dun" ("blacke, sootie, sable, darke, obscure," JF, s.v. "Negriccio") *pall* ("a long robe, also the black velvet laid over a Corps," EC2). *Night* is also *thick* ("Intimate, Familiar," JJ) with *Lady Macbeth's* murderous conspiracy and serves as her *pall* (i.e., accomplice; a *pall* is "A companion. One who generally accompanies another," FG).

59. *my keene Knife... Wound it makes.* *Macbeths Wife* envisions herself murdering *Duncan* with a *keene* ("sharpe," JP) *Knife*, but ultimately *Macbeth* will do the actual killing (cf. II.ii.7, 16–18, and 20).

As a "murderer" (i.e., copulator; the word "has a sexual implication," JA, p. 147), *Macbeths Wife* imagines herself in the male role: her *Knife* ("Penis," FR) is *keene* (i.e., erect; EP defines *keene* as "Sexually ardent or excited," but *keene* literally means "sharp-pointed," JF, s.v. "Pezzuto"). Thus, her *Knife makes* ("mate[s] with," OED) *the Wound* ("vagina," GW). Cf. *unsex me*, line 48, above.

Nor Heaven peepe through the Blanket of the darke,   [60]

To cry, hold, hold.

Enter Macbeth.   [I.v.4]

Great Glamys, worthy Cawdor,

Greater then both, by the all-haile hereafter,

Thy Letters have transported me beyond   [65]

This ignorant present, and I feele now

The future in the instant.

Macb.   My dearest Love,

Duncan comes here to Night.

Lady.   And when goes hence?   [70]

Macb.   To morrow, as he purposes.

Lady.   O never,

Shall Sunne that Morrow see.

Your Face, my *Thane*, is as a Booke, where men

May reade strange matters, to beguile the time.   [75]

Looke like the time, beare welcome in your Eye,

Your Hand, your Tongue: looke like th' innocent flower,

But be the Serpent under't. He that's comming,

60. ***Nor Heaven peepe through... the darke.*** *The Blanket* (literally a "coverlet for a bed," JM, s.v. "Fraçáda") *of the darke* will impede the ability of *Heaven* (God and the heavenly powers; also the sun) to *peepe* ("to prye," "to spie, to looke narrowly, to peere, to watch," JF, s.v. "Guatare"), thus preventing discovery of the murderous scheme.

So that *Heaven* will not *peepe* ("complain," "pule," JJ), *darke* must *Blanket* (cover, conceal) the "blunket" ("skiecolour with specks of graie," TT, s.v. "Graie"). The murder must be performed before the *peepe* ("the daune," "morne or breake of daie," JF, s.v. "Albóre") can "peepe out as the day in a morning, or the Sunne over a mountaine," "shew, present, or manifest himselfe" (RC, s.v. "Paroir"). Should *Heaven* perceive that *Lady Macbeth* is "Blank" ("sheepish, guilty," ND), her plot would be "blunkit" ("Injured by mismanagement, or by some mischievous contrivance," JJ).

61. ***To cry, hold.*** To *cry hold* is to "Stop. The allusion is to the old military tournaments; when the umpires wished to stop the contest they cried out 'Hold!'" (DPF).

64. ***all-haile.*** See note: *All haile*, I.iii.54.

66. ***ignorant.*** "Blinde: darke: unknowen: uncertaine," "privie: hidden: invisible: hard to be knowen" (TT, s.v. "Cæcus").

67. ***The future in the instant.*** *In the instant* ("present time," JB, q.v.), *Macbeth's Wife* "feels" ("perceive[s]," "become[s] aware of," OED) *The future* "at an *instant*" ("at hand," RC, s.v. "Presentement"). She also feels that *The future* presents an *instant* ("Urgent entreaty," OED) to seize the opportunity afforded at this *instant* ("point, moment," RC, q.v.).

74–75. ***Your Face... beguile the time.*** *Macbeth* must not allow *men* to *reade* (discern) *strange* ("extreme," "abnormal," OED) *matters* (subjects of thought) in his *Face*. Should he do so, he will reveal that he is *strange* (spelling variant of "strong": "Flagrantly guilty," OED) of *strange* ("strong": "Of a crime, evil quality, etc.: Gross, flagrant," OED) *matters* (affairs, business). He will thus deprive himself of his best opportunity to murder *Duncan*, for he will *beguile* ("cheat," "disappoint," "foil," OED) *the time* ("the favourable, convenient, or fitting point of time for doing something; the right moment or occasion; opportunity," OED).

76. ***Looke like the time.*** The expression means "to disguise one's true feelings." Cf. Samuel Daniel's *The Civile Wares*:

> He drawes a Traverse 'twixt his greevances;
> Lookes like the time: his eye made not report
> Of what he felt within: nor was he lesse
> Then usually he was, in every part;
> Wore a cleere face, upon a clowdy hart.

77–78. ***looke like th' innocent flower... Serpent under't.*** Proverbial: "Wee are to take most heede of those that come with fairest shewes and pretences to us: for under the sweetest flowers lie commonly hidde the most venemous serpents" (Henry Finch, *An Exposition of the Song of Solomon*). Also cf. *Romeo and Juliet*, III.ii.: "O Serpent heart hid with a flowring face."

Must be provided for: and you shall put

This Nights great Businesse into my dispatch,   [80]

Which shall to all our Nights, and Dayes to come,

Give solely soveraigne sway, and Masterdome.

Macb.   We will speake further.

Lady.   Onely looke up cleare:

To alter favor, ever is to feare: [85]

Leave all the rest to me.

Exeunt.

79–80. *put This Nights great Businesse into my dispatch.* Shakespeare follows Holinshed in making *Macbeths Wife* the principal planner of the murder. In Holinshed, the assassination of King Duff is masterminded by Donwalde's wife, who "shewed him [Donwalde] the meanes whereby he might soonest accomplishe it."

Macbeths Wife enjoins her husband to *put This Nights great* (important, weighty) *Businesse into* her *dispatch* ("action, deed, worke, execution," "achievement," RC, s.v. "Exploict"). *Macbeths Wife* will make a *dispatch* ("cleering the hands of," "a riddance," RC, s.v. "Desfaicte") of *Duncan* by bringing about his *dispatch* ("departure," JM, s.v. "desEmbaráço")—i.e., his death.

Macbeths Wife intends to "unsex" herself (line 48, above) and thus *dis-* (a prefix meaning "To strip of, free or rid of, to bereave or deprive of the possession of," OED) *patch* ("The female pudendum," F&H). Due to her newly-claimed androgyny, *Macbeths Wife* feels she herself has the "balls" to effect *This great* (i.e., erect; see note: *great*, line 18, above) *Businesse* ("penis," GW2). She knows *This Nights Businesse* ("sexual intercourse," EP; also sexual satisfaction, JH) of "screwing" *Duncan* cannot make her *great* ("Pregnant," OED), but it can make her *great* (high ranking, eminent). Cf. and see notes: I.vi.22–26 and II.iii.150–151.

82. *solely soveraigne sway, and Masterdome.* *Macbeths Wife* imagines that *Duncan's* murder will *solely* (only, merely) result in *Macbeth's* attainment of *soveraigne* ("Majestick, Princely, pertaining to a King," TB, s.v. "Regal") *sway* ("Commaund, power, authoritie," "rule," RC, s.v. "Command") *and Masterdome* ("absolute control; dominion, supremacy," OED). *Macbeth*, on the other hand, fears there will be additional consequences; cf. and see notes: I.vii.5–32.

84–85. *Onely looke up cleare... feare.* *Macbeth's Onely* (sole) responsibility in preparation for the murder is to (a) *looke up* ("cheer up, take courage, be cheerful," OED) *cleare* ("Manifestly, evidently," OED); and/or (b) *looke up* ("appeare," JM, s.v. "Assomár") *cleare* ("pure, sincere, without malice, or ill will: courteous, innocent, friendlie," TT, s.v. "Candĭdus"). *Macbeth* must continue to show *favor* ("friendly regard, goodwill," OED) to his guests, for he will arouse suspicion if he is *To alter* ("to be variable, not to be as one was," JM, s.v. "mudár Hito") and *alter* ("change," EC2) his *favor* ("countenance, face," OED). Consequently, he will *ever* (a) *feare* (feel alarmed or afraid); (b) *feare* ("frighten," OED) others; and/or (c) *feare* (be "deter[red] from a course of conduct," OED). Cf. lines 74–78, above.

Act I, scene vi

Scena Sexta.   [1]

Hoboyes, and Torches. Enter King, Malcolme,

Donalbaine, Banquo, Lenox, Macduff,

Rosse, Angus, and Attendants.   [I.vi.1]

Notes I.vi.

2. *Hoboyes.* A "hoboy" is "A lowd instrument of Musicke" (RC, s.v. "Naquaire") of the oboe class, but "It would be a mistake to equate the sixteenth-century English hoboy (hautbois, howeboie) with the modern oboe or even to suggest it was a direct precursor… it was associated with 'loud' (outdoor) music" (Christopher Wilson and Michela Calore, *Music in Shakespeare: A Dictionary*, q.v.). The playing of this instrument "always implies a certain special importance in the music, and is generally connected with a Royal banquet, masque, or procession… Hautboys represented very nearly the climax of power to 17th century ears" (Edward Woodall Naylor, *Shakespeare and Music*, pp. 175–176).

Ostensibly, members of *Macbeth's* household play the *Hoboyes* to honor *Duncan's* entrance into the castle (see note: II.iii.30), but this musical effect was in fact made by the playhouse musicians, who were seated backstage or in the musicians' gallery over the stage.

2. *Torches.* In the theatre of Shakespeare's time, both day and night scenes were presented under more-or-less universal lighting conditions (sunlight at outdoor playhouses, and sunlight shining through the windows and/or uniform candlelight at indoor playhouses). Therefore, although the *King* supposedly arrives at the *Macbeths'* castle after sunset, the stage would have been brightly lit, and the *Torches* (i.e., supernumerary characters carrying *Torches*) serve as a visual reminder that this scene occurs after dark.

2. *Enter King.* The *King* arrives at the gates of *Macbeth's* castle, where *Macbeths Wife* greets him and conducts him within (lines 16–43, below). As Matthew Johnson observes in *Behind the Castle Gate* (p. 72), the *King's* entering the castle as a guest invokes a

> set of social and cultural connotations… One trusts one's host not to abuse the rules of hospitality. The architecture of the gate acts as a series of visual reminders and frames for that trust. The first action of the guest is to walk or ride up, under the view of the battlements, arrowslits and gunports, stand under the marchicolations of the gate, and wait for entry. The body of the guest is… deliberately made vulnerable, and this vulnerability is accentuated upon entry.

Cf. and see note: *loved Mansonry*, line 10, below.

King.   This Castle hath a pleasant seat,   [5]

         The ayre nimbly and sweetly recommends it selfe

         Unto our gentle sences.

Banq.   This Guest of Summer,

         The Temple-haunting Barlet does approve,

         By his loved Mansonry, that the Heavens breath   [10]

         Smells wooingly here: no Jutty frieze,

         Buttrice, nor Coigne of Vantage, but this Bird

         Hath made his pendant Bed, and procreant Cradle,

         Where they must breed, and haunt: I have observ'd

         The ayre is delicate.   [15]

5–15. ***This Castle... The ayre is delicate.*** The *Macbeths* have chosen *a pleasant* ("comfortable," JM, s.v. "Améno"; "wel husbanded and appointed," JF, s.v. "Ornatus") *seat* ("a site, a situation," JF, s.v. "Sito") on which to build their *Castle. The ayre* (atmosphere, wind) *nimbly* ("handsomely, gracefully," RC, s.v. "Dextrement") *and sweetly* ("softly, smoothly; mildly, graciously, courteously, lovingly," RC, s.v. "Doucement") *recommends it selfe Unto* the *King's gentle* ("tractable, patient, quiet, still, amiable," JF, s.v. "Placido") *sences* (physical perceptions and sensations). *Banquo* agrees that *The ayre* ("Outward appearance, impression, or look; apparent character or manner," OED) of the place *is delicate* ("Delightful, charming, pleasant, nice," OED).

The ayre is also *delicate* ("wanton," TT, s.v. "Dēlĭcātus"), as befits a *Castle* ("vagina," GW2) with *a pleasant* ("gamesome," RC, s.v. "Joyeux") *seat* ("vulva," GW; a *seat* is literally a "A Place," OED; "place" means the genitals; see note: *place*, I.vii.72). *The ayre nimbly* ("lustily," RC, s.v. "Alaigrement") *and sweetly* ("wantonly," RC, s.v. "Delicatement") *recommends it selfe Unto* one's *gentle* (with play on "genital") *sences* ("sensuality," EP; "sensual nature," GW2).

The *Macbeths* have succeeded in making their *ayre* (i.e., "iyre" or "ire": anger, wrath) seem *gentle* ("without malice, faithfull, sincere," RC, s.v. "Bonnaire"). The *King* places himself in the *Macbeths'* power due to his *gentle* ("easie to be ruled or vanquished, weake," TT, s.v. "Făcĭlis") *sences* (wits, intelligence, understanding) and *delicate* ("softe," "that can not decerne thinges," TE, s.v. "Blax") *ayre* ("manner," DPF). Thus, the *King* makes himself into *a pleasant* ("A jester, a clown, a fool," OED) and a *seat* (i.e., an "ass"; literally "all that parte of the bodie wheron one sitteth, the buttocks, the hinder parts, the fundament," TT, s.v. "Sĕdes"). Cf. and see note: *An absolute Trust*, I.iv.19; and *loved Mansonry*, line 10.

8–9. *This Guest of Summer… Barlet.* *Barlet* is traditionally regarded as a typographical error for "marlet," a variant of "martlet" which means both "the swift" and "the house martin" (OED). *Banquo's* description of the *Barlet* as *Temple-haunting* suggests that the martin is the bird intended (Shakespeare also describes this bird's habit of nesting on walls in *The Merchant of Venice*, II.ix.: "the Martlet / Builds in the weather on the outward wall"). That the bird is a *Guest of Summer* also argues in favor of the martin. In *The Guide Into Tongues*, John Minsheu fancifully conjectures an etymology for "Martinets, Martins, Martelets, or Martens": "they are called Martlets or Martens, because they come unto us about the end of March, and goe away before S[aint] Martins day, that is about the twelfth of November, by reason of cold" (q.v.).

Yet another argument in favor of the martin is that this bird would be active during the *King's* late arrival (cf. and see note: *Torches*, line 2, above): "In the dusk of evening the Martins may often be seen flying about at so late an hour, that their bodies are almost invisible in the dim and fading twilight, and their presence is only indicated by the white patches upon their backs, which reflect every fading ray" (John George Wood, *Birds*, p. 118).

The martin also holds a more sinister aspect. In *Masque of Queenes*, Ben Jonson explains that the witches' "little Martin is he that cals them to their conventicles, which is done in a humane voice." In *Wits Miserie*, Thomas Lodge warns that "This Divell if he fall acquainted with you… he ties you to Martinet their familiar, maketh you honour Sathan in forme of a Bull, binding you to horrible and abhominable crimes."

In fairness to Shakespeare's much-maligned typesetters, it should also be said that *Barlet* might not be a misprint. According to OED, the earlier form of "marlet" was "merlet," which in addition to being a type of bird means "A battlement of a wall" (RC, q.v.). It is conceivable that the bird known as the "merlet" (or "marlet," "martlet," "martin," and "martinet") drew its name from its habit of nesting in "merlets," or high exterior walls. If so, then evidence for *Barlet* as a bona fide variant of "marlet" is arguably found in John Grange's 1577 *The Golden Aphroditis*. Grange twice uses "bartlet" for "merlet" (meaning "battlement") where he describes "the curious workemanship of the bartlets & turrets," and "The pinnacles and bartlettes of white free stone." Grange's "bartlets" and "bartlettes" strongly suggest that there is more to Shakespeare's *Barlet* than mere typesetter error.

9. *approve.* To *approve* means "to proove," "to confirme, to establish, to allow, to perswade or shew by reason, and example that it is good" (JF, s.v. "Probare").

10. *loved Mansonry.* The verb "manson" (variant of "mansion") means "To dwell, reside, or stay" (OED, s.v. "mansion"). In nouns formed from verbs, the suffix "-ary" means "belonging to or engaged in" (OED, q.v.); the suffix *-ry* is used to "denote the place where an employment is carried on, as *bakery, brewery, fishery, pottery*" (OED, s.v. "-ery"). *Mansonry* therefore means either (a) "dwelling in a place"; or (b) "the place where one resides." *Mansonry* may additionally play on (a) "mansionry" meaning an ecclesiastical residence (cf. *Temple-haunting*, line 9, above); and/or (b) *Manson* ("mansion") "aerie" (a nest).

The martin's *Mansonry* (i.e., its nest or its residing nearby) is *loved* because in popular superstition it is fortuitous for the bird to nest on one's house. Accordingly, it is extremely unlucky to harm the bird or its nest. In "Against Barbarity to Animals,"

Enter Lady.   [I.vi.2]

King.   See, see, our honor'd Hostesse:

              The Love that followes us, sometime is our trouble,

              Which still we thanke as Love. Herein I teach you,

              How you shall bid God-eyld us for your paines,   [20]

              And thanke us for your trouble.

Alexander Pope states that it is "ominous or unlucky to destroy some sorts of Birds, as *Swallows* and *Martins*; this Opinion might possibly arise from the Confidence these Birds seem to put in us by building under our Roofs, so that it is a kind of Violation of the Laws of Hospitality to murder them." The martin thus serves as an ironic symbol for the *King*, who makes himself a "martin" ("A jackass," DPF) by trusting to the *Macbeths'* hospitality. Cf. *Hostesse*, lines 17, 33, and 42, below; *Host*, line 40, below; and I.vii.18–20.

    11. **Smells.** To "smell" is (a) to emit an odor; and (b) "To have or exhibit a touch, tinge, or suggestion of something" (OED).

11. **wooingly.** *Wooingly* means (a) "Enticingly, alluringly" (OED); and/or (b) "Wantonly, impudently" (OED).

11. **Jutty.** The noun *Jutty* means "A penthouse," "part of a building that juttieth beyond, or leaneth over, the rest" (RC, s.v. "Soupenduë"). However, the absence of a comma after *Jutty* suggests that it is here an adjective meaning "jutting out." (OED dates *Jutty* in this sense from 1827, but dates "jetty" in the same sense from 1611.)

11. **frieze.** The "Cornice, the Crests, furniture, and finishing at the upper end of a Column or Pillar" (TB, s.v. "Frize").

12. **Buttrice.** "Buttresses" are "Staies for to beare up any building, or make it strong" (JB, q.v.).

12. **Coigne of Vantage.** A *Coigne* (in modern spelling, "quoin") is "an angle, nooke, or corner" (RC, s.v. "Coing"). When the house martin nests on buildings (see note: *Barlet*, line 9, above), its nest "is placed against the wall, under the gutter of the roof, in a corner of, or above windows, in fact anywhere where a projecting ledge affords some sort of shelter above it" (Charles Dixon, *The Nests and Eggs of British Birds*, p. 161). Martins will nest in each *Coigne of Vantage* (corner or nook that affords a *Vantage*, or opportunity) that is located in "A place *of Vantage*" ("an elevation," OED). Such a *Coigne* provides the birds a convenient place to "coyne" ("ingender, bring forth," TT, s.v. "Prōcūdo") their young. Cf. *procreant Cradle*, line 13, below.

13–14. **his pendant Bed... breed, and haunt.** According to popular tradition, the *Barlet* (a.k.a. "martin") cannot take flight from the ground. The bird therefore *must* (is obliged to) *haunt* ("frequent, resort often unto," RC, s.v. "Converser avec") an elevated *Cradle* (i.e., a bird's nest; a *Cradle* is literally "a basket-like grating or framework," OED) which is *pendant* ("Hanging; depending, suspended; stooping, declining, dangling or falling downwards," RC, q.v.). In *A Display of Heraldrie*, John Guillim explains that

> The *Martlet* or *Martinet*... hath legges so exceeding short, that they can by no meanes goe; and thereupon it seemeth the Grecians doe call them *Apodes, quasi sine pedibus*, not because they doe *want feet*, but because they have not such use of their *feet* as other *birds* have. And if perchance they fall upon the ground, they cannot raise themselves upon their feet as others doe, and so prepare themselves to flight. For this cause they are accustomed to make their *Nests* upon *Rockes* and other high places, from whence they may easily take their flight, by meanes of the support of the *aire*.

The martin's *procreant* ("Of, relating to, or enabling procreation," OED) *Cradle* (with probable play on *Cradle* meaning "The female pudendum," F&H, s.v. "monosyllable") is also the *Bed* (regarded as a place of lovemaking and childbirth) where the bird *must breed* (procreate, produce offspring).

18–21. **The Love that followes us... your trouble.** The *King's* presence creates *trouble* (labor, toil, exertion) for those such as the *Macbeths* who *Love* and "follow" (attend upon, accompany) him. Their affectionate efforts *sometime* give the *King trouble* (worry, distress), which he nevertheless thanks *as Love*. Because the *King* visits *Lady Macbeth* out of *Love*, she can likewise learn from the *King's* example to *bid* ("entreat, beg, ask, pray," OED) that *God-eyld* (a corruption of "God yield," where "yield" means to "reward, remunerate, recompense, repay," OED) the *King* for the *paines* she takes on his behalf. (The *King* probably uses *us, our*, and *we* to indicate solely himself, but he may speak collectively of all mankind; see note: *our*, V.v.28.)

Lady.   All our service,

In every point twice done, and then done double,

Were poore, and single Businesse, to contend

Against those Honors deepe, and broad,   [25]

Wherewith your Majestie loades our House:

For those of old, and the late Dignities,

Heap'd up to them, we rest your Ermites.

King.   Where's the Thane of Cawdor?

We courst him at the heeles, and had a purpose   [30]

To be his Purveyor: But he rides well,

And his great Love (sharpe as his Spurre) hath holp him

To his home before us: Faire and Noble Hostesse

We are your guest to night.

22–26. **All our service... our House.** If *All* the *Macbeths' service* ("discharge of any office or dutie, doing of worke," JM, s.v. "Ministério") were *done twice In every point* (detail), it would still be *poore* (paltry, insignificant) *and single* ("Slight, poor, trivial," OED, with play on *single* meaning "not double," TT, s.v. "Simple") *Businesse* (observance, diligence). The *Macbeths' service twice done* is nothing *to contend* ("to compare with"; also "to proove masteries, to sue one an other," TT, s.v. "Certo") *Against* ("Towards, with respect to, in regard to," OED) the *deepe* (important, significant) *and broad* ("ample, large, big, great, wide," TT, s.v. "Lātus") *Honors* that the *King* has bestowed upon them. These *Honors* are so *deepe* ("heavy," OED) that they are a *deepe* (serious, grave, solemn) "load" (burden).

In truth, *Lady Macbeth's service* is a *double* ("A trick," F&H). She and her husband are both *deepe* ("profoundly cunning, artful, or sly," OED) and *double* ("False, counterfeit, untrue, lying, deceiving, unfaithfull, trecherous," "hollow-harted," RC, s.v. "Fauls"). Their sole intention is to "serve" ("To maim; to wound; to punish," F&H) the *King*, and their seeming loyalty is a blind to "do him double" (i.e., deceive or betray him; cf. "thou diddest double and hadst a false intention before God," Sébastien Michaelis, *The Admirable History of the Possession and Conversion of a Penitent woman*).

Lady Macbeth ironically offers the *King* her *service* ("Sexual attentions," JH) when she welcomes him to her *House* (with play on *House* meaning "brothel"), for the *Macbeths* intend to do the *King double* (i.e., "screw" him; *double* is "allusive of copulation," GW2). The *Macbeths* plan *to contend* ("Struggle together, sexually," EC) and "serve" ("possess carnally," F&H, s.v. "Ride") the *King*, and their *deepe* ("A play on sexual ingression," JH) *and broad* (indecent, lewd) *Businesse* (copulation; see note: *Businesse,* I.v.80) will make the *King poore* (i.e., a "puer": L. for "boy," "catamite," FR) *and single* (i.e., "buggered"; see note: *single,* I.iii.158). The *Macbeths* will not fail to "do" ("rob and cheat," FG) the *King,* and they will "do" ("copulate with," EP) him *In every point* (i.e., "orifice"; a *point* is literally a "puncture; a minute hole, impression, or dot made by pricking," OED). Cf. and see note: *Unmannerly breech'd with gore,* II.iii.151.

The *King* does not realize that the *Macbeths* have a "load" (i.e., are "full of shit"; "load" alludes to the "bowels, full of undigested food or fæces," FR), so he is in for some *poore* (i.e., "shit"; *poore* is a variant of "pure": "dung," HH, p. 131) when the *Macbeths* "do [their] business" ("evacuate," F&H). The *King* should indeed expect *service* (i.e., a toilet; cf. JM's "Servício": "a privy, a close stoole") when he enters the *Macbeths' House* ("a privy," OED).

27–28. *For those of old… your Ermites.* *To* ("In addition to, besides," OED) the *Honors* (line 25, above) which the *King Heap'd up* ("increased, laide on," JM, s.v. "Cogolmádo") *of old* ("in old time, in time past," RC, s.v. "Anciennement"), he has "Up-heaped" ("well heaped on," RC, s.v. "Huvelot") the *Macbeths* with *late* (recent) *Dignities* ("Dignitie" means "Honour; renowne, reputation, credit, praise, glorie, fame," "promotion; also, an Honour; or, an honourable estate, inheritance, or title, bestowed by a Prince, or great Lord," RC, s.v. "Honneur").

In exchange, *Lady Macbeth* vows that she and her husband will *rest* (remain) the *King's Ermites* (hermits)—i.e., that they will always pray for him. Prayer was the chief work of the "hermite" ("one that hath forsaken the world and betaken himselfe to contemplation and godly life," JM, s.v. "Eremitáno"), who was usually sponsored by some wealthy patron. *Lady Macbeth's* statement is grimly ironic, for *Ermites* were expected to pray for the souls of dead benefactors as well as living.

30–33. *We courst him at the heeles… home before us.* *Macbeth* went in advance to serve as the *King's Purveyor* ("An Officer of the King or other great Personage, that provides Corn and other Victual for the house of him whose Officer he is; a Provider," TB, q.v.), but the *King had a purpose* (intention) *To be Macbeth's Purveyor* instead. The *King* therefore *courst* ("hyed, speeded, posted, gallopped," "hunted, chased, followed hard, hotly pursued," RC, s.v. "Couru") *Macbeth at the heeles* (in hot pursuit, close behind). The *sharpe* (eager, ardent, earnest) *Macbeth* nevertheless arrived first, for his *great Love holp* (helped) *him home as* quickly *as his sharpe* (cutting, keen-edged) *Spurre* ("A device for pricking the side of a horse in order to urge it forward, consisting of a small spike or spiked wheel attached to the rider's heel," OED).

Macbeth, however, is not motivated by *Love.* He is *sharpe* ("subtile," "wylie, craftie," JF, s.v. "Arguto") and driven by a *sharpe* ("Severe, merciless," OED) *Spurre* ("incentive, or incitement," OED). *Macbeth,* who plans to "screw" the *King, rides* (copulates, F&H) *well.* His *sharpe* ("Harde," "stiffe," TT, s.v. "Dūrus"; also "piercing, penetrating," "that will go or sinke in deepely," JM, s.v. "Penetrativo") *Spurre* ("pricke," TT, s.v. "Stimulus") easily brings him *home* (i.e., to sexual climax; see note: *homeward,* I.iii.32). Cf. and see note: I.vii.29–30.

La.	Your Servants ever,	[35]
	Have theirs, themselves, and what is theirs in compt,	
	To make their Audit at your Highnesse pleasure,	
	Still to returne your owne.	
King.	Give me your hand:	
	Conduct me to mine Host we love him highly,	[40]
	And shall continue, our Graces towards him.	
	By your leave Hostesse.	

Exeunt

35–38. **Your Servants ever... Still to returne your owne.** *Compt* (variant of "count" meaning "account," OED) is "The price that is given for a thing that is bought: hyre, value," "reward, monie" (TT, s.v. "Prĕtium"). *In compt* means "on account": "owing payment" or "in debt" (cf. Angel Day's *The English Secretorie*: "Remembring how manie waies I am beholding unto you, I remaine in accompt of your courtesies, rather studious to thinke on them, then anie waies able to requite them").

As the *King's Servants, Macbeth* and his wife *Have* (hold, possess) *theirs* ("those [persons] belonging to them," OED), *themselves, and what is theirs* (i.e., their property) *in compt* ("in debt" or "owing") to the *King* (cf. and see note: *your meere Owne,* IV.iii.104). Accordingly, the *Macbeths* must *make their Audit* (judicial settlement of accounts) *at the King's pleasure.* The *Macbeths* are required *Still* (always, on every occasion) *to returne* (repay, give back) the *King's owne,* which can mean (a) that which belongs to him; or (b) his "owing": "that which is owed [to him], a debt" (OED).

39–42. **Give me your hand... By your leave Hostesse.** The *King* says *By your leave* ("with your favor," "saving your displeasure," TT, s.v. "Pace") as he takes the *hand* of *Lady Macbeth,* who either leads or accompanies him into the castle. In *Gestures and Looks in Medieval Narrative* (pp. 48–49), John Anthony Burrow explains that

> The holding of hands takes two generally distinct forms. Either one person leads another 'by the hand,' or two people walk together 'hand in hand.' These actions differ in their significance. To lead someone by the hand is an act of courtesy by which the leader bestows honour on the led, most often when the leader is on his or her home ground and so can take the initiative with newly arrived guests and the like...
>
> Polite leading commonly involves some advantage, enjoyed by the leader but courteously yielded to the led. To go 'hand in hand' has a different significance, for the phrase implies no advantage on either side. The two parties treat each other as equals.

Either way, the *King* bestows an honor upon *Lady Macbeth.* If she leads the *King* by the *hand,* then he grants her a superior position as his *Hostesse.* If she walks *hand* in *hand* with the *King,* then he grants her the status of an equal.

40. **highly.** *Highly* means (a) "greatly, intensely, extremely, very, much" (OED); and (b) "Nobly, honourablie, royallie, magnificallie," "with much commendation, greatlie, with wordes of great honour: with a majestie, solemnely, like a lorde or great man: with a great gravitie or majestie" (TT, s.v. "Magnĭfĭcē").

41. **Graces.** A "grace" is "a thankful gifte" (TT, s.v. "Chărisma").

Act I, scene vii

Scena Septima.   [1]

Ho-boyes. Torches.

Enter a Sewer, and divers Servants with Dishes and Service

over the Stage. Then enter Macbeth.   [I.vii.1]

Macb.   If it were done, when 'tis done, then 'twer well,   [5]

It were done quickly: If th' Assassination

Could trammell up the Consequence, and catch

With his surcease, Successe: that but this blow

Might be the be all, and the end all. Heere,

Notes I.vii.

3–4. Enter a Sewer... over the Stage. According to TB (q.v.), the title of *Sewer* is applied to him that issues or comes in before the meat of the King or other great Personage, and placeth it upon the Table... I have heard of an old French book containing the Officers of the King of Englands Court, as it was anciently governed, wherein he, whom we now call Sewer, was called Asseour, which comes from the Fr. (Asseoir) to set, settle or place, wherein his Office in setting down the meat is well expressed. And Sewer, as it signifies an Officer, is by Fleta Latined Assessor, a setter down.
Here, the *Sewer* precedes *Servants* who carry both *Dishes* ("platters or plates," JF, s.v. "Piatti"; also the food served upon such plates) and *Service* ("a course of dishes at table," RC, s.v. "Més"). They pass *over the Stage*, which might mean (a) *over* ("across from side to side," OED) *the* main *Stage* platform; or (b) *over* ("Above," OED) *the* main *Stage* platform on the balcony of the tiring-house facade situated at the rear of the stage. The *Sewer* and the *Servants* are not given specific exit cues, so they may pass back and forth in the background throughout the scene. Their presence dramatically underscores the fact that *Macbeth* and *Lady Macbeth* are surrounded by others as they plan *Duncane's* murder, so they are in continual danger of discovery.
5–6. If it were done, when 'tis done... quickly. *If it* (i.e., *Duncane's* murder) has no unforeseen consequences and *were done* (ended, finished) *when 'tis done* (executed, performed), *then 'twer well It were done quickly* (without delay). However, *Macbeth* fears that this will not be the case (cf. and see notes through line 32, below).

6–7. **If th' Assassination... the Consequence.** As a verb, to *trammell* is "to catche fysshe or byrdes" (JP, q.v.). As a noun, a *trammell* is a "net for Partridges" (RC, s.v. "Tramail") or a "Drag-net, or Draw-net for fish" (RC, s.v. "Trameau"). There are three aspects of the *trammell* that are especially apposite to *Macbeth's* analogy. When used to catch birds, the *trammell* (1) is used in ambush; (2) is used at night; and (3) requires at least two people to use it effectively. As described by Richard Blome in *The Gentlemans Recreation,*

> The use of this Net is thus; a little after Sunset go into some Field, or place where
> you think to find sport, and there hide your self, and you will soon know if there
> be any [birds] by their Calling... be sure to observe exactly the place where they
> roost, by making some Mark at a distance, to the end you may not be to seek
> the place in the dark, Then prepare two strait light Poles which must be as long
> as the Net is broad... This Sport cannot well be performed without one to assist
> you... When the Partridges rise both must let go their hands, and let the Net
> fall on the ground upon them... This way is good only in dark Nights.

Macbeth wishes that *th' Assassination* (murder) *Could trammell up* (catch as in a net) *the Consequence* (result, outcome) of his own kingship as securely as *Duncane's* corpse will be "trammeled up" (wrapped up in his shroud; to "trammel" is "To bind up a corpse," OED). *Macbeth* plans to murder *Duncane* for the *Consequence* ("attaining, atchieving, obtaining," JM, s.v. "Conseguimiénto") of his own *Consequence* ("Importance in rank and position, social distinction," OED), and he hopes that *th' Assassination* will have no further *Consequence* (negative effect). At the same time, *Macbeth* fears the loss of his own *Consequence* (i.e., offspring; *Consequence* is literally "issue," "a succession, continuance, or unintermitted course of things," RC, s.v. "Suitte"). Cf. *Successe,* line 8, below; and see note: *murth'ring,* I.v.55.

7–9. **catch With his surcease... the end all.** *His* was formerly used as the third person genitive pronoun of both "he" and "it" (OED). Therefore, *his surcease* might mean (a) *his* (i.e., "its," referring to *th' Assassination* in line 6, above) *surcease* (termination, coming to an end); or (b) *his* (i.e., *Duncane's*) *surcease* (end, death). The sense and syntax suggest that *his* refers to *th' Assassination: Macbeth* hopes that *With his* (its) *surcease th' Assassination* will *catch* ("intangle, insnare, inwrap, in a net," RC, s.v. "Enrether"; cf. *trammell,* line 7, above) *Successe,* which means (a) "prosperitie, good luck" (JF, s.v. "Succésso"); (b) the "end of a thing" (JF, s.v. "Fine"); and/or (c) "Succession as of heirs, rulers, etc." (OED).

Macbeth also hopes *that but* (only, solely) *this blow* (stroke, attack) *Might be the be all* ("That which is or constitutes the whole; the whole being," OED), *and the end all.* Although OED considers *end all* to be a noun meaning "That which 'ends all'" (q.v.), *end* might be a noun and *all* an adjective: *Macbeth* hopes that his *end* ("intended result of an action; an aim, purpose," OED), which is *Duncane's end* (death), will be *all* (adjectively used to mean "the whole extent," OED). However, *Macbeth* fears that murdering *Duncane* will be not *the end* but the beginning of his difficulties. Cf. the proverb, "He does ill that does not all; the end crownes the worke" (RC, s.v. "Mal fait qui ne parfait").

Macbeth also hesitates to act because the *Witches'* prophecy foretells that his *Successe* (succession to *Duncane's* throne) will mean the *surcease* (end) of his *Successe* (posterity, children; see note: *successe,* I.iii.150). *Macbeth's blow* ("Sexual stroke or thrust," EP) *Might be all,* for his *catch* (penis; see note: *catch,* I.v.18) will *catch* (engender; see note: *catch,* I.v.18) no *sequence* ("issue," OED) in the *Con* (i.e., "cunt").

But heere, upon this Banke and Schoole of time,   [10]

Wee'ld jumpe the life to come. But in these Cases,

10–11. *But heere, upon this Banke... the life to come.* *Schoole* (which was also spelled "shoal," "schole," "scull," "schule," and "scholl") was dialectally pronounced similarly (or perhaps identically) to "shoal," "scale," "scull," "shell," and "shale," all of which are here encompassed by *Schoole* (see HH, pp. 227–229; and cf. OED's spelling variants for "school," "shoal," "shell," "scale," "shale," and "skull").

In "the vast Seas of time" (Francis Bacon, *Of the Proficience and Advancement of Learning*), *Macbeth's time* (lifetime) is a temporary *Banke* ("sandie hill in the sea, against which the waves doe breake," RC, s.v. "Banc") *and* "shoal" ("shelfe, or hill of sand, appearing above water," JF, s.v. "Assablissement"). *But* (only) *heere* (i.e., in the "*heere* and now"), *this Banke* ("platform," OED) briefly affords a *time* (occasion, opportunity) during which *Macbeth* can *jumpe* ("bound, on, or over," RC, s.v. "Franchir") a "scale" ("A rung or step of a ladder," OED) on the "scale of life" (i.e., the "ladder of life"; see note: I.iv.29). The present *time* (occasion) gives him the chance to immediately *jumpe* ("pass abruptly from one thing or state to another, with omission of intermediate stages," OED) into *the life to come* (i.e., his destined sovereignty). Cf. and see notes: I.iv.60–62; and lines 29–32, below.

Macbeth nevertheless remembers that, because man is both corporeal and spiritual (see note: *sightlesse substances*, I.v.56), "We must not fix our whole attention on these transitory blessings, but must make use of them as ladders, that, being raised to heaven, we may enjoy eternal and immortal blessings" (John Calvin, *Calvin's Bible Commentaries: Isaiah, Part IV*). As John Spencer explains in *Things New and Old*,

> HE that is to climb up some high ladder, must not think, that setting his Foot upon the lowest rownd, he can skip over all the rest and be at the top, without evident danger to himself: Such is the course of our life, just like a Ladder of many rownds set up to some high place: the first step is (or of necessity should be) the thought of God and goodnesse; and the last step, the full assurance of Heaven; but there are in the middle many other steps, as of means, consideration, deliberation, &c. how to love God above all things, and our Neighbours as our selves, and how to demean our selves in the midst of a crooked and froward generation; which if we miss, and step over, no marvel if we never come to the top, but perish in the mid-way to all Eternity.

The ultimate challenge of *Macbeth's time* (mortal existence) is to safely navigate his "vessel" (ship, body containing the soul) into a safe "scale" ("A landing-place," "A seaport town; a trading port," OED from 1682) in *the life to come* (the afterlife). "Banks" and "shoals," which figuratively represent occasions for sin, present dire obstacles to finding a safe "passage out of the swift river of time, into the boundless and bottom-less ocean of eternity" (John Flavel, *The Fountain of Life*). In the soul's journey through *time*, "vertue is so necessarie, that like as a cunning Pylot in a ship, so she sits in the fraile vessell of mans bodie, that but for her guidance, wold either be dashed in peeces against the rockes of affliction, or sinck in the sandes of a thousand temptations" (Joseph Hall, *Two Guides to a good Life*). Cf. "His soule's the pilot, who through various seas / Of time and fortune brings him to the port / Of endlesse quiet" (Thomas Nabbes, *Microcosmus*).

Considered in its spiritual aspect, *Macbeth's time* is a *Banke* ("a stoole, a bench," JM, s.v. "Bánco") in a *Schoole* ("studying place," JF, s.v. "Ginnasio"), for it is man's duty "to beleeve in God, and to serve him; and this vow being thus made, it is the will of God he should be tempted, that in the schoole of temptation he might learn to prac-tise his baptisme" (William Perkins, *The Combat Betweene Christ and the Divell dis-played*). Cf. *teach*, line 12, below; and *Instructions* and *taught*, line 13, below.

This time also serves as a *Banke* ("a Seat or Bench of Judgment," Thomas Blount, *Nomo-Lexikon*) that determines each soul's sentence in *the life to come.* "A just weight and ballance are the Lords" (Proverbs 16:11), and on doomsday God's "shell" ("A scale of a balance," OED) and "scale" ("The pan, or each of the pans, of a balance," OED) will weigh each *life* "with a pair of balances; and the soul and the good deeds in the one balance, and the faults and the evil deeds in the other" (Francis Bacon, *Collection of Apophthegms New and Old*). Cf. *Cases*, line 11 below; *judgement*, line 12, below; *Jus-tice*, line 14, below; and *pleade*, line 23, below; and cf. and see note: *breefe Candle*, V.v.29.

Even so, if *Macbeth* were certain that he *Could trammell up the Consequence* (line 7, above) as readily as he could catch a "shoal" ("A flock of birds," OED) or a "shole of fish" ("a companie of fish togither," JM, s.v. "Cardúme") in a "shale" ("A mesh of a net," OED), then he would willingly *jumpe* ("hazard," OED) *the life to come* (his future state of salvation or damnation). Without further consideration, he would immedi-ately *jumpe* ("seize upon, whether forcibly or by stealth," F&H) *the life to come* (i.e., the kingship).

Traditionally, *time* "is represented as an old man, quite bald, with the exception of a single lock of hair on the forehead" (DPF), but *time* ("occasion," OED) is pic-tured as "A famous old hag, quite bald behind" (DPF, s.v. "occasion"). "Times antient bawde, opportunity" (William Rowley, *All's Lost by Lust*) is here figured as a procuress who runs a "vaulting *Schoole*" ("A bawdy-house," FG) on the *Banke* ("The south side of the Thames opposite London [also called *Bankside*], and the brothel-quarter located there," OED). The bawd *time* ("occasion") provides a "shell" ("female pudendum," F&H) that *Macbeth* can "scale" (mount sexually, F&H). In a bid for "potency" (power, sexual ability), *Macbeth* is eager to seize this "occasion" (vagina, FR; literally "a case," OED) and *jumpe* ("coit athletically and vigorously with," EP) *the life* ("vulva," FR) *to* ("in order to," OED) *come* (experience orgasm, ejaculate).

However, *Macbeth* fears that in so doing he might be made (a) a *But* ("An object at which ridicule, scorn, or abuse, is aimed," OED); (b) a *But* (literally "A buttock," OED) and a *Banke* (an "arse," literally "a seat," FR); and/or (c) a "skul" (i.e., a "bug-ger"; a "skul" is literally "A scullion," JJ; a "scullion" is a "Whore; linked to foul anal smells," FR, who notes that "In sculling, the oar is worked over the stern or rear"). Cf. "the dark-backward and Abisme of Time" (*The Tempest*, I.ii.; the "backward" is "The hinder part of the body," OED; "the anus," JH).

We still have judgement heere, that we but teach

Bloody Instructions, which being taught, returne

To plague th' Inventer, this even-handed Justice

Commends th' Ingredience of our poyson'd Challice   [15]

To our owne lips. Hee's heere in double trust;

First, as I am his Kinsman, and his Subject,

Strong both against the Deed: Then, as his Host,

Who should against his Murtherer shut the doore,

Not beare the knife my selfe. Besides, this *Duncane*   [20]

Hath borne his Faculties so meeke; hath bin

12–14. **We still have judgement... plague th' Inventer.** The notion is ancient. Cf. Psalms 7:15–16: "He made a pit and digged it, and is fallen into the ditch which he made. His mischiefe shall returne upon his owne head, and his violent dealing shall come downe upon his owne pate."

Macbeth doubts the certainty of divine *judgement* (punishment, sentence); cf. line 11, above. Nevertheless, he believes that in harming others *We still* ("invariably" or "yet," OED) *have judgement heere* (in this world, in this life), *that* ("since, seeing that"; also "in that, in the fact that," OED) *we but* (only) *teach Bloody* (cruel, bloodthirsty) *Instructions* (lessons). These *being taught* will *returne To plague* ("to scourge, to punish, to whip," JF, s.v. "Flagellare"; "to hurt, to torment," JF, s.v. "Piagere") *th' Inventer* ("forger, maker, framer, composer," RC, s.v. "Forgeur"; also "a plotter, or practiser of plots," JM, s.v. "Inventór"). Cf. and see note: III.iv.157.

13–16. **returne... To our owne lips.** Holinshed uses the same figure when he describes *Macbeth's* troubled state of mind after *Duncane's* murder: "For the pricke of conscience (as it chaunceth ever in tyrantes, and suche as attayne to any astate by unrightuous meanes) caused him ever to feare, least he should be served of the same cuppe, as he had ministred to his predecessour."

The goddess *Justice* (a.k.a. "Nemesis") was depicted carrying a level balance to signify that she was *even-handed* ("Fair, evenly-balanced; free of bias or preference," OED). *Justice* was also "Drawn with Wings, standing on a Wheel" (Randle Holme, *The Academy of Armory*), and *Macbeth* fears that *Justice* will invariably *returne* ("turn again," OED) her "wheel" (an instrument of torture that signifies "Punishment it selfe, inflicted uppon malefactors," TW, q.v.). Thus, *Justice Commends* ("deliver[s]," EC, s.v. "Betake"; "give[s] one charge," "commit[s] unto the care, of," RC, s.v. "Recommander") *th' Ingredience* ("that which goeth into the making of a thing," HC, q.v.) *of our poyson'd Challice* ("a cup," JF, s.v. "Calice") *To our owne lips.* The *Challice* itself also signifies "Punishment and Affliction" (TDL), as in Psalms 11:6: "Upon the wicked hee shall raine snares, fire and brimstone, and an horrible tempest: this shall be the portion of their cup." Cf. and see note: II.iii.126–127.

16. **double.** See note: *double,* I.vi.23.

17–18. **his Kinsman... his Host.** The ancient law of hospitality was considered sacred and inviolable, so *Macbeth's* duty as the *King's Host* is as great as that of *Kinsman* and *Subject.*

18. **the Deed.** *Deed* is a Scottish variant of "death," *Deed* being "The nothern form of *death* n., formerly in regular use with Northern writers (*dede*), and still dialectal in Scotch" (OED). Cf. JJ's "Dede, Deid": "Death" and "The cause of death."

20. **beare.** With possible play on "bare" meaning "to unsheathe a weapon" (OED).

21. **Faculties.** "Faculty" means (a) "powre, authoritie, might, puissance, or jurisdiction, abilitie, strength, office, rule, governement, dominion" (JF, s.v. "Podestà"); (b) "A profession," "vocation, calling" (RC, s.v. "Profession"); (c) "The intellect," "understanding, apprehension, capacitie; judgement, knowledge, discretion" (RC, s.v. "Intellect"); and (d) the "power of feeling, smelling, &c." (RC, s.v. "Sentive").

21. **meeke.** As a religious man, *Duncane* carried his duties *meeke* (humbly, mildly, mercifully; *meeke* is an adverb as well as an adjective, OED). However, being *meeke* was not necessarily an advantage to a medieval king; see note: *our Captaines,* I.ii.40.

So cleere in his great Office, that his Vertues

Will pleade like Angels, Trumpet-tongu'd against

The deepe damnation of his taking off:

And Pitty, like a naked New-borne-Babe,   [25]

Striding the blast, or Heavens Cherubin, hors'd

Upon the sightlesse Curriors of the Ayre,

---

22. **cleere.** *Cleere* can mean (a) "cleane, unspotted, uncorrupted," "innocent, simple, honest, upright, sincere" (RC, s.v. "Pur"); and (b) "famous, noble in renowne, excellent" (TT, s.v. "Illustris").

22–24. **his Vertues Will pleade like Angels... his taking off.** The *Trumpet*, the traditional instrument of *Angels*, symbolizes God's prophetic voice and His judgment (particularly the Last Judgment when "the trumpet shall sound, and the dead shall be raised incorruptible," 1 Corinthians 15:52).

Try as he might, *Macbeth* cannot quite dismiss the threat of divine justice. He fears that *Duncane's Vertues* (the seven heavenly *Vertues* of "Faith, Hope, Charity, Prudence, Justice, Fortitude, and Temperance," DPF) *Will pleade* ("argue, or open, a cause before a Judge," "sue, contend, goe to law," RC, s.v. "Plaider") *like Angels against* (in opposition to; also "In the opposite scale; on the other side; as a counter-balance to," OED) *The deepe* (heinous) *damnation* ("sin incurring or deserving damnation," OED) *of Duncane's taking off* ("remov[al] by death," OED). Cf. and see notes: *Banke and Schoole*, line 10, above; and II.ii.78–80.

In addition, the *Trumpet* is a "Symbol of virility" (FR; the symbolism perhaps arises from "horn" meaning "an erection of the penis," F&H). *Macbeth* hopes to "fuck" *Duncane* and effect his *taking off* (phallic flaccidity; to "take off" is "To reduce a man's amorousness, especially by causing him an orgasm," EP), but *Macbeth* suspects that "impotence" (sterility, lack of sexual ability) will be the price he must pay for "potence" (power, authority). *Macbeth* fears that he cannot match the "virtue" (virility, HH, p. 113) of *Duncane's* "angel" ("angle": "The penis," F&H, s.v. "Prick") and "tongue" ("Penis," FR). In attempting to use *Duncane* like a *deepe* (with allusion to genital capacity; see note: *deepe*, I.vi.25) *damnation* ("whore or bawd," GW2), *Macbeth* might end up getting "fucked" himself. Cf. and see notes: lines 29–32, below.

25–27. *And Pitty... the sightlesse Curriors of the Ayre.* The imagery evokes many biblical passages, including 2 Samuel 22:11 ("And he rode upon a Cherub, and did flie: and hee was seene upon the wings of the winde"); and Psalms 104:3–4 ("who maketh the cloudes his charet: who walketh upon the wings of the wind. Who maketh his Angels spirits: his ministers a flaming fire"). TB defines *Cherubin* as

> the second of the nine Quires or Ranks of Angels mentioned in Scripture, so called of their sublime knowledge, or illuminated understanding. In Scripture God is said to sit on the Cherubins; because he over-reaches and is above all understanding. They also are said to bear and draw his Chariot: to signifie all his proceedings to be according to wisdom; and to be full of eys, to certifie Gods knowledge to penetrate into all secresies, and all to be open before him. They are set forth only with heads and wings without bodies: whereby is noti-fyed, that greatest understanding is found in spiritual and incorporeal crea-tures, and that over-great corporal cares are impediments to profound knowl-edge.

In Renaissance art, *Cherubin* were often pictured as *naked* infants, so *Pitty* (com-passion, sympathy) is possibly here personified as one of *Heavens Cherubin* (cf. "turne the Fiend Fury into the Cherubin Pity," George Rivers, *The Heroinae*). If so, then line 25 begins a new thought, and *Pitty* is the subject: *Pitty like* (in the form or likeness of) *a naked* (used "to connote a newborn child's vulnerability or innocence," OED) *New-borne-Babe Shall blow the horrid deed in every eye* (line 28, below).

Conversely, *Pitty* might be a verb meaning "To move to pity, excite the compas-sion of" (OED). If so, then line 25 continues the thought from line 22, above, and *Vertues* is the subject: *Duncane's Vertues Will pleade like Angels, And Pitty* (excite com-passion, arouse *Pitty*) *like* (in the same manner as; also "In a like degree; equally [to]," OED) *a naked New-borne-Babe.*

Either way, the *naked New-borne-Babe* is *Striding* (straddling) *the blast* ("curse," OED), which is delivered in the form of (a) a *blast* ("a winde," JF, s.v. "Afflato"), which "denotes Divine Wrath and vengeance, as a strong Wind overthrows whats before it, and inflames the Fire" (TDL); (b) a *blast* (the "sound in an instrument," TT, s.v. "Flāmen"), which signifies divine judgment (cf. and see note: *Trumpet-tongu'd,* line 23, above); and/or (c) a *blast* ("The sudden stroke of lightning, a thunder-bolt," OED), which "by a metaphor signifies the bright or furbisht blade of a Lance or Sword which shines and terrifies like lightning... To denote the Anger of God, a glittering Sword is attributed to him" (TDL).

The *sightlesse* (invisible) *Curriors* ("speedie messenger[s]," RC, s.v. "Poste"; also "horse-rider[s]," RC, s.v. "Courrier") *of the Ayre* are, of course, angels ("Angel" derives from Gk. "angelos": "messenger"), who were sometimes figured as *sightlesse* (without sight, blind) because they look on God, who is "Cloath'd with such light as blindes the angel's eye" (Giles Fletcher, "A Description of Mercy").

Biblically, "the Angels are the Lords chariots and horse, and the Lord himselfe is their rider" (Andrew Willet, *Hexapla in Genesin & Exodum*). By "horses" are "meant the windes or the cloudes... or the Host of Angels, who are Gods Horse-men" (Gio-vanni Diodati, *Pious Annotations upon the Holy Bible*), and "when Angels are figured out with winges, and are said to be clothed with winde or fire, it signifieth nothing else unto us, but that they are swift and ready to execute the will of God" (Sébastien Michaelis, *The Admirable History of the Possession and Conversion of a Penitent woman*).

Cf. and see notes: *sightlesse substances,* I.v.56; and II.ii.78–80.

Shall blow the horrid deed in every eye,

That teares shall drowne the winde. I have no Spurre

To pricke the sides of my intent, but onely   [30]

Vaulting Ambition, which ore-leapes it selfe,

And falles on th' other.

Enter Lady.   [I.vii.2]

How now? What Newes?

La.   He has almost supt: why have you left the chamber?   [35]

Mac.   Hath he ask'd for me?

La.   Know you not, he ha's?

Mac.   We will proceed no further in this Businesse:

He hath Honour'd me of late, and I have bought

Golden Opinions from all sorts of people,   [40]

---

28. **blow the horrid deed in every eye.** *Blow*, which euphemistically means "to damn" (F&H), corresponds to the multiple significations of *blast* (line 26, above) as: (a) "to breath or draw breth," "Also to fill with winde" (JF, s.v. "afflare"); (b) "to sound a signal on an instrument; to blaze abroad as by a trumpet" (F&H); and (c) "To shatter, destroy, or otherwise act upon by means of explosion" (OED).

Duncane possesses *Vertues* (virility, sexual ability; see note: line 22, above) able to *blow* ("To explode, and thus to inject semen into," JH, s.v. "blow up") *in every eye* ("pudendum"; also "anus," FR) *the deed* ("death": "sexual orgasm," JH; see note: *Deed,* line 18, above). By contrast, *Macbeth's* sinful ambition is capable only of a *horrid* (with play on *horrid* / "whored") *deed* ("copulation," TR). Cf. and see notes: lines 29–32, below.

29. **teares.** With possible play on *teares* as (a) "tare[s]": "very small particle[s]" (OED); (b) "rage[s] or passion[s]," "violent flurr[ies]" (OED); and (c) semen (JA, p. 142).

29. **drowne.** To *drowne* is (a) "to plunge or overwhelme in the water" (JF, s.v. "Sommérgere"); (b) "overwhelm, to overpower, by rising above like a flood; to immerse or smother; to overpower (sound) by greater loudness" (OED); and (c) "allusive of coitus" (GW2).

29. **winde.** Either *Duncane's Vertues* (line 22, above), *Pitty* (line 25, above), *or Heavens Cherubin* (line 26, above) will arouse such *winde* ("rage," OED) as to overpower *Macbeth's winde* ("Vain imagination or conceit," OED).

The *winde* was "regularly figured as wanton" (GW) and also "as fructifier" (GW2). *Duncane's Vertues* (i.e., sexual potency; see note: line 22, above) will arouse *winde* ("rage": "Violent desire or lust; burning sexual passion," OED) that will overpower *Macbeth's* ability to *winde* (copulate, JH).

29–32. **I have no Spurre... falles on th' other.** In his 1578 *Thesaurus Linguae Romanae & Britannicae*, Thomas Cooper defines "Desultor" as "A vaulter that leapeth up and downe from a horse," and "Desultores" as "Horsemen that in battaile had two horses, and quickly would chaunge horses, and leape from one to an other." The ability to "vault" (leap onto a horse's back) was essential to a mounted combatant.

As a soldier, *Macbeth* is an accomplished "vaulter," but he is no match for the formidable horsemen who serve as *Duncane's* champions (lines 26–27, above). Besides, *Macbeth* has *no Spurre* ("provocation; any thing that incenseth, stirreth, or urgeth forward," RC, s.v. "Esguillon") *To pricke* ("provoke, or drive forward, to move, to urge, to instigate, to presse or egge on," JF, s.v. "Spíngere") *the sides of* his *intent* ("a will, a desire, a wish, a longing, a purpose," JF, s.v. "Vóglia"), which is here figured as the flanks of a horse. *Macbeth* can claim only *Vaulting* ("Desultorious": "unconstant, mutable," TB, q.v.) *Ambition* ("Unlawfull, or immoderate desire of soveraignty," JB, q.v.). Such *Vaulting* (overreaching) *Ambition* ("Excessively high aims that reveal one is an ass," FR) might "ore-leap" (leap too far, overreach) *it selfe* in the same way that a "vaulter" *ore-leapes* the saddle and (a) *falles* ("fall[s] down," OED) *on th' other* ("the second," OED) horse; and/or (b) *falles on th' other* (the ass; see note: *other*, I.iii.17).

The prophecy predicts that *Macbeth* will leave behind no heir. He therefore has *no Spurre* (penis; a "spur" is "a pricke," TT, s.v. "Stimulus") *To pricke* (with obvious pun) *the sides* (loins, organs of generation, OED) *of* his *intent* (allusive of sexual probing or the genitals; a *tent* is literally "A probe," OED; also see note: *purpose*, I.v.53). *Vaulting* ("copulat[ing]," F&H) *Ambition* (i.e., lust or desire for "potency"; literally "desire to rise to high position," OED) usually *ore-leapes it selfe* (i.e., "fucks itself"; *ore* was pronounced identically to "whore"; to *leape* is "To mount, coitally," EC). If *Macbeth falles* (sins or yields to temptation; also "copulate[s]," JH), he might "fall," meaning (a) be disgraced or discredited, come to nothing; and (b) become impotent (to "fall" is literally "To lose the erect position," OED; cf. and see note: *fall downe*, I.iv.61). Paradoxically, *Macbeth's* lack of progeny is a direct result of his *Vaulting* (i.e., "riding" or "fucking"), for "Continuall riding weakneth the strength of the loynes, the kidneis and the spermatick parts... That much riding may bee a cause of barrennesse" (Helkia Crooke, *Mikrokosmographia*).

Also see notes: I.iii.152–153 and III.ii.22.

35. **chamber.** I.e., "a great hall, or dining chamber" (JF, s.v. "Salona").

38. **Businesse.** *Businesse* means (a) "doings, affaire, dealings in matters, trafficking, and plotting one with another" (RC, s.v. "Facendes"); and (b) copulation (see note: *Businesse*, I.v.80).

39–40. **I have bought... all sorts of people.** *Macbeth's* recent victories have *bought* ("obtain[ed], gain[ed], procure[d], in exchange for something else, or by making some sacrifice," OED) *Golden* ("by a metaphor, shining, beautifull, goodlie, rich, pretious, amiable or excellent," TT, s.v. "Aŭrĕus") *Opinions from all sorts of people* (persons of different temperaments and social standing).

Which would be worne now in their newest glosse,

Not cast aside so soone.

La.   Was the hope drunke,

Wherein you drest your selfe? Hath it slept since?

And wakes it now to looke so greene, and pale,   [45]

At what it did so freely? From this time,

Such I account thy love. Art thou affear'd

To be the same in thine owne Act, and Valour,

As thou art in desire? Would'st thou have that

Which thou esteem'st the Ornament of Life,   [50]

And live a Coward in thine owne Esteeme?

Letting I dare not, wait upon I would,

Like the poore Cat i'th' Addage.

---

41. **would be.** Formerly, *would* was "Used where *should* is now the normal aux-iliary" (OED). *Would be* therefore means "ought to be."

41. **glosse.** "A luster," "a shining, or glistening; a gracefull bright colour" (RC, s.v. "Lustre").

43–47. **Was the hope drunke... Such I account thy love.** *Macbeth* prefers to "wear" (enjoy) his newly-won *Golden Opinions* (line 40, above), so he abandons the regal *hope* (expectation, desire) *Wherein* he formerly *drest* (clothed, attired) himself. *Lady Macbeth* thinks her husband's *hope* ("trust, confidence," RC, s.v. "Espoir") must have been *drunke* ("bowsed, bibbed, tipled, swilled, quaffed; sucked up; received, or soaked in," RC, s.v. "Beu"), for "drunkennes... puts into man a marveilous confident hopes, so that it dareth fight with any man without weapon, whom sobriety durst not encounter with, though well armed" (Richard Rogers, *A Commentary upon the Whole Booke of Judges*). Having *slept*, *Macbeth's hope* (resolution) has evaporated along with his intoxication.

Macbeth was merely *drunke* (inebriated) *Wherein* ("In, at, during, or in the course of which time," OED) he *drest* (applied himself, turned his attention to) his regal *hope*. *Now*, *it* (i.e., his *hope*) *wakes* from drunken slumber *to looke* (appear) *greene* (sickly). Also, *it wakes to pale* (become *pale* through fear or shock) *At what it* formerly *did so freely* ("willingly, without constraint; boldly, without feare," RC, s.v. "Librement").

From this time forward, *Lady Macbeth* will *account* her husband's *love* (affection, sexual passion) as no better than *hope* (i.e., lust or phallic erection; *hope* "connotes potency, fruitfulness: penis, testes," FR) bestowed by alcohol. *Lady Macbeth* suggests that her husband cannot "dress" ("rise," "erect," OED) without artificial stimulation, for he is *greene* ("tender," "undeveloped," OED) *and pale* (where "paleness may suggest sexual fatigue," JH). Just like his *hope*, *Macbeth's love* is *Such* (i.e., "sick": "Effeminate," FR; L. *sic* means "such"). Cf. "demure Boyes… they fall into a kinde of Male Greene-sicknesse: and then, when they marry, they get Wenches. They are generally Fooles, and Cowards" (*2 Henry IV*, IV.iii.).

47–49. **affear'd… in desire.** *Macbeth* is *affear'd* (afraid) to match his *desire* (longing, expectation) with his *Act* (action, deeds) *and Valour*, which means (a) courage; (b) "Worth or worthiness in respect of manly qualities or attributes" (OED); and (c) "Worth or importance due to personal qualities or to rank" (OED). He also lacks the *Valour* (potency; see note: *Valours*, I.ii.25) to manifest his *desire* (sexual appetite, lust) in the *Act* (coïtus; see note: *Act*, I.iii.146).

49–51. **Would'st thou have… thine owne Esteeme.** *Ornament* means "a decking, a beautifying, a trimming, a garnishing. Also honor, dignitie, promotion, praise or commendation, and setting foorth, a gracing or embellishing of any thing" (JF, s.v. "Ornamento"). *Ornament of Life* means (a) wealth, possessions, or affluent worldly conditions (cf. "How are they naturally of levelling humours, and envy others whatever they enjoy of estates, houses, or ornaments of life," John Gauden, *A Discourse of Auxiliary Beauty*); and/or (b) qualities or virtues that elevate human existence to a meaningful level (cf. "What if you had not been brought up to pray, or to read, or to any needful trade, or ornament of life," Richard Baxter, *The Life of Faith*).

Macbeth "would have" (wishes to have) *that* which he "esteems" (judges, considers) *the Ornament of Life* (i.e., sovereignty), but he cannot possess this *And live a Coward* ("cullion, scowndrell, base fellow, faint-hearted companion," RC, s.v. "Coyon"; also "one that eats his Words, or unsaies what he said," ND, s.v. "Recreant") *in* his *owne Esteeme* ("estimation, account, valuation or reputation, or regard," JF, s.v. "Stima").

Moreover, if *Macbeth* wishes his *Life* ("Penis," FR) to obtain *the Ornament* ("female pudendum," F&H), then he cannot *live a Coward* (an impotent or effeminate man, FR; cf. RC's entry at "Pestri d'eau froide": "Effeminate, cowardlie, white-livered, without spirit, vigor, mettall"; also cf. JM's entry at "Pusilánimo": "a coward, a dastard, a meacoke"; a "meacock" is an effeminate man, GW2, s.v. "peacock"). *Macbeth* must therefore raise his *owne Esteeme* (i.e., his "standing," with quibble on phallic erection).

52. **wait upon.** Accompany.

53. **the poore Cat i'th' Addage.** *Lady Macbeth* refers to *th' Addage* ("proverbe," "short wittie saying, a common saying, an old said saw," JF, s.v. "Provérbio") that "The Cat would eat Fish but dares not wet his Feet" (John Hawkins, *The English School-Master Compleated*).

Macb.   Prythee peace:

I dare do all that may become a man,   [55]

Who dares do more, is none.

La.   What Beast was't then

That made you breake this enterprize to me?

When you durst do it, then you were a man:

And to be more then what you were, you would   [60]

Be so much more the man. Nor time, nor place

Did then adhere, and yet you would make both:

They have made themselves, and that their fitnesse now

Do's unmake you. I have given Sucke, and know

How tender 'tis to love the Babe that milkes me,   [65]

I would, while it was smyling in my Face,

Have pluckt my Nipple from his Bonelesse Gummes,

55–56. *I dare do all... is none.* Macbeth will *dare* to *do all that may become* (befit, be suitable to) *a man*. Whoever *dares* to *do more* than that *is none* (i.e., no man at all). Cf. III.iv.126, and "Be that you are, That is a woman; if you be more, you'r none" (*Measure for Measure*, II.iv.).

57. **What Beast.** If *Macbeth* thinks murdering the *King* would not *become a man* (line 55, above), then perhaps the suggestion was made by the *Beast* (the Devil or antichrist). Either that, or *Macbeth* himself is a *Beast*, which means (a) a brutal, stupid man ruled by animal instincts; and (b) "A eunuch" (FR).

58. *breake.* "To break a matter to a person" means "To be the first to impart it, and to do so cautiously and by piecemeal" (DPF).

58. *enterprize.* "An adventurous acte" (TT, s.v. "Ausum"); also "an usurpation, or incroachment upon" (RC, s.v. "Entreprinse").

60–61. *to be more... so much more the man.* Lady Macbeth's statement is at odds with prevailing opinion, for ambition was viewed as a symptom of pride (a deadly sin). To desire *to be more* than what one was constituted an affront to God and under-mined the very fabric of society. See notes: I.iv.29–30; and *Ambition*, I.v.19.

62. *adhere.* To *adhere* is "to side, or take part with" (RC, s.v. "Adherer").

63–64. *their fitnesse now Do's unmake you.* The *fitnesse* ("aptnesse, meetnesse," "conveniencie, sutablenesse," RC, s.v. "Aptitude") of *time* and *place* (line 61, above) to murder *Duncane* should "make" ("raise," "promote," OED) *Macbeth*, but instead the opportunity "unmakes him" ("deprive[s him] of a particular rank or station," "ruin[s] or destroy[s him]," OED).

Macbeth's wavering causes him to *unmake* ("alter in nature," OED) and lose his manly *fitnesse* ("Suitability, aptness, aptitude for love-making," EP). Thus, *Macbeth* "unmakes" himself (i.e., renders himself impotent; *un-* is a prefix "expressing reversal or deprivation," OED; to "make" is to "achieve sexually," EC). Cf. *it makes him*, II.iii.42.

64–65. *I have given Sucke... milkes me.* The historical *Lady Macbeth* and her first husband, GilleComgáin (d. 1032), together "had one son, Lulach... There may have been other sons who died, or indeed daughters who survived, but if so their names have not been recorded" (Rosalind K. Marshall, *Scottish Queens*, p. 3). However, Shake-speare probably did not know this as his only source was Holinshed. As drawn by Shakespeare, the *Macbeths* are clearly childless, so if *Lady Macbeth* has *given Sucke* it must have been to now-deceased children of *Macbeth's*.

However, *Lady Macbeth* may not speak of suckling infants, for *Sucke* can mean (a) "vaginal suction" (GW2; to *Sucke* is literally "To pump," FG); and (b) to "commit fellatio" (JA, pp. 130–131; L. "fello" means "suck milk from; fellate, practice fellatio," LD). *Lady Macbeth* knows *How tender* ("delicate," "wanton, womanlie," TT, s.v. "Mollìcellus") *'tis to love* ("fondle, caress," OED) and "milk" ("cause male ejaculation," EC) *the Babe* (i.e., penis; "Small boys are sometimes likened to the penis," JA, p. 65).

In inciting her husband to murder, *Lady Macbeth* also "give[s] sucke unto" him ("deceive[s], gull[s], ride[s], bring[s him] into a fools Paradise; use[s him] like a child," RC, s.v. "Embabouïner"; this sense still survives in the modern "sucker").

67. *pluckt my Nipple... Bonelesse Gummes.* An infant has *Gummes* that are *Bonelesse* (without "bone" or teeth), but *Lady Macbeth* implies that her husband is a "gum-sucker" ("A fool," F&H) who is *Bonelesse* ("Wanting 'backbone,' without 'sta-mina,'" OED, which dates this sense from 1882; but cf. Richard Niccols' 1627 *The Beggers Ape*: "Wee must provide for helpe without delay / Or bonelesse leave the Court and runne away").

Lady Macbeth inverts the sexual imagery by suggesting that she herself possesses the masculine characteristics of a *Nipple* ("penis. This depends on the idea of semen as milk," GW2) and "pluck" (i.e., virility; "pluck" is literally "Courage," FG; see note: *brave*, I.ii.22). At the same time, she implies that her husband is a "pussy" who lacks the ability to "pluck" (copulate, F&H, s.v. "ride"). Because *Macbeth* lacks "gum" ("semen," JH), when in the *Gummes* (either mouth or vagina; cf. *Sucke*, line 64, above) he is *Bonelesse* (i.e., impotent; "bone" alludes to the erect penis, GW2; "Marrowbone" is "The penis," F&H). Bone marrow was considered a "seminal source" (GW), for "Plato in his Timaeus defineth Seede to be A defluxion of the spinall marrow... whence it is that the common people think that the braines and marrow of the bones do engen-der much seed" (Helkiah Crooke, *Mikrokosmographia*). Also see note: *Braine*, I.iii.173; and cf. *Thy bones are marrowlesse*, III.iv.120.

67. *his.* I.e., "its" (see note: *his*, line 8, above).

And dasht the Braines out, had I so sworne

As you have done to this.

Macb.   If we should faile?   [70]

Lady.   We faile?

But screw your courage to the sticking place,

And wee'le not fayle: when *Duncan* is asleepe,

(Whereto the rather shall his dayes hard Journey

Soundly invite him) his two Chamberlaines   [75]

Will I with Wine, and Wassell, so convince,

---

68. **dasht the Braines out.** *Braines* can allude to the male genitals and semen (see note: *Braine*, I.iii.73), so there is possible play on "dash" as ejaculation or copulation (to "dash" is "to strike vehemently, to thrust into," TT, s.v. "Illīdo"; "A dash of Rain" is "a sudden, short, impetuous pouring down," ND).

68–69. **had I so sworne... to this.** Oaths were considered sacred and inviolable, so *Lady Macbeth* perversely argues that *Macbeth* is morally obligated to commit murder because he has *sworne* to do so.

72–73. ***But screw your courage to the sticking place... fayle.*** OED cites Shakespeare's usage here as the first instance of *sticking place* meaning "The place in which a thing stops and holds fast," and states that the phrase is thereafter used "Only in echoes of the Shakespeare example" (q.v.). However, it is extremely doubtful that Shakespeare intended *sticking place* in this sense.

To "stick" means "To kill (an animal, esp. a pig) by thrusting a knife into its throat" (OED). The *sticking place* is the jugular, the *place* on the neck where one should "stick" (thrust in) the knife in order to slaughter an animal (OED misdates *sticking place* meaning "the jugulum" from 1615, but the term dates from at least a generation earlier; cf. Barnabe Googe's 1577 *Foure Bookes of Husbandry*: "then cut the Dewlappe two inches behind the sticking place, to the brestwarde, and cut it alongstwyse about two or three inches, and pull the Dewlappe with thy finger"). To *screw* literally means "To insert or fix one thing in, into, on, to, or upon another or two things together by a turning or twisting movement" (OED). If *Macbeth* is to *screw* (thrust, twist) the knife into *Duncane's sticking place* (throat, jugular vein), he cannot "stick" ("doubt, feare, or stagger," TT, s.v. "Hæsĭto"). He must *screw* ("fix firmly," OED) his *courage to the place* of *sticking* ("staggering, or doubting," Jean de Renou, *A Medical Dispensatory*, s.v. "Hæsitation").

Lady Macbeth seeks to sexually reassure her husband after questioning his manhood (lines 50–51 and 57–68, above). She promises that he will not *fayle* ("slacken, hang flagging downeward," "fall downe, by weakenesse," "growe loose, feeble, weake," RC, s.v. "Alachir") if he can *But* (only) *screw* (attach or penetrate as with a *screw*, with obvious bawdy play on *screw* meaning "copulate," F&H) his *courage* (phallic erection; see note: *brave*, I.ii.22) *to the sticking* ("copulat[ing]," F&H) *place* ("privities," F&H).

74. ***Whereto.*** To which.

74. ***the rather.*** *The rather* means "all the more quickly, all the sooner"; also "the more readily" (OED).

75. ***Soundly.*** Given *Lady Macbeth's* intention to "stick *Duncane* like a pig" (see note: *sticking place*, line 72, above), *Soundly* probably plays on "sounder": "a Company of Swine" (ND). Cf. *Swinish*, line 79, below; *drenched*, line 80, below; and *guilt*, line 83, below.

75–76. ***his two Chamberlaines... convince.*** In Holinshed's account of the murder of King Duff, the king

> got him into his pryvie chamber, only with two of his chamberlaynes, who having brought him to bedde came foorth againe, and then fell to banqueting with Donewald and his wife, who had prepared divers delicate dishes, and sundry sorts of drinke for theyr arere [i.e., "late"] supper or collation [i.e., "evening repast"], whereat they sat up so long, till they had charged theyr stomakes with suche full gorges, that theyr heades were no sooner got to the pyllow, but a sleepe they were so fast, that a man might have removed the chamber over them, rather than to have awaked then out of theyr drunken sleepe.

Lady Macbeth plans to *convince* ("To overcome, to vanquish," TT, s.v. "Convinco") Duncan's *Chamberlaines* ("servant[s] that awayteth in the chamber," "grome[s] of the chamber," TE, s.v. "Cubicularius") *with Wine, and Wassell* (spiced ale; also the drinking of healths; TB gives the word as deriving from "our ancient Saxon Language, Waes heal... which is, according to our present Speech, Be of health"). Once the *Chamberlaines* are drunk, *Lady Macbeth* can easily *convince* ("convict," JF, s.v. "Convincere") them of *Duncane's* murder.

That Memorie, the Warder of the Braine,

Shall be a Fume, and the Receit of Reason

A Lymbeck onely: when in Swinish sleepe,

Their drenched Natures lyes as in a Death,   [80]

What cannot you and I performe upon

Th' unguarded *Duncan*? What not put upon

His spungie Officers? who shall beare the guilt

Of our great quell.

Macb.   Bring forth Men-Children onely: [85]

For thy undaunted Mettle should compose

Nothing but Males. Will it not be receiv'd,

When we have mark'd with blood those sleepie two

Of his owne Chamber, and us'd their very Daggers,

That they have don't?   [90]

77–79. **Memorie, the Warder of the Braine... A Lymbeck onely.** A person's
Memorie ("understanding, intelligence," "knowledge, sence," JF, s.v. "Intelligentià")
serves as a *Warder* ("a defender," "a protector, a shielder," JF, s.v. "Difensore"; also "a
Sentinell, or watch-tower in a castle, or fortresse," RC, s.v. "Guette") *of the Braine*. As
John Banister explains in *A Needfull, new, and necessarie treatise of Chyrurgerie,*
in a Citie there is but one governour (if it be well ruled) and that in mans bodie
is reason, the Prince is placed on high, for perill of rebellion, as here reason
inhabiteth the braine, the prince hath his watchers and guarde, so hathe the
bodie memorie as chief councellour with the other senses for his guarde, retaining wrath in his harte and concupiscense in the Liver, like Pensioners, to repulse

all injuries… which foresee, and let all commotions or tumultes, els the inferiour savage members, would sone scale the Tower and dislodge reason their Prince.
Cf. and see notes: I.iii.157–160.

In a drunk person, *Memorie* becomes a *Fume* (a "steame; a vapor, an exhalation," RC, s.v. "Fumée"), for "drunkennesse is caused by many fumes, which comming into the braine doe stupifie the same, and hinder all the operations of the immortall soule" (Daniel Dent, *A Sermon Against Drunkennes*). The rising of these intoxicating "fumes" from the stomach to the *Braine* was often likened to the distillation of spirits in *A Lymbeck* ("a still," JF, s.v. "Alambico"). Thus, the *Receit of Reason* (i.e., the *Braine* or brain-case; a *Receit* is literally "any vessell to receive a thing in," JB, s.v. "Receptacle") serves as "the upper part of a Lymbecke, wherein the vapours are gathered" (RC, s.v. "Cloche").

79–80. ***Swinish… drenched Natures.*** *Lady Macbeth* plans to make *Duncan's Swinish* ("beastlie, filthie," JF, s.v. "Porcino") *Chamberlaines* "swine-drunk" ("Beastly drunk," F&H). *Wine, and Wassell* (line 76, above) might make the *Chamberlaines drenched* (i.e., "drowned" or drunk), but for the plot to work the *Chamberlaines' Natures* (physical and mental powers) must be completely *drenched* ("overwhelmed," JM, s.v. "Sumído"). *Lady Macbeth* will therefore administer a "drench" ("A draught or dose of medicine administered to an animal," OED). She plans on "drenching" ("bedrugging," RC, s.v. "Droguement") the *Chamberlaines*, whom she considers no better than "Swine" ("A term of the utmost contempt," F&H). Cf. II.ii.9.

81–82. ***performe upon Th' unguarded Duncan.*** *Duncan* will be *unguarded* (unprotected and unsuspecting), so it will be easy for *Lady Macbeth* and her husband to *performe* ("carry out a design: generally a dishonest one," F&H). *Duncan* is so naive that they can easily *performe upon* (i.e., "Fuck"; literally "copulate [with]," F&H) him; cf. and see note: *Unmannerly breech'd with gore*, II.iii.151.

82. ***put upon.*** To *put upon* is to "attribute, impute," "to charge with" (RC, s.v. "Attribuer"), with possible play on *put* meaning copulate (F&H).

83. ***spungie Officers.*** *Duncan's Officers* are *spungie* ("that will sucke up, thirstie, like unto or resembling a spunge," JF, s.v. "Spongoso") and are therefore willing to "spunge" ("drink at others Cost," ND).

83. ***guilt.*** *Guilt* possibly plays on "gilt" meaning "A young sow or female pig" (OED). Cf. *sticking*, line 72, above; *Soundly*, line 75, above; *Swinish*, line 79, above; and *drenched*, line 80, above.

84. ***quell.*** Murder or slaughter.

86–87. ***thy undaunted Mettle… Nothing but Males.*** *Lady Macbeth's Mettle* (character; also "Audacitie, boldnesse, hardinesse, courage," RC, s.v. "Audace") is *undaunted*, which can mean (a) "dreadlesse, couragious" (RC, s.v. "Resolu"); (b) "dreadfull, to bee feared, terrible" (JF, s.v. "Formidabile"); (c) "manly" (JF, s.v. "Strénuo"); and/or (d) "licentious" (JF, s.v. "Baldanzoso"). *Lady Macbeth* has more than enough *Mettle* (i.e., "balls"; literally "semen," FG) to make up for her husband's lack, so her *Mettle* (i.e., vagina; literally "the breech of a Great Gun," EC2) *should compose* ("breed," "make," RC, s.v. "Concréer") *Nothing but Males*.

87. ***receiv'd.*** "Taken," "perceived, understood" (TT, s.v. "Perceptus"). Also see note: *receive*, line 91, below.

88. ***mark'd.*** *Mark'd* means both (a) "Anointed, spotted, besmeared" (TT, s.v. "Lǐtus"); and (b) "accused, defamed" (JF, s.v. "Notato").

88–89. ***two Of his owne Chamber.*** See note: *Chamberlaines*, line 75, above.

Lady.   Who dares receive it other,

As we shall make our Griefes and Clamor rore,

Upon his Death?

Macb.   I am settled, and bend up

Each corporall Agent to this terrible Feat.   [95]

Away, and mock the time with fairest show,

False Face must hide what the false Heart doth know.

Exeunt.

91. ***Who dares receive it other.*** No one dare *receive* (perceive) *it* (the murder) *other* ("In another way, otherwise," OED) for fear of (a) being made an *other* (i.e., an ass; see note: *other*, I.iii.17); and/or (b) being "buggered," or forced to *receive* ("admit a man coitally," GW2) *it* ("the penis," F&H; also "Sexual intercourse," OED) in the *other* (i.e., the ass; see note: *other*, I.iii.17).

92. ***we shall make our Griefes... rore.*** Upon *Duncan's* death, the *Macbeths shall make* their *Griefes* (sorrows, miseries) *and Clamor* ("pitifull crying out," JF, s.v. "Strido") *rore* ("grone or waile," "make lamentable noise," "be sorie, lament, or mourne," TT, s.v. "Gĕmo").

Also, in "buggering" *Duncan*, the *Macbeths* will give him *Griefes* ("bowel-pains," FR), *Clamor* (i.e., intestinal wind or farting; *Clamor* is literally "a rumbling," "cracking," RC, s.v. "Bruit"), and *rore* ("The sounds of evacuations and farting," FR, s.v. "roaring"; Shakespeare "makes the association [of farting] with buggery," FR, s.v. "Fart").

94–95. ***I am settled... this terrible Feat.*** *Macbeth* is now *settled* (decided, determined) to *bend* ("apply, devote, incline, render," RC, s.v. "s'Addonner") *up Each corporall* (bodily) *Agent* (means of ability, power) *to this terrible Feat* ("An evil deed; a crime," OED).

Figuratively, to *bend up* is "To strain every nerve, brace or wind oneself up, nerve oneself" (OED), a sense which derives from *bend up* meaning "To constrain or bring into tension by a string... In later times associated with the curved shape into which the bow is brought" (OED). *Macbeth* is determined to *bend up* his "bow" (penis; "The metaphor of the bow can be classified as a metaphor from weaponry... It was the capacity of the strings to tauten and relax which lay behind these double entendres," JA, p. 21). *Macbeth* "rises" to his wife's challenge that he "be a man" and makes himself *settled* (literally "stable, firme," JF, s.v. "Stabilire"). To achieve *this Feat* (sexual intercourse, JH, s.v. "Done feats"), *Macbeth* requires *Each corporall Agent* (i.e., his genitals and the generative power of his semen, for in procreative terms "Mans Seed is the agent and womans Seed the patient," Jane Sharp, *The Midwives Book*). In other words, *Macbeth* must *bend up* his *Each* (i.e., penis; an "eche" is literally "A taper," OED).

96–97. ***mock the time... the false Heart doth know.*** Cf. I.v.74–78 and 84–85; and III.ii.43–44.

Act II, scene i

Actus Secundus. Scena Prima.   [1]

Enter Banquo, and Fleance, with a Torch

before him.   [II.i.1]

Banq.	How goes the Night, Boy?	
Fleance.	The Moone is downe: I have not heard the	[5]
	Clock.	
Banq.	And she goes downe at Twelve.	
Fleance.	I take't, 'tis later, Sir.	
Banq.	Hold, take my Sword:	
	There's Husbandry in Heaven,	[10]
	Their Candles are all out: take thee that too.	
	A heavie Summons lyes like Lead upon me,	

Notes II.i.

2. **Fleance, with a Torch.** *Fleance* is *Banquo's* legendary son (see notes: *Your Children shall be Kings*, I.iii.95; *Fleans, flye*, III.iii.29; and *A shew of eight Kings*, IV.i.138). Although *a Torch* might refer to a servant carrying *a Torch* (cf. *Torches*, I.vi.2), *Fleance* himself probably carries *a Torch* to light his father's way (cf. III.iii.22).

4. **Boy.** In Shakespeare's time, a professional acting company included a number of *Boy* apprentices who were learning the acting trade. Shakespeare went out of his way to include parts for these young apprentices, such as the roles of *Fleance* and *Macduffe's Son*, who appears in IV.ii.

5. **The Moone is downe.** The disappearance of *The Moone* and the stars (lines 10–11, below) has ominous significance, for these are the "powers of heaven" ("The Heavens, or Celestiall Orbes and Sphears, being exceeding firme and strong creatures, and exercising great strength upon these inferiour earthly bodies," TW). Cf. and see note: *Powers*, line 14, below. Also cf. I.iv.62–63 and I.v.57–61.

6. **Clock.** A *Clock* that strikes the hour was common in Shakespeare's England but is an anachronism in eleventh-century Scotland. Although a medieval castle had "a watch tower with an alarm bell... It was not till the 14th century that clocks were placed in belfries" (*The Encyclopedia Americana*, s.v. "Belfry"). Cf. lines 45–46, below; and II.iii.98 and 105–106.

9–11. **Hold... take thee that too.** Gentlemen in Shakespeare's time customarily wore both *Sword* (i.e., rapier) and dagger. Before retiring for the evening, *Banquo* entrusts both weapons to the care of his son. *Banquo's* removing his weapons might indicate (a) his trust in *Macbeth* (see note: *Enter King*, I.vi.2); or (b) his distrust of himself (see note: *cursed thoughts*, line 14, below).

10–11. **There's Husbandry in Heaven... all out.** The inhabitants of *Heaven* demonstrate "good husbandrie" ("thriftines, sparingnes, saving," "frugalitie or moderation in living," TT, s.v. "Parcitas") by putting *out Their Candles* (i.e., the stars).

12. **heavie.** Both (a) "drowzie, dull," "sleepie" (JF, s.v. "Letargico"); and (b) "greivous, painefull, sore, daungerous, burdenous" (TT, s.v. "Grăvis").

12. **Summons.** Both death and sleep issue an unavoidable *Summons* ("A bidding," "inviting," RC, s.v. "Semonce"). Cf. lines 79–80, below.

And yet I would not sleepe:

Mercifull Powers, restraine in me the cursed thoughts

That Nature gives way to in repose.   [15]

Enter Macbeth, and a Servant with a Torch.   [II.i.2]

Give me my Sword: who's there?

Macb.   A Friend.

Banq.   What Sir, not yet at rest? the King's a bed.

He hath beene in unusuall Pleasure,   [20]

And sent forth great Largesse to your Offices.

This Diamond he greetes your Wife withall,

--- · ------------------------ ·· --

13–15. ***I would not sleepe... in repose.*** Holinshed reports that *Banquo* was complicit in *Duncan's* murder: *Macbeth* "communicating his purposed intent with his trustie frendes, amongst whom Banquho was the chiefest, upon confidence of theyr promised ayde, he slewe the king at Envernes, (or as some say at Botgosuane,) in the .vi. yeare of his reygne" (RH). However, as *Banquo* was the mythical ancestor of Shakespeare's patron, James I (cf. and see note: *Your Children shall be Kings*, I.iii.95), Shakespeare allows *Banquo* no closer to regicide than the admission that he has *cursed* ("treacherous, villainous, knavish, wicked, cruel, bad, lewde, ungodlie, unnaturall," JF, s.v. "Sceleráto") *thoughts*.

Shakespeare's *Banquo would not* (does not desire to) *sleepe* because he recognizes the moral danger posed by such *thoughts*. *In repose* (rest, slumber), man's *Nature* (physical and mental ability) will more easily "give way" ("make way; leave the way clear"; also "allow free scope, opportunity, or liberty of action," OED) to its inherently evil *Nature* (innate character or constitution). As William Perkins explains in *A Discourse of the Damned Art of Witchcraft*, man's *thoughts in repose* are especially likely to be *cursed*,

> For of dreames there be three sorts, Divine, Naturall, and Diabolicall. Divine, are those which come from God: Naturall, which proceede from a mans owne nature, and arise from the qualitie and constitution of the bodie: Diabolicall, which are caused by the suggestion of the devill... by naturall dreames a man may gesse at the corruption of his owne heart and know to what sinnes he is

most naturally inclined. For looke what men doe ordinarily in the day time conceive and imagine in their corrupt hearts, of the same, for the most part, they doe corruptly dreame in the night... It hath beene granted in all ages for a truth, that Satan can frame dreames in the brayne of man... the dreame that comes from God, is alwaies agreeable to his revealed will, and representeth nothing contrarie to the same, in whole or in part: whereas those that proceed from nature, doe savour of nature, and bee agreeable to mans corruption, which is repugnant unto Gods will. And those that are suggested by Satan, are of the same nature; the generall scope whereof is to crosse the will of God, and to withdrawe the heart from obedience thereunto... Whereas therefore men in their sleepes have dreames, they must take them commonly to be naturall, & withall know that they may be diabolicall, or mixt partly of the one kind, partly of the other.

Banquo has already had disturbing dreams of this "natural / diabolical" nature; cf. line 29, below. Also see notes: *fantasticall*, I.iii.157; and *false Creation*, line 53, below.

14. **Mercifull Powers.** For fear that evil forces will assault his dreams, *Banquo* appeals to the *Mercifull* (compassionate, favorable) *Powers* ("the third order of the second Hierarchy of Angels, so called by reason of their peculiar Jurisdiction over fiends, and all infernal spirits," TB, q.v.).

17. **Give me my Sword.** *Banquo* is startled by the newcomers, whose identity he cannot discern in the darkness. He calls for the return of his *Sword*, which he has given to his son (line 9, above). This action has ironic counterpoint in III.iii.22–31, where an unwary *Banquo* is ambushed and killed before he can draw his weapon.

20. **He hath beene in unusuall Pleasure.** The *King hath beene in unusuall* ("Extraordinarie, unwoonted," "out of custome, against the common, fashion," RC, s.v. "Extraordinaire") *Pleasure* (i.e., generosity; a *Pleasure* is "A benefit, favour," "good office, good turne," RC, s.v. "Benefice"; to *Pleasure* is to "doo a good turne in way of thankfulnes," RC2, s.v. "gratifie").

21–22. **sent forth great Largesse... your Wife.** In Holinshed's account of Donwald's murder of King Duff,

It chaunced, that the king upon the day before he purposed to departe forth of the Castell, was long in his oratorie at his prayers, and there continued till it was late in the night, at the last comming foorth he called suche afore him, as had faithfully served him in pursute and apprehention of the rebelles, and giving them hartie thankes, he bestowed sundry honorable giftes amongst them, of the which number Donwald was one, as he that had bene ever accompted a moste faithfull servant to the king.

The *King* has *sent forth great Largesse* ("bounty, liberality; handfuls of money cast among people, or a Donative bestowed on Souldiers," TB, q.v.) *to Macbeth's Offices* (either "a group of officials collectively" or "The parts of a house, or buildings attached to a house, specially devoted to household work or service," OED).

The *King* also gives a *Diamond* to *Macbeth's Wife*. The gift is ironic in that the *Diamond* is a symbol of fidelity and innocence, but the *Diamond* reflects *Lady Macbeth's* own "adamant" ("hard as an Adamant or Diamond, invincible," TB, s.v. "Adamantine") nature. The *Diamond* "is the hardest of all stones, insomuch that it cutteth glasse, and yieldeth neither to stroke of hammer nor fire, for which cause the Greekes name it Adamas, which in their tongue signifieth Invincible" (JB, s.v. "Adamant"; "Diamond and adamant are originally the same word," DPF). Cf. *undaunted Mettle*, I.vii.86.

22. **withall.** See note: *withall*, I.iii.63.

By the name of most kind Hostesse,

And shut up in measurelesse content.

Mac.   Being unprepar'd,   [25]

Our will became the servant to defect,

Which else should free have wrought.

Banq.   All's well.

I dreamt last Night of the three weyward Sisters:

To you they have shew'd some truth.   [30]

Macb.   I thinke not of them:

Yet when we can entreat an houre to serve,

We would spend it in some words upon that Businesse,

If you would graunt the time.

Banq.   At your kind'st leysure.   [35]

Macb.   If you shall cleave to my consent,

When 'tis, it shall make Honor for you.

24. ***shut up in measurelesse content.*** The *King* is now *shut up* ("retired, solitary," TB, s.v. "Recluse") *in measurelesse* (infinite, immeasurable) *content* ("rest, quietnes, repose, ease, peace," JF, s.v. "Réquie").

25–27. ***Being unprepar'd… should free have wrought.*** On the *King's* behalf, the *will* (desire, intention) of *Macbeth* and his *Wife should* ("would"; *should* was used "in the second and third persons, where *would* is now normal," OED) *free* (without constraint or fault) *have wrought* ("set on worke," TT, s.v. "Opĕrātus"; also "performed," "atchieved, compassed; finished, accomplished," RC, s.v. "Faict"). Because the *Macbeths* were *unprepar'd* ("Unprovided, unreadie," TT, s.v. "Inexpēditus") for the *King's* visit, their *free will* became a *servant* ("one that oweth service or that is in bondage and subjection, a slave," JF, s.v. "Servor") *to defect* ("lacke, want," RC, s.v. "Manque").

29. ***I dreamt last Night… Sisters.*** *Banquo* is assailed by evil thoughts, but he does his best to resist them (cf. and see note: *cursed thoughts*, line 14, above).

Banquo's stating that he *dreamt last Night of the three weyward Sisters* is a chronological inconsistency (see note: *the day of successe*, I.v.3).

29. ***the three weyward Sisters.*** See note: *weyward Sisters*, I.iii.36.

30. ***shew'd some truth.*** In their prediction that *Macbeth* should become *Thane of Cawdor* (I.iii.55), the *Witches* have *shew'd* ("reported, uttered, declared, told," JF, s.v. "Reláto") *some* (a portion, a little) *truth*. Nevertheless, their prophecies are highly suspect (see note: *can the Devill speake true*, I.iii.120), and *Banquo's* probing comment suggests that he fears for the state of *Macbeth's* soul as well as his own.

32. ***entreat.*** "To induce" (OED).

33. ***would.*** *Would* possibly here means "should." See note: *would*, I.vii.41.

33. ***Businesse.*** "A subject or topic of consideration or discussion" (OED).

35. ***At your kind'st leysure.*** *Banquo* downplays his own interest in the *Witches'* prophecy, stating that he is willing to discuss it whenever *Macbeth* is *At leysure* ("hath little to doe," RC, s.v. "Ocieux"). *Kind'st* here means "[most] favourably disposed to" (OED, s.v. "kind") or "[most] agreeable" (OED, s.v. "kindly").

36–37. ***If you shall cleave… make Honor for you.*** In an attempt to learn *Banquo's* feelings without revealing his own, *Macbeth* makes a deliberately ambiguous statement. *Macbeth* hopes that *Banquo shall* (is willing or able to, OED) *cleave* ("be joyned to," "agree," "holde faste one to an other," TT, s.v. "Cŏhærĕo") *to Macbeth's consent* ("Feeling, opinion," OED), but *Macbeth* does not explicitly state what his own feelings and opinions are.

Macbeth might mean that if he and *Banquo* are of *consent* ("of one mind or pourpose," TE, s.v. "Consensio") in agreeing that the *Witches'* prophecy is evil, then *When 'tis* (i.e., *When* they can find the time to express such opinions) *it shall* (will) *make Honor for Banquo* (i.e., be to his credit). On the other hand, *Macbeth* might invite *Banquo* to join his *consent* ("conspiracie," TT, s.v. "Consensĭo"). If *Banquo* will *cleave to* ("side, or take part with," RC, s.v. "Adherer") *Macbeth's consent* (election to sovereignty; "a declaration of *consent*" is "a giving of ones voice in election," JF, s.v. "Soffragatione"), then *When 'tis* (i.e., *When Macbeth* becomes king) *it shall make Honor* ("glorie, promotion," "a reward given to a man," TT, q.v.; also "a title," JF, s.v. "Nome") *for Banquo*.

Banq.   So I lose none,

In seeking to augment it, but still keepe

My Bosome franchis'd, and Allegeance cleare,   [40]

I shall be counsail'd.

Macb.   Good repose the while.

Banq.   Thankes Sir: the like to you.

Exit Banquo {and Fleance}.   [II.i.3]

Macb.   Goe bid thy Mistresse, when my drinke is ready,   [45]

She strike upon the Bell. Get thee to bed.

Exit {Servant}.   [II.i.4]

38–41. ***So I lose none... I shall be counsail'd.*** *So* ("On condition that, provided that," OED) *Banquo* loses no honor *In seeking to augment* ("To increase or adde to," TT, s.v. "Adaūgĕo") *it, Banquo* is willing to *be counsail'd* ("advised," JM, s.v. "aConsejádo"). *Banquo* wishes *still* (always, on all occasions) to *keepe* his *Bosome* ("inward mind, or thought; the height, or depth of the heart, or affection," RC, s.v. "Sein") both (a) "enfranchized" ("free, cleere," JM, s.v. "Líbero"); and (b) "affranchised" (freed from obligation). He also desires to *keepe* his *Allegeance* ("Obedience of a subject to his Prince," JB) *cleare* (faultless, blameless; see note: *cleere*, I.vii.22).

Banquo's statement is as equivocal as *Macbeth's*, for he does not explicitly state to whom he owes *Allegeance* (*Duncane* or *Macbeth*). *Banquo's* words can be construed to mean (a) that he is unwilling to *be counsail'd* in any undertaking that will cause him to lose "honor" (integrity, self-respect); or (b) provided that *Banquo lose* no honor (i.e., that there is little or no risk of being caught), he is willing to *be counsail'd* ("moved to believe or do a thing," "perswaded," JF, s.v. "Persuaso") to join *Macbeth's* conspiracy in order to gain "honor" (advancement, promotion, status).

42. ***the while.*** *The while* means "in the meantime, meanwhile" (OED).

45–46. ***bid thy Mistresse... strike upon the Bell.*** *Macbeth's Wife* will supposedly *strike upon the Bell* (i.e., the castle's alarum bell; see note: *Clock*, line 6, above) *when Macbeth's drinke is ready* (see note: *Possets*, II.ii.9). This is obviously the signal that she has made all *ready* for *Macbeth* to *strike* ("lance or cut a vein," OED; cf. and see note: *sticking*, I.vii.72). Cf. lines 77–78, below; I.vii.75–82; and II.ii.7–11.

The Bell supposedly wards off evil spirits (see note: *Knell*, line 79, below) and symbolically represents the voice of God, "its shape a link with the celestial vault" (JT). It is therefore a particularly perverse signal to use in committing a murder.

On another level, the shape of *the Bell* makes it "suggestive of coitus" and the "vagina" (GW2). Given the *Macbeths'* plan to "fuck" the *King*, *the Bell* is an appropriate signal for *Macbeth* to *strike* ("copulate," F&H).

Is this a Dagger, which I see before me,

The Handle toward my Hand? Come, let me clutch thee:

I have thee not, and yet I see thee still.   [50]

Art thou not fatall Vision, sensible

To feeling, as to sight? or art thou but

A Dagger of the Minde, a false Creation,

Proceeding from the heat-oppressed Braine?

I see thee yet, in forme as palpable,   [55]

As this which now I draw.

Thou marshall'st me the way that I was going,

And such an Instrument I was to use.

Mine Eyes are made the fooles o'th' other Sences,

Or else worth all the rest: I see thee still;   [60]

48–54. **Is this a Dagger... the heat-oppressed Braine.** *Macbeth's Minde* (genitals and semen; see note: *Braine*, I.iii.173) may lack legitimate heirs, but its *heat* ("Sexual passion," JH) engenders a *false* ("spurious": "illegitimate, bastard, adulterous," OED) *Creation* ("An offspring, petigree, or birth," TT, s.v. "Orīgo"). *Macbeth's sight* perceives this *fatall* (prodigious or deadly; see note: *fatall*, I.v.46) *Vision* ("sight, apparition, or a phantasie," RC2, q.v.), which manifests in the form of *a Dagger* ("a destructive symbol," JT, s.v. "knife"; also a phallic symbol; *Dagger* means "The penis," F&H, s.v. "prick"). *Macbeth* wonders if this *Vision* is also *sensible* ("That may bee felt or perceived," JB, q.v.) *To feeling* ("handling, touching," RC, s.v. "Tastonnant").

Hallucinations and visions were attributed to the *heat* of the *Braine*, for "Aristotle cleerely confesseth, that when the braine is excessively heated, many thereby attaine the knowledge of things to come, (as were the Sibils) which Aristotle sayth, growes not by reason of any disease, but thorow the inequalitie of the naturall heat" (Juan

Huarte, *Examen de ingenios*). To early audiences, *Macbeth's false* ("That which is voyd of truth, being unsound and counterfeit," TW) *Creation* ("work of imagination," OED) *Proceeding from the heat-oppressed Braine* would indicate that he is (a) insane, for it was believed that "madnes is caused by a hot distemper of the braine" (Walter Bruel, *Praxis Medicinae*); (b) drunk, for intoxication (which was considered to be a temporary form of madness) was supposedly caused by fumes which rose to the head and heated the *Braine* (see note: *Fume*, I.vii.78); and/or (c) in the Devil's power.

Shakespeare's contemporaries did not automatically attribute insanity to supernatural origins. Nevertheless, the insane were considered vulnerable to diabolical influences, for "oftentimes the divell deludes them, and takes his opportunity to suggest and represent such vaine objects to sicke melancholy men, and such as are ill affected... and by that meanes makes them to overthrow the temperature of their bodies, and hazard their soules" (Robert Burton, *Anatomy of Melancholy*). As William Perkins explains in *The Combat Betweene Christ and the Divell displayed*,

> the divel hath visions wherby he deludes the understanding... These visions the Divell shewes to men sometime sleeping, and sometime waking; even as the Lord doth shew his visions to his owne servants. The visions of Satan shewed to men sleeping are called dreames... His visions shewed to men waking, are to such as have crazed braines... Heerein the Divell sheweth great power and skill in that he can represent unto the eie in his counterfet visions such strange and admirable sights.

Also see notes: *fantasticall*, I.iii.157; *cursed thoughts*, line 14, above; and lines 59–60, below.

55. **palpable.** "Which may be seene or felt, manifest" (HC).

56. **As this which now I draw.** The actor playing *Macbeth* would here *draw* (unsheath) his own dagger, which resembles the knife which is "drawn" ("pictured, printed, figured," RC, s.v. "Formé"; "pourtrayed, counterfeited, resembled, represented," RC, s.v. "Effigié") before his eyes. Cf. *Ayre-drawne-Dagger*, III.iv.80.

57. **Thou marshall'st me... going.** The visionary dagger servers to "marshall" ("to appoint, to direct, to will, to command," JF, s.v. "Ordinare") *Macbeth* in *the way* (direction; also moral path) *that he was* already *going*—i.e., towards his becoming a "marshall" ("a hangman, an executioner," JF, s.v. "Agozzino"). Cf. *Hangmans hands*, II.ii.38.

59–60. **Mine Eyes are made the fooles... worth all the rest.** If the dagger really exists and *Macbeth's Eyes* alone show him the truth, then his *Eyes* are *worth all the rest* of his *other Sences*. However, as *th' other Sences* cannot perceive the dagger at all, it might be unreal. If so, *Macbeth's Eyes are made the fooles* (dupes, laughingstocks) *o'th' other Sences*.

All of the *Sences* were considered untrustworthy, but the *Eyes* and ears were held to be especially subject to diabolical infiltration. As William Perkins explains in *The Combat Betweene Christ and the Divell displayed*, Satan can

> represent unto the eie of man strange and marvellous things... Hence we must learne to have speciall care in the good ordering of all the outward senses of our bodies, specially the two senses of learning, seeing and hearing; for by them the Divell can cunningly convey his temptations into our hearts: the senses (specially these two) are the windowes of the heart and soule, and if we keepe them not well, Satan will be sure to convay some evill into us.

Macbeth's subsequent auditory hallucinations (II.ii.46 and 53–55) also give evidence that the visionary dagger is diabolical.

And on thy Blade, and Dudgeon, Gouts of Blood,

Which was not so before. There's no such thing:

It is the bloody Businesse, which informes

Thus to mine Eyes. Now o're the one halfe World

Nature seemes dead, and wicked Dreames abuse   [65]

The Curtain'd sleepe: Witchcraft celebrates

Pale *Heccats* Offrings: and wither'd Murther,

Alarum'd by his Centinell, the Wolfe,

Whose howle's his Watch, thus with his stealthy pace,

---

61. **Dudgeon.** "The handle of a dagger, at one time made of box-wood root, called dudgeon-wood" (DPF). This type of knife was popular in Scotland: cf. RC's "Dague à roëlles. A Scottish dagger; or Dudgeon haft dagger" (q.v.).

61. **Gouts of Blood.** According to OED, "gout" is a variant of "gote" meaning "a stream" (q.v.). However, in contemporary pronunciation "ou" (as in the modern "house") was interchangeable with "u" (as in the modern "hunt"; see HK, pp. 244–249). Therefore, "gout" probably plays on "gut" meaning both (a) "An outflow" (cf. TB's "Guttulous": "pertaining to a drop, full of drops"); and (b) "The contents of the abdominal cavity; the bowels, entrails" (OED).

62. **There's no such thing.** See notes: lines 48–54 and 59–60, above.

63. **the bloody Businesse... informes.** *The bloody Businesse* (i.e., the murderous task at hand) causes *Macbeth* to "inform" ("To shape or forme," "to imagine and conceive in the mind," TT, s.v. "Informo") the "Informe" ("ouglie, rude," RC, q.v.) "form" ("image," OED) of a *bloody* dagger.

64–65. **o're the one halfe World... dead.** *Nature seemes dead* (i.e., sleep encompasses) *the one halfe World* ("hemisphere," OED), for "Day is the presence of light in one halfe of the world, and night the absence of it in the other" (Edward Leigh, *A Treatise of Divinity*).

The one halfe World might also refer to mortal human existence, for "Bodies scarce make up a moity or half part of the world; but Spirits, even by themselves, have or possess their moity, and indeed the whole world" (Jean Baptiste van Helmont, "Of the Magnetick or Attractive Curing of Wounds"). Also see note: *sightlesse substances,* I.v.56.

65–66. **wicked Dreames abuse The Curtain'd sleepe.** *Wicked* (evil) *Dreames* were thought to *abuse* ("To mocke, to deceive, to frustrate," TT, s.v. "Dēlūdo") mortals while they *sleepe* (see notes: *cursed thoughts*, line 14, above; and *false Creation*, line 53, above). Also, while men *sleepe* they are subject to (or themselves commit) *abuse* (illicit or unlawful sexual acts, FR) in their *wicked* ("amorous, wanton," F&H) *Dreames*. Cf. and see note: III.iv.178–179.

The metaphor of *sleepe* drawing the "curtains" (used for both the eyelids and darkness) was common. The figure probably derives from "Curtaines" meaning "hangings for beds" (RC, s.v. "Courtinages"); cf. "My eyes are going to bed, and leaden sleep / Doth draw the curtains o'er them" (James Shirley, *The School of Complement*).

66–67. **Witchcraft celebrates... wither'd Murther.** *Pale* ("faint in lustre, dim," OED) *Heccat* is the moon, for *Heccat* was "A triple deity, called Phoebe or the Moon in heaven, Diana on the earth, and Hecate or Proserpine in hell. She is described as having three heads — one of a horse, one of a dog, and one of a lion. Her offerings consisted of dogs, honey, and black lambs... She presided over magic and enchantments, taught sorcery and witchcraft" (DPF).

Shakespeare's contemporaries viewed all pagan deities, including *Heccat*, as demons, for "what was Diana, Mercurie, & Saturne, but Sathan and his fellowes, which coloured and shrowded them selves under such names and titles among the blinde and prophane Gentiles?" (Henry Holland, *A Treatise Against Witchcraft*; also see note: *we three*, I.i.3). *Heccat* was further associated with *Witchcraft* (satanic worship) due to her incarnation as the Queen of Hell. In *Masque of Queenes*, Ben Jonson notes that "Hecate... was beleev'd to governe in witchcraft; and is remembred in all their invocations," and RS states that "certain wicked women following Satans provocations, being seduced by the illusion of Devils, believe and profess, that in the night times they ride abroad with Diana, the goddess of the Pagans."

Murther is possibly a direct object of the transitive verb *celebrates* in line 66 (*Witchcraft celebrates wither'd Murther*). *Witchraft celebrates* (publicly or ritually performs) *Offrings* ("sacrifice[s]," JF, s.v. "Immolatione") of dogs and lambs to *Heccat*, but *Witchcraft* also *celebrates wither'd* ("tainted, rotten," JF, s.v. "Rancio"; "putrified, corrupted," RC, s.v. "Fané") *Murther*, for "The witches of Scithia offered men in sacrifice unto Diana" (Henry Holland, *A Treatise Against Witchcraft*).

It is also possible that *Murther* is the subject of the next clause (*wither'd Murther Moves like a Ghost*); see notes: lines 67–71, below.

67–69. **wither'd Murther, Alarum'd by... his Watch.** *Murther* ("A murderer, an assassin," OED) is traditionally associated with (or figured as) *the Wolfe*, which signifies "ferocity, cunning, rapacity, cruelty and evil... the wolf in myth, folklore and fairy tale is a famous predator... Christian symbolism of the Good Shepherd (Christ) and his sheep (the faithful) naturally made the predatory wolf a symbol of Satan and heresy" (JT). *The Wolfe* is also a "figure of devouring, destructive sexuality" (GW); hence the comparison to *Tarquins ravishing sides* in line 70, below (see note).

Murther might here be the subject. If so, then *Murther* (either the act of murder or the murderer) is *Alarum'd* ("rouse[d] to action, urge[d] on, incite[d]," OED) *by his Centinell* ("one that watcheth in the night or wardeth in the day, a watchman," JM, s.v. "Centinéla"), *the Wolfe. The Wolfe's howle* ("prolonged and mournful cry," OED) serves as *his* (the *Wolfe's*) *Watch* ("signal," OED).

Alternatively, *Wolfe* could be the subject. If so, then *the Wolfe* is *Alarum'd* (warned or called to action) by the "howl" of *his Centinell* (another member of his pack), for wolves "howl over long distances to call each other to help, to warn of intruders, or to ask to be joined in a hunt" (Ruth Bjorklund, *Wolves*, p. 20).

With *Tarquins* ravishing sides, towards his designe   [70]

Moves like a Ghost. Thou sowre and firme-set Earth

Heare not my steps, which they may walke, for feare

Thy very stones prate of my where-about,

And take the present horror from the time,

Which now sutes with it. Whiles I threat, he lives: [75]

Words to the heat of deedes too cold breath gives.

A Bell rings.

I goe, and it is done: the Bell invites me.

Heare it not, *Duncan*, for it is a Knell,

That summons thee to Heaven, or to Hell.   [80]

Exit {Macbeth}.

69–71. *with his stealthy pace... Moves like a Ghost.* A son of the last King of Rome, the Roman general *Tarquin* (Sextus Tarquinius) is perhaps best known for *ravishing* (raping) "Lucretia, a notable chaste Roman Lady, albe[it] Sextus Tarquinius by force did ravish: which fact so moved her Father and kindred, that they with the helpe of the people, expeld the lecherous King and all his stocke for ever out of Rome" (HC; Shakespeare treats this story at length in *The Rape of Lucrece*).

Despite the metaphorical embellishment, the passage's main thought is quite simple. Either *the Wolfe* (line 68, above) or *Murther* (line 67, above) *with his stealthy pace Moves like a Ghost towards his designe* ("purpose, project, privat intention, or determination," RC, s.v. "Desing").

Both *the Wolfe* and *Murther* are *ravishing* ("that seizes upon prey; rapacious," OED), so the *stealthy pace* of either may be said to "side" ("rival, equal, match"; also "keep alongside," OED) *With Tarquin's ravishing* ("the snatching or taking away a thing violently," TB, s.v. "Rapture"). The *sides* ("The flankes," RC, s.v. "Iles") of both *Wolfe* and *Murther* move as swiftly and eagerly as *Tarquins ravishing* ("rap[ing], violat[ing]," OED) *sides* (loins, genitals; see note: *sides*, I.vii.30).

71–72. *Thou sowre and firme-set Earth... steps.* The *Earth* is quite obviously comprised of *sowre* ("Mud," OED, s.v. "sore"), but *Macbeth* aptly describes the *Earth* as *sowre* ("cruell, bitter, severe," JF, s.v. "Acerbo"; "frowning, lowring," RC, s.v. "Affreux") because it, like *Macbeth* himself, is *sowre* ("melancholie," "sad," RC, s.v. "Saturnien"). Contemporary scientific doctrine held that all matter was composed of four elements: *Earth*, air, fire, and water. These four elements manifested in the human body as the four humors which determined a person's physical and mental condition: "The humors in man are foure, first Blood, which is of the nature of the Aire, and sweete in taste. Secondly, Fleame, which is of the nature of water, and wallowish in taste. Thirdly, Choller, which is of the nature of fire and bitter in tast. And lastly, Melancholly which is of the nature of the earth, and sowre in taste" (Gervase Markham, *Verus Pater*).

Macbeth appeals to (a) the *firme-set* (stable, solid) *Earth* beneath his feet; and (b) himself as a mortal human being comprised of *Earth* (for "the LORD God formed man of the dust of the ground," Genesis 2:7). Moreover, *Macbeth* hopes he himself can be as "Sourd" ("deaf," EC2) as the *Earth*. He closes his ears (see note: *th' other Sences*, line 59, above) and his eyes (I.iv.64–65), for should he *Heare* ("listen to judicially in a court of law," OED) his own *steps* (course of action) he would not be *firme-set* (resolute, determined). Cf. II.ii.95–97.

71–75. **Earth, Heare not my steps... now sutes with it.** *Which* can mean "that": "so that" (OED). *Macbeth* entreats the *Earth* not to *Heare* his *steps*, *which* (so that) *they* (his steps) *may* (have ability or permission to) *walke*.

Alternatively, *which* might here be used as "The ordinary relative pronoun introducing an additional statement about the antecedent" (OED). If *Earth* is the antecedent, then *Macbeth* desires the deafness of the *Earth*, *which* his steps *may walke* upon without fear.

Walke is also a variant spelling of "wake" (OED), so *Macbeth* possibly enjoins the *Earth* not to *Heare* his *steps*, *which* (the *Earth*) *they* (his steps) *may* "wake."

If the *Earth* hears *Macbeth's steps*, its *stones* might *prate* ("chat," "prattle," "babble," "tittle tattle," JF, s.v. "Chiacchiarare") and reveal *Macbeth's where-about* (position, location). *Macbeth* cannot *walke* (go forward, make progress) if the *stones walke* ("spread abroad," "circulate, spread, pass from one person to another," OED) his location.

The noise of *Macbeth's steps* on the *stones* will break the silence *And take* (remove) *from the time the present* ("Of to daie, of this day or time," TT, s.v. "Hŏdĭernus") *horror* (i.e., silence; literally "a dreadfull sound," TT, q.v.), *Which now sutes with it*. The noise will also shatter *Macbeth's horror* ("reverent feare," JF, s.v. "Horrore"), which is *present* ("in sight, in view; at hand, hard by; in presence," RC, q.v.).

75. **Whiles.** Whilst.

75. **threat.** Both (a) to threaten; and (b) "To dispute, contend; to quarrel, wrangle" (OED, s.v. "threte").

76. **Words... too cold breath gives.** In order to achieve his goal, *Macbeth* cannot "blow hot and cold" (be "inconsistent, vacillating," F&H). If *Macbeth* "use[s] too many *Words*" ("talk[s] overmuch," RC, s.v. "Babiller"), his *breath* (speech) will make *cold* ("faint or out of courage," TT, s.v. "Frīgĕo"; "slowe, slack, remisse, nothing earnest," TT, s.v. "Frīgĭdus") *the heat* ("fervencie; eagrenesse, earnestnesse, vehemencie," RC, s.v. "Ardeur") of his *deedes*. Cf. the proverb "Many words few, or no blowes; they seldome strike home that threaten, or talke, much" (RC, s.v. "Mordre").

77–79. **A Bell rings... a Knell.** The same *Bell* which gives the signal that all is in readiness for the murder (cf. lines 45–46, above) also serves as the *King's Knell* (a "tolling for the dead," JF, s.v. "Suono a mórto"). The "Passing Bell is the hallowed bell which used to be rung when persons were *in extremis*, to scare away evil spirits which were supposed to lurk about the dying, to pounce on the soul while passing from the body to its resting-place. A secondary object was to announce to the neighbourhood the fact that all good Christians might offer up a prayer for the safe passage of the dying person into Paradise" (DPF).

78. **invites.** To "invite" is "to provoke, to chalenge, to defie one to fight," "to call a far off, to call foorth, to stire" (JF, s.v. "Provocare"); also to "intice, allure unto" (RC, s.v. "Attirer").

Act II, scene ii

Scena Secunda.   [1]

   Enter Lady.   [II.ii.1]

La.   That which hath made them drunk, hath made me bold:

           What hath quench'd them, hath given me fire.

           Hearke, peace: it was the Owle that shriek'd,   [5]

           The fatall Bell-man, which gives the stern'st good-night.

           He is about it, the Doores are open:

           And the surfeted Groomes doe mock their charge

Notes II.ii.

   3. **That which hath made... me bold.** *Lady Macbeth* has been drinking with the *Chamberlaines* (cf. and see note: I.vii.75–76), but *That which hath made them drunk, hath made* her *bold* ("fearelesse, hardie, dreadlesse; confident, secure," RC, s.v. "Asseuré"; see note: *drunke*, I.vii.43). The alchohol (and/or the thrill of the crime) has also made her *bold* ("lewde," TT, s.v. "Impröbŭlus"; a *bold* woman is "free from the restrains of female modesty," EP).

   4. **What hath quench'd them... fire.** *What hath quench'd* ("slake[d] the thirst [of]," JF, s.v. "Dissetare") the *King's Chamberlaines* has also *quench'd* ("put out, and overcom," TW) *them.* The "quencher" ("drink," F&H) is a "quencher" ("A destroyer, one that stinteth and maketh an end of a thing, a suppressour," TT, s.v. "Extructor"), for the drunken *Chamberlaines* will be *quench'd* ("killed: slaine, dead, utterlie perished or come to nought," TT, s.v. "Extinctus") when they are blamed for the *King's* murder.

   The alcohol has not *quench'd* ("Either somewhat to slake the heate of the fire, or else wholy to put it out," TW) but *given fire* (i.e., "set on fire": "encourage[d]," "give[n] boldnes," TT, s.v. "Accendo") to *Lady Macbeth.* The drink may have *quench'd* ("extinguish[d] the fire of sexual passion [in]," JH) the *Chamberlaines,* but it has *given Lady Macbeth fire* ("Fierce sexual heat," EC).

   5–6. **Hearke... the stern'st good-night.** Startled by an unexpected noise, *Lady*

Macbeth might "hark" ("whisper," JJ) as she cries *Hearke* ("Listen!"). She initially fears that the plot has gone awry (cf. lines 14–16, below), but she then realizes that *it was only the Owle that shriek'd.*

As a nocturnal bird, *the Owle* was likened to "a common Bellman, which in the dead of night goes round about a Citie, tinkling, and telling of the houres" (RC, s.v. "Resveilleur"; cf. Edmund Spenser's *The Faerie Queene*: "What time the native Belman of the night / the bird that warned Peter of his fall / First rings his silver Bell t'each sleepy wight, / That should their mindes up to devotion call").

"Before the new police force was established, watchmen or bellmen used to parade the streets at night" (DPF), so the *Bell-man* would give a very "stern" ("rigorous; rough, sharpe, hard; pitilesse, untractable, inexorable," RC, s.v. "Severe") *good-night* to any suspicious characters caught lingering in the streets. The *good-night* of *the Owle* would be even sterner, for in popular belief "The crieng of the Owle by night, betokeneth death" (Stephen Bateman, *Batman uppon Bartholome*). The *Bell-man* is as *fatall* (deadly, fateful; see note: *fatall*, I.v.46) as *the Owle* because "Formerly a bellman announced deaths, and called on the faithful to pray for the souls of the departed" (OED).

7. **He is about it.** *Macbeth* is *about it* (busied with killing *Duncan*) offstage. Holinshed gives no details of *Duncan's* murder, stating simply that *Macbeth* "slewe the king at Envernes, (or as some say at Botgosuane,) in the .vi. yeare of his reygne." In framing *Duncan's* murder, Shakespeare additionally draws upon Holinshed's account of Donewalde's murder of King Duff (although in that story Donewalde does not do the killing himself):

> Then Donewalde though he abhorred the act greatly in his harte, yet through instigation of his wife, he called foure of his servants unto him (whom he had made privie to his wicked intent before, and framed to his purpose with large giftes) and now declaring unto them, after what sorte they should worke the feate, they gladly obeyed his instructions, and speedely going about the murder, they enter the chamber (in which the king lay) a litle before cockes crow, where they secretely cut his throte as he lay sleeping, without any buskling at all.

If Shakespeare follows Holinshed, then this scene is set either (a) between midnight and three o'clock in the morning (see note: *the second Cock*, II.iii.34); or (b) just before dawn, proverbially the darkest part of night; cf. I.v.57–61.

7. **the Doores are open.** *Lady Macbeth* thinks that the murder of *Duncan* provides an *open* "Doore" ("Opportunity or occasion of doing much good," TW). By making certain that *the Doores* to the *King's* chamber *are open*, *Lady Macbeth* has "open[ed] a door for" ("furnish[ed] opportunity or facility for," OED) her husband.

Ironically, *Doores* also signify "all hindrances, inward and outward, to keep Christ from entering" (TW). Cf. and see note: *Knocke within*, line 73, below.

8. **surfeted.** The *Groomes* suffer from "surfetting" ("Drunkennesse, or all sickenesse proceeding of too much drinking," TT, s.v. "Crapula"), but they have also committed a "surfet" ("an oversight, a fault," JF, s.v. "Eccésso") in allowing themselves to be duped by the *Macbeths*.

8. **Groomes.** "A Groome of the Chamber" is "one that waits in the chamber, to dresse his Master, or Mistresse" (RC, s.v. "Attourneur").

8. **charge.** *Charge* means (a) "keeping, custodie" (JF, s.v. "Custódia"); (b) "an office, a dutie" (JF, s.v. "Officio"); and/or (c) "A thing or person entrusted to the care or management of any one" (OED).

With Snores. I have drugg'd their Possets,

That Death and Nature doe contend about them,   [10]

Whether they live, or dye.

Enter Macbeth.   [II.ii.2]

Macb.   Who's there? what hoa?

Lady.   Alack, I am afraid they have awak'd,

And 'tis not done: th' attempt, and not the deed,   [15]

Confounds us: hearke: I lay'd their Daggers ready,

He could not misse 'em. Had he not resembled

My Father as he slept, I had don't.

My Husband?

Macb.   I have done the deed: [20]

Didst thou not heare a noyse?

Lady.   I heard the Owle schreame, and the Crickets cry.

Did not you speake?

Macb.   When?

Lady.   Now.   [25]

Macb.   As I descended?

Lady.   I.

Macb.   Hearke, who lyes i'th' second Chamber?

Lady.   *Donalbaine.*

9. ***Possets.*** A "posset" is "a drink taken before going to bed; it was milk curdled with wine" (DPF); *Possets* were "popular as a restorative, or as a preparative" (GW2); cf. lines 3–4, above. In *Klinike, or The Diet of the Diseased*, James Hart gives the basic recipe for Scottish *Possets*: "In Scotland, the better sort make their posset onely of milke and white wine, with a little sugar and cinnamon, which they drinke, and give away the curd, which is the best way of using it, and least hurtfull to health."

10–11. ***Death and Nature doe contend… live, or dye.*** *Lady Macbeth* has drugged the *Groomes* so strongly that *Death and Nature* (life, personified as "Mother *Nature*") *doe contend* ("fight," "debate of," "trie by battaile," TT, s.v. "Dēcerno") *about* ("Concerning, regarding," OED) *them* to determine *Whether they* will *live, or dye.* At stake is the *Groomes' Nature* ("vital or physical powers," OED).

12–19. ***Enter Macbeth… My Husband.*** The stage of the early modern playhouse was brightly lit regardless of whether the dramatic action was set during the day or night (see note: *Torches*, I.vi.2). Therefore, *Macbeth* is fully visible to the audience when he cries out upon entering the stage (lines 12–13), and he remains in view while *Lady Macbeth* delivers her confidence to the audience (lines 14–18).

Macbeth asks *Who's there* because (a) he hears some imaginary noise (cf. line 46, below); or (b) he discerns the presence of someone nearby, although in the "dark" he does not know whom. Similarly, *Lady Macbeth* hears her husband's outcry in line 13, but she cannot see him in the "dark." She does not actually discern his presence until line 19.

15–16. ***th' attempt… Confounds us.*** The *Macbeths* can divert blame from themselves after they have accomplished *the deed* (i.e., *Duncan's* death; see note: *the Deed*, I.vii.18). However, if they are caught in *th' attempt* ("action," RC, s.v. "Entreprinse") of *th' attempt* ("personal assault made upon a person's life," OED), then they will be "confounded" ("utterly ruined," RC, s.v. "Accablé"). Paradoxically, *Lady Macbeth* does not realize that it is not *th' attempt* ("Temptation," OED) but *the deed* itself which *Confounds* them ("brings [them] to perdition," OED).

In seeking to "screw" the *King*, if the *Macbeths* are caught in *th' attempt* ("sexual assault," JH) without accomplishing *the deed* (coïtus; see note: *deed*, I.vii.28), they will themselves be "confounded" (i.e., "fucked"; "confound" in its sense of "mix, mingle" is used of sexual acts, JA, p. 180).

18. ***had.*** Would have.

22. ***Crickets cry.*** In folklore, the *cry* of "Crickets seem the watch of death" (John Dryden, *Oedipus*). Nevertheless, like the *Barlet* (I.vi.9), it was considered unlucky to kill *Crickets*, for "such an act is a breach of hospitality, the little insect invariably taking refuge in houses" (Edwin and Mona Radford, *Encyclopedia of Superstitions*).

23. ***Did not you speake.*** *Lady Macbeth* did, in fact, hear her husband *speake* (lines 13–14, above).

26. ***As I descended.*** *Macbeth* has *descended* (come down) from the *King's* upstairs chamber, but he has also *descended* ("come down ideally, mentally, or morally," "stoop[ed] to something unworthy," OED).

27. ***I.*** Shakespeare denotes the word "aye" (yes) with the letter *I*, which accurately reflects its pronunciation.

28. ***Hearke… th' second Chamber.*** *Macbeth* cries *Hearke* ("Listen!") because he hears (or imagines) a noise coming from *th' second Chamber* (the *Chamber* adjoining or next to the *King's*). After killing *Duncan*, *Macbeth* was startled by noises coming from this *second Chamber*; cf. lines 32–38, below.

Mac.   This is a sorry sight.   [30]

Lady.   A foolish thought, to say a sorry sight.

Macb.   There's one did laugh in's sleepe,

              And one cry'd Murther, that they did wake each other:

              I stood, and heard them: But they did say their Prayers,

              And addrest them againe to sleepe.   [35]

Lady.   There are two lodg'd together.

Macb.   One cry'd God blesse us, and Amen the other,

              As they had seene me with these Hangmans hands:

              Listning their feare, I could not say Amen,

              When they did say God blesse us.   [40]

Lady.   Consider it not so deepely.

Mac.   But wherefore could not I pronounce Amen?

              I had most need of Blessing, and Amen stuck in my throat.

30. ***This is a sorry sight.*** The murder has caused *Macbeth* to be *sorry* ("to be grieved, to forethinke, to be ashamed of, to wish a thing had never beene done, to be miscontented," JF, s.v. "Pentire").

This is a demonstrative pronoun indicating that the thing spoken of is in close proximity, so the *sorry* (pitiful; also "Vile, mean, worthless," FG) *sight* ("shocking, repulsive, or ridiculous spectacle," OED) that *Macbeth* speaks of is actually present. *This sorry* (with play on "sore" as a "sorrel or reddish colour," JJ) *sight* that *Macbeth* speaks of is the blood on the daggers and/or his own hands.

Although the audience can clearly see *Macbeth's* bloody hands, this scene supposedly takes place in darkness (cf. and see note: lines 12–19, above). *Lady Macbeth* does not react to the presence of the daggers until line 60, below, so she either (a) cannot see them in the dark; or (b) does not immediately recognize the blunder that *Macbeth* has made in removing them from the scene of the crime.

32–34. ***There's one did laugh… I stood, and heard them.*** After killing *Duncan, Macbeth stood* ("remained," RC, s.v. "Esté") *and heard* (listened to) a conversation between the occupants of *th' second Chamber* (line 28, above), *one* of whom *cry'd Murther* while the other *did laugh in's sleepe.* Superstition holds that "to laugh or smile in thy slepe declareth sadnes" (Thomas Hill, *The Moste pleasaunte Arte of the Interpretation of Dreames*). To dream of *Murther* has various significations, but here the dream obviously gives literal warning of death.

34. ***they did say their Prayers.*** To *say* one's *Prayers* was a protection against evil (see note: *God blesse us*, line 37, below).

35. ***addrest.*** Either (a) "prepared" (JF, s.v. "Presto"); or (b) "begun, entered into" (RC, s.v. "Acheminé").

35. ***them.*** "As reflexive pron[oun] = themselves" (OED).

36. ***There are two lodg'd together.*** Whereas *Macbeth* is concerned with the ominous nature of his guests' dreams and prayers (lines 32–34, above, and lines 37–40 and 42–43, below), *Lady Macbeth* seeks only to explain the presence of a second person *lodg'd* (sleeping; to "lodge" means to "sleep," OED) in the second chamber after initially stating that *Donalbaine* was its only occupant (line 29, above).

37–43. ***One cry'd God blesse us… Amen stuck in my throat.*** *God blesse us* was spoken to ward off all forms of evil (including demons, witches, and the Devil himself), for "In the name of God all knees do bow down, both in heaven, in earth, and under the earth… the damned spirts and devils in hell do quake at his name" (Thomas Cranmer, *Catechismus*). *Amen* was similarly used (cf. "Let me say Amen betimes, least the divell crosse my praier," *The Merchant of Venice*, III.i.). *Donalbaine* and the other person sleeping in the chamber next to *Duncan's* (probably *Malcolme*; cf. II.iii.128) unconsciously discern the presence of a nearby threatening evil — i.e., *Macbeth. Macbeth* himself *could not pronounce Amen* because "if a man be conscious to himselfe, of any sinne, that is unrepented of, such a man cannot pray" (John Preston, *The Saints Daily Exercise*). Cf. "God heareth not sinners" (John 9:31).

38. ***Hangmans hands.*** Strictly speaking, hanging is a bloodless form of execution. However, in a broad sense a "hangman" is "a headsman, an executioner" (JF, s.v. "Manegoldo"). Cf. TE's "Carnifex": "a boucher of men, or hangman, that cutteth theym in pieces."

42. ***wherefore.*** *Wherefore* means "why, for what cause" (TT, s.v. "Cur").

Lady.   These deeds must not be thought

               After these wayes: so, it will make us mad.   [45]

Macb.   Me thought I heard a voyce cry, Sleep no more:

               Macbeth does murther Sleepe, the innocent Sleepe,

               Sleepe that knits up the ravel'd Sleeve of Care,

               The death of each dayes Life, sore Labors Bath,

               Balme of hurt Mindes, great Natures second Course,   [50]

               Chiefe nourisher in Life's Feast.

Lady.   What doe you meane?

---

44. ***thought.*** "Esteemed," "supposed; held, reputed; prised, valued; respected, regarded," "judged; weighed, considered" (RC, s.v. "Estimé").

45. ***After these wayes.*** In this manner.

45. ***it will make us mad.*** A guilty conscience supposedly led to despair, which in turn led to infirmity of mind. Madness was thus considered a form of divine vengeance, as Robert Burton explains in *Anatomy of Melancholy*:

> The principall agent and procurer of this mischiefe is the Devill, those whom God forsakes the Divell by his permission layes hold on. Sometimes he persecutes them with that worme of conscience as he did *Judas*, *Saul* and others. The Poets call it *Nemesis*, but it is indeed Gods just judgement... and those God not still assists, the Divell is ready to try and to torment, still seeking whom he may devoure... His ordinary engine by which he produceth this effects, is the melancholy humour it selfe, which is *Balneum Diaboli*, the Divels bath; and as in *Saul* these evill spirits get in as it were and take possession of us... that Divel that then told thee that it was a light sinne or no sinne at all, now aggravates on the other side, and telleth thee that it is a most irremissible offence, as hee did *Cain* and *Judas*, to bring them to despaire.

Cf. and see notes: I.iii.157–160; and *sowre*, II.i.71.

Evidently, *Lady Macbeth* does not realize that her husband is already *mad*. Cf. and see notes: *heat-oppressed Braine*, II.i.54; and *I heard a voyce cry*, line 46, below.

46. ***Me thought.*** "It seemed to me." "Methinks" means "it seems to me; here *me*

is the dat[ive] case, and *thinks* is an impers[onal] verb from M[iddle] E[nglish] *thinken*, to seem" (Walter Skeat, *A Concise Etymological Dictionary of the English Language*, q.v.).

46. *I heard a voyce cry.* The hearing of voices is a symptom of mental illness which, according to contemporary medical and religious doctrine, indicates "Strange stings and prickes of conscience, vexing men with continuall expectation of some evil to come" (TW, s.v. "Voices"). These delusions were attributed to both natural and diabolical causes, for although "illusions of voices... proceed most part from a corrupt Imagination," nevertheless "evil spirits... take all opportunities of humours decayed, or otherwise to pervert the soule of a man" (Robert Burton, *Anatomy of Melancholy*). Cf. and see notes: *fantasticall*, I.iii.157; II.i.48–54 and 59–60; and III.ii.14–15.

46–55. *Sleep no more... sleepe no more.* In *Anatomy of Melancholy*, Robert Burton attributes a lack of *sleepe* to "horror of conscience, fearefull dreames, and visions," for the conscience-stricken

> are in great paine and horror of minde, distraction of soule, restlesse, full of continuall feares, cares, torments, anxieties, they can neither eat, drinke, nor sleep... Their sleepe is, if it be any, unquiet, subject to fearefull dreames, and terrors... And so for the most part it is with them all, they thinke they heare and see visions, conferre with Divels, that they are tormented, and in hel fire already damned quite.

47–49. *Sleepe... The death of each dayes Life.* Sleepe *knits up* ("conclude[s]," "make[s] a conclusion, epilogue, or finall end of," RC, s.v. "Epiloguer") *each dayes Life.* Sleepe can also "knit up" ("wrap up," TT, s.v. "Collīgo"; "bind," RC, s.v. "Enlier") *the ravel'd* ("Untwisted, unwoven," "disordered," RC, s.v. "Desfilé") "sleave" ("the knotted or entangled part of thread or silk," DPF) *of Care.* In other words, *Sleepe* untangles *each dayes* chaotic thread of *Life* spun by the "Three Fates" (see note: *we three*, I.i.3).

By "knitting up" (rewinding, binding up) the "sleave" ("the raw edge of woven articles," DPF) *of Care* (i.e., the thread or fabric of *Life*; *Care* is "Perh[aps] the same word as *cary*": "Some textile fabric," OED), *Sleepe* "knits up" (ends, finishes) *Care* ("industrie, labour, paines," RC, s.v. "Soing"; also "fretfulnesse, perplexitie or anguish of mind," RC, s.v. "Solicitude").

49. *sore Labors Bath.* Sleep serves as a *Bath* for (a) *sore* (painful; also dirty; see note: *sowre*, II.i.71) *Labor* (work, exertion); and (b) *sore* ("Sorrowful," JJ, s.v. "sair") *Labor* ("Care, sorow, pensivenes, thought, regarde," TT, s.v. "Cūra"). As man "dies" and is "reborn" each day after passing through life's *sore* (with play on *sore* meaning "vulva," GW) *Labor* (childbirth), sleep provides a *Bath* ("The water of baptism," OED).

50. *Balme of hurt Mindes.* Sleep was commonly regarded as a *Balme* ("An excellent medicine for a greene wound, and divers other purposes," HC) for *hurt Mindes.* Cf. "Sleepe is paines easiest salve, and doth fullfill / All offices of death, except to kill" (John Donne, "The Storme"). Also cf. V.iii.52–57.

50–51. *Natures second Course... Life's Feast.* As the most substantial *Course* of a *Feast*, the *second Course* was the *Chiefe* (principal, most important) *nourisher* ("fosterer," "feeder," "susteiner," JM, s.v. "Alimentadór"). The notion of sleep as a *nourisher* of *Life* was scientific as well as poetic: "certaine it is, (as it is commonly beleeved) that Sleepe doth Nourish much; Both for that the Spirits doe lesse spend the Nourishment in Sleepe, than when living Creatures are awake: And because... it helpeth to thrust out the Nourishment into the Parts" (Francis Bacon and William Rawley, *Sylva Sylvarum*).

Macb.   Still it cry'd, Sleepe no more to all the House:

Glamis hath murther'd Sleepe, and therefore *Cawdor*

Shall sleepe no more: *Macbeth* shall sleepe no more.   [55]

Lady.   Who was it, that thus cry'd? why worthy *Thane*,

You doe unbend your Noble strength, to thinke

So braine-sickly of things: Goe get some Water,

And wash this filthie Witnesse from your Hand.

Why did you bring these Daggers from the place?   [60]

They must lye there: goe carry them, and smeare

The sleepie Groomes with blood.

Macb.   Ile goe no more:

I am afraid, to thinke what I have done:

Looke on't againe, I dare not.   [65]

Lady.   Infirme of purpose:

Give me the Daggers: the sleeping, and the dead,

Are but as Pictures: 'tis the Eye of Childhood,

That feares a painted Devill. If he doe bleed,

Ile guild the Faces of the Groomes withall,   [70]

For it must seeme their Guilt.

---

53. **all the House.** With play on *House* meaning (a) the occupants of a dwelling; and (b) "A theatre, playhouse," "the audience or attendance at a theatre" (OED). See note: *Here's a Farmer,* II.iii.9.

57–58. *You doe unbend your Noble strength... braine-sickly.* One who is "Brainesicke" is "wilde brained, cock brained, heady, altogether following his owne counsell, obstinate, and one that will not be perswaded by another: disposed to be mad" (TT, s.v. "Cĕrĕbrōsus"). *Macbeth's braine-sickly* thoughts *doe unbend* (weaken or cause him to abandon) his *Noble* ("valiant, hardie, couragious, full of prowes," RC, s.v. "Próde") *strength* ("force, might, power, stoutnes, and constancie of minde," TT, s.v. "nervus").

Macbeth's wild thoughts cause him to lose his "Bend" ("power, as *Beyond my bend, i.e.* my means or power. The allusion is to a bow or spring; if strained beyond its bending power, it breaks," DPF). Cf. RC's "Debendade": "an unbending; a violent loosing, or letting go, as of an arrow out of a bow. À la debendade. Confusedly; without order, or array; also, violently, or furiously."

Also, *Macbeth's* "sick" ("Effeminate," FR) *braine* (genitalia; see note: *Braine,* I.iii.173) causes his *Noble* ("High, loftie," "upright," TT, s.v. "Celsus") *strength* ("potency": "Ability to achieve erection or ejaculation in sexual intercourse; virility," OED) to *unbend* ("to slacken, to weaken," JF, s.v. "Allasciare"). Cf. and see note: *bend up,* I.vii.94.

58–59. *Goe get some Water... your Hand.* Cf. lines 77–80 and 87, below; and V.i.30–37, 52–53, and 63.

59. *filthie.* *Filthie* means (a) "soiled or stainid with som unclene thing" (TE, s.v. "Squalleo"); (b) "grizly, gastly, horrible and horride to looke upon" (JF, s.v. "Scuarcóia"); and (c) "dishonest, shamefull" (TT, s.v. "Inhŏnestus").

59–61. *Witnesse... lye.* The blood on *Macbeth's* hands is damning *Witnesse* ("evidence," TT, s.v. "Testĭmonium"), but if the *Daggers lye* (rest, remain) at the scene of the crime, they will *lye* ("speake false," JM, s.v. "Mintir"). Thus, each weapon will serve as a false *Witnesse* ("a deponent, or one that gives in evidence," RC, s.v. "Tesmoing") against *Duncan's Groomes.* Cf. *subborned,* II.iv.35.

60. *these Daggers.* Lady Macbeth now notices that her husband has removed the murder weapons from the scene of the crime. See note: *This is a sorry sight,* line 30, above.

61. *carry.* To "bring from one place to another, to conveigh, to transferre" (TT, s.v. "Transfĕro").

62. *sleepie.* *Sleepie* means "drouzie, slumbring," "sluggish, heavie, lumpish" (JF, s.v. "Sonacchioso").

66. *Infirme of purpose.* Lady Macbeth says that (a) her husband is *Infirme* ("irresolute," OED) *of purpose* (determination, intention); and (b) *Infirme* ("Impotent," RC, s.v. "Impuissant"; "weake, feeble, unable," RC, s.v. "enferme") *of purpose* (genitals, sexual ability; see note: *purpose,* I.v.53).

67–68. *the sleeping... Are but as Pictures.* Lady Macbeth does not fear to look upon *the dead* because she has seen *the sleeping,* and sleep is *but* the "picture" ("likenes or resemblance or patterne of any thing," JF, s.v. "Simolacro") of death. Cf. II.iii.101–102.

69. *painted.* With play on *painted* meaning (a) "Fancied, or conceived in mind; fained, imagined" (RC, s.v. "Phantasié"); (b) "counterfeited" (TT, s.v. "Fūcātus"); and (c) covered or coated in liquid (OED).

70–71. *guild... Guilt.* *Guilt* ("fault, blame," JF, s.v. "Culpa") puns "gild" ("To smear with blood," OED). To *guild* also means "to laie over with golde" (TT, s.v. "Dĕauro"), and *Guilt* means "adorned with gold" (JF, s.v. "Orato"). Cf. and see note: *Golden Blood,* II.iii.147.

Exit {Lady}.   [II.ii.3]

Knocke within.

Macb.   Whence is that knocking?

How is't with me, when every noyse appalls me?   [75]

What Hands are here? hah: they pluck out mine Eyes.

Will all great *Neptunes* Ocean wash this blood

Cleane from my Hand? no: this my Hand will rather

The multitudinous Seas incarnardine,

Making the Greene one, Red.   [80]

Enter Lady.   [II.ii.4]

Lady.   My Hands are of your colour: but I shame

To weare a Heart so white.

---

73. **Knocke within.** Biblically, the *Knocke* signifies "Gods calling and inviting of us, by his word & Spirit calling to our consciences to be let in and entertained, that hee may dwell with us for ever. Rev. 3, 20. I stand at the doore and Knocke. This is Gods Knocking at the Gates of our Hearts" (TW). Cf. I.iii.154–155.

In real life, of course, someone who must *Knocke* to gain entry would be "without" (outside), not *within* (inside). However, in the early modern playhouse the backstage area was located *within* (inside) the tiring-house situated at the rear of the stage. This *Knocke* is ostensibly made by *Macduff* and *Lenox*, who must *Knocke* repeatedly to gain entrance to the castle (lines 84, 90, and 96, below; and II.iii.3, 7, 12, 18, 23, and 28). As this scene flows into the next, Shakespeare dramatically telescopes time. The murder supposedly occurs just before dawn or in the wee hours of the morning (see note: *He is about it*, line 7, above), but it is far later when *Macduff* and *Lenox* enter the castle (cf. II.iii.32–33 and 59–60).

74. **Whence.** *Whence* means "of or from what place" (RC, s.v. "D'où").

75. **appalls.** To "apall" is to "dash out of courage," "vexe, trouble, or strike to the heart" (TT, s.v. "Percello"); also "To discourage, unharten, feare, frighten," "put into doubt, drive out of hart, bring out of conceit, with his owne fortune, or worth" (RC, s.v. "Descourager").

76. **What Hands are here... Eyes.** Cf. Matthew 5:29–30: "And if thy right eie offend thee, plucke it out, and cast it from thee. For it is profitable for thee that one of thy members should perish, and not that thy whole body should be cast into hell. And if thy right hand offend thee, cut it off, and cast it from thee." Also cf. 2 Samuel 22:21: "The LORD rewarded mee according to my righteousnesse: according to the cleannesse of my hands"; and 2 Samuel 22:25: "the LORD hath recompensed me, according to my righteousnsse: according to my cleannesse in his eye sight."

76. **hah.** Hah has many significations, including "a word of chiding, as we say to dogs, hagh? what?" (JF, s.v. "HA").

77. **Neptunes Ocean.** *Neptune* is "In Roman religion and mythology: the god of the sea, corresponding to the Greek Poseidon. Also in allusive use, or as a personification of the sea" (OED).

78–80. **this my Hand... the Greene one, Red.** Although *The Seas* are *multitudinous* ("that hath a great company or number," TB), they are nevertheless all *one*: "the Sea is gathering of water, multiplyed by divers places and names: but by continuation is one Sea... The Sea is head and receipt of Rivers, and fountaine of showers, and the thing whereby people farre a sunder may come together" (Stephen Bateman, *Batman uppon Bartholome*). Figuratively, the "ocean as a whole, as opposed to the concept of the drop of water, is a symbol of universal life as opposed to the particular... It is regarded traditionally as the source of the generation of all life" (JC, s.v. "ocean").

Revelation 16:3–6 predicts that *The multitudinous Seas*, which together form *one Greene* ocean, will become *Red* at the time of the Last Judgment:

> And the second Angel powred out his viall upon the sea, and it became as the blood of a dead man: and every living soule died in the sea. And the third Angel powred out his viall upon the rivers and fountaines of waters, & they became blood. And I heard the Angel of the waters say, Thou art righteous, O Lord, which art, and wast, and shalt be, because thou hast judged thus: For they have shedde the blood of Saints and Prophets, and thou hast given them blood to drinke: for they are worthy.

Revelation foretells that at the end time the "multitude" (large number) of creatures living in *The Seas* will die. Also at this time, the "multitude" of deceased souls will unite with their mortal remains: "And the sea gave up the dead which were in it: and death and hell delivered up the dead which were in them: and they were judged every man according to their works" (Revelation 20:13).

Macbeth realizes that the blood on his *Hand* marks him as one of the sinners who will bring down God's terrible wrath upon all living things. On doomsday, *Macbeth's* guilt will cause *The Seas* to (a) "incarnadine" ("redden," OED) and become "carnation" ("light rosy pink, but sometimes used for a deeper crimson colour," OED); and (b) "incarnate" ("make fleshie," "fill up with, flesh," RC, s.v. "Incarner") when the souls of all those buried at sea once again "incarnate" (manifest in their physical bodies; "Carnation" means both "flesh-colour" and "Incarnation," OED; cf. TB's "Incarnation": "the bringing on of flesh, a being made of flesh, an assuming flesh. An Incarnate colour is a Carnation colour, a flesh color, or of the colour of our Damask Rose"). Cf. and see notes: I.vii.22–29.

82. **shame.** "To blush, or be ashamed at" (RC, s.v. "Vergongner").

83. **Heart so white.** *Macbeth's Heart* ("the seat of moral courage," DPF) is *white* ("Pale, pallid, esp. from fear," OED). See note: *Milke*, I.v.17; and cf. *pale-hearted Feare*, IV.i.104.

Knocke.

I heare a knocking at the South entry: [85]

Retyre we to our Chamber:

A little Water cleares us of this deed.

How easie is it then? your Constancie

Hath left you unattended.

Knocke.   [90]

Hearke, more knocking.

Get on your Night-Gowne, least occasion call us,

And shew us to be Watchers: be not lost

So poorely in your thoughts.

Macb.   To know my deed,   [95]

Knocke.

'Twere best not know my selfe.

Wake *Duncan* with thy knocking:

I would thou could'st.

Exeunt.   [100]

87. *A little Water cleares us of this deed.* Cf. lines 77–80, above; and V.i.30–37, 52–53, and 63.

88–89. *your Constancie... unattended.* *Macbeth* is usually "attended" ("accompanied; followed," RC, s.v. "Convoyé") by his *Constancie* ("stedfastnes, perseverance," JF, s.v. "Costanza"; also "certainetie, surenesse, assurednesse," RC, s.v. "Fermeté"), but now it has *left* (departed from, abandoned) him. *Lady Macbeth* also implies that her husband has lost his *Constancie* (i.e., potency; literally "Stablenes," "firmenes," "hardenes," TT, s.v. "Firmĭtas").

92. *occasion.* Necessity occasioned by circumstances.

93. *Watchers.* A "watcher" is (a) "One who keeps awake at night" (OED); and (b) a reprobate (to "watch" is to "contrive mischief," OED).

93. *lost.* "Having the mental powers impaired" (OED).

94. *poorely.* Both (a) "without courage"; and (b) "in a manner unworthy of one's position" (OED). Also see note: *poore*, I.vi.24.

95–97. *To know my deed... my selfe.* For "A tree by hys fruite men truly shall knowe, / And dedes what man is, doo perfectly showe" (John Hall, *The Courte of Vertu*).

98. *Wake Duncan with thy knocking.* *Macbeth* speaks to the person who is *knocking.* He entreats the unknown visitor to *Wake* (rouse, awaken) *Duncan.*

Act II, scene iii

Scena Tertia.   [1]

Enter a Porter.   [II.iii.1]

Knocking within.

Porter.   Here's a knocking indeede: if a man were

               Porter of Hell Gate, hee should have old turning the   [5]

               Key.

Knock.

               Knock, Knock, Knock. Who's there

               i'th' name of *Belzebub*? Here's a Farmer, that hang'd

               himselfe on th' expectation of Plentie: Come in time, have [10]

               Napkins enow about you, here you'le sweat for't.

Knock.

               Knock, knock. Who's there in th' other Devils Name?

--- · ---

Notes II.iii.

   2–6. **a Porter... turning the Key.** "As the Gates of Paradise were garded by the
Cherubins... so Hell gates are warded by Porters for [that] purpose, by the Divell and
his Angels" (Samuel Gardiner, *Doomes-Day Booke*).
   This human *Porter*, who was carousing late into the night (line 34, below), is now
in a semi-inebriated and/or semi-conscious state. He imagines himself as *a Porter of
Hell Gate* (probably due to his need to "dam": "To urine," JJ; cf. *Urine*, line 38, below;
and cf. and see notes: *stealing*, line 21, below; *Lye*, line 45, below; and *Legges*, line 50,
below). Countless damned souls "knock" on *Hell Gate*, so its *Porter* would certainly
have old (i.e., be "Of long practice or experience," OED) *turning the Key*.

Also, *a Porter* ("Pimp. Both are doorkeepers and keepers of the keys," FR) *of Hell* ("the female pudendum," F&H) *should have old* (i.e., grow weary) putting *the Key* ("The penis," F&H) into the *Gate* ("The vulva," EP) and *turning* (engaging in a "turn," or an "act of coition," F&H).

3. **within.** See notes: *within*, I.ii.2 and II.ii.73.

9. **Belzebub.** *Belzebub* is "An Hebrew word compounded of Bel, which in that language signifieth an Idoll, and Zebub, a Fly: so that Belzebub signifieth the Idoll of Flies: notwithstanding commonly it is taken for the divell" (JB, q.v.).

9–26. **Here's a Farmer... some of all Professions.** A basic principle of modern "method acting," a performance style developed by Constantin Stanislavsky and the Moscow Art School at the turn of the twentieth century, is that the actor must ignore his audience. In a modern proscenium theatre, this is quite easy to do because the stage is brightly lit and the audience sits in the dark. Moreover, the actor is exposed to the audience on only one side. The usual "box set" surrounds the actor on three sides (stage left, stage right, and upstage), and he mentally constructs an imaginary "fourth wall" across the proscenium opening (downstage) to sever himself from the real world and place himself entirely in the world of the play.

The "theatre in the round" architecture of the early modern playhouse, in which actors and audience were equally lit, prohibited any such division. Actors would freely acknowledge, respond to, and interact with the people who surrounded them on all sides (see *Introduction*, p. 18, note 3). When the *Porter* states *Here's a Farmer*, he points out *a Farmer* in the theatre's audience, which was typically comprised of people *of all Professions*. He similarly "recognizes" other individual audience members when he spots *an Equivocator* (line 14) and *an English Taylor* (lines 20–21).

9–10. **a Farmer... th' expectation of Plentie.** The avaricious *Farmer* was a stereo-typical figure, as in *No-Body, and Some-Body*:

> His Barnes are full, and when the Cormorants
> And welthy Farmers hoord up all the graine
> He empties all his garners to the poore
> Under the stretcht prise that the Market yeelds.

This hoarding *Farmer* speculated crop prices would rise due to a dearth, but he *hang'd himselfe* when there was instead *th' expectation of Plentie* ("aboundance, fertilitie, fruit-fulnes," JF, s.v. "Ubertà"). The *Farmer* was consigned to Hell because his suicide (or, as it was customarily termed, "self-murder") placed him in violation of the sixth commandment, "Thou shalt not kill" (Exodus 20:13).

10–11. **Come in time... you'le sweat for't.** The *Farmer*, who *hang'd himselfe* (lines 9–10, above), has *in time* ("fitly, oportunely," JF, s.v. "Atempo") *Come* to Hell wearing a "napkin" (i.e., a noose; a "napkin" is literally "a neckerchief," OED; cf. F&H's "neck-cloth": "a halter"). Although the *Farmer* might *have Napkins* ("pocket handkerchief[s]," EC) *enow* (plural of "enough") to wipe his *sweat*, here in Hell he will nevertheless *sweat* ("suffer," "pay the penalty," F&H).

13. **th' other Devils Name.** The *Porter's* inability to remember any *other Devils Name* besides *Belzebub* indicates his drowsy and/or inebriated state, for the *Devils* "name is Legion" (Mark 5:9). In Shakespeare's time, the average person would have known that "The devill hath divers names, he is called Diabolus, Daemon, (& of Plato Cacodaemon) Sathan, Lucifer, Leviathan, Mammon, Asmodeus, Beelzebub, Baal, Berith, Belphegor, & Astaroth" (Robert Allott, *Wits Theater of the little World*).

Faith here's an Equivocator, that could sweare in both

the Scales against eyther Scale, who committed Treason   [15]

enough for Gods sake, yet could not equivocate to Hea-

ven: oh come in, Equivocator.

Knock.

Knock,

Knock, Knock. Who's there? 'Faith here's an English   [20]

Taylor come hither, for stealing out of a French Hose:

Come in Taylor, here you may rost your Goose.

Knock.

---

14. **Faith.** "In faith" is an expression meaning "truelie, as God me helpe: certain-lie, doubtles, in deede" (TT, s.v. "Hercle").

14–17. **an Equivocator... equivocate to Heaven.** "Equivocation" means both (a) "a double, divers and doubtful signification of a word or speech" (TB, q.v.); and (b) "A speech or answere made, with a secret meaning reserved in ones mind" (JB, q.v.).

The "Doctrine of Equivocation" came very much to the fore at around the time that *Macbeth* was written. In the autumn of 1605, the conspirators of the Gunpowder Plot attempted to blow up the House of Lords in order to assassinate James I (as well as most of the government). In 1606, those involved in the plot were tried and executed, as was the Jesuit priest Father Henry Garnet, confessor to some of the conspirators. Garnet was the suspected author of an anonymous tract entitled "A Treatise of Equivocation: wherein is largely discussed The Question whether a Catholicke or any other person before a magistrate beyng demaunded upon his oath whether a Prieste were in such a place, may (notwithstanding his perfect knowledge to the contrary) without Perjury and securely in conscience answere, No, with this secret meaning reserved in his mynde, That he was not there so that any man is bounde to detect it." The main object of the treatise was to furnish "scrupulous or conscientious Catholics with a system of concealment, by the use of which the discovery of Seminary Priests and Jesuits might be prevented, and judicial examination baffled" (David Jardine, Introduction to *A Treatise of Equivocation*, p. xvii).

Even though this *Equivocator* (i.e., perjurer) *could sweare* ("take a corporall oath," TT, s.v. "Sacramentare") *in both the Scales* (pans of a balance, the symbol of justice) *against eyther Scale* (i.e., *eyther* side in a legal proceeding), *yet* he *could not equivocate to Heaven.* The *Equivocator* was damned to Hell because, by lying under oath, he had broken the third commandment: "Thou shalt not take the Name of the LORD thy God in vaine" (Exodus 20:7).

20–21. **an English Taylor... a French Hose.** This *Taylor*, who while alive kept his own private "hell" ("A taylor's repository for his stolen goods," FG), was *stealing* cloth *out* from that purchased by his customer to make *Hose* ("A mans breeches," TT, s.v. "Sublīgācŭlum"). As François de Calvi explains in *The History of Theeves*, very often

> The Taylor steales, demanding a third part of cloth more then needes to make a suit; and when hee that causeth it to be made, suspecting his honestie, would bee present at the cutting of it out, he troubles him, and so dazles his sight, with the often turning and winding the breadth and length of the piece, that he makes his senses become dull, with his long attention; in the meane time, the Taylor taking his opportunity, casts the cloth into a false pleat under the sheares, and so cuts it out as single, when the piece is double, whereby hee makes a great gaine; besides what he extracts out of silver or gold Lace, Buttons, Silke and the like; of which, a good part hee condemnes to his Hell, from whence there is no redemption.

In *Anatomie of Abuses*, Phillip Stubbes describes *French Hose* as being

> of two divers makings, for the common french-hose... contayneth length, breadth, and sidenes sufficient, and is made very round. The other contayneth neither length, breadth nor sidenes, (beeing not past a quarter of a yarde side) wherof some be paned, cut and drawne out with costly ornaments, with Canions annexed reaching down beneath their knees.

This *Taylor* was such a skilled thief that he could even steal cloth from the minimal amount required to make tight-fitting *French Hose.* Nevertheless, he has ended up in Hell for breaking the eighth commandment: "Thou shalt not steale" (Exodus 20:15).

HK gives "steal" and "stale" as homonyms (p. 148), so the *Taylor* might also be guilty of "staling" ("urinat[ing]," OED) *out of a French* ("Syphilitic," JH) *Hose* ("Penis. Lit[erally] a flexible tube or pipe for conveying liquids," FR). Cf. and see note: *rost your Goose*, line 22, below.

France was also regarded as a hotbed of sodomy (FR), so the new arrival might be *an English* ("a pun on "ingle-ish," HK pp. 104–105; an "ingle" is a catamite; see note: *single*, I.iii.158) *Taylor* (i.e., sodomite; the "tail" is the "Arse," F&H; to "tail" is to copulate, F&H, s.v. "ride"). Thus, he is guilty of *stealing* (illicit sexual acts, JA, p. 167; "Thievery was linked to sodomy," FR, s.v. "Thief").

22. **here you may rost your Goose.** On the downside, the *Taylor* is in Hell, so his *"Goose* is cooked" (he is ruined, F&H). On the upside, in Hell there is plenty of fire in which the *Taylor* can rost ("heat much," RC, s.v. "Brasiller") his *Goose* ("a smoothing iron used to press down the seams, for which purpose it must be heated," FG).

Also, the *Goose* ("penis," GW2) of this *Taylor* (fornicator and/or bugger; see note: *Taylor*, line 21, above) is "roasted" (poxed, GW2) with a *Goose* (i.e., venereal sore; "a winchester goose" is an "impostume about the privie members," JF, s.v. "Pannocchia"). The *Taylor* should therefore feel right at home in Hell, for he is familiar with "fire" (venereal infection, JH).

Knock, Knock. Never at quiet: What are you? but this

place is too cold for Hell. Ile Devill-Porter it no further: [25]

I had thought to have let in some of all Professions, that

goe the Primrose way to th' everlasting Bonfire.

Knock.

Anon, anon, I pray you remember the Porter.

{Porter opens the door.}   [30]

Enter Macduff, and Lenox.   [II.iii.2]

Macd.   Was it so late, friend, ere you went to Bed,

        That you doe lye so late?

Port.   Faith Sir, we were carowsing till the second Cock:

        And Drinke, Sir, is a great provoker of three things.   [35]

Macd.   What three things does Drinke especially

        provoke?

24–25. *this place is too cold for Hell.* "The paynes of Hel are many and of divers sortes, The firste payne is the payne of fyre. The seconde is the payne of colde. Of these two our Lorde speaketh in the gospell, where he sayeth: there shal be weping & wailing with gnashing of teeth, which is by reason of the colde" (Pope Innocent III, *The Mirror of Mans lyfe*). In the bleak morning air, the drowsy *Porter* comes to his senses as he realizes that *this place is too cold* even *for Hell.*

The *Porter* also accuses the audience of being *cold* ("apathetic," OED). There may also be play on both *place* and *Hell* as the vagina (see notes: *place*, I.vii.72; and *Hell*, line 5, above), and on *cold* meaning "sexually frigid" (EP).

25. **Devill-Porter.** See note: *Porter of Hell Gate*, line 5, above.

26. **all Professions.** "Profession" can mean (a) "qualitie, vocation" (RC, q.v.); (b) "A religious system, denomination, or body" (OED); and/or (c) "The trade of whoring" (EC); cf. and see note: *Porter*, line 5, above.

27. **the Primrose way... Bonfire.** The *Primrose* ("A curious corruption of the French *primeverole*, Italian *primeverola*, compounds of the Latin *primavera* [first spring flower]... The flower is no rose at all," DPF) was a symbol of "Wanton pleasure" (JT). In following "the Primrose path of dalliance" (*Hamlet*, I.iii.), the *Taylor's* "fire" (lust; see note: *fire*, II.ii.4) and *Bonfire* ("penis," F&H, s.v. "Prick") has led him to Hell's *everlasting Bonfire* (literally "a fire made of bones," DPF). The *Taylor* may also have ended up with *fire* (venereal disease; see note: *rost your Goose*, line 22, above) in his "bone" (penis; see note: *Bonelesse*, I.vii.67).

29. **Anon.** The *Porter* tells whoever is knocking at the gate that he is coming *Anon* ("by and by, in all the hast, forthwith," TT, s.v. "Ilico").

29. **I pray you remember the Porter.** The *Porter* reminds that audience that they should always *remember* ("give a gratuity to, tip," OED) *the Porter.*

30. **Porter opens the door.** *Lady Macbeth* herself greeted *Duncan* when he arrived at the castle (I.vi.16), but *Macduff* and *Lenox* are received by a humble *Porter*, who would certainly not open the main gate to admit such routine visitors. As Matthew Johnson explains in *Behind the Castle Gate* (p. 71),

> Entry to the castle was graded carefully according to social status, and might be manipulated according to the occasion. While high-status visitors might have the great doors thrown open, the battlements above lined with the bodies of retainers bearing the livery of the lord, and a fanfare of trumpets, others might enter through a wicket gate, or smaller gate set within the larger doors... The simple action of entering the castle, then, was set up as a stage-setting for a very careful social grading of the visitor.

In the early modern playhouse, the small "wicket gate" that the *Porter* now opens would have been represented by a door in the tiring-house wall at the rear of the stage.

33. **lye so late.** *Lye*, which here means "sleep," sets up a string of puns on urine (see notes through line 51, below).

34. **carowsing.** To "carouse" means "to Drink hard, or Quaff heartily" (ND).

34. **the second Cock.** Tradition holds that roosters crow thrice during the night: between twelve and one A.M.; at three A.M.; and again at sunrise. Therefore, *the second Cock* means three A.M.

To hear a *Cock* crow in the dead of night is a very ill omen (and in some folklore specifically foretells impending death). This ancient superstition may originate in (or perhaps even predate) Mark 14:72: "And the second time the cocke crew: and Peter called to minde the word that Jesus said unto him, Before the cocke crow twise, thou shalt denie me thrise. And when he thought thereon, he wept."

35. **provoker.** With play on "provoke" meaning to (a) "moove, cause, stirre, incourage, or incite" (TT, s.v. "Incĭto"); (b) "stimulate or induce a physical action, reaction, condition, etc." (OED); and (c) "excite sexually" (EP).

35. **three things.** The *three things* of which the *Porter* speaks are probably "the male genitals, penis and testicles" (FR; cf. the modern "three point landing," "three prong plug," "playing three to one," etc.).

Port.   Marry, Sir, Nose-painting, Sleepe, and Urine.

Lecherie, Sir, it provokes, and unprovokes: it provokes

the desire, but it takes away the performance. Therefore   [40]

much Drinke may be said to be an Equivocator with Le-

cherie: it makes him, and it marres him; it sets him on,

and it takes him off; it perswades him, and dis-heartens

him; makes him stand too, and not stand too: in conclu-

sion, equivocates him in a sleepe, and giving him the Lye,   [45]

leaves him.

Macd.   I beleeve, Drinke gave thee the Lye last Night.

Port.   That it did, Sir, i'the very Throat on me: but I

requited him for his Lye, and (I thinke) being too strong

for him, though he tooke up my Legges sometime, yet I   [50]

made a Shift to cast him.

---

38. **Marry.** "An oath, meaning by Mary, the Virgin" (DPF).

38–39. **Nose-painting... Lecherie.** The drunkard is figured with a red *Nose* because broken capillaries on the *Nose* are a stereotypical side effect of chronic alcoholism. As alcohol also encourages *Lecherie*, it tempts a man's *Nose* (i.e., penis) to "paint" (go whoring; "paint" is "allusive of prostitutes," GW; also see note: *Painted*, V.vii.77).

39. **provokes, and unprovokes.** See note: *provoker*, line 35, above.

40. **desire.** Lust; sexual appetite.

40. **performance.** "Effective virility; sexual potency" (EP).

42. **it makes him, and it marres him.** Drink *makes* a man (i.e., gives him an erection; to "make" is literally "To give rise to," OED) and gives him the ability to "make" ("mate," OED). However, drink also *marres* a man (sexually hinders him; to "mar" is literally to "do fatal or destructive bodily harm," OED), for "Wine... taken moderately, raiseth the spirits, and provokes a desire of Venery: but if it be drunke in great abundance, it then workes the contrary effect and takes away all such thoughts" (Jacques Ferrand, *Erotomania*). Furthermore, "a drunkard as a man besides himselfe is unmeete for generation; because it is likely that his procreation shall be unequall, crooked and unstable, as well in members as in maners" (Jacques Hurault, *Politicke, Moral, and Martial Discourses*).

42–43. *it sets him on, and it takes him off.* Drink can "set on" ("eg on," "pro-voke," JF, s.v. "Aizzare") a man to "set on" ("seek the satisfaction of his desire to coit," EP), but drink also *takes him off* (diverts, distracts, or dissuades him) and *takes him off* ("reduce[s] [his] amorousness," EP).

43. *perswades.* Sexually seduces (JH, s.v. "Persuasions").

43. *dis-heartens.* "Heart" alludes to virility and phallic erection (see note: *Heart,* I.iii.154), so to "dishearten" a man is to "abate his sexual urgency" (EP).

44. *stand too, and not stand too.* Drink gives a man the courage to *stand too* ("apply [him]self manfully," OED), but too much drink has the opposite effect. Also, regarding a man's "courage" (sexual ability, phallic erection; see note: *brave,* I.ii.22), drink causes him to both *stand too* (achieve an erection, EP), *and not stand too* (i.e., become sexually unable).

45–46. *eqivocates him in a sleepe… leaves him.* Drink gives a man *the Lye* (*a sleepe* or period of rest) and *equivocates* ("lies": places or prostrates) *him in* (into) *a sleepe.* Drink also *equivocates* ("lies" or utters untruths; see note: *Equivocator,* line 14, above) by giving a man fanciful dreams, for "dreames arise of the fulnesse of the bellie and excesse of drinke" (Andrew Willet, *Hexapla in Genesin & Exodum*). Although drink will "give the lye" ("speake falsely," John Florio, *Queen Anna's New World of Words,* s.v. "Mentíre") to a man when he is *in a sleepe,* invariably drink *leaves* a man when it gives *him the Lye* (urine, OED). Cf. lines 36–38, above.

47–48. *Drinke gave thee the Lye… i'the very Throat.* When *Drinke* "*gave* the *Porter the Lye*" (accused him of lying), it *gave* him *the Lye* (uttered falsehoods; see note: *giving him the Lye,* line 45, above). Thus, *Drinke* "lied in his *Throat*" ("lie[d] foully or infamously," OED).

When the *Porter* took *Drinke* down his *Throat,* it *gave* him *the Lye* because it (a) caused him to *Lye,* or sleep; (b) *gave* him *Lye* (urine) in his *Throat* (penis, JA, p. 33); (c) "fucked" him (*Lye* means "to copulate with," JH; cf. the modern "lay"); and/or (d) made him "piss-proud" ("Having a false erection," FG); cf. lines 40–44, above.

48. *on.* "Of" (OED).

48–51. *I requited him for his Lye… cast him.* The code of the duello demanded that a man who was "given the lie" (i.e., called a liar) defend his honor in combat: "When one party insulted or accused another of a dishonorable deed, the accused had to respond by 'giving the lie,' that is by stating loudly and clearly, 'You lie in the throat.' The original speaker then denied the lie by formally challenging the other to a duel" (Edward Muir, *Ritual in Early Modern Europe,* p. 150).

Drinke is here personified as the *Porter's* opponent, who was *strong* ("Powerful or formidable as a combatant," OED) because he was *strong* ("Of a liquor: Containing a large proportion of spirit or alcohol," OED). *Drinke tooke up* the *Porter's Legges* in that it (a) "f[ou]ght at the leg," or "t[ook] unfair advantages: it being held unfair by back-sword players to strike at the leg" (FG, s.v. "leg"); (b) made him "take to his legs," or run away; (c) made him too intoxicated to stand (cf. F&H's "cut one's leg": "to get drunk"); and/or (d) caused him to "leg" ("To piss," F&H).

Nevertheless, the *Porter* proved the stronger combatant and *requited* (repaid, rec-ompensed) *Drinke for his Lye* (both falsehood and urine). The *Porter* was ultimately victorious over *Drinke* because he *made a Shift* (a "trick to deliver one from any difficulty, or danger near at hand," ND, s.v. "Expedient") *to cast* ("overthrow, defeat," OED) *him.* The *Porter* prevailed over *Drinke* because he *made a Shift* ("removal," OED) and *cast* (vomited, OED) *him.*

Enter Macbeth.   [II.iii.3]

Macd.   Is thy Master stirring?

Our knocking ha's awak'd him: here he comes.

Lenox.   Good morrow, Noble Sir.   [55]

Macb.   Good morrow both.

Macd.   Is the King stirring, worthy *Thane*?

Macb.   Not yet.

Macd.   He did command me to call timely on him,

I have almost slipt the houre.   [60]

Macb.   Ile bring you to him.

Macd.   I know this is a joyfull trouble to you:

But yet 'tis one.

Macb.   The labour we delight in, Physicks paine:

This is the Doore.   [65]

Macd.   Ile make so bold to call, for 'tis my limitted

service.

Exit Macduffe.   [II.iii.4]

Lenox.   Goes the King hence to day?

Macb.   He does: he did appoint so.   [70]

Lenox.   The Night ha's been unruly:

Where we lay, our Chimneys were blowne downe,

57–58. **Is the King stirring... Not yet.** *The King Is Not yet stirring* (active, moving; also "leaving one's place," "going out of doors," OED), but shortly he will be *stirring* (raising, inciting) a *stirring* ("a tumult, an uprore," JF, s.v. "Suscitatione").

59. **timely.** Both (a) "earely" (JF, s.v. "Abuon hora"); and (b) "in fit season, in due or good time" (TT, s.v. "Mātūrē"). Cf. *in time*, line 10, above.

60. **almost slipt the houre.** *Slipt* can mean (a) "Failed," "missed" (RC, s.v. "Failli"); (b) "neglected, forgotten" (JF, s.v. "Pretermesso"); and (c) overslept (cf. JJ's "slippery": "Sleepy, overpowered with sleep"). *Macduff* has *almost slipt the houre* not through his own negligence but because he was left locked outside for an extended period of time. Cf. lines 32–33, above; and see note: *Knocke within*, II.ii.73.

62–63. **a joyfull trouble... yet 'tis one.** The *trouble* (exertion, toil) that *Macbeth* has taken on the *King's* behalf is *joyfull*, but it remains a *trouble yet* (nevertheless). Cf. I.vi.19–21.

64. **Physicks.** Alleviates; treats medicinally.

64. **paine.** With play on *paine* meaning (a) bodily suffering arising from illness; and (b) "Trouble taken in accomplishing or attempting something; difficulty" (OED).

66. **limitted.** *Limitted* means "prescribed, appointed" (TT, s.v. "Fīnītus").

70. **appoint.** Both (a) "To bidde, will, charge, or commaund, to cause or make: to wish or desire: to decree, ordaine" (TT, s.v. "Iŭbĕo"); and (b) "to set downe a day, to prefixe a day, to agree on a day or time, to doe a thing" (JM, s.v. "Aplazár").

71. **unruly.** "Violent"; also "Stormy" (OED).

72. **lay.** Both (a) lodged; and (b) slept.

72. **Chimneys.** *Chimneys* were the "traditional focus... of communication with supernatural forces" (JT). As such, they were regarded as a means of entrance and egress for the Devil, witches, and evil spirits.

The unnatural tempest is drawn from Holinshed: see note: *things strange*, II.iv.5.

And (as they say) lamentings heard i'th' Ayre;

Strange Schreemes of Death,

And Prophecying, with Accents terrible,   [75]

Of dyre Combustion, and confus'd events,

New hatch'd toth' wofull time.

The obscure Bird clamor'd the live-long Night.

Some say, the Earth was Fevorous,

And did shake.   [80]

Macb.   'Twas a rough Night.

Lenox.   My young remembrance cannot paralell

A fellow to it.

Enter Macduff.   [II.iii.5]

Macd.   O horror, horror, horror,   [85]

Tongue nor Heart cannot conceive, nor name thee.

{*Macb. & Len.*}   What's the matter?

Macd.   Confusion now hath made his Master-peece:

73–75. **lamentings... Prophecying.** Either (a) *lamentings* ("bewailings, moanings, complaints," JF, s.v. "Laménti"), which were *Strange Schreemes of Death,* were *heard, And* these *lamentings* were *Prophecying* (foretelling things to come); or (b) *Strange* *lamentings And Prophecying* ("soothsaying, foretelling," JF, s.v. "Vacicinatione") were *heard.*

75. **Accents.** That which gave "accent" (emphasis) to the "accent" (inflected speech) of the disembodied voices was possibly an "accent" ("a thunder, a rumbling," JF, s.v. "Tuóno").

76. **dyre Combustion.** *Combustion* means (a) "burning, or consuming with fire; also, a tumult" (RC, q.v.); and/or (b) "Obscuration of a planet or star by proximity to the sun" (OED), which "Many times in change of the Air… shews the higher Winds, and great Storms" (Nicholas Cox, *The Gentleman's Recreation*).

Astrologically speaking, when a planet is in *Combustion* "its influence is then said to be burnt up, or destroyed… In horary questions, when a planet is combust, it signifies the person to be in great fear and danger from some superior person, who… will finally overpower or greatly injure him" (James Wilson and Oliver Ames Goold, *Complete Dictionary of Astrology*). This *dyre* ("cruel, terrible, vigorous," TB) *Combustion* probably indicates the waning of *Duncan's* influence and the ascent of *Macbeth's*, but it might also (a) signify *Macbeth's* fear that *Banquo's* progeny will eclipse him; or (b) presage *Macduff's* overpowering *Macbeth.* Cf. and see note: *predominance,* II.iv.11.

76–77. **confus'd events, New hatch'd toth' wofull time.** The *Prophecying* (line 75, above) announces the onset of *confus'd* ("Troublous, angrie, full of contention," "seditious," TT, s.v. "Turbŭlentus") *events* which have been *New* ("Newly, recently, lately; a short time previously, just before," OED) *hatch'd* ("br[ought] to maturity or full development, esp. by a covert or clandestine process," OED). These *confus'd events* have been *hatch'd* (brought forth, "as a byrde that is come out of the egge," TE, s.v. "Effœtus") *toth' wofull time.*

78. **obscure Bird.** The *obscure* ("frequenting the darkness," OED) *Bird* is probably the owl, whose "clamor" ("skreeke," "pitifull crying out," JF, s.v. "Strido") traditionally foretells death. See note: *Owle,* II.ii.5; and cf. OED's "nightbird": "A bird that is chiefly (or only) heard or seen at night; *esp.* an owl."

78. **live-long.** Whole, entire.

79–80. **the Earth was Fevorous, And did shake.** Man was considered to be a microcosm (little world) which mirrored the macrocosm (large world), so physicians would "oft-times define a Feaver to be an Earth-quake of the Microcosm" (Jean Baptiste van Helmont, "That the three first Principles of the Chymists, nor the Essences of the same, are not of, or do not belong unto the Army of Diseases"). That *the Earth* itself *was Fevorous, And did shake* indicates great disruption in the world order, for "That an Earthquake signifies Political Commotions and Change of Affairs, is obvious to any one" (Henry More, *An Enquiry into the Mystery of Iniquity*). Moreover, "terrible earthquakes… are commonly prodigies and fore-runners of Gods wrath to bee inflicted upon the Land where they happen" (David Person, *Varieties*).

82. **My young remembrance.** Although this line seemingly indicates that *Lenox* is *young,* *Lenox's* own description of *young* men in V.ii.13–15 suggests the opposite. *Lenox* himself is not necessarily *young,* for he might speak solely of his *remembrance* of *young* ("recent," OED) events.

82. **paralell.** To *paralell* is to "compare or match" (TB, q.v.).

88. **Confusion.** *Confusion* can mean (a) "chaos" (RC, q.v.); (b) "ruine, havoke or utter destruction" (JF, s.v. "Storminio"); (c) "corruption" (JM, s.v. "Cohondimiénto"); (d) "Perverting of order and peace: or disorder" (TW, q.v.); and/or (e) "when people are without a Prince or Ruler; lack of Government" (TB, s.v. "Anarchy").

Most sacrilegious Murther hath broke ope

The Lords anoynted Temple, and stole thence   [90]

The Life o'th' Building.

Macb.   What is't you say, the Life?

Lenox.   Meane you his Majestie?

Macd.   Approch the Chamber, and destroy your sight

With a new *Gorgon*. Doe not bid me speake: [95]

See, and then speake your selves: awake, awake,

Exeunt Macbeth and Lenox.   [II.iii.6]

Ring the Alarum Bell: Murther, and Treason,

{*Exit Porter.*}   [II.iii.7]

Banquo, and *Donalbaine*: *Malcolme* awake,   [100]

Shake off this Downey sleepe, Deaths counterfeit,

And looke on Death it selfe: up, up, and see

The great Doomes Image: *Malcolme, Banquo,*

As from your Graves rise up, and walke like Sprights,

To countenance this horror. Ring the Bell.   [105]

Bell rings. Enter Lady.   [II.iii.8]

Lady.   What's the Businesse?

89–91. *sacrilegious Murther... The Life o'th' Building.* Biblically, the *Temple* signifies "The bodies and soules of the faithfull, wherein God dwelleth, as in an house or Temple" (TW, q.v.). Cf. "your body is the Temple of the holy Ghost which is in you" (1 Corinthians 6:19); "ye are the Temple of the living God" (2 Corinthians 6:16); and "Yee are Gods building" (1 Corinthians 3:9).

Murther is "sacrilege" (a "hainous or detestable offence," JF, s.v. "Sacrilégio") under any circumstances. However, *Murther* has specifically committed "sacrilege" ("theft, or taking away of things out of a Church or an holy or consecrated place," TT, s.v. "Sacrĭlĕgium") by stealing *The Life* from *The Lords anoynted* ("Consecrated, sacred," OED) *Temple*—i.e., *Duncan's* body. At his coronation, *Duncan* would have been *anoynted* ("seasoned with oyle," RC, s.v. "Huilé") on his "temples" ("the sides of the head betweene the eyes, and eares," RC, q.v.) to signify that he was *The Lords anoynted* ("a king by 'divine right,'" OED; see note: I.iv.29–30). Now, *Duncan's Temple* (body, forehead) is *broke ope* and *anoynted* ("Imbrued, defiled, smeered, beraied," TT, s.v. "Oblĭtus") with blood. Cf. line 147, below.

94–95. *destroy your sight With a new Gorgon.* The *sight* (shocking spectacle) of the *King's* mutilated corpse is a *Gorgon* ("Anything unusually hideous," DPF) which can *destroy* the *sight* (vision) as effectively as the "Gorgons, Medusa, Sthenio and Euryale (Phorcys's Daughters) who had snakes instead of hair, and killed men with their looks" (EC2). The *Gorgon* "is symbolic of conditions beyond the endurance of the conscious mind, slaying him who contemplates it" (JC).

98–106. *Ring the Alarum Bell... Bell rings.* No supernumerary characters appear in this scene, so logically *Macduff's* command to *Ring the Alarum Bell* must be directed to the *Porter*. If the *Porter* exits immediately after the order is first given in line 98, he could plausibly ascend to the top of the tower where the *Alarum Bell* is located (see note: *Clock*, II.i.6) in time to *Ring the Bell* when *Macduff* gives the command for the second time (lines 105–106).

101. *Downey.* *Downey* can mean (a) "soft as downe; full of, or filled with, downe" (RC, s.v. "Duvetté"); and (b) "Bed. *Gone to the downy*, gone to bed. Bed being stuffed with down" (DPF).

101. *sleepe, Deaths counterfeit.* *Sleepe* is indeed the *counterfeit* ("an image or likenesse in forme, a similitude," JF, s.v. "Imágine") of *Death*, for in Greek mythology *sleepe* ("Hypnos") was the twin brother of *Death* ("Thanatos"), both born of Mother Night ("Nyx").

103–105. *The great Doomes Image... this horror.* The *Image* (sight, vision) of *Duncan's* murder presents an *Image* ("likenes, semblance," TT, s.v. "Spĕcies") of the day of God's *great Doome* ("A sentence pronounced: a judgement," JB, q.v.), the day on which "the trumpet shall sound, and the dead shall be raised incorruptible" (1 Corinthians 15:52; also see note: *incarnardine*, II.ii.79). *Malcolme* and *Banquo* can only *countenance* ("endure," "suffer," "abide," "beare, or tolerate with pacience," JF, s.v. "Sostentare") *this horror* if they *walke* ("of a dead person: to return as a ghost," OED) *like* the *Sprights* ("disembodied spirit[s]," "ghost[s]," OED) who on *Doomes*-day will return to their bodies and *rise up* from their *Graves*.

107. *Businesse.* A "ruffling in a common weale," "a storme or trouble of adversitie, daunger, or perill, a commotion" (TT, s.v. "Tempestas").

That such a hideous Trumpet calls to parley

The sleepers of the House? speake, speake.

Macd.   O gentle Lady,   [110]

'Tis not for you to heare what I can speake:

The repetition in a Womans eare,

Would murther as it fell.

Enter Banquo.   [II.iii.9]

O *Banquo, Banquo*, Our Royall Master's murther'd.   [115]

Lady.   Woe, alas:

What, in our House?

Ban.   Too cruell, any where.

Deare *Duff*, I prythee contradict thy selfe,

And say, it is not so.   [120]

Enter Macbeth, Lenox, and Rosse.   [II.iii.10]

Macb.   Had I but dy'd an houre before this chance,

I had liv'd a blessed time: for from this instant,

There's nothing serious in Mortalitie:

All is but Toyes: Renowne and Grace is dead,   [125]

108. ***Trumpet calls to parley.*** The *Bell* (line 106, above) serves as a *Trumpet,* the usual instrument that summoned people *to parley* (to "speake togither of grave matters," JM, s.v. "Parlamentár"). Cf. RC's "Chamade": "The sounding of Trumpets; a call, or summon by the sound of Trumpets; and hence; Sonner la chamade. To sound a parley; also, to summon, challenge, call on" (q.v.). Also see note: *great Doomes,* line 103, above.

109. ***sleepers.*** A "sleeper" is (a) one who sleeps; and/or (b) "a drouser, a lazie boodie, a sluggard" (JF, s.v. "Dormacchione").

117–118. ***in our House... Too cruell, any where.*** The manner of *Duncan's* death would be *Too cruell* ("bloudie, bloudthirstie, bloudie minded," RC, s.v. "Cruel") *any where,* but it is especially so in the *House* of (supposed) friends.

119. ***Deare Duff... contradict thy selfe.*** Banquo hopes that *Duff* (i.e., *Macduff*) will *contradict* himself by saying that his news is *Duff* ("worthless or spurious," OED from 1781).

122–124. ***Had I but dy'd an houre before... Mortalitie.*** Macbeth says that *Had* he *but dy'd an houre before this chance* ("unfortunate event, mishap, mischance," OED), he would have *liv'd* (existed during) *a blessed* ("blissefull," RC, s.v. "Benict") *time* (era, period). Now, *There's nothing serious* (important) *in* either *Mortalitie* (mortal existence, life) or *Mortalitie* (death).

From this time forward, *Mortalitie* (life) can hold nothing *serious* (sincere, earnest), for in order to conceal his guilt Macbeth must lie for the rest of his life. Had *Macbeth but dy'd an houre before,* he would not have had the *chance* (opportunity) to murder *Duncan.* He would therefore have *liv'd a time* (period of existence, life-time) that was *blessed* ("in the estate of an happy life, which consists in Gods love and favour," TW). *Macbeth's Mortalitie* (life, existence) can no longer be *serious* ("religious," OED), for now *There's nothing serious* (of great importance, of large consequence) *in Mortalitie,* which means (a) "Deadliness, power to kill" (OED); and/or (b) "The quality in a sin of being mortal" (OED; a "Mortal sinne" is "so called, because it kills the soul; and robs it of the spiritual life of grace," TB, s.v. "Venial").

125. ***Toyes.*** Both (a) "trifles, vanities, trash" (JF, s.v. "Zaccarélle"); and (b) "fibs," "lyes," "tales to gull asses with" (RC, s.v. "Bourdes"). Cf. *serious,* line 124, above.

The Wine of Life is drawne, and the meere Lees

Is left this Vault, to brag of.

Enter Malcolme and Donalbaine.   [II.iii.11]

Donal.   What is amisse?

Macb.   You are, and doe not know't: [130]

The Spring, the Head, the Fountaine of your Blood

Is stopt, the very Source of it is stopt.

Macd.   Your Royall Father's murther'd.

Mal.   Oh, by whom?

Lenox.   Those of his Chamber, as it seem'd, had don't: [135]

Their Hands and Faces were all badg'd with blood,

So were their Daggers, which unwip'd, we found

Upon their Pillowes: they star'd, and were distracted,

No mans Life was to be trusted with them.

126–127. ***The Wine of Life... to brag of.*** Due to its red color, *Wine* is a symbol of blood and "of vital force, joy, spiritual blessing, healing, salvation, truth, and transformation… wine was linked with fertility and life after death" (JT). *Duncan's* death has *drawne* ("Drayned; exhausted, emptied," RC, s.v. "Espuisé") *The Wine of Life* (i.e., his blood) from the *Vault* (i.e., his body; literally a "celler, or such like underground roome, arched over head," RC, s.v. "Hypogée"; cf. "The hollow concave of our bodies vaultes," Thomas Middleton, *The Wisdome of Solomon Paraphrased*). Consequently, *this Vault* (earthly life underneath the *Vault*, or over-hanging canopy of Heaven) contains nothing but *Lees* (literally the "dregges, or thicke substance of any thing setled in the bottome," TT, s.v. "Fæx," but figuratively used for the "Basest part, 'dregs,' 'refuse,'" OED).

Duncan's murder has also *drawne The Wine of Life* (spirit, vital force) from *Macbeth*, so nothing *Is left this* (i.e., *Macbeth's*) *Vault* (body) *to brag* (boast) *of* but *the meere Lees. Macbeth* speaks of his sorrow (whether genuine or feigned) at *Duncan's* passing, for the heavy "melancholy" humor in blood was likened to the *Lees of Wine*: "Of this melancholy there be two sorts; one that digested by our liver swimmeth like oyle above water... which lasteth but for an houre... the other sinketh downe to the bottome like the lees of the wine, and that corrupteth all the blood, and is the causer of lunacie" (Thomas Nashe, *The Terrors of the night*). Such melancholic *Lees* would indeed make *Macbeth drawne* ("withered; wasted, consumed," RC, s.v. "Espuisé").

In stating the nothing is left to him but *the meere Lees* (with possible play on *Lees* meaning "Untruth, falsehood, lying," OED, s.v. "lease"), *Macbeth* acknowledges that he has lost *The Wine of Life* (i.e., eternal salvation; *Wine* signifies "The bloud of Christ shed to death, rejoycing the faithfull Soule, as the Wine doth the heart," TW, q.v.). Biblically, "the Cup signifies its part of the cross and castigation, which God in his own time distributes or gives out to every one: So the dregs of that draught do signifie the most bitter part of the calamity or punishment" (TDL). Cf. "For in the hand of the LORD there is a cup, and the wine is red: it is full of mixture, and he powreth out of the same: but the dregges thereof all the wicked of the earth shall wring them out, and drinke them" (Psalms 75:8); and Zephaniah 1:12: "I wil search Jerusalem with candles, and punish the men that are setled on their lees" ("that is, such as with great security, tranquillity, and self conceited firmness stick close to their wickedness, mocking and deriding both God and Men," TDL). Also cf. and see note: *Challice*, I.vii.15.

Due to his unholy pact with the powers of darkness, *Macbeth* is also *drawne* (drained of semen, JH; literally "drayned," "without sap, without moisture," RC, s.v. "Essuccé"). *Macbeth's Vault* (literally "An act of vaulting," OED, but figuratively used for the sexual act; see note: *Vaulting*, I.vii.31) is now empty of *Wine* ("semen," FR). His *brag* (genitals, FR; a "Braguette" is "A codpeece," RC, q.v.) can *brag* (boast) *of* nothing but *the meere Lees* ("allusive of seminal fluid," JH, s.v. "Dance"). Cf. and see notes: I.iii.21, 152–153, and 173; I.vii.29–32; III.i.75–84; IV.i.141; and V.iii.29–30.

129. **amisse.** With play on *amisse* meaning (a) awry, out of order; and (b) "loste" (TE, s.v. "Amissus"); one who is "lost" is "greatlie tormented" (TT, s.v. "Dēperdĭtus") and "Forlorne," "in a desperate or miserable taking" (RC, s.v. "Esperdu").

132. **stopt.** To "stop" is "to dam up" (JF, s.v. "Turare") or to "stay the current of" (RC, s.v. "Donner barres à").

135–136. ***Those of his Chamber... badg'd with blood.*** The servants *of Duncan's Chamber* would have worn a "Cognizance" ("a badge of Armes upon a Servingman or Watermans sleeve," TB, q.v.). Similarly, the *blood* they wore was a "Cognizance" ("confession of a thing done," TB, q.v.). Cf. and see note: *Steep'd in the Colours of their Trade*, line 150, below.

138. **star'd.** A person who *star'd* would "looke about him amazedly, or madly" (RC, s.v. "Enroullir les yeux").

138. **distracted.** *Distracted* means "mad, franticke, out of his wits" (JB, s.v. "Fanaticall").

Macb.	O, yet I doe repent me of my furie, [140]
	That I did kill them.
Macd.	Wherefore did you so?
Macb.	Who can be wise, amaz'd, temp'rate, & furious,
	Loyall, and Neutrall, in a moment? No man:
	Th' expedition of my violent Love [145]
	Out-run the pawser, Reason. Here lay *Duncan*,
	His Silver skinne, lac'd with His Golden Blood,

---

140. **furie.** In *furie* ("madnesse, rage, anger," TT, s.v. "Fŭrŏr"), *Macbeth* extracted vengeance like one of "The furies of hell, punishing evill men after their death for their wicked doings" (TT, s.v. "Fŭrĭe").

141. **I did kill them.** *Macbeth's* slaughtering of *Duncan's Chamberlaines* is drawn from Holinshed's account of Donewald's murder of King Duff:

> Donewald... in the morning when the noyse was reysed in the kings chamber how the king was slaine, his body conveyed away, and the bed all berayed with bloud, he with the watche ran thither as though he had knowen nothing of the mater, and breaking into the chamber, and finding cakes of bloud in the bed & on the floore about the sides of it, he foorthwith slewe the chamberlaynes, as giltie of that haynous murder... he burdened the chamberlaines whom he had slaine with al the fault, they having the keyes of the gates committed to their keeping al the night, and therefore it could not be otherwise (sayde he) but that they were of counsel in the committing of that moste detestable murder.

142. **Wherefore.** See note: *wherefore*, II.ii.42.

143. **wise.** *Wise* means "prudent, circumspect, which advisedlie provideth, what he ought, or what he hath to doe," "considered" (TT, s.v. "Circunspēctus").

143. **amaz'd.** *Amaz'd* can mean (a) "Skared," "astonied; wilde, or ghastlie of looke; also, disturbed, moved; altered, distempered, or put into passion" (RC, s.v. "Effaré"); and/or (b) "that feeleth nothing, that lacketh his senses: foolish, that perceiveth nothing" (TT, s.v. "Stŭpĭdus").

143. **temp'rate.** *Temp'rate* can mean (a) "Tempered, moderated, well governed" (RC, s.v. "Attrempé"); (b) "patient" (JF, s.v. "Moderato"); and/or (c) "well advised" (TE).

143. **furious.** See note: *furie*, line 140, above.

144. **Neutrall.** To "be neutrall" is "to take neither part, to be indifferent" (JF, s.v. "Neutrare").

144. **in a moment.** *In* the same *moment*; at the same time.

145–146. **Th' expedition... the pawser, Reason.** In acting swiftly, *Macbeth* allowed himself to be ruled by his heart rather than his head. His *Reason* was a *pawser* (a "lingerer, deferrer, delayer; one thats long about a businesse; a man of no dispatch," RC, s.v. "Musard") that was easily *Out-run* ("run" is a past tense of "run") by *Th' expedition* ("quicknes," "nimblenes or speed," JF, s.v. "Speditione") *of* his *violent* (intense, powerful) *Love.* Cf. I.vi.31–33.

147. **His Silver skinne... Golden Blood.** Superficially, this line contains a sartorial metaphor ("silver lace" and "gold lace" were used in high fashion of the time; see note: *an English Taylor*, lines 20–21, above). Cf. *breech'd* and *gore*, line 151, below; and *piece of worke*, line 167, below.

Symbolically, *Silver* denotes purity and also "The cheefest and choisest persons in a Kingdome, as Princes, Rulers, and Priests" (TW). "Gold" is "A metal of perfection, symbolically divine through its universal association with the sun... Its associated emblematic qualities range from purity, refinement, spiritual enlightenment, truth, harmony and wisdom to earthy power and glory, majesty, nobility and wealth" (JT).

Duncan's Silver ("Having the whiteness or lustre of silver; silvery," OED) *skinne* was *lac'd* (i.e., "lesed": "damaged, injured," OED) and *lac'd* ("Diversified with streaks of colour," OED) by *His Blood*, which is described as *Golden* because it is (a) valuable (*Blood* is "The vital fluid; hence, the vital principle, that upon which life depends; life," OED); and (b) the luminous red color of "red gold" (pure gold, OED; cf. JM's "Arroxár": "to make to shine or glister like gold, to make looke red," and JF's "Rutilo, shining red like gold, ruddie").

A "lace" is also a "cord, line, string, thread, or tie" (OED). The imagery and phrasing evoke Ecclesiastes 12:7–8 as given in the 1568 Bishops' Bible: "Or ever the silver lace be taken away, or the golden well be broken: Or the pot be broken at the well, and the wheele broken upon the cesterne. Then shall the dust be turned agayne unto earth from whence it came, and the spirite shall returne unto God who gave it." A marginal note in the Bishops' Bible explains that the "*Silver* lace" is "The marowe in the backe bone," but the "*Silver* lace" (or, as it is variously termed, the "*Silver* cord" or "*Silver* thread") also represents "the hidden bond which joins man to his Origin and to his End" (JC). It is that which "links body and spirit... In art, Fortune holds a cord representing mortal life, cut at whim" (JT, s.v. "Cord"). Cf. and see notes: *Golden Round*, I.v.29; *broke ope The Lords anoynted Temple*, lines 89–90, above; and *marrowlesse*, III.iv.120.

And his gash'd Stabs, look'd like a Breach in Nature,

For Ruines wastfull entrance: there the Murtherers,

Steep'd in the Colours of their Trade; their Daggers   [150]

Unmannerly breech'd with gore: who could refraine,

That had a heart to love; and in that heart,

Courage, to make's love knowne?

148–149. *his gash'd Stabs... Ruines wastfull entrance.* Generally speaking, murder is *a Breach* (violation, infraction) *in Nature* ("humanity, humanness," OED), but a *Breach* is specifically a gap broken through a fortified wall. *Duncan's gash'd* ("jagged, hacked," RC, s.v. "Chiqueté") *Stabs* (stab wounds) are "a breach made by assault" ("a gap," JF, s.v. "Apertura") *in his Nature* (bodily substance, OED). Through this *Breach*, *Ruine* ("havock, destruction, slaughter," JF, s.v. "Eccidio"; also "death," "decay of man or beast," JF, s.v. "Occaso") has made *wastfull* (destroying, devastating; also "That causes bodily waste or decay," OED) *entrance.*

Also, *Duncan's gash'd* (with play on "gash" meaning "The female pudendum," F&H) *Stabs* ("The innuendo is specifically to violent sexual ingression," JH, s.v. "Stab") allowed *Ruine* a means of *entrance* (sexual ingression, JH). *Duncan's* bloody wounds *look'd like a Breach* ("female pudendum," F&H, s.v. "monosyllable") *in* ("During," "In the process of," OED) *Nature* (menstruation; see note: *Nature,* I.v.52).

Also cf. and see note: *Against the use of Nature,* I.iii.155.

149–150. *Murtherers... the Colours of their Trade.* In Shakespeare's London, each "livery company" (*Trade* guild) had its own distinct *Colours.* These were incorporated into the guild's official "livery" (uniform) and its armorial bearings, which guild members often wore on their uniforms in the form of a badge (cf. *badg'd,* line 136, above). Therefore, a man's *Trade* was instantly identifiable from the *Colours* that he wore. *Macbeth* claims to have recognized *Duncan's* two *Chamberlaines* as *Murtherers* because they were *Steep'd* ("soked, seasoned in, throughly wet, or moistned," RC, s.v. "Abbreuvé") *in the Colours of their Trade*—i.e., *Duncan's* blood.

150–151. *their Daggers Unmannerly breech'd with gore.* *Breech'd with gore* possibly refers to *gore* ("foule and rotten blood," TT, s.v. "Tābum") clotted within the "breach," or blood groove, on the *Daggers* (cf. JM's "Mélla": "a gap or breach in a knife, sword, or other thing").

Breech'd can also mean "having hosen on" (JF, s.v. "Bracato"), so the *Murtherers' Daggers* might be *Unmannerly* (i.e., slovenly or untidily; cf. TB's "Grobianism": "slovenliness, unmannerly parts or precepts") *breech'd* (covered, clothed) *with gore* ("clothes, dress," TR; *gore* "appears to be the same with *gear,* dress, from the Saxon *gearwa,*" JJ).

The "breech" is also the "arse, tayle" (RC, s.v. "Vezon"), and the "dagger" is a phallic symbol (see note: *Dagger,* II.i.48). Shakespeare uses "Buggery" as a "metaphor for betrayal or murder, especially within families or nations, for a politically heretical or an unnatural act" (FR, q.v.). These *Unmannerly* ("Not manly," FR, s.v. "unmannered") *Murtherers* have "buggered" *Duncan.* Their *Unmannerly* ("wicked, lewd," JM, s.v. "desComedído"; "wanton, unchast, lascivious," RC, s.v. "Immodeste") *Daggers* (penises) have *breech'd* (penetrated, violated) *Duncan's* "breech" (anus). Thus, *their Daggers* are *breech'd with gore* ("Dung, fæces," OED); cf. Fr. "pousse-crotte" ("push-shit"): a homosexual.

151. *refraine.* To *refraine* is (a) to "forbeare," "to hold off, beare backe, restraine himselfe" (RC, s.v. "Se garder de"); and (b) "To withold oneself from sexual intercourse" (EP). *Macbeth* could not resist "buggering" the murderers just as they had "buggered" *Duncan*; cf. *breech'd,* line 151, above.

Lady.   Helpe me hence, hoa.

Macd.   Looke to the Lady.   [155]

Mal.   Why doe we hold our tongues,

           That most may clayme this argument for ours?

Donal.   What should be spoken here,

           Where our Fate hid in an augure hole,

           May rush, and seize us? Let's away,   [160]

           Our Teares are not yet brew'd.

Mal.   Nor our strong Sorrow

           Upon the foot of Motion.

Banq.   Looke to the Lady:

           And when we have our naked Frailties hid,   [165]

           That suffer in exposure; let us meet,

           And question this most bloody piece of worke,

154–164. ***Helpe me hence, hoa... Looke to the Lady.*** There are no servants, attendants, or other supernumeraries on stage during this scene, so the only people available
to *Helpe the Lady* when she is overcome are the named characters. Of these, *Lenox* and
Rosse have no lines from this point forward, so they could conceivably assist *the Lady*
from the stage when she asks to be helped *hence* ("from this place," TT, s.v. "Hinc").
However, it is more probable that all the characters (except *Malcolme* and *Donalbaine*)
rush to *the Lady's* aid, and that she remains onstage until the general *Exeunt* in line 177,
below. *Banquo's* repetition of *Macduff's* command to *Looke to* (care for) *the Lady* is probably directed at *Macbeth*, who would be the logical person to *Looke to* his wife.

157. ***argument.*** An *argument* is (a) "a theame," "a matter supposed to be written
or spoken of, a subject or grounde to speake or write of" (JF, s.v. "Thema"); and (b)
"A Prognostication, fore-telling, fore-shewing," "signe, of a future thing; a guessing,
by signes, of things to come" (RC, s.v. "Prognostication"; to "argue" is "to betoken,
indicate," OED). Cf. *augure*, line 159, below.

159. ***our Fate hid in an augure hole.*** *An augure* is "An instrument to bore with, a smal percer" (TT, s.v. "Cestrum"); *an augure hole* is literally "an hole bored or made with an auger" (TT, s.v. "Fŏrāmen"). Figuratively, *an augure hole* is any inconspicuous place, particularly one regarded as the *hole* ("hiding-place," OED) of vermin (including those of the human variety; cf. "Oh, what shal become of swearers, drunkards, whoremongers, & such like, in that day! They shall seeke to creepe into an auger hole, to hide their heads," Arthur Dent, *The Plaine Mans Pathway to Heaven*).

Donalbaine fears that his father's *Fate* ("Death," OED) is *an augure* ("a fore token, presage, prophecie, forewarning," TT, q.v.) and a *Fate* ("An oracle or portent of doom," OED) which foreshadows his own *Fate* (predestined future state).

There is possible additional play on *augure* meaning "penis" (cf. and see note: *all's*, I.ii.21), and on *hole* meaning "The *rectum*; short for arse-hole" (F&H). Cf. and see note: *their Daggers Unmannerly breech'd with gore*, lines 150–151, above.

161–163. ***Our Teares... the foot of Motion.*** *Malcolme* and *Donalbaine* recognize that their father's murder is only the beginning of their troubles, so their *strong* ("Hard to bear, rigorous, grievous," OED) *Sorrow* ("affliction"; also "lamenting or mourning," OED) is not yet fully *Upon the foot of Motion* (i.e., underway or in *Motion*). Neither is their *Sorrow* ("tears," "weeping," OED) yet *Upon the foot* (i.e., the worst or bitterest part; literally "That which sinks to and lies upon the bottom; bottoms, dregs," OED; cf. *Lees*, line 126, above) *of Motion* ("emotion; passion," OED). Whoever *brew'd* ("devised, plotted, contrived," RC, s.v. "Brassé") *Duncan's Teares* ("torn part[s] or place[s]," "rent[s] or fissure[s]," OED) probably has worse in store. Therefore, his children's *Teares are not yet brew'd* (of a beverage: fully steeped, infused, or fermented). In time to come, their *Teares* ("Calamity and sorrow, the cause of Teares," TW) will be even more *strong* ("Of an infusion, solution, etc.: Having a large preponderance of the solid ingredient or of the flavouring element; having little dilution," OED; cf. and see note: *strong*, line 49, above).

165–166. ***naked Frailties... exposure.*** Those on the scene have rushed out into the chill morning air before being fully dressed (cf. *this place is too cold for Hell*, lines 24–25, above). Therefore, they *suffer in exposure* (an "unsheltered or undefended condition," OED) due to their *naked* (unclothed, uncovered) *Frailties* (i.e., mortal physical bodies; cf. "I know that I shall rise out of the earth at the latter day; and that I shall bee clothed againe in my frailtie, as my Saviour was at his resurrection in his owne flesh," Thomas Dekker, *Foure Birds of Noahs Arke*).

Duncan's murder also emphasizes that (a) *naked* ("exposed & laid open to shame, reproach, and contempt," TW) *Frailties* (moral weaknesses, liabilities to sin) *suffer in exposure* ("the unmasking or 'showing up' of an error, fraud, or evil," OED); and (b) when *naked* ("Such as want the favour and protection of God, which is our best covering," TW), mankind will *suffer* from "frailtie" ("Mortalitie," "subjection unto death," RC, s.v. "Mortalité").

165. ***hid.*** *Hid* can mean (a) "concealed" (JF, s.v. "Secréto"); (b) "Clad, or clothed" (RC, s.v. "Affublé"); and/or (c) "defended" (TT, s.v. "Protectus").

167. ***question.*** Both (a) to "examine," "make inquisition after" (RC, s.v. "s'Enquester"); and (b) "to discuss" (OED).

167. ***piece of worke.*** A *piece of worke* is (a) a deed or action; and (b) any sewn article (particularly one involving "work": "needlework, embroidery," OED). Cf. and see notes: lines 147 and 150–151, above.

To know it further. Feares and scruples shake us:

In the great Hand of God I stand, and thence,

Against the undivulg'd pretence, I fight   [170]

Of Treasonous Mallice.

Macd.   And so doe I.

All.   So all.

Macb.   Let's briefly put on manly readinesse,

And meet i'th' Hall together.   [175]

All.   Well contented.

Exeunt. {*Manet Malcolme and Donalbaine.*}   [II.iii.12]

Malc.   What will you doe?

Let's not consort with them:

To shew an unfelt Sorrow, is an Office   [180]

Which the false man do's easie.

Ile to England.

Don.   To Ireland, I:

Our seperated fortune shall keepe us both the safer:

Where we are, there's Daggers in mens smiles;   [185]

The neere in blood, the neerer bloody.

168. **scruples.** A "scruple" is (a) a "suspicion" (OED); (b) "A doubt," "mistrust, suspence" (RC, s.v. "Doubte"); and (c) a "difficultie" (JB, q.v.).

169–171. **In the great Hand of God... Treasonous Mallice.** *Banquo* (a) is "Under the hand of God" ("defended by the great power and providence of God," TW, q.v.); (b) considers himself a *Hand of God* ("An Instrument or ministry by which God doth any thing," TW, s.v. "Hands"); and/or (c) stands *In the great Hand of God* ("Gods blessings, protection, and deliverances," TW, s.v. "Hands"). *Thence* ("from there," OED), *Against* ("In resistance to, in defence or protection from"; also "in anticipation of, in preparation for," OED) *the* unknown murderer's *undivulg'd* (hidden, unrevealed) *pretence* ("intention, purpose," RC, s.v. "Attainte"), *Banquo* fights *Of* (variant of "off," OED) *Treasonous Mallice* ("treacherie, knaverie, falsehood," RC, s.v. "Malice").

174. **briefly.** "Verie speedelie, hastilie, swiftlie" (TT, s.v. "Cursim").

174. **put on manly readinesse.** Both (a) *put on* (assume, adopt) *manly* ("great, wise, strong, hardy," TT, s.v. "Masculus"; also "valiant, stout, couragious, bold," JF, s.v. "Strénuo") *readinesse* ("prowesse, valour," RC, s.v. "Appertise"); and (b) *put on* (place clothing on one's body, don) *manly* ("fierce and warlike," TT, s.v. "Fortis") *readinesse* (i.e., attire; cf. "ready": "properly dressed or attired; in a fit state for public appearance," OED).

176. **contented.** Both (a) agreed; and (b) "Willing, ready" (OED).

179. **consort.** "To accompanie, associate," "joyne in fellowship" (RC, s.v. "Compagnonner").

180–181. **To shew an unfelt Sorrow... easie.** A *false* ("Treacherous, traiterous," "deceitful, craftie, disloyal," TT, s.v. "Perfidiōsus") *man* can easily perform the *Office* ("a thing that ought to be done: honour done to one, homage," TT, s.v. "Officium") of showing an *unfelt Sorrow*. Cf. I.vii.92–93 and 96–97.

182–183. **to England... To Ireland.** Holinshed relates that

> Malcolme Cammore and Donald Bane the sonnes of king Duncane, for feare of theyr lives (whiche they might well know that Makbeth would seeke to bring to end for his more sure confirmation in the astate) fled into Cumberland, where Malcolme remained til time that S[aint] Edward the sonne of king Etheldred recovered the dominion of England from the Danish power, the whiche Edward receyved Malcolme by way of moste freendly entertaynement, but Donald passed over into Ireland, where he was tenderly cherished by the king of that lande.

186. **The neere... the neerer bloody.** Those who are *neere* ("Nearer in kinship," OED) *in blood* (*blood* relationship, family connection) to the *King* have the best claim to the throne. Therefore, they are *the neerer* ("more likely," TT, s.v. "Prŏpior") *bloody* (blood-thirsty, murderous).

Malcolme and Donalbaine, who are most *neere in blood* to the *King*, logically conclude that they will be the assassin's next victims. As the *King's* next of kin, they will be *the neerer* (sooner) *bloody* (bleeding, wounded).

Malc.   This murtherous Shaft that's shot,

Hath not yet lighted: and our safest way,

Is to avoid the ayme. Therefore to Horse,

And let us not be daintie of leave-taking,   [190]

But shift away: there's warrant in that Theft,

Which steales it selfe, when there's no mercie left.

Exeunt.

187–189. ***This murtherous Shaft... avoid the ayme.*** *Malcolme* realizes that if the murderer's *ayme* ("Endeavour or Design," ND) is to claim the throne, then the *King's* children are the next logical targets. The *murtherous Shaft* ("arrow of the long-bow," DPF) *that's shot Hath not yet lighted* (fallen, struck, landed), so the *safest way* (course of action) *Is* to move out of range and thus *avoid the ayme* ("The direction or pointing of a missile at that which it is intended to strike," OED).

To avoid being "buggered" like their father (cf. and see note: *Unmannerly breech'd with gore,* line 151, above), *Malcolme* and *Donalbaine* must *avoid* the *shot* ("seminal emission," JH, s.v. "shoot") from *This murtherous* (i.e., lustful or wanton; see note: *murth'ring,* I.v.55) *Shaft* ("penis," OED). The chances are good that the *King's* children are the murderer's next *ayme* ("A thing aimed at; a mark, or butt," OED), so they must take care if they are *to avoid* an *ayme* ("mark": "Penis... Lit[erally] the target or butt, of which the *prick* is the centre," FR) in *the ayme* ("butt": "buttocks," EP). Cf. and see note: *bend up,* I.vii.94.

190. ***daintie of.*** Fastidious or overly-particular about.

191–192. ***shift away... no mercie.*** *Theft* is "without *warrant*" ("unlawful," TB, s.v. "Illicitous"), so one who *steales* is held under *warrant* ("A writ or order issued by some executive authority, empowering a ministerial officer to make an arrest," OED). In order to *shift away* ("free himselfe," RC, s.v. "Eschapper"), a thief must either (a) gain *mercie* ("compassionate treatment in a case where severity is merited or expected, esp. in giving legal judgment or passing sentence," OED); (b) make a *warrant* ("a baile, a suretie," JF, s.v. "Sodatore"); or (c) *shift* ("deceive," "use tricks, deale cunningly, proceed by sleights," RC, s.v. "Ruser") in order to *shift away* ("to escape or run away," "to breake prison, to winde ones neck out of the halter," JF, s.v. "Scalappiare").

However, *Malcolme* has *warrant* (authorization, freedom from blame or legal responsibility) to "steal [himself]" ("withdraw [him]self secretly or quietly," OED), for in so doing the *Theft* (i.e., *Malcolme* himself; *Theft* is literally the stolen article, "That which is or has been stolen," OED) merely *steales it selfe.* Moreover, *Malcolme's* "steeling" (hardening, strengthening) himself provides *warrant* ("safeguard, protection, defence," OED) from his enemies, who are surely without *mercie* (compassion, pity; also "duties of Charity towardes our Neighbour," TW).

There is possible additional play on "steal" meaning "The shaft or stem of an arrow" (OED), and on *warrant* meaning a knot to secure the line of a bow (OED). Cf. lines 187–189, above.

Act II, scene iv

Scena Quarta.   [1]

Enter Rosse, with an Old man.   [II.iv.1]

Old man.   Threescore and ten I can remember well,

Within the Volume of which Time, I have seene

Houres dreadfull, and things strange: but this sore Night   [5]

Hath trifled former knowings.

Rosse.   Ha, good Father,

Thou seest the Heavens, as troubled with mans Act,

Threatens his bloody Stage: byth' Clock 'tis Day,

And yet darke Night strangles the travailing Lampe: [10]

Is't Nights predominance, or the Dayes shame,

Notes II.iv.

2–3. **an Old man... remember well.** The *Old man* must be older than *Three-score and ten* (i.e., seventy; a *score* is twenty), for he can *well remember* past events for that number of years.

4. **Volume.** With play on *Volume* meaning (a) space or amount; and (b) "a booke" (TE, s.v. "Volumen"). Cf. and see note: I.iii.174–176.

5. **dreadfull.** *Dreadfull* means "horrible, scrowfull, deadlie, heavie, darke, clowdie, stinking, hidde, naughtie, foule, filthie, troublous or stormie: ill and lothsome, unluckie, cruell" (TT, s.v. "Ater"); also "daungerous, to be feared" (TT, s.v. "Formīdō-lōsus").

5–24. **things strange... they eate each other.** Shakespeare draws this series of *strange* (prodigious; unnatural) *things* from Holinshed, who reports that following the murder of King Duffe

> For the space of .vi. moneths togither after this haynous murder thus commit-
> ted, there appeared no sunne by day, nor Moone by night in any parte of the
> realme, but stil was the skie covered with continual clowdes, and sometimes

suche outragious windes arose with lightnings and tempestes, that the people were in great feare of present destruction… undoubtedly almightie God shewed himselfe thereby to be offended moste highly for that wicked murther of king Duffe… Monstrous sightes also that were seene within the Scottishe kingdome that yeare were these, horses in Lothian being of singuler beautie and swiftnesse, did eate their owne flesh, & would in no wise taste any other meate… There was a Sparhauke also strangled by an Owle… all men understood that the abhominable murder of king Duffe was the cause hereof.

5. *sore.* Sore means (a) "painful"; (b) "Sorrowful"; (c) "Violent"; and (d) "Heavy, oppressive, severe" (JJ).

6. *trifled former knowings.* The *Old man* says that the past night's *knowings* (i.e., portents or omens; *knowings* are literally "sign[s]," "indication[s]," OED) have *trifled* (rendered insignificant, or made into "trifles": "things of small estimation," TT, s.v. "Affãnïæ") all his *former knowings* (experiences, OED).

7. *Father.* Generally used for "an elder" (F&H).

8–10. *the Heavens… the travailing Lampe.* The *Heavens* (God and his angels, the occupants of *the Heavens*) are *troubled* ("made angrie, provoked," TT, s.v. "Concĭtus") *with mans Act* (the actions of mankind). Consequently, they "threaten" ("give ominous indication of impending evil," "declare [their] intention of injuring or punishing," OED) *his bloody Stage* (the location in which events occur; also a "course of action," OED). *Byth' Clock 'tis Day, And yet darke Night strangles* (smothers, stifles) *the travailing* ("traveling"; "travail" and "travel" were interchangeably pronounced, HK, p. 268) *Lampe* (i.e., the sun). In order to "travel," the sun must now (a) "travail" (labor, exert great effort); and (b) endure "Travaile" ("Troubles, dangers and evils, which happen in ones journey," TW).

In ancient myth, the sun god (a.k.a. "Helios," "Phoebus," "Sol," and "Apollo") traveled through the sky in a chariot drawn by fiery winged steeds. Now, the horses who pull this flaming chariot suffer from the *strangles* ("A disease in horses and other animals, characterized by inflamed swellings in the throat," OED). Consequently, *the travailing Lampe* of Day is blotted out by "The Strangles" ("the thicke humor which young horses void at their narells; also, foame, or a foamie slime," RC, s.v. "Gourme"; cf. "the Sunne… / …breaking through the foule and ugly mists / Of vapours, that did seeme to strangle him," *1 Henry IV*, I.ii.). *Duncan's* murder is doubtless the cause of this unnatural darkness, for "to se the Sune darkened, signifyeth the perill or danger of a king" (Thomas Hill, *The Moste pleasaunte Arte of the Interpretation of Dreames*).

The actor playing *Rosse* stands on a *Stage* ("skaffold for players to play upon," JF, s.v. "Proscenio") that is brightly lit (see note: *Torches*, I.vi.2), so he describes lighting conditions opposite to those of his actual environment. The actor playing *Rosse* can clearly see the people in the audience (see note: *Here's a Farmer*, II.iii.9), and when he looks up towards *the Heavens* (the ceiling or canopy over the stage, which was elaborately painted with a representation of the heavenly constellations) he discerns that the "gods" ("the occupants of the gallery at a theatre," F&H) are *troubled* by the dramatic events which have transpired during this *Act* ("part of a play," RC, s.v. "Catastrophe").

9. *byth' Clock.* See note: *Clock*, II.i.6.

11. *predominance.* A "predominant" person or thing "ruleth or beareth sway" (JB, q.v.); the word was used especially "with reference to the supposed influence… of planets" (OED). *Predominance* also means "A person's besetting sin; a sin or weakness which dominates a person's moral character" (OED).

That Darknesse does the face of Earth intombe,

When living Light should kisse it?

Old man.   'Tis unnaturall,

Even like the deed that's done: On Tuesday last,   [15]

A Faulcon towring in her pride of place,

Was by a Mowsing Owle hawkt at, and kill'd.

Rosse.   And *Duncans* Horses,

(A thing most strange, and certaine)

Beauteous, and swift, the Minions of their Race,   [20]

Turn'd wilde in nature, broke their stalls, flong out,

Contending 'gainst Obedience, as they would

Make Warre with Mankinde.

Old man.   'Tis said, they eate each other.

Rosse.   They did so: [25]

To th' amazement of mine eyes that look'd upon't.

Enter Macduffe.   [II.iv.2]

Heere comes the good *Macduffe*.

How goes the world Sir, now?

Macd.   Why see you not?   [30]

Ross.   Is't known who did this more then bloody deed?

Macd.   Those that *Macbeth* hath slaine.

12. *intombe.* To "burie, or laie in a grave" (JF, s.v. "Tombare").

14–15. *unnaturall... the deed that's done.* Because *the deed that's done* (i.e., the murder of the *King*) is *unnaturall* ("Wicked, ungodly," "accursed," TT, s.v. "Scĕlĕrātus"), the state of the world is *unnaturall* ("woondrous, that giveth a strange signe or token," JF, s.v. "Prodigioso"). Also see notes: *Against the use of Nature*, I.iii.155; *deed*, I.vii.28; and *Unmannerly breech'd with gore*, II.iii.151.

15. **On Tuesday last.** If these ominous events have been ongoing since *Tuesday last*, at least several days have elapsed since the *King's* murder. In Holinshed, the unnatural events following the murder of King Duff continue for a full year; see note: *things strange*, line 5, above.

16–17. *A Faulcon towring... kill'd.* The natural world was thought to adhere to a strict hierarchical order (see note: I.iv.29–30), and the animals' behavior reflects the chaos and upheaval in the human realm. Normally, *A Faulcon* (a symbol of "Superiority, aspiration, spirit, light and liberty... a solar emblem of victory," JT) would "tower" ("sore on High," ND) *in pride of place* ("the most prominent or important position," OED). However, while she "towers" ("mount[s] up, as a hawk, so as to be able to swoop down on the quarry," OED) *in pride of place* ("the high position or pitch to which a falcon or other bird of prey rises before swooping down on its prey," OED), she is *hawkt at* (flown at, attacked as by a hawk) *and kill'd by a* lowly *Mowsing* ("loving Mice; hunting after Mice," RC, s.v. "Sourien") *Owle.*

18–20. *Horses... the Minions of their Race.* As an adjective, "minion" means "Proper, feate, pretie, fine, trimme, well fashioned," "hansome, well made," (TT, s.v. "Concinnus"). Shakespeare might here use *Minions* as a noun meaning "those which are the handsomest or best made," but those *Horses* which are *the Minions* (i.e., studs; a "minion" is literally "a lover or paramour," EC) *of their Race* ("A breed of horses; a herd of horses, *esp.* one kept for breeding," OED) would in any case be the finest examples.

21. *flong out.* "Flinging" is "A horses kicking, winsing, yerking, striking," "flying out with the heeles" (RC, s.v. "Ruade"); to "fling" is "To kicke, spurne, wince," "let flye, yerke out behind, or with the heeles; also, to be stubborne, disobedient, obstinate, or, obstinate in disobedience" (RC, s.v. "Calcitrer"). To "fling out" also means "to goe out hastely, to conveigh himselfe quickelie: to turne awaie or cast of[f]" (TT, s.v. "Ejĭcĭo").

23. *Make Warre.* In antiquity, the horse was "dedicated to Mars, and the sudden appearance of a horse was thought to be an omen of war... the horse is a symbol pertaining to Man's baser forces" (JC).

26. *amazement.* "Extreme feare, dread; anxietie, or perplexitie of mind" (RC, s.v. "Transe").

29–30. *How goes the world... see you not.* *Macduffe* thinks that *Rosse* can easily *see* for himself *How the world goes* ("how events shape themselves," OED) simply by observing the ill omens surrounding him (lines 3–26, above).

Ross.	Alas the day,	
	What good could they pretend?	
Macd.	They were subborned,	[35]
	Malcolme, and *Donalbaine* the Kings two Sonnes	
	Are stolne away and fled, which puts upon them	
	Suspition of the deed.	
Rosse.	'Gainst Nature still,	
	Thriftlesse Ambition, that will raven up	[40]
	Thine owne lives meanes: Then 'tis most like,	
	The Soveraignty will fall upon *Macbeth*.	
Macd.	He is already nam'd, and gone to Scone	
	To be invested.	
Rosse.	Where is *Duncans* body?	[45]
Macd.	Carried to Colmekill,	
	The Sacred Store-house of his Predecessors,	
	And Guardian of their Bones.	
Rosse.	Will you to Scone?	
Macd.	No Cosin, Ile to Fife.	[50]

34–35. ***What good could they pretend... subborned.*** *Rosse* cannot perceive *What good* (benefit, profit) the *King's* servants *could* possibly *pretend* ("lay claime to, aime at," RC, s.v. "Pretendre") in committing regicide. In response, *Macduffe* explains that

Duncan's Chamberlaines were *subborned* ("corrupt[ed]," "bribe[d]," TB, s.v. "Suborn") by some other guilty party.

Macduffe might also voice a suspicion that the facts of *Duncan's* murder are not as they seem. The *Chamberlaines* were possibly *subborned* (i.e., falsely accused; "to sub-orne" is to "brynge in a false wytnesse," TE, s.v. "Suborno"; cf. *Witnesse,* II.ii.59). While the true perpetrator escaped, the *Chamberlaines* were innocent scapegoats who were *subborned* ("put in place of another," JM, s.v. "Suppuésto"; to "subborn" is to "coun-terfeit, foist or thrust in false things among; or in stead of, true," RC, s.v. "Supposer").

36–37. ***Malcolme, and Donalbaine... Are stolne away.*** See note: II.iii.182–183; and cf. II.iii.191–192.

40. ***Thriftlesse.*** "Unprofitable, worthless, useless" (OED).

40. ***Ambition.*** See notes: *Ambition,* I.v.19 and I.vii.31.

40. ***raven.*** To *raven* is "To devour," "to swill, to stuffe or fill himselfe with: to drowne, or give himselfe too much, or to all, &c. to cast in as it were into a great streame or bottomlesse pitte, where it is like to be swallowed" (TT, s.v. "Ingurgĭto").

43. ***nam'd.*** *Malcolme* is *Duncan's* rightful heir by selection (cf. I.iv.48–50), but *Malcolme's* flight has placed him under suspicion of patricide. The aristocracy has there-fore *nam'd* (nominated or elected) *Macbeth* to be king. (According to Holinshed, *Mac-beth* enlisted the support of the nobility before murdering *Duncan*; see notes: *cursed thoughts,* II.i.14; and *invested,* line 44, below).

43–44. ***gone to Scone To be invested.*** *Scone* is a village in central Scotland whose abbey once contained "the stone called the Regall of Scotland, upon which the kings of Scotland were wont to sitte, at the time of their coronations for a throne" (RH). "Edward I removed to London, and placed in Westminster Abbey, the great stone upon which the kings of Scotland were wont to be crowned. This stone is still preserved, and forms the support of Edward the Confessor's chair, which the British monarchs occupy at their coronation" (DPF).

Holinshed's *Macbeth* did not act alone in murdering *Duncan* but was *invested* ("clothe[d] with or in the insignia of an office," "install[ed] in an office or rank with the customary rites or ceremonies," OED) with the foreknowledge and consent of the nobility (see note: *cursed thoughts,* II.i.14). After murdering *Duncan, Macbeth* "Then having a companie about him of such as he had made privie to his enterpryce, he caused himselfe to be proclaymed king, and foorthwith went unto Scone, where by common consent, he receyved the investure of the kingdome according to the accus-tomed maner" (RH).

46–47. ***Colmekill... Store-house of his Predecessors.*** The "Isle of Colmkil (oth-erwise called Iona)" (RH), which lies off the western coast of Scotland, was the tradi-tional burying ground of the Scottish kings. Holinshed states that "The bodie of Duncane was firste conveyed unto Elgyne, and there buried in kingly wise, but after-wardes it was removed and conveyed unto Colmekill, and there layd in a sepulture amongst his predecessours."

Colmekill is named after Saint Columba (A.D. 521–597), a missionary who founded an abbey there is 563. The Celtic form of L. "Columba" ("dove") is "colum" or "colm"; "cill" can mean either "a burying ground" or "a church" (Neil McAlpine and John Mackenzie, *A Pronouncing Gaelic Dictionary*). Therefore, "colum cille" (or *Colmekill*) can mean (a) "dove of the church"; or (b) "burial ground of Saint Columba" (Iona, where the saint is buried). *Colmekill* should not be confused with *Saint Colmes ynch* (I.ii.76).

Rosse.   Well, I will thither.

Macd.   Well may you see things wel done there: Adieu

              Least our old Robes sit easier then our new.

Rosse.   Farewell, Father.

Old M.   Gods benyson go with you, and with those   [55]

              That would make good of bad, and Friends of Foes.

  Exeunt omnes

51–52. **Well... wel done.** *Macduffe* plays on *Well* meaning (a) "bee it as it bee will" (RC, s.v. "Ainsi comme ainsi"); (b) properly, appropriately; and (c) "in a way which is morally good" (OED).

53. **Least our old Robes... our new.** Members of the aristocracy wore ceremonial *Robes* to the monarch's coronation, at which they were expected to swear an official oath of allegiance to the sovereign. In the English coronation ceremony, the "oath of Homage," which has remained unchanged since medieval times, "is as follows:—'I, N[ame], Duke {or Earl, etc.} of N[ame], become your Liege man of Life and Limb and of earthly worship; and faith and truth shall bear unto you, to live and die against all manner of folks. So help me God'" (Leopold G. Wickham Legg, Introduction to *English Coronation Records*, p. lvi).

To avoid taking such an oath, *Macduffe* plans to *sit* ("To disregard, neglect, pay no heed or attention to," OED) *Macbeth's* coronation. He returns home to *Fife Least* (for fear that) their *old Robes* (i.e., the nobility's loyalty to the *old* king) *sit* (befit or suit them) *easier* (more comfortably or satisfactorily) *then* their *new* (i.e., their loyalty to the *new* king, *Macbeth*). Cf. I.iii.122.

55. **benyson.** "A benediction," "blessing; a wishing of all good lucke unto" (RC, s.v. "Benediction").

Act III, scene i

Actus Tertius. Scena Prima.   [1]

Enter Banquo.   [III.i.1]

Banq.   Thou hast it now, King, Cawdor, Glamis, all,

             As the weyard Women promis'd, and I feare

             Thou playd'st most fowly for't: yet it was saide   [5]

             It should not stand in thy Posterity,

             But that my selfe should be the Roote, and Father

             Of many Kings. If there come truth from them,

             As upon thee Macbeth, their Speeches shine,

             Why by the verities on thee made good,   [10]

             May they not be my Oracles as well,

             And set me up in hope. But hush, no more.

Senit sounded. Enter Macbeth as King, Lady{,} Lenox,

Rosse, Lords, and Attendants.   [III.i.2]

Macb.   Heere's our chiefe Guest.   [15]

La.   If he had beene forgotten,

             It had bene as a gap in our great Feast,

             And all-thing unbecomming.

Notes III.i.

3. **Thou hast it now.** Banquo's statement suggests that Macbeth has recently been crowned. However, this scene takes place on the same day as Banquo's murder (cf. lines 19–20, 35–36, and 161, below), so at least ten years have passed since Duncan's murder. According to Holinshed, Macbeth, who ascended the throne in 1040, was initially

a good king who "set his whole intention to maintayne justice, and to punishe all enor-
mities and abuses, whiche had chaunced through the feeble and slouthfull administration of Duncane... governing the realme for the space of tenne yeares in equall
justice." It was not until after *Macbeth* had ruled for a decade that "he beganne to shewe
what he was, in steede of equitie practising crueltie" (RH).

4. **weyard Women.** See note: *weyward Sisters*, I.iii.36.

6–8. **It should not stand... many Kings.** The prophecy foretold that *It* (i.e., the
kingship) *should* (formerly used for both "shall" and "would," OED) *not stand* (remain,
continue) *in Macbeth's Posterity* ("children," "offspring," TT, s.v. "Postĕri"), *But that
Banquo should be the Roote* ("the beginning or foundation," TT, s.v. "Stirps"), *and
Father* ("ancestor"; also "originator," OED) *Of many Kings* (see note: *Your Children
shall be Kings*, I.iii.95).

Macbeth will not be *Father* to *Posterity* because *It* (i.e., his penis; see note: *it*,
I.vii.91) cannot *stand* (become erect; see note: *stand too*, II.iii.44). By contrast, *Banquo* possesses a good *Roote* ("Either penis or penis erectus," EP).

8–9. **If there come truth... their Speeches shine.** *If there come truth from* the
Witches to *Banquo As* (in the same way that, to the same extent that) *their Speeches*
(statements) *shine* ("be evident or manifest," TT, s.v. "Dīlūcĕo") *upon* (regarding, in
respect to) *Macbeth*, then *Banquo* expects fortune to *shine upon* ("look favourably upon,
be favourable to," OED) him as well.

10. **verities.** A "veritie" is "a true tale, a true matter" (JF, s.v. "Vero").

11–12. **my Oracles... set me up in hope.** Initially, *Banquo* suspected that the *Witches*
were *Oracles* (i.e., that they "talked out their asses"; FR posits that "oracle" was heard
as L. "ora": to speak," + "cul": the fundament). Now, however, *Banquo* considers the
possibility that the *Witches* are perhaps true *Oracles* ("vehicle[s] or medium[s] of divine
communication," OED). Their speeches might be *Oracles* ("Answer[s] given by God,"
"Prophesie[s] or Prediction[s]," TB, q.v.) *And set* him *up* (establish him) *in hope* (confidence, expectation). As *Banquo* has been promised royal progeny, he sees no reason why
these *Oracles* ("cunt[s]," F&H, s.v. "monosyllable") should not *set* him *up* ("cause [him]
an erection," JH, s.v. "set up") *in hope* (virility, fertility; see note: *hope*, I.vii.43).

12. **hush, no more.** If *Banquo* were alone in his thoughts, he would have no need
to *hush* upon *Macbeth's* approach. However, *Banquo* must *hush* because he is talking
to the audience. See note: *Here's a Farmer*, II.iii.9.

13. **Senit.** A *Senit* is a ceremonial trumpet call: "In Tudor England, the sennet was
reserved for personages of the highest rank" (Christopher Wilson and Michela Calore,
Music in Shakespeare: A Dictionary, q.v.). *Senit* is seemingly derived "from *sonare*, and thus
the spelling ought to be *sonnet*, not *sennet*. But other forms are found —*Synnet*, *Signet*,
Signate, which may be proper derivatives of *signum*, and thus make this trumpet call 'a
signal,' instead of 'a sounding'" (Edward Woodall Naylor, *Shakespeare and Music*, p. 178).

15–17. **our chiefe Guest... our great Feast.** *Banquo* is *Macbeth's chiefe* ("principall, of the first ranke," RC, s.v. "Cardinal"; also "honorable," "eminent, excellent,"
RC, s.v. "Haut") *Guest* at tonight's *Feast*. The *Feast* represents an attempt by *Macbeth*
to maintain good relations with the aristocracy: "Makbeth after the departure thus of
Duncanes sonnes used great liberalitie towardes the nobles of the realme, thereby to
winne their favour" (RH). However, this *Feast* in *Banquo's* honor also has a darker purpose. See note: *two Murtherers*, line 88, below.

17. **a gap.** Both (a) a "hole" (JF, s.v. "Buca"); and (b) "a flawe" (JF, s.v. "Sfendimento").

18. **all-thing.** *All-thing* is used in the same way as the modern "everything."

Macb.	To night we hold a solemne Supper sir,
	And Ile request your presence. [20]
Banq.	Let your Highnesse
	Command upon me, to the which my duties
	Are with a most indissoluble tye
	For ever knit.
Macb.	Ride you this afternoone? [25]
Ban.	I, my good Lord.
Macb.	We should have else desir'd your good advice
	(Which still hath been both grave, and prosperous)
	In this dayes Councell: but wee'le take to morrow.
	Is't farre you ride? [30]
Ban.	As farre, my Lord, as will fill up the time
	'Twixt this, and Supper. Goe not my Horse the better,
	I must become a borrower of the Night,
	For a darke houre, or twaine.
Macb.	Faile not our Feast. [35]
Ban.	My Lord, I will not.
Macb.	We heare our bloody Cozens are bestow'd
	In England, and in Ireland, not confessing
	Their cruell Parricide, filling their hearers
	With strange invention. But of that to morrow, [40]
	When therewithall, we shall have cause of State,
	Craving us joyntly. Hye you to Horse:

19. *solemne.* Ceremonial; celebratory.

23. *indissoluble.* Something *indissoluble* "cannot be untied, loosed or undone" (EC2).

28. *still.* At all times; on all occasions.

28. *grave.* *Banquo's* advice has hitherto been *grave* ("Earnest," "of importance and weight, necessarie," TT, s.v. "Sērius"), but he will shortly be in a *grave* ("a toumbe: a sepulchre," TT, s.v. "Bustum").

28. *prosperous.* *Prosperous* can mean (a) "Right, apt," "convenient," "diligent" (TT, s.v. "Dexter"); (b) "sincere," "eloquent" (TT, s.v. "Candĭdus"); and/or (c) "profitable," "gainefull" (JF, s.v. "Utile").

29. *take to morrow.* Perhaps (a) resume again *to morrow* (to *take* is "To begin or start afresh after leaving off," OED); or (b) find time *to morrow* (to *take* is "to seize an opportunity," OED).

34. *twaine.* Two.

37–38. *our bloody Cozens… Ireland. Malcolme* and *Donalbaine are bestow'd* ("lodge[d]," "put up," OED) *In England, and in Ireland* (cf. and see note: II.iii. 182–183), where they are hospitably and honorably received (to "bestow" is "to set much by, to esteeme or account," RC, s.v. "Tribuire"; *bestow'd* also means "provided for," RC, s.v. "Appané").

39. *Parricide.* Both (a) "a killing or killer of Father, Mother, or any of near kin" (EC2); and (b) "the action or crime of killing the ruler of or betraying one's country" (OED).

40. *invention.* "A fictitious statement or story; a fabrication, fiction, figment" (OED).

41. *therewithall.* "Along with or together with that; besides, or in addition to that" (OED).

41. *cause.* "A matter of concern, an affair, business" (OED).

42. *Craving.* Demanding.

Adieu, till you returne at Night.

Goes *Fleance* with you?

Ban.	I, my good Lord: our time does call upon's.	[45]

Macb.	I wish your Horses swift, and sure of foot:

And so I doe commend you to their backs.

Farwell.

Exit Banquo.	[III.i.3]

Let every man be master of his time,   [50]

Till seven at Night, to make societie

The sweeter welcome:

We will keepe our selfe till Supper time alone:

While then, God be with you.

{*Exeunt. Manet Macbeth and a Servant.*}	[III.i.4] [55]

Sirrha, a word with you: Attend those men

Our pleasure?

Servant.	They are, my Lord, without the Pallace

Gate.

Macb.	Bring them before us.	[60]

Exit Servant.	[III.i.5]

To be thus, is nothing, but to be safely thus:

Our feares in *Banquo* sticke deepe,

53. *We will keepe our selfe... alone.* *Macbeth* will not *keepe* himself *alone till Supper time* but will instead meet with hired murderers. Notably, *Macbeth* formally dismisses his *Wife* along with the rest of the court; cf. III.ii.5–6 and 14.

54. *While.* "Up to the time that; till, until" (OED).

54. *God be with you.* *God be with you* means "farewell" (TB, s.v. "Vale"; the phrase is the ancestor of the modern "Good-bye").

56. *Sirrha.* A form of address used to those of inferior rank.

58. *without.* Outside.

62. *To be thus, is nothing, but to be safely thus.* *To be thus* (i.e., *To be* king) *is nothing, but to be* (i.e., "without being"; *but* means "If not, unless, except," OED) *thus safely* ("securely," JM, s.v. "Seguraménte"; "Without perill or punishment," TT, s.v. "Tūtō").

63. *Our feares in Banquo sticke deepe.* *Macbeth's feares in Banquo sticke deepe,* meaning (a) take *deepe* root, attain a firm hold; and (b) pierce *deepe,* or cut to the quick. According to Holinshed, "The woordes also of the three weird sisters, wold not out of his [*Macbeth's*] mind, which as they promised him the kingdome, so lykewise did they promise it at the same time, unto the posteritie of Banquho." *Macbeth* therefore *feares* that *Banquo* will *sticke* (i.e., "fuck"; see note: *sticking,* I.vii.72) him *deepe* (see note: *deepe,* I.vi.25).

And in his Royaltie of Nature reignes that

Which would be fear'd. 'Tis much he dares,   [65]

And to that dauntlesse temper of his Minde,

He hath a Wisdome, that doth guide his Valour,

To act in safetie. There is none but he,

Whose being I doe feare: and under him,

My *Genius* is rebuk'd, as it is said   [70]

Mark Anthonies was by *Cæsar*. He chid the Sisters,

When first they put the Name of King upon me,

And bad them speake to him. Then Prophet-like,

They hayl'd him Father to a Line of Kings.

Upon my Head they plac'd a fruitlesse Crowne,   [75]

And put a barren Scepter in my Gripe,

Thence to be wrencht with an unlineall Hand,

No Sonne of mine succeeding: if't be so,

For *Banquo's* Issue have I fil'd my Minde,

For them, the gracious *Duncan* have I murther'd,   [80]

64. **Royaltie of Nature.** *Macbeth* fears the *Royaltie* ("kinglines, loyaltie, uprightnes, sinceritie, honestie," JM, s.v. "Realità") *of Banquo's Nature* (temperament, innate disposition). He also fears the *Royaltie* (i.e., virility or sexual capability; *Royaltie* contains "an innuendo of violent pelvic movements during copulation," JF, s.v. "Royal"; to "roil" is literally "To move about vigorously," OED) *of Banquo's Nature* (genitals and semen; see notes: *Nature,* I.ii.17 and I.v.52).

64. **reignes.** With play on *reignes* meaning (a) kidneys, regarded as the seat of sexual passion (cf. and see note: *neer'st,* line 145, below); and (b) "loins" (OED).

66. **dauntlesse temper of his Minde.** *Macbeth* dreads (a) the *dauntlesse* (bold, fearless) *temper* (constitution, quality) *of Banquo's Minde* (disposition, intellect); and (b) the *dauntlesse* (sexually potent; see note: *brave,* I.ii.22) *temper* (i.e., hardness; to "temper" steel is to harden it) *of Banquo's Minde* (penis; see note: *Braine,* I.iii.173). Cf. and see note: *undaunted Mettle,* I.vii.86.

69. **being.** With play on *being* meaning both (a) person; and (b) existence.

69–71. **under him, My Genius is rebuk'd... Cæsar.** *Genius* means "a good or evil Angel, the spirit of man, nature it self, natural inclination" (TB, q.v.). The genii of antiquity "were attendant spirits. Everyone had two of these tutelaries from his cradle to his grave... The Romans maintained that two genii attended every man from birth to death — one good and the other evil. Good luck was brought about by the agency of 'his good genius,' and ill luck by that of his 'evil genius'" (DPF).

Thomas North's 1579 translation of Plutarch's *Lives of the Noble Grecians and Romanes* relates that

> a soothsayer or astronomer of Ægypt... told Antonius plainly, that his fortune (which of it selfe was excellent good, and very great) was altogether bleamished, and obscured by Cæsars fortune: and therefore he counselled him utterly to leave his company, and to get him as farre from him as he could. For thy Demon said he, (that is to say, the good angell and spirit that kepeth thee) is affraied of his: and being coragious & high when he is alone, becometh fearefull and timerous when he commeth neere unto the other.

75–78. **Upon my Head... No Sonne of mine succeeding.** Due to *Macbeth's Gripe* ("violent seisure," RC, s.v. "Rafflade") of the *Scepter* ("Monarchie, kingdome, absolute rule, Soveraigntie in chiefe," RC, s.v. "Sceptre"), he suffers from "griping" ("a pinching or gnawing at the hart," JF, s.v. "Pizzicuore"; "a tormenting," TT, s.v. "Torsio"). The prophecy predicts that *Macbeth* will be *fruitlesse* ("sterill, barren, dry," "that cannot ingender, without generation, yeelding or bringing nothing," JF, s.v. "Sterile") and therefore *fruitlesse* ("childlesse," JM, s.v. "Machórra"). His *Head* ("Prepuce. More freq[ently] the testes or scrotum," FR) and *Crowne* (genitals; see note: *Crowne,* I.v.49) are *fruitlesse* ("Withered, faded, consumed," "deprived of force," RC, s.v. "Aganni"), so *Macbeth* has gained nothing but *a barren* ("sterill," JF, s.v. "Infecondo"; "saplesse," "withered, without moysture, or juice," JF, s.v. "Secco") *Scepter* ("phallus," TR). *Macbeth* will have *No Sonne succeeding,* so the sovereignty is destined *to be wrencht* ("wrested," "extorted," JF, s.v. "Storciuto") from his own "line" (descendants, race) *with* (by) *an unlineall Hand* ("allusive of penis," GW2).

79. **For Banquo's Issue have I fil'd my Minde.** For *Banquo's Issue, Macbeth* has (a) *fil'd* ("defile[d]," "fowle[d], soyle[d]," RC, s.v. "Deturper") his *Minde* (intellectual and spiritual existence); and (b) *fil'd* ("shave[d] off," TB, s.v. "Delimate"; "trimmed, made smooth," RC, s.v. "Deturper") his *Minde* (genitals; see note: *Braine,* I.iii.173). Cf. and see note: *the frame of things dis-joynt,* III.ii.22.

Put Rancours in the Vessell of my Peace

Onely for them, and mine eternall Jewell

Given to the common Enemie of Man,

To make them Kings, the Seedes of *Banquo* Kings.

Rather then so, come Fate into the Lyst,   [85]

And champion me to th' utterance.

Who's there?

Enter Servant, and two Murtherers.   [III.i.6]

Now goe to the Doore, and stay there till we call.

Exit Servant.   [III.i.7] [90]

Was it not yesterday we spoke together?

{*1.*} *Murth.* It was, so please your Highnesse.

Macb.   Well then,

Now have you consider'd of my speeches:

Know, that it was he, in the times past,   [95]

Which held you so under fortune,

Which you thought had been our innocent selfe.

This I made good to you, in our last conference,

---

81. ***Put Rancours in the Vessell of my Peace.*** The *Peace* ("That sweete and comfortable quietnesse and tranquility of Conscience, which is the immediate fruite of our attonement with God," TW) of *Macbeth's Vessell* (body as enclosing the soul) is disturbed by "rancor" ("spite, rage, vexation, disdaine, yrkesomnes, swelling, malice, venome," JF, s.v. "Aschio").

Also, *Macbeth* has *Put* "rancor" ("Rammishnes, rottennes of things mouldie or vinewed," TT, s.v. "Rancor"; "festring," JF, s.v. "Lividézza") *in the Vessell* ("genitals," GW2; the "Naturall Instruments, which receive & containe the matter of generation," TW) *of* his *Peace* (i.e., his "piece" or penis; see note: *peace*, I.v.53). Cf. and see notes: I.iii.152–153; and *the yellow Leafe*, V.iii.30.

82–83. *eternall Jewell… the common Enemie of Man.* The *eternall Jewell* which *Macbeth* has sacrificed *to the Enemie* ("the Devil," OED) might be (a) his *eternall* soul (cf. "Think upon your owne poore soule the greatest jewell that ever God committed to you," Gervase Babington, *A profitable Exposition of the Lords Prayer*); or (b) his *eternall* salvation (cf. "the losse of eternall salvation, the which pretious jewell they cary in these weake vessels," Thomas Morton, *A Treatise of the threefolde state of man*).

In his bargain with the powers of darkness, *Macbeth* has also *Given* up his *Jewell* ("man's genitals," GW2) to be "buggered" by the Devil's *common* ("whorish," GW) *Enemie* ("penis," F&H, s.v. "prick").

84. *Seedes.* See note: *Seedes*, I.iii.64.

85–86. *come Fate… champion me to th' utterance.* The official function of the king's *champion* is described in *The Chronicle of John Hardyng*: "At the seconde course came into that hall, sir Robert Democke the kynges champion, making a proclama-cion, that whosoever woulde saye that kyng Richarde was not lawfullye kyng, he would fight with hym at the utteraunce, and threwe downe his gauntlet." The king's *cham-pion* would challenge anyone who disputed the monarch's claim to the crown to fight *to th' utterance* (to the utmost, to the death; cf. RC's "Combatre à oultrance": "To fight at sharpe, to fight it out, or to the uttermost; not to spare one another in fighting").

Macbeth calls upon *Fate* ("something destined or suitable," DPF; also "Death," OED) to *come into the Lyst* (the "place rayled in for a combat," RC, s.v. "Estacade") *And champion* him *to th' utterance*—i.e., to kill *Banquo* and his issue, who stand as rival claimants to the throne.

The "joust" was also "a familiar euphemism or substitute term for coition" (TR, q.v.). If *Fate* (i.e., "death" or orgasm; see note: *Death*, line 132, below) comes to *Mac-beth's* aid, he can "screw" *Banquo to th' utterance* (a "Pun on seminal emission," FR, s.v. "utter"; to "utter" is "To put or thrust forth, shoot or urge out; to discharge, emit, eject," OED). Then, *Macbeth* need not fear being "added to the *Lyst*" (i.e., castrated; literally "added to the list of geldings in training," F&H, q.v.).

88. *two Murtherers.* The hired *Murtherers* appear in Holinshed, who relates that *Macbeth*

> willed therefore the same Banquho with his sonne named Fleaunce, to come to a supper that he had prepared for them, which was in deede, as he had devised, present death at the handes of certaine murtherers, whome he hyred to execute that deede, appoynting them to meete with the same Banquho and his sonne without the palayce as they returned to theyr lodgings, and there to slea them, so that he woulde not have his house slaundered, but that in time to come he might cleare himselfe, if any thing were layde to his charge upon any suspition that might arise.

The appearance of *Banquo's* ghost at the feast (III.iv.48) does not occur in Holinshed, but for Shakespeare it is simply too good a dramatic opportunity to pass up. Shake-speare therefore has *Banquo* and *Fleance* attacked before they arrive at *Macbeth's* cas-tle, not as they depart.

95. *he. Banquo.*

Past in probation with you:

How you were borne in hand, how crost: [100]

The Instruments: who wrought with them:

And all things else, that might

To halfe a Soule, and to a Notion craz'd,

Say, Thus did *Banquo*.

1.Murth.   You made it knowne to us.   [105]

Macb.   I did so:

And went further, which is now

Our point of second meeting.

Doe you finde your patience so predominant,

In your nature, that you can let this goe?   [110]

Are you so Gospell'd, to pray for this good man,

And for his Issue, whose heavie hand

Hath bow'd you to the Grave, and begger'd

Yours for ever?

1.Murth.   We are men, my Liege.   [115]

99. ***Past in probation.*** *Past* ("confirmed"; "determined or decided," OED) *in probation* ("A proofe, a tryall," JB, q.v.; "approbation, proving," RC, q.v.).

100. ***borne in hand.*** "Delude[d], abuse[d] with false pretences" (OED).

101. ***Instruments.*** "Instrument" can mean (a) "An Agent," "one thats imployed in a businesse" (RC, s.v. "Faciendaire"); (b) "Evidence" (RC, q.v.); and/or (c) "meanes" (RC, s.v. "Attrapoire").

103. ***halfe a Soule.*** A *halfe a Soule* is a half-wit (*Soule* is used of the "Intellectual or spiritual power; high development of the mental faculties," OED).

Soule is also synonymous with "spirit" meaning "semen" (see note: *Spirits*, I.v.27), so *halfe a Soule* means an effeminate or impotent man (FR, s.v. "half," who notes that "Plato's half-men [sought] their other halves for completion"). Cf. "The Boy is Plyable to all my wishes, / 'Tis a half Soul bred in the Lag of Love, / And Spiritless as the Desire which got him" (John Bancroft, *King Edward the Third*). Also cf. and see notes: *bow'd you* and *begger'd*, line 113, below.

103. ***Notion.*** "Knowledge"; also "intelligence, understanding" (RC, s.v. "Cognoissance").

109. ***predominant.*** See note: *predominance*, II.iv.11.

110. ***let this goe.*** *Let this goe* can mean (a) permit *this* to continue; and/or (b) ignore or forget *this*.

111. ***Are you so Gospell'd.*** *So* instructed in the "Gospel" ("the word of God," TB, q.v.) as to "Love your enemies, blesse them that curse you, doe good to them that hate you, and pray for them which despitefully use you, and persecute you" (Matthew 5:44).

113. ***bow'd you.*** I.e., "made you impotent" and/or "buggered you" ("bow" alludes to the penis; see note: *bend up*, I.vii.94; *bow'd* is a synonym of "bent," which alludes to the position of the passive partner in sodomy, JA, p. 191).

113. ***begger'd.*** "Beggar" is used "euphemistically for bugger" (OED).

Macb.   I, in the Catalogue ye goe for men,

As Hounds, and Greyhounds, Mungrels, Spaniels, Curres,

Showghes, Water-Rugs, and Demy-Wolves are clipt

All by the Name of Dogges: the valued file

Distinguishes the swift, the slow, the subtle,   [120]

The House-keeper, the Hunter, every one

According to the gift, which bounteous Nature

Hath in him clos'd: whereby he does receive

116–122. *in the Catalogue ye goe for men… the gift.* All breeds *in the Catalogue* ("A roll, a bill, a register of names or other things," JB) *goe for* ("[are] accounted or valued as," OED) *Dogges*, so all breeds are accordingly *clipt* ("Cleped": "called, named," TB, q.v.) *by* that *Name* (title). Only a *valued* (that which indicates value or worth) *file* ("a register, a record," JF, s.v. "Registro"; also a "label": "a supplementary note, comment, or clause," OED) *Distinguishes every one According to* its natural *gift* (talent, ability).

Macbeth taunts the *Murtherers* by saying that they may *goe for* ("pass as," OED) *men*, but in reality they are *clipt* (castrated, FR; *clipt* means "cut off," "pared, curtalled, cut short, abridged, maymed, mangled, unperfect," JF, s.v. "Troncato") and lack *the gift* ("genitals," FR). *Macbeth* also implies that the *Murtherers* are *Dogges* (sodomites or eunuchs, FR, who cfs. Deuteronomy 23:18: "Thou shalt not bring the hire of a whore, or the price of a dogge into the house of the LORD thy God for any vow: for even both these are abomination unto the LORD thy God").

This passage was possibly inspired by Holinshed, who devotes an entire chapter to "English Dogges" and boasts that "There is no country that may (as I take it) compare with ours in number, excellencie, and diversitie of Dogges." Nevertheless, when used *for men*, "dog" is "a most degrading expression" (DPF). In general, a "dog" is "a churlish knave" (TT, s.v. "Cănis"), but each of the different *Dogges* mentioned by *Macbeth* has a specific derogatory application (see notes).

117. *Hounds, and Greyhounds.* Holinshed extols the "Greyhounde, cherished for hys strength and swiftnesse" and classifies several types of "Hounds… the foremoste excelleth in perfite smelling, the seconde in quicke espying, the third in swiftnesse and quicknesse, the fourth in smelling and nimblenesse. &c. & the last in subtilty and deceitfulnesse."

A "hound" is also "A mean, contemptible fellow; a scoundrel; a filthy sneak" (F&H). "Hound" can also mean a libertine: cf. RC's "Levron": "A young, or little, Greyhound; also, a young wanton fellow that (as a young Greyhound) minds nothing but pleasure."

117. **Mungrels.** A dog of "Mongrell" breed is "halfe the one halfe the other" (RC, s.v. "Mestif"). In human terms, a "mongrel" is "a Hanger on among the Cheats, a Spunger. Of a Mongrel-race or Breed, a Curr or Man of a base, ungenerous Breed" (ND). *Mungrels* also alludes to effeminate or homosexual men; cf. JF's "Mongrellino": "an effeminate, wanton, coy, fond smell-feast, a spruce-fellow."

117. **Spaniels.** A "spaniel" is a "Spanish dog" (DPF). Holinshed explains that many varieties of dog "are commonly called Spanyels… the common name for all is Spanniell, as if these kindes of Dogges had bene brought hyther out of Spaine." "Spaniel" also means "A parasite" (F&H) and is associated with "farting and arse-licking" (FR).

117. **Curres.** A "cur" is "a Dog of a mungrel Breed, good for nothing" (ND) and "is figuratively used to signify a surly fellow" (FG). A "cur" is also an impotent or effeminate man (a "cur" is "A cut or curtailed dog," FG; "cut" means "Castrated," OED).

118. **Showghes.** *Showghes* are "A kind of lap-dog, said to have been originally brought from Iceland" (OED). *Showghes* was probably pronounced "shuffs" or "chuffs" (cf. OED's spelling variants of "showgh" as "shough"; "chuff" as "chough"; and "rough" as "rowghe"; for dialectal substitution of "ch" for "sh," see HH, pp. 317–318; and for interchangeability of "gh" and "f," see HK, p. 207). If so, there is possible play on (a) "chuffe" meaning "a pild, bald, filthie, snudging, snuffing, miserable, pinching, sparing, base-minded companion" (JF, s.v. "Spilórcio"); and/or (b) "chuff" meaning "The buttocks or backside; the anus" (OED, which describes the word as "Of uncertain origin" dating from 1945; however, OED gives "chuff" meaning "A cheek swollen or puffed with fat" from 1530).

118. **Water-Rugs.** A "rug" is "a garment of shag" (JJ, s.v. "Rauchan"). Hence, a "water-rug" is "A shaggy breed of water-dog" (OED, which gives Shakespeare's usage here as the only example).

As applied to a man, a *Rug* is a "ruffian" ("anyone behaving roughly or severely," "a pimp," "a bawdy-house bully," F&H). Cf. TT's "Lachne": "Rug, shaghaire, or ruffen," and JF's "Lacno": "a dogs name, as we say a shaghaire or ruffian." Also cf. and see note: *shagge-ear'd*, IV.ii.100.

In addition, *Rug* can mean "The pubic hair, esp. of a woman," "the female external genitals" (OED); *Water* can allude to either semen or the female sexual secretions (JA, p. 92).

118. **Demy-Wolves.** *Demy* (half) *Wolves* are "Dogges ingendered of wolves and dogs" (TT, s.v. "Cracutæ"); Holinshed mentions "other Dogges… bredde betweene a bytche & a Woolfe." *Wolves* is also used for (a) "Unregenerate men, which be of a fierce and cruell disposition, like Wolves" (TW); and (b) "whoremonger[s]" (GW2, s.v. "wolf"); also see note: *Wolfe*, II.i.68.

120. **Distinguishes.** To "distinguish" is "To put a difference between things" (JB, q.v.); "to particularize" (JF, s.v. "Particolare").

121. **House-keeper.** "A dog kept to guard the house; a watch-dog" (OED). As applied to a man, *House-keeper* possibly alludes to the *keeper* ("Pimp," FR) of a *House* (brothel); cf. and see note: *Water-Rugs*, line 118, above.

121. **Hunter.** "A dog used in or adapted for hunting" (OED). The "hunt" was "symbolic of sexual pursuit" (TR), so *Hunter* means both "wencher" (GW2, s.v. "woodman") and "penis" (FR, s.v. "Prick").

Particular addition, from the Bill,

That writes them all alike: and so of men.   [125]

Now, if you have a station in the file,

Not i'th' worst ranke of Manhood, say't,

And I will put that Businesse in your Bosomes,

Whose execution takes your Enemie off,

Grapples you to the heart; and love of us,   [130]

Who weare our Health but sickly in his Life,

Which in his Death were perfect.

2.*Murth.*   I am one, my Liege,

Whom the vile Blowes and Buffets of the World

Hath so incens'd, that I am recklesse what I doe,   [135]

To spight the World.

1.*Murth.*   And I another,

So wearie with Disasters, tugg'd with Fortune,

That I would set my Life on any Chance,

To mend it, or be rid on't.   [140]

Macb.   Both of you know *Banquo* was your Enemie.

{2.} *Murth.* True, my Lord.

124–125. **Particular addition, from the Bill... alike.** The Bill ("short memo-randum," "description of a thing, in writing," RC, s.v. "Escripteu"), like the *Catalogue* (line 116, above), *writes* (records in writing, depicts) *all* dogs *alike*. Neither gives any *Particular* (specially detailed; "To particularize" is "to distinguish, or sever from others; to name specially," RC, s.v. "Particulariser") *addition* ("An appendix," "labell," RC, s.v. "Appendice").

If the *Murtherers* are true men, then they have received *Particular* (with allusion to the "particle" or "particula": "penis," JA, p. 45) *addition* ("Something which is added or joined to another thing," OED) *from the Bill* ("penis," GW2; literally "a kind of broadsword" or "a halberd," OED). Cf. Sonnet 20:

> And for a woman wert thou first created,
> Till nature as she wrought thee fell a dotinge,
> And by addition me of thee defeated,
> By adding one thing to my purpose nothing.

124. *from.* Apart from.

126. *a station in the file.* Both (a) *a station* ("position... in a scale of estimation or dignity," OED) *in the file* (catalog, list; see note: *file,* line 119, above); and (b) *a station* ("a stande or standing place," JF, s.v. "Stazzo") *in the file* ("A row of persons, animals, or things placed one behind the other," OED); cf. *ranke,* line 127, below.

127. *ranke.* With play on *ranke* meaning (a) status, position in a hierarchy; (b) a row or line; (c) "whatever is Stale, Corrupt, or Tainted, and Stinks" (ND); and (d) "sexually dirty; obscene" (EP). Cf. *Rancours,* line 81, above.

127. *Manhood.* *Manhood* can mean (a) "mans estate" (HC, s.v. "Virilitie"); (b) "integritie; worth," "desert, merit" (RC, s.v. "Vertu"); (c) "virility, sexual prowess" (JH); and/or (d) "the male organ" (JA, p. 69).

128–130. *I will put that Businesse... love of us.* The *Businesse* (matter) *that Macbeth will put* in the *Murtherers' Bosomes* (i.e., entrust to their confidence) is the *execution* (putting to death) of *Banquo.* Its *execution* (carrying out) will "grapple" (join, fasten) the *Murtherers to Macbeth's heart and love,* and also take their *Enemie off* (kill him).

This *execution* (sexual act; see note; *execution,* I.ii.24) gives the *Murtherers* the chance to prove that they are capable of *Businesse* (coïtus; see note: *Businesse,* I.v.80). In "buggering" *Banquo,* the *Murtherers* can "grapple" (copulate vigorously, JH) *to the heart* (i.e., "arse"; see note: *Heart,* I.iii.154) and "take off" their *Enemie* (i.e., abate phallic erection by achieving orgasm; see notes: *takes him off,* II.iii.43; and *Enemie,* line 83, above).

131–132. *our Health but sickly... perfect.* *Banquo's Life* (with probable play on *Life* as the genitals; see note: *Life,* I.vii.50) makes *Macbeth's* (a) *Health* ("Spiritual, moral, or mental soundness or well-being," OED) *sickly* ("crazed," JF, s.v. "Tristanzuolo"); (b) *Health* ("Well-being, welfare, safety," OED) *sickly* ("unsound," RC, s.v. "Oultré"); and (c) *Health* (i.e., virility; literally "Soundness of body; that condition in which its functions are duly and efficiently discharged," OED) *sickly* (impotent; see note: *braine-sickly,* II.ii.58). *Macbeth* thinks he will again be *perfect* ("Whole, sound," JB, s.v. "Intire"; "of sound mind, sane," OED) if he can bring about *Banquo's Death.* Achieving this *Death* ("sexual orgasm," JH) will also demonstrate that *Macbeth* is *perfect* (virile, sexually potent; something *perfect* is "Completely formed," OED; also see note: *imperfect,* I.iii.76).

138. *Disasters.* *Disasters* means "misfortune[s]," "misadventure[s], hard chance[s]" (RC, s.v. "Desastre").

138. *tugg'd with Fortune.* The *First Murtherer* has been *tugg'd* ("broken, beaten," JF, s.v. "Cozzonato"; "havockt, spoiled, defeated, crusht, crazed," JF, s.v. "Romputo") *with* (by) *Fortune.* This extremely fickle and promiscuous goddess (see note: *Fortune,* I.ii.20) has also *tugg'd* him (i.e., "fucked" him; to "tug" is to "copulate," GW2).

Macb.	So is he mine: and in such bloody distance,
	That every minute of his being, thrusts
	Against my neer'st of Life: and though I could [145]
	With bare-fac'd power sweepe him from my sight,
	And bid my will avouch it; yet I must not,
	For certaine friends that are both his, and mine,
	Whose loves I may not drop, but wayle his fall,
	Who I my selfe struck downe: and thence it is, [150]
	That I to your assistance doe make love,
	Masking the Businesse from the common Eye,
	For sundry weightie Reasons.
2.Murth.	We shall, my Lord,
	Performe what you command us. [155]
1.Murth.	Though our Lives —
Macb.	Your Spirits shine through you.
	Within this houre, at most,
	I will advise you where to plant your selves,
	Acquaint you with the perfect Spy o'th' time, [160]
	The moment on't, for't must be done to Night,
	And something from the Pallace: always thought,

143–145. ***in such bloody distance... neer'st of Life.*** *Banquo* stands *in bloody distance* (in fencing, the space in which it is possible for one combatant to strike another) and *thrusts Against* (lunges at, stabs at) *Macbeth's neer'st of Life*, meaning (a) his *neer'st* blood relations (cf. II.iii.186); and/or (b) his heart or vital organs (cf. "they have with their arrowes of blasphemy shotte thorough & boared the Lord to the very neerest place of his life," Edward Topsell, *The Reward of Religion*). Therefore, *Macbeth* feels "thrust at" ("provoked, inforced: vexed," TT, s.v. "Impulsus").

Banquo also attempts to "screw" and "castrate" *Macbeth*: he *thrusts* ("A fencing metaphor for a penis-thrust," EP) *Against Macbeth's neer'st of Life* (i.e., his virility and genitals, "neer" means "loin" and also "kidney," OED; the kidneys were regarded as the seat of sexual desire, JA, p. 92; also see note: *Life*, I.vii.50).

146. ***bare-fac'd.*** "Unconcealed, undisguised" (OED).

147. ***bid my will avouch it.*** As an absolute monarch, *Macbeth* need only *bid* ("proclaim, announce," OED) that *Banquo's* death is his *will* (desire, wish) in order to *avouch* ("warrant, authorize," RC, s.v. "Advouër") *it*.

151. ***make love.*** Court; attempt to win the favor of.

156–157. ***Though our Lives... shine through you.*** The *First Murtherer* begins to say that he and his companion are willing to kill *Banquo* even *Though* they should lose their *Lives*. *Macbeth* feels no need for these words to be said, because the *Murtherers' Spirits* (courageous dispositions; also sexual capacities; see note: *Spirits*, I.v.27) *shine through* them (i.e., are transparently evident; to *shine through* is "to be transparent," JF, s.v. "Trasparére"; also see note: *shine*, line 9, above). *Macbeth's* praise of the *Murtherers* darkly recalls Matthew 5:15–16 (cf. and see note: V.v.28–29).

160. ***the perfect Spy o'th' time.*** *Macbeth* has enlisted other agents besides these two *Murtherers* (cf. III.iv.167–168). He has at his disposal a *Spy* (one who secretly observes others in order to collect information) who is *perfect* ("thoroughly knowledgeable," OED) "of" ("with," "regarding," OED) *th' time* (opportunity, occasion) to murder *Banquo* and *Fleance*.

162. ***something from.*** At some distance away *from*.

162. ***always thought.*** *Thought* (considered, planned) in "all ways."

That I require a clearenesse; and with him,

To leave no Rubs nor Botches in the Worke:

Fleans, his Sonne, that keepes him companie,   [165]

Whose absence is no lesse materiall to me,

Then is his Fathers, must embrace the fate

Of that darke houre: resolve your selves apart,

Ile come to you anon.

{2.} *Murth*. We are resolv'd, my Lord.   [170]

Macb.   Ile call upon you straight: abide within,

{*Exit Murtherers*.}   [III.i.8]

It is concluded: *Banquo*, thy Soules flight,

If it finde Heaven, must finde it out to Night.

{*Exit Macbeth*.}   [175]

163. **clearenesse.** Freedom from blame (cf. and see note: *cleere*, I.vii.22). Holinshed reports that *Macbeth* employed hired assassins so that he himself would be "clear" of suspicion (see note: *two Murtherers*, line 88, above).

163–168. **and with him... that darke houre.** *To leave no Rubs* (flaws; "rough or uneven feature[s]," OED) *nor Botches* ("blemish[s] resulting from unskilful workmanship," OED) *in the Worke, Banquo's Sonne Fleans must with* his father *embrace the fate Of that darke houre* (i.e., the *houre* when *Banquo* meets his *fate*). Should the *Murtherers* allow *Banquo* or *Fleans* to "rub" ("run away," FG), *the Worke* will be but a "botching piece of worke" ("a bungling," JF, s.v. "Taccola").

Macbeth wants to "rub" (i.e., "screw"; "rub" is used "of coital friction," GW2) *Banquo*, not "screw himself" (to "rub" is "To masturbate," F&H). It is therefore essential that *the Worke* (sexual labor, copulation, JA, p. 156) *leave no Botches* ("impostumes about the share, or members," TT, s.v. "Būbōnes") *nor Rubs* (i.e., syphilitic sores on the penis or testicles; a "rub" is literally "an uneven, or ill pollished part of a pretious stone, which in a curious eye disgraces all the rest," RC, s.v. "Saut"). Cf. *Rancours in the Vessell of my Peace*, line 81, above; and *Jewell*, line 82, above.

168. **resolve.** Determine; decide on a matter.

Act III, scene ii

Scena Secunda.   [1]

Enter Macbeths Lady, and a Servant.   [III.ii.1]

Lady.   Is *Banquo* gone from Court?

Servant.   I, Madame, but returnes againe to Night.

Lady.   Say to the King, I would attend his leysure,   [5]

             For a few words.

Servant.   Madame, I will.

Exit {Servant}.   [III.ii.2]

Lady.   Nought's had, all's spent,

             Where our desire is got without content: [10]

             'Tis safer, to be that which we destroy,

             Then by destruction dwell in doubtfull joy.

Enter Macbeth.   [III.ii.3]

             How now, my Lord, why doe you keepe alone?

             Of sorryest Fancies your Companions making,   [15]

             Using those Thoughts, which should indeed have dy'd

             With them they thinke on: things without all remedie

             Should be without regard: what's done, is done.

Notes III.ii.

9–10. ***Nought's had... without content.*** *Where our desire* ("object of desire; that which one desires or longs for," OED) *is got* (gained) *without content* (satisfaction, pleasure), *all's spent* (expended; exhausted) and *Nought* (nothing) *is had*.

The *Macbeths* have gained sovereignty, but *Nought* ("sexual intercourse," EP, s.v. "do naught with") *is had* (over and done). The couple are *without content*, meaning (a) "Sexual satisfaction" (FR); and/or (b) children (*content* literally means "A thing contained," OED, here with allusion to a child contained in the womb). The couple cannot *content* (gratify) their *desire* (sexual appetite, lust) because *Macbeth's all* (penis; see note: *all's*, I.ii.21) *is spent* (depleted of semen, EC, s.v. "spend"). *Macbeth* can no longer *tent* (i.e., sexually penetrate; literally "probe," OED) his wife's *con* (i.e., "cunt"), so the couple have merely *got* (gained) *desire* ("Longing for something lost or missed; regret," OED).

11–12. ***'Tis safer... doubtfull joy.*** These lines suggest that *Macbeths Lady*, like her husband, entertains thoughts of suicide. Cf. lines 26–27, below; and V.vii.135–137.

12. ***doubtfull.*** *Doubtfull* means (a) "fearfull," "hanging in doubt or suspence" (TT, s.v. "Suspensus"); and (b) "uncertaine: sometime double, also two edged, or cutting on both sides: that hath a handle on both sides, or two heades or faces, daungerous" (TT, s.v. "Anceps").

14–15. ***keepe alone... sorryest Fancies.*** Because *Macbeth* suffers from "Melancholie" ("sadnesse, pensivenesse, heavinesse, thoughtfullnesse, care-taking; solitarinesse, retyrednesse," RC, q.v.), he tends to *keepe alone* and indulge his *sorryest* (saddest or most worthless) *Fancies* (flights of fancy, imaginings). In *Anatomy of Melancholy*, Robert Burton explains that melancholy is dangerous to mental health because it often

> degenerates into madnesse... those men... [who] are commonly sad & solitary, and that continually, & in excesse, more then ordinary suspitious, more fearefull, and have long, sore, and most corrupt Imaginations; cold and black, bashfull and so solitary, that... they will endure no company, they dreame of graves still, and dead men, & thinke themselves bewitched or dead: if it be extreme they think they heare hideous noyses, see and talke with blacke men, & converse familarly with divels... or that they are possessed by them, that some body talkes to them, or within them.

Cf. and see notes: I.iii.157–160; II.i.53–54 and 71–72; II.ii.46; and III.iv.48.

16. ***Using.*** Entertaining.

16. ***Thoughts.*** "Thought" is "Anxiety or distress of mind; solicitude; grief, sorrow, trouble, care, vexation" (OED).

17. ***without.*** Beyond.

18. ***what's done, is done.*** Proverbial. Cf. V.i.68–69.

Macb. We have scorch'd the Snake, not kill'd it:

Shee'le close, and be her selfe, whilest our poore Mallice   [20]

Remaines in danger of her former Tooth.

But let the frame of things dis-joynt,

Both the Worlds suffer,

Ere we will eate our Meale in feare, and sleepe

In the affliction of these terrible Dreames,   [25]

That shake us Nightly: Better be with the dead,

Whom we, to gayne our peace, have sent to peace,

19–21. **We have scorch'd the Snake... her former Tooth.** According to folk belief, "though all a serpents body be mangled, unlesse his head be cut off, (which he cunningly hides) by a kind of attractive power and vigor one part will come to another againe" (Thomas Adams, *The Happines of the Church*). *Macbeth* fears that *the Snake* is *not kill'd* but only *scorch'd* ("slash[ed] with a knife," OED), so *Shee'le* again *close* ("consolidate," "fasten together," RC, s.v. "Soulder") *and be her selfe*.

Macbeth's Mallice (malicious intent, power to do harm) is a *poore* adversary when pitted against the *Tooth* (destructive ability) of *the Snake* ("a dominant symbol of chaos, evil, sin, temptation or deceit," JT; the *Tooth* of *the Snake* "is put for hostile invasion, spoil, and tearing in peices," TDL). However, it is probably not *Macbeth's Mallice* (hostility) but his *Mallice* ("Bodily disease," "trouble or restlessness of mind," JJ) which *Remaines in danger of her* (*the Snake's*, figured as the embodiment of treachery) *former Tooth* (i.e., the *Tooth* of which she was formerly possessed).

Macbeth has reason to fear that *Banquo* is a *Snake* ("a secret plotter, a hidden foe," F&H) who seeks to *close* (i.e., "screw" him; to *close* is literally to fornicate or indulge lust, FR). *Macbeth* also fears that his *Mallice* ("Testicles," FR, who conjectures play on L. "malus": "apple") and *Mallice* (i.e., his penis and potency; cf. L. "malus": "tall pole, upright pole," LD) are *in danger* of being made *poore* ("of low condition, faint, feeble, small," TT, s.v. "Hŭmĭlis"; also see note: *poore*, I.vi.24). *Macbeth* is terrified of *Banquo's Tooth* ("allusive of penis," GW) and *Snake* (penis, GW).

Although *the Snake* is an obvious phallic symbol, *Macbeth* might refer to *the Snake* as feminine because "she" was used "of certain animals... the names of which have a quasi-grammatical feminine gender exc[ept] when a male is specifically referred to"

(OED). *Macbeth* might also refer to *the Snake* as feminine because in medieval and Renaissance art the serpent who first tempted Eve in the Garden of Eden was often depicted with a woman's face (Gertrude Grace Sill, *A Handbook of Symbols in Christian Art*, p. 25).

22–26. *let the frame of things dis-joynt... shake us Nightly.* Every night, *Macbeth* "shakes" ("quake[s] with fear," OED) from *the affliction of terrible Dreames.* His *frame* ("constitution of the Body," EC2, s.v. "Corporature") is made to *suffer* as though it were *dis-joynt* ("put out of joynt," RC, s.v. "Delocher"; "dismembred," RC, s.v. "Emembré") on a *frame* ("rack": "An instrument of torture, usually consisting of a frame on which the victim was stretched by turning two rollers fastened at each end to the wrists and ankles," OED). Cf. *torture of the Minde*, line 28, below.

Macbeth would do anything to escape this anguish, even if it means creating *dis-joynt* ("A disjointed or out-of-joint condition," OED) in *the frame* ("heaven, earth," OED). *Ere* (before) *Macbeth will eate* his *Meale in feare, and sleepe In the affliction* ("torture," "torment, racking," JF, s.v. "Scémpio") *of terrible Dreames*, he will *let Both the Worlds suffer* (endure, undergo) *the frame* ("rack": "intense pain or anguish," OED) *of things* (circumstances, events) *dis-joynt* ("disordered," "confounded," JF, s.v. "Scommesso"; "Broken, destroyed," TT, s.v. "Lăbĕfactus"). He will even *let the frame of things* (the established structure of the universe) *dis-joynt* ("go out of joint," "come in pieces," OED) and *let Both the Worlds suffer* ("be killed or destroyed," OED).

Both the Worlds might refer to (a) *Both* the temporal and spiritual worlds (cf. and see note: *the one halfe World*, II.i.64); or (b) *Both* the microcosm (the "little world" of *Macbeth's* own physical and mental existence) and the macrocosm (the "big world," or outer universe; cf. "For now both the worlds, that is to say, the great world that contayneth all, and man whyche is the little world contayned therein, waxe both olde, and drawe towards an ende," Pope Innocent III, *The Mirror of Mans lyfe*).

These terrible Dreames also (a) *shake* (i.e., "fuck"; see note: *Shakes*, I.iii.158) *Macbeth* and cause him to *suffer* ("Be a pathic, one upon whom sodomy is practiced," FR); (b) cause *Macbeth* to *shake* (i.e., become impotent; see note: *Shakes*, I.iii.158); and/or (c) make *Macbeth's frame* (body) *dis-joynt* ("disjoined": "Disunited, separated, parted," OED) *of* (from) his *things* (genitals, EP). In *Malleus Maleficarum* (p. 58), Heinrich Institoris and Jakob Sprenger explain that *Witches* possess the ability to cast an

> Illusion so that the Male Organ appears to be entirely removed and separate from the Body... although, it is no illusion in the opinion of the sufferer. For his imagination can really and actually believe that something is not present, since by none of his exterior senses, such as sight or touch, can he perceive that it is present.

Also cf. and see note: I.iii.152–153.

24. *we... our.* *Macbeth* speaks solely of himself. Both *we* and *our* are here used as royal singular pronouns.

26–27. *Better be with the dead... sent to peace.* The notion was proverbial: cf. "That life is better life past fearing death, / Then that which lives to feare" (*Measure for Measure*, V.i.). However, *Macbeth's* words suggest that he is contemplating suicide. In order *to gayne* his *peace* (security), he thinks it *Better* to *be with the dead* (i.e., Duncan), *Whom Macbeth sent to peace* (the repose of death). Cf. and see note: *Scorpions*, line 46, below.

Ironically, *Macbeth's* actions have not resulted in the *gayne* but the loss of his *peace* (i.e., his "piece" or penis; see note: *peace*, I.v.53).

Then on the torture of the Minde to lye

In restlesse extasie.

Duncane is in his Grave: [30]

After Lifes fitfull Fever, he sleepes well,

Treason ha's done his worst: nor Steele, nor Poyson,

Mallice domestique, forraine Levie, nothing,

Can touch him further.

Lady.   Come on: [35]

Gentle my Lord, sleeke o're your rugged Lookes,

Be bright and Joviall among your Guests to Night.

Macb.   So shall I Love, and so I pray be you:

Let your remembrance apply to Banquo,

Present him Eminence, both with Eye and Tongue: [40]

Unsafe the while, that wee must lave

Our Honors in these flattering streames,

And make our Faces Vizards to our Hearts,

Disguising what they are.

---

28. **the torture of the Minde.** *Macbeth* endures *the torture* ("a racke, an engine to torment," JF, s.v. "Tormento"; also "a racking," RC, q.v.) *of the Minde*. This *torture* arises from melancholy, the *torture* (a homonym or near-homonym of "tartar"; see HK, p. 271) *of the Minde.* "Tartar" as a term for "the deposit of wine, means infernal stuff, being derived from the word *Tartaros*... Paracelsus says, It is so called because it produces oil, water, tincture, and salt, which burn the patient as the fires of Tartarus burn" (DPF). Cf. and see note: *Lees,* II.iii.126.

29. **restlesse.** *Restlesse* can mean (a) "active, busie, turbulent, ever stirring" (RC, s.v. "Irrequiet"); (b) "unquiet, without rest" (JM, s.v. "inQuiéto"); (c) "full of trou-

ble" (TT, s.v. "Irrĕquĭĕtus"); and (d) "uncertaine what to doe, doubtfull" (TT, s.v. "Fluctŭans").

29. *extasie. Extasie* derives from Gk. "eckstasis" which means "to stand out of (the body or mind)" (DPF). To be in a state of *extasie* means "to lose one's wits, to be beside oneself" (DPF).

31. *fitfull.* Full of "fits," which can mean (a) "transitory state[s] of activity"; (b) "capricious impulse[s], humour[s], mood[s]"; (c) "painful, terrible, or exciting experience[s]"; (d) "severe but transitory attack[s] (of illness)"; and/or (e) "paroxysm[s] of lunacy" (OED).

31. *Fever.* With play on *Fever* as "A state of intense nervous excitement, agitation" (OED).

32. *his.* Its (see note: *his*, I.vii.8).

33. *Mallice domestique.* Both (a) *Mallice* (hostile action or activity) *domestique* ("Of or pertaining to one's own country or nation; not foreign, internal, inland," OED); and (b) *Mallice* ("Guile, deceit, cousenage, trumperie, treacherie, knaverie, falsehood, shifting," RC, s.v. "Malice") *domestique* ("of our household," RC, q.v.). See note: *Cousin*, I.ii.30.

33. *forraine.* With play on *forraine* meaning both (a) "of another country" (RC2); and (b) "Not of one's household or family" (OED).

33. *Levie.* Both (a) "The action of enrolling or collecting men for war"; and (b) "A body of men enrolled" (OED).

34. *touch.* To "strike, to smite, to hit, to moove or grieve" (JF, s.v. "Tocare"); to "hurt or offer the least violence" (TW).

36. *sleeke o're your rugged Lookes. Macbeth's Lookes* (appearance and facial expressions; also glances) are *rugged*, which can mean (a) "rough and unpleasant" (TT, s.v. "Confrăgōsus"); (b) "churlish, austere, surly, severe" (RC, s.v. "Aspre"); and/or (c) "full of wrinckles" (RC, s.v. "Se Cameloter"). In order to *sleeke* ("to entice, to flatter," JF, s.v. "Allecchiare") his guests, *Macbeth* must *sleeke* ("unwrinkle," "smooth," JF, s.v. "Discrespare") his *rugged Lookes*.

39. *remembrance. Remembrance* means "consideration, regard, mindefulnes, heede" (TT, s.v. "Animadversione").

39. *apply.* Give attention to; devote especially.

40. *Eminence.* Homage, honor.

41. *Unsafe the while.* I.e., "as long as we are *Unsafe*" (see note: *the while*, II.i.42).

41–44. *lave Our Honors… Disguising what they are.* The *Macbeths must make* their *Faces* (countenances) *Vizards* (masks) *to* their *Hearts* (true thoughts and feelings, with probable play on "arts" meaning "cunning tricks"). In order to disguise *what they are*, they must (a) *lave* ("pour out," OED) their *Honors* ("expression[s] of high estimation," OED) *in flattering* ("guildefull, deceitfull," TT, s.v. "Captātōratius") *streames* (i.e., *streames* of words); and/or (b) *lave* ("wash," OED) their *Honors* (reputations) *in flattering* ("faire spoken: friendlie: pleasant: gentle: courteous: alluring: merie: delectable: fawning: sweete, pretie," TT, s.v. "Blandus") *streames*.

To *Macbeth*, selling their *Hearts* (with probable play on *Hearts* as "arse"; see note: *Heart*, I.iii.154) and using false *Faces* makes them no better than *Vizards* (i.e., prostitutes, who commonly wore *Vizards*, or masks; a "visor-mask" is "a harlot," F&H). Just like *Vizards* (whores), the *Macbeths must lave* ("wash": "fuck," EC) their soiled *Honors* (sexual purity) *in flattering* ("pimp[ing] or prostitut[ing]," FR; also copulating, F&H, s.v. "greens") *streames* (with possible play on seminal emission; cf. F&H's "Stream's Town": "The female pudendum").

Lady.   You must leave this.   [45]

Macb.   O, full of Scorpions is my Minde, deare Wife:

Thou know'st, that *Banquo* and his *Fleans* lives.

Lady.   But in them, Natures Coppie's not eterne.

Macb.   There's comfort yet, they are assaileable,

Then be thou jocund: ere the Bat hath flowne   [50]

His Cloyster'd flight, ere to black *Heccats* summons

The shard-borne Beetle, with his drowsie hums,

Hath rung Nights yawning Peale,

There shall be done a deed of dreadfull note.

Lady.   What's to be done?   [55]

46. ***full of Scorpions is my Minde.*** The "Scorpion" is "A venemous worme with seven feet, bearing his sting in his taile; with which hee striketh mischievously" (JB, q.v.); "The intense pain caused by the sting of the scorpion (situated at the point of the tail) is proverbial" (OED). The scorpion is also "an emblem of treachery" (JC) and represents "Death, chastisement, retribution" (JT). *Macbeth's Minde* is tormented not only on the rack (see note: *torture of the Minde,* line 28, above) but also with *Scorpions* ("Whips armed with metal or knotted cords," DPF).

Macbeth apparently contemplates suicide, for according to ancient legend *Scorpions* possessed a "suicidal tendency. It was long believed that the scorpion, if trapped and faced with imminent death, or even captivity, would kill itself with its sting" (Chris Andrews, *Poetry and Cosmonogy,* p. 101).

48. ***Natures Coppie's not eterne.*** *Banquo* and *Fleans* hold a limited "lease on life" governed by the terms of a *Coppie* (a "Copyhold Estate": "Land which a tenant holds [or rather, held] without any deed of transfer in his own possession. His only document is a copy of the roll made by the steward of the manor from the court-roll kept in the manor-house," DPF). The duration of a *Coppie* was *not eterne* (without an expiration date), for the tenant of a copyhold occupied land only "at the will of the lord according to the custom of the manor" (OED).

Moreover, should the *Natures* (genitals, semen; see notes: *Nature,* I.ii.17 and I.v.52) of *Banquo* and *Fleans* produce "copies" (reproductions of themselves, descendants) from the "copy-hold" ("female pudendum; Cunt," F&H), such "copies" are not *eterne* (immortal).

This line provides the only hint that *Macbeth* has informed his wife of the prediction that *Banquo's* descendants will become kings. If *Macbeths Lady* knows of this, however, she expresses no anxiety over it in the visible course of the play.

50. ***jocund.*** "Merrie, pleasant" (JB, q.v.).

50–51. ***the Bat... Cloyster'd flight.*** *The Bat* is "Widely a symbol of fear and superstition, associated with death, night, and, in Judeo-Christian tradition, idolatry or Satanism. Bats can also signify madness" (JT). Here, *the Bat* takes *His flight* from a *Cloyster* ("Anie manner of thing, wherewith any thing is enclosed," TT, s.v. "Claustrum"), which is probably a *Cloyster* ("a monasterie, a convent, a nunnerie, a religious house," JF, s.v. "Monastério").

51. ***to.*** "In accordance with" (OED).

51. ***Heccats.*** See note: *Heccats,* II.i.67.

52. ***shard-borne Beetle.*** A *shard* is "A patch of cow-dung" (OED). The *shard-borne Beetle* is "the black flie, bred commonly in Dung, called a Beetle" (TB, s.v. "Scarabee"). "Flies generally symbolize evil and pestilence" (JT); also see note: *Belzebub,* II.iii.9.

53. ***yawning.*** *Yawning* can mean (a) sleepy; (b) "That opens the mouth wide, esp. in order to swallow or devour something" (OED); (c) "negligent, slothfull, idle, careles" (TT, s.v. "Oscĭtans"); and (d) moaning (a *yawning* is "an unpleasant open sounde," TT, s.v. "Hĭātus").

53. ***Peale.*** A "knell," a "toule upon the bels" (JF, s.v. "Tocco di campana").

54. ***note.*** Distinction or importance, with play on *note* meaning (a) "A musical tone," "A tune, a song; a melody; a strain of music" (OED); and/or (b) "A distinctive cry, call, or sound" (OED). Cf. *hums,* line 52, above; *rung,* line 53, above; and *yawning Peale,* line 53, above.

Macb.   Be innocent of the knowledge, dearest Chuck,

Till thou applaud the deed: Come, seeling Night,

Skarfe up the tender Eye of pittifull Day,

And with thy bloodie and invisible Hand

Cancell and teare to pieces that great Bond,   [60]

Which keepes me pale. Light thickens,

And the Crow makes Wing toth' Rookie Wood:

Good things of Day begin to droope, and drowse,

Whiles Nights black Agents to their Prey's doe rowse.

Thou marvell'st at my words: but hold thee still,   [65]

Things bad begun, make strong themselves by ill:

So prythee goe with me.

Exeunt.

56. **dearest Chuck.** Although *Chuck* is "a term of endearment" (FG), this form of address stands in stark contrast to *my dearest Partner of Greatnesse* (I.v.11–12). The appellation becomes yet more degrading in light of the fact that *Chuck* means to copulate (F&H, s.v. "Ride").

57–60. **seeling... that great Bond.** *Night* will be able to "seele, or sow up, the eye-lids; (& thence also) to hoodwinke, blind, keepe in darknesse, deprive of sight" (RC, s.v. "Siller les yeux") and *Skarfe* ("binde," "hoodwinke," JF, s.v. "Lenzare") *up the tender* (affectionate, kind) *Eye of pittifull* ("Merciful," "that hath pitie or compassion, that is sorie for an others ill: tender harted," TT, s.v. "Misĕricors") *Day.* Thus, the "ceiling" (canopy, curtain) of *Night* provides cover for *Macbeth's* evil actions. Cf. I.iv.62–63 and I.v.57–61.

Macbeth now makes a "sealing" ("A covenant made, or contract passed, betweene partie & partie, under seale," RC, s.v. "Seellé") with *Night* to *Cancell and teare to pieces* the *great Bond* ("covenant," "deed," OED) of *Banquo's* and *Fleans' 'bond of life'* (*The Life and Death of Richard III*, IV.iv.); cf. *Natures Coppie's*, line 48, above. The lives of *Banquo* and his son are the *Bond* ("a force which enslaves the mind through the affections or passion," OED) *Which keepes Macbeth* (a) *pale* (i.e., imprisoned; "pale" is a synonym of *Bond* meaning "a boundary," OED; cf. III.iv.31–32); and (b) *pale* (i.e., impotent; *pale* literally means "without spirit," OED; see notes: *spirit,* I.ii.70, and *Spirits,* I.v.27); cf. and see note: *greene, and pale,* I.vii.45.

61. **thickens.** Becomes dark or misty (OED).

62. **th' Rookie Wood.** *Th' Rookie Wood* can mean (a) "the misty or dark wood. The verb *reek* (to emit vapour) had the preterite *roke, rook,* or *roak*" (DPF); (b) the *Wood* frequented by "rooks" (crows; in popular superstition, rooks are an omen of death; see note: *Raven,* I.v.45); and/or (c) the *Wood* where the "rooks" (i.e., murderers; a "rook" is "a disreputable, greedy, garrulous, or slovenly person," OED) will "rook" ("Cheat or play the Knave," ND) and create a "rook" ("A disturbance, a sort of uproar," JJ).

63. **droope.** Both (a) "to slumber" (JF, s.v. "Dormacchiare"); and (b) "to vanish out of sight," "to fade away" (JF, s.v. "Suanire").

64. **Nights black Agents.** An "agent" is a "Doer, also a dealer for another" (EC2). The *Nights black Agents* are "Divels, which doe appeare in the night, in the forme of divers Beastes" (Pierre le Loyer, *A Treatise of Specters*). It was believed that "such Spirits... can likewise shew themselves as Lions, Wolves, Tygers, Bears, and all other cruel or ravenous Beasts" (RS).

64. **rowse.** To "awaken," "to stir up" (JF, s.v. "Adestare"); also "to undenne, to unkenell, or fetch forth from any corner" (JF, s.v. "Scopare").

65. **hold thee still.** To *hold still* is "to hold one's peace, refrain from speaking" (OED).

Act III, scene iii

Scena Tertia.   [1]

Enter three Murtherers.   [III.iii.1]

{1. Mur.}   But who did bid thee joyne with us?

{3. Mur.}   Macbeth.

{2. Mur.}   He needes not our mistrust, since he delivers   [5]

               Our Offices, and what we have to doe,

               To the direction just.

{1. Mur.}   Then stand with us:

               The West yet glimmers with some streakes of Day.

               Now spurres the lated Traveller apace,   [10]

               To gayne the timely Inne, end neere approches

               The subject of our Watch.

{3. Mur.}   Hearke, I heare Horses.

Banquo within.   Give us a Light there, hoa.

{2. Mur.}   Then 'tis hee: [15]

               The rest, that are within the note of expectation,

               Alreadie are i'th' Court.

{1. Mur.}   His Horses goe about.

{3. Mur.}   Almost a mile: but he does usually,

               So all men doe, from hence toth' Pallace Gate   [20]

               Make it their Walke.

Notes III.iii.

2. **three Murtherers.** In the original production, the *three Murtherers* were possibly portrayed by the same *three* (male) actors who portrayed the *three Witches.*

3–4. **But who did bid thee… Macbeth.** Evidently, the *Third Murtherer*, who best knows the courtiers and their movements (lines 16–21, below), is the *perfect Spy o'th' time* mentioned in III.i.160. The *Third Murtherer* must introduce himself to his accomplices because *Macbeth* was apparently too distracted to do so.

5. **He.** The *Third Murtherer.*

5. **delivers.** "Deliver" can mean (a) "To tell, relate, report" (RC, s.v. "Raconter"); (b) "to informe" (JM, s.v. "Informár"); and (c) "To give," "conferre on," "put into the hands of" (RC, s.v. "Livrer").

6. **Offices.** Prescribed duties.

7. **To the direction just.** *Just* ("exactly"; "appropriate; suitable," OED) *To* ("In accordance with," OED) *Macbeth's direction* ("order," JM, s.v. "Aderéço"; "instruction," RC, q.v.).

10. **the lated Traveller.** *The lated* ("last, lag," "hindmost of all," JF, s.v. "Sezzaio") *Traveller* is *Banquo*, who is the last to arrive at the feast. Cf. lines 15–17, below.

11. **the timely Inne.** This *Inne* is *timely* ("opportune," OED; "convenient," RC, s.v. "Opportun") because it is located within walking distance of the palace and horses can conveniently be stabled there. *Banquo* and *Fleans* send their horses on to the *Inne* (line 18, below) while they continue on foot to the castle (lines 19–21, below).

11. **end.** "The death (of a person)" (OED).

14. **within.** See notes: *within*, I.ii.2 and II.ii.73.

14. **a Light.** This *Light*, supplied by off-stage and unseen attendants, is the same *Torch* brought onto the stage by *Fleans* in line 22, below. This *Light* allows the *Murtherers* (who are supposedly hidden in the dark, despite the fact that they are clearly visible on the brightly-lit stage) to accurately target their victims. However, *Fleans* is able to escape when the *Light* goes out in the scuffle (cf. line 32, below).

16. **the note of expectation.** The list of expected guests.

18. **His Horses goe about.** Obviously, *Banquo's Horses* must *goe about* (in a circuitous route) out of sight due to the impossibility of bringing real *Horses* onto the stage.

Enter Banquo and Fleans, with a Torch.   [III.iii.2]

{*2. Mur.*}   A Light, a Light.

{*3. Mur.*}   'Tis hee.

{*1. Mur.*}   Stand too't.   [25]

Ban.   It will be Rayne to Night.

{*1. Mur.*}   Let it come downe.

Ban.   O, Trecherie!

              Flye good *Fleans*, flye, flye, flye,

              Thou may'st revenge. O Slave!   [30]

   {*Banquo dies. Exit Fleans.*}   [III.iii.3]

{*3. Mur.*}   Who did strike out the Light?

{*1. Mur.*}   Was't not the way?

{*3. Mur.*}   There's but one downe: the Sonne is fled.

{*2. Mur.*}   We have lost   [35]

              Best halfe of our Affaire.

{*1. Mur.*}   Well, let's away, and say how much is done.

   Exeunt.

29. ***Fleans, flye.*** Holinshed reports that "It chaunced yet, by the benefite of the darke night, that though the father were slaine, the son yet by the helpe of almightie God reserving him to better fortune, escaped that daunger, & afterwardes... to avoyde further perill he fledde into Wales."

Fleans (whose name is derived from "flean," Anglo-Saxon for "to *flye*") never really existed (see note: *Your Children shall be Kings*, I.iii.95), but in Shakespeare's time *Banquo* and his son *Fleans* were believed to be ancestors of the Stuart line (see note: *A shew of eight Kings*, IV.i.138).

31. ***Banquo dies.*** The theatre of Shakespeare's time had neither lighting black-outs nor a proscenium curtain (see note: *Here's a Farmer*, II.iii.9), so *Banquo's* corpse would either (a) be carried or dragged from the stage in full view of the audience; or (b) fall or be thrown somewhere out of sight, possibly into the trap-door or the "dis-covery space" located at the rear of the stage.

32–33. ***Who did strike out the Light.*** The *First Murtherer* extinguished *the Light* during their attack, allowing *Fleans* to escape in the darkness. See note: *Fleans, flye*, line 29, above.

36. ***Best halfe.*** Possibly "more than *halfe*," but *Best* can also mean "most appro-priate or desirable" (OED).

Act III, scene iv

Scæna Quarta.   [1]

Banquet prepar'd. Enter Macbeth, Lady, Rosse, Lenox,

Lords, and Attendants.   [III.iv.1]

Macb.	You know your owne degrees, sit downe:
	At first and last, the hearty welcome. [5]
Lords.	Thankes to your Majesty.
Macb.	Our selfe will mingle with Society,
	And play the humble Host:
	Our Hostesse keepes her State, but in best time
	We will require her welcome. [10]
La.	Pronounce it for me Sir, to all our Friends,
	For my heart speakes, they are welcome.

Enter first Murtherer.   [III.iv.2]

Macb.	See they encounter thee with their harts thanks
	Both sides are even: heere Ile sit i'th' mid'st, [15]
	Be large in mirth, anon wee'l drinke a Measure
	The Table round. There's blood upon thy face.
{1.} Mur.	'Tis Banquo's then.
Macb.	'Tis better thee without, then he within.
	Is he dispatch'd? [20]

Notes III.iv.

4–5. *your owne degrees... the hearty welcome.* Shakespeare's contemporaries viewed the entire world, including human society, as a divinely-ordained hierarchy (see note: I.iv.29–30). Great pains were taken to observe *degrees* ("rankes," "the states of people in a common wealth, as the clergie, the nobles, the gentlemen, and the commons," JF, s.v. "Ordini"), so people dining together were seated in order of their *degrees* from highest to lowest. *Macbeth* gives *the hearty welcome At* ("to," OED) those *first* ("foremost in position, rank, or importance," OED) *and last* ("at the end of a series arranged in order of rank or estimation; lowest," OED).

7–9. *mingle with Society... keepes her State.* Macbeth will *mingle* (mix, freely interact) *with Society* ("A congregation, an assemblie," "company," TT, s.v. "Congrĕ-gătĭo"). By contrast, *Lady Macbeth keepes her State*, meaning that she (a) maintains *her State* ("dignitie; ranke, degree," "pompe of great persons," RC, s.v. "Estat"); and/or (b) remains in her "seate of state where a king sitteth, an imperiall seate, a seate of majestie, a throne or seate royall" (JF, s.v. "Sóglio").

9. *in best time.* At the *best* or most opportune moment (cf. "now hee came late, but in best time for her," Mary Wroth, *The Countesse of Mountgomeries Urania*).

10. *require.* Ask for.

10. *welcome.* "A welcoming salute" (OED).

11. *Pronounce.* To "declare openly" (TE, s.v. "Pronuntio"); "to proclaime" (TT, s.v. "Ostendo").

11. *Sir.* Variant form of "Sire" (OED).

12–15. *my heart speakes... Both sides are even.* Lady Macbeth gives *welcome* to her guests from her *heart*, and her guests *encounter* ("meet," "address," OED) *Lady Macbeth with their harts thanks.* Therefore, *Both sides are even* ("Having no balance or debt on either side," OED).

16. *large.* Unrestrained.

16–17. *wee'l drinke a Measure... There's blood upon thy face.* The *Table round* ("In turn or succession among a group of people [in early use esp. one seated at a table]; so as to include each person of a group," OED), *Macbeth* plans to *drinke a Measure* (i.e., quantity of wine) from *a Measure* ("A wine vessell," TT, s.v. "Cădus"). Before he can do so, he steps aside to speak to the *first Murtherer.*

19. *'Tis better thee without... within.* *'Tis better* for *Banquo's* blood to be *without* (on the outside of) the *first Murtherer* than to be *within* (inside) *Banquo.*

{*1.*} *Mur.*   My Lord his throat is cut, that I did for him.

Mac.   Thou art the best o'th' Cut-throats,

        Yet hee's good that did the like for *Fleans*:

        If thou did'st it, thou art the Non-pareill.

{*1.*} *Mur.*   Most Royall Sir   [25]

        Fleans is scap'd.

Macb.   Then comes my Fit againe:

        I had else beene perfect;

        Whole as the Marble, founded as the Rocke,

        As broad, and generall, as the casing Ayre: [30]

        But now I am cabin'd, crib'd, confin'd, bound in

        To sawcy doubts, and feares. But *Banquo's* safe?

{*1.*} *Mur.*   I, my good Lord: safe in a ditch he bides,

        With twenty trenched gashes on his head;

        The least a Death to Nature.   [35]

22–24. **Thou art the best... the Non-pareill.** Any assassin who killed *Fleans* would be on equal footing with the *first Murtherer*, who as *Banquo's* killer is *the best o'th' Cut-throats*. If the *first Murtherer* has managed to kill both *Fleans* and *Banquo*, then he is *the Non-pareill* ("A person who or thing which has no equal; an unrivalled or unique person or thing," OED).

27. **Fit.** An attack of mental instability or insanity (see note: *fitfull*, III.ii.31).

28. **perfect.** *Perfect* means (a) whole, mentally or physically healthy; and/or (b) sexually potent (see notes: *imperfect*, I.iii.76; and *perfect*, III.i.132).

29. **Whole as the Marble.** The deaths of *Banquo* and *Fleans* would ensure that *Macbeth* is *Whole* (steadfast, firm) *as Marble*. In general, *Marble* is a symbol of strength,

permanence, and power, but *Macbeth* probably thinks specifically of the "Stone of Scone," the piece of *Marble* that serves as "a sacred token for the stablishment of the Scottishe kingdome… Upon this stone… the Scottishe kings were used to sit, when they receyved the investure of the kingdome" (RH). Cf. and see note: *Scone*, II.iv.43.

The deaths of *Banquo* and *Fleans* would also ensure that *Macbeth* is (a) *Whole* ("Sound, sane," OED) and in possession of his "marbles" ("Mental faculties; brains; common sense," OED from 1902); and (b) *Whole* ("Having all its parts or elements; having no part or element wanting," OED) and in possession of his "marbles" ("testes," F&H).

29. **founded as the Rocke.** *Macbeth* hoped to be *founded* ("grounded, established," TT, s.v. "Fundātus") *as the Rocke* (which "by a Metaphor denotes a firm, stable, or secure place from dangers, and consequently Refuge and Protection," TDL). He also hoped to be *founded* (i.e., sexually potent; *founded* means "erected," RC, s.v. "Edifié").

30–32. **As broad… To sawcy doubts, and feares.** If *Fleans* were dead, *Macbeth* would be *As broad* ("Unrestrained, kept within no narrow bound," OED) *and generall* ("universal": "In every part or place," OED) *as the casing* (surrounding) *Ayre*. However, *Banquo's Ayre* ("heir") *Fleans* has escaped, and to *Macbeth Fleans'* liberty is *casing* ("enclosing in a case," "put[ting] up in a case or box," "incasing," OED). The continuing threat posed by *Banquo's* "cabin" ("litter," OED) has *cabin'd* ("shut up or confine[d]," OED) *Macbeth* as if in a "cabin" ("a cell," JF, s.v. "Capanna"). *Macbeth* is now *crib'd* ("confine[d] within a small space or narrow limits," OED) and *confin'd* (restrained, shut up). He is also *bound in* ("tied," "alied," TT, s.v. "Dēvinctus"; also "bounden": "In bondage, subject," OED) *To sawcy* ("impudent, bold, presuming," F&H) *doubts, and feares.*

Macbeth also has *doubts* as to his "sauce" ("semen," FR), and he *feares* that his *broad* (i.e., penis; literally "A goad, prick, pointed instrument," OED, s.v. "brod") will never again be *broad* (i.e., erect; literally extended at full length). *Macbeth* despairs of being *generall* ("whole" or "entire": "Sexually potent. Lit[erally] not castrated," FR), for to *Macbeth Banquo's* "heir" is *casing* (with play on "case" meaning "female pudendum, cunt," F&H, s.v. "monosyllable"). *Fleans* makes *Macbeth* feel *cabin'd* (i.e., like a "pussy"; the "cabin" is the "vagina," GW2), and *confin'd* as if in the *con* (i.e., "cunt"). *Macbeth* also *feares* that he has lost his "balls," for he is now *crib'd* as in a "crib" ("an oxe-stall in a stable," JF, s.v. "Presépio"; an ox is a castrated bull).

Also, *Banquo's casing* "heir" makes *Macbeth* feel "like shit" (*casing* is cow dung, OED). *Macbeth* is *confin'd* ("constipate[d]," OED) and *bound* ("Confined in the bowels," OED) *as* "fine" ("excrement," FR) in the "fine" ("Buttocks," FR; the "fine" is literally "the end"). Cf. *stoole*, line 86, below; *push us from our stooles*, line 104, below; and V.iii.27–28.

32. **safe.** The murdered *Banquo* is not *safe* ("unhurt, uninjured, unharmed," OED), but he is most certainly *safe* ("not likely to cause harm or injury," OED).

34–35. **twenty trenched gashes… Death to Nature.** The *twenty trenched* (cut, hacked) *gashes on Banquo's head* have (a) *trenched* ("undermined," JF, s.v. "Cavádo") him; and (b) made him *trenched* ("bur[ied] in a trench," OED); cf. line 33, above.

The "score" (*twenty*) of *trenched gashes on Banquo's head* (penis, prepuce; see note: *Head*, III.i.75) has served to "score" him ("cut" or castrate him, FR). These *trenched gashes* (with play on both "trench" and "gash" as "The female pudendum," F&H) are the *Death* of *Banquo's Nature* (genitals, semen, and reproductive ability; see notes: *Nature*, I.ii.17 and I.v.52). Cf. II.iii.148.

Macb.   Thankes for that:

There the growne Serpent lyes, the worme that's fled

Hath Nature that in time will Venom breed,

No teeth for th' present. Get thee gone, to morrow

Wee'l heare our selves againe.   [40]

Exit {First} Murderer.   [III.iv.3]

Lady.   My Royall Lord,

You do not give the Cheere, the Feast is sold

That is not often vouch'd, while 'tis a making:

'Tis given, with welcome: to feede were best at home: [45]

From thence, the sawce to meate is Ceremony,

Meeting were bare without it.

Enter the Ghost of Banquo, and sits in Macbeths place.   [III.iv.4]

Macb.   Sweet Remembrancer:

Now good digestion waite on Appetite,   [50]

And health on both.

Lenox.   May't please your Highnesse sit.

37–39. **the growne Serpent... No teeth.** Cf. and see note: III.ii.19–21.
37. **worme.** Serpent, with possible play on *worme* meaning "penis" (F&H).
39–40. **to morrow... our selves againe.** *Macbeth* says either (a) *Wee (Macbeth*

and the *first Murtherer*) will *heare* (listen to) *our selves* (i.e., each other) *againe to mor-row*; or (b) *Wee* (*Macbeth* only, using *Wee* as the royal pronoun) will *heare* ("give audi-ence to," OED) the *first Murtherer againe to morrow* when *Wee* are *againe our selves* (i.e., "when I am *againe* myself"). The plural *our selves* (as opposed to "our self") favors the former interpretation: cf. *Macbeth's* use of "our self" to mean solely himself in III.i.53 and line 7, above.

43–47. *You do not give the Cheere... bare without it.* Macbeth does *not* (a) *give* his guests *the Cheere* ("Kindly welcome or reception, hospitable entertainment," OED) at *the Cheere* ("a feast, a merriment," JM, s.v. "Fiésta"); and/or (b) *give the Cheere* ("a salutation before drinking," OED from 1919). *Lady Macbeth* admonishes her husband, "For it is not... to eat and drinke simply, that we invite one another, but for to eat and drinke together for companie and good-fellowship" (Plutarch, *Morals*). A *Feast* (meal, banquet) *That is not often vouch'd* ("pledged": "give[n] assurance or promise of friendship or allegiance by the act of drinking together," OED) *while 'tis a making* (in progress) *is sold*, which can mean (a) "Cheapened," "bargained, coped, or agreed for" (RC, s.v. "Marchandé"); (b) "vulgare and of the common sort" (JF, s.v. "Vendibile"); and/or (c) "mercenarie" (JF, s.v. "Vendereccio").

Just as *meate* ("foode, or whatsoever else is to be eaten," JF, s.v. "Epulie") needs *sawce* ("condiment, seasoning for meat," RC, s.v. "Sauce"), *Meeting* ("Companie with other: an assemblie," "resorting together," TT, s.v. "Congrĕssĭo") needs *Ceremony* ("a custome, a course or order," "an accustomed maner of doing," JF, s.v. "Rito"; also "courtesy, politeness, or civility," OED). Otherwise, *meate* is *bare* ("poore," "defective," JF, s.v. "Povero"), and *Meeting* is *bare* ("voide, emptie," TT, s.v. "Nūdus").

Meeting (gathering together) without such *sawce* ("that seasoneth, or maketh pleasaunt," TT, s.v. "Condīmentum") is as *bare* ("barren, sterile," TT, s.v. "Jējūnus") as *Meeting* ("Coitus," FR) when the *meate* ("the penis"; also "the female pudendum," F&H) has no *sawce* (semen; see note: *sawcy*, line 32, above). The *Cheere* and *Feast* are "soled" (defiled, sullied) when they are *sold* like a *Feast* ("sexual banquet," GW), or like *Cheere* (sexual intercourse, FR) *That is not vouch'd* ("pledged": "b[ound] by or as by a pledge," OED) *while 'tis a making* (with play on "making" meaning "mat[ing]," OED).

48. *the Ghost of Banquo.* In a play abounding with supernatural forces, it might be difficult for modern readers to recognize that *the Ghost of Banquo* is not an appari-tion but a hallucination. By this point in the play, original audiences would have under-stood *Macbeth* to be insane due to his prior hallucinations (II.i.48–62; II.ii.46 and 53) and his own confessions of mental instability (I.iii.157–159; III.i.79, 81, and 131; III.ii.24–29 and 46; and lines 27–28, above). That *the Ghost* is imaginary is further evidenced by the fact that (a) it comes and goes with *Macbeth's* passions; and (b) it never speaks, as do all other ghosts in Shakespeare's Folio plays (viz. the ghost of *Ham-let* the elder in *Hamlet*; the ghost of *Cæsar* in *Julius Cæsar*; the ghosts of *Richard's* vic-tims in *The Life and Death of Richard III*; and the ghosts of *Posthumus'* family in *Cymbeline*). Also see note: III.ii.14–15.

49. *Remembrancer.* In seeing to *Macbeth's* "debt," *Lady Macbeth* is not only a *Remembrancer* ("A person who reminds another or others of a thing," OED) but also serves as "the Kings Remembrancer, who entreth in his office all recognisanses taken before the Barons, and maketh bonds for any of the Kings debts, or for appearance or observing of orders, and maketh proces for the breach of them" (Edward Phillips, *The New World of English Words*, s.v. "Remembrancers").

Macb.	Here had we now our Countries Honor, roof'd,
	Were the grac'd person of our *Banquo* present:
	Who, may I rather challenge for unkindnesse, [55]
	Then pitty for Mischance.
Rosse.	His absence (Sir)
	Layes blame upon his promise. Pleas't your Highnesse
	To grace us with your Royall Company?
Macb.	The Table's full. [60]
Lenox.	Heere is a place reserv'd Sir.
Macb.	Where?
Lenox.	Heere my good Lord.
	What is't that moves your Highnesse?
Macb.	Which of you have done this? [65]
Lords.	What, my good Lord?
Macb.	Thou canst not say I did it: never shake
	Thy goary lockes at me.
Rosse.	Gentlemen rise, his Highnesse is not well.
Lady.	Sit worthy Friends: my Lord is often thus, [70]
	And hath beene from his youth. Pray you keepe Seat,
	The fit is momentary, upon a thought
	He will againe be well. If much you note him
	You shall offend him, and extend his Passion,
	Feed, and regard him not. Are you a man? [75]

53–54. ***our Countries Honor, roof'd… Banquo present.*** *Macbeth* says that *Were the grac'd* ("Endowed with grace," OED; also "Favoured," "loved, cherished," RC, s.v. "Favorisé") *person of Banquo present*, then his (a) *Countries Honor* (glory, renown) would be *roof'd* ("Heaped full," "fullfilled, accomplished," RC, s.v. "Comblé"); and/or (b) *Countries Honor* (i.e., the nobility; *Honor* is literally "one who or that which does honour or credit," OED) would be *roof'd* ("dwell[ing] under one roof," OED).

Also, if *Banquo's grac'd* (virile or genitally well endowed; see note: *Grace*, I.iii.61) *person* (with possible play on person as the "human genitals," OED, which dates from 1824) *Were present*, then the *Honor* (chastity, sexual purity) of the "country" (with play on "cunt") would bee *roof'd* (i.e., "screwed"; to "rough" is to copulate, F&H, s.v. "ride"; "roof" also puns "ruff" meaning "Female pudendum," FR; for pronunciation of "roof" as "ruff," see HK, p. 238).

55. ***challenge.*** To "accuse of, charge with, call in question for, an offence" (RC, s.v. "Chalenger").

64. ***moves.*** Angers, troubles, or excites.

67–68. ***never shake Thy goary lockes at me.*** Gestures of shaking the *lockes* (literally "tufts of haires," JF, s.v. "Berli") can express "feelings of anger and scorn. They can also express distress or sorrow" (John Anthony Burrow, *Gestures and Looks in Medieval Narrative*, p. 62). Cf. RC's "Bransler la teste": "To shake the head; a gesture denoting mockerie, or contempt; (We say of one that shaketh his head, it seemes he is not verie well pleased.)" *Macbeth* interprets *Banquo's shake* of his *goary* (bloody) *lockes* as a scornful insult to his manhood: to "Shake the head connotes castration, impotence" (FR, s.v. "Shake").

72. ***upon.*** "Within the space of," "in the course of" (OED).

74. ***offend.*** Both (a) "to doe amisse, to displease, discontent" (TT, s.v. "Offendo"); and (b) to "injure," "hurt" (RC, s.v. "Injurier").

74. ***Passion.*** *Passion* can mean (a) "sicknes" (TT, s.v. "Affectus"); (b) a "symptome, concurring with some disease offending the bodie, and bringing it out of temper" (JF, s.v. "Passióne"); (c) "suffering, griefe" (RC2, q.v.); (d) "disquietnes of minde thorough anie affection" (TT, s.v. "Fluctus"); and (e) "a wild or vehement rage" (TT, s.v. "Impĕtus").

Macb.	I, and a bold one, that dare looke on that
	Which might appall the Divell.
La.	O proper stuffe:
	This is the very painting of your feare:
	This is the Ayre-drawne-Dagger which you said [80]
	Led you to *Duncan*. O, these flawes and starts
	(Impostors to true feare) would well become
	A womans story, at a Winters fire
	Authoriz'd by her Grandam: shame it selfe,
	Why do you make such faces? When all's done [85]
	You looke but on a stoole.
Macb.	Prythee see there:
	Behold, looke, loe, how say you:
	Why what care I, if thou canst nod, speake too.
	If Charnell houses, and our Graves must send [90]
	Those that we bury, backe; our Monuments
	Shall be the Mawes of Kytes.

---

77. **appall.** Both (a) terrify (see note: *appalls*, II.ii.75); and (b) make pale.

78. **O proper stuffe.** Lady Macbeth (a) considers her husband's ravings *proper* ("thorough, complete; perfect," OED) *stuffe* ("Nonsense, idle, ridiculous, impertinent Talk," ND); (b) contemptuously praises her husband by saying that he is made of *proper* ("singular, excellent," TT, s.v. "Præcĭpuus") *stuffe* ("solid qualities of intellect or character," OED); and/or (c) implies that her husband is an *O* (i.e., a "pussy"; literally the "pudend," JH) who lacks a *proper* ("able," TT, s.v. "Idōnĕus") "prop" ("penis," GW2; literally a "stick, rod, pole, stake, beam, or other rigid support," OED) with *stuffe* ("seminal fluid," F&H, s.v. "cream").

79. **painting.** *Painting* can mean (a) "a painted picture or likeness" (OED); and

(b) "false colouring, counterfaite colour: deceit: falsehood," "dissimulation, covie, guile, colourable deceit" (TT, s.v. "Fūcus").

80. *Ayre-drawne-Dagger.* *Lady Macbeth* tries to convince her husband that his current vision is no more substantial than his prior hallucination of an *Ayre-drawne-Dagger* (cf. and see note: *Dagger of the Minde*, II.i.53; also see note: *the Ghost of Banquo*, line 48, above). The *Dagger* was *Ayre-drawne*, which can mean (a) *drawne* ("Very cunningly made, & as it were wrought with a painters pensill: painted," TT, s.v. "Pergrăphĭcus") in the *Ayre*; and/or (b) *drawne* ("Of a sword: Pulled out of the sheath, naked," OED).

81. *flawes.* *Lady Macbeth* thinks that her husband is (a) "flawed" ("Crazed," RC, s.v. "Fellé"; "A flaw" is a "craze, or small cracke," RC, s.v. "Felure"); (b) "Flawd" ("Drunk," FG); (c) "blowing hot air" or "full of wind" (a "flaw" is a "sodaine blast of winde, a boystrous storme or tempest," JF, s.v. "Turbine"); (d) acting like a "pussy" ("flaw" means "vagina," GW2); and/or (e) acting like an "ass[hole]" (a "flaw" is literally "a chinke, a cleft, a cranie, a gap," JF, s.v. "Sfendimento").

81. *starts.* *Starts* are "sudden fit[s] of passion," "outburst[s]" (OED). Also see notes: *start*, I.iii.57; and *starting*, V.i.46–47.

82. *Impostors to true feare.* "Impostor" and "imposture" were interchangeably spelled (OED) and identically pronounced (HK, p. 271). Therefore, *Macbeth's flawes and starts* (line 81 above) are (a) merely "impostures" ("illusion[s]; fantasie[s], false vision[s]," "mockerie[s], or gullerie[s]," "tricke[s] of forgerie[s], put upon dull, or dazeled eyes," RC, s.v. "Illusion") *to* ("of" or "as compared with," OED) *true feare*; and/or (b) *Impostors* ("lyer[s], cogger[s], foister[s], deceiver[s]," "dissembler[s]," "abuser[s] of people with false tales, or shewes," RC, s.v. "Joncheur") *to* ("That goes, or takes one, or causes one to go, to," OED) *true feare*.

84. *Authoriz'd.* "Advowed, avouched," "allowed of" (RC, s.v. "Advoué").

84. *Grandam.* A *Grandam* is "An old woman" (OED). In stating that her husband's behavior only befits a *Grandam* (i.e., asshole, FR, who notes that "anus" is L. for "old woman"), *Lady Macbeth* also implies that he is "full of shit." Cf. and see note: *stoole*, line 86, below.

84. *shame it selfe.* *Macbeth's* conduct is (a) *shame* ("infamie, dishonor," JF, s.v. "Vergogna") *it selfe*; and (b) worthy only of a man who has been "shamed" ("castrate[d]," FR; *shame* is literally "disgrace"; see note: *Grace*, I.iii.61).

85–86. *make such faces… on a stoole.* *Macbeth* makes *faces* while he "looks" (gazes, casts his glace) *but* (only) *on* an empty *stoole* ("a chair, a seate," TT, s.v. "Sella"). In so doing, he "looks" (appears) "full of *stoole*" ("excrement," RC, s.v. "Selle"). *Macbeth* is "making an ass of himself" like a *but* (backside; also a laughing-stock; see note: *But*, I.vii.10) that makes *faces* ("Fæces," FR; also see note: *fac'd*, I.ii.26) *on a stoole* ("A chamber pot," TT, s.v. "Lăsănum"). There is probable additional play on *such* meaning the posteriors (see note: *such*, line 140, below).

89. *nod.* To *nod* is "to shake the head" (JM, s.v. "Cabeceár"). Cf. and see note: *shake Thy goary lockes*, lines 67–68, above.

90–92. *If Charnell houses… the Mawes of Kytes.* *If Charnell houses* ("place[s] to lay sculles, and bones of dead men in," JB, q.v.) *and our Graves must send backe Those that we bury*, then we would not honor corpses with decent burial. Instead, *our Monuments* ("tombe[s], grave[s], or sepulchre[s]," JF, s.v. "Monumento") *Shall be* (will come to be) *the Mawes* ("gargill[s] or throte hole[s]," JF, s.v. "Ventricchio"; "stomack gut[s]," JF, s.v. "Duodeno") *of Kytes* (birds of prey, buzzards).

{*Exit Ghost.*}   [III.iv.5]

La.   What? quite unmann'd in folly.

Macb.   If I stand heere, I saw him.   [95]

La.   Fie for shame.

Macb.   Blood hath bene shed ere now, i'th' olden time

               Ere humane Statute purg'd the gentle Weale:

               I, and since too, Murthers have bene perform'd

               Too terrible for the eare. The times has bene,   [100]

               That when the Braines were out, the man would dye,

               And there an end: But now they rise againe

               With twenty mortall murthers on their crownes,

               And push us from our stooles. This is more strange

               Then such a murther is.   [105]

La.   My worthy Lord

               Your Noble Friends do lacke you.

---

94. ***unmann'd in folly.*** *Macbeth's folly* ("madnesse," TT, s.v. "Amentĭa") has
unmann'd him, meaning it has made him (a) subject to "unmanlinesse" ("cowardise,"
"faintheartednesse," RC, s.v. "Lascheté"); (b) "unmannerly" ("not sober," JB, s.v.
"Immodest"; "unreasonable," RC, s.v. "Importun"); (c) "unmannerllie" ("Rude,"

"uncivill," RC, s.v. "Rude"); and/or (d) "unmanlie, effeminate" (RC, s.v. "Lasche"). Cf. and see note: *Unmannerly,* II.iii.151.

96. ***Fie for shame.*** *Lady Macbeth* thinks her husband is behaving (a) like a "pussy" (the *Fie for shame* is "The female pudendum," F&H); and/or (b) like a "piece of shit" or an "ass[hole]" (see note: *Fye,* V.i.38).

97–99. ***Blood hath bene shed... and since too.*** *Humane* (used interchangeably with "human"; see note: *humane,* I.v.17) *Statute* ("a lawe, a decree, a determination, a thing certainly determined and appointed, an ordinance," JF, s.v. "Statuto") has *purg'd* ("cleansed," "clarified, purified," RC, s.v. "Appuré") *the gentle* ("gentil[e]": "Pertaining to a nation," OED; *gentle* and "gentile" were homonyms, HK, p. 109) *Weale* (state, commonwealth). Nevertheless, *Blood hath bene shed* both *ere* (before) *and since* (after; from that time).

As an absolute monarch, *Macbeth* easily could have *purg'd* his realm of *Banquo* through *Statute* ("A law or decree made by a sovereign," OED; cf. III.i.145–147), but he instead opted to "purge" the body politic of *Banquo* as he would a disease from the human body. Contemporary medical doctrine held that sickness was caused by an imbalance of the four bodily "humors" (viz. blood, phlegm, choler, and melancholy), and the excess humors were dispelled when patients were *purg'd* ("freed from impurity," OED) by the letting of *Blood.* To effect the *Weale* ("Welfare, well-being," OED) of the *Weale* (body politic), *Macbeth* thinks *Blood shed* (i.e., bloodletting) an effective "purge" ("A purgative medicine or treatment," OED).

Moreover, *Macbeth* considers himself *purg'd* ("Excused," "justified, delivered from imputation, discharged of blame," RC, s.v. "Deculpé") in the shedding of *Banquo's Blood,* for *Banquo* plagued the *gentle* (with play on "genital") *Weale* ("wheel": "Female pudendum," JH) of the body politic like a *Weale* (i.e., a syphilitic sore; literally a "blister, skab, itch, or tetter," JF, s.v. "Broffolétta"). Cf. V.ii.35–37 and V.iii.70–71.

100. ***The times has bene.*** *Times* ("the age now or then present," OED) is here singular: cf. "There had beene good store of Laymens blood shed already, and now the times is comming to have Clergie mens shed" (Richard Baker, *A Chronicle of the Kings of England*).

101. ***Braines... dye.*** With possible play on *Braines* as semen (see note: *Braine,* I.iii.173) and *dye* meaning "To experience a sexual orgasm" (EP).

103. ***twenty mortall murthers.*** Cf. and see note: *twenty trenched gashes,* line 34, above.

103. ***crownes.*** With play on "crown" meaning (a) the "skonce of ones head" (JF, s.v. "Cuticágna"), "the midst of the skull" (JF, s.v. "Mesocraneo"); (b) "A Diadem," a "wreath for the head of a King" (RC, s.v. "Diademe"); and (c) the genitals (see note: *Crowne,* I.v.49).

104. ***push us from our stooles.*** The *Ghost of Banquo* has (a) "pushed" ("shove[d]," JF, s.v. "Urtare") *Macbeth from* his "stool" (chair, seat) at the banquet table (line 48, above); (b) "pushed" (i.e., "fucked"; to *push* is "To copulate," F&H) *Macbeth* by "pushing" him *from* his "stool" (a "throne," "a chair of authority, state, or office," OED); (c) "pushed" *Macbeth* (i.e., afflicted him with hemorrhoids or syphilitic sores; a "push" is "a blister," JM, s.v. "Chicón"; cf. *Weale,* line 98, above) in the "stool" (i.e., the "seat" or "arse"); and/or (d) treated *Macbeth* "like shit" by "push[ing]"("exert[ing] muscular pressure internally," OED) him like "stool" (fæces; see note: *stoole,* line 86, above). Cf. V.iii.27–28.

107. ***lacke.*** "To perceive the absence of; to miss" (OED).

Macb.   I do forget:

Do not muse at me my most worthy Friends,

I have a strange infirmity, which is nothing   [110]

To those that know me. Come, love and health to all,

Then Ile sit downe: Give me some Wine, fill full:

Enter Ghost.   [III.iv.6]

I drinke to th' generall joy o'th' whole Table,

And to our deere Friend *Banquo*, whom we misse: [115]

Would he were heere: to all, and him we thirst,

And all to all.

Lords.   Our duties, and the pledge.

Mac.   Avant, & quit my sight, let the earth hide thee:

Thy bones are marrowlesse, thy blood is cold: [120]

Thou hast no speculation in those eyes

Which thou dost glare with.

La.   Thinke of this good Peeres

But as a thing of Custome: 'Tis no other,

Onely it spoyles the pleasure of the time.   [125]

Macb.   What man dare, I dare:

Approach thou like the rugged Russian Beare,

The arm'd Rhinoceros, or th' Hircan Tiger,

108. *I do forget.* Macbeth loses his grip on reality to the point that he tends to *forget* his actual surroundings. Cf. and see note: *What is the night*, line 161, below.

109. *muse.* To "wonder, or gaze at" (RC, s.v. "Amuser").

110. *infirmity.* A "crazinesse; also, maladie, sicknesse" (RC, s.v. "Infirmité"). Also see note: *Infirme*, II.ii.66.

116. *to all, and him we thirst.* Macbeth does *thirst* ("desire to drinke," TE, s.v. "Sitis") *to all*, including *him* that they *thirst* ("wish, or long for," RC, s.v. "Convoiter")— i.e., *Banquo.*

117. *all to all.* Macbeth might simply pledge *all* (everything) *to all* (everyone), but the phrase seems to carry the sense "to reciprocate to each one in kind." Cf. "they are fain to become weak to the weak, and all to all" (John Everard, *The Gospel-Treasury Opened*).

119. *Avant.* *Avant* means "be gone; fie upon it" (RC, s.v. "Avalisque"); "get you packing" (RC, s.v. "Vie foüet, & au vent"); RC further notes that the word is "Used… in the driving away of a dog," s.v. "Devant").

120. *Thy bones are marrowlesse.* *Bones* are a "symbol of life as seen in the character of a seed… embracing both the tree and its inner, hidden, and inviolable heart" (JC). The "marrow" was traditionally regarded as "The seat of a person's vitality and strength" (OED; also see note: *lac'd*, II.iii.147). If *Banquo's bones are marrowlesse*, then he is (a) "deprive[d] of marrow" ("bereave[d] of strength," RC, s.v. "Esmoëller"); and (b) impotent or sterile ("marrow" is "semen," EP; also see note: *Bonelesse*, I.vii.67).

120. *thy blood is cold.* Banquo's (a) *blood* ("vital fluid," "life," OED) *is cold* ("cold in death, dead," OED); and (b) *blood* ("semen," GW; also sexual aptitude; see note: *bloody*, I.ii.24) *is cold* (frigid, sexually unable; see note: *cold*, II.iii.25).

121. *speculation.* "The faculty or power of seeing; sight, vision, *esp.* intelligent or comprehending vision" (OED).

124. *of Custome.* Usual, commonplace, ordinary.

125. *Onely it spoyles.* I.e., "*it* merely *spoyles.*"

125. *the time.* The moment.

127. *like.* In the form or likeness of.

127. *rugged Russian Beare.* *Rugged* can mean (a) "brizly, hairie, grizly, rough," "shaggie" (JF, s.v. "Setoloso"); and (b) "fierce, cruell" (JM, s.v. "Aspero"). The *Russian Beare*, like the *Hircan Tiger* (line 128, below), was regarded as particularly savage.

128. *arm'd Rhinoceros.* An *arm'd* animal is "Furnished with horns, teeth, etc., or protected by natural mail" (OED). The *Rhinoceros* is not only *arm'd* with his horn but also "armed with manifold strong, hard, & thick skales" (Thomas Blundeville, *M. Blundeville His Exercises*).

128. *Hircan Tiger.* "Hyrcania" is "part of Asia, bordering South on Armenia" (EC2). The "Tyger" is "a truculent beast, and the swiftest of all other beasts… but of all, the Hircan Tyger is the most cruelst" (HC). Also see note: *Tiger*, I.iii.10.

Take any shape but that, and my firme Nerves

Shall never tremble. Or be alive againe,   [130]

And dare me to the Desart with thy Sword:

If trembling I inhabit then, protest mee

The Baby of a Girle. Hence horrible shadow,

Unreall mock'ry hence.

{Exit Ghost.}   [III.iv.7] [135]

                            Why so, being gone

I am a man againe: pray you sit still.

La.   You have displac'd the mirth,

Broke the good meeting, with most admir'd disorder.

Macb.   Can such things be,   [140]

And overcome us like a Summers Clowd,

Without our speciall wonder? You make me strange

Even to the disposition that I owe,

When now I thinke you can behold such sights,

And keepe the naturall Rubie of your Cheekes,   [145]

When mine is blanch'd with feare.

Rosse. What sights, my Lord?

La.   I pray you speake not: he growes worse & worse

Question enrages him: at once, goodnight.

Stand not upon the order of your going,   [150]

But go at once.

129. **shape.** *Macbeth* fears *Banquo's* (a) *shape* ("imaginary, spectral, or ethereal form," OED); and (b) *shape* ("sexual organs," OED).

129–130. **my firme Nerves Shall never tremble.** Were *Macbeth* confronted with any adversary except the *Ghost of Banquo*, his *firme* ("constant, stedfast," JF, s.v. "Costante") *Nerves* ("Sinew[s], strength, force, power, stoutness, and constancy of minde," TB, s.v. "Nerve") would *never tremble* ("shake for feare," TT, s.v. "Contrĕmisco"). Moreover, his *firme* ("stiffe, hard," JF, s.v. "Sólido"; "vigorous, strong, lustie," "able," JF, s.v. "Vigoroso") "nerve" ("penis," GW2) would *never tremble* ("waver," "falter," "quiver," JF, s.v. "Titubare"; "shake": "lose stability, become weakened," OED).

131. **Desart... Sword.** The *Desart* is "Commonly an image of sterility" (JT). *Macbeth* would never tolerate insults to his manhood from any live adversary, and he would resolutely defy them with his *Sword* ("Penis," EP).

132. **If trembling I inhabit.** I.e., "If I dwell in fear."

132. **protest.** To *protest* is (a) to "declare openly" (RC2, q.v.); (b) "to crie out oftentimes, or to speake lowde" (TT, s.v. "Clāmĭro"); and (c) "to swear, to averre, to avouch" (JF, s.v. "Asseverare").

133. **Baby of a Girle.** I.e., "a childes babie, or puppet" (JF, s.v. "Poppara"). A *Baby* is "A child's doll" (OED).

133–134. **shadow, Unreall mock'ry.** Even in his terror, *Macbeth* realizes that the *shadow* ("ghost," JF, s.v. "Ombra") of *Banquo* is merely a *shadow* ("An unreal appearance; a delusive semblance or image," OED). Hence, he calls it an *Unreall mock'ry* ("An illusion; fantasie, false vision," RC, s.v. "Illusion"; "a deceitful thing," RC2, s.v. "delusion"). See note: *the Ghost of Banquo*, line 48, above.

138. **displac'd.** *Displac'd* can mean (a) "overturned" (HC); (b) "banished" (OED); and (c) "put out of joynt" (RC, s.v. "Disloqué").

139. **admir'd.** *Admir'd* means "wondered at" (RC, s.v. "Admiré").

140–141. **Can such things be... a Summers Clowd.** Such things as the *Ghost of Banquo* (a) *overcome Macbeth* ("take [him] by surprise," OED); (b) *overcome* ("subdue, vanquish," RC, s.v. "Debeller"; "undoe; breake; defeat, discomfit," "ruine, destroy, overthrow," RC, s.v. "Desfaire") *Macbeth*; and/or (c) *overcome* (spread over, cover, come upon, overtake) *Macbeth* "As oft in summer tide, / blacke cloudes do dimme the sonne, / And straight againe in clearest skye / his restles steedes do ronne" (Arthur Broke, *The Tragicall Historye of Romeus and Juliet*).

Such things also put *Macbeth* "under *a Clowd*" ("Under suspicion, in disrepute," DPF) and cause him to be *overcome* ("proved guiltie," RC2, s.v. "convict"). By being "in the clouds" ("In dreamland, entertaining visionary notions," DPF), *Macbeth* "buggers himself": he is *overcome* ("overcome sexually," EC, s.v. "come over") by *things* (genitals; see note: *things*, III.ii.22) in the *such* ("anal area," FR, who holds it to be a pun on L. "tale": "such"). Also see note: *Such*, I.vii.47.

142–144. **You make me strange... such sights.** When *Macbeth* thinks how others *can behold such sights* (terrible visions; see note: *sight*, II.ii.30) with equanimity, it "makes him strange" ("distant or unfriendly," OED) *Even to* his own *disposition* (mental and physical constitution and capabilities).

145. **naturall Rubie of your Cheekes.** *Lady Macbeth's Cheekes* are "Ruby-face" ("very red," ND), but this is due to consternation, not her *naturall* constitution.

150. **the order of your going.** See note: *your owne degrees*, line 4, above.

151. **at once.** Both (a) "Immediately, straightway" (OED); and (b) "together," "simultaneously" (OED).

Len.	Good night, and better health
	Attend his Majesty.
La.	A kinde goodnight to all.

{*Exeunt. Manet Macbeth and Lady Macbeth.*}   [III.iv.8] [155]

Macb.	It will have blood they say:	
	Blood will have Blood:	
	Stones have beene knowne to move, & Trees to speake:	
	Augures, and understood Relations, have	
	By Maggot Pyes, & Choughes, & Rookes brought forth	[160]
	The secret'st man of Blood. What is the night?	
La.	Almost at oddes with morning, which is which.	
Macb.	How say'st thou that *Macduff* denies his person	
	At our great bidding.	
La.	Did you send to him Sir?	[165]

---

157. **Blood will have Blood.** According to popular belief, "Whoso shall man bereave of vitall breath, / His life shall be abridg'd with cruell death. / Blood will have blood, whoso shall cut mans life, / His also shall be cut with blooudy knife" (Francis Sabie, *Adams Complaint*). The origin is Genesis 9:6: "Who so sheddeth mans blood, by man shall his blood be shed."

In *A Godly and Learned Exposition of Christs Sermon in the Mount*, William Perkins explains that this proverb also speaks of the spiritual consequences of bloodshed:

we may observe this rule of Gods justice in the punishment of sinne: namely, to reward men in their kind, punishing them in the same things wherein they offend... And experience shewes, that blood will have blood; for though the murtherer escape the hands of the civill Judge, yet the terror & vengeance of God doth ordinarily pursue him to destruction.

158–161. ***Stones have beene knowne to move... man of Blood.*** "Folklore is rife with stories about stones that move of their own volition" (Gary R. Varner, *Menhirs, Dolmen and Circles of Stone*, p. 35). Perhaps the most famous of moving *Stones* is that which, according to Matthew 27:2 and Mark 16:4, moved from the entrance to Christ's tomb, but there are far too many accounts of moving *Stones* to know which particular one (if any) Shakespeare had in mind. Perhaps *Macbeth* refers to the moving *Stones* of Scottish folklore documented by Robert Kirk in *The Secret Commonwealth*. Kirk explains that many believe "those Creatures that move invisibly in a House, and cast huge great Stones, but do no much Hurt... to be Souls that have not attained their Rest, thorough a vehement Desire of revealing a Murther or notable Injurie done or received."

Along the same lines, many ancient ballads and folktales contain the motif of murdered souls speaking from within *Trees*, or from within birds such as *Maggot Pyes* ("magpie[s]," OED), *Choughes* ("jacke daw[s]," "jay[s]," JM, s.v. "Grája"), *& Rookes* ("white-billed Crow[s]," RC, s.v. "Freux"), all of which are highly vocal members of the crow family (cf. and see notes: *Raven*, I.v.45; and *Rookie*, III.ii.62).

Since time immemorial, these *Augures* ("auguries": omens, portents) *and understood* ("made known or patent," OED) *Relations* ("declaration[s]," "shewing[s]," "signifying[s]," RC, s.v. "Declaration") *have brought forth* (revealed, *brought* to light) *The secret'st* (most stealthy or clandestine) *man of Blood* ("murderer," OED). Cf. Habakkuk 2:10–11: "Thou hast consulted shame to thy house, by cutting off many people, and hast sinned against thy soule. For the stone shall crie out of the wall, and the beame out of the timber shall answere it."

161. ***What is the night.*** *Macbeth's* abrupt question *What is the night* (i.e., "What time is it?") reveals that he loses touch with reality during his fits of mania. See note: *the Ghost of Banquo*, line 48, above; and cf. I.iii.161–173.

162. ***at oddes.*** To "set at oddes" is "to begin a quarrell" (RC, s.v. "Campane").

163–164. ***Macduff denies his person... bidding.*** Macbeth gave *bidding* (command) that *Macduff* should come to court, but *Macduff* does not comply because he is in fear of his life. According to Holinshed, *Macduff* aroused *Macbeth's* ire when *Macbeth*

buylded a strong Castell on the top of an high hill cleped Dunsinnane situate in Gowry, ten myles from Perth... Makbeth beeing once determined to have the worke go forwarde, caused the Thanes of eche shire within the Realme, to come and helpe towardes that building, eche man hys course about. At the last when the turne fell unto Makduffe Thane of Fife to buylde his part, he sent workmen with all needfull provision, and commaunded them to shew suche diligence in every behalfe, that no occasion might bee given for the king to finde fault with him, in that he came not himselfe as other had done, which he refused to do for doubt least the king bearing him (as he partly understoode) no great good will, woulde lay violent handes upon him, as he had done uppon dyverse other. Shortly after, Makbeth comming to behold howe the worke went forwarde, and bycause hee found not Makduffe there, he was sore offended, and sayde, I perceyve this man will never obey my commaundements.

Cf. II.iv.49–50; and see note: II.iv.53.

165. ***Sir.*** See note: *Sir*, line 11, above.

Macb.   I heare it by the way: But I will send:

There's not a one of them but in his house

I keepe a Servant Feed. I will to morrow

(And betimes I will) to the weyard Sisters.

More shall they speake: for now I am bent to know   [170]

By the worst meanes, the worst, for mine owne good,

All causes shall give way. I am in blood

Stept in so farre, that should I wade no more,

Returning were as tedious as go ore:

Strange things I have in head, that will to hand,   [175]

Which must be acted, ere they may be scand.

166. ***by the way.*** *By the way* can mean (a) "Incidently; by chaunce, by occasion" (RC, s.v. "Incidemment"); (b) "secretly" (JF, s.v. "Alla fuggita"); and (c) "by meanes" (JF, s.v. "Per via").

167–168. ***There's not a one... a Servant Feed.*** *Feed* means "bribe[d]" (OED). According to Holinshed, "Makbeth had in everie noble mans house, one slie fellow or other in fee with him, to reveale all that was said or doone within the same, by which slight he oppressed the most part of the nobles of his realme."

168–169. ***I will... to the weyard Sisters.*** *Macbeth's* first encounter with the *weyard Sisters* seemingly happened by chance. However, this statement suggests that *Macbeth* knows where to find them, and that he has consulted with them since their first meeting. *Shakespeare* here conflates Holinshed's *weyard Sisters* with Holinshed's "certain wysardes, in whose wordes he [*Macbeth*] put great confidence." See notes: *the worst meanes*, line 171, below; *Trade, and Trafficke*, III.v.7; and *Beware Macduffe*, IV.i.85.

169. ***betimes.*** *Betimes* can mean (a) early; (b) "quickelie, with the soonest" (TT, s.v. "Mātūrē"); and (c) "In good time, in due time; while there is yet time, before it is too late" (OED).

169. ***weyard Sisters.*** See note: *weyward Sisters*, I.iii.36.

171. ***the worst meanes, the worst.*** To gain knowledge of *the worst* events that may befall him, *Macbeth* plans to use the *Witches*, who are *the worst meanes* ("intermediary agent[s]," OED). As a *meanes* ("bribe," OED), *Macbeth* might give the *Witches meanes* ("sexual intercourse," OED, s.v. "mean"). Cf. and see notes: lines 178–179, below; *Trade, and Trafficke*, III.v.7; and *Loves for his owne ends*, III.v.16.

171–172. ***for mine owne good... give way.*** *Macbeth* will undertake *All causes* ("affair[s], business," OED; "mission[s]," "object[s] or project[s]," DPF) if they will *give way* ("make way; leave the way clear," OED) to his *owne good*. *Macbeth* is even willing to use "cause" ("sexual business," JH) as a "cause" (variant of "causey": "a row of stepping stones," "A Highway," OED) to his *owne good*.

172–174. ***I am in blood Stept in so farre... go ore.*** The *Returning* that *Macbeth* speaks of is his willingness "To repent, as when a sinner which hath erred from the way of Gods Commaundements, doth come home againe by unfained repentance" (TW, s.v. "to Returne"). Cf. "But I am in / So farre in blood, that sinne will pluck on sinne" (*The Life and Death of Richard III*, IV.ii.).

175–176. ***Strange things I have in head... scand.*** *Macbeth* has *Strange* (unusual and/or violent) *things in* his *head that will to hand* (i.e., *that will* be put into action). These *must be acted* (carried out, accomplished) *ere* (before) *they may be* (a) *scand* ("perceive[d], discern[ed]," OED) by others; and/or (b) *scand* (examined, considered, or interpreted). *Macbeth* also warns the audience not to "scan" ("pass judgement on," "form an opinion of," OED) his thoughts and deeds until they are *acted* (performed, dramatically presented).

La.   You lacke the season of all Natures, sleepe.

Macb.   Come, wee'l to sleepe: My strange & self-abuse

           Is the initiate feare, that wants hard use:

           We are yet but yong indeed.   [180]

       Exeunt.

177–178. *You lacke the season… wee'l to sleepe.* *Sleepe* was believed to (a) *season* ("moderate, alleviate, temper," OED) *all Natures* (constitutions and dispositions); and (b) *season* ("preserve," RC, s.v. "Confire") *all Natures* (living things); cf. and see notes: II.ii.50–51. *Lady Macbeth* attributes her husband's crazed fits to a *lacke* of *sleepe*, for "if men lacke sleepe long, frensie disturbeth both reason and remembrance" (Thomas Bilson, *The Survey of Christs Sufferings for Mans redemption*).

Macbeth has suffered from chronic insomnia for about ten years now (cf. II.ii.46–51 and 53–55; also see note: *Thou hast it now*, III.i.3). It is therefore highly unlikely that he can go to *sleepe* simply by going to bed. However, despite his sexual difficulties, *Macbeth* may yet attempt to *season* ("bring into a healthy condition," OED) his *Nature* (genitals, semen, and/or libido; see notes: *Nature*, I.ii.17 and I.v.52). *Macbeth* yet hopes to *sleepe* (an age-old euphemism for sexual intercourse), for perhaps he can still *season* ("Impregnate, copulate with," FR) his wife.

178–179. *My strange & self-abuse… hard use.* *Macbeth* suffers from *strange* (unfamiliar, unaccustomed) *& self-abuse* ("Self-deception," OED; the "and" indicates that *self-abuse* is not here one word: both *strange* and *self* are adjectives describing *abuse*). *Macbeth* is only an *initiate* ("A beginner, a novice," OED) in *feare*, so his *initiate* ("newly introduced," OED) *feare wants* (lacks) *hard* ("Inured, hardened, obdurate," OED) *use* (customary employment).

Macbeth, who suffers from impotence, also *wants hard* (allusive of penis erectus, EP) *use* ("Sexual enjoyment," EP). Nevertheless, he might undergo *strange* (i.e., lewd; "The bawdy sense is rung on the term, 'Stranger' = whore, and 'strange' = an adjective used to describe a sexually promiscuous woman," JH, s.v. "Home-things") *self-abuse* ("Masturbation," OED, which dates from 1728; however, OED records *abuse* meaning "Violation, defilement" from 1586; also see note: *abuse*, II.i.65).

Macbeth's self-abuse might occur unconsciously via assault by a succubus ("A demon in female form supposed to have carnal intercourse with men in their sleep," OED). For the witch, "increasing the devil's progeny is one of her chief goals" (Hans Peter Broedel, *The Malleus Maleficarum and the Construction of Witchcraft*, p. 26), but demonic impregnation required a human intermediary. Because it "was a necessary condition of their spiritual natures that demons could not generate human offspring… succubi received semen from their human partners and then used this as incubi to inseminate women" (ibid., p. 44). An involuntary emission could be construed as evidence that *Macbeth* was attacked by succubi, for "Such demons, as in the incubus and succubus notions of world literature, are 'impregnated' by one's sperm emitted during sleep and give birth to more demons and spirits" (David M. Feldman, *Birth Control in Jewish Law*, p. 117).

Cf. and see notes: *the worst meanes*, line 171, above; *Trade, and Trafficke*, III.v.7; and *Loves for his owne ends*, III.v.16.

180. *We are yet but yong indeed.* *Macbeth* perhaps uses *We* as the royal pronoun referring solely to himself. If so, he attributes his fear to the fact that he is *indeed* ("Certainlie, surelie, without dout, without faile, truely, verely," TT, s.v. "Certē") *yong* ("newly or recently initiated; inexperienced, or having little experience; unpractised; 'raw,'" OED).

On the other hand, *Macbeth* might use *We* as the plural pronoun referring to both himself and his wife. If so, then he yet hopes for fertile and satisfying love-making, for they are *yet but yong indeed* (i.e., youthful and vigorous enough for the "deed," or sexual intercourse; see note: *deed*, I.vii.28).

Act III, scene v

Scena Quinta.

Thunder. Enter the three Witches, meeting

Hecat.   [III.v.1]

{*Witch 1.*}   Why how now *Hecat*, you looke angerly?

Hec.   Have I not reason (Beldams) as you are?   [5]

               Sawcy, and over-bold, how did you dare

               To Trade, and Trafficke with *Macbeth*,

               In Riddles, and Affaires of death;

               And I the Mistris of your Charmes,

               The close contriver of all harmes,   [10]

               Was never call'd to beare my part,

               Or shew the glory of our Art?

               And which is worse, all you have done

               Hath bene but for a wayward Sonne,

               Spightfull, and wrathfull, who (as others do)   [15]

               Loves for his owne ends, not for you.

               But make amends now: Get you gon,

               And at the pit of Acheron

Notes III.v.

3. **Hecat.** For *Hecat's* association with witchcraft, see note: *Heccats*, II.i.67.
4. **angerly.** *Angerly* can mean (a) "Threatning, menacing" (TT, s.v. "Mĭnans");
and (b) "chafing, fuming," "displeased" (TT, s.v. "Indignans").

5. *Beldams.* A "beldam" is (a) "an old hag," a "witch-walking by night" (JF, s.v. "Versiera"); and (b) an "old trot, over-ridden jade" (RC, s.v. "Une vieille loudiere").

5. *as you are.* I.e., "that you are."

6–7. *Sawcy... Trade, and Trafficke with Macbeth. Hecat* thinks the *Witches Sawcy* ("Froward, malapert," "wayward," "arrogent," TT, s.v. "Prŏtervus") *and over-bold* ("impudent, shamelesse," JF, s.v. "Impudénte"). They *Trade* ("buy and sell," "cheapen, bargaine, cope, or agree for," RC, s.v. "Marchander") *and Trafficke* ("deal in merchandise"; also "cousen, deceive, beguile," RC, s.v. "Trafiquer") *with Macbeth In Riddles* ("darke question[s]," "obscure, and mysticall demaund[s]," RC, s.v. "Enigme") *and Affaires* ("busines," "negotiations, dooings, dealings," JF, s.v. "Facende") *of death* ("Bloodshed, slaughter, murder," OED).

The *Witches* are also *Sawcy* ("Insolent in a bawdy or lascivious way," EC) *and over-bold* ("licentious, luxurious, sensual, wanton, given to pleasures," JF, s.v. "Licentioso"). They *Trade* ("engage in sexual business," EC) *and Trafficke* ("deal in sex," GW2) *with Macbeth In Riddles* (with "innuendo of sexual ingression," JH; the bawdy sense derives from "riddle" meaning "to make holes in something," OED) *and Affaires* ("sexual intrigue[s]," GW2) *of death* (orgasm; see note: *Death*, III.i.132). Cf. and see note: *Loves for his owne ends*, line 16, below.

10. *close.* "Secret, hidden" (TT, s.v. "Cēlātus").

10. *contriver.* Both (a) "An Architect; a Governour, Overseer, director; a chiefe deviser" (RC, s.v. "Architecte"); and (b) "a schemer, plotter" (OED).

12. *Art. Art* can mean "trade, craft, misterie, occupation; also, skill, cunning, workmanship; also, craft, subtiltie, deceit, guile" (RC, q.v.).

14. *wayward.* See note: *weyward*, I.iii.36.

16. *Loves for his owne ends. Witches*, who allegedly possessed rapacious sex drives, relentlessly sought *Love* (sexual intercourse) in order to bear children who could be ritually sacrificed or raised in the Devil's service. Paradoxically, *Witches* were thought to curse men with impotence as a way to compel them into a sexual relationship, for "enchantments permitted a man to perform sexually only with a witch" (Hans Peter Broedel, *The Malleus Maleficarum and the Construction of Witchcraft*, p. 191).

It is uncertain whether *Macbeth's* sexual interaction with the *Witches* is a matter of coercion or commerce (cf. *Trade, and Trafficke*, line 7, above). Moreover, there is considerable debate as to whether Shakespeare truly intended *Macbeth* to have a sexual relationship with the *Witches*, for many scholars believe that this scene was written and inserted by Thomas Middleton while revising the play (see note: *Come away*, line 40, below). However, there are also other passages (e.g. III.iv.168–171 and 178–179) which seemingly imply that *Macbeth's* relationship with the *Witches* has a sexual aspect.

18. *pit of Acheron.* Located in northern Greece, *Acheron* is the "'River of Sorrows' (Greek, *achos roös*); one of the five rivers of the infernal regions" (DPF). *Acheron*, "because it flows partly underground, was believed to be one of the five rivers linking this world to the underworld realm of the dead. The name Acheron was sometimes used to refer to the underworld itself" (JT). The *pit of Acheron* is therefore a *pit* ("a cave, a den, a caverne," JF, s.v. "Caverna"; "a deepe darke dungeon," "Also a streame running violently in some low valley making a hideous noise with the downefall," JF, s.v. "Burrato") containing an entrance to Hell. (This extaordinary entrance to the underworld seemingly has a very ordinary door; cf. and see notes: IV.i.50 and 166).

Meete me i'th' Morning: thither he

Will come, to know his Destinie.   [20]

Your Vessels, and your Spels provide,

Your Charmes, and every thing beside;

I am for th' Ayre: This night Ile spend

Unto a dismall, and a Fatall end.

Great businesse must be wrought ere Noone.   [25]

Upon the Corner of the Moone

There hangs a vap'rous drop, profound,

Ile catch it ere it come to ground;

And that distill'd by Magicke slights,

Shall raise such Artificiall Sprights,   [30]

As by the strength of their illusion,

Shall draw him on to his Confusion.

He shall spurne Fate, scorne Death, and beare

His hopes 'bove Wisedome, Grace, and Feare:

And you all know, Security   [35]

Is Mortals cheefest Enemie.

Musicke, and a Song.

Hearke, I am call'd: my little Spirit see

Sits in a Foggy cloud, and stayes for me.

23. *I am for th' Ayre.* *Hecat* is a spirit of *th' Ayre* (see notes: *we three*, I.i.3; *Thunder, Lightning, or in Raine*, I.i.4; and *Heccats*, II.i.67). Also, as the lyrics of the *Come away* song clearly show (see note: line 40, below), *Hecat* exits the stage by flying through *th' Ayre*.

24. *dismall.* Dismall means "tragicall," "deadly, dolorous, cruel, outragious, belonging to tragedies" (JF, s.v. "Trágico").

24. *Fatall.* See note: *fatall*, I.v.46.

25. *businesse.* Both (a) mayhem; and (b) sexual intercourse. See notes: *Businesse*, I.v.80 and II.iii.107.

26–28. *Upon the Corner… come to ground.* A *profound* ("high, loftie," JM, s.v. "Alto") *vap'rous* ("thin, moist, which may be voided out by the pores," JB, s.v. "Halituous") *drop hangs Upon the Corner of the Moone* (i.e., the tip of the horned moon; cf. Thomas Cooper's *Thesaurus Linguae Romanae & Britannicae*: "Cornua lunaria": "The poynts or corners of the moone"). The crescent *Moone* symbolizes the bow of *Hecat* in her incarnation as the virgin huntress Diana (see note: *Heccats*, II.i.67).

In classical mythology, the *Moone* goddess *Hecat* possessed great knowledge of poisons. *The Moone* itself was supposedly covered with poisonous foam which would *drop* down "on plants, from which it could be collected as 'moon-juice' (*virus lunare*) and used for magical purposes" (Daniel Ogden, *Magic, Witchcraft, and Ghosts in the Greek and Roman Worlds*, p. 239). The *Moone drop* is very potent, but its magic will be especially powerful if *Hecat* can *catch it ere it come to ground.*

29. *slights.* Slights are "devises," "deceits, cunning shifts or tricks" (JF, s.v. "Artificii").

30. *Artificiall.* Artificiall can mean (a) "according to arte" (JF, s.v. "Artificiale"); (b) "wittie, subtile: cunning: crafty" (TT, s.v. "Artĭfĭcĭōsus"); and/or (c) "counterfait or fained" (JF, s.v. "Fattito").

30. *Sprights.* Supernatural beings (OED). Also see note: *Sprights*, II.iii.104.

32. *Confusion.* Confusion can mean (a) "ruine, havoke or utter destruction" (JF, s.v. "Stormino"); (b) "perdition" (OED); and (c) "The casting downe of the conscience before God and man for some sin" (TW).

33. *beare.* "To entertain, harbour, cherish (a feeling)" (OED).

34. *hopes.* Feelings of confidence (see note: *hope*, I.vii.43).

35–36. *Security Is Mortals cheefest Enemie.* Security means "Surenesse, assurance, trust, confidence," "boldnesse, hardinesse" (RC, s.v. "Asseurance"); *cheefest* means "The auncientest of them all," "first" (TT, s.v. "Antīquissĭmus"). Cf. and see note: *Macbeth Is ripe for shaking*, IV.iii.278–279.

37. *Musicke, and a Song.* This *Musicke and Song*, which are distinct from the song in line 40, below, are a ritualistic incantation undertaken by *Hecat* and the *Witches* before she is called away (line 38, below). Cf. IV.i.161–162.

38–39. *my little Spirit… stayes for me.* This *little Spirit* might be the "martin" who serves as the Devil's messenger (see note: *Barlet*, I.vi.9). However, the *Spirit* could also be *Hecat's* familiar, the "Spirit like a Cat" who will descend during the *Come away* song (see note: line 40, below).

Sing within. Come away, come away, &c.   [40]

{Exit Hecat.}   [III.v.2]

{Witch 1.}   Come, let's make hast, shee'l soone be

       Backe againe.

Exeunt.

---

    40. Sing within… come away, &c. William Davenant's 1664 adaptation of *Macbeth* contains lyrics for both *Come away* and *Blacke Spirits* (IV.i.47). Davenant was generally considered the author of these lyrics until 1778, when Isaac Reed discovered Thomas Middleton's manuscript play *The Witch*. Davenant's lyrics are obviously based on those found in Middleton's play, which was commissioned and staged by the King's Men sometime around 1609–1616.

    Accordingly, many scholars conjecture that this entire scene, along with the *Blacke Spirits* song and certain other passages in the play, were written and inserted by Middleton during an early revival. However, as Shakespeare and Middleton are known collaborators on other plays, even if the songs are Middleton's they might have appeared in *Macbeth* from the beginning. Moreover, as *Macbeth* probably pre-dates *The Witch* (see note: *three Witches*, I.i.2), it is also possible that Middleton "borrowed" the songs from *Macbeth* and inserted them into his own play. Yet another possibility is that both Middleton and Shakespeare "borrowed" the songs from some other source which is as yet unknown.

    Although it is uncertain who wrote these songs or when, the Folio's compilers clearly considered them to be a legitimate part of the script. Evidently, all or part of both *Come away* and *Blacke Spirits* were included in the play at an early point in its production history.

    The original music for *Come away* was probably written by Robert Johnson (ca. 1583–ca. 1634), who composed many other songs for Shakespeare's company. The melody possibly survives in John Stafford Smith's 1812 *Musica Antiqua*, which prints an arrangement for *Come away* that Smith describes as "The original Music in the Witches scene in Middleton's comedy 'The Witch.'" Smith further claims that this music was transcribed "From a MS. of that age in the Editor's possession." (For Johnson's authorship and the provenance of Smith's arrangement, see John P. Cutts' "The Original Music to Middleton's *The Witch*").

    The lyrics from Thomas Middleton's *The Witch*, along with the surrounding dialogue, are as follows:

Hec.	hye thee home with 'em
	looke well to the House to night; I am for aloft.
Fire.	Aloft (quoth you?) I would you would breake yor
	neck once, that I might have all quickly: hark: hark Mother.
	they are above the Steeple alredy, flying over your head
	with a noyse of *Musitians*
Hec.	they are they indeed: help: help me: I'm too late els.

Song:

in the aire.	*Come away: Come away:*
	Hecat: Heccat, Come away
Hec.	*I come, I come, I come, I come,*
	with all the speed I may,
	with all the speed I may.
	wher's Stadlin?
in the aire	*Heere*
{Hec.}	*wher's Puckle*
in the aire	*heere*
	And Hoppo too, and Hellwaine too
	we lack but you; we lack but you,
	Come away, make up the count
Hecc.	*I will but noynt, and then I mount.*

A Spirit like a Cat descends.

above	*Ther's one comes downe to fetch his dues*
	a kisse, a Coll, a Sip of Blood
	and why thou staist so long
	I muse, I muse.
	Since the Air's so sweet, and good.
Hec.	*Oh art thou come*
	what newes: what newes?
{above}	*All goes still to our delight,*
	Either come, or els
	Refuse: Refuse:
Hec.	*Now I am furnishd for the Flight.*
Fire:	hark, hark, the Catt sings a brave Treble in her owne Language.

going up.

Hec.	*Now I goe, now I flie,*
	Malkin my sweete Spirit, and I.
	Oh what a daintie pleasure 'tis
	to ride in the Aire
	when the Moone shines faire
	and sing, and daunce, and toy, and kiss;
	Over Woods, high Rocks, and Mountaines,
	Over Seas, our Mistris Fountaines,
	Over Steepe Towres, and Turretts,
	we fly by night, 'mongst troopes of Spiritts,
	No Ring of Bells, to our Eares sounds
	No howles of Woolves, no yelps of Hounds.
	No, not the noyse of waters-breache
	or Cannons throat, our height can reache.
above.	*No Ring of Bells &c.*
Fire.	Well Mother, I thank your kindnes: You must be gambolling i'th Aire; and leave me to walk here, like a Foole, and a Mortall.
Exit.	

Act III, scene vi

Scæna Sexta.   [1]

Enter Lenox, and another Lord.   [III.vi.1]

Lenox.   My former Speeches,

                    Have but hit your Thoughts

                    Which can interpret farther: Onely I say   [5]

                    Things have bin strangely borne. The gracious *Duncan*

                    Was pittied of *Macbeth*: marry he was dead:

                    And the right valiant *Banquo* walk'd too late,

                    Whom you may say (if't please you) *Fleans* kill'd,

                    For *Fleans* fled: Men must not walke too late.   [10]

                    Who cannot want the thought, how monstrous

                    It was for *Malcolme*, and for *Donalbane*

                    To kill their gracious Father? Damned Fact,

                    How it did greeve *Macbeth*? Did he not straight

                    In pious rage, the two delinquents teare,   [15]

                    That were the Slaves of drinke, and thralles of sleepe?

                    Was not that Nobly done? I, and wisely too:

                    For 'twould have anger'd any heart alive

                    To heare the men deny't. So that I say,

                    He ha's borne all things well, and I do thinke,   [20]

Notes III.vi.

4. *hit.* Coincided; agreed with (OED).

4. *Thoughts.* Fears and suspicions (see notes: *Thoughts,* III.ii.16; and *thinke,* V.i.81).

5. *interpret.* To "consider" (TT, s.v. "Verto"); to "give the signification: to judge or count," "to take and understand" (TT, s.v. "Interprĕtor").

5. *Onely I say.* I.e., "*I Onely say.*"

6. *borne.* Managed; carried out.

7. *pittied of.* Lamented by.

7. *he was dead. He was dead* possibly means "*he was* killed." *Dead* is a verb meaning "to cause to die; to put to death, kill, slay, destroy" (OED).

10. *Fleans fled.* See note: *Fleans, flye,* III.iii.29.

10. *walke.* To "go from place to place; to journey, wander" (OED).

11. *want.* Lack; be without.

13. *Fact.* "A grievous offence, a crime" (TT, s.v. "Căpĭtăl").

15. *teare.* "To rend," "mangle, dismember" (RC, s.v. "Dechirer").

16. *thralles.* "Subject[s], vassall[s]" (RC, s.v. "Subject").

That had he *Duncans* Sonnes under his Key,

(As, and't please Heaven he shall not) they should finde

What 'twere to kill a Father: So should *Fleans.*

But peace; for from broad words, and cause he fayl'd

His presence at the Tyrants Feast, I heare   [25]

Macduffe lives in disgrace. Sir, can you tell

Where he bestowes himselfe?

Lord.   The Sonnes of *Duncane*

(From whom this Tyrant holds the due of Birth)

Lives in the English Court, and is receyv'd   [30]

Of the most Pious *Edward*, with such grace,

That the malevolence of Fortune, nothing

Takes from his high respect. Thither *Macduffe*

Is gone, to pray the Holy King, upon his ayd

To wake Northumberland, and warlike *Seyward,*   [35]

---

21. **had he... under his Key.** If *Macbeth had Duncans Sonnes under* (subject to) *his Key* ("Great authority and power," TW), he would not hesitate to keep them (a) "under locke and key" ("locked up close," RC, s.v. "Enfermé"); and (b) "screw" them, or keep them *under his Key* (penis; see note: *Key*, II.iii.6).

22. **As.** Equivalent to "which" (OED).

22. **and't.** If it.

24. **But peace... broad words.** *Lenox* does not wish to speak too freely for fear of getting himself into trouble like *Macduff*, who aroused *Macbeth's* anger *from broad* ("Plainspoken, outspoken," OED; also "spreading largely abroad," TT, s.v. "Pătŭlus") *words.*

24. **cause.** Because.

24. **fayl'd.** *Fayl'd* means "omit[ted]" (RC, s.v. "Faillir"); "omit[ted]" means "neglect[ed]" (OED). "Fail" also carries the sense "to do amisse, not to doe that we ought" (TT, s.v. "Pecco").

25. **Tyrants.** A "tyrant" is (a) "A cruell Prince, One that ruleth unjustly" (JB, q.v.); and (b) "a usurper" (OED).

27. **bestowes.** To "bestowe" is "to withdrawe," "to hide himselfe" (TT, s.v. "Conjĭcĭo"). Also see note: *bestow'd*, III.i.37.

28–30. **The Sonnes of Duncane… English Court.** As only *Malcolme* has gone to England, *Sonnes* might be a typographical error for "Sonne." Cf. and see note: II.iii.182–183.

29. **holds.** Witholds.

29. **due of Birth.** Birthright; that which is *due* (owing) to one by *Birth*.

31. **Of.** By.

31–34. **Pious Edward… Holy King.** The *Pious* and *Holy King* is *Edward* the Confessor (ca. 1003–1066), who was canonized in 1161 (*Edward* was a layman; the "Confessor" of his title means "One who avows his religion in the face of danger, and adheres to it under persecution and torture, but does not suffer martyrdom," OED). Holinshed describes *King Edward* as

> wholly gyven to a devoute trade of life, charitable to the poore, and very liber-
> all, namely to Hospitalles and houses of Religion… As hath bin thought he was
> enspired with the gift of Prophecie, and also to have hadde the gift of healing
> infirmities and diseases. Namely, he used to help those that were vexed with the
> disease, commonly called the Kyngs evill, and left that vertue as it were a por-
> tion of inheritance unto his successors the Kyngs of this Realm.

32–33. **nothing Takes.** Detracts nothing.

33–34. **Thither Macduffe Is gone.** Holinshed relates that by the time *Macbeth* attacked *Macduffe's* castle (see note: *The Castle of Macduff*, IV.i.186), "Makduffe was alreadie escaped out of daunger and gotten into England unto Malcolme Canmore, to trie what purchas he might make by meanes of his support to revenge the slaughter so cruelly executed on his wife, his children, and other friends."

34–35. **upon his ayd… warlike Seyward.** Warlike ("Valiant in armes, fierce," "martiall: apte to warre," TT, s.v. "Bellĭcōsus") *Seyward* is Siward Digera ("the strong"), Earl of *Northumberland* (d. 1055). Holinshed relates that *Malcolme* was restored to the throne after *Seyward's* army vanquished *Macbeth*:

> Malcolme the sonne of Duncane next inheritour to the crowne of Scotlande
> being within age, was by the nobles of Scotlande delivered as warde to the cus-
> tome of this king Edwarde, during whose minoritie one Makebeth a Scot trayter-
> ously usurped the crowne of Scotland, against whom this king Edward made
> warre in which the said Makebeth was overcome and slayn…
>
> About the thirtenth yeare of King Edwardes raigne… or rather about the nine-
> teenth or twentith yere as should appeare by the Scottishe Writers, Siward the
> noble Earle of Northumberlande with a great power of Horsemenne went into
> Scotland, and in battell put to flight Mackbeth that had usurped the Crowne of
> Scotland, and that done, placed Malcolme surnamed Camoyr, the son of Dun-
> cane, sometime King of Scotlande, in the governement of that Realme, who
> afterward slew the sayd Macbeth, and then raigned in quiet.

According to Shakespeare, *Seyward* is *Malcolme's* uncle (V.ii.5 and V.vi.7), but Holinshed says *Sewyard* was *Malcolme's* grandfather (see note: *Prince of Cumberland*, I.iv.50). In any case, *Seyward* is closely related to *Malcolme*, so he is willing *To wake* (rouse) *Northumberland* (i.e., the inhabitants of *Northumberland*) to *Malcolme's ayd*. Because *Seyward* is one of *Edward's* supporters, *Edward* will in turn *ayd Malcolme*.

That by the helpe of these (with him above

To ratifie the Worke) we may againe

Give to our Tables meate, sleepe to our Nights:

Free from our Feasts, and Banquets bloody knives;

Do faithfull Homage, and receive free Honors,   [40]

All which we pine for now. And this report

Hath so exasperate their King, that hee

Prepares for some attempt of Warre.

Len.   Sent he to *Macduffe?*

Lord.   He did: and with an absolute Sir, not I   [45]

The clowdy Messenger turnes me his backe,

And hums; as who should say, you'l rue the time

That clogges me with this Answer.

Lenox.   And that well might

Advise him to a Caution, t' hold what distance   [50]

His wisedome can provide. Some holy Angell

Flye to the Court of England, and unfold

His Message ere he come, that a swift blessing

May soone returne to this our suffering Country,

Under a hand accurs'd.   [55]

Lord.   Ile send my Prayers with him.

Exeunt

37–39. *we may againe… bloody knives.* The *Lord* hopes that he and his compatriots *may againe Free* (rid, relieve) their *Feasts and Banquets from bloody knives.* He probably alludes to *Banquo's* murder, but *Macbeth* reputedly "committed many horrible slaughters and murthers, both as well of the nobles as commons, for the which he was hated right mortally of all his liege people" (RH).

40. *receive free Honors.* Receive *Honors* (rewards, titles) that are *free*, meaning (a) "noble, honourable"; and/or (b) "Guiltless, innocent" (OED).

41–42. *this report Hath so exasperate their King.* Their *King* is *Edward*, the *King* of the English. *Edward* is *exasperate* (used as a past participle without the "-d" suffix; hence = "exasperated") by the *report* ("Rumour," "tidings, newes," TT, s.v. "Rūmor"; also "common or open talke," TT, s.v. "Prædīcmatio") of *Macbeth's* evil doings in Scotland.

44–45. *Sent he… He did.* Macbeth *Sent Macduffe* an explicit order to come to court; cf. III.iv.163–166.

45–48. *with an absolute Sir, not I… this Answer.* When the *Messenger* delivers *Macbeth's* command that *Macduffe* should come to court, *Macduffe* responds *with an absolute* ("plaine, open, flat," RC, s.v. "Formel") *Sir, not I.* Then, *The clowdy* (gloomy, angry) *Messenger turnes his backe* on *Macduffe And hums* ("mumble[s]," F&H) *as who should say* (i.e., "as if to say") *you'l rue* (regret) *the time That clogges* ("fetter[s]," "shackle[s]," JF, s.v. "Pastoiare") *me with this Answer.* Macbeth does not treat the bearers of bad news very well (cf. V.iii.13–25 and V.v.41–51), so the *Messenger* presumably looks forward to the time when *Macbeth* will extract his vengeance on *Macduffe.*

Turnes me his backe is a grammatical construction known as an "ethical dative," which Shakespeare and his contemporaries used "to imply that a person, other than the subject or object, has an indirect interest in the fact stated" (OED; the dative still survives in modern English, but generally now a direct interest is expressed: e.g., "I sing me a song" or "He catches him some fish"). The general idea is that the *Lord* empathizes with *Macduffe.*

50. *Advise.* Both (a) "to counsell" (JF, s.v. "Consigliare"); and (b) "To warne" (TT, s.v. "Admŏnĕo").

50. *a Caution.* Caution means (a) "great heedfulnesse, or warie cariage in [a] thing" (JB, q.v.); and (b) "provision; foresight," "heed," "regard," "consideration" (RC, s.v. "Prouvoyance").

52. *unfold.* To "declare at large" (JB, q.v.); to "tell, to shew plainly" (TT, s.v. "Explīco").

56. *Ile send my Prayers with him.* Macduffe puts himself in danger by going to England, where he might be mistaken for an agent of *Macbeth.* Cf. and see notes: IV.iii.22 and 30–32.

Act IV, scene i

Actus Quartus. Scena Prima.   [1]

Thunder. Enter the three Witches.   [IV.i.1]

{Witch 1.}   Thrice the brinded Cat hath mew'd.

{Witch 2.}   Thrice, and once the Hedge-Pigge whin'd.

{Witch 3.}   Harpier cries, 'tis time, 'tis time.   [5]

{Witch 1.}   Round about the Caldron go:

                  In the poysond Entrailes throw

                  Toad, that under cold stone,

                  Dayes and Nights, ha's thirty one:

                  Sweltred Venom sleeping got,   [10]

                  Boyle thou first i'th' charmed pot.

All {Witches}.   Double, double, toile and trouble;

                  Fire burne, and Cauldron bubble.

Notes IV.i.

3. **brinded.** A variant of "Brindled": "Streaked, tabby, marked with streaks" (OED).

4. **Hedge-Pigge.** As a nocturnal animal, the *Hedge-Pigge* (hedgehog) is a traditional *Witches'* familiar. Supposedly "The inward disposition of this beast, appeareth to bee very crafty and full of suttlety" (Edward Topsell, *The Historie of Foure-Footed Beastes*).

The *Hedge-Pigge* is also "a symbol of sexual bestiality" and "heresy: 'buggery' meant both 'abominable heresy' and 'sodomy'" (FR, q.v., who interprets the *Hedge-Pigge* to be *Macbeth* himself, with whom the *Second Witch* shares a telepathic empathy; cf. lines 48–51, below). Also cf. and see notes: *Unmannerly breech'd with gore*, II.iii.151; and *A deed without a name*, line 54, below.

5. **Harpier.** This familiar is either (a) a "harpy" ("A fabulous monster, rapacious and filthy, having a woman's face and body and a bird's wings and claws, and supposed

to act as a minister of divine vengeance," OED); or (B) a crab (cf. JJ's "harper-crab": "Tammy Harper": "the crab called Cancer araneus").

6. ***Round about.*** See note: *about*, I.iii.38.

6–36. ***the Caldron... th' Ingredience of our Cawdron.*** A symbol of transformation and germination, *the Caldron* in ancient times was associated with the womb of Mother Earth. Like many pagan symbols, *the Caldron* took on a more sinister aspect in Christian tradition, coming to represent "the baser forces of nature" (JC) as well as "The female pudendum" (F&H, s.v. "Monosyllable"). This *Caldron*, which was undoubtedly a large and spectacular stage property, was most likely raised onto the stage via the trap door (cf. *Why sinkes that Caldron*, line 131, below).

For the outrageous *Ingredience* of *th' charmed pot*, Shakespeare, like other fiction writers of his time, drew on ancient tradition, popular superstition, and his own imagination. In Thomas Middleton's *The Witch*, Hecat and her coven concoct a potion containing "the Blood of a Bat," "Libbards Bane," "the Juice of Toad: the Oile of Adder," and "three ounces of the red-haird wench." The witches in Ben Jonson's *Masque of Queenes* brew up "the eyes of the Owl," "Batts wing," "The Basiliskes bloud, and the Vipers skin," "The Fig-tree wild, that growes on tombes," "Hemlock, Henbane, Adderstongue, / Night-shade, Moone-wort, Libbards-bane," and the "sinew" and "haire" of "A Murderer... hung in chaines." Although these magical recipes might seem extraordinary, none of them offers much of anything new. Cf. the account of "The Witch of Thessalia" in the *Pharsalia* of Lucan (Marcus Annaeus Lucanus, A.D. 39–65):

> Then to her prayer.
> First through his gaping bosom blood she pours
> Still fervent, washing from his wounds the gore.
> Then copious poisons from the moon distils
> Mixed with all monstrous things which Nature's pangs
> Bring to untimely birth; the froth from dogs
> Stricken with madness, foaming at the stream;
> A lynx's entrails: and the knot that grows
> Upon the fell hyaena; flesh of stags
> Fed upon serpents; and the sucking fish
> Which holds the vessel back though eastern winds
> Make bend the canvas; dragon's eyes; and stones
> That sound beneath the brooding eagle's wings.
> Nor Araby's viper, nor the ocean snake
> Who in the Red Sea waters guards the shell,
> Are wanting; nor the slough on Libyan sands
> By horned reptile cast; nor ashes fail
> Snatched from an altar where the Phoenix died.
> And viler poisons many, which herself
> Has made, she adds, whereto no name is given:
> Pestiferous leaves pregnant with magic chants
> And blades of grass which in their primal growth
> Her cursed mouth had slimed.

7. ***the poysond Entrailes.*** *The poysond Entrailes* are perhaps (a) *Entrailes* that are *poysond* ("poisonous, venomous," OED); (b) the *Entrailes* of a person or animal who has been *poysond* ("killed by poison," OED); or (c) *Entrailes* ("applicable to the female internal pudenda or to the anus / rectum," JA, p. 95) which are *poysond* (sexually tainted or "pox[ed]," GW).

{*Witch 2.*}   Fillet of a Fenny Snake,

In the Cauldron boyle and bake: [15]

Eye of Newt, and Toe of Frogge,

Wooll of Bat, and Tongue of Dogge:

Adders Forke, and Blinde-wormes Sting,

Lizards legge, and Howlets wing:

For a Charme of powrefull trouble,   [20]

Like a Hell-broth, boyle and bubble.

All {*Witches*}.   Double, double, toyle and trouble,

Fire burne, and Cauldron bubble.

{*Witch 3.*}   Scale of Dragon, Tooth of Wolfe,

---

8. ***Toad, that under cold stone.*** In Ben Jonson's *Masque of Queenes*, one of the witches boasts: "I Went to the Toad breedes under the wall, / I charm'd him out, and he came at my call." In a marginal note, Jonson explains that toads "by the confessions of Witches, and testimonie of Writers, are of principall use in their witchcraft." Cf. and see note: *Padock*, I.i.12.

This *Toad*, like Jonson's in *Masque of Queenes*, has apparently sprung of its own accord from the dirt *under* a *cold stone*. Toads were supposedly "Creatures, which are generated of putrefaction" which "Nature brings forth of her own accord, without any seed of the same kind... Toads are generated of dirt, and of womens flowers" (Giambattista della Porta, *Natural Magick*).

Cold is here disyllabic, which suggests Scottish pronunciation (the Scots form is "cauld," JJ).

10. ***Sweltred Venom sleeping got.*** This *Venom* (poison, infection) has possibly

been (a) *Sweltred* (exuded as venom, OED) from "The Jawes of a Toade (sweating & foaming out poyson)" (Thomas Dekker, *The Dead Tearme*); or (b) *Sweltred* ("sweat[ed] profusely," OED) from the skin of a *sleeping* plague victim, who subsequently *Sweltred* ("die[d]," JJ, s.v. "Swelt"). Cf. "The crystals of lead are admirably good to be used in the plague for to provoke sweating and expel the venome out of the body" (John Glauber, *A Description of New Philosophical Furnaces*).

12. **Double, double, toile and trouble.** The *Witches* stir up *Double* (treacherous, deceitful; see note: *double*, I.vi.23) *toile* ("pining griefe, passion or paine of bodie and minde," JF, s.v. "Stento") *and trouble* ("Calamitie, miserie, wretchednesse," "much woe; misfortune, adversitie; mischiefe, extreame hurt, or damage," RC, s.v. "Calamité"). The *Witches Double* (increase twofold) *toile and trouble*, and then *double* it again (thus increasing it fourfold). Cf. *doubly redoubled*, I.ii.46.

14. **Fillet.** *Fillet* can mean (a) "The Flank" (JJ); (b) "The 'string' of the tongue" (OED); (c) "A band of fibre, whether muscle or nerve; a flap of flesh" (OED); and/or (d) "A coloured band or stripe" (OED).

14. **Fenny Snake.** *Fenny* can mean (a) "waterish," "marrish, that which is of the river, or pertaining to the river" (JF, s.v. "Fluviale"); and (b) dwelling in "fen" ("excrement," OED). Cf. "where will the Snake make her nest, but in the rytchest dunge" (Austin Saker, *Narbonus*).

15. **bake.** "To form into a cake or mass; to cake" (OED).

16. **Newt.** An "Eft, or a Lizard" (JF, s.v. "Leguro"). RS gives the brain of a *Newt* as one of the magical ingredients "which are said to procure love, and are exhibited in poison loving cups."

16. **Frogge.** An ancient fertility symbol, the *Frogge* in Christian tradition "has been given a devilish significance, and has sometimes been likened to heretics… it conveys the repulsive aspect of sin" (George Wells Ferguson, *Signs & Symbols in Christian Art*).

17. **Bat.** For the evil associations of the *Bat*, see note: *Bat*, III.ii.50.

18. **Adders.** *Adders* "are a craftie & subtill venomous beast, biting suddenly them that passe by them… Adders, especially deafe Adders, signifie unrepentant wicked men, and also discord" (Edward Topsell, *The Historie of Serpents*). Cf. I.v.77–78.

18. **Forke.** "The forked tongue of a snake" (OED).

18. **Blinde-wormes Sting.** The *Sting* ("the fang or venom-tooth of a poisonous serpent," OED) of a "blindworme" ("sloworme," JF, s.v. "Cecilie"; OED defines "slow-worm" as "A small harmless scincoid lizard, *Anguis fragilis*," but notes that "the word is used to render various Latin names of serpents and lizards"). In *The Historie of Serpents*, Edward Topsell explains that *Blinde-wormes* take their name

> because of the dimnes of the sight thereof… It is harmelesse except being pro-
> voked, yet many times when an Oxe or a Cow downe in the pasture, if it chaunce
> to lye upon one of these Slow-wormes, it byteth the beast, & if remedy be not
> had, there followeth mortalitie or death, for the poyson thereof is very strong.

19. **Lizards.** *Lizards* were used in everyday medicine. JB defines a *Lizard* as "A little beast much like our Euet, but without poyson, breeding in Italy & other hot countries. The dung of this beast is good to take away spots in the eye, & cleereth the sight. And the head thereof being bruised and laid to, draweth out thorns, or any thing sticking within the flesh" (q.v.).

19. **Howlets.** "An Howlet" (pronounced "owlet") is "the little Horne-Owle" (RC, s.v. "Huette"). Also see note: *Owle*, II.ii.5.

Witches Mummey, Maw, and Gulfe   [25]

Of the ravin'd salt Sea sharke:

Roote of Hemlocke, digg'd i'th' darke:

Liver of Blaspheming Jew,

Gall of Goate, and Slippes of Yew,

Sliver'd in the Moones Ecclipse: [30]

Nose of Turke, and Tartars lips:

Finger of Birth-strangled Babe,

Ditch-deliver'd by a Drab,

Make the Grewell thicke, and slab.

Adde thereto a Tigers Chawdron,   [35]

For th' Ingredience of our Cawdron.

All {*Witches*}.   Double, double, toyle and trouble,

Fire burne, and Cauldron bubble.

---

25. **Mummey.** *Mummey* was a common ingredient used in mainstream medicine. TB defines "Mummie" as

> a thing like pitch sold by Apothecaries; It is hot in the second degree, and good against all brusings, spitting of blood, and divers other diseases: There are two kinds of it, the one is digged out of the Graves, in Arabia and Syria, of those bodies that were embalmed, and is called Arabian Mummie. The second kind is onely an equal mixture of the Jews Lime and Bitumen.

25. **Maw.** *Maw* can mean (a) the stomach or gullet (see note: *Mawes*, III.iv.92); and/or (b) "The womb" (OED).

25–26. **Gulfe Of the ravin'd salt Sea sharke.** Either (a) the *Gulfe* ("throat boll, or windpipe," JM, s.v. "Tragadéro") of a *ravin'd* (ravenously hungry or gorged) *salt Sea sharke* ("a fish whose teeth are like a sawe," JF, s.v. "Citaro"); or (b) the *Gulfe* ("vagina," GW2; cf. JF's "Golfo di setalia, the rugged or brislie gulfe, a womans privities") of a *ravin'd* (sexually rough; see note: *Raven*, I.v.45) *salt* ("Wanton, amorous," F&H) *Sea* (i.e., "fornicating"; to "see" is "To copulate," F&H) *sharke* ("predatory member of the brothel trade," GW2).

27. **Hemlocke.** A powerful sedative and hallucinogen, *Hemlocke* ("a venemous herb," EC2) was widely used in contemporary medicine. In *The English Physician*, Nicholas Culpeper warns that "If any shall through mistake eat the Herb Hemlock instead of Parsly, or the Root instead of a Parsnip (both which it is very like) whereby hapneth a kind of Phrensie, or Perturbation of the senses, as if they were stupified or drunk."

28. **Liver.** The *Liver* was formerly "believed to be the seat of passion" (JH).

28. **Blaspheming Jew.** "Blasphemy" is "A word uttered unto the reproch of God, of his Religion, of his Word, Ordinances, Creatures, or Workes" (TW). A great many Renaissance Christians believed in "the blasphemous wickednesse of the Jewes, that would never receive the doctrine, that Christ was the son of God" (Nicholas Byfield, *A Commentary upon the Three First Chapters of the First Epistle generall of St. Peter*).

29. **Slippes.** *Slippes* are "young twig[s] or branch[es]" (TT, s.v. "Surcŭlus").

29. **Yew.** The *Yew* tree was a symbol of death, loss, and grief. In popular superstition, the *Yew* was highly unlucky, and the *Yew* was considered "so venimous, as whosoever did but sleepe under the shade of this tree, or did eat of that mortiferous fruit, he forthwith died" (Pierre d'Avity, *The Estates, Empires, & Principallities Of The World*).

30. **Sliver'd.** Cut or split off.

30. **the Moones Ecclipse.** An *Ecclipse* is "Almost universally an ill omen — symbolically the death of light, suggesting cosmic disorder" (JT).

31. **Turke, and Tartars.** The *Turke* (generally used to mean a "Muslim," OED) and "the Scythians who are commonly called the Tartarians" (Giles Fletcher, *Israel Redux*) were both considered to be "Enemies of the policied world of Christendome" (Thomas Lodge, *Wits Miserie*).

32–33. **Finger of Birth-strangled Babe... Drab.** This *Babe* was *strangled* at *Birth* by its own mother, a *Drab* ("A nasty, sluttish whore," FG) who *deliver'd* (gave birth to) it in a *Ditch*. In *Discovery of Witchcraft*, Reginald Scot remarks that *Witches* supposedly
> make ointments of the bowels and members of children, whereby they ride in the air, and accomplish all their desires. So as, if there be any children unbaptised, or not guarded with the signe of the crosse, or orizons; then the witches may and do catch them from their mothers sides in the night, or out of their cradles, or otherwise kill them with their ceremonies; and after buriall steal them out of their graves, and seeth them in a caldron, untill their flesh be made potable. Of the thickest whereof they make ointments, whereby they ride in the air, but the thinner potion they put into flaggons, whereof whosoever drinketh, observing certain ceremonies, immediately becommeth a master or rather a mistresse in that practise and faculty.

34. **Grewell.** The *Witches* have made this *Grewell* ("Potage," JB, q.v), which contains human ingredients (lines 25, 28, 31, and 32, above), not only to anoint themselves but also for consumption. *Witches* were believed to "eat the flesh and drink the bloud of men and children openly" (RS), cannibalism at the *Witches'* Sabbath being "expressly a diabolic parody of the Eucharist" (Hans Peter Broedel, *The Malleus Maleficarum and the Construction of Witchcraft*, p. 128).

34. **slab.** "Semi-solid; viscid" (OED).

35. **Chawdron.** "Entrails of a beast, esp. as used for food" (OED).

{*Witch 2.*}   Coole it with a Baboones blood,

Then the Charme is firme and good.   [40]

Enter Hecat, and the other three Witches.   [IV.i.2]

Hec.   O well done: I commend your paines,

And every one shall share i'th' gaines:

And now about the Cauldron sing

Like Elves and Fairies in a Ring,   [45]

Inchanting all that you put in.

Musicke and a Song. Blacke Spirits, &c.

{*Witch 2.*}   By the pricking of my Thumbes,

Something wicked this way comes:

Open Lockes, who ever knockes.   [50]

Enter Macbeth.   [IV.i.3]

Macb.   How now you secret, black, & midnight Hags?

What is't you do?

---

39. **Baboones.** *Baboones* "are evill manered and natured, wherfore also they are picturd to signifie wrath, they are so unapeasable. The Latins use them adjectively to signifie any angry, stubborn, froward, or ravening man" (Edward Topsell, *The Historie of Foure-Footed Beastes*).

41. **Enter Hecat, and the other three Witches.** Including *Hecat*, this stage direction brings the total number of *Witches* to seven. *Hecat and the other three Witches* are given no specific exit, so they remain on stage and actively participate in the scene until all of the *Witches* vanish in line 162, below.

45. *Elves and Fairies.* Formerly thought of as fearsome supernatural agents, an "elf" was an "imp" or "demon" (OED), while "those whome wee at this day doe call Fees, and the Italians Fate, in English the Fayries... were of the nature and number of divels" (Pierre le Loyer, *A Treatise of Specters*).

47. *Musicke and a Song. Blacke Spirits, &c.* The *Blacke Spirits Song* appears in Thomas Middleton's *The Witch* as follows:

> *A Charme Song: about a Vessell.*
> Black Spiritts, and white: Red Spiritts, and Gray,
> Mingle, Mingle, Mingle, you that mingle may.
> Titty, Tiffin: keepe it stiff in
> Fire-Drake, Puckey, make it Luckey.
> Liand, Robin, you must bob in
> Round, a-round, about, about
> All ill come runing-in, all Good keepe-out.

The song's lyricist evidently drew inspiration from Reginald Scot's *Discovery of Witchcraft*, which tells of "he-spirits and she-spirits, Titty and Tiffin, Suckin and Pidgin, Liard and Robin, &c. his white-spirits and black-spirits, gray-spirits and red-spirits."

For the connection between the music in *Macbeth* and Thomas Middleton's *The Witch*, see note: *Come away*, III.v.40.

48–49. *By the pricking of my Thumbes... comes.* Many contemporary witchcraft tracts relate stories of *Witches* offering their blood to the Devil, commonly from their *Thumbes* (see note: *Pilots Thumbe*, I.iii.31). The *Second Witch's pricking* ("cutting, launcing, piercing," RC, s.v. "Elancement") *of* her own *Thumbes* is part of a magical invocation to summon *Something wicked this way*. The *Something wicked* that approaches at the *Witch's* behest might be the apparitions that will shortly manifest (lines 80, 93, and 107, below), but the *Something wicked* could also be *Macbeth* himself.

50. *Open Lockes, who ever knockes.* Assisted by their familiars, *Witches* supposedly possessed the power to *Open Lockes*: "The Spirits of the Air of Wednesday are subject to the South-west-winde: their nature is... to open locks or bolts" (Heinrich Cornelius Agrippa von Nettesheim, *Fourth Book of Occult Philosophy*). *Witches* were so strongly associated with the opening of *Lockes* that in the vernacular "The Black Arte is picking of Lockes... the Charm is he that doth the feate" (Robert Greene, *The Second Part of Conny-Catching*).

The *Witches* have assembled at *the Pit of Acheron* (III.v.18), a locale that presumably has neither doors nor *Lockes*. However, as elaborate sets were not employed on the stage of the early modern playhouse, *Macbeth* would gain entry to the *Pit of Acheron* via one the permanent (and very ordinary) doors built into the tiring-house wall located at the back of the stage. There is no stage direction to indicate that *Macbeth* actually *knockes* to gain entry, so the *Second Witch* magically unfastens the *Lockes* and causes the door to fly *Open* in anticipation of *Macbeth's* arrival.

52. *black, & midnight. Black* means "Having dark or deadly purposes, malignant; pertaining to or involving death, deadly; baneful, disastrous, sinister" (OED); *midnight* means "As dark as midnight" (OED). *Witches* supposedly convened at *midnight* to celebrate the "*black* art" (satanic worship; see note: *three Witches*, I.i.2).

Black is also a "common adj[ective] for vulva and anus" (FR, s.v. "gown"), so there is possible additional play on *black* meaning "shit[ty]" (cf. "out olde rotten witche, As white as midnightes arsehole," Anonymous, *The Historie of Jacob and Esau*).

All {*Witches*}.   A deed without a name.

Macb.   I conjure you, by that which you Professe,   [55]

                (How ere you come to know it) answer me:

                Though you untye the Windes, and let them fight

                Against the Churches: Though the yesty Waves

                Confound and swallow Navigation up:

                Though bladed Corne be lodg'd, & Trees blown downe,   [60]

                Though Castles topple on their Warders heads:

                Though Pallaces, and Pyramids do slope

                Their heads to their Foundations: Though the treasure

                Of Natures Germaine, tumble altogether,

                Even till destruction sicken: Answer me   [65]

                To what I aske you.

---

54. ***A deed without a name.*** The *deed without a name* could be any heresy too unthinkable for words, but "The unspeakable, not to be named sexual activity has traditionally been sodomy" (FR). *Witches* were imagined as perverting the laws of God and nature (see note: *about*, I.iii.38), so in mating with demons *Witches* would supposedly "contaminate themselves with Sodomy" (Sébastien Michaelis, *The Admirable History of the Possession and Conversion of a Penitent woman*). In addition, "There were suggestions that the demon could perform coitus and pederasty (i.e. Sodomy) at once, with a third member in his lovers mouth" (Michael Ford, *Luciferian Witchcraft*, p. 101).

55. ***I conjure you, by that which you Professe.*** To *conjure* means to (a) "beseech earnestly, intreat vehemently" (RC, s.v. "Conjurer"); (b) "invoke by supernatural power" (OED); and (c) "bind by oath, or under a great penalty" (JB). *Macbeth* "conjures" the *Witches by that which* they *Professe* ("acknowledge or formally recognize as an object of faith or belief," OED)—i.e., the powers of darkness.

57. ***Though you untye the Windes.*** *Witches* supposedly possessed the power to *untye* ("loose," "sette at libertie," "release," TT, s.v. "Laxo") *the Windes*, which were associated with diabolical forces (see note: *Thunder and Lightning*, I.i.2).

In biblical metaphor, "because vehement winds are hurtful, therefore Enemies which annoy and commit devastations on the Earth are called by this appellation, especially the East-wind, which blasts Corn, and suffers it not to ripen, and if ripe, scatters and blows it down" (TDL). Cf. and see note: *bladed Corne*, line 60, below.

58–59. *yesty Waves... swallow Navigation up.* The *yesty* ("yeasty": "Foamy, frothy, like troubled water," OED) *Waves* "of the Sea denote Calamities and Punishments, because they rush upon us and are noxious, as the Waves are troublesome to Ships and Seamen" (TDL). *Macbeth* is determined to proceed despite a calamity of biblical proportions, one in which (a) the *Waves Confound* ("spoile," "ruine," "destroy," J.F., s.v. "Tracassare") *and swallow up Nagivation* ("the sea-faring trade," JF, s.v. Marinarezza"; "Also, a Navie, or Fleet," RC, s.v. "Navigage") *up*; and/or (b) the *Waves Confound* ("meddle, or mingle together," "make confuselie one of all," TT, s.v. "Confúndo") *up* and return to a state of chaos. Cf. and see note: *tumble altogether*, line 64, below.

60. *Though bladed Corne be lodg'd.* Bladed *Corne* is *Corne* "in the blade" ("as yet only blade or leaf, not yet in the ear," OED). The "lodging" ("throw[ing] down on the ground, lay[ing] flat," OED) of *bladed Corne* "by a Metaphore... signifieth any manner of great trouble, affliction, adversitie, or miserie that overthroweth a man or bringeth him under foote" (Niels Hemmingsen, *A Postill, or Exposition of the Gospels*, s.v. "Calamitie").

As in Mark 4:28 ("For the earth bringeth foorth fruite of herselfe, first the blade, then the eare, after that the full corne in the eare"), the *bladed Corne* represents the early stages of spiritual enlightenment, so its destruction signifies the Devil's blighting influence on the soul. In *Sathans Sowing Season*, William Est explains that

> Sathan is the infatigable enemy of mankinde, and that this is his perpetuall practise, by all meanes to worke our destruction. And that he may the better effect this, hee laboureth chiefly to supresse the first beginnings of godlilines, to corrupt the very seed, and to choke up the corne in the blade, that it never may growe to maturity and ripenesse.

61–63. *Though Castles topple... their Foundations.* Macbeth imagines an earthquake (a manifestation of God's avenging fury; cf. and see note: II.iii.79–80) in which *Castles topple on* the *heads* of *their Warders* (guards or keepers). The *heads* ("top[s], summit[s], upper end[s]," OED) of *Pallaces, and Pyramids* ("steeple[s] or pillar[s], broad and square beneath, and sharpe above," JB) *do slope* ("go a slope or a sconce, or a skew," "go sidelin," "stagger or go reeling," JF, s.v. "Scansare") *to their Foundations.*

63–65. *Though the treasure... destruction sicken.* Leviticus 19:19 dictates that "Thou shalt not sow thy field with mingled seed." The prohibitions of Leviticus are interpreted in many diverse ways, but a "widely accepted view of the rules concerning mixtures is that they offend against the ordering of nature as laid out in the creation story in Genesis 1" (Calum Carmichael, *Law, Legend, and Incest in the Bible: Leviticus 18–20*, p. 90). Should *the treasure* ("Heavenly and Eternal good things," TDL) *Of Natures Germaine* (seed) *tumble* ("jumble," "disorder," "marre by mingling together," "make a troublesome hotchpotch," RC, s.v. "Brouiller") *altogether* (into one mass or body), the world would suffer *destruction*. Creation would *tumble* ("overturne," JF, s.v. "Sconuólgere"; "fall downe," TT, s.v. "Vóluto") *altogether* (entirely, wholly) because it would return to chaos, the state in which it existed prior to God's giving form to the universe.

Macbeth imagines such great perversion of the natural order that the *treasure* ("genitals," GW2; also "semen," GW) *Of Natures Germaine* ("brother[s] or sister[s]," OED; "neere of kinne, of all-one race," RC, q.v.) will *tumble* ("copulate," EP) *altogether, Even till destruction* itself *sicken* ("feel faint with horror or nausea," OED).

{*Witch 1.*}   Speake.

{*Witch 2.*}   Demand.

{*Witch 3.*}   Wee'l answer.

{*Witch 1.*}   Say, if th'hadst rather heare it from our mouthes,   [70]

                   Or from our Masters.

Macb.   Call 'em: let me see 'em.

{*Witch 1.*}   Powre in Sowes blood, that hath eaten

                   Her nine Farrow: Greaze that's sweaten

                   From the Murderers Gibbet, throw   [75]

                   Into the Flame.

All {*Witches*}. Come high or low:

                   Thy Selfe and Office deaftly show.

    Thunder.

71–86. **our Masters... dismisse me.** The seeming contradiction of the *Witches* controlling the demons while the demons are at the same time the *Witches' Masters* is explained in Robert Filmer's *An Advertisement to the Jury-Men of England, Touching Witches*:

> the Witch as a slave binds himselfe by Vow to believe in the Devill, and to give him either Body, or Soule, or both under his hand Writing, or some part of his Bloud. The Divell promiseth to be ready at his vassals command to appeare in the likenesse of any Creature, to consult, and to aid him for the procuring of Pleasure, Honour, Wealth, or Preferment, to goe for him, to carry him any whither, and doe any command. Whereby we see the Devill is not to have benefit of his bargaine till the Death of the Witch, in the meane time he is to appeare alwayes at the Witches command, to go for him, to carry him any whither, and to doe any command, which argues the Devill to be the Witches slave and not the Witch the Divells.

Also see note: *He will not be commanded*, line 90, below.

73–74. **Sowes blood... Farrow.** *Sowes* have long been recognized as loving and attentive mothers and consequently symbolize "motherhood, fertility, prosperity, and happiness" (JT). Therefore, it would be extremely unnatural for a *Sowe* to eat her own *Farrow* (young pigs). The act was considered so abominable that King Kenneth II of Scotland (ca. 954–995) passed a law that "If a sow eate hir pigs, let hir be stoned to death, and buried, so that no man eate of hir flesh" (RH).

74. **nine.** See note: *nine*, I.iii.25.

74–75. **Greaze... Murderers Gibbet.** This *Greaze* ("fat," RC2; "oily or fatty matter in general," OED) has been *sweaten* ("sweated": "ooze[d] out like sweat," "exude[d]," OED) by the rotting corpse of a *Murderer* hung *From the Gibbet* ("an upright post with projecting arm from which the bodies of criminals were hung in chains or irons after execution," OED).

The suffix *-en* is the "ending of the past participle of many strong verbs" (OED), but *sweaten* is deliberately substituted for "sweated" in order to form a rhyme with *eaten* (line 73, above).

77–81. **Come high or low... unknowne power.** The entire universe, including Heaven and Hell, was thought to adhere to a strict hierarchy in which there were creatures *high* and *low*: "There are nine severall orders of angels in heaven: therefore nine severall orders of divels in hell" (John Deacon and John Walker, *A Summarie Answere to al the Material Points in any of Master Darel His Bookes*). As William Gouge explains in *The Whole Armour of God*, there are

> divers and distinct orders of Divells, one subordinate to another: as among men there be divers orders, some Kings, some Dukes, Earles, Barons, &c. Thus they make the Divell, mentioned before, the head and Monarch of all the rest: Principallities under him: powers under them, and so in the rest... The first title is Principallities, or governments: so termed, because they have great rule, power, and dominion, not so much over other Divells, as over wicked men. The second is powers, to shew that their principallitie is not a meere titular matter, but is armeed with power, so as with their powerfull government, they are able to doe great matters.

Cf. and see note: *Mercifull Powers*, II.i.14.

78. **deaftly.** *Deaftly* means "finely, neatly," "elegantly" (JM, s.v. "Garridaménte").

1. *Apparation, an Armed Head.*   [IV.i.4] [80]

Macb.   Tell me, thou unknowne power.

{*Witch 1.*}   He knowes thy thought:

                Heare his speech, but say thou nought.

1 *Appar.*   *Macbeth, Macbeth, Macbeth*:

                Beware *Macduffe*,   [85]

                Beware the Thane of Fife: dismisse me. Enough.

{*1st Apparation*} *Descends.*   [IV.i.5]

Macb.   What ere thou art, for thy good caution, thanks

                Thou hast harp'd my feare aright. But one word more.

{*Witch 1.*}   He will not be commanded: heere's another   [90]

                More potent then the first.

Thunder.

2 *Apparition, a Bloody Childe.*   [IV.i.6]

2 *Appar.*   *Macbeth, Macbeth, Macbeth.*

Macb.   Had I three eares, Il'd heare thee.   [95]

80–87. *1. Apparition, an Armed Head... Descends.* Although the words of the *Apparations* are equivocal, their visions are truthful. The *First Apparation* represents *Macbeth's Head*, which will be severed by *Macduffe* (V.vii.116). *Macbeth* does not recognize that this unearthly *Head* has his own face because it is "armed with a helmet" (RC, s.v. "Heaumé").

The built-in levels of the early modern stage (the space under the stage, the stage itself, and the balcony and "heavens" up above) symbolically corresponded to the regions of Hell, earthly existence, and Heaven. The first three diabolical apparitions (lines 80, 93, and 107) appear from under the stage, arising through the center of the cauldron via the trap door underneath it, and descending through the trap door when they disappear (lines 87, 100, and 117). By contrast, the *shew of eight Kings* (line 138, below) might take place on the balcony, which would indicate that the succession of *Banquo's* progeny is divinely ordained.

82. *He knowes thy thought.* Just as the Devil held no true power of prophecy (see notes: *why doe you start*, I.iii.57; and *prediction*, I.iii.61), neither could he read men's minds. In *An Exposition of the Lords Prayer*, William Burton states that it is impossible for Satan to

> know the thoughts of the heart... that is proper to GOD onely, who is called the searcher of the heart: but the divell doth conjecture of mens thoughts by outward signes... He observeth what every man doth most busie himselfe about, and by the outwarde fruite hee judgeth of the inwarde roote which is in the heart, and when hee knoweth the heart, he infecteth it, that it may bring forth evill actions.

Therefore, the Devil only *knowes Macbeth's thought* because the evil which he himself has planted there outwardly manifests in *Macbeth's* behavior. Cf. *harped*, line 89, below.

85–116. *Beware Macduffe... come against him.* Holinshed relates that *Macbeth* learned of certain wysardes, in whose wordes he put great confidence, (for that the prophecie had happened so right, whiche the three Fayries or weird sisters had declared unto him) how that he ought to take heede of Makduffe, who in tymes to come should seeke to destroy him. And surely hereupon had he put Makduffe to death, but that a certaine witch whom he had in great trust, had told that he should never be slain with man borne of any woman, nor vanquished till the wood of Bernane, came to the Castell of Dunsinnane. By this prophecie Makbeth put all feare out of his heart, supposing hee might doe what hee would, without any feare to be punished for the same, for by the one prophesie he beleeved it was unpossible for any man to vanquish him, and by the other unpossible to slea him. This vaine hope caused him to doe manye outragious things, to the grievous oppression of his subjects.

88. *caution.* A *caution* is (a) a "warning, putting in minde, or taking heede" (RC2, q.v.); and (b) "an assurance: an obligation, a bill of ones hand or bond of assurance: a taking heed, a testament or promise in writing" (TT, s.v. "Cautĭo"). Cf. *Bond of Fate*, line 103, below.

89. *harp'd.* To "harpe at" is "To guesse," "to speake at random, or onely by conjecture" (RC, s.v. "parler à tastons").

90. *He will not be commanded.* In *A Discourse of the subtill Practises of Devilles by Witches and Sorcerers*, George Gifford states that

> The conjurer estemeth him selfe to be a great Lord and commaunder even of devils, and in deed hath no power to do any thing further then Satan is willing and receiveth power from God, and moveth his wicked heart to deale in. This great bynder and commaunder of Devils, hath his own soule bound and commaunded by them, and is in miserable and vile captivity.

91–93. *More potent... a Bloody Childe.* The *Second Apparition* of *a Bloody Childe* represents *Macduffe*, who *was from his Mothers womb Untimely ript* (V.vii.66–67). *Macduffe* is indeed *More potent* ("Mighty, strong, able," JB) than *Macbeth*, who was depicted in the *First Apparition*.

94–95. *Macbeth, Macbeth, Macbeth... Il'd heare thee.* To "hear with both ears" is an expression meaning to listen with full attention (cf. "I must heare him with both eares, & beleve hym also," Thomas Wilson, *A Discourse uppon usurye*). The *Second Apparition* calls *Macbeth's* name *three* times, and *Macbeth* sarcastically responds by saying that he could not *heare* ("listen," "give ear," OED) any better even if he *Had three eares*.

2 *Appar.*	Be bloody, bold, & resolute:
	Laugh to scorne
	The powre of man: For none of woman borne
	Shall harme *Macbeth*.

{*2nd Apparition*} *Descends.*   [IV.i.7] [100]

Mac.	Then live *Macduffe*: what need I feare of thee?
	But yet Ile make assurance: double sure,
	And take a Bond of Fate: thou shalt not live,
	That I may tell pale-hearted Feare, it lies;
	And sleepe in spight of Thunder. [105]

Thunder

3 *Apparation, a Childe Crowned, with a Tree in his hand.*   [IV.i.8]

	What is this, that rises like the issue of a King,
	And weares upon his Baby-brow, the round
	And top of Soveraignty? [110]
All {*Witches*}.	Listen, but speake not too't.
3 *Appar.*	Be Lyon metled, proud, and take no care:
	Who chafes, who frets, or where Conspirers are:
	Macbeth shall never vanquish'd be, untill
	Great Byrnam Wood, to high Dunsmane Hill [115]
	Shall come against him.

98–99. ***none of woman borne Shall harme Macbeth.*** See notes: *Beware Macduffe*, line 85, above; and V.vii.66–67.

102–103. ***Ile make assurance... a Bond of Fate.*** The second prophecy gives *Macbeth* cause for *assurance* ("Audacity, brazen self-confidence," DPF). Nevertheless, *Macbeth* wishes to be *double* (an adverb meaning "doubly": "in two ways or respects; twice, twice over," OED) *sure* ("without doubt," TT, s.v. "Certus") that he is *sure* ("safe, out of daunger, defended from perill," TT, s.v. "Tūtus"). In order to "give himself *assurance*" ("make [himself] sure or certain," JB, s.v. "Assecure") that *Macduffe* can never harm him, *Macbeth* seeks *assurance* ("securitie for a debt," RC, s.v. "Garnissement"; "a pledge," JM, s.v. "Catión"). By killing *Macduffe*, *Macbeth* will *take a Bond* ("take securitie or warrantise," RC, s.v. "Exciper"; make "a demaunding for the performance of covenants," RC, s.v. "Stipulation") *of* ("from," OED) *Fate* ("Death," OED).

103. ***thou.*** I.e., *Macduffe.*

105. ***Thunder.*** *Thunder* "is a witnesse of Gods power, and serveth to strike terrour and feare in men; that the godly may bee humbled, and the better subdued unto God; and the wicked confounded and left without excuse" (TW). Cf. and see note: *blast,* I.vii.26.

107. ***3. Apparation... a Tree in his hand.*** The *Third Apparation* represents *Malcolme,* the *Childe* of *Duncane. Malcolme* will defeat *Macbeth* by using the foliage of *Byrnam Wood* (line 115, below) to camouflage the approach of his army (V.iv.10–13), after which he will be *Crowned* King of Scotland.

109–110. ***weares... round And top of Soveraignty.*** The *round* is the "crown" (cf. *Golden Round,* I.v.29), which signifies that the infant *weares* ("possess[es] and enjoy[s]," HH, p. 117) the *top* ("The highest pitch or degree," OED) *of Soveraignty.*

112. ***Lyon metled.*** *Macbeth* should possess the "mettle" ("stoutnesse, courage," "boldnesse, resolution, hardinesse," RC, s.v. "Animosité") of a *Lyon,* a traditional symbol of "royal authority, strength, courage" as well as "cruelty, ferocity, and death" (JT).

112–113. ***take no care... who frets.*** *Macbeth* should *take no care* (give no regard, take no heed of) *Who* is "in a chafe" ("Angrie, troubled, offended, greatly mooved," TT, s.v. "Irātus") or *who frets* ("rage[s]"; is "angrie, raging, or furious," JF, s.v. "Stizzarsi").

115. ***high Dunsmane Hill.*** According to Holinshed, *Macbeth* "buylded a strong Castell on the top of an high hill cleped Dunsinnane situate in Gowry, ten myles from Perth." (Although *Dunsmane* might be a typographical error for "Dunsinane," it could be a bona-fide variant: a similar spelling occurs in Holinshed where he describes "Dunsman castell builded.")

{*3rd Apparation Descends.*}   [IV.i.9]

Macb.   That will never bee:

Who can impresse the Forrest, bid the Tree

Unfixe his earth-bound Root? Sweet boadments, good: [120]

Rebellious dead, rise never till the Wood

Of Byrnan rise, and our high plac'd *Macbeth*

Shall live the Lease of Nature, pay his breath

To time, and mortall Custome. Yet my Hart

Throbs to know one thing: Tell me, if your Art   [125]

Can tell so much: Shall *Banquo's* issue ever

Reigne in this Kingdome?

All {*Witches*}.   Seeke to know no more.

Macb.   I will be satisfied. Deny me this,

And an eternall Curse fall on you: Let me know.   [130]

Why sinkes that Caldron? & what noise is this?

    Hoboyes

{*Witch 1.*}   Shew.

            {*Witch 2.*}   {*Witch 3.*}

            Shew.   Shew.   [135]

All {*Witches*}.   Shew his Eyes, and greeve his Hart,

Come like shadowes, so depart.

119. **impresse.** To "force authoritatively into service" (OED).

120. **boadments.** Omens, prophecies, or predictions.

121–122. **Rebellious dead... Byrnan rise.** Those who are *Rebellious* ("seditious," "mutinous," JF, s.v. "Seditioso") against *Macbeth* will *never rise* ("take up arms," "make an attack," OED) *till the Wood Of Byrnan rise*—i.e., not *till* doomsday, when the *dead* shall *rise* ("return to life," "come back from the dead," OED). Cf. and see note: *cracke of Doome*, line 145, below.

122. **high plac'd.** *Macbeth* is *high plac'd* in that he (a) holds a *high* (exalted, important) "place" ("social rank or status," OED); and (b) dwells in a *high* ("far up; having a lofty position," OED) "place" (location). Cf. and see note: *high Dunsmane Hill*, line 115, above.

123–124. **Lease of Nature... mortall Custome.** *Macbeth's* "*Lease* on life" will not expire prematurely, for he will only *pay* (deliver, hand over) *his breath* (life, spirit) to *pay* ("discharge a debt," "satisfy a creditor," JJ) those to whom his debt is due. His only creditors are the *time* ("prescribed or allotted term," OED) of his *time* ("period of one's life, life-time," OED), and the "customary" (usual) natural death which is the *Custome* ("a rent and yearly revenue," TT, s.v. "Vectīgal") of all who are *mortall*. Cf. "Since his lifes calender is out of date, / And deaths new-yeare exactes his custom'd fee, / No more a man, nor mortall now is hee" (Charles Fitz-Geffry, *Sir Francis Drake, His Honorable lifes commendation, and his Tragicall Deathes lamentation*). Also cf. *Natures Coppie's*, III.ii.48.

131. **Why sinkes that Caldron.** The earth opens up as the *Caldron sinkes* ("descend[s] into hell," OED). In the early modern playhouse, this special effect would have been accomplished by lowering the *Caldron* through the trap door on the stage.

131. **noise.** Both (a) a "dinne"; and (b) "a tune, musicke, melodie" (RC, s.v. "Son").

132. **Hoboyes.** See note: *Hoboyes*, I.vi.2.

137. **Come like shadowes, so depart.** The *Witches* enjoin the spirits to *Come like* (in the form of) *shadowes* (apparitions or visions; see note: *shadow*, III.iv.133), and to *depart so* ("in that style or fashion," OED).

A shew of eight Kings, and Banquo last, with a glasse

in his hand.   [IV.i.10]

Macb.   Thou art too like the Spirit of *Banquo*: Down: [140]

Thy Crowne do's seare mine Eye-bals. And thy haire

Thou other Gold-bound-brow, is like the first:

A third, is like the former. Filthy Hagges,

Why do you shew me this?— A fourth? Start eyes!

---

138. *A shew of eight Kings*. *Banquo* and his son *Fleans* were not, in fact, real people (see note: *Your Children shall be Kings*, I.iii.95). Nevertheless, Holinshed meticu-
lously traces the royal descendants of these mythical forefathers of the Stuart line,
relating that

> Fleaunce... fled into Wales, where shortly after by his curteous and amiable
> behaviour, he grew into such favour and estimation with the prince of that coun-
> trey... at length also he came into such familiar acquaintance with the sayd
> princes daughter, that she of courtesie in the ende suffred him to get hir with
> childe: whiche being once understood, hyr father the prince conceyved such
> hatefull displeasure towardes Fleaunce, that he finally slewe him, and helde his
> daughter in moste vile estate of servitude, for that she had consented to be on
> this wise defloured by a straunger.
>
> At the last yet, she was delivered of a sonne named Walter, who within few
> yeares proved a man of greater courage and valiancie, than any other had com-
> monly bene founde, although he had no better bringing up than (by his graun-
> dfathers appointment) amongst the baser sorte of people... It chaunced that
> falling out with one of his companions, after many taunting woordes which
> passed betwixt them, the other to his reproch objected that he was a bastard, &
> begotten in unlawfull bed, wherewith being sore kindled, in his raging furie he
> ran upon him & slew him out of hand.
>
> Then was he glad to flee out of Wales, and comming into Scotland to seeke
> some frendshippe there, he happened into the companie of suche Englishmen,
> as were come thither with Queene Margaret, & behaved himself so soberly in
> all his demeanour, that within a while he was highly esteemed amongst them.
>
> Not long after by such meanes atteyning to the degree of high reputation, he
> was sent with a great power of men into the Westerne Isles, into Galloway, and
> other partes of the realme, to deliver the same of the tirannie and injurious
> oppression there exercised by divers misgoverned persons: which enterpryse
> according to his commission, he atchieved with such prudent policie & man-

hoode, that immediatly upon his returne to the court, he was made lord Steward of Scotland, with assignement to receyve the kings rents & dueties out of all the partes of the realme.

    This Walter Stewarde… had issue .ii. sonnes, the one named Alexander… and the other named Robert Steward… Alexander Steward… had divers mo sonnes, as John & James… John Stewarde, after the death of his brother James, maried the heyre of Bonkill a virgine of great beautie, and had by hyr Walter Steward that inherited the landes of Bonkill, Ranfrew, Rothessay, Bute, & Stewartoune… He maried Marjorie Bruce daughter to king Robert Bruce, by whom he had issue king Robert the second of that name.

Therefore, Robert II (1316–1390) is the first of the *eight Kings* of Scotland who appears as a *shew* ("A phantasmal appearance; an apparition," OED) in this *shew* ("a pageant, masque, procession, or similar display on a large scale," OED). The others are: Robert III (ca. 1337–1406); James I (1394–1437); James II (1430–1460); James III (ca. 1451–1488); James IV (1473–1513); James V (1512–1542); and James VI (1566–1625), for whom *The Tragedie of Macbeth* was written (see note: *three Witches*, I.i.2).

In point of fact, James VI was not the eighth but the ninth Scottish monarch directly descended from Robert II, but Shakespeare purposely omits Mary I (1542–1587), the daughter of James V. Due to Mary's Catholicism, sexual escapades, and political intrigues, she was not very popular with many Englishman, many Scotsmen, or her own son, James VI (who became king at the age of one when the Scottish nobility forced his mother to abdicate). Mary was imprisoned and eventually executed by her cousin, Elizabeth I of England. The "Virgin Queen" Elizabeth had no children of her own, so upon her death her cousin James VI of Scotland became James I of England. See note: *trebble Scepters*, line 149, below.

    138–147. *Banquo last, with a glasse… beares a glasse.* As indicated by the stage direction of lines 138–139 and *Macbeth's* description in line 147, both *Banquo* and the eighth *King* hold *a glasse* ("A glass mirror, a looking-glass," OED; mirrors were used in divination to predict future events). These two mirrors, if held facing each other with the *Kings* between them, would create the optical illusion of an infinite *Line* of *Kings* stretching *out to'th' cracke of Doome* (line 145).

    140. *Spirit.* With play on *Spirit* meaning (a) "A person considered in relation to his character or disposition" (OED); (b) an erect penis (see note: *spirit*, I.ii.70); and (c) semen (see note: *Spirits*, I.v.27).

    140. *Down.* With play on *Down* meaning to "abate an erection" (GW2, s.v. "take down").

    141. *Thy Crowne do's seare mine Eye-bals.* *Macbeth's Eye-bals* are "seared" (blighted, burned) by the sight of *Banquo's* descendants wearing the *Crowne*. The *Kings'* existence testifies to the virility of *Banquo's Crowne* (genitals; see note: *Crowne*, I.v.49) and also causes *Macbeth's Eye-bals* ("testes," FR) to *seare* ("dry up," "wither away," OED).

    141–142. *thy haire Thou other.* *Haire* was pronounced identically to "air" and "heir." The *other* ("That follows the first; second," OED) "heir" has inherited his predecessor's "air" (demeanor, bearing) as well as his *haire* ("In general, hairs represent energy… Hairs also signify fertility," JC).

    143. *former.* With play on *former* meaning (a) "that goeth, or is set, before" (RC, s.v. "Anterieur"); (b) "a senior, an ancestor," "a preceding man," (JF, s.v. "Priore"); and (c) "One who forms or gives form to something" (OED).

What will the Line stretch out to'th' cracke of Doome?   [145]

Another yet? A seaventh? Ile see no more:

And yet the eight appeares, who beares a glasse,

Which shewes me many more: and some I see,

That two-fold Balles, and trebble Scepters carry.

Horrible sight: Now I see 'tis true,   [150]

For the Blood-bolter'd *Banquo* smiles upon me,

And points at them for his. What? is this so?

{*Witch 1.*}   I Sir, all this is so. But why

Stands *Macbeth* thus amazedly?

Come Sisters, cheere we up his sprights,   [155]

And shew the best of our delights.

Ile Charme the Ayre to give a sound,

While you performe your Antique round:

That this great King may kindly say,

Our duties, did his welcome pay.   [160]

Musicke.

---

145. **will the Line stretch out... Doome.** *Banquo's Line* (race, descendants) *will stretch out to'th' cracke* ("the roar... of a trumpet," OED) *of Doome* ("judgement," RC, s.v. "Jugement") — i.e., until doomsday, when "the trumpet shall sound, and the dead shall be raised incorruptible" (1 Corinthians 15:52).

If *Banquo's Line* (pronounced as "loin," HK, p. 125; "loins" are "the pubic regions of male lovers, with obvious emphasis on their penises," JH, s.v. "lines") can *stretch out* (with innuendo of phallic erection, FR) *to'th' cracke* ("The female pudendum," F&H) *of Doome,* then it is certainly long enough to "bugger" *Macbeth* in *th' cracke* (i.e., the "cracker": "Arse," ND). Given the connection between sodomy and flatulence (see note: *rore,* I.vii.92), *Macbeth* probably imagines *th' cracke of Doome* as a *cracke* ("fart; scape, tayle-shot," RC, s.v. "Pet").

Macbeth also entertains the notion that *th' cracke of Doome* is merely a *cracke* ("boast, brag," OED; also "A lie," F&H) made by a *cracke* ("crazy person, or soft-head," F&H). Cf. V.v.32–34.

147. **the eight.** *Eight* is a spelling variant of "eighth" (OED). In Shakespeare's time, a terminal "th" was pronounced as a "t" (HK, p. 320), so *eight* and "eighth" were pronounced identically. Cf. the Folio's spelling of the play entitled "*The Famous History of the Life of King Henry the Eight.*"

148–149. **some I see... trebble Scepters carry.** *Some* of *Banquo's* descendants *carry two-fold Balles* ("golden orb[s] carried as part of a monarch's regalia," OED), which might signify (a) the *two* coronation ceremonies of James VI of Scotland and I of England (the first at Scone in Scotland, the second at Westminster in England); or (b) James' rule over the *two* islands of Great Britain and Ireland.

The *trebble Scepters* indicate that *some* of *Banquo's* progeny will rule as does James VI, "whose hand a thre-fold scepter swayes...[and] keps three kingdoms in so still a peace" (William Mure, "The Kings Majestie came to Hamilton on Monday the XXVIII July [1617]"). The three kingdoms are probably England, Scotland, and Ireland. However, as James maintained a claim to the French throne, the *trebble Scepters* might represent Great Britain, Ireland, and France.

Obviously, *Banquo's* descendants also confirm the potency of his *two-fold Balles* ("two testicles," FR), *and trebble Scepters* (allusive of the male genitalia; see notes: *three things,* II.iii.35; and *Scepter,* III.i.76).

151. **the Blood-bolter'd Banquo.** *Banquo,* who is covered with *Blood,* is *bolter'd* ("balter[ed]": "clot[ted] or clog[ged] with anything sticky," OED). Also, his hair is *bolter'd* ("balter[ed]": "tangle[d]," "mat[ted]," OED) by *Blood* (cf. *goary lockes,* III.iv.68). Nevertheless, *Banquo's* "bolt" ("Penis," FR; literally "A blunt arrow," FG) has *bolter'd* ("tumble[d] about," OED, where "tumble" means copulate; see note: *tumble,* line 64, above). Consequently, *Banquo* is *bolter'd* (i.e., "bolstered": supported, assisted, upheld) by his *Blood* (descendants, progeny). (OED omits both "bolter" and "bolster" as spelling variants of "ba[u]lter," but cf. "Me thinks I see them with their bolstred haire," Anonymous, *The Lamentable and True Tragedie of M. Arden of Feversham in Kent*).

155. **sprights.** Variant of "spirits" (OED).

157. **the Ayre.** With play on *Ayre* meaning "a melody."

157. **a sound.** "A song," "a tune," "melodie" (TT, s.v. "Cantus").

158. **Antique round.** The *Witches* will dance a *round* (circular dance) that is *Antique* (variant spelling of "antic": "grotesque, bizarre, uncouthly ludicrous," OED). See note: *about,* I.iii.38.

159–160. **kindly... did his welcome pay.** The *Witches pay* their *duties* ("payment[s] due," OED) to *Macbeth kindly* (properly, suitably) by performing a dance. *Macbeth* has not outwardly given the *Witches* a particularly warm *welcome* (cf. lines 52, 129–130, and 143, above), but he has certainly welcomed their evil into his heart. Cf. and see notes: *insane Root,* I.iii.93; *Thought,* I.iii.157; and *He knowes thy thought,* line 82, above.

The Witches Dance, and vanish.   [IV.i.11]

Macb.   Where are they? Gone?

Let this pernitious houre,

Stand aye accursed in the Kalender.   [165]

Come in, without there.

Enter Lenox.   [IV.i.12]

Lenox.   What's your Graces will.

Macb.   Saw you the Weyard Sisters?

Lenox.   No my Lord.   [170]

Macb.   Came they not by you?

Lenox.   No indeed my Lord.

Macb.   Infected be the Ayre whereon they ride,

And damn'd all those that trust them. I did heare

The gallopping of Horse. Who was't came by?   [175]

Len.   'Tis two or three my Lord, that bring you word:

Macduff is fled to England.

Macb.   Fled to England?

Len.   I, my good Lord.

Macb.   Time, thou anticipat'st my dread exploits: [180]

The flighty purpose never is o're-tooke

Unlesse the deed go with it. From this moment,

162. **Witches Dance.** It was believed that "at these magicall assemblies, the witches never faile to dance; and in their dance they sing these words; Har har, devill devill, dance here, dance here, play here, play here, Sabbath, sabbath. And whiles they sing and dance, every one hath a broom in her hand, and holdeth it up aloft" (RS). Cf. and see note: *about,* I.iii.38.

165. **aye.** In the Folio, Shakespeare never uses the spelling *aye* to indicate the word that means "yes" (see note: *I,* II.ii.27). *Aye* means "Ever, always, continually" (OED, which notes that the "word rhymes, in the literary speech, and in all the dialects, with the group *bay, day, gay, hay, may, way*").

166. **Come in, without.** *Lenox* has been waiting *without* (outside) the place where *Macbeth* has met with the *Witches*. On the early modern stage, *Lenox* would actually have waited "within" the tiring-house. See notes: *within,* I.ii.2; and *Open Lockes,* line 50, above.

173. **Infected be the Ayre... ride.** If the *Witches* departed by natural means, they would have passed *Lenox* on their way out. Because *Lenox* did not see them, they must have ridden on *the Ayre* (which *Witches* were thought to literally "infect"; cf. and see note: *filthie ayre,* I.i.13).

177. **Macduff is fled to England.** *Lenox* has known for some time that *Macduff is fled to England* (cf. III.vi.26–34 and 51–53), but he only relays this information to *Macbeth* after others have officially delivered the news.

180–182. **Time, thou anticipat'st... the deed go with it.** By hesitating, *Macbeth* has allowed *Macduff* to escape beyond his reach. Because *Macbeth* delayed killing *Macduff,* *Time* has "anticipated" ("prevented," RC, s.v. "Anticipé") *Macbeth's dread* (fearful, terrible) *exploits* ("Carrying[s] out, execution[s], performance[s]," OED). *Macbeth* now knows that *The flighty* ("Swift, quicke," "speedie, nimble," RC, s.v. "Viste") *purpose* (aim, object) is always "in flight" ("running away," JM, s.v. "Fŭga"). It *is never o're-tooke* ("reached unto, gotten, purchased, obtained, compassed," JM, s.v. "Alcançádo") *Unlesse the deed* ("doing, performance," OED) *go with* ("accompanie," "keepe fellowshippe with," TT, s.v. "Cŏmĭtor") *it.*

The very firstlings of my heart shall be

The firstlings of my hand. And even now

To Crown my thoughts with Acts: be it thoght & done: [185]

The Castle of *Macduff*, I will surprize.

Seize upon Fife; give to th' edge o'th' Sword

His Wife, his Babes, and all unfortunate Soules

That trace him in his Line. No boasting like a Foole,

This deed Ile do, before this purpose coole,   [190]

But no more sights. Where are these Gentlemen?

Come bring me where they are.

Exeunt

183–184. ***firstlings of my heart... hand.*** The *firstlings* ("The first fruites of the yeare, that are offered unto God," TT, s.v. "Prĭmĭtiæ") are God's due as per Proverbs 3:9: "Honour the LORD with thy substance, and with the first fruits of all thine increase." *Macbeth* has long since abandoned God, but he here renounces even the sovereignty of his own reason. From now own, the *firstlings of* his *heart* (regarded as the seat of passion and desire) will immediately spring to his *hand* without any intervention from moderating reason or conscience.

186. ***The Castle of Macduff, I will surprize.*** According to Holinshed, when *Macbeth* was

> advertised whereabout Makduffe went, he came hastily wyth a great power into Fife, and forthwith besieged the Castell where Makduffe dwelled, trusting to have found him therin. They that kept the house, without any resistance opened the gates, and suffred him to enter, mistrusting none evill. But neverthelesse Makbeth most cruelly caused the wife and children of Makduffe, with all other whom he found in that castell, to be slaine.

189. ***trace.*** Follow.

191. ***sights.*** *Sights* can mean (a) "Mental or spiritual vision[s]" (OED); (b) horrifying spectacles (see note: *sight*, II.ii.30); and/or (c) "Care[s] or sorrow[s]; grief[s]; trouble[s] of any kind" (OED, s.v. "site").

191. ***these Gentlemen.*** *These Gentlemen* are the *two or three* messengers who have brought word of *Macduff's* flight to England (lines 176–177, above).

Act IV, scene ii

Scena Secunda.   [1]

Enter Macduffes Wife, her Son, and Rosse.   [IV.ii.1]

Wife.   What had he done, to make him fly the Land?

Rosse.   You must have patience Madam.

Wife.   He had none: [5]

                  His flight was madnesse: when our Actions do not,

                  Our feares do make us Traitors.

Rosse.   You know not

                  Whether it was his wisedome, or his feare.

Wife.   Wisedom? to leave his wife, to leave his Babes,   [10]

                  His Mansion, and his Titles, in a place

                  From whence himselfe do's flye? He loves us not,

                  He wants the naturall touch. For the poore Wren

                  (The most diminitive of Birds) will fight,

                  Her yong ones in her Nest, against the Owle: [15]

                  All is the Feare, and nothing is the Love;

                  As little is the Wisedome, where the flight

                  So runnes against all reason.

Rosse.   My deerest Cooz,

                  I pray you schoole your selfe. But for your Husband,   [20]

Notes IV.ii.

6–7. *when our Actions do not... make us Traitors.* Although *Macduffe's Actions* (deeds) *do not make* him a *Traitor* to his country, his *feares* have made him a *Traitor* to his family. Cf. lines 56–59, below.

11. *Mansion.* "An house," "habitation, dwelling, place of aboade" (RC, s.v. "Domicile").

11. *Titles.* A "title" is an "an interest or propertie in, a thing; a mans due; that which either he hath, or should have" (RC, s.v. "Droict").

13. *naturall touch.* A *touch* ("feeling," JF, s.v. "Tocco") that is *naturall* ("bred in by nature," TT, s.v. "Ingĕnĭtus"; "good, honest, just and righteous," TT, s.v. "pius").

13–15. *the poore Wren... the Owle.* *Macduffes Wife* thinks her husband has disgraced himself, for even the *diminitive* ("Little," "Petty," HC, q.v.) *Wren* will defend its *yong ones against the Owle*, a fierce predator. (Although heartfelt, *Macduffes Wife's* metaphor has no basis in ornithology: *the Owle* hunts other birds in flight, not in the *Nest*.)

20. *schoole.* Both (a) "To discipline" (RC, s.v. "Discipliner"); and (b) "To checke," "reprove" (RC, s.v. "Rabroüer").

He is Noble, Wise, Judicious, and best knowes

The fits o'th' Season. I dare not speake much further,

But cruell are the times, when we are Traitors

And do not know our selves: when we hold Rumor

From what we feare, yet know not what we feare,   [25]

But floate upon a wilde and violent Sea

Each way, and move. I take my leave of you:

22. *fits.* *Fits* can mean (a) "Opportunitie[s]," "convenience[s] of time and place" (TT, s.v. "Opportūnĭtas"); (b) "hardship[s], danger[s]" (OED); and/or (c) lunacies, insanities (see note: *fitfull*, III.ii.31).

22. *Season.* The current time; this occasion.

23–24. *when we are Traitors... know our selves.* *Macduffe* does not *know* ("perceive, acknowledge, or understand," OED) that he is a "traitor" to either his country or to his family.

24–27. *when we hold Rumor... Each way, and move.* Modern readers accustomed to standardized spelling tend to perceive *Rumor* solely as "General talk, report, or hearsay, not based upon definite knowledge" (OED). However, it is highly unlikely that this sense comes into play in this passage.

Rumor is here a variant spelling of "roomer," an old nautical term meaning "Farther off; at or to a greater distance" (*Lloyd's Encyclopædic Dictionary*, q.v.). "Roomer" was used to describe the movements of a ship specifically when a vessel was (a) forced off-course (cf. "there came such a storme, that the ship was forced with wether to goe roomer 800. miles," Richard Hakluyt, *The Principal Navigations, Voyages, Traffiques and Discoveries of the English Nation*); and (b) under threat and forced to take evasive action (cf. "it putte our shippes at sea in no small perill: for having mountaines of fleeting Ise on every side, we went romer for one, & loofed for another, some scraped us, & some happily escaped us," George Best, *A True Discourse of the late voyages of discoverie*).

Rosse's nautical metaphor is particularly apt, for *Macduffe* has been forced to *fly the Land* (line 3, above) in order *t' hold what distance His wisedome can provide* (III.vi.50–51). *Macduffes Wife* considers her husband's flight an act of betrayal, but *Rosse* reminds her that *Macduffe* had little choice in the matter. In order to avoid immediate destruction, *Macduffe* must *hold* "roomer" (abruptly change direction, or travel far off-course like a ship carried by an adverse wind).

The instinct for self-preservation causes us to *hold* "roomer" (flee or change direction in order to escape) *From what we feare.* However, if *we know* (understand) *not what we feare* (i.e., are unsure of our enemy's next move, or exactly from which direction the next attack will come), then *we* are apt to be "at sea" ("Puzzled," F&H). In such a state, *we* imagine threats coming from all directions and so constantly *hold* "roomer" (change course, or "tack about before the wind," *Lloyd's Encyclopædic Dictionary*). Like a ship *upon a wilde* ("cruel, terrible, fierce," TT, s.v. "Fĕrus") *and violent* ("rough, stormy, tempestuous," OED) *Sea,* we are "adrift" ("driven at random by the winds," DPF). Because *we* cannot control our course, *we floate* ("vacillate, waver," OED; "move unsteadily to and fro like an object on the surface of a liquid," OED) *Each* (every) *way, and move,* which means (a) "To depart, start off" (OED); (b) "to change from one place, position, or situation to another; to shift, remove" (OED); (c) "To keep in continuous or regular motion" (OED); and (d) "to be unstable, or unsure" (TE, s.v. "Vacillo").

(Although the nautical term "roomer" was in common use from the sixteenth through the nineteenth centuries, OED completely omits this word, defining "roomer" only as "A lodger who occupies a room or rooms without board" dating from 1859. OED also omits "roomer" as a variant spelling of *Rumor,* but examples of this are also readily found. The etymology of "roomer" is unknown, but, as sailors inevitably think of their ships as female, it is possible that the word arose from a terse command to "Room her," or "Room 'er"—i.e., "Give her more room.")

Shall not be long but Ile be heere againe:

Things at the worst will cease, or else climbe upward,

To what they were before. My pretty Cosine,   [30]

Blessing upon you.

Wife.   Father'd he is,

And yet hee's Father-lesse.

Rosse.   I am so much a Foole, should I stay longer

It would be my disgrace, and your discomfort.   [35]

I take my leave at once.

Exit Rosse.   [IV.ii.2]

Wife.   Sirra, your Fathers dead,

And what will you do now? How will you live?

Son.   As Birds do Mother.   [40]

Wife.   What with Wormes, and Flyes?

Son.   With what I get I meane, and so do they.

Wife.   Poore Bird,

Thou'dst never Feare the Net, nor Lime,

The Pitfall, nor the Gin.   [45]

Son.   Why should I Mother?

Poore Birds they are not set for:

My Father is not dead for all your saying.

28–35. *Ile be heere againe... your discomfort.* *Rosse* is on his way to join *Macduffe* in *England*, so he hopes to soon *be heere againe* as part of an invading army (cf. IV.iii.211–218). Should *Rosse* not join the effort to overthrow *Macbeth*, *It would be* his *disgrace* (dishonor, with possible play on *disgace* as emasculation; see notes: *Grace*, I.iii.61; and *shame*, III.iv.84). *Rosse* thinks that *Macduffes Wife* and children are safe from *Macbeth* because they pose no threat to him. However, if *Macbeth* learns that *Macduffes Wife* harbors *Rosse*, *It would be* her *discomfort* ("misfortune," "Griefe, sorrow, trouble," RC, "Desconvenuë"; *discomfort* was also "confused with 'discomfit'": "undoing," OED).

29. *Things at the worst will cease.* Proverbial: cf. "Things at the worst, the proverbe saith will mend / why should not then my sorrowes have an end" (Henry Chillester, *Youthes Witte*).

30–31. *My pretty Cosine, Blessing.* *Rosse* offers *Blessing* to *Macduffe's Son*, who is *pretty* ("Little, small," "young," RC, s.v. "Petit").

32–33. *Father'd he is... Father-lesse.* *Macduffe's Son* is *Father-lesse* (lacking a father) just as if he were not *Father'd* (i.e., a bastard, an unrecognized illegitimate child).

40–42. *As Birds do... With what I get.* *Macduffe's Son* puts his trust in providence in accordance with Matthew 6:26: "Behold the foules of the aire: for they sow not, neither do they reape, nor gather into barnes, yet our heavenly father feedeth them."

43–45. *Poore Bird, Thou'dst never Feare... the Gin.* Proverbially, "Th'old bird is not (easily) intrapped" (RC, s.v. "Vieil oiseau ne se prend à reths"), but *Macduffe's Son* is a young and *Poore* ("hapless," OED) *Bird* ("A young man, youngster, child, son," OED). Because he is innocent, he does not suspect *The Pitfall* ("A hidden or unsuspected danger," OED), *nor the Gin* ("a deceit or subtill craft," TT, s.v. "Transenna"; "Some secret assault of an enemy," TW, s.v. "snare"). *Macduffe's Son* will therefore *never Feare the Net*, *nor Lime* ("A viscous sticky substance prepared from the bark of the holly and used for catching small birds," OED), *The Pitfall* ("A trap for catching birds, in which a trapdoor falls over a cavity or hollow," OED), *nor the Gin* ("a snare or nooze, to catch Birds," ND).

The words of *Macduffes Wife* recall Ecclesiastes 9:12: "as the birds are caught in the snare; so are the sonnes of men snared in an evill time, when it falleth suddenly upon them."

47. *Poore Birds they are not set for.* Traps *are set for* valuable *Birds*, *not for Poore* (worthless) ones. Therefore, as a *Poore Bird*, *Macduffe's Son* feels he has no need to fear.

Wife.   Yes, he is dead:

How wilt thou do for a Father?   [50]

Son.   Nay how will you do for a Husband?

Wife.   Why I can buy me twenty at any Market.

Son.   Then you'l by 'em to sell againe.

Wife.   Thou speak'st withall thy wit,

And yet I'faith with wit enough for thee.   [55]

Son.   Was my Father a Traitor, Mother?

Wife.   I, that he was.

Son.   What is a Traitor?

Wife.   Why one that sweares, and lyes.

Son.   And be all Traitors, that do so.   [60]

Wife.   Every one that do's so, is a Traitor,

And must be hang'd.

Son.   And must they all be hang'd, that swear and lye?

Wife.   Every one.

Son.   Who must hang them?   [65]

Wife.   Why, the honest men.

Son.   Then the Liars and Swearers are Fools: for there

are Lyars and Swearers enow, to beate the honest men,

and hang up them.

52–53. *buy me twenty… sell againe.* A woman (a) who bought husbands in such great quantity would want them only for resale; or (b) could not *buy* so many husbands without "selling" ("betray[ing]," F&H) some of 'em.

54–55. *Thou speak'st withall thy wit… enough for thee.* In an attempt at *wit* (cleverness), *Macduffe's Son* has exhausted his small store of *wit* (intellect); cf. "tis pittie a foole cannot have a little witte, but hee will spende it all in a fewe wordes" (Nicholas Breton, *A Poste With a packet of madde Letters*). Nevertheless, *Macduffes Wife* must admit that her *Son* has *wit enough* (sufficient for his purpose).

58–59. *a Traitor… sweares, and lyes.* Technically, *Macduffe* is not *a Traitor* to *Macbeth* because he has not sworn allegiance to him (see note: II.iv.53). *Macduffe* has, however, sworn a marital vow to his wife, which she now considers broken.

68. *enow.* See note: *enow*, II.iii.11.

Wife.	Now God helpe thee, poore Monkie: [70]
	But how wilt thou do for a Father?
Son.	If he were dead, youl'd weepe for him: if you
	would not, it were a good signe, that I should quickely
	have a new Father.
Wife.	Poore pratler, how thou talk'st? [75]

Enter a Messenger.   [IV.ii.3]

Mes.	Blesse you faire Dame: I am not to you known,
	Though in your state of Honor I am perfect;
	I doubt some danger do's approach you neerely.
	If you will take a homely mans advice, [80]
	Be not found heere: Hence with your little ones
	To fright you thus. Me thinkes I am too savage:
	To do worse to you, were fell Cruelty,
	Which is too nie your person. Heaven preserve you,
	I dare abide no longer. [85]

Exit Messenger   [IV.ii.4]

Wife.	Whether should I flye?
	I have done no harme. But I remember now
	I am in this earthly world: where to do harme
	Is often laudable, to do good sometime [90]

70. **Monkie.** *Monkie* is (a) "an endearment" (F&H); (b) "the Devil; an imp of mischief. Hence, a meddlesome child" (DPF); and (c) "a ninnie, a foole" (JF, s.v. "Babbione").

78. **state of Honor.** Either her (a) *state* (social position) *of Honor* (exalted rank); or (b) *state* (condition) *of Honor* (virtue, purity)—i.e. her lack of treachery.

78. **perfect.** Thoroughly acquainted (cf. and see note: *perfect*, III.i.160).

79. **doubt.** Fear.

80. **homely.** "Plaine," "ordinarie" (RC, s.v. "Gobier"); "poor," "simple," "of the common sorte" (TT, s.v. "Plēbēiūs").

82. **fright.** Possibly here used in the sense "To scare away" (OED).

82. **Me thinkes.** See note: *Me thought*, II.ii.46.

83. **To do worse to you.** This line suggests that the *Messenger* is a renegade member of the party sent to attack *Macduffe's* castle.

Accounted dangerous folly. Why then (alas)

Do I put up that womanly defence,

To say I have done no harme?

What are these faces?

Enter Murtherers.   [IV.ii.5] [95]

{*1.*} *Mur.*   Where is your Husband?

Wife.   I hope in no place so unsanctified,

          Where such as thou may'st finde him.

{*1.*} *Mur.*   He's a Traitor.

Son.   Thou ly'st thou shagge-ear'd Villaine.   [100]

{*1.*} *Mur.*   What you Egge?

          Yong fry of Treachery?

Son.   He ha's kill'd me Mother,

          Run away I pray you.

{*Son dies.*} *Exit* {*Macduffes Wife*} *crying Murther.*   [105]

{*Exeunt.*}

92. **womanly.** Both (a) "Of a woman, of the female kinde" (TT, s.v. "Foemĭnĕus"); and (b) "Unapt to warre, cowardous or weake," "timerous, fearefull, without heart or courage" (TT, s.v. "Imbellis").

94. **faces.** A "face" is "By metonymy: a person" (OED), particularly one with "face" ("boldness," "impudence," F&H).

97. **no place so unsanctified.** I.e., Hell.

100. **shagge-ear'd Villaine.** The initial "h" of "hair" was dropped, making it a homonym of "ear" (see HK, pp. 111 and 113). It is therefore possible that *Macduffe's Son* calls the *First Murtherer* "a shaghaire or ruffian" (JF, s.v. "Lacno"; cf. and see note: *Water-Rugs*, III.i.118). In implying that the *First Murtherer* is a "ruffian," *Macduffe's Son* might mean that he is (a) "The devil" (FG); (b) "wanton," "brutal," or "violent" (F&H, q.v.); and/or (c) a "prick" ("ruffian" literally means "The penis," F&H, s.v. "Prick").

On the other hand, *Macduffe's Son* may indeed call the *First Murtherer shagge-ear'd*, for "The haires thicke growing about the temple and eares: doth denote that person (of experience knowne) to be of an hot nature, and prone to the veneriall act... The haires which are within the eares, if they be many, thick, and long, argueth an ernest mind in the desire of the actuall lust of the body" (Thomas Hill, *A Pleasant History: Declaring the whole Art of Phisiognomy*).

Macduffe's Son might also imply that the *First Murtherer* is a *Villaine* (i.e., an "ass"; *Villaine* is a synonym of "hind," which means both a "peasant" and the "back part") who "shags" ("copulate[s]," FG) in the "ear" (i.e., the "eeres" or "erse": "arse").

101–102. **you Egge, Yong fry of Treachery.** Proverbially, "an evill Bird layeth an ill Egge, the Cat will after her kind, an ill Tree cannot bring foorth good fruit, the young Crab goeth crooked like the Damme, the young Cocke croweth as the old, and it is a verie rare matter to see children tread out of the pathes of their Parents" (Joseph Swetnam, *The Araignment of Lewd, Idle, Froward, and unconstant women*). Therefore, as an *Egge* ("a young person," OED) engendered from *Macduffe's Egge* ("testicle," GW2), *Macduffe's Son* is by default guilty of *Treachery*.

Also, *Macduffe's Son*, who is the *fry* ("Offspring, progeny," OED) of *Macduffe's fry* ("seed," OED), has "egged" ("provoke[d]," OED) the *First Murtherer*. In response, the *First Murtherer* calls *Macduffe's Son* a "fried *Egge*," for "fryed egges be worst of all, for they engender ill humours" (Thomas Coghan, *The Haven of Health*).

105–106. **Son dies... Exeunt.** *Macduffe's Son* obviously cannot remove himself from the stage after he *dies*. He may fall within the curtains of the discovery space at the rear of the stage, or his corpse might be carried off by his mother or dragged off by one of the *Murtherers*.

Act IV, scene iii

Scæna Tertia.   [1]

Enter Malcolme and Macduffe.   [IV.iii.1]

Mal.	Let us seeke out some desolate shade, & there
	Weepe our sad bosomes empty.

Macd.   Let us rather   [5]

Hold fast the mortall Sword: and like good men,

Bestride our downfall Birthdome: each new Morne,

New Widdowes howle, new Orphans cry, new sorowes

Strike heaven on the face, that it resounds

As if it felt with Scotland, and yell'd out   [10]

Like Syllable of Dolour.

Mal.   What I beleeve, Ile waile;

What know, beleeve; and what I can redresse,

As I shall finde the time to friend: I wil.

What you have spoke, it may be so perchance.   [15]

This Tyrant, whose sole name blisters our tongues,

Was once thought honest: you have lov'd him well,

He hath not touch'd you yet. I am yong, but something

You may discerne of him through me, and wisedome

To offer up a weake, poore innocent Lambe   [20]

T' appease an angry God.

Notes IV.iii.

2–4. *Enter Malcolme and Macduffe... sad bosomes empty.* In crafting this encounter between *Malcolme and Macduffe*, Shakespeare closely follows Holinshed, who reports that upon *Macduffe's*

> comming unto Malcolme, he declared into what great miserie the estate of Scotlande was brought, by the detestable cruelties exercysed by the tyranne Makbeth, having committed many horrible slaughters and murthers, both as well of the nobles as commons, for the which he was hated right mortally of all his liege people, desiring nothing more than to be delivered of that intollerable and moste heavie yoke of thraldome, whiche they susteyned at suche a caytifes handes.
>
> Malcolme hearing Makduffes words which he uttred in right lamentable sort, for pure compassion and very ruth [i.e., "pity"] that pearced his sorowfull hart, bewayling the miserable state of his country, he fetched a deepe sigh, which Makduffe perceyving, began to fall most earnestly in hande wyth him, to enterprise the delivering of the Scottishe people out of the hands of so cruell and bloudie a tyraunt, as Makbeth by too many plaine experiments did shew himselfe to be, which was an easie matter for him to bring to passe, considering not only the good tytle he had, but also the earnest desire of the people to have some occasion ministred, wherby they might be revenged of those notable injuries, which they dayly susteyned by the outragious crueltie of Makbeths misgovernance.

6. *mortall.* Deadly.

7. *Bestride.* To *Bestride* is "To stand over in order to defend"; to "protect, support" (OED).

7. *downfall.* *Downfall* means "Falling down, descending" (OED). As the terminal "-en" was not strictly requisite in early modern English, *downfall* is not necessarily a typographical error for "downfallen" (cf. Shakespeare's use of "forgot" where modern syntax prefers "forgotten": "I feare my Thisbies promise is forgot," *Midsommer Nights Dreame*, V.i.).

7. *Birthdome.* The suffix *-dom[e]* denotes a "domain, realm" (OED). *Birthdome* therefore means "the realm of our *Birth.*"

9. *Strike heaven on the face.* Openly insults or tempts the vengeance of *heaven*.

9–11. *heaven... Like Syllable of Dolour.* Because *Scotland* is not "Soleable" ("Which may be comforted," HC) in its *Dolour* (sorrow or anger), in sympathy *heaven resounds* (echoes) with *Like Syllable* ("exact or precise words," OED).

14. *time.* Opportunity or occasion.

14. *to friend.* "To act as a friend," "to assist, help" (OED).

16. *whose sole name blisters our tongues.* Popular superstition held that liars were afflicted with *blisters* on their *tongues*. *Macbeth* is so false that even pronouncing his *sole* (lone, mere) *name* causes *tongues* to blister.

18–21. *He hath not touch'd you... an angry God.* Although *Malcolme is yong*, he has already suffered a great deal at *Macbeth's* hands. *Macbeth hath not yet touch'd* (injured; see note: *touch*, III.ii.34) *Macduffe*, but nevertheless *Macduffe* may *discerne* ("finde out," "come to the knowledge and understanding of a thing," "see & perceive," TT, s.v. "Dēprĕhendo") *something of Macbeth through* (by means of) *Macbeth's* dealings with *Malcolme*. In order to avoid the same kind of abuse, *Macduffe* might *discerne wisedome To offer up a weake, poore innocent Lambe* (i.e., *Malcolme*) *T'appease an angry God* (i.e., *Macbeth*).

Macd.   I am not treacherous.

Malc.   But *Macbeth* is.

A good and vertuous Nature may recoyle

In an Imperiall charge. But I shall crave your pardon: [25]

That which you are, my thoughts cannot transpose;

Angels are bright still, though the brightest fell.

Though all things foule, would wear the brows of grace

Yet Grace must still looke so.

Macd.   I have lost my Hopes.   [30]

Malc.   Perchance even there

Where I did finde my doubts.

Why in that rawnesse left you Wife, and Childe?

Those precious Motives, those strong knots of Love,

Without leave-taking. I pray you,   [35]

Let not my Jealousies, be your Dishonors,

But mine owne Safeties: you may be rightly just,

What ever I shall thinke.

Macd.   Bleed, bleed poore Country,

Great Tyrrany, lay thou thy basis sure,   [40]

For goodnesse dare not check thee: wear thou thy wrongs,

The Title, is affear'd. Far thee well Lord,

---

22. ***I am not treacherous.*** According to Holinshed, "Though Malcolme was right sorowfull for the oppression of his Countreymen the Scottes, in maner as Makduffe

had declared, yet doubting whether he were come as one that ment unfaynedly as hee spake, or else as sent from Makbeth to betray him, he thought to have some further triall." To determine whether *Macduffe's* motives are sincere, *Malcolme* subsequently accuses himself of many vices. If *Macduffe* encourages *Malcolme* to return to Scotland despite the latter's extreme self-recriminations, *Malcolme* will know that *Macduffe* is *treacherous.* (For *Malcolme's* description of his own character flaws as given by Holinshed, see notes: *Voluptuousnesse,* line 73, below; *Avarice,* line 92, below; and *The Kingbecoming Graces,* line 106, below.)

24–25. **A good and vertuous Nature... Imperiall charge.** A man's *good and vertuous Nature* might (a) *recoyle* ("degenerate," OED) *In* ("In the hands of; in the control or power of," OED) *an Imperiall* ("royall, majesticall," JF, s.v. "Imperiale") *charge* ("precept, injunction, mandate, order," OED); and/or (b) *recoyle* ("retraite or give ground," JF, s.v. "Rinculare") *In* ("during," OED) *an Imperiall charge* ("impetuous attack or onset," OED).

26. **thoughts.** Opinions; also worries and suspicions (see notes: *Thoughts,* III.ii.16; and *thinke,* V.i.81).

26. **transpose.** "To change or alter the order of a thing" (JB, q.v.).

27–29. **Angels are bright still... looke so.** Even the fallen angel "Sathan himselfe is transformed into an Angel of light" (2 Corinthians 11:14). True *Angels still looke bright* because they *are bright still,* but *things foule* ("Morally or spiritually polluted; abominable, detestable, wicked," OED) *still* (nevertheless) *looke* (appear) *to wear the brows* ("Fronting aspect[s], countenance[s]," OED) *of grace* (divine virtue).

30–32. **lost my Hopes... finde my doubts.** If *Macduffe's Hopes* were to betray *Malcolme,* then *Malcolme's doubts* (fears) and *Macduffe's Hopes* are one and the same.

33. **Why in that rawnesse... Childe.** Because *Macduffe* has left his *Wife and Childe* in *Macbeth's* power, *Malcolme* suspects that *Macduffe* is in league with *Macbeth.* For *Macduffe* to leave his family undefended would be very "raw," which means (a) "unexperienced, ignorant" (RC, s.v. "Malusité"); and (b) "Cruell, without pitie, outragious, fell, fierce, sower in countenance, terrible," "heinous, verie greevous" (TT, s.v. "Atrox").

Malcolme also alludes to the diseased state of the body politic: in medical terminology, *rawnesse* is "ill digestion" (JB, s.v. "Cruditie") as well as "abrasion, excoriation" (OED). Cf. V.ii.35–37 and V.iii.65–71.

34. **Motives.** A "motive" is "a moving reason, argument, or cause; an incitement, inducement, or provocation unto a thing" (RC, s.v. "Motif").

34. **knots of Love.** *Knots of Love* are "tie[s] or bond[s] of love" (OED, s.v. "love-knot").

36. **Jealousies.** Suspicions.

37. **Safeties.** Both (a) "Suretie[s]," "securitie[s], assurance[s]" (RC, s.v. "Sureté"); and (b) "protection[s], defence[s]" (RC, s.v. "Sauveté").

37. **rightly.** "Truly, indeed" (TT, s.v. "Vērē").

37. **just.** "Faithfull, loyall, trustie, sure," "earnest" (TT, s.v. "Fĭdēlis").

40–42. **Tyrany... The Title, is affear'd.** *Malcolme* is the "good" ("right, proper," "Valid," OED) King of Scotland, but he *dare not check* (restrain, challenge) the tyrant (usurper) *Macbeth.* Because *The Title* (i.e., *Malcolme,* who holds legitimate *Title* to the crown) *is affear'd* (afraid to take action on his own behalf), *The Title* (claim) of *Tyrany* (i.e., the usurper *Macbeth*) is "affeered" ("settle[d], confirm[ed]," OED). Therefore, *Tyrany* may *wear* (carry, maintain) its *wrongs* (injustices, abuses) without hindrance, and *lay* (set down, establish) its *basis* (foundation) *sure* ("Securely, safely"; "without risk of failure," OED).

I would not be the Villaine that thou think'st,

For the whole Space that's in the Tyrants Graspe,

And the rich East to boot.   [45]

Mal.   Be not offended:

I speake not as in absolute feare of you:

I thinke our Country sinkes beneath the yoake,

It weepes, it bleeds, and each new day a gash

Is added to her wounds. I thinke withall,   [50]

There would be hands uplifted in my right:

And heere from gracious England have I offer

Of goodly thousands. But for all this,

When I shall treade upon the Tyrants head,

Or weare it on my Sword; yet my poore Country   [55]

Shall have more vices then it had before,

More suffer, and more sundry wayes then ever,

By him that shall succeede.

Macd.   What should he be?

Mal.   It is my selfe I meane: in whom I know   [60]

All the particulars of Vice so grafted,

That when they shall be open'd, blacke *Macbeth*

Will seeme as pure as Snow, and the poore State

44–45. *For the whole Space… And the rich East.* I.e., not for anything; not at any price.

45. *to boot. To boot* means "moreover, besides, over and besides" (RC, s.v. "Advenant").

48. *the yoake. The yoake* is "An Instrument of Wood or Iron, to joyne men, or Oxen, or other creatures together; serving, eyther to tame, or to punish" (TW). Figuratively, *the yoake* represents "The cruell bondage, wherein Tyrants keepe Gods people" (TW).

50. *withall. Withall* means "also, moreover, besides" (JF, s.v. "Anche").

52. *gracious England. England* (*Edward*, the King of *England*) is *gracious* in that he is (a) pious, godly; and (b) generous, courteous. See note: *Pious Edward*, III.vi.31.

53. *for.* Notwithstanding.

54–55. *treade upon the Tyrants head… my Sword. Malcolme* implies that *Macbeth* is the "Serpent" ("Sathan," TW). The source is Genesis 3:14–15:

> And the LORD God said unto the Serpent, Because thou hast done this, thou art cursed above all cattel, and above every beast of the field: upon thy belly shalt thou goe, and dust shalt thou eate, all the dayes of thy life. And I will put enmitie betweene thee and the woman, and betweene thy seed and her seed: it shall bruise thy head, and thou shalt bruise his heele.

To kill a serpent, however, one must do more than simply *treade upon* its *head*. In popular belief, the only way to kill a snake was to sever its *head* (see note: III.ii.19–21). Cf. V.vii.116.

57. *sundry.* Both (a) "Divers, differing" (RC, s.v. "Divers"); and (b) "manifold" (JF, s.v. "Parechii").

61. *the particulars of Vice so grafted.* "Grafting" is literally "A joyning of a science or graft so neerely & firmely into a stocke, as that it become one with it" (TW). *Malcolme* is inseparable from *the particulars* ("part[s], division[s], or section[s]," OED) *of* his *Vice* (sins, moral failings) because they are *grafted* (inseparably connected, joined as one).

Also, *Malcolme's Vice* ("penis," FR) is addicted to "grafting" ("sexual ingression and copulation," JH). His *particulars* (i.e., male genitals; see note: *Particular*, III.i.124) are inseparable from *Vice* ("fornication," FR; a *Vice* is literally "A screw," OED).

62–63. *open'd… as pure as Snow. Malcolme's Vice* is *grafted* (line 61, above), so it will inevitably "open" to full bloom. If *Malcolme's* sins are *open'd* (allowed to proceed unhindered), when they are *open'd* (revealed, disclosed to view) *Macbeth* will seem *as pure as Snow.* Cf. "their root shall be rottennes, and their blossome shall goe up as dust: because they have cast away the Lawe of the LORD of hosts" (Isaiah 5:24); and "Such root (we say, such tree) such fruit" (RC, s.v. "Telle racine telle fueille"). Also cf. and see notes: *insane Root*, I.iii.93; and V.iii.29–30.

Esteeme him as a Lambe, being compar'd

With my confinelesse harmes.   [65]

Macd.   Not in the Legions

Of horrid Hell, can come a Divell more damn'd

In evils, to top *Macbeth*.

Mal.   I grant him Bloody,

Luxurious, Avaricious, False, Deceitfull,   [70]

Sodaine, Malicious, smacking of every sinne

That ha's a name. But there's no bottome, none

In my Voluptuousnesse: Your Wives, your Daughters,

Your Matrons, and your Maides, could not fill up

The Cesterne of my Lust, and my Desire   [75]

All continent Impediments would ore-beare

That did oppose my will. Better *Macbeth*,

Then such an one to reigne.

Macd.   Boundlesse intemperance

In Nature is a Tyranny: It hath beene   [80]

Th' untimely emptying of the happy Throne,

And fall of many Kings. But feare not yet

To take upon you what is yours: you may

Convey your pleasures in a spacious plenty,

And yet seeme cold. The time you may so hoodwinke: [85]

65. *confinelesse.* Without "confines": "limits, bounds," (JF, s.v. "Confini"). For possible sexual double entendre, see note: *confin'd*, III.iv.31.

70. *Luxurious.* "Riotous, wanton, leacherous" (JB).

71. *Sodaine. Sodaine* means "quick, swift, violent, vehement, ravenous, cruell" (TT, s.v. "Răpĭdus").

71. *smacking.* Savoring or tasting (see note: *smack*, I.ii.52), with possible additional play on "smack" meaning an "act of coition; coit with" (GW2).

71–72. *every sinne That ha's a name. Macbeth* is guilty of *every sinne That ha's a name*, and some that do not. Cf. and see notes: *Unmannerly breech'd with gore*, II.iii.151; *Hedge-Pigge*, IV.i.4; and *A deed without a name*, IV.i.54.

72. *bottome.* With possible play on *bottome* as the "pubic region" (GW2).

73–89. *my Voluptuousnesse… Finding it so inclinde.* In an attempt to assess *Macduffe's* sincerity, *Malcolme* accuses himself of *Voluptuousnesse* ("lecherie, wickednes, naughtines, lewdnes," TT, s.v. "Nēquĭtia"). Holinshed relates that when *Macduffe* implored *Malcolme* to claim the throne, *Malcolme*

> answered as followeth. I am truly right sorie for the miserie chaunced to my Countrey of Scotlande, but though I have never so great affection to relieve thee same, yet by reason of certaine incurable vyces, whiche raigne in me, I am nothing meete thereto: First suche immoderate lust and voluptuous sensualitie (the abhominable fountaine of all vyces) foloweth me, that if I were made king of Scots, I shoulde seeke to deflower your Maydes and matrones in such wise, that mine intemperancie shoulde bee more importable unto you, than the bloudie tyrannie of Makbeth now is.
>
> Hereunto Makduffe answered: this surely is a very evill fault, for many noble Princes and Kings have lost both lyves and Kingdomes for the same, neverthelesse there are women ynowe in Scotlande, and therefore follow my counsell, make thy selfe king, and I shall convey the matter so wisely, that thou shalt be so satisfied at thy pleasure in such secrete wise, that no man shall be aware therof.

75. *Cesterne.* A *Cesterne* is "a vessel set in the ground, wherein they gather rain water to keep, any hollow Vault" (TB, s.v. "Cisterne"). *Cesterne* is here used to mean "An unfilled container" (EC), with possible play on *Cesterne* meaning "vagina" (GW).

75–77. *my Desire… oppose my will. Malcolme's* sexual *Desire would ore-beare* ("overwhelm," "overcome"; also "bear down, thrust, push, or drive over by weight or physical force," OED) the *continent* ("chaste, pure, honest," "undefiled," TT, s.v. "Castus") *Impediments* ("obstacle[s]," "hinderance[s]," "opposition[s]," JF, s.v. "Ostacolo") of *All* women *That did oppose* (resist, fight against) his *will* ("sexual desire," EP; also "penis," EC).

79. *intemperance.* Sexual excess.

80. *Nature.* Allusive of the genitals, sexual desire, and semen (see notes: *Nature*, I.ii.17 and I.v.52).

80. *Tyranny.* "Violent or lawless action; violence, outrage, villany" (OED).

84 . *Convey.* Both (a) to "conduct" (JF, s.v. "Conviare"); and (b) "To steale" (JB, s.v. "Embezill").

84. *pleasures.* "Sexual pleasures" (JH).

84. *plenty. Plenty* means (a) "abundance" (JB, s.v. "affluence"); and (b) sexual intercourse (FR, who holds it a pun on "copia" and "copulate").

85. *cold.* Chaste or sexually disinclined (see note: *cold*, II.iii.25).

85. *hoodwinke.* To *hoodwinke* literally means "to blindfold" (JF, s.v. "Bendare"). Figuratively, to *hoodwinke* means "to deceive" (RC, s.v. "Baffoüer").

We have willing Dames enough: there cannot be

That Vulture in you, to devoure so many

As will to Greatnesse dedicate themselves,

Finding it so inclinde.

Mal.   With this, there growes   [90]

In my most ill-composd Affection, such

A stanchlesse Avarice, that were I King,

I should cut off the Nobles for their Lands,

Desire his Jewels, and this others House,

And my more-having, would be as a Sawce   [95]

To make me hunger more, that I should forge

Quarrels unjust against the Good and Loyall,

Destroying them for wealth.

Macd.   This Avarice

stickes deeper: growes with more pernicious roote   [100]

Then Summer-seeming Lust: and it hath bin

The Sword of our slaine Kings: yet do not feare,

Scotland hath Foysons, to fill up your will

Of your meere Owne. All these are portable,

With other Graces weigh'd.   [105]

87. **Vulture.** The *Vulture* is used as a "metaphor for opportunistic greed" (JT) as well as "voracious sexual appetite" (GW).

88. **Greatnesse.** *Greatnesse* is "Eminence of rank or station" (OED), with probable play on *Greatnesse* as large penis size (*Greatnesse* literally means "great bulk," OED; also see note: *great*, I.v.18).

89. **inclinde.** "Inclined or disposed to love-making" (EP).

91. **Affection.** "Covetousnes, lust, desire, dishonest love" (TT, s.v. "Cŭpĭdĭtās").

92. **stanchlesse.** Insatiable; unquenchable ("Stanched" means "slaked, quenched," RC, s.v. "Estanché").

92–105. **Avarice... With other Graces weigh'd.** Holinshed reports that after *Macduffe* forgave *Malcolme's* lust (a deadly sin), *Malcolme* next accused himself of *Avarice* (also a deadly sin):

> Then saide Malcolme, I am also the moste avaritious creature on the earth, so that if I were king, I should seeke so many wayes to get lands and goodes, that I woulde slea the most part of all the nobles of Scotland by surmised accusations, to the end I might enjoy their lands, goods, and possessions... Therefore sayth Malcolme, suffer me to remaine where I am, least if I attaine to the regiment of your realme, mine inquenchable avarice may prove such, that ye would thinke the displeasures which now grieve you, should seeme easie in respect of the unmeasurable outrage, whiche might ensue through my comming amongst you.
>
> Makduffe to this made answere, how it was a farre worse fault than the other, for avarice is the roote of all mischiefe, and for that crime the most part of our kings have bene slain & brought to their finall ende. Yet notwithstanding follow my counsel, and take upon thee the crowne, there is golde and riches inough in Scotlande to satisfie thy greedie desire.

96. **forge.** Both (a) "To invent," "to devise," "contrive; imagine" (RC, s.v. "Inventer"); and (b) "To make a manifest lie: to fayne that is not true" (TT, s.v. "Ementĭor").

100. **stickes deeper.** See note: *sticke deepe*, III.i.63.

101. **Summer-seeming.** It is *seeming* (suitable, fitting) to "seem" ("Copulate," FR) in *Summer* (symbolic of youthful vigor).

102. **The Sword.** The "cause of death or destruction"; a "destroying agency" (OED).

103. **Foysons.** "Foison" means "Store, plentie, abundance, great fullnesse" (RC, q.v.).

104. **your meere Owne.** *Your meere Owne* means "what is entirely *your Owne*." In a feudal society ruled by an absolute monarch, "no man hath any property in his goods but as the King pleaseth: no owner of ought he hath, but his King by the right God hath given him, may take from him all hee hath, and dispose of it for his owne use" (William Prynne, *The Aphorismes of the Kingdome*).

104. **portable.** *Portable* means "that may be carried, tolerable" (JF, s.v. "Portabile").

Mal.	But I have none. The King-becoming Graces,
	As Justice, Verity, Temp'rance, Stablenesse,
	Bounty, Perseverance, Mercy, Lowlinesse,
	Devotion, Patience, Courage, Fortitude,
	I have no rellish of them, but abound [110]
	In the division of each severall Crime,
	Acting it many wayes. Nay, had I powre, I should
	Poure the sweet Milke of Concord, into Hell,
	Uprore the universall peace, confound
	All unity on earth. [115]
Macd.	O Scotland, Scotland.
Mal.	If such a one be fit to governe, speake:
	I am as I have spoken.
Mac.	Fit to govern? No not to live. O Nation miserable!
	With an untitled Tyrant, bloody Sceptred, [120]
	When shalt thou see thy wholsome dayes againe?
	Since that the truest Issue of thy Throne
	By his owne Interdiction stands accust,
	And do's blaspheme his breed? Thy Royall Father

106–130. *The King-becoming Graces… Thy hope ends heere.* Holinshed relates that after *Macduffe* forgave *Malcolme* for both lust and avarice,

> Then sayde Malcolme againe, I am furthermore inclined to dissimulation, telling of leasings [i.e., "lies"] and all other kinds of deceyt, so that I naturally rejoyce in nothing so muche as to betray and deceyve suche, as put any trust or confidence in my wordes. Then sith there is nothing that more becommeth a prince than constancie, veritie, truth, and justice, with the other laudable felowship of those faire and noble vertues which are comprehended onely in soothfastnesse, & that lying utterly overthroweth the same, you see how unable I am to governe any province or region: and therfore sith you have remedies to cloke and hide al the rest of my other vices, I pray you find shift to cloke this vice amongst the residue.
>
> Then sayd Makduffe: this yet is the worst of all, and there I leave thee, and therefore say, oh ye unhappie & miserable Scottishmen which are thus scourged with so many and sundrie calamities, eche one above other. Ye have one cursed and wicked tyrant that nowe raignes over you, without any right or tytle, oppressing you with his most bloudie crueltie: This other that hath the right to the crowne, is so replete with the inconstant behaviour and manifest vices of English men, that he is nothing worthie to enjoy it: for by his owne confession he is not onely avaritious, and given to unsatiable lust, but so false a traytour withall, that no trust is to be had to any worde he speaketh. Adue Scotlande, for now I account my selfe a banished man for ever without comfort or consolation: and with those words the teares trickled down his cheekes right abundantly.

107. *Verity.* "Truth" (JB, q.v.).

108. *Bounty. Bounty* can mean (a) "Goodnesse, honestie, sinceritie, vertue, uprightnesse" (RC, s.v. "Bonté"); and (b) "freenes in giving or bestowing" (TT, s.v. "Līberālītas").

110. *rellish.* "Savour, or true Taste of any thing" (ND, s.v. "Gust").

111. *division.* With play on *division* meaning (a) "distribution, disposing of a thing into sundrie members, parcells, or portions" (RC, q.v.); and (b) "A florid melodic passage" (OED). Cf. *Concord,* line 113, below.

113. *Milke.* "The graces of the holy Spirite, which are as necessary to a heavenly life, as Milke is to this naturall life" (TW).

113. *Concord. Concord* is (a) "Amitie, friendship, love, kindnesse, good will" (RC, s.v. "Amitié"); and (b) "harmonie" (RC, s.v. "Concorde").

114. *Uprore.* To *Uprore* is "To throw into confusion" (OED). *Uprore* "is not compounded of *up* and *roar,* but is the German *auf-ruhren* (to stir up)" (DPF).

121. *wholsome.* "Sound or healthful," "spiritually sound, or bringing health to the soule" (TW).

123. *Interdiction.* An *Interdiction* is a "prohibition, injunction; also, (in Law) a determination, or order in Court, for the possession of a thing in controversie" (RC, s.v. "Interdict").

123. *accust. Accust* is either (a) a phonetic spelling of "accused" ("charged with an offence, or trespasse," RC, s.v. "Calengé"); or (b) a typographical error for "accurst."

124. *blaspheme.* "To curse" (RC, s.v. "Mauldire"). Also see note: *Blaspheming,* IV.i.28.

124. *breed.* A "race, a stocke, a linage" (TT, s.v. "Prōles").

Was a most Sainted-King: the Queene that bore thee,   [125]

Oftner upon her knees, then on her feet,

Dy'de every day she liv'd. Fare thee well,

These Evils thou repeat'st upon thy selfe,

Hath banish'd me from Scotland. O my Brest,

Thy hope ends heere.   [130]

Mal.   *Macduff*, this Noble passion

Childe of integrity, hath from my soule

Wip'd the blacke Scruples, reconcil'd my thoughts

To thy good Truth, and Honor. Divellish *Macbeth*,

By many of these traines, hath sought to win me   [135]

Into his power: and modest Wisedome pluckes me

From over-credulous hast: but God above

Deale betweene thee and me; For even now

I put my selfe to thy Direction, and

Unspeake mine owne detraction. Heere abjure   [140]

The taints, and blames I laide upon my selfe,

For strangers to my Nature. I am yet

Unknowne to Woman, never was forsworne,

Scarsely have coveted what was mine owne.

At no time broke my Faith, would not betray   [145]

125–127. ***the Queene... Dy'de every day she liv'd.*** Christian doctrine teaches that "the truely wise indeed, guided by grace, have the time of their dissolution continually before their eyes, and in a holy meditation of death, prepare themselves to die daily... Such as thus prepare themselves, have never any feare to die; but in their hearts wish to be dissolved, and to be with Christ" (John Norden, *A Pensive Soules delight*). Cf. "And why stand we in jeopardy every houre? I protest by your rejoycing which I have in Christ Jesus our Lord, I die dayly" (1 Corinthians 15:30–31); "For if ye live after the flesh, ye shall die: but if ye through the spirit doe mortifie the deeds of the body, ye shall live" (Romans 8:13); and "Mortifie therefore your members which are upon the earth: fornication, uncleannesse, inordinate affection, evill concupiscence, and covetousnesse, which is idolatrie" (Colossians 3:5).

131–149. ***this Noble passion... to command.*** Holinshed states that when *Macduffe* was readie to depart, Malcolme tooke him by the sleeve, and sayde, Be of good comfort Makduffe, for I have none of these vices before remembred, but have jested with thee in this maner, only to prove thy mind: for diverse tymes heretofore, hath Makbeth sought by this maner of meanes to bring me into his handes, but the more slow I have shewed my self to condiscend to thy motion and request, the more diligence shall I use in accomplishing the same.

Incontinently hereupon they embraced eche other, and promising to bee faythfull the one to the other, they fell in consultation, howe they might best provide for al their businesse, to bring the same to good effect.

133. ***Scruples.*** See note: *scruples*, II.iii.168.

135. ***traines.*** A "Traine" is (a) "a plot, practise, conspiracie, devise" (RC, q.v.); and (b) "a trappe" (JP).

136. ***modest.*** *Modest* means "sober," "temperate, well advised," "well in his wits" (JF, s.v. "Sóbrio").

136. ***pluckes.*** To "pluck" is to "hold or draw back" (TT, s.v. "Subdūco"); to "stay one from doeing of a thing" (TT, s.v. "Rĕflecto").

139. ***Direction.*** *Direction* is (a) "instruction," "teaching, tutoring" (JF, s.v. "Instruction"); and (b) "guiding," "governement, rule" (TT, s.v. "Mŏdĕrāmen").

140. ***abjure.*** To "forsweare; denie with an oath" (RC, s.v. "Abjurer").

The Devill to his Fellow, and delight

No lesse in truth then life. My first false speaking

Was this upon my selfe. What I am truly

Is thine, and my poore Countries to command:

Whither indeed, before they heere approach   [150]

Old *Seyward* with ten thousand warlike men

Already at a point, was setting foorth:

Now wee'l together, and the chance of goodnesse

Be like our warranted Quarrell. Why are you silent?

Macd.   Such welcome, and unwelcom things at once   [155]

'Tis hard to reconcile.

Enter a Doctor.   [IV.iii.2]

Mal.   Well, more anon. Comes the King forth

I pray you?

150–152. ***Whither indeed... was setting foorth.*** *Whither* means "To which place" (OED) and refers to *my poore Countrie* (line 149, above). If *they* is a typographical error for "thy," then the passage reads: *Whither* (to Scotland) *indeed, before* "thy" (*Macduffe's*) *approach heere* (*Edward's* court in England), *Old Seyward, with* his *warlike men, was setting foorth.*

However, *they* may be printed correctly. If *heere* means "this place," then the passage reads: *Whither* (to Scotland) *indeed, Old Seyward with* his *warlike men was setting foorth before they* (*Seyward* and his army) *approach heere* (*Edward's* court). (The pairing of *was* with the plural pronoun *they* is irrelevant: "Levelling of *was* to the plural is chiefly a northern feature in Middle English and the 16th cent[ury], but from the 17th cent[ury] onwards it is attested widely as a minority variant... Levelling of *were* to the singular is also found in a number of regional and nonstandard varieties," OED; cf. V.iii.16–18).

Heere also means "In the matter before us or in question" (OED), and *approach* means "Nearer advance of an enemy; offensive or hostile movement" (OED). The passage may therefore read: *Whither* (to Scotland) *indeed, Old Seyward with* his *warlike men was setting foorth before they* (*Seyward* and his army) *approach* (invade, make an attack on *Macbeth's* forces) *heere* (in the matter in question, or *Malcolme's* claim to the throne).

In addition, in Shakespeare's time *heere* rhymed with "air" (HK, pp. 178, 207, and 308; the initial "h" in *heere* was dropped, and the vowel was not pronounced identically to today's). Therefore, early audiences may have heard the words *they heere* as *they* "yare" (which means both "Ready, prepared" and "Quickly, without delay, promptly, immediately, soon," OED).

In any case, *Malcolme* says that *Seyward's* forces have already set out for Scotland.

151. ***Old Seyward with ten thousand warlike men.*** Cf. and see note: *warlike Seyward,* III.vi.35.

152. ***at a point.*** *At a point* can mean (a) "Determined," "agreed, accorded" (RC, s.v. "Appointé"); and/or (b) "ready," "at hand" (JM, s.v. "Apíque").

153–154. ***the chance of goodnesse... Quarrell.*** *Malcolme* hopes that *the chance* ("The falling out or happening of events," "fortune, luck," OED) *of* (belonging to, springing from) *goodnesse* ("The benefites which come from Gods goodnesse," "His most infinite holinesse and justice," TW) will "belike" ("be pleased with," OED) their *warranted* (justified, sanctioned) *Quarrell.*

Doct.	I Sir: there are a crew of wretched Soules	[160]
	That stay his Cure: their malady convinces	
	The great assay of Art. But at his touch,	
	Such sanctity hath Heaven given his hand,	
	They presently amend.	

    Exit {Doctor}.   [IV.iii.3] [165]

Mal.	I thanke you Doctor.	
Macd.	What's the Disease he meanes?	
Mal.	Tis call'd the Evill.	
	A most myraculous worke in this good King,	
	Which often since my heere remaine in England,	[170]
	I have seene him do: How he solicites heaven	
	Himselfe best knowes: but strangely visited people	
	All swolne and Ulcerous, pittifull to the eye,	
	The meere dispaire of Surgery, he cures,	
	Hanging a golden stampe about their neckes,	[175]
	Put on with holy Prayers, and 'tis spoken	
	To the succeeding Royalty he leaves	
	The healing Benediction. With this strange vertue,	
	He hath a heavenly guift of Prophesie,	
	And sundry Blessings hang about his Throne,	[180]
	That speake him full of Grace.	

160–175. *a crew of wretched Soules... a golden stampe.* The *Doctor* describes a *wretched crew* ("flock of people," JF, s.v. "Cappanella"; also a "rout, rable," JF, s.v. "Troupe") *visited* (afflicted) with *the Evill* (scrofula, "a disease called the Kings evill, a wen or swelling in the necke," JF, s.v. "Scrofole"). *Their malady convinces* ("conquere[s]," "overcome[s]," "vanquish[es]," TT, s.v. "Expugno") *The great assay* ("attempt," "triall," JF, s.v. "Saggiata"; also "experiment, experience," RC, s.v. "Preuve") *of Art* (human skill). Therefore, these people are *The meere* (absolute, downright) *dispaire* ("That which causes despair, or about which there is no hope," OED) *of Surgery* ("the Art of curing wounds," EC2). Luckily, *Edward* the Confessor possessed *Such sanctity* (holiness) that he could cure this *Disease* with his *touch*, a gift which he supposedly passed on to all his successors (see note: *Pious Edward*, III.vi.31).

The practice of *Hanging a golden stampe* (coin) *about* the *neckes* of scrofula victims is anachronistic for the reign of *Edward* the Confessor, but the ritual was current during the reign of James I. *Edward* informally touched for *the Evill*, but "Henry VII... established a set ceremonial, and instituted the custom of touching the sore with a gold angel noble, afterwards given to the sufferer, and worn on a ribbon round his neck" (William Tate, *The Parish Chest*, p. 157). (These lines were evidently inserted to flatter James, by whose time the ceremony of touching for *the Evill* had acquired cult status.)

161. *stay.* Await.

170. *remaine.* "A stay in a place; a sojourn" (OED).

178. *vertue.* *Vertue* can mean (a) "Power to doe," "ability, faculty" (TT, s.v. "Făcultas"); and (b) "the soveraintie or devine power and majestie" (TT, s.v. "Nūmen").

179. *heavenly guift of Prophesie.* See note: *Pious Edward*, III.vi.31.

181. *speake.* Reveal; demonstrate.

Enter Rosse.   [IV.iii.4]

Macd.   See who comes heere.

Malc.   My Countryman: but yet I know him not.

Macd.   My ever gentle Cozen, welcome hither.   [185]

Malc.   I know him now. Good God betimes remove

            The meanes that makes us Strangers.

Rosse.   Sir, Amen.

Macd.   Stands Scotland where it did?

Rosse.   Alas poore Countrey,   [190]

            Almost affraid to know it selfe. It cannot

            Be call'd our Mother, but our Grave; where nothing

            But who knowes nothing, is once seene to smile:

            Where sighes, and groanes, and shrieks that rent the ayre

            Are made, not mark'd: Where violent sorrow seemes   [195]

            A Moderne extasie: The Deadmans knell,

            Is there scarse ask'd for who, and good mens lives

            Expire before the Flowers in their Caps,

            Dying, or ere they sicken.

Macd.   Oh Relation; too nice, and yet too true.   [200]

Malc.   What's the newest griefe?

Rosse.   That of an houres age, doth hisse the speaker,

            Each minute teemes a new one.

184. *My Countryman... know him not.* From a distance, *Malcolme* identifies *Rosse* as his *Countryman* by his distinctly Scottish dress (which the King's Men would have made great effort to recreate for their performance before their patron, King James VI of Scotland and I of England). However, *Malcolme* (a) does not *know* (recognize) *Rosse* because it has been more than ten years since the two have seen each other (see note: *Thou hast it now*, III.i.3); or (b) does not *know* (understand, clearly perceive) *Rosse* to be a friend until *Macduffe* greets him as his ally.

186. *betimes.* See note: *betimes*, III.iv.169.

188. *Sir.* See note: *Sir*, III.iv.11.

192–193. *where nothing But who knowes nothing... smile.* In Scotland, *nothing But who* ("except one who," OED) *knowes nothing* (i.e., a complete ignoramus or an idiot) *is once* (on any occasion) *seene to smile.*

194. *rent.* To "teare in peeces," "breake a sunder" (TT, s.v. "Dīlănĭo").

196. *Moderne.* Everyday; commonplace.

196. *extasie.* See note: *extasie*, III.ii.29.

196. *The Deadmans knell.* See note: *Knell*, II.i.79.

198. *Expire before the Flowers in their Caps. Flowers* were worn *in Caps* as a sign of joy and celebration. In Scotland, such causes for happiness are very short-lived.

199. *or ere.* Before ever; before even (OED).

200. *Relation.* See note: *Relations*, III.iv.159.

200. *nice.* Both (a) "Simple" (JJ); and (b) "precise" (ND).

201–203. *the newest griefe... a new one.* When *Each minute teemes* ("pour[s] out," EC2) *a new griefe* (injury, sorrow), a *griefe of an houres age* is very old news indeed. Therefore, *the speaker* of such news can expect (a) "To be hissed at, to have no hearing given him" (TT, s.v. "Explōdor"); and (b) to be "disgraced, driven away with hissing" (RC, s.v. "Explaudé").

Macd.   How do's my Wife?

Rosse.   Why well.   [205]

Macd.   And all my Children?

Rosse.   Well too.

Macd.   The Tyrant ha's not batter'd at their peace?

Rosse.   No, they were wel at peace, when I did leave 'em

Macd.   Be not a niggard of your speech: How gos't?   [210]

Rosse.   When I came hither to transport the Tydings

Which I have heavily borne, there ran a Rumour

Of many worthy Fellowes, that were out,

Which was to my beleefe witnest the rather,

For that I saw the Tyrants Power a-foot.   [215]

Now is the time of helpe: your eye in Scotland

Would create Soldiours, make our women fight,

To doffe their dire distresses.

Malc.   Bee't their comfort

We are comming thither: Gracious England hath   [220]

Lent us good *Seyward*, and ten thousand men,

An older, and a better Souldier, none

That Christendome gives out.

205–207. **well... Well too.** *Macduffe's* family is *well* because they are (a) in their *well*, or grave (a *well* is a "pit bored or dug in the ground," OED); and/or (b) under the "welle" ("Green sward," JJ, q.v.).

208. **The Tyrant ha's not batter'd at their peace.** To "batter" means (a) to "breake down with an engine of warre, called a Ramme" (TT, s.v. "Arīēto"); and (b) "to laie siege unto" (JF, s.v. "Oppugnare"). *Macduffe* envisions his family secured in their impenetrable castle and thus able to withstand a long siege, but unfortunately the gates were opened to *Macbeth's* assassins (see note: *The Castle of Macduff*, IV.i.186).

The "Battering-Ram" is also "a symbol of penetration, that is, of an ambivalent force capable of either fertilizing or destroying" (JC, q.v.). *Macbeth*, who is a *Tyrant* (i.e., a "prick"; cf. JF's "tirante": "breeches or hosen in pedlers French or rogues language"), has *batter'd* (i.e., "screwed"; to "batter down" is "to achieve a forced or violent sexual ingression," JH) *Macduffe's* family. *Macbeth* did not hesitate to "batter" ("Assail sexually," FR) *their* "piece" ("Genitals," FR). Cf. F&H's "battering-piece": "The penis" (s.v. "Prick").

210. **niggard.** A "miser" (JF, s.v. "Avaro"); "a sparing man" (TT, s.v. "Cimbicus").

213. **many worthy Fellowes, that were out.** These *worthy* (valiant, brave; see note: *worthy*, I.ii.30) *Fellowes* (men of the common people) *were out* ("on an expedition; at war, on a field of battle," OED) in a domestic uprising against *Macbeth*. See note: *Since his Majesty went into the Field*, V.i.7.

214. **witnest.** "Testified," "prooved by witnes" (TT, s.v. "Attestātus"); "affirmed, verified" (RC, s.v. "Averé").

214. **the rather.** The sooner (see note: *the rather*, I.vii.74).

216. **your eye.** *Your eye* means *your* (a) supervision or attention (OED); or (b) person; *eye* is used for "The whole man, by Sinecdoche" (TW).

218. **doffe.** *Doffe* "is do-off" (DPF).

Rosse.   Would I could answer

This comfort with the like. But I have words   [225]

That would be howl'd out in the desert ayre,

Where hearing should not latch them.

Macd.   What concerne they,

The generall cause, or is it a Fee-griefe

Due to some single brest?   [230]

Rosse.   No minde that's honest

But in it shares some woe, though the maine part

Pertaines to you alone.

Macd.   If it be mine

Keepe it not from me, quickly let me have it.   [235]

Rosse.   Let not your eares dispise my tongue for ever,

Which shall possesse them with the heaviest sound

That ever yet they heard.

Macd.   Humh: I guesse at it.

Rosse.   Your Castle is surpriz'd: your Wife, and Babes   [240]

Savagely slaughter'd: To relate the manner

Were on the Quarry of these murther'd Deere

To adde the death of you.

Malc.   Mercifull Heaven:

What man, ne're pull your hat upon your browes: [245]

226. **would be.** Should be.

227. **latch.** To "catch" or "receive"; also "to grasp with the mind, to comprehend" (OED).

229. **Fee-griefe.** A *Fee-griefe* is one held "in fee" ("as one's absolute and rightful possession," OED). There is additional play on *Fee* meaning "a subsidie or imposition of any payment, an equall or like paine in recompence of a hurt" (JF, s.v. "Taglione"). Cf. *Due*, line 230, below.

237. **possesse.** To "apprise of, acquaint with" (OED).

239. **Humh.** *Humh* is here used to express (a) a sharp intake of breath (cf. Fr. "Humer": "to fetch, or draw in, as the breath, or with the breath," RC, q.v.); or (b) an inarticulate expression of grief (cf. TE's "Emutio": "to humme or make anye other sowne lyke a man that is dumme"). Cf. *Give sorrow words*, line 246, below.

242. **Quarry of these murther'd Deere.** *Quarry* "signifies among Hunters a reward given to Hounds after they have hunted, or the Venison which is taken by hunting" (TB), with play on *Deere / "dear"* (beloved persons).

245. **pull your hat upon your browes.** A stereotypical gesture of sorrow. Evidently, the *hat* was pulled down *upon* the *browes* in order to hide weeping: cf. "With that the Knight turning his head, pluckt his hat to his eyes to hide the teares that trickled down his face" (Thomas Deloney, *The Gentile Craft, The second Part*); and "Come, come, be merry Sir; doe as mourners doe at Funerals, weare your Hat in your eyes, and Laugh in your heart" (William Rowley, *A New Wonder, A Woman Never Vext*).

Give sorrow words; the griefe that do's not speake,

Whispers the o're-fraught heart, and bids it breake.

Macd.   My Children too?

Ro.   Wife, Children, Servants, all that could be found.

Macd.   And I must be from thence? My wife kil'd too?   [250]

Rosse.   I have said.

Malc.   Be comforted.

Let's make us Med'cines of our great Revenge,

To cure this deadly greefe.

Macd.   He ha's no Children. All my pretty ones?   [255]

Did you say All? Oh Hell-Kite! All?

What, All my pretty Chickens, and their Damme

At one fell swoope?

Malc.   Dispute it like a man.

Macd.   I shall do so: [260]

But I must also feele it as a man;

I cannot but remember such things were

That were most precious to me: Did heaven looke on,

And would not take their part? Sinfull *Macduff*,

They were all strooke for thee: Naught that I am,   [265]

Not for their owne demerits, but for mine

Fell slaughter on their soules: Heaven rest them now.

246–247. ***Give sorrow words... bids it breake.*** The sentiment was common: cf. "No greater ease of heart then griefes to tell, / It daunteth all the dolours of our mind, / Our carefull hearts thereby great comfort find" (John Higgins, *The Falles of Unfortunate Princes*). Although cliché, the adage was nevertheless grounded in medical wisdom. In *Anatomy of Melancholy*, Robert Burton recommends that

> our best way for ease is to impart our misery to some friend, not to smother it up in our own brest... and that which was most offensive to us, a cause of feare and grief... another hell, when as wee shall but impart it to some discreet, trusty and loving friend, is instantly removed by counsell happily, wisdome, perswasion, advise, his good meanes, which we could not otherwise apply unto our selves... the simple narration many times easeth our distressed minde, and in the midst and greatest extremities so many have bin relieved by exonerating themselves to a faithfull friend.

Also see note: *keepe alone*, III.ii.14.

247. ***Whispers.*** To "whisper" is "To suggest secretly to the mind" (OED).

255. ***He ha's no Children.*** *He* refers to *Macbeth*. *Macduffe* contemplates that (a) a man with his own *Children* could never so mercilessly slaughter another man's; and/or (b) *Macduffe* can never extract equal vengeance on *Macbeth*, because to do so *Macduffe* would need to kill *Macbeth's* own *Children*.

256–264. ***Hell-Kite... would not take their part.*** *Macduffe's* expressions of grief might sound trite (and perhaps even comical) to modern ears, but original audiences would have heard his words in the context of Matthew 23:37: "I have gathered thy children together, even as a hen gathereth her chickens under her wings." This is "A metaphor taken from Birds or Fowl, especially Hens, who gather their Chickens under them, cherish them, and protect them from being seized upon, by Kites or other Birds of prey" (TDL).

In calling his family *Chickens*, *Macduffe* refers to them as innocent and God-fearing people. Biblically, predators such as the *Kite* ("Buzzard," RC, s.v. "Bousant") signify "Uncleane and filthy men" (TW, s.v. "Hatefull birds"). However, the *Hell-Kite* is "that slie Puttocke sathan" (Thomas Nash, *Christs Teares Over Jerusalem*), for "The Kite hath (as one observes) as it were an aking tooth at the Chickens, fain would he make a prey of them: so would the Devil of Believers" (TDL). *Macduffe* envisions *Macbeth* as the *Hell-Kite*, the Devil incarnate, who has destroyed *All* his *pretty Chickens and their Damme* (mother) *At one fell* ("bloudie, cruell," "bloudthirstie, mercilesse," JF, s.v. "Sanguinoso") *swoope* ("the sudden pouncing of a bird of prey from a height upon its quarry," OED).

In protecting the faithful, supposedly "Christ knows how to preserve them, by gathering them all under his Wings. Soul, fear not, if thou art under the Protection of the Lord Jesus Christ, thou art in safety from all temporal and spiritual dangers" (TDL). *Macduffe* therefore wonders that *heaven would looke on* his family's distress *And not take their part*. However, even in the face of personal tragedy, *Macduffe* never doubts a divine presence as does *Macbeth*; cf. V.v.28–29 and 32–34.

259. ***Dispute.*** Both (a) to "debate, or reason of a thing" (TT, s.v. "Discepto"); and (b) "To fight, contend, assault, or strive," "be contrary or against" (TT, s.v. "Pugno").

265. ***Naught.*** Both (a) "Nothing" (TT, s.v. "Nĭhĭlum"); and (b) "Wicked," "cast out of Gods favour" (TT, s.v. "Rĕprŏbus").

Mal.   Be this the Whetstone of your sword, let griefe

Convert to anger: blunt not the heart, enrage it.

Macd.   O I could play the woman with mine eyes,   [270]

And Braggart with my tongue. But gentle Heavens,

Cut short all intermission: Front to Front,

Bring thou this Fiend of Scotland, and my selfe

Within my Swords length set him, if he scape

Heaven forgive him too.   [275]

Mal.   This time goes manly:

Come go we to the King, our Power is ready,

Our lacke is nothing but our leave. *Macbeth*

Is ripe for shaking, and the Powres above

Put on their Instruments: Receive what cheere you may,   [280]

The Night is long, that never findes the Day.

Exeunt

272. *intermission.* A "delay of time, a letting passe" (JF, s.v. "Intermissióne").

272. *Front to Front.* A *Front* is "a forhead, a brow, the space or forefront of a squadron or battell" (JF, s.v. "Fronte"); to *Front* is "to meete face to face" (JF, s.v. "Frontare").

275. *Heaven forgive him too.* If *Macduffe* fails to kill *Macbeth*, he will consider it an unpardonable sin. *Macduffe* will therefore need God's forgiveness as much as *Macbeth*, so he will entreat *Heaven* to *forgive* them both.

276. *manly.* "Valiantlie, stoutlie, manfully, boldly, with a courage," "quicklie, with great diligence" (TT, s.v. "Strēnuē").

278. *Our lacke is nothing but our leave.* Perhaps *Malcolme* and his companions (a) have no *lacke* ("need, scarcitie, wante," TT, s.v. "Inŏpĭa") except their *leave* ("licence to depart," TT, s.v. "Mission") from King *Edward*; or (b) are guilty of a *lacke* ("A default, fault, offence, defect," RC, s.v. "Default") only if they give their *leave* ("sufferance, permission," JF, s.v. "Licentia") for things in Scotland to continue as they are.

278–279. *Macbeth Is ripe for shaking.* An allusion to Nahum 3:12: "All thy strong holds shall be like fig trees with the first ripe figs: if they bee shaken, they shall even fall into the mouth of the eater." The over-confident *Macbeth Is ripe* (ready, due) *for shaking* ("ruine," "overthrow," JF, s.v. "Scóssa"), for "Securitie is like a Calme before an Earthquake: you know it is said of Laish, it was a secure people, and you know how they fared: They were so secure, that when an enemie came against them, it was like the shaking of a Fig-tree that hath ripe Figges on it, which being shaken, the Figges fall into their mouth" (John Preston, *A Sermon Preached at a Generall Fast before the Commons-House Of Parliament: The Second Of July, 1625*).

In *An Herbal for the Bible*, Levinus Lemnius interprets this verse to mean that even the seemingly invincible cannot escape God's vengeance:

> The Prophet Nahum advouching all humane helps to be vaine, weake and help-lesse, and all Fortresses, Holdes, Castels, Towers, Skonses, Munitions, Rampiers, & Bulwarks to be unable to stande against God, compareth them to ripe Figs, which if they be never so little shaken, fal downe... Whereby he meaneth, that all their strength, power & force shal be confounded and brought to nothing, by the mightie hand of God.

Cf. and see notes: III.v.35–36; and V.iii.11–12 and 29–30.

279–280. *the Powres above Put on their Instruments.* *Malcolme* entreats *the Powres above* (where "power" means both an army and a defending angel; see note: *Powers*, II.i.14) to (a) *Put on* ("forward, set forward, further," "hasten," "advance, prefer, promote," RC, s.v. "Avancer") *their Instruments* ("Agent[s]," RC, s.v. "Faciendaire"); and (b) *Put on* (don) *their Instruments* ("Armour," "weapons," TT, s.v. "Arma"; "all store for warres," TT, s.v. "Armāmenta").

281. *The Night is long... the Day.* Proverbially, "Yet ne'r was Night so long, but did give place / At length to cheerly Day" (Joseph Beaumont, *Psyche, or Loves Mysterie*). *Malcolme* believes that their suffering must inevitably end, and he believes that time is near.

Act V, scene i

Actus Quintus. Scena Prima.   [1]

Enter a Doctor of Physicke, and a Wayting

Gentlewoman.   [V.i.1]

Doct.   I have too Nights watch'd with you, but can

             perceive no truth in your report. When was it shee last   [5]

             walk'd?

Gent.   Since his Majesty went into the Field, I have

             seene her rise from her bed, throw her Night-Gown up-

             pon her, unlocke her Closset, take foorth paper, folde it,

             write upon't, read it, afterwards Seale it, and againe re-   [10]

             turne to bed; yet all this while in a most fast sleepe.

Doct.   A great perturbation in Nature, to receyve at

             once the benefit of sleep, and do the effects of watching.

             In this slumbry agitation, besides her walking, and other

             actuall performances, what (at any time) have you heard   [15]

             her say?

Gent.   That Sir, which I will not report after her.

Notes V.i.

2. **Doctor of Physicke.** *Physicke* is "medicine, helping, or curing" (RC2, q.v.); a *Doctor* is "he that hath taken the highest degree in Divinity, Physick, Civil-law or Musick" (EC2, q.v.). One need not have a degree of any sort to practice medicine in

Shakespeare's time, so a *Doctor of Physicke* was a highly educated and skilled medical man.

4. *watch'd.* Both (a) observed; and (b) remained awake.

6. *walk'd.* To "walk" is "to walk in one's sleep" (OED).

7. *Since his Majesty went into the Field.* Although *Malcolme* and *Macduffe's* forces have not yet arrived in Scotland, *Macbeth* has already gone *into the Field* ("battlefield," OED) to suppress domestic uprisings. According to Holinshed, upon hearing of *Malcolme's* imminent invasion

> the nobles drew into two severall factions, the one taking part with Makbeth, and the other with Malcolme. Hereupon ensued oftentymes sundrie bickerings, and diverse light skirmishes, for those that were of Malcolmes side, woulde not jeoparde to joyne with their enimies in a pight field [i.e., "pitched battle"], tyll his comming out of England to their support. But after that Makbeth perceived his enimies power to encrease, by such ayde as came to them forth of England with his adversarie Malcolme, he reculed backe into Fife, there purposing to abide in campe fortified, at the Castell of Dunsinane, and to fight with his enimies, if they ment to pursue him.

8–11. *rise from her bed... in a most fast sleepe.* Lady Macbeth's nocturnal ramblings stand in contrast to her husband's waking (yet equally unconscious) fits of mania (see note: *What is the night*, III.iv.161). *Lady Macbeth* outwardly has control of her passions, but she cannot escape her own conscience while asleep. In *Anatomy of Melancholy*, Robert Burton attributes sleep disorders such as somnambulism primarily to one's own tainted imagination, explaining that

> sleepers, which by reason of abundance of humors and concurse of vapours troubling the Phantasie, imagine many times absurd and prodigious things... when there is nothing but a concourse of bad humours, which trouble the Phantasie. This is likewise evident in such as walke in the night in their sleep, and doe strange feats: these vapours move the Phantasie, the Phantasie the Appetite, which moving the animall spirits, causeth the body to walke up and downe, as if they were awake.

Burton goes on to advise that "Against fearefull and troublesome dreames... the best remedy is not to meditate or think in the day time of any terrible objects." Also see notes: *fantasticall*, I.iii.157; *cursed thoughts*, II.i.14; *mad*, II.ii.45; and *Blood will have Blood*, III.iv.157.

9. *Closset.* A "cabinet," "a casket" (JF, s.v. "Cabinetto").

9–10. *take foorth paper... Seale it.* Envelopes were not in common use until the mid-nineteenth century, so in order to *Seale* ("fasten a folded letter or other document with melted wax or some other plastic material and impress a seal upon this, so that opening is impossible unless the seal is broken," OED) the letters which she unconsciously writes, *Lady Macbeth* must first *folde* the *paper* to mark the margins.

12. *perturbation.* "Passion," "trouble, or affliction; also, a motion, disposition, inclination, or affection, of the mind; also, an accident, or symtome concurring with some disease to th'offence, or distemperature, of the bodie" (RC, s.v. "Passion").

13. *effects.* *Effects* are "working[s], operation[s]" (TT, s.v. "Vis").

13. *watching.* Waking.

14. *agitation.* *Agitation* is "motion," "mooving" as well as "perturbation of the minde" (JF, s.v. "Agitatione").

15. *actuall.* *Actuall* means "in act, or shewing it selfe in deed" (RC, q.v.).

Doct.   You may to me, and 'tis most meet you should.

Gent.   Neither to you, nor any one, having no witnesse

to confirme my speech.   [20]

Enter Lady, with a Taper.   [V.i.2]

Lo you, heere she comes: This is her very guise, and up-

on my life fast asleepe: observe her, stand close.

Doct.   How came she by that light?

Gent.   Why it stood by her: she ha's light by her con-   [25]

tinually, 'tis her command.

Doct.   You see her eyes are open.

Gent.   I, but their sense are shut.

Doct.   What is it she do's now?

Looke how she rubbes her hands.   [30]

Gent.   It is an accustom'd action with her, to seeme

thus washing her hands: I have knowne her continue in

this a quarter of an houre.

---

18. **meet.** Appropriate.

19–20. **no witnesse to confirme my speech.** The *Gentlewoman* has already heard *Lady Macbeth's* unconscious confessions, but she is reluctant to accuse the queen of murder without a *witnesse*. To make such an accusation in medieval Scotland would be suicidal, *witnesse* or no. However, Shakespeare may recall a law of his own time: a statute of Elizabeth I dictated that "no person or persons, shalbe hereafter indited or arraigned for any offence or offences made treason... unlesse the same offence & offences of treason & misprision of treason aforesaid, be proved by the testimonie, deposition, & oth of two lawful and sufficient witnesses" (*Anno Primo Reginæ Elizabethæ*).

21. ***Taper.*** Unlike the torches carried in I.vi.2, I.vii.2, II.i.2, and II.i.16, this *Taper* is not simply a token indication of darkness on a brightly lit stage (see note: *Torches*, I.vi.2). If Shakespeare included this prop merely to indicate that the scene takes place at night, then the *Taper* would logically be carried by either the *Doctor* or the *Gentlewoman*, who, unlike *Lady Macbeth*, have use of their vision (cf. and see note: *their sense are shut*, line 28, below).

Very soon after entering the stage, *Lady Macbeth rubbes her hands* (line 30, below). To perform this action, she must put down the lighted *Taper*, and on the bare stage of the early modern playhouse the only place to do so is on the floor. When *Lady Macbeth* stoops to set down the *Taper*, from her crouched position she "sees" spots of blood (lines 34 and 37) not only on her hands but also on the floor. *Lady Macbeth*, at least in her mind, has returned to "the scene of the crime." According to ancient superstition, "When blood was shed untimely, especially innocent blood, it brought a curse with it... Numerous stories are still told of indelible blood stains that cannot be washed out, no matter how often they are scrubbed or scraped. Always they return to give silent testimony of the crime committed there" (Edwin and Mona Augusta Radford, *The Encyclopedia of Superstitions*, s.v. "blood").

22. ***Lo.*** "Looke, see," "behold, there" (RC, s.v. "Voilà").

22. ***guise.*** "A manner, fashion," "behaviour: a custome" (TT, s.v. "Mōs").

23–28. ***observe her, stand close... their sense are shut.*** According to contemporary medical belief, "vapours stopping the conduits of the senses, doe cause sleep" (Robert Basset, *Curiosities or The Cabinet of Nature*; also see note: *rise from her bed*, line 8, above). As Théophraste Renaudot explains in *A General Collection of Discourses of the Virtuosi of France*, in sleepwalkers

> though sense be hindred in sleep, yet motion is not... For the hinder part of the head, destinated to motion, is full of abundance of spirits, especially at the beginning of the Spinal Marrow, where there is a very apparent Cavity which cannot be stop'd by vapours, as the anterior part of the head is, in which the organs of the senses are, which being stop'd by vapours can have no perception during sleep... 'tis impossible for one not awake to see, because visible objects make a more lively impression in their organ then any other; and a man asleep is not distinguish'd from another but by cessation of the sense of seeing.

During sleep, the outward *sense* (faculty of perception) of the two eyes *are shut*, so *Lady Macbeth* cannot perceive her actual surroundings. Although she is mobile, she is guided not by sensory input but by her unconscious mind, for "though in sleepe the common sense, and so the outward senses are all bound, yet the phantasie and memory doe not cease, but being now freed from the attendance upon the intelligences of them, or the outward senses, as if they were at more liberty, they are exercised more freely" (Nicholas Byfield, *A Commentary: Or, Sermons Upon the Second Chapter of the First Epistle of Saint Peter*).

Because *Lady Macbeth* cannot see the *Gentlewoman* and the *Doctor*, they have no need to *stand close* ("concealed," TT, s.v. "Occultātus"). Rather, the *Gentlewoman* instructs the *Doctor* to *stand close* ("neere," RC, s.v. "Espez") to *Lady Macbeth* in order to better *observe* her. *Lady Macbeth* then unconsciously interacts with the *Doctor* and the *Gentlewoman*, who stand within arm's length. Cf. and see notes: *my Lord*, line 38, below; *No more o'that*, line 45, below; *Heere's the smell of the blood still*, line 52, below; *The hart is sorely charg'd*, line 55, below; and *give me your hand*, line 68, below.

Lad.   Yet heere's a spot.

Doct.   Heark, she speaks, I will set downe what comes   [35]

from her, to satisfie my remembrance the more strongly.

La.   Out damned spot: out I say. One: Two: Why

then 'tis time to doo't: Hell is murky. Fye, my Lord, fie,

a Souldier, and affear'd? what need we feare? who knowes

it, when none can call our powre to accompt: yet who   [40]

would have thought the olde man to have had so much

blood in him.

Doct.   Do you marke that?

Lad.   The Thane of Fife, had a wife: where is she now?

What will these hands ne're be cleane? No more o'that   [45]

my Lord, no more o'that: you marre all with this star-

ting.

35–36. ***I will set downe what comes from her... strongly.*** In order *to satisfie* ("set free from doubt or uncertainty," OED) his *remembrance the more strongly* ("Forcibly, effectually," "throughly, pithily, with efficacie, to purpose," RC, s.v. "Efficacement"), the *Doctor* pulls out pencil and paper and begins to *set downe* ("put down in writing," "write out," OED) *Lady Macbeth's* words. Unlike the *Gentlewoman*, the *Doctor* has not yet heard *Lady Macbeth's* confessions, so he does not necessarily suspect that her malady springs from criminal guilt. He attempts to record *what comes from her* in order to diagnose the cause of her malady, not to gather evidence against her. According to Robert Burton's *Anatomy of Melancholy*, in cases where

the Patient of himselfe is not able to resist, or overcome these heart-eating passions, his friend; or Physitian must be ready to supply that which is wanting... If he conceale his grievances, and will not be knowne of them. They must observe by his lookes, gestures, motions, phantasy, what it is that offends him, and then to apply remedies unto him: many are instantly cured, when their mindes are satisfied... No better way to satisfie, then to remove the object, cause, occasion, if by any Art or meanes possibly we may finde it out.

37–45. *Out damned spot... will these hands ne're be cleane.* Cf. II.ii.58–59, 77–83, and 87–88; and see note: *Taper*, line 21, above.

37. *One: Two.* The usual interpretation of these words is that *Lady Macbeth* remembers hearing the clock strike *Two* just prior to *Duncan's* murder. This cannot be the case, because (a) *the Clock goes downe at Twelve* (II.i.5–7); and (b) *Lady Macbeth* herself was to *strike upon the Bell* to signal that all was in readiness for the murder (II.i.45–46 and 77–78). *Lady Macbeth* might here (a) recall her own striking of the bell *Two* times; or (b) envision each of *Duncan's Two* grooms passing into unconsciousness *One* after the other (cf. II.ii.8–11).

38. *Hell is murky.* *Lady Macbeth* might say that *Hell is* (a) *murky* ("obscure, darke, unknowen," "dim, blacke, not shining, mistie, hard to finde, hidden, secret, diffuse, close and secret, hard to be understood," JF, s.v. "Oscuro"); or (b) "mirky" ("Smiling, hearty, merry, pleased," JJ). In either case, *Lady Macbeth's* statement does not necessarily express fear. If *murky* means the former, then *Lady Macbeth* might simply say that *Hell* is incomprehensible and thus irrelevant.

38. *Fye.* *Fye* is an expession of disapproval "akin to 'shit'" (FR). *Fye* literally means "dung" and the "orificium ana'le" (DPF).

38. *my Lord.* In Shakespeare's time, professional actors presented plays with a bare minimum of rehearsal. Moreover, they did not receive a complete copy of the script but worked from cue-scripts which contained only their own cues and lines (see *Introduction*, p. 9, and *Textual Preparation*, p. 402). Actors working under these performance conditions must have followed very simple guidelines for blocking and action, so an actor would generally address his speech towards the person named in it (e.g., *worthy Thane*, I.ii.60; *Macbeth*, I.iii.54; and *Hecat*, III.v.4). In the absence of such spoken titles, the common-sense rule of thumb is for the actor to respond to the character who delivers his cue (Patrick Tucker, *Secrets of Acting Shakespeare: The Original Approach*, p. 263). *Lady Macbeth* therefore speaks directly to the *Doctor* (the character who speaks her cue line), whom she mistakes for her *Lord* (husband). She again speaks directly to the *Doctor* in lines 44, 63, and 67, below.

40. *accompt.* *Accompt* "is in the common lawe taken for a writte or action brought against a man, that by meanes of office or businesse undertaken, is to render an account unto another: as a bailife toward his Master, a guardian in socage toward his ward, & such others" (John Cowell, *The Interpreter: or Booke Containing the Signification of Words*, q.v.). As absolute monarchs, the *Macbeths* must make *accompt* to no one.

44. *The Thane of Fife... where is she now?* *Macbeth* launched his attack on *Macduffe's* family immediately after visiting the *Witches* (cf. IV.i.183–190), so it is doubtful whether *Lady Macbeth* knew of *Macbeth's* plans in advance. Nevertheless, she clearly knows of (and feels guilty for) the murder of *Macduffes Wife*.

45. *cleane.* Figuratively, *cleane* means "free from the guilt and curse of sin" (TW).

45–47. *No more o'that... this starting.* *Lady Macbeth* confuses the *Doctor's* starting ("Fearing sore, or beeing amazed," TT, s.v. "Păvĭtans"; "violent quaking, shrugging, or trembling," RC, s.v. "Tremoussement") with her husband's *starting* ("a suddaine, violent, and unexpected passion," RC, s.v. "Boutade") (a) following *Duncan's* murder (II.ii.46–65 and 82–99); and/or (b) upon seeing *the Ghost of Banquo* (III.iv.48–93 and 113–135).

Doct.   Go too, go too:

You have knowne what you should not.

Gent.   She ha's spoke what shee should not, I am sure   [50]

of that: Heaven knowes what she ha's knowne.

La.   Heere's the smell of the blood still: all the per-

fumes of Arabia will not sweeten this little hand.

Oh, oh, oh.

Doct.   What a sigh is there? The hart is sorely charg'd.   [55]

Gent.   I would not have such a heart in my bosome,

for the dignity of the whole body.

Doct.   Well, well, well.

Gent.   Pray God it be sir.

48. ***Go too, go too.*** *Go too* can mean (a) "how now?" (JF, s.v. "Ombè"); (b) "well now," "Now then" (RC, s.v. "Or"); and/or (c) "away in the name of god" (JF, s.v. "Orsu col nome di Dio").

49. ***You have knowne what you should not.*** The *Doctor*, who has finally recognized the import of *Lady Macbeth's* words, admonishes her directly (see note: *my Lord*, line 38, above).

52. ***Heere's the smell of the blood still.*** The phrase "*Here is* calls attention to what the speaker has, brings, offers, or discovers; = there is here, see or behold here" (OED). *Lady Macbeth* calls attention to *the smell of the blood* on her hands by thrusting them under the nose of the *Gentlewoman* (the character who spoke her cue line; see note: *my Lord*, line 38, above).

52–53. ***all the perfumes of Arabia... this little hand.*** A "perfume" is a "substance which emits a pleasant smell when burned; incense" (OED). Two of the most widely sought *perfumes of Arabia* were "frankincense, which is a Gumme, growing in Arabia" (JB, s.v. "Olibanum"), and "Myrrhe," which JB defines as a

> Gumme brought out of Arabia... and is often used in Physicke, being of an opening, cleansing, and dissolving nature. Poets feine that Myrrhe, first came by reason of a kings daughter, named Murrha, who for a grievous crime committed, was by the Gods turned into a little Tree, out of the branches wherof this Gumme still droppeth in manner of teares, as a token of her repentant sorrowe.

According to JT (s.v. "Incense"), *the perfumes of Arabia* symbolize

> purity, virtue, sweetness, and prayer. From the earliest times, the burning of aromatic resins, woods, dried plants or fruits has been one of the most universal of all religious acts... Frankincense and myrrh, two of the Magi's gifts to Christ, were highly valuable throughout the Near East and Mediterranean world. These and other forms of incense were burned for ritual purification, a tradition inherited by the Church.

Thus, *Lady Macbeth* expresses her despair of redemption. Cf. *Tropologia*, in which Thomas De Laune states that in the Bible

> Christ is called A *Bundle of Myrrhe*... Of which, abundance grows in Arabia; Myrrh is indeed bitter, but most fragrant, and of singular profit, in cleansing and healing of Wounds, in expelling corrupt humors out of the Body, in easing pains or griefs, in comforting the heart, and most effectual in preserving the body from putrefaction. All which may be most fairly accommodated and improved in paralells applyed to our blessed Saviours passion... Other Myrrh may be bought for Money... All the Riches of both the Indies can't purchase one drain of this Divine Myrrh.

54. ***Oh, oh, oh.*** "The sound of one that sobbeth, weepeth, howleth, or cryeth out in weeping" (TT, s.v. "Oh, oh, oh, oh").

55. ***sigh.*** Both (a) "a wearie breath, a sob, a gaspe" (JF, s.v. "Sospiro"); and (b) "A wayling or lamenting, a mourning: a pitifull grone" (TT, s.v. "Gĕmitus").

55. ***The hart is sorely charg'd.*** The *Doctor* feels *Lady Macbeth's* pulse and determines that her *hart is sorely* ("In such a manner as to cause great pain or bodily injury; severely," OED) *charg'd* ("burdened, fraighted, loaded, laden, taxed," JM, s.v. "Cargád"). He also suspects that her *hart is sorely* ("To a great extent; in a high degree," OED) *charg'd* ("accused of, a crime," RC, s.v. "Accoulpé"; "guiltie," JM, s.v. "Réo").

57. ***dignity.*** "Noblenesse, greatnesse of power, authoritie" (TT, s.v. "Amplĭtūdo"); "Majestie, lordlines," "prerogative royall" (TT, s.v. "Mājestas").

Doct.   This disease is beyond my practise: yet I have   [60]

         knowne those which have walkt in their sleep, who have

         dyed holily in their beds.

Lad.   Wash your hands, put on your Night-Gowne,

         looke not so pale: I tell you yet againe *Banquo*'s buried;

         he cannot come out on's grave.   [65]

Doct.   Even so?

Lady.   To bed, to bed: there's knocking at the gate:

         Come, come, come, come, give me your hand: What's

         done, cannot be undone. To bed, to bed, to bed.

Exit Lady.   [V.i.3] [70]

Doct.   Will she go now to bed?

Gent.   Directly.

Doct.   Foule whisp'rings are abroad: unnaturall deeds

         Do breed unnaturall troubles: infected mindes

         To their deafe pillowes will discharge their Secrets: [75]

         More needs she the Divine, then the Physitian:

---

60. **practise.** Both (a) "experience" (RC, s.v. "Practique"); and (b) "occupation" (RC, s.v. "Usage"). Cf. line 76, below.
    60–62. ***I have knowne those… dyed holily in their beds.*** Walking in one's *sleep*

was not necessarily a symptom of wicked thoughts or deeds, but it could be interpreted as such (see note: *a most fast sleepe*, line 11, above). Moreover, sleepwalking was (and is) extremely dangerous. As James Hart warns in *Klinike, or The Diet of the Diseased*, in individuals

> such as during their naturall sleepe, yet perform such actions as are commonly performed by such as are awake... the bonds of the senses, passages of the spirits, and impediments of motion being removed, they performe workes proper to those that are awake; as to climbe up to the tops of houses, to walke upon narrow beames and bridges, and many other such actions without any feare or danger, which if they were awake they durst never doe: and all this by reason this discerning facultie of the common sense is yet at rest, not acknowledging nor discerning any danger, unlesse by loud houping and crying the party be awaked out of sleep. If they be suddenly awaked, then are they in danger of sudden precipitation, or falling downe head long, all the spirits and powers of the body then leaving the extreme parts hands and feet, and flying to succour the feeble heart now assaulted with no small feare.

Nevertheless, the terrified *Doctor* reasons that it is perhaps best to ignore *Lady Macbeth's* nocturnal ramblings. She may yet live a long time, and die of natural causes *holily* ("Devoutly, relgiously," "with feare of conscience," RC, s.v. "Devotement") *in* her bed.

63. **Wash your hands, put on your Night-Gowne.** Cf. II.ii.86–94.

64. **Banquo's buried.** *Lady Macbeth's* thoughts jump immediately from the murder of *Duncan* to the murder of *Banquo*.

66. **Even so.** "Is it so?" (TT, s.v. "Siccĭně").

67. **there's knocking at the gate.** Cf. and see note: *Knocke within*, II.ii.73.

68–69. **give me your hand... to bed.** *Lady Macbeth*, imagining the *Doctor* as her husband, grabs him by the *hand* and attempts to drag him off *to bed*.

68–69. **What's done, cannot be undone.** Proverbial. Cf. "that is done, is done, it can not be called backe agayne" (Hughe Latimer, *The seconde Sermon of Maister Hughe Latimer*). Cf. III.ii.17–18.

72. **Directly.** Immediately.

73–74. **Foule whisp'rings are abroad... unnaturall troubles.** Regarding the *unnaturall deeds* of *Macbeth* and his wife, *Foule whisp'rings* ("rumour[s]," "malicious insinuation[s], secret slander[s] or detraction[s]," OED) *are abroad* ("In public, so as to be widely known, believed," OED). These have led to *whisp'rings* ("secret speech[es] or communication[s]," TB, s.v. "Cryptology") *abroad* ("out of one's own country; in or into foreign lands," OED) inviting a foreign invasion (cf. III.vi.41–43; and IV.iii.5–7, 51–53, and 150–152). As a consequence of the monarchs' *unnaturall troubles* ("Harm[s], injur[ies], offence[s]," OED), Scotland is threatened by *unnaturall troubles* ("mutinie[s]; tumult[s], sedition[s], insurrection[s], uprore[s]," RC, s.v. "Mutinerie").

75. **To their deafe pillowes... their Secrets.** It was considered necessary to "discharge" ("give vent to words, feelings," OED) in order to be (a) "discharged" ("disburdened," RC, s.v. "Deschargé"); cf. and see note: *Give sorrow words*, IV.iii.246; and (b) "discharged" ("absolved, pardoned, forgiven," RC, s.v. "abSuélto"). *Lady Macbeth* has long since lost the confidence of her husband (cf. III.ii.55–57), so now she can confide in no one except her *deafe* pillow.

76. **Divine.** A "preacher of divinitie, a professor of divinitie or holie things" (JF, s.v. "Theólogo").

God, God forgive us all. Looke after her,

Remove from her the meanes of all annoyance,

And still keepe eyes upon her: So goodnight,

My minde she ha's mated, and amaz'd my sight.   [80]

I thinke, but dare not speake.

Gent.   Good night good Doctor.

Exeunt.

78. ***Remove... all annoyance.*** *Annoyance* can mean (a) "vexation of minde, a fault, or a trespas, or guilt of conscience" (RC, s.v. "Ricadia"); (b) "paine, griefe, sicknesse" (RC, s.v. "Mau"); and/or (c) "hurt, offence," "damage... In Law it is, where any man erects any wall, stops any water, or doth any thing upon his own ground to the unlawful hurt or annoyance of his neighbors" (TB, s.v. "Nusance").

The *Doctor* instructs the *Gentlewoman* to *Remove the meanes of all annoyance from Lady Macbeth* because he recognizes that her condition is dangerous to both herself and others. In *Anatomy of Melancoly*, Robert Burton recommends that in treating those who suffer

> Perturbations of the minde... bad objects are to be removed, and all such persons in whose companies they be not well pleased... that their mindes be quietly pacified, vaine conceipts diverted, if it be possible, with terrors, cares, fixed studies, cogitations, and whatsoever it is that shall any way molest or trouble the minde, because that otherwise there is no good to be done.

One such *meanes of annoyance* is the lighted candle, which *Lady Macbeth* has probably left behind on the stage (cf. lines 68–70, above). The candle is a *meanes of annoyance* in that it allows *Lady Macbeth* to imagine that she "sees" her way through the castle (see note: *Taper*, line 21, above).

79. ***still.*** At all times.

80. ***mated.*** *Mated* can mean (a) "Deaded," "quelled, subdued, overcome" (TT, s.v. "Mat"); and (b) "amazed, affrighted, astonished, terrified, danted" (JF, s.v. "Sbigottito").

81. ***thinke.*** To "suspect" (OED).

Act V, scene ii

Scena Secunda.   [1]

Drum and Colours. Enter Menteth, Cathnes,

Angus, Lenox, Soldiers.   [V.ii.1]

Ment.	The English powre is neere, led on by *Malcolm*,
	His Unkle *Seyward*, and the good *Macduff.* [5]
	Revenges burne in them: for their deere causes
	Would to the bleeding, and the grim Alarme
	Excite the mortified man.
Ang.	Neere Byrnan wood
	Shall we well meet them, that way are they comming. [10]
Cath.	Who knowes if *Donalbane* be with his brother?
Len.	For certaine Sir, he is not: I have a File
	Of all the Gentry; there is *Seywards* Sonne,
	And many unruffe youths, that even now
	Protest their first of Manhood. [15]
Ment.	What do's the Tyrant.
Cath.	Great Dunsinane he strongly Fortifies:
	Some say hee's mad: Others, that lesser hate him,
	Do call it valiant Fury, but for certaine

Notes V.ii.

2. **Colours.** *Colours* signifies both the battle-flag and the soldiers who serve under it. Cf. RC's "Enseigne": "an Ensigne, Standard, or Banner; the Colours under which a Band, or Companie of footmen serve; also, the Band, or Companie it selfe."

2–3. **Menteth, Cathnes, Angus.** Shakespeare drew these characters' titles from Holinshed's list of Scottish earldoms that were created following *Malcolme's* accession. See note: *Henceforth be Earles*, V.vii.129.

4–5. **The English powre... His Unkle Seyward.** Holinshed reports that *The English powre* (army) was *led on by Seyward*, but Holinshed states that *Seyward* was *Malcolme's* grandfather, not his *Unkle* (see note: *Prince of Cumberland*, I.iv.50).

6. **deere.** *Deere* can mean (a) "Glorious, noble, honourable, worthy"; (b) "important"; and/or (c) "Heartfelt; hearty; hence earnest" (OED).

6. **causes.** "Cause" can mean (a) "reason for action, motive"; (b) "Matter in dispute," "affair to be decided"; (c) "charge, accusation"; and/or (d) "a movement which calls forth the efforts of its supporters" (OED).

7. **Alarme.** A call to arms (see note: *Alarum*, I.ii.2).

8. **mortified.** *Mortified* can mean (a) "dead and senseles" (TT, s.v. "Gangræna"); (b) "decayed" (RC, s.v. "Amati"); (c) "quailed, allayed, abated in vigor" (RC, s.v. "Emmati"); and/or (d) "dead to sin or worldly desires; having the appetites and passions in subjection; prompted by a spirit of religious self-mortification; ascetic, unworldly" (OED).

10. **well.** "With courage and spirit; gallantly, bravely" (OED).

12. **File.** See note: *file*, III.i.119.

14–15. **unruffe youths... first of Manhood.** The *youths* are *unruffe* ("not rough") in that they are (a) "not rough-chinned; unbearded" (OED); (b) "untaught, not exercised or traded in a thing, nothing expert or cunning, that knoweth not how" (TT, s.v. "Rŭdis"); (c) not "Cruell in countenance, and menacing" (TT, s.v. "Trŭcŭlentus"); and/or (d) not "dangerous to medle with" (TT, s.v. "Sĕvērus").

Nevertheless, these *youths Protest* ("claim, demand," OED) *their* (a) *first* ("elements or rudiments"; "beginning," OED) *of Manhood* (manliness and/or merit; see note: *Manhood*, III.i.127); and/or (b) *first* ("*ellipt*[*ical*] for 'the first of the season,'" OED) *of Manhood* ("valour, prowesse," RC, s.v. "Vertu"; "courage, valiancie," JF, s.v. "Virilità") — i.e., they claim the right to warfare as *Manhood's* "first fruit" ("the first products of a man's work or endeavour," OED).

18. **hee's mad.** *Macbeth* is indeed *mad* and has been so for quite some time. Cf. and see notes: II.i.48–54; II.ii.45–46 and 57–58; III.iv.48 and 177–178; and V.v.32–34.

19. **Fury.** A "vehemencie," "a sodaine motion, a rage, a pange, a passion" (JF, s.v. "Impeto").

| | He cannot buckle his distemper'd cause | [20] |
| | Within the belt of Rule. |

Ang.   Now do's he feele

His secret Murthers sticking on his hands,

Now minutely Revolts upbraid his Faith-breach:

Those he commands, move onely in command,   [25]

Nothing in love: Now do's he feele his Title

Hang loose about him, like a Giants Robe

Upon a dwarfish Theefe.

Ment.   Who then shall blame

His pester'd Senses to recoyle, and start,   [30]

When all that is within him, do's condemne

It selfe, for being there.

20–21. *He cannot buckle... the belt of Rule.* Macbeth cannot (a) *buckle* ("limit, enclose," OED) *his distemper'd* ("disordered, intemperate," JF, s.v. "Intemperato") *cause* (enterprise, undertaking) *Within the belt* (compass) *of Rule* ("Good order and discipline," OED); and/or (b) *buckle* ("grapple with," F&H) *his distemper'd* ("Crasie," EC2; "vexed," "perturbed in mind," JF, s.v. "Passionato") *cause* ("Disease, sickness," OED) *Within the belt* (i.e., mental control; to *belt* is "To gird, metaph[orically] used in relation to the mind," JJ) *of Rule* ("Moderation, temperance," TT, s.v. "Mŏdĕrāmen"). *Macbeth's* lack *of Rule* ("a settled well-regulated state or condition," OED) is so extreme that *He cannot* even *buckle* ("claspe," "hooke," RC, s.v. "Aggraffer") his *belt* ("arming girdle, or sword girdle," RC, s.v. "Balthée"). Cf. and see notes: *Bring me no more Reports*, V.iii.3; and *Give me my Armor*, V.iii.42.

It is now obvious to everyone that *Macbeth* suffers from "impotencie" ("unablenes to rule or order," TT, s.v. "Impŏtentĭa") and that his *cause* (sexual ability; see note: *causes*, III.iv.172) is *distemper'd* ("faint, feeble, weake," RC, s.v. "Ohié"). *He cannot buckle* (copulate, JH) *Within the belt* (synonymous with "zone": "vaginal region," GW2), because *Within the belt* ("male pubic region," JH, s.v. "Squeez'd out at the buccal") he has no *Rule* ("powre, strength, puissance," JF, s.v. "Potentia"). Cf. "And buckle in a waste most fathomlesse, / With spannes and inches so diminutive" (*Troylus and Cressida*, II.i.).

23. *sticking on his hands.* Macbeth can no longer shift the blame for his crimes onto anyone else, so his guilt is now *sticking on his* own *hands.* Cf. II.ii.76–80.

24. *minutely.* Occurring each minute.

24. *Faith-breach.* I.e., a "breach of faith": "disloyaltie, tretcherie, treason," "false dealing" (John Florio, *Queen Anna's New World of Words*, s.v. "Perfídia").

25. *move onely in command.* Those in *Macbeth's* army *move* ("go forward, march, advance," OED) *onely in* ("in the control or power of," OED) *command* ("coercion," OED; "an injunction," "imposition or charge," JF, s.v. "Ingiontione"). *Macbeth's* followers are therefore prone to desertion (cf. V.iii.3; and V.vii.36–37 and 41–42).

27–28. *a Giants Robe... a dwarfish Theefe.* Due to their stunted growth, dwarfs symbolically represent "human ignorance or blind instinct. They can also be associated with the symbolism of the fool as an inversion of the king, a role sometimes played by dwarfs at court" (JT). Cf. I.iii.122.

30. *pester'd.* Pester'd can mean (a) "troubled" (HC, q.v.); (b) "perplexed" (RC, s.v. "Envelopé"); (c) "in a maze, at his wits end" (RC, s.v. "Perplex"); (d) "intrapped; caught, or confined, within a trap" (RC, s.v. "Entrapé"); and/or (e) "invironed on all sides, with dangerous mischiefes," "afflicted which way soever he turne him" (RC, s.v. "Couché"). Cf. III.iv.31–32.

30. *recoyle.* See note: *recoyle*, IV.iii.24.

30. *start.* See notes: *start*, I.iii.57; and *starting*, V.i.46–47.

31–32. *When all that is within him... being there.* Cf. II.ii.95–97.

Cath.   Well, march we on,

To give Obedience, where 'tis truly ow'd:

Meet we the Med'cine of the sickly Weale,   [35]

And with him poure we in our Countries purge,

Each drop of us.

Lenox.   Or so much as it needes,

To dew the Soveraigne Flower, and drowne the Weeds:

Make we our March towards Birnan.   [40]

Exeunt marching.

35–39. *the Med'cine of the sickly Weale... Soveraigne Flower.* The *Weale* (health, well-being) *of the Weale* (commonwealth, body politic) is *sickly* ("crazie, queasie, distempered, ill disposed of bodie," RC, s.v. "Maladif"). Therefore, *Malcolme* must serve as a *Med'cine* ("A medical practitioner," OED) and administer a *Med'cine* ("a remedy, a redresse," JF, s.v. "Remédio"). *With him in* their *Countries purge* ("cleansing," JF, s.v. "Purga"), those faithful to *Malcolme* will *poure* ("cast out largely," "spend exceedingly," TT, s.v. "Profundo") *Each drop* of blood *of* ("from," "out of," OED) themselves. *Each drop* ("fall": "death," OED) in this bloodletting will help to heal their country. Cf. and see notes: III.iv.97–98 and V.iii.70–71.

As a *Med'cine* to cure *the sickly Weale, Malcolme* is a *Soveraigne* ("Of remedies, etc.: Efficacious or potent in a superlative degree," OED) *Flower* ("The bloom of certain plants used in Medicine," OED). In order to "due" ("endow, invest, endue," OED) *Malcolme* with his "due" (proper, rightful) title of *Soveraigne* (king), *Lenox* and his companions will *dew* ("bedew, wet gently, moisten faire and softly," RC, s.v. "Rosoyer") this *Soveraigne Flower* with their own blood.

39. **Weeds.** *Macbeth* and *Lady Macbeth*, who are figured as *Weeds* ("Generic for sorryness or worthlessness," F&H).

Act V, scene iii

Scæna Tertia.   [1]

Enter Macbeth, Doctor, and Attendants.   [V.iii.1]

Macb.   Bring me no more Reports, let them flye all:

Till Byrnane wood remove to Dunsinane,

I cannot taint with Feare. What's the Boy *Malcolme?*   [5]

Was he not borne of woman? The Spirits that know

All mortall Consequences, have pronounc'd me thus:

Feare not *Macbeth*, no man that's borne of woman

Shall ere have power upon thee. Then fly false Thanes,

And mingle with the English Epicures,   [10]

The minde I sway by, and the heart I beare,

Shall never sagge with doubt, nor shake with feare.

Notes V.iii.

3–39. **Bring me no more Reports... What Newes more.** *Macbeth's* mind has broken down to the point that he is no longer an effective leader. He puts his faith in prophecy and refuses important *Reports*, but he soon changes his mind and impatiently calls *Seyton* to demand more *Newes* (lines 26, 27, and 36, below). Also see note: *The minde I sway by*, line 11, below.

3. **let them flye all.** The commanders and soldiers who appeared in the previous scene were originally part of *Macbeth's* army. These former supporters *flye* ("abhor, detest, loath extreamly, have in abhomination; utterly disagree from," RC, s.v. "Abhorrer") *Macbeth*, so they *flye* ("forsake, run from," RC, s.v. "Refuir") him and *flye* ("run over hurriedly," OED) to join *Malcolme's* forces.

5. **taint.** Both (a) "To lose vigour or courage; to become weak or faint; to wither, fade"; and (b) "to corrupt, contaminate, deprave" (OED).

5. **the Boy Malcolme.** Almost two decades have passed since *Malcolme* fled to England (see notes: *Thou hast it now*, III.i.3; and *Macbeths head*, V.vii.116). Although *Macbeth* has aged considerably (cf. lines 29–30, below), in Shakespeare's rather inconsistent timeline *Malcolme* remains a young man.

6–7. **The Spirits that know All mortall Consequences.** *The* diabolical *Spirits* with whom *Macbeth* has conversed do not truly *know All mortall* "consequence" ("That which followeth after," HC; the "unintermitted course of things," RC, s.v. "Suitte"), but *Macbeth* has been fully drawn in by the Devil's lies. Cf. and see notes: *why doe you start*, I.iii.57; *prediction*, I.iii.61; and *He knowes thy thought*, IV.i.82.

7. **pronounc'd.** To "pronounce" is (a) "To prophesie," "to tell or foretell things to come" (TT, s.v. "Prŏfãris"); and (b) to "adjudge, order, decree," "to give sentence, deliver his opinion, pronounce an award" (RC, s.v. "Sententier"). Also see note: *Pronounce*, III.iv.11.

9–10. **flye false Thanes... English Epicures.** An "Epicure" is (a) "One given to excesse of gluttonie" (HC); and (b) "One who gives himself up to sensual pleasure" (OED), "one alwaies saucily craving, violent and importunate, lecherous, a wanton riotous banquetor" (JF, s.v. "Procace"). Holinshed accuses the *English* of infecting Scotland with Epicureanism, relating that after *Malcolme* returned from exile with his *English* followers

> such outrageous riot entred at this time, and began to growe in use amongst the Scottishmen, togither with the language and maners of the English nation... the nature of man is so prone & ready to embrace all kinds of vice, that where the Scottishe people before had no knowledge nor understanding of fine fare or riotous surfet, yet after they had once tasted the sweet poisoned bait thereof, there was now no meane to be found to restrain theyr licorous desires.

Macbeth does not care if his traitorous *Thanes* (a) *flye* (desert him) *And mingle* (associate, keep company) *with the English Epicures* (gluttons); and/or (b) *flye* (copulate, GW2) *And mingle* ("Copulate; esp. homosexually," FR; to *mingle* is literally "to cleave, that they be one body," TT, s.v. "Adcorpŏro") *with the English Epicures* (lechers).

11–12. **The minde I sway by... sagge with doubt.** Although *Macbeth* believes that *The minde* he "sways" ("governe[s], rule[s], commaund[s]," RC, s.v. "Gouverner") *by* is firm, he has long since begun to *sway* ("vacillate," OED). *Macbeth* asserts that *doubt* will never make him *sagge* ("drift, deviate insensibly," OED), but he is decidedly incoherent. At first he has no *Feare* (lines 5 and 8, above), then he is *sick at hart* (line 26, below), then he is again *not affraid* (line 75, below). The once formidable *Macbeth* is now incapable of even the simple task of donning his armor (see note: *Give me my Armor*, line 42, below). In *Anatomy of Melancholy*, Robert Burton gives erratic behavior such as that exhibited by *Macbeth* as one of melancholy's unmistakable "Symptomes or signes in the Mind":

> Inconstant they are in all their actions, unapt to resolve of any businesse, they will and will not, perswaded to and fro upon every small occasion, or word spoken... in most things wavering, unable to deliberat through feare... Now prodigall, and then covetous, they doe, and by & by repent them of that which they have done, soone weary, and still seeking change, erected and dejected in an instant, animated to undertake, and upon a word spoken againe discouraged.

Despite clear evidence to the contrary, *Macbeth* continues to allege his own "potency" (both military might and sexual power; see note: I.ii.45–46). He refuses to acknowledge that it is possible for his *heart* (phallic erection; see note: *Heart*, I.iii.154) to *sagge* ("To droop; to sink or hang down loosely," OED). Instead, *Macbeth* persists in his belief that his *minde* (penis; see note: *Braine*, I.iii.173) can *sway* (achieve erection; HH notes that a "sway" is a pump handle, and that "Shakespeare's verb 'swayes' has reference to the smooth upward movement of some such lever," p. 328).

Enter Servant.   [V.iii.2]

> The divell damne thee blacke, thou cream-fac'd Loone:
>
> Where got'st thou that Goose-looke.   [15]

Ser.   There is ten thousand.

Macb.   Geese Villaine?

Ser.   Souldiers Sir.

Macb.   Go pricke thy face, and over-red thy feare

> Thou Lilly-liver'd Boy. What Soldiers, Patch?   [20]
>
> Death of thy Soule, those Linnen cheekes of thine
>
> Are Counsailers to feare. What Soldiers Whay-face?

Ser.   The English Force, so please you.

Macb.   Take thy face hence.

{*Exit Servant.*}   [V.iii.3] [25]

> Seyton, I am sick at hart,
>
> When I behold: *Seyton*, I say, this push
>
> Will cheere me ever, or dis-eate me now.

---

14. **The divell damne thee... Loone.** *Macbeth* calls the *Servant*, who is white with
fear, a *cream-fac'd Loone* ("A country bumkin, or clown," FG). To darken the *Servant's*
"white" (fearful) complexion, the *divell* should *damne* him and burn him in Hell until
blacke ("Sootie," "smoakie," RC, s.v. "Fuligineux").

In addition, *Macbeth* insults the *Servant* by implying that he is willing to "play
the *Loone*" ("play the whore," F&H) with his "lune" ("moon": "backside," GW2). The
Servant therefore has *cream* ("seminal fluid," F&H) in his "face" (ass; see not: *fac'd*,
I.ii.26). For this, the *divell* should *damne* (i.e., "screw"; see note: *damned*, I.ii.20) him
blacke (i.e., in the anus; see note: *black,* IV.i.52). Also see note: *damnation*, I.vii.24.

15. **Goose-looke.** The *Servant's* fear makes him appear as white as a *Goose*
(emblematic of cowardice). The *Servant* also looks like (a) a *Goose* ("A foole; asse," RC,
s.v. "Fol"); and (b) a *Goose* ("Prostitute," JH).

19–20. *pricke thy face… Thou Lilly-liver'd Boy.* The *Servant* is *Lilly-liver'd* ("Pale Visag'd," ND, s.v. "White-liver'd"), which indicates that he is a *Lilly-liver'd* ("cowardly, dastardly," F&H) *Boy* ("a worthless fellow, a knave, a rogue, a wretch," OED). If the *Servant* cannot *over-red* ("overpower," "master," "subdue," JJ, s.v. "red") his *feare*, then he should *pricke* ("pierce full of holes," JF, s.v. "Sforare"; "launce, cut," RC, s.v. "Eslancer") his *face* and *over-red* ("cover over with red," "cover with blood," OED) his pallor.

The *Servant* is also a *Boy* ("catamite," FR), so he is *Lilly-* ("a term of abuse, esp. of a man to imply lack of masculinity," OED) *liver'd* (the seat of sexual passion; see note: *Liver,* IV.i.28). He should *pricke* (with obvious bawdy implication) and *over-red* (i.e., cover with "blood," or semen; see note: *blood,* III.iv.120) his *face* (rear end; see note: *fac'd,* I.ii.26).

20. *Patch.* A *Patch* is (a) "A fool; so called from the motley or patched dress worn by licensed fools" (DPF); (b) "The female pudendum" (F&H); and (c) a mercury plaster used to treat syphilitic sores (JH).

21. *Death of thy Soule.* *Macbeth* curses the *Servant* with *Death of* the *Soule* ("Eternal Death and damnation of soule and body in Hell, as the first Death is the dissolution of the soule and body," TW, s.v. "second Death"). *Macbeth* also implies that the *Servant* should get "fucked up the ass": *Soule* alludes to the buttocks ("sole" literally means "bottom"), and *Death* means orgasm (see note: *Death,* III.i.132).

21–22. *those Linnen cheekes… Counsailers to feare.* Because the *Servant's cheekes Are* white as *Linnen* ("Cloth woven from flax," OED), they serve as *Counsailers* ("perswader[s]," "inducer[s]," JF, s.v. "Persuasore") *to feare* ("terrour, dread," TT, s.v. "Terror").

Also, the *Servant's Linnen* ("suggestive of underclothing, hence of sex," GW2) *cheekes* ("posteriors," F&H) are *Counsailers* (i.e. whores; literally sellers of *Coun* or "cunt") *to feare* (i.e., "to fere": "to mate," OED; a "fere" is "a bed-fellow," EP).

22. *Whay-face.* The *Servant* has (a) a *face* (complexion, countenance) as white as *Whay* ("The serum or watery part of milk which remains after the separation of the curd by coagulation," OED); and (b) a *face* (backside; see note: *fac'd,* I.ii.26) containing or covered with *Whay* ("sexual fluid," GW2).

26. *sick at hart.* I.e., "heart-sick": "depressed and despondent, esp. through 'hope deferred' or continued trouble" (OED).

27–28. *this push Will… dis-eate me now.* *Cheere* and "chair" were pronounced identically (HK, pp. 98 and 179). If *Macbeth* is victorious, *this push* ("violent meeting, or conflict," RC, s.v. "Heurt") *Will* (a) *ever* (eternally, perpetually) *cheere* ("revive," "comfort," "put into heart," RC, s.v. "Rafreschir"; "encourage, embolden," TT, s.v. "Hortor") him; and (b) "chair" him ("install [him] in a chair of authority," OED) for *ever* on the "chair" ("throne," OED).

On the other hand, *this push* might "disseat" (remove from a seat, unseat) *Macbeth,* which would expose the prophecies as mere "deceit" ("Guile," "trumperie, craft, treacherie, falsehood," TT, s.v. "Dŏlus"; OED records "deceit" as a verb meaning "To construct deceitfully, to forge" from 1484).

In other words, *Macbeth* must now "shit or get off the pot" ("take action or make a decision, or else allow another person to do so," OED from 1939, s.v. "pot"). *This push* (contraction of the bowels; see note: *push,* III.iv.104) might *ever cheere Macbeth* (i.e., allow him to *cheere,* or defecate, FR, who cfs. RC's "Chier": "To shite," "goe to the stoole, doe that which no bodie can doe for him"). Conversely, *this push* could *dis-eate* (unseat) his "seat" (posteriors; also "anus," JH) from the "seat" and "chair" (both are synonyms of "throne": "Toilet seat," "chamber-pot," FR). Cf. *push us from our stooles,* III.iv.104.

I have liv'd long enough: my way of life

Is falne into the Seare, the yellow Leafe,   [30]

And that which should accompany Old-Age,

As Honor, Love, Obedience, Troopes of Friends,

I must not looke to have: but in their steed,

Curses, not lowd but deepe, Mouth-honor, breath

Which the poore heart would faine deny, and dare not.   [35]

Seyton?

  Enter Seyton.   [V.iii.4]

Sey.   What's your gracious pleasure?

Macb.   What Newes more?

Sey.   All is confirm'd my Lord, which was reported.   [40]

29–34. *my way of life... Mouth-honor.* "The falling leaves of autumn are an ancient metaphor for mortality and the passage of time" (JT), and *Macbeth's way of life* ("event and successe of [his] course of life," TW, s.v. "their Way") *Is falne into the Seare* (dry, withered), *the yellow* (symbolic of age and decay) *Leafe*. Moreover, *Macbeth's* mind is now as a *Leafe* ("page of a booke," JF, s.v. "Faccia") which is *yellow* (symbolic of "jealousy, envy, melancholy," F&H, and also "inconstancy... Judas in mediæval pictures is arrayed in yellow," DPF). Cf. I.iii.174–176.

Macbeth, who is now in his fifties (see notes: *King*, I.ii.2; *Thou hast it now*, III.i.3; and *Macbeths head*, V.vii.116), has reached "the autumne or fall of the leafe" (JF, s.v. "Autunno"). The "time that fruits be ripe... is at the fall of the leafe" (Thomas Hayne, *The Times, Places, and Persons of the holie Scripture*), so *Macbeth* should now reap the "fruit" of his life's endeavors. However, he harvests not *Honor, Love, Obedience, Troopes* ("companies of souldiours," RC, s.v. "Desbandade"; "squadrons," JF, s.v. "Asquadra") *of Friends* (supporters in his cause), but only *deepe* (*deepe*-rooted, profound; also "Awful, dread, stern," OED) *Curses*. His few remaining followers pay him only *Mouth-honor* (i.e., "Honour with the lips": "Outwardly with the mouth and gesture, without true Faith and love," TW).

Biblically, the blessed man "shalbe like a tree planted by the rivers of water, that bringeth foorth his fruit in his season, his leafe also shall not wither, and whatsoever he doeth shall prosper. The ungodly are not so" (Psalms 1:3–4). To the unrighteous, God will "send a faintness into their hearts in the lands of their enemies, and the sound of a shaken leafe shall chase them, and they shall flee, as fleeing from a sword: and they shall fall, when no one pursueth" (Leviticus 26:36). In stating that his *way of life Is falne into the yellow Leafe*, *Macbeth* acknowledges that he cannot escape his guilt, for as "Scripture teacheth us in Leviticus, saying, That the wicked shall tremble at the fall of the leafe of a tree... this violence of mans conscience commeth from God, who causeth his enemies to feele his judgement and fury in such sort, that they cannot abide it, but are constrained to condemne themselves" (Pierre de La Primaudaye, *The French Academie*). Cf. IV.iii.61 and 278–279.

Macbeth also considers the prospect of divine retribution in the life to come, for "Surely as the fall of the leafe is a token of Winter approaching: so the falling away of the wicked in this life, is a foretoken of that endlesse winter of fearefull wrath, which from God is to come upon them" (William Cowper, *Anatomie of a Christian Man*).

In addition, *Macbeth's way* ("Health, condition, state," F&H) *of life* (i.e., his penis; see note: *Life*, I.vii.50) *Is falne* ("indicating detumescence," GW; also see note: *fall downe*, I.iv.61) *into the Seare* (impotent; cf. and see note: *seare*, IV.i.141), *the yellow Leafe* ("an innuendo of venereal disease, and, quite possibly, to a resulting loss of the penis," JH, s.v. "fall of the Leaf"). Cf. and see notes: *Rancours in the Vessell of my Peace*, III.i.81; and *the frame of things dis-joynt*, III.ii.22.

35. *poore heart.* A *poore* (worthless) person (*heart* is "Put for the person," OED).

35. *deny.* "To refuse," "cast off, renounce, forsake" (RC, s.v. "Refuser").

36. *Seyton.* Holinshed gives *Seyton* as one of the surnames created after *Malcolme's* coronation: "Many new surnames were taken up at this time... as Cauder, Lokart, Gordon, Seyton... with many other that had possessions given to them." Although anachronistic in *Macbeth's* Scotland, "the Setons of Touch... held the office of hereditary armour-bearers to the king" (William Anderson, *The Scottish Nation*, p. 437). "*Seyton*" also puns "Satan."

Macb.	Ile fight, till from my bones, my flesh be hackt.
	Give me my Armor.
Seyt.	'Tis not needed yet.
Macb.	Ile put it on:
	Send out moe Horses, skirre the Country round, [45]
	Hang those that talke of Feare. Give me mine Armor:
	How do's your Patient, Doctor?
Doct.	Not so sicke my Lord,
	As she is troubled with thicke-comming Fancies
	That keepe her from her rest. [50]
Macb.	Cure of that:
	Can'st thou not Minister to a minde diseas'd,
	Plucke from the Memory a rooted Sorrow,
	Raze out the written troubles of the Braine,
	And with some sweet Oblivious Antidote [55]
	Cleanse the stufft bosome, of that perillous stuffe
	Which weighes upon the heart?

42–74. ***Give me my Armor… Bring it after me.*** Macbeth's mental state has deteriorated to the point that he cannot even decide whether to put on his *Armor*. Macbeth asks *Seyton* to help him arm (lines 42 and 44), then he immediately orders *Seyton* to instead convey messages to his commanders in the field (lines 45–46). *Macbeth* negates that order by again requesting his *Armor* (line 46), but, by distractedly talking to the *Doctor* (lines 47–60 and 65–73), he makes it impossible for *Seyton* to dress him. After once more ordering *Seyton* to *put* his *Armour on* (line 61), *Macbeth* directly sends *Seyton* away to carry out the orders which he gave previously (lines 45–46). Once *Seyton* is gone, *Macbeth* impatiently calls to another *Attendant* to *dispatch* (hurry, make haste) to help him prepare for battle (line 65), but in line 69 orders that his armor be pulled off. *Macbeth* then changes his mind one more time, commanding that his armor be brought *after* him (line 74).

45–46. *skirre… Hang those that talke of Feare.* Macbeth commands his agents to *skirre* ("ride rapidly through," OED) *the Country round*, which can mean (a) "all over"; (b) "by a roundabout or circuitous route"; or (c) "in the vicinity" (OED).

Skirre might also be a variant spelling of "scour" meaning "To move about hastily or energetically; *esp.* to range about in search of something, or in movements against a foe" (OED; cf. OED's spelling variants "scure" and "scurre"). Also, *Macbeth* wants to "scour" his army (i.e., quickly get rid of its worthless "shit"; cf. and see note: *scowre*, line 71, below) by hanging *those that talke of Feare.*

49–50. *thicke-comming Fancies… rest.* Lady Macbeth's guilt-ridden *Fancies* ("extravagant conceits, idle visions, odde imaginations," RC, s.v. "Fantosmeries") are now *thicke* (rapidly occurring; see note: *thick*, I.iii.108) during both her sleeping and waking hours. Cf. II.ii.53, and see notes: *fantasticall*, I.iii.157; *cursed thoughts*, II.i.14; *mad*, II.ii.45; *Blood will have Blood*, III.iv.157; and V.i.8–11.

51. *Cure of that.* To *Cure* is both (a) "To effect a cure"; and (b) "To take care of" (OED).

52–55. *Cans't thou not Minister… Oblivious Antidote.* Macbeth hopes that the *Doctor* can *Minister* (administer medicine, OED) *to a minde diseas'd* ("sickish, ill at ease, crazed, weake, feeble, unable," JF, s.v. "Inférmo"). *Lady Macbeth's Sorrow is rooted* ("having taken roote," JM, s.v. "Raygádo"; also "Inveterate, old, auncient, of long use," "setled by continuance," RC, s.v. "Inveteré"), but perhaps there is *some Oblivious* ("that maketh one forget," TT, s.v. "Oblīviōsus") *Antidote* ("a medicine or preservative against venome or poyson," TB, q.v.) to *Plucke* ("root up," RC, s.v. "Arracher"; "displant," "unplant," RC, s.v. "Desplanter") it *from the Memory.* Hopefully, this *Antidote* can *Raze* ("cut quite off, close by the root, cleane away," RC, s.v. "Raser"; also "deface, efface, blot," RC, s.v. "Canceler") *out the written troubles of the Braine.* Unfortunately, "The bodies wounds by medicines may be eased, / But griefes of mindes, by salves are not appeased" (Robert Greene, *The Scottish Historie of James the fourth*).

Lady Macbeth's mental and physical ailments are *rooted* (spring from, originate) in *Sorrow*, for "all the diseases of the body have their beginning from the minde… Sorow and griefe hath great power to weaken the ablest state of body: it doth (as Plato speaketh) exercise cruell tyranny… it teareth, it eateth, and utterly consumeth the mind, and body also" (Eleazar Duncon, *The Copy of a Letter written by E.D. Doctour of Physicke to a Gentleman*). Cf. and see notes: *insane Root*, I.iii.93; and *it will make us mad*, II.ii.45.

56. *stufft bosome.* With play on *stufft* meaning (a) "Stopped up, obstructed; said esp. of a bodily organ when diseased" (OED); and (b) "full" (JB, s.v. "Farced"). The figure was common: cf. TW's definition of "Thorny ground": "An heart stuffed with the cares of this World, which choake the seede of the word, as Thornes choake the Corne springing out of the ground."

Doct.   Therein the Patient

             Must minister to himselfe.

Macb.   Throw Physicke to the Dogs, Ile none of it.   [60]

             Come, put mine Armour on: give me my Staffe:

             Seyton, send out:

    {Exit Seyton.}   [V.iii.5]

             Doctor, the Thanes flye from me:

             Come sir, dispatch. If thou could'st Doctor, cast   [65]

             The Water of my Land, finde her Disease,

             And purge it to a sound and pristine Health,

             I would applaud thee to the very Eccho,

             That should applaud againe. Pull't off I say,

             What Rubarb, Cyme, or what Purgative drugge   [70]

             Would scowre these English hence: hear'st thou of them?

Doct.   I my good Lord: your Royall Preparation

             Makes us heare something.

58–59. *Therein the Patient Must minister to himselfe.* In *Anatomy of Melancholy*, Robert Burton advises that

> from the Patient himselfe, the first and chiefest remedy must be had… Whatsoever it is that runneth in our minds, vain conceit, be it pleasing or displeasing, which so much affects or troubleth us, by all possible meanes he must withstand it, expell those vaine, false, frivolous Imaginatious, absurd conceipts, vaine sorrowes, from which… this Disease primarily proceedes.

60. **Physicke.** With play on *Physicke* as both (a) the practice of medicine; and (b) "A cathartic, a purge, a laxative" (JH). Cf. lines 68–69, below.

61. **Staffe.** A *Staffe* is both (a) "a launce, a speare, a pike, a long poule" (JF, s.v. "Asta"); and (b) "a scepter, an officers sticke" (JF, s.v. "Bacchetta").

65–69. **cast The Water... applaud againe.** *Macbeth* thinks that his court physician is no exalted *Doctor of Physicke* (V.i.2) but merely a "*Water-Doctor*" ("a urine-inspecting physician: spec[ifically] a quack," F&H). Even so, *Macbeth* had hoped that the *Doctor* could *cast The Water* ("diagnose by means of the urine," F&H) in order to *purge* ("make cleane without guilt," TW) his wife's *Land* ("ground": "The divine essence or centre of the individual soul, in which mystic union lies," OED; also see note: *stufft bosome*, line 56, above). If the *Doctor* could do this, *Macbeth would applaud* him *to the very Eccho* ("appland [him] so loudly as to produce an echo," DPF).

Macbeth also hoped that the *Doctor* could *purge* ("heale or remedie," TT, s.v. "Purgo") his wife's *Land* (vagina, FR; cf. Fr. "Landie": "The deaw-lap in a womans Privities," RC). It was believed "that menstruous blood turned into melancholy... by putrefaction or adustion" (Robert Burton, *Anatomy of Melancholy*), so *Lady Macbeth* requires a *purge* ("purgation": "Menstruation; an instance of this; a menstrual discharge," OED) in order *to regain a sound and pristine* ("old, ancient, accustomed, wonted," TB, q.v.) *Health.* Cf. and see notes: I.v.50–52.

Macbeth also seeks to *cast* ("banish, reject, expell," "drive out," RC, s.v. "Forbannir") *The Water* ("Afflictions and troubles which threaten dangers, as Waters doe threaten drowning," TW) from his *Land* (kingdom). If the *Doctor* could *purge* (empty the bowels, OED) the invaders from the "bowels" ("The interior of anything; heart, centre," OED) of Scotland, *Macbeth would applaud* (fart, FR; literally "To clap": to make a hard explosive noise, OED) so loudly that even his *Eccho* ("flatus," FR) would produce an *Eccho* ("A rebounding or sounding backe of any noyse or voyse, in a wood, valley or hollow place," JB, q.v.) and *applaud* (fart) *againe.* Cf. and see note: lines 70–71, below.

70–71. **What Rubarb, Cyme... scowre these English hence.** *Macbeth* considers the *English* to be "shit" who afflict Scotland with "choler" ("a humor causing anger," RC2; "also a sicknes of the stomach, with a troblous flixe and vomite joyned with great daunger: the cholerike passion," TT, s.v. "Chŏlĕra"). *Macbeth's* country is therefore in need of a *Purgative* ("laxative," OED) *drugge* such as *Rubarb*, "A costly roote much used in Phisicke to purge choler" (JB). Barring that, perhaps the *English* can be "scoured" ("emptied, evacuated, voided," RC, s.v. "Desgorgé"; "purged," RC, s.v. "Purifié") *hence* by *Cyme* ("Cyma": "yonge colewortes," TE), for "Colewort being not throughly sodden, purgeth choler & keeps the body soluble" (Pliny the Elder, *The Historie of the World*).

(For further discussion of this passage, see *Introduction*, pp. 14–15. OED's dating of *Cyme* to 1725 is demonstrably incorrect, as is its assertion that *Cyme* is "an 18th cent[ury] adaptation of the ancient Latin" word "cyma." The L. "cyma" was anglicized to *Cyme* no later than the sixteenth century, as is clear from Thomas Cartwright's 1579 *An Hospitall for the diseased*: "For the Collike in the side. Take a small Woodden dishe, and putte therein firste colde Ashes, then laye upon theim hotte ymbers, without great coles, and there upon strewe a good quantitie of Cummenseede... for lacke of Cumminseede take red Sage, Camemell, Isope, Cyme, Peniriall, of like quantitie, and use it as the Cumminseede before.")

Macb.   Bring it after me:

I will not be affraid of Death and Bane,   [75]

Till Birnane Forrest come to Dunsinane.

{*Exeunt. Manet Doctor.*}   [V.iii.6]

Doct.   Were I from Dunsinane away, and cleere,

Profit againe should hardly draw me heere.

{*Exit Doctor.*}   [80]

75. **Bane.** *Bane* can mean (a) "Ruin, fatal mischief; woful or hapless fate; harm, woe" (OED); (b) "A slayer or murderer; one who causes the death or destruction of another" (OED); (c) "poyson; destruction" (EC2); and (d) "Death," "deceasse, or departure out of this life" (RC, s.v. "Mort").

78. **cleere.** Out of reach (OED).

Act V, scene iv

Scena Quarta.   [1]

Drum and Colours. Enter Malcolme, Seyward, Macduffe,

Seywards Sonne, Menteth, Cathnes, Angus,

{Lenox, Rosse,} and Soldiers Marching.   [V.iv.1]

Malc.   Cosins, I hope the dayes are neere at hand   [5]

That Chambers will be safe.

Ment.   We doubt it nothing.

{Seyw.}   What wood is this before us?

Ment.   The wood of Birnane.

Malc.   Let every Souldier hew him downe a Bough,   [10]

And bear't before him, thereby shall we shadow

The numbers of our Hoast, and make discovery

Erre in report of us.

Sold.   It shall be done.

{Seyw.}   We learne no other, but the confident Tyrant   [15]

Keepes still in Dunsinane, and will indure

Our setting downe befor't.

Malc.   'Tis his maine hope:

For where there is advantage to be given,

Both more and lesse have given him the Revolt,   [20]

Notes V.iv.

3. **Seywards Sonne.** Historically, his name was "Osbeorn."

5. **Cosins.** See note: *Cosins,* I.iii.144.

6. **Chambers will be safe.** *Malcolme* looks forward to the day when *Chambers* (bedrooms; also "private Lodgings," ND) *will be safe* from both (a) spies (cf. III.iv.167–168); and (b) murderous assassins (cf. II.iii.94–98 and IV.ii.95–106).

7. **nothing.** "Not at all, in no way" (OED).

10. **Let every Souldier hew him downe a Bough.** Holinshed states that Malcolme folowing hastily after Makbeth, came the night before the battaile unto Byrnan wood, and when his armie had rested a while there to refreshe them, hee commaunded everye man to get a bough of some tree or other of that wood in his hand, as bigge as he might beare, and to march forth therwith in such wise, that on the next morow they might come closely and without sight in thys manner within viewe of hys enimies.

11. **shadow.** To "hide, to keepe in silence, or from the knowledge of men, to make not to be seene" (TT, s.v. "Obscūro").

12. **discovery.** "Exploration, investigation, reconnoitring, reconnaissance" (OED).

15–17. **no other, but the confident Tyrant... befor't.** *No other but* (no one other than) *the confident* ("foolehardie, rash," TT, s.v. "Confidens"; "Bold, fearelesse, hardie, dreadlesse," RC, s.v. "Asseuré") *Tyrant* himself *Keepes* ("defend[s]," "watch[es]," or "lie[s] in wait," OED) *still in Dunsinane* castle. Reportedly, *Macbeth will indure* (permit, tolerate) his enemies to "set *downe*" ("encamp," OED) *befor't.* According to Holinshed,

after that Makbeth perceived his enimies power to encrease, by such ayde as came to them forth of England with his adversarie Malcolme, he reculed backe into Fife, there purposing to abide in campe fortified, at the Castell of Dunsinane, and to fight with his enimies, if they ment to pursue him, howbeit some of his friends advysed him, that it should be best for him, eyther to make some agreement with Malcolme, or else to flee with all speed into the Iles, and to take his treasure with him, to the ende he might wage sundrie great Princes of the realme to take his part, and retayne straungers, in whom he might better trust than in his owne subjectes, which stale dayly from him: but he had suche confidence in his prophecies, that he beleeved he shoulde never be vanquished, till Byrnane wood were brought to Dunsinnane, nor yet to be slaine with anye man, that should be or was borne of any woman.

18–20. **his maine hope... given him the Revolt.** *Macbeth's maine* ("Physical strength, force, or power," OED) is already greatly depleted, and he fears that on open ground what is left of his *maine* ("body of soldiers," OED) will desert him. *Where Macbeth* has *given Both more and lesse* (i.e., *Both* those of higher and lower rank) *advantage* ("faire opportunitie," RC, s.v. "s'endormir sur le rosty"), his followers *have given him the Revolt* ("flight," JF, s.v. "Vólta"; "change of allegiance," OED). Therefore, *Macbeth's maine* (chief, principle) *hope* (prospect) is to withdraw into *Dunsinane* castle.

And none serve with him, but constrained things,

Whose hearts are absent too.

Macd.   Let our just Censures

Attend the true event, and put we on

Industrious Souldiership.   [25]

{Seyw.}   The time approaches,

That will with due decision make us know

What we shall say we have, and what we owe:

Thoughts speculative, their unsure hopes relate,

But certaine issue, stroakes must arbitrate,   [30]

Towards which, advance the warre.

Exeunt marching

21. **constrained.** "Compelled, forced" (RC, s.v. "Compulsé").

23–25. **Let our just Censures... Industrious Souldiership.** *Malcolme's* army seemingly has a good chance of success, but *Macduffe* cautions his companions against over-confidence. Their *just* ("equitable"; also "accurate," OED) *Censures* ("judgement[s]," "opinion[s]," JB; also "ill report[s], or discommendation[s]," RC, s.v. "Blasme") of *Macbeth* and his followers must *Attend* (await) *the true* (actual, real) *event* ("successe," "comming to passe," JF, s.v. "Succésso"). *Malcolme* and his forces should therefore *put on* (assume, adopt) *Industrious* ("diligent, vigilant," RC, s.v. "Industrieux") *Souldiership.*

26–31. **The time approaches... advance the warre.** *The time approaches That* (which) *will with due* ("genuine, real, true," OED) *decision* ("determination, end of a controversie," RC, q.v.) teach *Malcolme's* soldiers *What* (i.e., *what* courage and strength) they truly *have* (possess) as opposed to *what* they merely *owe* ("own": "lay claim to," OED). *Speculative* ("contemplative," RC, s.v. "Speculativo") *Thoughts relate* (communicate) only *unsure hopes, But stroakes* ("battell[s], fight[s], bickering[s], skirmish[es]," RC, s.v. "Chamaillis") *must arbitrate* ("Determine," HC, s.v. "Censure") the *certaine* ("True," "undoubted," RC, s.v. "Vray") *issue* (outcome). *Towards which* (i.e., *Towards* this *time* of *decision,* or the *decision* itself), *Malcolme's* forces will now *advance* ("bring or carrie forth," TT, s.v. "Prověho"; "put forward," TT, s.v. "Prōtollo") *the warre* ("attack, invasion, assault"; also "Actual fighting, battle," OED).

Act V, scene v

Scena Quinta.   [1]

Enter Macbeth, Seyton, & Souldiers, with

Drum and Colours.   [V.v.1]

Macb.   Hang out our Banners on the outward walls,

              The Cry is still, they come: our Castles strength   [5]

              Will laugh a Siedge to scorne: Heere let them lye,

              Till Famine and the Ague eate them up:

              Were they not forc'd with those that should be ours,

              We might have met them darefull, beard to beard,

              And beate them backward home. What is that noyse?   [10]

A Cry within of Women.

Sey.   It is the cry of women, my good Lord.

      {*Exit Seyton.*}   [V.v.2]

Macb.   I have almost forgot the taste of Feares:

              The time ha's beene, my sences would have cool'd   [15]

              To heare a Night-shrieke, and my Fell of haire

              Would at a dismall Treatise rowze, and stirre

              As life were in't. I have supt full with horrors,

              Direnesse familiar to my slaughterous thoughts

              Cannot once start me. Wherefore was that cry?   [20]

Notes V.v.

4. ***Hang out our Banners.*** *Macbeth's Banners* were perhaps hung from the balcony at the rear of the stage during these lines, upon the entrance of *Malcolme's Army* in the next scene (V.vi.2–4), or during the ensuing *Alarums* (V.vi.18 or V.vii.23). The *Banners* would then be taken in when the castle is surrendered to *Malcolme* (V.vii.36–43), or during the *Alarum* immediately following (V.vii.44). The removal of the *Banners* would signal that *Macbeth* has suffered a decisive defeat.

5. ***Cry.*** Either (a) shouting; or (b) rumor.

6. ***laugh... to scorne.*** To *laugh to scorne* is "to mock, flowt, frump, scoffe, deride, jeast at" (RC, s.v. "se Mocquer").

6. ***Siedge.*** *Siedge* can mean (a) an "assault; batterie" (RC, s.v. "Oppugnation"); (b) "a beleaguring or compassing about" (TB, s.v. "Obsession"); (c) "a going to the stoole: a stoole" (TT, s.v. "Dējectĭo"); and/or (c) "the buttockes, arse, fundament, the hinder parts, or part of the bodie whereon we use to sit" (RC, q.v.). Cf. and see notes: V.iii.60 and 65–71.

7. ***Ague.*** A "fever" (RC2, q.v.).

8. ***forc'd.*** "Fortified, made strong against attack" (OED).

9–10. ***met them darefull... backward home.*** *Macbeth* must settle in for a siege because so many of his soldiers have defected to *Malcolme's* side. Otherwise, he *might have met* (confronted in battle) *Malcolme's* army *darefull* ("Full of daring or defiance," OED), *beard to beard* (i.e., face to face). With a full contingent of troops, *Macbeth* would have attacked the enemy on open ground *And beate* ("expell[ed] and drive[n] out with force," TT, s.v. "Quătĕfăcio") *them home backward* ("that hath lost ground, thats gone, or put, from the place he held; thats recoyled, thats retired," RC, s.v. "Desmarché").

Macbeth is certain that he is more "man" than the enemy, as would be clear if they *met beard to beard* (facial hair was considered a barometer of virility; *beard* also means "pubic hair," EP). *Macbeth* thinks he could easily *beate* ("Cudgel Sexually," FR) his enemies *home* (where *home* alludes to "forceful sexual ingression," JH, s.v. "Drive it home") *backward* (with "innuendo of sodomy," JH; the *backward* is the posteriors and anus; see note: *time*, I.vii.10).

15. ***my sences would have cool'd.*** I.e., "My blood would have run cold."

16. ***Night-shrieke.*** Cf. II.ii.5 and 21–22.

16. ***Fell of haire.*** *Fell* can mean (a) "a covering of any kind" (JJ, s.v. "Filsch"); and/or (b) the scalp (literally "The skin," RC, s.v. "Cuir"). Also cf. and see note: *unfixe my Heire*, I.iii.153.

17. ***dismall.*** "Unfortunate, unluckie, unhappie, dismall, ominous" (RC, s.v. "Infauste").

17. ***Treatise.*** A story; also "An entreaty" (OED).

19. ***Direnesse.*** "Dire" can mean (a) "cruell, fell, severe, austere, remorceles" (JF, s.v. "Diro"); and (b) "unhappy, unfortunate, unluckie, dismall, blacke" (JF, s.v. "Infausto").

20. ***once.*** On any occasion; under any circumstances.

20. ***start.*** See note: *start*, I.iii.57.

20. ***Wherefore.*** See note: *wherefore*, II.ii.42.

{*Enter Seyton.*}   [V.v.3]

Sey.   The Queene (my Lord) is dead.

Macb.   She should have dy'de heereafter;

                There would have beene a time for such a word:

                To morrow, and to morrow, and to morrow,   [25]

                Creepes in this petty pace from day to day,

                To the last Syllable of Recorded time:

---

22. **The Queene… is dead.** *The Queene is dead* either by (a) suicide (cf. III.ii.11–12 and V.vii.135–137); or (b) somnambulistic mishap (cf. and see note: V.i.60–62).

23–24. **She should have… a time for such a word.** *Should* and *would* were used interchangeably (see notes: *would*, I.vii.41; and *should*, II.i.27), so it is uncertain whether *Macbeth* expresses resignation or grief upon hearing of his wife's death. He might say that *She should* ("would": must inevitably) *have dy'de heereafter* ("in time to come, another daie," TT, s.v. "Postĕrĭŭs"), so *There would have beene* (must have had to be) *a time* (an occasion) for her death. On the other hand, he might say that *She should* (ought to) *have dy'de heereafter*, for *There would* ("should": ought to) *have beene a time* (a "fitting point of time," OED) for her death. The context favors the former interpretation: everyone must die, so the *word* (news) of someone's death will come *To morrow, and to morrow, and to morrow,* until *time* ends upon the *last Syllable* (lines 25–27, below); *all our yesterdayes* have shown that *all* life ends in *dusty death* (lines 28–29, below); and *death*, like life, ultimately means *nothing* (lines 30–34, below).

24. **word.** *Word* might simply mean a message or news, but *word* is also (a) a spelling variant and dialectal homonym of "world" (HH, p. 208); and (b) "the text of an actor's part" (OED). Cf. lines 30–32, below.

25–26. *To morrow... Creepes in this petty pace.* To "creep" is to "slide foorth like a serpent" (TT, s.v. "Prōserpo"); "to proceed or goe forward by litle and litle, to goe or slide on the bellie as serpens doe" (TT, s.v. "Serpo"). *Macbeth* envisions time as the Ouroboros (Gk. "tail eater"), "the forme of a Serpent, who continually with her taile in her mouth, turneth her selfe round with as great slownesse or leisure as is possible, shewing thereby that Time with a creeping and unseene pace, steales by little and little cleane from us" (Richard Linche, *The Fountaine of Ancient Fiction*). Also, the serpent "biting of its own taile... signifie[s] the virulencie and biting cares that accompany melancholie" (Alexander Ross, *Mystagogus Poeticus*). Proverbially "The happier our time is, the shorter while it lasteth" (John Bodenham and Nicholas Ling, *Politeuphuia*), so for the miserable *Macbeth* time *Creepes* (crawls slowly) along *in this petty* ("paultrie," RC, s.v. "Homonceau"; "Of little importance, insignificant, trivial," OED) *pace* ("A going, a maner of gate," TT, s.v. "Incessus").

Macbeth's life is completely *petty* (i.e., "shitty"; a *petty* is literally "An outside lavatory, a privy," OED from 1848). He sees nothing in his future but a *petty* (with play on "pet" meaning "An act of breaking wind; a fart," OED; cf. Fr. "peter": to fart) *pace* (i.e., "passage": "The action or an act of defecation," OED; *pace* was a homonym or near-homonym of "pass"; see HK, pp. 110 and 267, and cf. OED's spelling variants). *To morrow, and to morrow, and to morrow Creepes* (with possible play on L. "crepo": fart, JA, p. 249) along as meaninglessly as "wind" ("flatus"; also "something empty, vain, trifling, or unsubstantial," OED).

For additional scatological imagery in this speech, cf. and see notes: *Candle*, line 29, below; *poore*, line 30, below; *struts and frets*, line 31, below; *Tale*, line 32, below; and *sound and fury*, line 33, below.

27. *the last Syllable of Recorded time.* For early audiences, *Macbeth's* words would have called to mind "the doctrine of the last sillable, which is that transubstanciacion is done by myracle in an instaunt, at the sounde of the last sillable (um) in this sentence, Hoc est corpus meum... whensoever the wordes of consecration be fully pronounced, then is Christes body there" (Nicholas Ridley, *A brief declaracion of the Lordes Supper*). Catholics and Protestants fiercely debated whether transubstantiation was miraculous or merely symbolic, but in all Christian services its purpose "was to give prominence to, and in particular to harness, the power of the Real Presence of Christ, revealed at Mass as in no other event on earth until the Second Coming" (Andrew Kirkman, *The Cultural Life of the Early Polyphonic Mass*, p. 167). *Macbeth* anticipates *the last Syllable* ("The least portion or detail of speech or writing"; "the least mention, hint, or trace of something," OED) *of Recorded* (written, remembered) *time*, which will occur upon *the last Syllable*—i.e., the end of the world brought about by the second coming of Christ.

To "record" is also "To testify," "To bear witness" (OED). Therefore, *the last Syllable of Recorded* (witnessed, preserved by way of judicial testimony) *time* is that spoken of in Revelation 20:12: "And I sawe the dead, small and great, stand before God: and the books were opened: & an other booke was opened, which is the booke of life: and the dead were judged out of those things which were written in the books, according to their works." The "Bookes opened" signify "Mens Consciences, or records and Testimonies of every mans conscience, being unfolded and manifested through the mighty power of God, wherin (as in Bookes) are written all mens thoughtes, words, and workes" (TW, q.v.). Cf. and see note: *Banke and Schoole of time*, I.vii.10.

And all our yesterdayes, have lighted Fooles

The way to dusty death. Out, out, breefe Candle,

Life's but a walking Shadow, a poore Player,   [30]

That struts and frets his houre upon the Stage,

28–29. *all our yesterdayes... dusty death.* The enlightened follow the advice of Matthew 5:15–16: "Neither doe men light a candle, and put it under a bushell: but on a candlesticke, and it giveth light unto all that are in the house. Let your light so shine before men, that they may see your good workes, and glorifie your father which is in heaven." By contrast, *Fooles* follow "Ignis fatuus": "foolish fire. It is a kinde of light or exhalation seen in the night, seeming to go before, or to follow men, leading them out of their way to waters or other dangerous places, yet it hurts not, and is called Ignis fatuus, because it onely feareth fools" (TB, q.v.).

If *Macbeth* uses *our* to refer solely to himself, then he realizes that his *yesterdayes have* not *lighted* (illuminated) others to salvation by "shewing forth such lights, whereby others may walke in this darke world to the kingdome of heaven" (William Perkins, *A Godly and Learned Exposition or Commentarie upon the three first Chapters of the Revelation*). Because *Macbeth* has spent his life pursuing an "ignis fatuus" ("used allusively or fig[uratively] for any delusive guiding principle, hope, aim, etc.," OED), his *yesterdayes have* merely *lighted Fooles The way to dusty death* ("A separation of the whol man from Gods heavenly presence and glory, for ever," TW). *Macbeth's* poor example guides others to *dusty death* as effectively as an "Ignis fatuus, or foolish fire, with other Lights burning about graves, or such like fattie places where there is store of clammie or fat oylie substance for their matter" (John Swan, *Speculum Mundi*; ignis fatuus is often sighted at gravesites because it results from the spontaneous combustion of gases generated by rotting organic matter).

If *Macbeth* uses *our* as "relating to humanity or the body of Christians" (OED), then he here passes from unrepentance to unbelief. No "light" ("Holinesse of life," TW) leads to "light" ("glorious and blessed life in Heaven, which is endlesse," TW), so both life and *death* are *dusty* ("Mean, worthless, vile," OED). *All our yesterdayes*, whether lived virtuously or not, *have* merely *lighted* other *Fooles* such as ourselves *The way to dusty* ("rotten," RC, s.v. "Paperasses") *death*. Both saints and sinners end up as "dust" (the "mouldered remains of a dead body," OED), and the only "light" any of us can provide to others is the ignis fatuus emanating from *our* graves.

29. **Out, out, breefe Candle.** *Macbeth* cries *Out* ("An exclamation expressing grief, abhorrence, or indignant reproach," OED) upon the painful realization that life goes *Out* like a *breefe* ("of little length, of small continuance," RC, s.v. "Brief") *Candle* ("a symbol of individuated light, and consequently of the life of an individual as opposed to the cosmic and universal life," JC).

The light of each person's *Candle* (i.e., life) also serves as the *breefe* ("little writing, short declaration," RC, s.v. "Brevet") of the *breefe* ("summary of the facts of a case, with reference to the points of law supposed to be applicable to them, drawn up for the instruction of counsel conducting the case in court," OED) by which his life is judged. Cf. and see note: *the last Syllable of Recorded time*, line 27, above.

Unfortunately for *Macbeth*, his *Candle* (life) draws *Out* "shit" as fast and furious as does a *Candle* ("A bougie; a suppository," OED, which dates this sense from 1684, but cf. Thomas Adams' 1619 *The Happines of the Church*: "every frowne he makes, gives his Patron a vomite: and every candle of commendation a purge").

30. **Life's but a walking Shadow.** *Walking* ("The whole course or progresse of a mans life, from step to step, till he come to the end of his race," TW) is *but a Shadow* (something fleeting or ephemeral, OED). Cf. Psalms 39:5–6: "Behold thou hast made my dayes as it were an hand breadth long, & mine age is even as nothing before thee: truely every man is all [together] vanitie. Truely man walketh in a vayne shadow, truely he [and all his] do disquiet themselves in vayne" (Bishops' Bible).

Also, *Life's but* (a) *a walking* (haunting, spectrally manifesting) *Shadow* (ghost, apparition); (b) *a Shadow* (illusion, delusion) experienced while *walking* (sleepwalking, unconsciously acting); (c) a "living hell," or *a walking* (i.e., "waking"; "walk" is a variant of "wake," OED) *Shadow* (misery, unhappiness); and/or (d) *a walking* (i.e., insignificant; *walking* describes "an actor playing a small part with little or no speaking," OED from 1769) *Shadow* ("an actor or a play in contrast with the reality represented," OED).

30–31. **a poore Player, That struts and frets.** Humanity tends to "fret" ("to be light brained, to rave," "to be passionate, raging, and brainsicke," JF, s.v. "Smaniare") and to "fret" ("to be moodie, to be wrathful," JF, s.v. "Crocciare"). As a result, man will often "strut" ("contend, strive, quarrel, bluster," OED) and "fret" ("scoulde," "wrangle aloud that all may heare," JF, s.v. "Marinare") like a *poore* (insignificant or inferior) *Player* (actor) in performance.

Perhaps man outwardly *struts* ("pranck[s] it as a Turkie cocke," JF, s.v. "Arruffare"), because in truth his life is *poore* (i.e., "shitty"; see note: *poore*, I.vi.24). His "air" (empty talk; also "Gas generated in the stomach or bowels," FR) arises from *frets* ("pains in the stomach or bowels," OED) that cause his bowels to "strut" ("To distend, cause to swell or bulge, make protuberant; to puff out," OED).

And then is heard no more. It is a Tale

Told by an Ideot, full of sound and fury

Signifying nothing.

Enter a Messenger.   [V.v.4] [35]

        Thou com'st to use thy Tongue: thy Story quickly.

Mes.   Gracious my Lord,

I should report that which I say I saw,

But know not how to doo't.

Macb.   Well, say sir.   [40]

Mes.   As I did stand my watch upon the Hill

I look'd toward Byrnane, and anon me thought

The Wood began to move.

Macb.   Lyar, and Slave.

Mes.   Let me endure your wrath, if't be not so: [45]

Within this three Mile may you see it comming.

I say, a moving Grove.

Macb.   If thou speak'st false,

Upon the next Tree shall thou hang alive

Till Famine cling thee: If thy speech be sooth,   [50]

I care not if thou dost for me as much.

I pull in Resolution, and begin

32–34. *a Tale Told by an Ideot... Signifying nothing.* Traditionally, existence is regarded as *a Tale* ("a storie, a narration," JF, s.v. "Stória") told by God. Cf. John 1:1: "In the beginning was the Word, & the Word was with God, and the Word was God"; and the statement of Saint Clement of Alexandria (ca. 150–ca. 215) that "The Creation of the world is Gods Writing" (Gervase Babington, *Comfortable Notes Upon the bookes of Exodus and Leviticus*). By contrast, *Macbeth* sees existence not as divinely inscribed but as *a Tale* ("a lie," JF, s.v. "Fávola") pulled out of the "tail" ("arse," F&H) of *an Ideot* ("A layman": "A man who is not a cleric; one of the laity," OED). Life is such a terrible *Tale* ("jeast, mockerie," RC, s.v. "Mensonge") that it could only be authored by (a) *an Ideot* ("a professional fool or jester," OED); (b) *an Ideot* ("One that knowes nothing," JF, s.v. "Nescio"); or (c) *an Ideot* ("an asse," RC, s.v. "Fat").

Most in Shakespeare's audience believed that "It is a thing so evident, that there is a God; that whosoever denieth it, is (surely) out of his wit" (Martin Fotherby, *Atheomastix*), so *Macbeth's* nihilistic statements would have been interpreted as clear evidence of insanity. Moreover, because there can be no repentance without belief, *Macbeth's* denial of God would have been perceived as the Devils' greatest victory over his soul: "Sathan may and doth tempt us to Atheisme... his desire being to damne soules, and this being the most damning sinne that is: he doth use all meanes, to wipe out of the heart of man, all impression of the God-head" (Richard Capel, *Tenations*).

33. *sound.* Sound can mean (a) "a noise, a crash, a blustering or roaring" (TT, s.v. "Sŏnĭtus"); (b) "wynde, blaste, breathe" (TE, s.v. "Aer"); and/or (c) "The musical tone of the fart" (TR).

33. *fury.* Fury can mean (a) "madnesse, frenzie" (RC, s.v. "Furie"); (b) "sorow or griefe" (TT, s.v. "Stĭmŭlus"); (c) "fiercenesse, outragiousnesse; extreame wrath, anger, impatiencie" (RC, s.v. "Fureur"); and/or (d) excrement (literally "choler," JM, s.v. "Ardidéza"; see note: *scowre*, V.iii.71).

36. *thy Tongue... Story.* Whatever news the *Messenger* carries, *Macbeth* considers it to be just one more chapter in the *Tale Told by an Ideot* (lines 32–33, above).

38. *say.* Declare or suppose.

42. *me thought.* See note: *Me thought*, II.ii.46.

49. *next.* Nearest.

50. *cling.* Cling can mean (a) to "fasten, clinch, take hold" (JF, s.v. "Aggratticare"); and/or (b) to "shrink up, wither, decay" (OED).

50. *If thy speech be sooth.* See note: *say sooth*, I.ii.44.

52. *I pull in Resolution.* Now that the seemingly impossible events foretold in the prophecies have come to pass, *Macbeth* must *pull in* ("bridle, represse, maister, moderate, restrain, hold under, keepe short," RC, s.v. "Refrener") his *Resolution* ("conviction, certainty, positive knowledge," OED; also "stoutnesse, courage," "boldnesse, hardinesse," RC, s.v. "Animosité"). Nevertheless, he is determined to *pull in* ("gather up," "take," "receive," RC, s.v. "Retirer") the *Resolution* ("conclusion; end, issue, close," RC, s.v. "Conclusion"), even if it means his *Resolution* ("Death," OED).

To doubt th' Equivocation of the Fiend,

That lies like truth. Feare not, till Byrnane Wood

Do come to Dunsinane, and now a Wood   [55]

Comes toward Dunsinane. Arme, Arme, and out,

If this which he avouches, do's appeare,

There is nor flying hence, nor tarrying here.

I 'ginne to be a-weary of the Sun,

And wish th' estate o'th' world were now undon.   [60]

Ring the Alarum Bell, blow Winde, come wracke,

At least wee'l dye with Harnesse on our backe.

Exeunt

53–54. ***th' Equivocation... That lies like truth.*** See notes: *can the Devill speake true*, I.iii.120; and *Equivocator*, II.iii.14.

55–56. ***now a Wood Comes... Arme, and out.*** Instead of taking the safest course of action and settling in for *a Siedge* (line 6, above), *Macbeth* instead decides to *Arme* and go *out* to meet the camouflaged invaders. Holinshed relates that

> when Makbeth beheld them comming in this sort, hee first marveyled what the matter ment, but in the end remembred himselfe, that the prophecie which he had hearde long before that time, of the comming of Byrnane wood to Dunsinnane Castell, was likely to bee now fulfilled. Neverthelesse, he brought hys men in order of battell, and exhorted them to doe valiantly.

60. ***And wish th' estate o'th' world... undon.*** Macbeth wishes not only for the end of his own life but also that *th' estate* ("condition of existence," OED) *o'th' world* were now *undon* ("destroyed," "broken in peeces," TT, s.v. "Lăběfactātus"). Cf. III.ii.22–23.

61. ***Alarum Bell.*** See note: *Clock*, II.i.6.

61. ***Winde.*** A *Winde* is a "Whirlwind": "a violent or destructive agency; a confused and tumultuous process or condition" (OED). There is possible additional play on *Winde* as flatulence (see note: *pace*, line 26, above).

61. ***wracke.*** *Wracke* can mean (a) ruin, destruction, overthrow (cf. and see note: *wracke*, I.iii.129); (b) "rack": "torment, torture, affliction" (JF, s.v. "Tormento"; cf. and see note: *torture*, III.ii.28); (c) "A stroak, a blow" (JJ, s.v. "Rak"); and (d) "Retributive punishment; vengeance" (OED).

62. ***dye with Harnesse on our backe.*** *Harnesse* means "armour; weapons" (RC, s.v. "Armes"). "To die in *Harnesse*" means "To continue in one's work or occupation till death" (DPF). The expression is roughly equivalent to the modern "to die with one's boots on."

Act V, scene vi

Scena Sexta.   [1]

Drumme and Colours.

Enter Malcolme, Seyward, Macduffe, {Seywards Sonne, Lenox, Rosse,

Menteth, Cathnes, Angus,} and their Army, with Boughes.   [V.vi.1]

Mal.   Now neere enough: [5]

Your leavy Skreenes throw downe,

And shew like those you are: You (worthy Unkle)

Shall with my Cosin your right Noble Sonne

Leade our first Battell. Worthy *Macduffe*, and wee

Shall take upon's what else remaines to do,   [10]

According to our order.

{Seyw.}   Fare you well:

Do we but finde the Tyrants power to night,

Let us be beaten, if we cannot fight.

Macd.   Make all our Trumpets speak, give them all breath   [15]

Those clamorous Harbingers of Blood, & Death.

Exeunt

Alarums continued.   [V.vi.2]

Notes V.vi.

6. **leavy Skreenes.** *Malcolme Skreenes* (conceals, hides) his *leavy* (variant spelling of "levy": "A body of men enrolled," OED) with a *leavy* ("bushie, shrubbie," JF, s.v. "Cestuto"; "full of leaves," RC, s.v. "Fueilleux") "screen" ("Something interposed so as to conceal from view," OED). Cf. V.iv.10–13.

7. **shew.** Appear.

7. **worthy Unkle.** Seyward (cf. *Unkle Seyward,* V.ii.5).

9. **Battell.** *Battell* can mean (a) a "fight, skirmish" (JM, s.v. "Peléa"); and/or (b) "a battalion, a great squadron" (JF, s.v. "Peléa").

11. **order.** *Order* can mean (a) "an injunction," "an instruction" (JF, s.v. "Institutióne"); and/or (b) "a ranke, a forme," "a ray," "a fyle as souldiers now of late march in" (JF, s.v. "Ordine").

16. **Harbingers.** Forerunners (see note: *Herbenger,* I.iv.56).

18. **Alarums continued.** *Continued* means "continual, constant" (OED). One continuous battle sequence runs from this point until the *Retreat* of *Macbeth's* army in V.vii.90.

Act V, scene vii

Scena Septima. [1]

Enter Macbeth. [V.vii.1]

Macb.   They have tied me to a stake, I cannot flye,

But Beare-like I must fight the course. What's he

That was not borne of Woman? Such a one [5]

Am I to feare, or none.

Enter young Seyward. [V.vii.2]

Y.Sey.   What is thy name?

Macb.   Thou'lt be affraid to heare it.

Y.Sey.   No: though thou call'st thy selfe a hoter name [10]

Then any is in hell.

Macb.   My name's *Macbeth*.

Y.Sey.   The divell himselfe could not pronounce a Title

More hatefull to mine eare.

Macb.   No: nor more fearefull. [15]

Y.Sey.   Thou lyest abhorred Tyrant, with my Sword

Ile prove the lye thou speak'st.

Fight, and young Seyward slaine.

Macb.   Thou was't borne of woman;

But Swords I smile at, Weapons laugh to scorne, [20]

Brandish'd by man that's of a Woman borne.

Notes V.vii.

3–4. They have tied me... fight the course. *Macbeth* compares himself to a *Beare*, "A symbol of primitive brute force... The bear is viewed as a dark power in Christian and Islamic traditions: cruel, lustful, vengeful, greedy" (JT). Like a *Beare tied to a stake* in *Beare*-baiting, a blood-sport in which a captive *Beare* was "baited" (bitten, attacked, harassed) by vicious dogs, *Macbeth* has no other option but to *fight the course*, which means (a) each of the subsequent attacks made by the dogs in bear-baiting (OED); and (b) "the terme of time wherein any thing is finished" (JF, s.v. "Periodo").

10. hoter. *Hoter* plays on (a) "hot" meaning "dangerous" (OED); and/or (b) "haut" meaning "High, lofty, haughty" (OED).

15. fearefull. "Dreadfull, frightfull," "horrible" (RC, s.v. "Espoventable").

18. young Seyward slaine. *Young Seyward's* body is probably removed from the stage during the next *Alarums* (line 23, below); cf. lines 101–102, below.

Exit {Macbeth}.   [V.vii.3]

Alarums. Enter Macduffe.   [V.vii.4]

Macd.   That way the noise is: Tyrant shew thy face,

If thou beest slaine, and with no stroake of mine,   [25]

My Wife and Childrens Ghosts will haunt me still:

I cannot strike at wretched Kernes, whose armes

Are hyr'd to beare their Staves; either thou *Macbeth*,

Or else my Sword with an unbattered edge

I sheath againe undeeded. There thou should'st be,   [30]

By this great clatter, one of greatest note

Seemes bruited. Let me finde him Fortune,

And more I begge not.

Exit {Macduffe}. Alarums.   [V.vii.5]

Enter Malcolme and Seyward.   [V.vii.6] [35]

{Seyw.}   This way my Lord, the Castles gently rendred:

The Tyrants people, on both sides do fight,

The Noble Thanes do bravely in the Warre,

The day almost it selfe professes yours,

And little is to do.   [40]

Malc.   We have met with Foes

That strike beside us.

26. *still.* Always; on every occasion.

27–30. *I cannot strike... sheath againe undeeded.* *Macduffe cannot strike at wretched* (pitiful, trivial) *Kernes* (low-ranking mercenaries; see note: *Kernes,* I.ii.19) who have been *hyr'd to beare their Staves* ("poles, stakes," JF, s.v. "Pali"). He will *either strike at Macbeth, Or else sheath againe* the *edge* of his *Sword undeeded* (without "deeds," or valorous acts), and without having used it "to batter" ("To beat, punish, or strike," TT, s.v. "Verbĕro").

Macduffe's object is to claim *Macbeth's* life, which *Macduffe* feels is "deeded" (under a "deed": "an obligation or bond betweene two or more," TT, s.v. "Syngrăpha") to himself. If *Macduffe* fails to *strike at Macbeth,* he will *sheath againe* the *edge* of his *Sword undeeded*—i.e., without claiming his "deed" ("bond," "charter," JF, s.v. "Instruménto") on *Macbeth's* life. Cf. III.ii.48 and IV.i.122–124.

31–32. *By this great clatter... bruited.* *Macbeth* is *bruited* (i.e., defended by "brutes"; cf. *Kernes,* line 27, above), so the nearby *clatter* (crashing noise of battle; cf. JF's "Repicare": "to clatter or clash as armour doth") serves as *clatter* ("An idle or vague rumour," "Idle talk," JJ) to announce *Macbeth's* presence. However, *Macbeth's* being nearby is not merely *bruited* ("rumour[ed]," OED): his presence is *bruited* ("reported," RC, s.v. "Renommé"; "noise[d]," "disclose[d]," TT, s.v. "Vulgo") by "Bruit" ("a great sound, or noise; a rumbling, clamor," RC, q.v.).

36. *gently.* Gently means "curteouslie, willinglie, gladlie, sweetelie, graciouslie: without troubling or disquieting of any" (TT, s.v. "Cŏmĭtĕr").

36. *rendred.* "Given," "yeelded up" (TT, s.v. "Dēdĭtus").

37. *The Tyrants people, on both sides do fight.* Some of *The Tyrants people* ("troops, military forces," OED) have changed allegiance and *fight* on the opposite side. Cf. V.ii.25–26 and 33–34; V.iii.3 and 9–10; V.iv.19–20; V.v.8; and lines 41–42, below.

38. *bravely.* "Gallantly," "nobly, worthily" (RC, s.v. "Galemment").

38. *Warre.* See note: *warre,* V.iv.31.

39. *day.* Shakespeare condenses three years of warfare into a single *day* of battle. Although *Seyward* captured *Macbeth's* castle at *Dunsinane* in 1054, *Macbeth* was not killed until the battle at Lumphanon in 1057. Cf. lines 94 and 116, below.

39. *almost it selfe professes yours.* I.e., *almost* on its own *professes* (declares; acknowledges) *it selfe* to be *yours.*

41–42. *We have met... strike beside us.* Malcolme's forces have *met with Foes That* (a) have deserted *Macbeth's* army and *strike beside* (alongside) them (cf. line 37, above); and/or (b) *strike beside* ("By the side so as to miss," OED) them. Cf. "the blowes thou makst at me / Are quite besides, and those I offer at thee / Thou spreadst thine armes, and takst upon thine brest" (Francis Beaumont and John Fletcher, *The Maides Tragedy*).

{*Seyw.*}   Enter Sir, the Castle.

    Exeunt. Alarum   [V.vii.7]

    Enter Macbeth.   [V.vii.8] [45]

Macb.   Why should I play the Roman Foole, and dye

             On mine owne sword? whiles I see lives, the gashes

             Do better upon them.

    Enter Macduffe.   [V.vii.9]

Macd.   Turne Hell-hound, turne.   [50]

Macb.   Of all men else I have avoyded thee:

             But get thee backe, my soule is too much charg'd

             With blood of thine already.

Macd.   I have no words,

             My voice is in my Sword, thou bloodier Villaine   [55]

             Then tearmes can give thee out.

    Fight: Alarum   [V.vii.10]

Macb.   Thou loosest labour

             As easie may'st thou the intrenchant Ayre

             With thy keene Sword impresse, as make me bleed: [60]

             Let fall thy blade on vulnerable Crests,

             I beare a charmed Life, which must not yeeld

             To one of woman borne.

46–48. ***play the Roman Foole… Do better upon them.*** "The Stoicks say, that it is living according to Nature in a Wise man to take his leave of Life, even in the height of prosperity, if he do it opportunely, and in a Fool to prolong it, though he be miserable" (Michael de Montaigne, "Of the Inconstancy of our Actions"). *Macbeth* rejects this traditional *Roman* philosophy and refuses to *dye On* his *owne sword*, for *whiles* (during the time that) he sees other *lives* ("those who are alive, the living," OED), he thinks *the gashes Do better* (do more good) *upon them.*

Richard Burbadge, the leading actor of Shakespeare's company, originated both the title role in Shakespeare's *Macbeth* and the role of *the Roman Foole Brutus* who, after suffering defeat in battle, dies on his *owne sword* in Act V, scene v of Shakespeare's *Julius Cæsar.* In these lines, Richard Burbadge / *Macbeth* defiantly informs the audience that if they expect him to *dye On* his *owne sword* as he did when he played *Brutus,* they will be sadly disappointed.

50. ***Hell-hound.*** "A divell got loose," "or Furie broken out of hell; a divellish, horrible, or terrible fellow" (RC, s.v. "Diable deschaîné").

52. ***charg'd.*** Both (a) "laden, burdened, overcharged" (TT, s.v. "Onustus"); and (b) "accused, appeached" (RC, s.v. "Calengé"). Cf. and see note: *the last Syllable of Recorded time,* V.v.27.

55–56. ***bloodier Villaine Then tearmes… out.*** *Macbeth* is *bloodier Then tearmes* (words) *can give out.* He is also *bloodier Then tearmes* ("the flowers, fluxe, issue, or naturall purgation of women monthly," TT, s.v. "Menses").

58–61. ***Thou loosest labour… vulnerable Crests.*** It would be *As easie* to *impresse* (leave a mark on) *the intrenchant* ("Incapable of being cut," OED) *Ayre as* it would be to *make Macbeth bleed* ("make him pay dearly for something," "victimise him," DPF). Therefore, *Macduffe* "loses *labour*" ("labour[s] in vaine," RC, s.v. "Brique"; "imploy[s] his time to no purpose," RC, s.v. "Batre l'eau"). *Macbeth* advises *Macduffe* that he would do better to *Let* his *blade* (sword) *fall on* (attack) *vulnerable Crests* ("A bunch of feathers in a helmet," JF, s.v. "Crésta"; also a "Cognisaunce, or device, borne on the top of an helmet," RC, s.v. "Cymier").

In attacking *Macbeth, Macduffe* is just "fucking around." The *labour* (sexual exertion; see note: *labour'd,* I.iii.128) of *Macduffe's keene* (erect; see note: *keene,* I.v.59) *Sword* (penis; see note: *Sword,* III.iv.131) cannot *impresse* (sexually assault, JH, s.v. "light Impression") *the intrenchant* (with probable play on "trench" as the vagina; see note: *trenched,* III.iv.34) *Ayre. Macduffe* cannot "screw" *Macbeth* with his *blade* ("penis," F&H, s.v. "prick"), so he had best find more *vulnerable Crests* ("allusive of penis," GW; also the clitoris, JA, p. 98).

62. ***charmed Life.*** *Macbeth* believes that his *Life* is *charmed* ("Fortified, protected, rendered invulnerable, etc., by a spell or charm," OED), but it is in fact *charmed* ("bewitched," "forspoken, ill, unluckie, fatall, hard, darke," JF, s.v. "Adduggiato").

Macd.   Dispaire thy Charme,

And let the Angell whom thou still hast serv'd   [65]

Tell thee, *Macduffe* was from his Mothers womb

Untimely ript.

Macb.   Accursed be that tongue that tels mee so;

For it hath Cow'd my better part of man:

And be these Jugling Fiends no more beleev'd,   [70]

That palter with us in a double sence,

That keepe the word of promise to our eare,

And breake it to our hope. Ile not fight with thee.

Macd.   Then yeeld thee Coward,

And live to be the shew, and gaze o'th' time.   [75]

64. *Dispaire.* To *Dispaire* is "To distrust" (RC, s.v. "Se Desfier"); "To mistrust" (TT, s.v. "Diffido").

65. the Angell whom thou still hast serv'd. *The Angell whom Macbeth* has *still* (always) *serv'd* is Lucifer, for once "the Devil himself was of the Order of Seraphim" (RS). Also see note: *Genius*, III.i.70.

66–67. Macduffe was... Untimely ript. *Macduffe* explains that he *was Untimely* ("bred, borne, or brought forth, before a due time," RC, s.v. "Abortif") *ript* (cut away; also "unsowne," TT, s.v. "Dissūtus") *from his Mothers womb.* (*Macduffe's* words are usually interpreted to mean that he was prematurely delivered by cesarean section, but he could equally well say that he survived *his Mothers* attempt to abort him). In Holinshed, *Macbeth* confronts *Macduffe*

> saying, thou traytor, what meaneth it that thou shouldest thus in vaine follow me that am not appoynted to be slain by any creature that is borne of a woman, come on therefore, and receve thy rewarde which thou hast deserved for thy paynes, and therewithall he lyfted up his sworde thinking to have slaine him. But Makduffe quickly avoyding from his horse, ere he came at him, answered (with his naked sworde in his hande) saying: it is true Makbeth, and now shall thine insatiable crueltie have an ende, for I am even he that thy wysards have tolde the of, who was never borne of my mother, but ripped out of hir wombe: therewithall he stept unto him, & slue him in the place.

69. Cow'd my better part of man. *Macduffe's* revelation has (a) *Cow'd* (disheartened, discouraged, terrified) *Macbeth's* "better parte of man & woman that is the soule" (Henry Parker, *Dives et Pauper*); and (b) *Cow'd* ("clip[ped], cut short," OED) *Macbeth's better part* ("penis and testicles," JH). Cf. and see note: *Coward*, I.vii.51.

70–73. these Jugling Fiends... breake it to our hope. When *Macbeth* allowed *these Jugling* ("cousening or playing Legierdemain," TB, s.v. "Prestigiation") *Fiends* to *palter* ("to haggle, hucke, hedge," RC, s.v. "Harceler") *with* him over the price of his soul, he did not realize that the Devil was a "paltrer" ("a niggard, a great covetous man, a pinch penie," "a miser, a penie father," JF, s.v. "Avarone") and a "Poltry fellow, one that deals not squarely, but couseningly or dodgingly" (TB, s.v. "Poltron").

The *Fiends* promised that *Macbeth shall never vanquish'd be, untill Great Bynam Wood, to high Dunsmane Hill Shall come against him* (IV.i.114–116), and that *none of woman borne Shall harme Macbeth* (IV.i.98–99). Both statements are literally true, so the *Fiends* have kept their *word of promise* ("An indication of a future event or condition," OED) *to Macbeth's eare*. Nevertheless, they have broken their *word to Macbeth's hope* (expectation), for he believed such things to be impossible. Therefore, *these Jugling* (deceiving) *Fiends* have "fucked" *Macbeth* (*Jugling* means "copulation," JH).

74. yeeld thee Coward. If *Macbeth* is such a *Coward* that he will not fight (engage in combat), then he must *yeeld* ("resigne," "surrender," JF, s.v. "Cédere").

Also, if *Macbeth* is such a *Coward* (a castrated or impotent man; see note: *Coward*, I.vii.51) that he cannot engage in a "fight" ("a sexual encounter," JH), then he must *yeeld* ("submit sexually," JH). Also see note: *yeeld*, I.iii.152.

75. shew. *Macduffe* threatens to "make a *shew* of" *Macbeth* ("to exhibit [him] to public view; to expose [him] to public contempt," OED). *Macduffe* also threatens to *shew* (i.e., "screw"; to *shew* is to copulate, F&H, s.v. "ride") *Macbeth* and make him into a *shew* (i.e., a eunuch or bugger; *shew* alludes to "homosexuality, or something unnatural," FR). Cf. lines 76–78, below.

75. gaze. I.e., a "gazing stocke; a subject, or cause, for amusement," "A thing to wonder at" (RC, s.v. "Amusoire").

Wee'l have thee, as our rarer Monsters are

Painted upon a pole, and under-writ,

Heere may you see the Tyrant.

Macb.   I will not yeeld

To kisse the ground before young *Malcolmes* feet,   [80]

And to be baited with the Rabbles curse.

Though Byrnane wood be come to Dunsinane,

And thou oppos'd, being of no woman borne,

Yet I will try the last. Before my body,

I throw my warlike Shield: Lay on *Macduffe*,   [85]

And damn'd be him, that first cries hold, enough.

Exeunt fighting. Alarums.   [V.vii.11]

Enter {Macbeth & Macduffe} Fighting, and Macbeth slaine.   [V.vii.12]

{Exit Macduffe with Macbeth.}   [V.vii.13]

Retreat, and Flourish. Enter with Drumme and Colours,   [90]

Malcolm, Seyward, Rosse, Thanes, & Soldiers.   [V.vii.14]

76–78. **Wee'l have thee... Heere may you see the Tyrant.** To advertise their
wares or services, itinerant vendors and tradesmen would set up or carry *a pole upon*

which was hung a small *Painted* sign (cf. "Some carry painted Clothes on little Poles, / By which its known that such Men do catch Moles: / Others on Clothes some painted Rats have made, / Which notifies Rat-catching is their Trade," L. Meriton, "On London Cries"). Such *Painted* poles were also used at fairs to advertise that "Verie rare" ("not often seene," TT, s.v. "Perrārus") *Monsters* ("ugly or deformed person[s]," OED) were on display (cf. "Hang him out in a painted cloth for a monster," Henry Shirley, *The Martyr'd Souldier*). *Macduffe* threatens to display *Macbeth* like a side-show freak. A painting of *Macbeth* will advertise the attraction, and *under-writ* (written underneath) will be the words *Heere may you see the Tyrant*.

Macduffe also threatens to make *Macbeth* into a *rarer* (i.e., pathic; "rare" is a variant spelling of "rear" which means both "rare" and "The buttocks or backside," OED; for pronunciation, see HK, p. 208) *Monster* (i.e., eunuch; a "monster" is "any deformed creature, or misshapen thing that exceedeth, lacketh or is disordred in natural form," JF, s.v. "Móstro"). As such, *Macbeth* will be *Painted* (i.e., "fucked" as a whore, FR, who notes that "Cosmetic paint of 'fucus'... may have connoted 'fucks'") *upon a pole* ("penis," F&H). *Macbeth* will also be *writ* ("An innuendo of copulation and ejaculation," JH; to "rit" is "To cut or pierce with a sharp instrument," OED) *under* (i.e., in the buttocks; that which is *under* is literally "position[ed] at the bottom," OED; *under* also alludes to the inferior position in copulation, JH).

81. **baited with the Rabbles curse.** *Macbeth* refuses to be *baited* ("taunted," RC, s.v. "Apistolé") *with the Rabbles curse* ("malediction," "railing," "slaundring," JF, s.v. "Maladittione"). Cf. and see note: *Beare-like*, line 4, above.

"Baite" is also a spelling variant of "bate," an "apheitc form of abate" (OED). *Macbeth* refuses to be "[a]bated" ("beat[en] down," OED, with "innuendo of the seminal emission," JH) *with the Rabbles curse* ("penis," FR, who holds it a pun on Gk. "keras": "horn").

84. **try the last.** *Macbeth* will (a) *try* (test, put to the proof) *the last* ("the only remaining," OED) prophecy; (b) *try* ("strive," "fight with," "proove masteries," "sue one an other," "endevour," "enforce him selfe all that he can," TT, s.v. "Certo") "to *the last*" ("to the utmost," "up to or until the end," OED); and/or (c) *try* ("adventure, hazard, see what will happen," RC, s.v. "Espreuve") for *the last* ("Continuance, duration," OED).

85. **warlike.** See note: *warlike*, III.vi.35.

86. **cries hold.** See note: *cry, hold*, I.v.61.

87–90. **Alarums... Retreat.** As evidenced by the stage direction calling for *Alarums*, the climactic duel between *Macbeth* and *Macduffe* is just one small part of a large-scale battle sequence (see notes: *Alarum*, I.ii.2; and *Alarums continued*, V.vi.18). After *Macbeth* is *slaine*, his body is removed from the stage by *Macduffe*, or possibly by other *Souldiers* during the *Retreat* (withdrawal) of *Macbeth's* army ordered by the *Retreat* ("The signal to retreat in battle," OED).

90–91. **Flourish. Enter... Thanes, & Soldiers.** At least three separate groups here enter simultaneously. The *Flourish* announces the presence of *Malcolm* (see note: *Flourish*, I.iv.2), who enters with *Seyward* from within *Macbeth's* "castle" (a.k.a. the tiring-house at the rear of the stage); cf. lines 36 and 43–44, above. The second group is the *English powre* (V.ii.4) led by *Rosse*, who traveled with *Malcolm's* forces from Scotland; cf. 216–220 and 277. Any additional groups are the Scottish forces led by the other *Thanes*, which might include any or all of the following: *Menteth, Cathnes, Angus*, and/or *Lenox*; cf. V.ii.2–3.

Mal.	I would the Friends we misse, were safe arriv'd.
{*Seyw.*}	Some must go off: and yet by these I see,
	So great a day as this is cheapely bought.
Mal.	*Macduffe* is missing, and your Noble Sonne. [95]
Rosse.	Your son my Lord, ha's paid a souldiers debt,
	He onely liv'd but till he was a man,
	The which no sooner had his Prowesse confirm'd
	In the unshrinking station where he fought,
	But like a man he dy'de. [100]
{*Seyw.*}	Then he is dead?
Rosse.	I, and brought off the field: your cause of sorrow
	Must not be measur'd by his worth, for then
	It hath no end.
{*Seyw.*}	Had he his hurts before? [105]
Rosse.	I, on the Front.
{*Seyw.*}	Why then, Gods Soldier be he:
	Had I as many Sonnes, as I have haires,
	I would not wish them to a fairer death:
	And so his Knell is knoll'd. [110]
Mal.	Hee's worth more sorrow,
	And that Ile spend for him.

93. **go off.** Die.

93. **by these.** *By* the presence of *these* many *Soldiers* and commanders who have returned unharmed.

95. **Macduffe… and your Noble Sonne.** *Malcolm* quickly surveys his re-assembled troops and notices the absence of both *Macduffe* and *Seyward's Sonne.*

96–107. **a souldiers debt… Gods Soldier be he.** Figuratively, "God's soldiers" are the elect (cf. "They be Gods souldiours to fight for hys people, as s[aint] Paul sais. No man goes to warre on his owne wages," James Pilkington, *Aggeus and Abdias Prophetes*). Patriotic sentiment has long held that those who die in service to their country are also "God's soldiers." Cf. the 1588 tract *A Briefe Discoverie of Doctor Allens seditious drifts*:

> We do all owe God a death: how shall we better pay it, then in his quarrell? Our lives are all at our Princes commandement: how can they be better spent, then in her service? We are all borne for our countrey: why should we then refuse to die for our countrey? If we die in Gods quarrell, we shall live in his kingdome: If we die in our Princes service, we shall live in the memorie of all posteritie: If we die in defense of our countrey, our renowne shall live for ever.

97–100. **He onely liv'd… like a man he dy'de.** *Young Seyward fought* alongside others *In* an *unshrinking* ("Not shrinking or drawing back; unyielding, firm," OED) *station* (a "standing place, where men of warre or ships abide for a certaine time," TT, s.v. "Stătio"). His *Prowesse* ("Valiantnes, hardines, courage," "valour, stoutnes, noblenes, worthines," JF, s.v. "Prodezza") *no sooner had confirm'd* (affirmed, established) *he was a man But* (used "After *no sooner*, where modern use requires *than*," OED) *like a man he dy'de.* Cf. V.ii.13–15 and V.vi.7–9.

102. **cause.** Grounds, motivation.

105–109. **Had he his hurts before… a fairer death.** *Seyward* is relieved to hear that his son received *his hurts before* ("In front, in or on the anterior or fore side," OED), *on the Front* (either the anterior of his body or his forehead; see note: *Front,* IV.iii.272). Holinshed reports that

> in the foresaid battayle, in which Earle Siwarde vanquished the Scottes, one of Siwards sonnes chaunced to be slayne, whereof, though the father had good cause to be sorowfull, yet when he heard that he dyed of a wound which hee had receyved in fighting stoutely in the forepart of his body, and that with his face towarde the enimie, hee greatly rejoyced thereat, to heare that he died so manfully… I rejoyce (saith he) even with all my harte, for I woulde not wishe eyther to my sonne nor to my selfe, any other kind of death.

Alas, *Seyward* himself was not fated to die a valiant death on the battlefield. According to Holinshed,

> the noble Earle of Northumberlande Siwarde dyed of the flixe, of whome it is sayde, that when hee perceyved the houre of death to be at hand, he caused himselfe to be put in armour, and to be set up in his chayre, affirming, that a Knighte and a man of honor, oughte to die in that sorte, rather than lying on a couch like a feeble and faint harted creature: and sitting so uprighte in his chaire armed at all peeces, hee ended his life, and was buried at Yorke.

108. **haires.** With probable play on *haires* / "heirs." Cf. *unfixe my Heire,* I.iii.153.

{*Seyw.*}   He's worth no more,

They say he parted well, and paid his score,

And so God be with him. Here comes newer comfort.   [115]

Enter Macduffe, with Macbeths head.   [V.vii.15]

Macd.   Haile King, for so thou art.

Behold where stands

Th' Usurpers cursed head: the time is free:

I see thee compast with thy Kingdomes Pearle,   [120]

That speake my salutation in their minds:

Whose voyces I desire alowd with mine.

Haile King of Scotland.

All.   Haile King of Scotland.

Flourish.   [125]

Mal.   We shall not spend a large expence of time,

Before we reckon with your severall loves,

And make us even with you. My Thanes and Kinsmen

Henceforth be Earles, the first that ever Scotland

In such an Honor nam'd: What's more to do,   [130]

Which would be planted newly with the time,

As calling home our exil'd Friends abroad,

That fled the Snares of watchfull Tyranny,

114. **paid his score.** In giving his life for *Malcolm's* cause, *young Seyward* has "paid his score" ("requite[d] [his] obligation," OED) to God, king, and country. Cf. and see note: *a souldiers debt*, line 96, above.

116–119. **Enter Macduffe... Th' Usurpers cursed head.** *Macbeth's* head stands on a spear that has been planted in the ground by *Macduffe*. Holinshed relates that after slaying *Macbeth*, *Macduffe* "cutting his heade from the shoulders, hee set it upon a poll, and brought it unto Malcolme. This was the end of Makbeth, after he had raigned .xvii. yeares over the Scottishmen... He was slaine in the yeare of the incarnation 1057."

120. **compast with thy Kingdomes Pearle.** *Malcolm* is imagined as a precious stone *compast* (encircled, surrounded) *with* the nobility, who are *Pearle* (figuratively used for "virtuous or highly esteemed person[s]," OED). The metaphor was standard: cf. "the bright stars of Court, blest with the dailie beames and influences of the Regall Sunne, who like orient Pearles, serve to adorne the golden Diadem" (Samuel Garey, *Great Brittans little Calendar*). Cf. *Silver* and *Golden*, II.iii.147.

122. **voyces.** "Voice" can mean (a) "A suffrage voice, favour, election or consent, opinion or judgement" (TT, s.v. "Suffrāmagium"); and (b) "concord, agreement" (TT, s.v. "Concentĭo").

126. **expence.** *Expence* is (a) expenditure (OED); and/or (b) a possible variant of "expanse": "a widely extended space or area; a wide extent of anything" (OED).

127. **reckon.** "To go over or settle an account" (OED).

127. **severall.** Individual.

128. **even.** See note: *even*, III.iv.15.

129–130. **Henceforth be Earles... In such an Honor nam'd.** Holinshed relates that *Malcolm*

> Immediately after his coronation... called a Parliament at Forfair, in the which he rewarded them with landes and livings that had assisted him agaynst Makbeth, advauncing them to fees and offices as he saw cause, and commaunded that specially those that bare the surname of any office or landes, shoulde have and enjoye the same... Many of them that before were Thanes, were at this time made Earles, as Fife, Menteth, Atholl, Levenox, Murray, Cathnes, Rosse, and Angus. These were the first Earles that have beene heard of amongst the Scottishe men, (as their hystories make mention.)

Holinshed is, as usual, incorrect: in actual fact, "there were Earls in Scotland even before the time of Malcolm II" (JJ, s.v. "Thane"; Malcolm II was this *Malcolm's* great-grandfather; see note: *Cousin*, I.ii.30).

131. **planted.** Both (a) "Sowen," "begotten, borne" (TT, s.v. "Sătus"); and (b) "placed, setled, fixed," "limitted, appointed" (RC, s.v. "Assis").

131. **newly.** "Freshly" (TT, s.v. "Rĕcens"); "in a new sort or manner, contrarie to the olde fashion and custome" (TT, s.v. "Nŏvē").

Producing forth the cruell Ministers

Of this dead Butcher, and his Fiend-like Queene;   [135]

Who (as 'tis thought) by selfe and violent hands,

Tooke off her life. This, and what need full else

That call's upon us, by the Grace of Grace,

We will performe in measure, time, and place:

So thankes to all at once, and to each one,   [140]

Whom we invite, to see us Crown'd at Scone.

Flourish. Exeunt Omnes.

FINIS.

134. **Ministers.** See note: *Ministers*, I.v.55.

135. **Butcher.** *Macbeth* was a *Butcher*, meaning (a) "a murtherer," "a cutter of throtes" (JF, s.v. "Scannatore"); and (b) a bugger (FR; a "botcher" is "a tailor," F&H; see note *Taylor*, II.iii.21). Cf. and see note: *Unmannerly breech'd with gore*, II.iii.151.

137. **need full.** "Needful" was formerly written as two words. Cf. JF's "Edi mestiere, it is neede full, expedient, or necessarie."

138. **by the Grace of Grace.** *By the Grace* ("benefit," "pleasure, healpe, a good turne, favour," "kindnesse," TT, s.v. "Bĕnĕfĭcĭum") *of Grace* ("The free benefit of God," TW).

139. **measure.** "A proportion," "an equalnesse, when one thing answereth to an other" (TT, s.v. "Prōportio").

139. **time.** "The appointed, due, or proper time" (OED).

139. **place.** "A fitting time or juncture; an opportune moment, a suitable occasion; an opportunity" (OED).

141. **Crown'd at Scone.** See note: *Scone*, II.iv.43.

FINIS.

Textual Preparation

The First Folio of 1623 preserves Shakespeare's work intact with a bare minimum of errors.[1] Typesetter's errors (such as backwards, inverted, or upside-down letters, spacing inconsistencies, etc.) are easily recognizable

Enter Boy and Watch.
match. Lead Boy, which way ?

An obvious typographical error in the First Folio.

and have been corrected in this transcription.[2] Only categorically obvious typesetting errors are emended; no other textual errors (including errors in punctuation, spelling, or lineation) are assumed. Detection of any other errors as may occur is left to the capable discernment of the individual reader.

Given the overall integrity of the First Folio, all dialogue is preserved fully intact: the spelling, punctuation, capitalization and verse lineation (except in the case of simultaneous delivery) have not been altered in any way.

Minimal contextual adjustments have been made to present the First Folio text in a user-friendly format. These modifications exclusively address the following:

(I)   Variant character tags and speech prefixes;
(II) Discrepancies in entrances and exits;
(III) Act and scene division;
(IV) Font and
    i. Interchangeable vowels and consonants;
    ii. Ligatures;
(V)   Abbreviations;
(VI) Dual column format and
    i. Simultaneous dialogue;
    ii. Turned-up and turned-under lines.

(I) Variant character tags and speech prefixes.

Shakespearean characters often turn up in the First Folio under multiple aliases. For example, in *The Life and Death of Richard III*, a character appears whose full historical name and title is "Sir Thomas Stanley, Earl of Derby." This character's lines are sometimes assigned to *Derby* and sometimes to *Stanley*. Similarly, the historical character "Anthony Woodville, Lord Rivers" is tagged as both *Woodville* and *Rivers*.

In *The Tragedie of Romeo and Juliet*, *Juliet's* father is variously tagged as *Father, Capulet*, and *Old Capulet*; the comic servant as *Servant, Peter*, and *Clowne*; and *Juliet's* mother as *Mother, Madam, Wife, Lady, Old Lady*, and *Lady of the house*. Such a plethora of titles can be confusing to both reader and producer, because it is not immediately apparent that they belong to one single character. Therefore, for purposes of clarity, any character who appears under multiple names is assigned a uniform character tag. For example, in *Romeo and Juliet*, any lines spoken by *Juliet's* mother will be assigned to *Lady Capulet*.[3]

Sometimes, instead of the name of the character, the name of the actor who originally played the part is used in the Folio.[4] An example of this can be found in Act V, scene i of *A Midsommer Nights Dreame*:

> *Tawyer with a Trumpet before them.*
> *Enter Pyramus and Thisby, Wall, Moone-shine, and Lyon.*

Pyramus, Thisby, Wall, Moone-shine, and *Lyon* are all character names, but the mysterious "*Tawyer*" is the actual personage William Tawyer (or Tawier), a bit player and musician employed at the Globe Theatre.[5]

The names of two more prominent players turn up in *Much adoe about Nothing*:

> *Kem.*   Gods my life, where's the Sexton? let him write
> downe the Princes Officer *Coxcombe*: come, binde them
> thou naughty varlet.
> *Couley.* Away, you are an asse, you are an asse.

"*Kem[p]*" and "*Couley*" are William Kemp (or Kempt) and Richard Couley (or Cowly); both are included in the Folio's list of "Principall Actors." The appearance of Kemp and Couley's names in print allows scholars to identify them as the actors who originated the roles of *Dogberry* and *Borachio* respectively. However, to a reader trying to follow the story or to a company staging the play, this information is of no practical value whatsoever. Consequently, where they occur, actors' names are replaced with those of the characters.

(II) Discrepancies in entrances and exits.

In the First Folio, all entrances that will occur within a scene are sometimes lumped together at the beginning. In *The Merry Wives of Windsor*, the following characters are listed in the entrance at the top of Act I, scene i:

> *Enter Justice* Shallow, Slender, *Sir* Hugh Evans, *Master*
> Page, Falstoffe, Bardolph, Nym, Pistoll, Anne Page,
> *Mistresse* Ford, *Mistresse* Page, Simple.

However, for the first 69 lines of dialogue, only *Shallow, Slender,* and *Evans* speak. Moreover, these three characters talk about *Master Page, Falstoffe,* and *Anne Page* as if they are not actually present. *Master Page* does not speak until line 70, in dialogue that runs as follows:

> *Evan.* ... I will peat the doore for Mr.
> > *Page.* What hoa? Got-plesse your house heere.[6]
> *M.Page.* Who's there?

It is therefore reasonable to assume that *Master Page* does not enter onto the scene until he says "Who's there" after *Evans* "peats the door." Common sense is the largest factor in assigning an exact point for entrances and exits; if a character speaks a line of greeting or farewell, it is safe to assume that his entrance or exit falls at that point.

Sometimes a character is never assigned an entrance to a scene but is clearly present, as in Act I, scene iii of *The Life and Death of Richard III*:

> *Q.M.* Rivers and *Dorset,* you were standers by,
> And so wast thou, Lord *Hastings,* when my Sonne
> Was stab'd with bloody Daggers: God, I pray him,
> That none of you may live his naturall age,
> But by some unlook'd accident cut off.

Queene Margaret clearly speaks directly to other characters present: *Rivers, Dorset,* and *Lord Hastings.* However, *Hastings* is not given an entrance in the First Folio. Since *Hastings* also speaks during this scene, he obviously must be on stage. Therefore, his omission from the list of entering characters must be an error.[7] Similarly, sometimes a character is clearly absent from the stage but has not been instructed to exit.

Such inaccuracies are hardly noticeable to the reader but can prove greatly inconvenient for the producer. In order to make the scripts viable for production, every character has been assigned clear and precise entrance and exit cues.[8]

Other than entrances and exits, very few stage directions have been added. Such insertions are invasive and unnecessary; all that is truly required to grasp the stage business is simple attention to a line's content. *Hamlet*'s advice to "sute the Action to the Word, the Word to the Action" is tremendously apt.

Most stage directions are embedded in the dialogue itself. This system was highly practical, especially considering that the professional actor did not have the modern luxury of performing a single play for weeks or months on end. A public playhouse in Shakespeare's England had to continually serve up fresh fare in order to draw an audience. On average, ten different plays were presented in a two-week period. Old plays were revived and new plays intro-duced on an ongoing basis, and almost never was the same play repeated on two consecutive days. A leading actor would have as many as seventy-one dif-ferent roles in his repertoire; a supporting actor would of necessity have even more, as he would be expected to portray multiple characters within a single play.[9]

Under such circumstances, a prompter (or "book-holder") was always at hand to assist a player if he had trouble recalling his lines. Likewise, a player could not reasonably be expected to recall his blocking without some readily available memory aid. It is hardly difficult to recall the accompanying action to such lines as "I do embrace thee," "I kisse your Highnesse Hand," "poore gyrle she weepes," and so on.[10]

(III) Act and scene division.

Act and scene division of plays in the First Folio occurs somewhat hap-hazardly. Some plays are clearly broken down into acts and scenes; some into acts only; some are wholly lacking this division. Any act and scene division that appears in the Folio has been retained.

In addition, for the benefit of those staging the plays, scenes are further divided into French scenes (so named because of their use by 17th century French Dramatists). A new French scene begins each time a character or set of characters enters or leaves the stage. Act and scene numbers are printed in Roman numerals (in upper and lower case respectively); French scenes are printed in Arabic numerals. For example: Act three, scene two, French scene seven will appear in the right margin as [III.ii.7].

(IV) Font.

The original font(s) employed in the First Folio differ in some significant ways from contemporary fonts. Some alphabetical symbols (such as the long "s") are wholly obsolete and have been replaced with their modern equivalents:

As printed in the Folio	Herein transcribed as
ſiſters	sisters
kiſſe	kisse
ſoule	soule

i. Interchangeable vowels and consonants

The glyphs U, V, I, and J present much unnecessary confusion in direct transcription. Although their descendents still survive in modern typeface, these letters are not used in exactly the same way as were their Renaissance predecessors.

"U" and "V" did not originally represent different letters and came to be considered as such only comparatively recently in the evolution of the modern alphabet. The "U" form derives from the black letter tradition that originated in handwritten calligraphy; the "V" form is older and dates all the way back to Roman usage. The earliest printed texts employed one or the other exclusively, but over time both began to appear together.

When the First Folio was printed, the convention was to use "V" in the initial position and "U" in the median and terminal positions.[11] For the convenience of the modern reader, these transcriptions use "U" to designate the vowel and "V" to designate the consonant:

As printed in the Folio	Direct transcription	Herein printed
vn-vrg'd	vn-vrg'd	un-urg'd
vſe	vse	use
loue	loue	love

In addition, a modern "W" (double U) is substituted for "VV" (double V):

As printed in the Folio	Direct transcription	Herein printed
vvould	vvould	would

Likewise, "I" and "J" originated as the same letter, and in the First Folio "I" represents both vowel and consonant. In updating the font, "I" has been used for the vowel and "J" for the consonant:

As printed in the Folio	Direct transcription	Herein printed
iniurious	iniurious	injurious
Iuie	Iuie	Ivie
Iuſtice	Iustice	Justice

ii. Ligatures

Seventeenth-century printers employed ligatures (glyphs representing a combination of two or more characters) because they took less time to set and took up less room on the printed line. In modern usage, only a few ligatures (such as the "æ" in "Cæsar") have survived. Obsolete glyphs can therefore create something of a puzzle in direct transcription.

The most common enigma presented by these obsolete glyphs involves the letter "Y" and its predecessor, the Anglo-Saxon thorn. The thorn was a phonetic symbol that represented the "th" sound, both voiced (as in "*th*at") and unvoiced (as in "*th*ink"). By the late Renaissance, the thorn had disappeared except in ligatures employing its nearest equivalent in the standard typeset: the letter "Y."[12] The similarity between the two is clearly discernable in early Black Letter fonts.

Þ y

Left: **The Anglo-Saxon Thorn.** *Right:* **The letter "Y" in a Black Letter font.**

Words in the Folio that employ "Y" / thorn ligatures have been fully spelled out using modern typeface:

As printed in the Folio	Direct transcription	Herein printed
ẏ	yt	that
ẙ	yu	thou
ẙ	ye	the (or thee)

Other enigmatic ligatures involve the use of a tilde (˜) over vowels; the tilde stands for either "M" or "N" (exactly which must be determined from context):

As printed in the Folio	Direct transcription	Herein printed
thē	thē	them (or then)
mã	mã	man
thēſelues	thēselues	themselves

Only the most commonly used ligatures have been updated to modern font. Any other deviation has been retained, for any indiscriminate change can severely damage content. Consider the following lines from Act V, scene i of *A Midsommer Nights Dreame* as printed in modern editions:

> *Pir.* O grim-look'd night! O night with hue so black!
> O night, which ever art when day is not!
> O night, O night! alack, alack, alack,
> I fear my Thisby's promise is forgot!
> And thou, O wall, O sweet, O lovely wall,
> That stand'st between her father's ground and mine!
> Thou wall, O wall, O sweet and lovely wall,
> Show me thy chink, to blink through with mine eyne!

This speech as printed in the First Folio contains an important (and easily discernable) difference in the typeface:

> *Pir.* O grim lookt night, ô night with hue so blacke,
> O night, which ever art, when day is not:
> O night, ô night, alacke, alacke, alacke,
> I feare my *Thisbies* promise is forgot.
> And thou ô wall, thou sweet and lovely wall,
> That stands between her fathers ground and mine,
> Thou wall, ô wall, o sweet and lovely wall,
> Shew me thy chinke, to blinke through with mine eine.

The circumflex (^) over the "o" is not necessarily attributable to the type-setter's negligence or error. *Nick Bottome*, the character who portrays the role of *Piramus* in the play-within-a-play, is the consummate ham. It therefore follows that the "^" over the "o" could just as easily demonstrate *Bottome's* highly melodramatic inflection. Instead of substituting "O," the original "ô" is preserved in the belief that the original glyph far better reflects the substance of both speech and speaker.

(V) Abbreviations

As with ligatures, commonly used abbreviations are spelled out as full words:

As printed in the Folio	Direct transcription	Herein printed
Mʳ	Mr	Master
S.	S.	Saint
L.	L.	Lord

(VI) Dual column layout and simultaneous dialogue.

The First Folio was printed in a two-column format, a space-saving textual arrangement favored by many printers in an age when paper was highly expensive. Many books from the period, including the 1611 King James Bible, are laid out in this way.

i. Simultaneous dialogue

Isaac Jaggard and his employees were scrupulous in their composition and proofreading of the First Folio.[13] However, the printed work failed its original handwritten sources in one highly significant respect: all simultaneous dialogue was inadvertently erased.

It is a readily observable phenomenon in everyday life that two or more people will speak at once. It follows that dramatists, who seek, in Hamlet's words, to "hold as 'twer the Mirrour up to Nature," should also adopt overlapping speech as a theatrical device.

In modern scripts, simultaneous dialogue is easily recognizable because it is arranged in multiple columns across the width of the entire page. This multi-column arrangement was not unknown to Elizabethan dramatists. It is found in the 1616 Folio of Ben Jonson's works, where, in Act IV, scene v of *The Alchemist*, fully sixteen lines of concurrent dialogue are printed in two discrete columns. To remove any doubt whatsoever as to the congruity of these speeches, this dialogue is prefaced by the stage direction *"They speake together."*

If we could look over the shoulder of Shakespeare's book-holder, we would undoubtedly find numerous places where multiple characters speak at once. The apparent absence of simultaneous dialogue in the Folio is wholly attributable to its layout.

When Jaggard chose a dual-column layout for the Folio, he created a conundrum for his typesetters. Since the main body of sequential dialogue was already printed in side-by-side columns, it was impossible to further break down simultaneous dialogue into additional columns. In this situation, the compositors had no choice but to eliminate the multiple columns. When a compositor came upon multi-column (a.k.a. simultaneous) dialogue in a handwritten manuscript, he took the leftmost speech and placed it first in order in the column. Next, he took the speech immediately to its right and placed it underneath. This continued until all multiple columns had been distilled down into one. As a result, concurrent speeches deceptively appear as consecutive in the First Folio.

When the use of cue-scripts is taken into account, the most readily apparent clue as to simultaneous dialogue lies in what appears to be a "repeated" cue line. Consider the following lines from Act V, scene ii of *As you Like it* as printed within a single First Folio column:

> *Phe.* If this be so, why blame you me to love you?
> *Sil.* If this be so, why blame you me to love you?
> *Orl.* If this be so, why blame you me to love you?
> *Ros.* Why do you speake too, Why blame you mee to love you.

The actor who originally played *Rosalind* would not have the entire promptscript in hand. Instead, he would have only a part script in which his line and cue would run as follows:

> _____ to love you?
> Why do you speake too, Why blame you mee to love you.

Since the actor playing *Rosalind* will begin to speak as soon as he hears the cue "to love you," it follows that *Phebe*, *Silvius*, and *Orlando* deliver their lines simultaneously.

In passages where the dialogue doesn't make sense when delivered sequentially, the lines are probably overlapping. Take, for example, the following excerpt from Act I, scene i of *The Tragedie of Romeo and Juliet*:

> *Enter old Capulet in his Gowne, and his wife.*
> *Cap.*   What noise is this? Give me my long Sword ho.
> *Wife.*   A crutch, a crutch: why call you for a Sword?
> *Cap.*   My Sword I say: Old *Mountague* is come,
>   and flourishes his Blade in spight of me.
> *Enter old Mountague, & his wife.*

> *Moun.* Thou villaine *Capulet.* Hold me not, let me go
> 2. *Wife.* Thou shalt not stir a foote to seeke a Foe.

Upon critical examination, something seems amiss. If *Mountague* is not yet on stage, why should *Capulet* claim that "Old *Mountague* is come"? How can *Capulet* describe his enemy's actions if he is not yet in sight? The simple answer is, of course, that the patriarchs of the rival families enter onto the scene at the same time.

Sadly, no handwritten promptbook pages from Shakespeare's Folio plays survive, but the above lines would probably have been laid out in the original handwritten prompt-copy as follows:

Enter old Capulet in his Gowne, and his wife.	*Enter old Mountague, & his wife.*
Cap.	*Moun.*
What noise is this? Give me my long Sword ho.	Thou villaine *Capulet.* Hold me not, let me go
Wife.	2. *Wife.*
A crutch, a crutch: why call you for a Sword?	Thou shalt not stir a foote to seeke a Foe.
Cap.	
My Sword I say: Old *Mountague* is come And flourishes his Blade in spight of me.	

Admittedly, this textual arrangement is conjectural. However, it is absurd to slavishly and unquestioningly follow the columnar format set down by Jaggard and his associates in 1623. Such a practice serves only to preserve the mechanical limitations of the First Folio's printer, not the intentions of its author.[14] Many passages that initially seem redundant, nonsensical, or melodramatic make perfect sense when delivered simultaneously.[15] In order to restore working viability to Shakespeare's play scripts, some attempt must be made to accurately arrange dialogue as originally delivered in performance.[16]

ii. Turned-up and turned-under lines

The First Folio's columns were of limited width and accordingly limited the width of the text that could be placed within them. Consequently, lines that were too long were either turned up (had part of the text placed on the row above), as in *Measure for Measure*, Act V, scene i:

> *Isab.* Oh that it were as like as it is true. (speak'st,
> *Duk.* By heaven (fond wretch) thou knowst not what thou

Or turned under (had part of the text placed on the row beneath), as in Act I, scene ii of *Comedie of Errors*:

> *E.Dro.* What meane you sir, for God sake hold your
> Nay, and you will not sir, Ile take my heeles. (hands:

In the two examples above, the typesetter has inserted an opening parenthesis to indicate that the fractured text is truly one single line of iambic pentameter.[17] In all cases where parentheses mark a fracture, the text is herein adjusted to a single row. Therefore, the example immediately presented above will appear as:

> *E.Dro.* What meane you sir, for God sake hold your hands:
> Nay, and you will not sir, Ile take my heeles.

Parentheses are not universally employed to identify turned-up and turned-under lines in the Folio. They primarily occur on pages with tightly packed type, because there was simply no room to spill over a long line's excess text onto a row of its own. When the Folio's typesetters had the luxury of space, an extra-long line could be readily accommodated on two rows, as in *Alls Well, that Ends Well*, Act II, scene iii:

> *King.* Why then young *Bertram* take her shee's thy
> wife.

Although this speech is broken up onto two rows, scrutiny will reveal the line to be ten beats with a meter suspiciously akin to a regular line of iambic pentameter. Therefore, this is probably a turned-under verse line. Most editions would therefore place this line onto one single row, as follows:

> *King.* Why, then, young *Bertram*, take her; she's thy wife.

Such changes to lineation are not made herein, because such evidence, although suggestive, is not unarguably conclusive. Systematic "fixing" of fractured verse lines is ill-advised, because characters often switch back and forth between prose and verse, as in Act IV, scene I of *Twelfe Night, Or what you will*:

> *Enter Sebastian and Clowne*
>
> *Clo.* Will you make me beleeve, that I am not sent for   ← *The Clowne begins*
> you?   *the scene in prose*
>   *and continues in*
>   *prose throughout.*
>
> *Seb.* Go too, go too, thou art a foolish fellow,   ← *Sebastian begins the*
> Let me be cleere of thee.   *scene in verse.*
>
> *Clo.* Well held out yfaith: No, I do not know you,
> nor I am not sent to you by my Lady, to bid you come
> speake with her: nor your name is not Master *Cesario,*
> nor this is not my nose neyther: Nothing that is so, is so.
>
> *Seb.* I prethee vent thy folly some-where else, thou   ← *Sebastian switches to*
> know'st not me.   *prose in mid-speech.*
>
> *Clo.* Vent my folly: He has heard that word of some
> great man, and now applyes it to a foole. Vent my fol-
> ly: I am affraid this great lubber the World will prove a

Cockney: I prethee now ungird thy strangenes, and tell
me what I shall vent to my Lady? Shall I vent to hir that
thou art comming?

Seb. I prethee foolish greeke depart from me, there's   ← *Sebastian continues*
money for thee, if you tarry longer, I shall give worse   *the scene in prose.*
paiment.

It is important to know that such switches between verse and prose occur
and to understand their dramatic purpose: Shakespeare uses these switches to
mark important emotional transitions for the character.[18] Consequently, it is
often difficult to determine whether an initial lowercase letter indicates a fractured verse line or a switch between verse and prose. Consider the following
example from Act III, scene i of *The Life and Death of Richard III*:

> *Yorke.* I would that I might thanke you, as, as, you
> call me.

The words "call me" placed on a line of their own might be a sign that *Yorke*
lapses into prose. On the other hand, the lineation could just as easily denote a
turned-under alexandrine (an extra-long verse line consisting of twelve beats). In
this case, it is simply impossible to tell which was originally intended. Because
such ambiguity frequently occurs, the lineation is left intact. In such cases, the ultimate determination as to Shakespeare's intent justly lies with the individual.

Notes

1. In his preface to *Loves Labours Lost* (New Variorum edition, 1904), Dr. Horace Howard
Furness estimates that in the entire canon "there is only one obstinately refractory line, or
passage, in every eight hundred and eighty." In a play of approx. 3,000 lines, this equates
to 3.4 significant errors. Compare this to the thirty-one "corrections" (eleven to punctuation, ten to spelling, and ten to capitalization) made to eight lines of *2 Henry IV* illustrated
above (*Introduction*, p. 17).

2. For a list of textual corrections, see Appendix I. This textual preparation is intended
to be helpful to actors, directors, producers, students, teachers, and general readers. Those
researching the process and mechanics of 17th century printing in general, and of the First
Folio in particular, will find little of interest herein and will be better served by consulting
original Folios or facsimiles thereof.

3. Since these variant titles did not appear in the cue-scripts used by Shakespeare's players, they are completely non-essential to an actor's character interpretation. For those who
may find them of interest, however, variant character titles are preserved in Appendix IV.

4. Shakespeare was part owner of an established theatre with a long-standing resident
company. Consequently, he often wrote parts with specific actors in mind.

5. From his appearance in *Midsommer Nights Dreame*, Mr. Tawyer's employment with
the King's Men can be dated from as early as 1594. When he died in 1625, William Tawyer
was entered into the sexton's register of St. Savior's Church, Southwark, as "Mr. Heminges
man." Apparently, despite this long tenure, Tawyer never rose very high in the ranks of the
theatrical profession. Even with over thirty years' experience with Shakespeare's company,
his name is not among the First Folio's list of "Principall Actors."

6. The phonetic spellings are here indicative of *Evans'* Welsh accent.

7. Such omissions are easily explained when the "Foul Papers" are taken into account as source material. A Playwright scribbling away in a white heat would be most concerned with setting down dialogue as it played out in his head. Minor points, like precise moments for entrances and exits, could be added in later when a clean prompt-book was prepared.

8. For a list of emended entrances and exits, see Appendix II.

9. Based on Bernard Beckerman's analysis of Philip Henslowe's 1594–1597 box office records from *The Rose* (*Shakespeare at the Globe,* Collier, 1962).

10. For more on Shakespeare's embedded stage directions and the performing style of his company, see Ronald Watkins' *On Producing Shakespeare* (Citadel Press, 1950).

11. The earliest printed book to use "U" and "V" to delineate vowel from consonant respectively was printed in Italy in 1524 and was written by Gian Giorgio Trissino (1478–1550), a fervent orthographic reformer. Trissino even appealed to Pope Clement VII for the introduction of new letters into the Italian alphabet. As with all revolutionaries, it took time for his views to become widely adopted. The First Folio was printed, 99 years later, according to older convention.

12. The substitution of "Y" for the thorn also appears on Shakespeare's gravestone. His epitaph reads:

> GOOD FREND FOR IESVS SAKE FORBEARE,
> TO DIGG THE DVST ENCLOASED HEARE:
> BLEST BE YE MAN YT SPARES THES STONES
> AND CVRST BE HE YT MOVES MY BONES

Shakespeare's family obviously thought it more important to prevent his crypt from re-use (a very real possibility when demand exceeded supply for prime chapel burial space) than to extol his earthly accomplishments. Incidentally, Shakespeare had the honor of burial in Stratford-on-Avon's Holy Trinity Church not because of his fame but because he was a lay-rector of the parish. Tradition holds that he died on his 52nd birthday, April 23, 1616, after drinking too much with fellow-poets Ben Jonson and Michael Drayton. His true memorial was raised in the First Folio. In his dedication, Ben Jonson speaks of Shakespeare as "a Moniment, without a tombe, / And art alive still, while thy Booke doth live, / And we have wits to read, and praise to give," for "He was not of an age, but for all time!"

13. For illustration of the proofreading of the First Folio, see the Norton Facsimile, Appendix A.

14. At the time of writing (Winter 2011), not one single commercially available edition of any Shakespearean play has yet attempted to restore simultaneous dialogue.

15. For an in-depth exploration of simultaneousness in Shakespeare, see Richard Flatter's *Shakespeare's Producing Hand* (Greenwood Press, 1948).

16. Since this text restores simultaneous dialogue, for obvious reasons the "through" line numbering system established by Dr. Charlton Hinman is not herein employed.

17. A poetic meter frequently used by Shakespeare. Iambs are feet of poetry composed of an unstressed syllable followed by a stressed syllable; "pentameter" indicates there are five such feet in a verse line (from Gk. *penta,* five). The resulting verse line will therefore consist of ten alternating stressed and unstressed syllables. By no means does Shakespeare limit himself exclusively to regular iambic pentameter; departures from the norm indicate both rhythmic and expressive variation. For more on Shakespeare's irregular verse as reflective of a character's emotional state, see Flatter, pp. 25–54.

18. For more on Shakespeare's use of verse versus prose, see Doug Moston's introduction to *The First Folio of Shakespeare 1623* (Applause Books, 1995).

Appendix I

Typographical Errors Corrected
from the First Folio of 1623

Act, scene, line	*Herein printed*	*Originally printed*
I.iii.4	Swine	Swiue
II.iii.32	*Macd.*	*Macd:*
III.vi.36–37	(with him above To ratifie the Worke)	(with him above) To ratifie the Worke)
III.vi.50	t' hold	t hold
V.iii.67	pristine	pristiue
V.iv.10	*Malc.*	*Malc,*
V.v.48	false	fhsle
V.vii.17	speak'st	speak st

Appendix II

Stage Directions, Entrances and Exits
Emended from the First Folio of 1623

Act, scene, line	Herein printed	First Folio text
I.ii.2–4	*Alarum within. Enter King{,} Malcome, Donalbaine, Lenox, with attendants, meeting a bleeding Captaine.*	*Alarum within. Enter King Malcome, Donalbaine, Lenox, with attendants, meeting a bleeding Captaine.*
I.ii.53	*Exit Attendants with Captaine.*	No exit given
I.iv.66	*Exit {Macbeth}.*	*Exit.*
II.i.44	*Exit Banquo {and Fleance}.*	*Exit Banquo.*
II.i.47	*Exit {Servant}.*	*Exit.*
II.i.81	*Exit {Macbeth}.*	*Exit.*
II.ii.72	*Exit {Lady}.*	*Exit.*
II.iii.30	*Porter opens the door.*	No stage direction given
II.iii.99	*Exit Porter.*	No exit given
II.iii.177	*Exeunt. {Manet Malcolme and Donalbaine.}*	*Exeunt.*
III.i.13–14	*Senit sounded. Enter Macbeth as King, Lady{,} Lenox, Rosse, Lords, and Attendants.*	*Senit sounded. Enter Macbeth as King, Lady Lenox, Rosse, Lords, and Attendants.*
III.i.55	*Exeunt. Manet Macbeth and a Servant.*	*Exeunt Lords.*
III.i.172	*Exit Murtherers.*	No exit given
III.i.175	*Exit Macbeth.*	*Exeunt.*
III.ii.8	*Exit {Servant}.*	*Exit.*
III.iii.31	*Banquo dies.*	No stage direction given
III.iii.31	*Exit Fleans.*	No exit given
III.iv.41	*Exit {First} Murderer.*	*Exit Murderer.*
III.iv.93	*Exit Ghost.*	No exit given
III.iv.135	*Exit Ghost.*	No exit given

Act, scene, line	Herein printed	First Folio text
III.iv.155	*Exeunt. Manet Macbeth and Lady Macbeth.*	*Exit Lords.*
III.v.41	*Exit Hecat.*	No exit given
IV.i.87	*{1st Apparation} Descends.*	*He Descends.*
IV.i.100	*{2nd Apparition} Descends.*	*Descends.*
IV.i.117	*3rd Apparation Descends.*	*Descend.*
IV.ii.105	*Son dies.*	No stage direction given
IV.ii.105	*Exit {Macduffes Wife} crying Murther.*	*Exit crying Murther.*
IV.ii.106	*Exeunt.*	No exit given
IV.iii.165	*Exit {Doctor}.*	*Exit.*
V.iii.25	*Exit Servant.*	No exit given
V.iii.63	*Exit Seyton.*	No exit given
V.iii.77	*Exeunt. Manet Doctor.*	No exit given
V.iii.80	*Exit Doctor.*	*Exeunt.*
V.iv.2–4	*Drum and Colours. Enter Malcolme, Seyward, Macduffe, Seywards Sonne, Menteth, Cathnes, Angus, {Lenox, Rosse,} and Soldiers Marching.*	*Drum and Colours. Enter Malcolme, Seyward, Macduffe, Seywards Sonne, Menteth, Cathnes, Angus, and Soldiers Marching.*
V.v.2–3	*Enter Macbeth, Seyton, & Souldiers, with Drum and Colours.*	*Enter Macbeth, Seyton, & Souldiers, with, Drum and Colours.*
V.v.13	*Exit Seyton.*	No exit given
V.v.21	*Enter Seyton.*	No entrance given
V.vi.3–4	*Enter Malcolme, Seyward, Macduffe, {Seywards Sonne, Lenox, Rosse, Menteth, Cathnes, Angus,} and their Army, with Boughes.*	*Enter Malcolme, Seyward, Macduffe, and their Army, with Boughes.*
V.vii.22	*Exit {Macbeth}.*	*Exit.*
V.vii.34	*Exit {Macduffe}. Alarums.*	*Exit. Alarums.*
V.vii.88	*Enter {Macbeth & Macduffe} Fighting, and Macbeth slaine.*	*Enter Fighting, and Macbeth slaine.*
V.vii.89	*{Exit Macduffe with Macbeth.}*	No exit given

Appendix III

Lineation Emended from the First Folio of 1623

Act, scene, line	Originally printed
I.i.13–14	Both on line 13
I.iii.32–33	Both on line 32
I.iii.69–70	Printed sequentially: (1) 2*nd* *Witch's* line; (2) 3*rd* *Witch's* line
I.iii.85–86	Both on line 85
I.iii.183–184	Both on line 183
I.iv.65–66	Both on line 65
I.iv.71–72	Both on line 71
I.v.31–32	Both on line 32
I.v.43–44	Both on line 43
I.v.61–62	Both on line 61
I.v.86–87	Both on line 86
I.vi.15–16	Both on line 15
I.vi.42–43	Both on line 42
I.vii.32–33	Both on line 32
II.i.43–44	Both on line 43
II.i.46–47	Both on line 46
II.i.80–81	Both on line 80
II.ii.71–72	Both on line 71
II.ii.83–84	Both on line 83
II.ii.89–90	Both on line 89
II.ii.95–96	Both on line 95
II.ii.99–100	Both on line 99
II.iii.6–8	All on line 6
II.iii.11–12	Both on line 12
II.iii.17–19	All on line 17
II.iii.22–23	Both on line 22
II.iii.27–28	Both on line 27
II.iii.67–68	Both on line 67
II.iii.176–177	Both on line 176
III.i.48–49	Both on line 48

Act, scene, line	Originally printed
III.i.54–55	Both on line 54
III.i.60–61	Both on line 60
III.i.174–175	Both on line 174
III.ii.7–8	Both on line 7
III.ii.64–68	Both on line 67
III.iv.40–41	Both on line 40
III.iv.134 and 136	Both on line 134
III.iv.154–155	Both on line 154
III.iv.180–181	Both on line 180
III.v.43–44	Both on line 43
III.vi.56–57	Both on line 56
IV.i.78–79	Both on line 78
IV.i.91–92	Both on line 91
IV.i.99–100	Both on line 99
IV.i.105–106	Both on line 105
IV.i.116–117	Both on line 116
IV.i.131–132	Both on line 131
IV.i.134–135	Printed sequentially: (1) 2nd Witch's line; (2) 3rd Witch's line
IV.i.160–161	Both on line 160
IV.i.166–167	Both on line 166
IV.i.192–193	Both on line 192
IV.ii.36–37	Both on line 36
IV.ii.85–86	Both on line 85
IV.ii.104–105	Both on line 104
IV.iii.164–165	Both on line 164
IV.iii.281–282	Both on line 281
V.i.20–21	Both on line 20
V.i.82–83	Both on line 82
V.ii.40–41	Both on line 40
V.iii.24 and 26	Both on line 24
V.iii.62 and 64	Both on line 62
V.iii.79–80	Both on line 79
V.iv.31–32	Both on line 31
V.v.34–35	Both on line 34
V.v.62–63	Both on line 62
V.vi.16–17	Both on line 16
V.vii.21–22	Both on line 21
V.vii.33–34	Both on line 33
V.vii.43–44	Both on line 43
V.vii.56–57	Both on line 56
V.vii.124–125	Both on line 124

Appendix IV

Character Tags Emended from the First Folio of 1623

Act, scene, line	Herein printed	Originally printed
I.i.3	*Witch 1.*	1.
I.i.5	*Witch 2.*	2.
I.i.7	*Witch 3.*	3.
I.i.8	*Witch 1.*	1.
I.i.9	*Witch 2.*	2.
I.i.10	*Witch 3.*	3.
I.i.11	*Witch 1.*	1.
I.i.12	*All {Witches}.*	*All.*
I.iii.3	*Witch 1.*	1.
I.iii.4	*Witch 2.*	2.
I.iii.5	*Witch 3.*	3.
I.iii.6	*Witch 1.*	1.
I.iii.14	*Witch 2.*	2.
I.iii.15	*Witch 1.*	1.
I.iii.16	*Witch 3.*	3.
I.iii.17	*Witch 1.*	1.
I.iii.30	*Witch 2.*	2.
I.iii.31	*Witch 1.*	1.
I.iii.34	*Witch 3.*	3.
I.iii.36	*All {Witches}.*	*All.*
I.iii.54	*Witch 1.*	1.
I.iii.55	*Witch 2.*	2.
I.iii.56	*Witch 3.*	3.
I.iii.68	*Witch 1.*	1.
I.iii.69	*Witch 2.*	2.
I.iii.69	*Witch 3.*	3.
I.iii.71	*Witch 1.*	1.

Act, scene, line	Herein printed	Originally printed
I.iii.72	*Witch 2.*	2.
I.iii.73	*Witch 3.*	3.
I.iii.75	*Witch 1.*	1.
I.v.3	*Lady.*	Lady.
II.iii.87	*Macb. & Len.*	Macb. and Lenox.
III.i.142	*{2.} Murth.*	Murth.
III.i.170	*{2.} Murth.*	Murth.
III.iii.3	*1. Mur.*	1.
III.iii.4	*3. Mur.*	3.
III.iii.5	*2. Mur.*	2.
III.iii.8	*1. Mur.*	1.
III.iii.13	*3. Mur.*	3.
III.iii.15	*2. Mur.*	2.
III.iii.18	*1. Mur.*	1.
III.iii.19	*3. Mur.*	3.
III.iii.23	*2. Mur.*	2.
III.iii.24	*3. Mur.*	3.
III.iii.25	*1. Mur.*	1.
III.iii.27	*1. Mur.*	1.
III.iii.32	*3. Mur.*	3.
III.iii.33	*1. Mur.*	1.
III.iii.34	*3. Mur.*	3.
III.iii.35	*2. Mur.*	2.
III.iii.37	*1. Mur.*	1.
III.iv.18	*{1.} Mur.*	Mur.
III.iv.21	*{1.} Mur.*	Mur.
III.iv.25	*{1.} Mur.*	Mur.
III.iv.33	*{1.} Mur.*	Mur.
III.v.4	*Witch 1.*	1.
III.v.42	*Witch 1.*	1
IV.i.3	*Witch 1.*	1
IV.i.4	*Witch 2.*	2
IV.i.5	*Witch 3.*	3
IV.i.6	*Witch 1.*	1
IV.i.12	*All {Witches}.*	All.
IV.i.14	*Witch 2.*	2
IV.i.22	*All {Witches}.*	All.
IV.i.24	*Witch 3.*	3
IV.i.37	*All {Witches}.*	All.
IV.i.39	*Witch 2.*	2

Act, scene, line	Herein printed	Originally printed
IV.i.48	*Witch 2.*	2
IV.i.54	*All {Witches}.*	*All.*
IV.i.67	*Witch 1.*	1
IV.i.68	*Witch 2.*	2
IV.i.69	*Witch 3.*	3
IV.i.70	*Witch 1.*	1
IV.i.73	*Witch 1.*	1
IV.i.77	*All {Witches}.*	*All.*
IV.i.82	*Witch 1.*	1
IV.i.90	*Witch 1.*	1
IV.i.111	*All {Witches}.*	*All.*
IV.i.128	*All {Witches}.*	*All.*
IV.i.133	*Witch 1.*	1
IV.i.134	*Witch 2.*	2
IV.i.134	*Witch 3.*	3
IV.i.136	*All {Witches}.*	*All.*
IV.i.153	*Witch 1.*	1
IV.ii.96	*{1.} Mur.*	*Mur.*
IV.ii.99	*{1.} Mur.*	*Mur.*
IV.ii.101	*{1.} Mur.*	*Mur.*
V.iv.8	*Seyw.*	*Syew.*
V.iv.15	*Seyw.*	*Syw.*
V.iv.26	*Seyw.*	*Sey.*
V.vi.12	*Seyw.*	*Sey.*
V.vii.36	*Seyw.*	*Sey.*
V.vii.43	*Seyw.*	*Sey.*
V.vii.93	*Seyw.*	*Sey.*
V.vii.101	*Seyw.*	*Sey.*
V.vii.105	*Seyw.*	*Sey.*
V.vii.107	*Seyw.*	*Sey.*
V.vii.113	*Seyw.*	*Sey.*

Bibliography

Key Reference Works

Adams, J.N. *The Latin Sexual Vocabulary.* Baltimore: Johns Hopkins University Press, 1982.

Blount, Thomas. *Glossographia, or A dictionary, interpreting all such hard words, whether Hebrew, Greek, Latin, Italian, Spanish, French, Teutonick, Belgick, British or Saxon; as are now used in our refined English tongue.* London: Tho. Newcomb, 1656.

Brewer, Ebenzer Cobham. *Dictionary of Phrase and Fable.* London: Cassell and Company, 1900.

Bullokar, John. *An English Expositior: teaching the interpretation of the hardest words in our language.* London: John Legatt, 1616.

Cawdrey, Robert. *A table alphabeticall, conteyning and teaching the true writing, and understanding of hard usuall English wordes, borrowed from the Hebrew, Greeke, Latine, or French, &c.* London: J.R. for Edmund Weaver, 1604.

Cirlot, Juan Eduardo. *A Dictionary of Symbols.* Translated by Jack Sage. Mineola, NY: Dover Publications, 2002.

Cockeram, Henry. *The English Dictionarie.* London: For Edmund Weaver, 1623.

Coles, Elisha. *An English Dictionary: Explaining The difficult Terms that are used in Divinity, Husbandry, Physick, Phylosophy, Law, Navigation, Mathematicks, and other Arts and Sciences.* Clark, NJ: The Lawbook Exchange, 2006.

Colman, E.A.M. *The dramatic use of Bawdy in Shakespeare.* London: Longman, 1974.

Cotgrave, Randle. *A dictionarie of the French and English tongues.* London: Adam Islip, 1611.

De Laune, Thomas. *Tropologia, Or, A Key to Open Scripture Metaphors.* London: John Richardson and John Darby for Enoch Prosser, 1681.

Elyot, Thomas. *The Dictionary of syr Thomas Eliot knyght.* London: Thomas Berthelet, 1538.

Farmer, John S., and William E. Henley. *Slang and its Analogues.* New York: Scribner & Welford, 1890.

Florio, John. *A worlde of wordes, or most copious, dictionarie in Italian and English, collected by John Florio.* London: Arnold Hatfield for Edw. Blount, 1598.

Grose, Frances. *Lexicon Balatronicum: A Dictionary of Buckish Slang, University Wit, and Pickpocket Eloquence.* London: For C. Chappell, 1811.

Henke, James T. *Courtesans and Cuckolds: A Glossary of Renaissance Dramatic Bawdy (exclusive of Shakespeare).* New York: Garland, 1979.

Holinshed, Raphael. *The Firste volume of the Chronicles of England, Scotlande, and Irelande.* London: For John Hunne, 1577.

Hulme, Hilda M. *Explorations in Shakespeare's Language.* London: Longmans, Green & Co., 1962.

Jamieson, John. *An Etymological Dictionary of the Scottish Language.* 2 vols. Edinburgh: Printed at the University Press for W. Creech (etc.), 1808.

Kökeritz, Helge. *Shakespeare's Pronunciation.* New Haven: Yale University Press, 1953.

"Latin Dictionary and Grammar Aid." University of Notre Dame. http://archives.nd.edu/latgramm.htm (accessed 2011–12).

Minsheu, John. *A dictionarie in Spanish and English, first published into the English tongue by Ric. Percivale* Gent. Edited by Richard Percivale. London: Edm. Bollifant, 1599.

A New Dictionary of the Terms Ancient and Modern of the Canting Crew, in its several Tribes of Gypsies, Beggers, Thieves, Cheats, &c. London: For W. Hawes, P. Gilbourne and W. Davis, 1690[?].

Palsgrave, John. *Lesclarcissement de la langue francoyse compose par maistre Johan Palsgrave Angloyse natyf de Londres, et gradue de Paris.* London[?]: Richard Pynson and Johan Haukyns, 1530.

Partridge, Eric. *Shakespeare's Bawdy.* London: Routledge & Kegan Paul Ltd., 1947.

Ross, Thomas W. *Chaucer's Bawdy.* New York: E. P. Dutton, 1972.

Rubinstein, Frankie. *A Dictionary of Shakespeare's Sexual Puns and Their Significance.* London: MacMillan, 1984.

Scot, Reginald. *The Discovery of Witchcraft.* London: For Andrew Clark, 1665.

Simpson, J.A., and E.S.C. Weiner, eds. *Oxford English Dictionary.* 2nd ed. Oxford: Clarendon Press, 1989.

Thomas, Thomas. *Dictionarium Linguae Latinae et Anglicanae.* Canterbury: Richard Boyle, 1587.

Tresidder, Jack, ed. *The Complete Dictionary of Symbols.* San Francisco: Chronicle Books, 2005.

Williams, Gordon. *A Dictionary of Sexual Language and Imagery in Shakespearean and Stuart Literature.* London: Athlone Press, 1994.

_____. *A Glossary of Shakespeare's Sexual Language.* London: Athlone Press, 1997.

Wilson, Thomas. *A Christian Dictionarie, Opening the signification of the chiefe wordes dispersed generally through Holie Scriptures of the Old and New Testament, tending to increase Christian knowledge.* London: William Jaggard, 1612.

Other Reference Works

Adams, Thomas. *The Happines of the Church.* London: G.P. for John Grismand, 1619.

_____. *The Works of Thomas Adams.* Edited by Joseph Angus. Vol. 2. London: James Nisbet and Co., 1862.

Ady, Thomas. *A Perfect Discovery of Witches.* London: For R.I., 1661.

Allott, Robert. *Wits Theater of the little World.* London: James Roberts for Nicholas Ling, 1600.

Anderson, William. *The Scottish Nation.* Vol. 3. London: A. Fullarton & Co., 1863.

Andrews, Chris. *Poetry and Cosmogony: Science in the Writing of Queneau and Ponge.* Amsterdam: Rodopi, 1999.

Anno Primo Reginæ Elizabethæ. London: Richard Jugge and John Cawood, 1559.

Aristotle's Compleat and Experience'd Midwife: In Two Parts. London: 1700.

Ascham, Roger. *Toxophilus: 1545.* Edited by Edward Arber. London: 1869.

Atsma, Aaron J., ed. "Theoi Greek Mythology." The Theoi Project. http://www.theoi.com/ (accessed 2011–2012).

Augustine, Saint, Bishop of Hippo. *A Little Pamphlet of Saint Augustine entituled the Ladder of Paradise.* Translated by T.W. London: For Edward Aggas, 1580.

Babington, Gervase. *Comfortable Notes Upon the bookes of Exodus and Leviticus.* London: For Thomas Chard, 1604.

_____. *A profitable Exposition of the Lords Prayer.* London: Thomas Orwin for Thomas Charde, 1588.

Bacon, Francis. *Collection of Apophthegms New and Old.* Whitefish, MT: Kessinger Publishing, 1994.

_____. *The Philosophical Works of Francis Bacon.* Edited by John M. Robertson. New York: E.P. Dutton & Co., 1905.

_____, and William Rawley. *Sylva Sylvarum: or A Naturall Historie.* London: John Haviland for William Lee, 1635.

Baker, Richard. *A Chronicle of the Kings of England.* London: For Daniel Frere, 1643.

Bancroft, John. *King Edward the Third.* London: For J. Hindmarsh (etc.), 1691.

Banister, John. *A Needfull, new, and necessarie treatise of Chyrurgerie.* London: Thomas Marshe, 1575.

Basset, Robert. *Curiosities or The Cabinet of Nature.* London: N. and J. Okes, 1637.

Bateman, Stephen. *Batman uppon Bartholome.* London: Thomas East, 1582.

Baxter, Richard. *The Practical Works of Richard Baxter.* Vol. 3. London: George Virtue, 1838.

Beaumont, Francis, and John Fletcher. *The Maides Tragedy.* London: For Richard Higgenbotham, 1619.

Beaumont, Joseph. *Psyche, or Loves Mysterie.* London: John Dawson for George Boddington, 1648.

Beckerman, Bernard. *Shakespeare at the Globe 1599–1609.* New York: Collier, 1962.

Benguerel, G. *Thomas Middleton, Part I.* Nordhausen, 1870.

Berry, Herbert. *The Boar's Head Playhouse.* Cranbury, NJ: Associated University Presses, 1986.

Best, George. *Three Voyages of Martin Frobisher.* Edited by Richard Collinson. London: Hakluyt Society, 1867.

The Bible: That is, The Holy Scriptures Conteined in the Olde and Newe Testament. London: Christopher Barker, 1587.

Bilson, Thomas. *The Survey of Christs Sufferings for Mans redemption: And of His Descent to Hades or Hel for our deliverance.* London: Melchisedech Bradwood for John Bill, 1604.

Bjorklund, Ruth. *Wolves.* Tarrytown, NY: Marshall Cavendish Benchmark, 2009.

Blome, Richard. *The Gentlemans Recreation.* London: S. Roycroft for Richard Blome, 1686.

Blount, Thomas. *Nomo-Lexikon, A Law Dictionary.* Clark, NJ: The Lawbook Exchange, 2005.

Blundeville, Thomas. *M. Blundeville His Exercises.* London: John Windet, 1594.

Bodenham, John, and Nicholas Ling. *Politeuphuia: Wits Common wealth.* London: J. Roberts for Nicholas Ling, 1600.

Bolton, Robert. *A Discourse About the State of True Happinesse.* London: Felix Kyngston for Edmund Weaver, 1611.

The Booke of common praier and administration of the sacramentes and other rites and ceremonies in the Churche of Englande. London: Richard Jugge and John Cawode, 1559.

Bovet, Richard. *Pandaemonium.* London: For Thomas Parkhurst, 1684.

Bowdler, Thomas, ed. *The Family Shakespeare in Ten Volumes.* London: For Longman, Hurst, Rees, Orme, and Brown, 1818.

Breton, Nicholas. *A Poste With a packet of madde Letters. The second part.* London: R. B. for John Browne, and John Smethicke, 1606.

Broedel, Hans Peter. *The Malleus Maleficarum and the Construction of Witchcraft: Theology and Popular Belief.* Manchester: Manchester University Press, 2003.

Broke, Arthur. *The Tragicall Historye of Romeus and Juliet.* London: Richard Tottill, 1562.

Brooke, C.F. Tucker, ed. *The Shakespeare Apocrypha.* Oxford: Clarendon Press, 1918.

Brown, Meg Lota, and Kari Boyd McBride. *Women's Roles in the Renaissance.* Westport, CT: Greenwood Press, 2005.

Bruel, Walter. *Praxis Medicinae.* London: John Norton for William Sheares, 1642.

Brydall, John. *Decus & Tutamen, or a prospect of the laws of England.* London: G. Sawbridge, W. Rawlins, and S. Roycroft, 1679.

Bullen, A.H., ed. *A Collection of Old English Plays.* Vol. 1. London: Wyman & Sons, 1882.

Bullinger, Heinrich. *Fiftie Godlie and Learned Sermons.* London: For Ralphe Newberrie, 1577.

Bulwer, John. *Chirologia.* Whitefish, MT: Kessinger Publishing, 2003.

Burford, E.J. *The Orrible Synne: A Look at London Lechery from Roman to Cromwellian Times.* London: Calder & Boyars, 1973.

Burrow, John Anthony. *Gestures and Looks in Medieval Narrative.* Cambridge: Cambridge University Press, 2002.

Burton, Robert. *The Anatomy of Melancholy, what it is.* Oxford: John Lichfield and James Short for Henry Cripp, 1621.

Burton, William. *A Commentary On Antoninus His Itinerary.* London: For Thomas Roycroft, 1658.

_____. *An Exposition of the Lords Prayer.* London: The Widdow Orwin for Thomas Man, 1594.

Butler, Christopher. *Number Symbolism.* London: Routledge & Kegan Paul, 1970.

Byfield, Nicholas. *A Commentary: Or, Ser-*

mons *Upon the Second Chapter of the First Epistle of Saint Peter*. London: Humfrey Lownes for George Latham, 1623.

_____. *A Commentary upon the Three First Chapters of the First Epistle generall of St. Peter*. London: Miles Flesher and Robert Young, 1637.

Calvin, John. *Calvin's Bible Commentaries: Isaiah, Part IV*. Translated by John King. Charleston, SC: Forgotten Books, 2007.

Camden, William. *Annales: The True and Royall History of the famous Empresse Elizabeth*. London: For Benjamin Fisher, 1625.

Cannon, John, and Anne Hargreaves. *Kings and Queens of Britain*. Oxford: Oxford University Press, 2009.

Capel, Richard. *Tentations: Their Nature, Danger, Cure*. London: Richard Badger, 1633.

Carmichael, Calum M. *Law, Legend, and Incest in the Bible: Leviticus 18–20*. Ithaca, NY: Cornell University Press, 1997.

Cartwright, Thomas. *An Hospitall for the diseased*. London: For Edward White, 1579.

Cerasano, S.P., ed. *Medieval and Renaissance Drama in England*. Vol. 20. Cranbury, NJ: Associated University Press, 2007.

Chillester, Henry. *Youthes Witte, Or The Witte of Grene Youth*. London: John Wolfe, 1581.

Clare, Israel Smith, ed. *The Middle Ages and the Reformation*. Vol. 5 of *Library of Universal History*. New York: R.S. Peale and J.A. Hill, 1898.

_____, ed. *Medieval History — Continued*. Vol. 7 of *Library of Universal History*. New York: Union Book Company, 1906.

Cocker, Mark, and Richard Mabey. *Birds Britannica*. London: Chatto & Windus, 2005.

Coghan, Thomas. *The Haven of Health*. London: Anne Griffin for Roger Ball, 1636.

Coignet, Matthieu. *Politique Discourses upon Trueth and Lying*. Translated by Edward Hoby. London: Ralfe Newberie, 1586.

Collier, John Payne. *Memoirs of the Principal Actors in the Plays of Shakespeare*. London: For The Shakespeare Society, 1846.

Cooper, Thomas. *Thesaurus Linguae Romanae & Britannicae*. London: Henry Denham, 1578.

Corbin, Peter, and Douglas Sedge, eds. *Three Jacobean Witchcraft Plays*. Manchester: Manchester University Press, 1986.

Cowell, John. *The Interpreter: or Booke Containing the Signification of Words*. Cambridge: John Legate, 1607.

Cowper, William. *Anatomie of a Christian Man*. London: Thomas Snodham for John Budge, 1611.

Cox, Nicholas. *The Gentleman's Recreation In Four Parts, Viz. Hunting, Hawking, Fowling, Fishing*. 3rd ed. London: Joseph Phillips and Henry Rodes, 1686.

Craig, John. *A Short Summe of the whole Catechisme*. London: John Wolfe for Thomas Manne, 1583.

Cranmer, Thomas. *Writings of the Rev. Dr. Thomas Cranmer, Archbishop of Canterbury and Martyr, 1556*. Philadelphia: Presbyterian Board of Publication, 1842.

Crooke, Helkiah. *Mikrokosmographia: A Description of the Body of Man*. London: William Jaggard, 1615.

Culpepper, Nicholas. *The English Physitian*. London: Peter Cole, 1652.

Cunningham, Peter, ed. *Extracts from the Accounts of the Revels at Court, in the Reigns of Queen Elizabeth and James I, from the Original Office Books of the Masters and Yeomen*. London: For The Shakespeare Society, 1842.

Cutts, John P. "The Original Music to Middleton's 'The Witch.'" *Shakespeare Quarterly* 7, no. 2 (Spring, 1956): 203–209.

Daniel, Samuel. *The Civile Wares betweene the Howses of Lancaster and Yorke*. London: Simon Watersonne, 1609.

Daniels, Cora Linn, and Charles McClellan Stevans. *Encyclopaedia of Superstitions, Folklore, and the Occult Sciences of the World*. 3 vols. Milwaukee, WI: J.H. Yewdale and Sons, 1906.

Dante Alighieri. *The Divine Comedy of Dante Alighieri: Inferno*. Translated by Robert M. Durling. Edited by Robert M. Durling and Robert Turner. Oxford: Oxford University Press, 1996.

Davenant, William. *Macbeth, A Tragedy: With all the Alterations, Amendments, Additions, And New Songs. As it is now Acted at the Dukes Theatre*. London: For A. Clark (etc.), 1674.

Davison, Peter, ed. *The First Quarto of King Richard III*. New York: Press Syndicate of the University of Cambridge, 1996.

d'Avity, Pierre. *The Estates, Empires, & Principallities of the World*. London: Adam Islip for Mathewe Lownes and John Bill, 1615.

Day, Angel. *The English Secretorie*. London: Robert Walde-grave, 1586.

Deacon, John, and John Walker. *Dialogicall Discourses of Spirits and Divels*. Amsterdam: Theatrum Orbis Terrarum, 1976.

_____. *A Summarie Answere to al the Material Points in any of Master Darel His Bookes*. London: George Bishop, 1601.

de Calvi, Francois. *Histoire Des Larrons, or the History of Theeves*. Translated by Paul Godwin. London: John Raworth, 1638.

Dekker, Thomas. *The Dramatic Works of Thomas Dekker*. Edited by Richard Herne Shepherd. Vol. 4. London: John Pearson, 1873.

_____. *The Non-Dramatic Works of Thomas Dekker*. Edited by Alexander B. Grosart. Vol. 5. London: Hazell, Watson, & Veney, Ltd., 1886.

de La Primaudaye, Pierre. *The French Academie*. London: John Legat, 1618.

_____. *The Second Part of the French Academie*. London: G. Bishop, Ralph Newbery, R. Barker, 1594.

della Porta, Giambattista. *Natural Magick*. London: For Thomas Young and Samuel Speed, 1658.

Deloney, Thomas. *The Gentile Craft, The second Part*. London: Elizabeth Purslow, 1639.

de Montaigne, Michael. *Essays of Michael Seigneur de Montaigne*. Translated by Charles Cotton. London: For T. Basset, M. Gilliflower, and W. Hensman, 1685.

Dent, Arthur. *The Plaine Mans Path-way to Heaven*. London: For Edward Bishop, 1607.

Dent, Daniel. *A Sermon Against Drunkennes*. Cambridge: Printed by the Printers to the Universitie of Cambridge, 1628.

Dent, Robert William. *Shakespeare's Proverbial Language: An Index*. Berkeley: University of California Press, 1981.

de Renou, Jean. *A Medical Dispensatory*. Translated by Richard Tomlinson. London: J. Streater and J. Cotterel, 1657.

Diodati, Giovanni. *Pious Annotations upon the Holy Bible*. London: T.B. for Nicholas Fussell, 1643.

Dixon, Charles. *The Nests and Eggs of British Birds*. London: Chapman and Hall, 1894.

Donne, John. *Poems, By J. D. With Elegies on the Authors Death*. London: M. F. for John Marriot, 1633.

Drayton, Michael. *Poems: By Michaell Draiton Esquire*. London: Valentine Simmes for N. Ling, 1605.

Dryden, John. *The Works of John Dryden*. Edited by Maximillian E. Novak. Vol. 13. Berkeley: University of California Press, 1984.

Duncon, Eleazar. *The Copy of a Letter written by E.D. Doctour of Physicke to a Gentleman*. London: Melchisedech Bradwood, 1606.

The Encyclopedia Americana: A Library of Universal Knowledge. Vol. 3. New York: The Encyclopedia Americana Corporation, 1918.

Est, William. *Sathans Sowing Season*. London: Nicholas Okes for Richard Bonian, 1611.

Everard, John. *The Gospel-Treasury Opened*. London: John Owsley for Rapha Harford, 1657.

Ewing, William, and John E. H. Thomson. *The Temple Dictionary of the Bible*. London: J.M. Dent & Sons, 1910.

Farr, Edward, ed. *Select Poetry, Chiefly Sacred, of the Reign of King James the First*. Cambridge: Cambridge University Press, 1847.

Feldman, David Michael. *Birth Control in Jewish Law: Marital Relations, Contraception, and Abortion As Set Forth in the Classic Texts of Jewish Law*. Northvale, NJ: Jason Aronson, Inc., 1998.

Ferguson, George Wells. *Signs & Symbols in Christian Art*. Oxford: Oxford University Press, 1961.

Ferguson, William. *The Identity of the Scottish Nation: An Historic Quest*. Edinburgh: Edinburgh University Press, 1999.

Ferrand, Jacques. *Erotomania or A treatise discoursing of the essence, causes, symptomes, prognosticks, and cure of love, or erotique melancholy*. Translated by Edmund Chilmead. Oxford: L. Lichfield, 1640.

Filmer, Robert. *An Advertisement to the Jury-Men of England, Touching Witches*. London: J.G. for Richard Royston, 1653.

Finch, Henry. *An Exposition of the Song of Solomon: called Canticles*. London: John Beale, 1615.

Firth, C.H., and R.S. Rait, eds. *Acts and Ordinances of the Interregnum, 1642–1660*. 3 vols. London: H.M.S.O., 1911.

Fitz-Geffry, Charles. *Sir Francis Drake His Honorable lifes commendation, and his Tragicall Deathes lamentation*. Oxford: Joseph Barnes, 1596.

Flatter, Richard. *Shakespeare's Producing Hand: A Study of His Marks of Expression to be Found in the First Folio*. New York: W.W. Norton, 1948.

Flavel, John. *The Whole Works of the Reverend Mr. John Flavel, Late Minister at Dartmouth in Devon*. Vol. 1. London: For D. Midwinter (etc.), 1740.

Fletcher, Giles. *Israel Redux: Or the Restauration of Israel, Exhibited in Two short Treatises*. London: S. Streater for John Hancock, 1677.

Florio, John. *Florio his Firste fruites*. Amsterdam: Theatrum Orbis Terrarum, 1969.

_____. *Queen Anna's New World of Words, 1611*. Menston, England: Scolar Press, 1968.

Fludd, Robert. *Mosaicall Philosophy: Grounded upon the Essentiall Truth or Eternal Sapience*. London: For Humphrey Moseley, 1659.

Ford, Michael. *Luciferian Witchcraft*. Houston, TX: Succubus Pubishing, 2005.

Fotherby, Martin. *Atheomastix*. London: Nicholas Okes, 1622.

Foxe, John. *Actes and monuments*. London: John Day, 1563.

Fraunce, Abraham. *The Third part of the Countesse of Pembrokes Yuychurch*. London: For Thomas Woodcocke, 1592.

Friar, Stephen, and John Ferguson. *Basic Heraldry*. New York: W. W. Norton & Co., 1993.

Gardiner, Samuel. *Doomes-Day Booke: Or, An Alarum for Atheistes, A Watchword for Worldlinges, A Caveat for Christians*. London: Edward Allde for Nicholas Ling, 1606.

Garey, Samuel. *Great Brittans little Calendar*. London: John Beale for Henry Fetherstone, and John Parker, 1618.

Gauden, John. *A Discourse of Auxiliary Beauty*. London: For R. Royston, 1656.

G.D. *A Briefe Discoverie of Doctor Allens seditious drifts*. London: J. Wolfe for Francis Coldock, 1588.

Gifford, George. *A Discourse of the subtill Practises of Devilles by Witches and Sorcers*. London: For Toby Cooke, 1587.

Glauber, Johann Rudolf. *A Description of New Philosophical Furnaces*. London: Richard Coats, for Tho. Williams, 1651.

Godwin, Thomas. *Moses and Aaron: Civil and Ecclesiastical Rites, Used by the Ancient Hebrews*. London: For R. Scot (etc.), 1685.

Googe, Barnabe. *Foure Bookes of Husbandry*. London: Richard Watkins, 1577.

Gouge, William. *The Whole Armour of God*. London: John Beale, 1619.

Grange, John. *The Golden Aphroditis*. London: Henry Bynneman, 1577.

Greene, Robert. *The Scottish Historie of James the fourth, slaine at Flodden*. London: Thomas Creede, 1598.

_____. *The Second Part of Conny-Catching*. London: John Wolfe for William Wright, 1591.

Guillim, John. *A Display of Heraldrie*. London: William Hall for Raphe Mab, 1611.

Hakluyt, Richard. *Hakluyt's Voyages*. London: J.M. Dent & Co., 1907.

Hall, James. *Dictionary of Subjects and Symbols in Art*. 2nd ed. Oxford: Westview Press, 2007.

Hall, John. *The Courte of Vertu*. London: Thomas Marshe, 1565.

Hall, Joseph. *Two Guides to a good Life*. London: W. Jaggard, 1604.

Hall, Thomas. *A Practical and Polemical Commentary*. London: E. Tyler for John Starkey, 1658.

Halliwell-Phillipps, J.O. *Outlines of the Life of Shakespeare*. 3rd ed. London: Longman, 1883.

_____, ed. *The works of William Shakespeare: in reduced facsimile from the famous first folio edition of 1623*. London: Chatto and Windus, 1876.

Hansen, Mark Hillary, ed. *Kings, Rulers, and Statesmen*. New York: Sterling Publishing, 2005.

Hardyng, John, and Richard Grafton. *The Chronicle of John Hardyng*. Edited by Henry Ellis. London: For F.C. and J. Rivington (etc.), 1812.

Harrison, G.B., ed. *Dæmonologie By King James The First (1597) and Newes From Scotland (1591)*. Oxford: Bodley Head, 1924.

Hart, James. *Klinike, or The Diet of the Diseased*. London: John Beale for Robert Allot, 1633.

Hawkins, John. *The English School-Master Compleated*. London: A. and I. Dawks for the Company of Stationers, 1692.

Hawkins, Richard. *The Hawkins' Voyages During the Reigns of Henry VIII, Queen Elizabeth, and James I*. Edited by Clements R. Markham. London: Hakluyt Society, 1878.

Hayne, Thomas. *The Times, Places, and Persons of the holie Scripture*. London: Thomas Purfoot for Richard Ockould, 1607.

Hemmingsen, Niels. *A Postill, or Exposition of the Gospels that are usually red in the churches of God, upon the Sundayes and Feast dayes of Saincts*. Translated by Arthur Golding. London: Henry Bynneman for Lucas Harrison and George Byshop, 1569.

Herrick, Robert. *The Poetical Works of Robert Herrick*. Edited by George Saintsbury. Vol. 2. London: George Bell & Sons, 1893.

Heywood, Thomas. *The English Traveller*. London: Robert Raworth, 1633.

_____. *The Hierarchie of the blessed Angells*. Amsterdam: Theatrum Orbis Terrarum, 1973.

Higgins, John. *The Falles of Unfortunate Princes*. London: F. K. for William Aspley, 1619.

Hill, Thomas. *The Contemplation of Mankinde*. London: Henry Denham for William Seres, 1571.

_____. *The Moste pleasaunte Arte of the Interpretation of Dreames*. London: Thomas Marsh, 1576.

_____. *A Pleasant History: Declaring the whole Art of Phisiognomy*. London: W. Jaggard, 1613.

Hinman, Charlton, ed. *The Norton Facsimile: The First Folio of Shakespeare*. New York: Norton, 1968.

The Historie of Jacob and Esau. London: Henrie Bynneman, 1568.

Holder, Joseph B., ed. *Birds*. Vol. 2 of *Animate Creation* by John George Wood. New York: Selmar Hess, 1898.

Holland, Henry. *A Treatise Against Witchcraft*. Cambridge: John Legatt, 1590.

Holme, Randle. *The Academy of Armory*. Chester: Printed for the Author, 1688.

The Holy Bible, King James Version, a reprint of the edition of 1611. Peabody, MA: Hendrickson, 2003.

Hopper, Vincent Foster. *Medieval Number Symbolism: Its Sources, Meaning, and Influence on Thought and Expression*. Mineola, NY: Dover Publications, 2000.

Huarte, Juan. *Examen de ingenios. The Examination of mens Wits*. Translated by Richard Carew. London: Adam Islip for Richard Watkins, 1594.

Hunter, Robert. *Lloyd's Encyclopædic Dictionary*. Vol. 6. London: Edward Lloyd, Ltd., 1895.

Hurault, Jacques. *Politicke, Moral, and Martial Discourses*. Translated by Arthur Golding. London: Adam Islip, 1595.

Idel, Moshe. *Ascensions on High in Jewish Mysticism: Pillars, Lines, Ladders*. Budapest: Central European University Press, 2005.

Innocent III, Pope. *The Mirror of Mans lyfe*. Translated by Henry Kirton. London: Henry Bynneman, 1576.

Institoris, Heinrich, and Jakob Sprenger. *The Malleus Maleficarum of Heinrich Kramer and James Sprenger*. Edited and Translated by Montague Summers. Mineola, NY: Dover Publications, 1971.

Johnson, Matthew. *Behind the Castle Gate: From Medieval to Renaissance*. New York: Routledge, 2002.

Johnston, James B. *Place-names of Scotland*. Edinburgh: Neill and Company, Ltd. for David Douglas, 1903.

Jonson, Ben. *The Workes of Benjamin Jonson.* London: Will. Stansby, 1616.

_____. *The Workes of Benjamin Jonson.* London: Richard Bishop, 1640.

Kachru, Braj B., Yamuna Kachru, and Cecil L. Nelson, eds. *The Handbook of World Englishes.* Chichester, West Sussex, UK: Blackwell Publishing, 2009.

Kinnaston, Francis. *Leoline and Sydanis.* London: Ric. Hearne, 1642.

Kirk, Robert. *The Secret Commonwealth of Elves, Fauns & Fairies.* Edited by Andrew Lang. London: David Nutt, 1893.

Kirkman, Andrew. *The Cultural Life of the Early Polyphonic Mass.* Cambridge: Cambridge University Press, 2010.

Koch, John T. *Celtic Culture: A Historical Encyclopedia.* 5 vols. Santa Barbara, CA: ABC-CLIO, 2006.

The Lamentable and True Tragedie of M. Arden of Feversham In Kent. London: Elizabeth Allde for Edward White, 1592.

Laslett, Peter. *The World We Have Lost: England Before the Industrial Age.* New York: Scribner's, 1965.

Latimer, Hughe. *The seconde Sermon of Maister Hughe Latimer.* London: Jhon Day and Wylliam Seres, 1549.

Lavater, Ludwig. *Lewes Lavater: Of Ghosts and Spirits Walking By Night 1572.* Whitefish, MT: Kessinger Publishing, 2003.

Lee, Sidney, ed. *Dictionary of National Biography.* 2nd ed. London: Smith, Elder, & Co., 1906.

Legg, Leopold G. Wickham. *English Coronation Records.* Westminster: Archibald Constable & Co. Ltd., 1901.

Leigh, Edward. *A Treatise of Divinity.* London: E. Griffin for William Lee, 1646.

le Loyer, Pierre. *A Treatise of Specters or straunge Sights, Visions and Apparitions appearing sensibly unto men.* Translated by Zachary Jones. London: Valentine Simmes for Mathew Lownes, 1605.

Lemnius, Levinus. *An Herbal for the Bible.* Translated by Thomas Newton. London: Edmund Bollifant, 1587.

_____. *The Touchstone of Complexions.* Translated by Thomas Newton. London: Thomas Marsh, 1576.

Linche, Richard. *The Fountaine of Ancient Fiction.* London: Adam Islip, 1599.

Lodge, Thomas. *The Complete Works of Thomas Lodge.* Vol. 4. Glasgow: Robert Anderson for the Hunterian Club, 1883.

_____. *Wits Miserie, and the Worlds Madnesse: Discovering the Devils Incarnat of this Age.* London: Adam Islip, 1596.

Lucan. *The Pharsalia of Lucan.* Translated by Edward Ridley. London: Longmans, Green, and Co., 1896.

Malines, Gerard. *Consuetudo, vel, Lex Mercatoria: Or, The Ancient Law-Merchant.* London: J. Redmayne for T. Basset and R. Smith, 1685.

Markham, Gervase. *Verus Pater, Or A bundell of Truths.* London: Nicholas Okes for Thomas Langley, 1622.

Marshall, Rosalind K. *Scottish Queens, 1034–1714.* East Linton, Scotland: Tuckwell, 2003.

Martin, Gregory et al., eds. *The Second Tome of the Holie Bible.* Doway, France: 1610.

Mayhew, A.L. and Walter W. Skeat. *A Concise Dictionary of Middle English.* Whitefish, MT: Kessinger Publishing, 2004.

McAlpine, Neil, and John Mackenzie. *A Pronouncing Gaelic Dictionary.* 5th ed. Edinburgh: Maclachlan & Stewart, 1866.

Melling, John Kennedy. *Discovering London's Guilds and Liveries.* Princes Risborough, UK: Shire Publications, 2003.

Melville, James. *Ane Fruitful and Comfortable Exhortatioun anent Death.* Edinburgh: Robert Walde-grave, 1597.

Meres, Francis. *Wits Common Wealth: The Second Part.* London: William Stansby, 1634.

Meriton, L. "Of London Cries." In *Pecuniae obediunt Omnia: Money Masters all Things,* 95–99. London and Westminster: The Booksellers of London and Westminster, 1698.

Michaelis, Sébastien. *The Admirable History of the Possession and Conversion of a Penitent woman.* London: F. Kingston for William Aspley, 1613.

Middleton, Thomas. *The Wisdome of Solomon Paraphrased.* London: Valentine Sems, 1597.

_____. *The Witch.* Edited by L. Drees and Henry de Vocht. Louvain, Belgium: Librairie Universitaire: Ch. Uystpruyst, 1945.

Minsheu, John. *Ductor in Linguas, The Guide Into Tongues*. London: John Browne, 1617.

More, Henry. *The Theological Works of the most Pious and Learned Henry More, D.D.* London: Joseph Downing, 1708.

Morton, Thomas, of Berwick. *A Treatise of the threefolde state of man*. London: For Robert Dexter and Raph Jackeson, 1596.

Moston, Doug, ed. *The First Folio of Shakespeare*. New York: Applause, 1994.

Muir, Edward. *Ritual in Early Modern Europe*. 2nd ed. Cambridge: Cambridge University Press, 2005.

Mure, William. "The Kings Majestie came to Hamilton on Monday the XXVIII July [1617]." In *The Works of Sir William Mure of Rowallan*, edited by William Tough, Vol. 1, 41–44. Edinburgh: Scottish Text Society, 1898.

Nabbes, Thomas. *The Works of Thomas Nabbes*. 2 vols. New York: Benjamin Blom, 1968.

Nashe, Thomas. *Christs Teares Over Jerusalem*. London: For Thomas Thorp, 1613.

_____. *Pierce Penniless's Supplication To The Devil*. Edited by J. Payne Collier. London: For The Shakespeare Society, 1842.

_____. *The Works of Thomas Nashe*. Edited by Ronald B. McKerrow. Vol. 1. London: A.H. Bullen, 1904.

_____. *The Works of Thomas Nashe*. Edited by Ronald B. McKerrow. Vol. 3. London: A.H. Bullen, 1905.

Naylor, Edward Woodall. *Shakespeare and Music*. London: J.M. Dent & Co., 1896.

Niccols, Richard. *The Beggers Ape*. Whitefish, MT: Kessinger Publishing, 2004.

No-Body, and Some-Body. London: For John Trundle, 1606.

Norden, John. *A Pensive Soules delight*. London: Will. Stansby for John Busby, 1615.

Ogden, Daniel. *Magic, Witchcraft, and Ghosts in the Greek and Roman Worlds*. New York: Oxford University Press, 2002.

Olson, Oscar Ludvig. *The Relation of the Hrolfs Saga Kraka and the Bjarkarimur to Beowolf*. Chicago: University of Chicago, 1916.

Opie, Iona, and Moira Tatem. *A Dictionary of Superstitions*. New York: Barnes & Noble, 1999.

Painter, William. *The Palace of Pleasure*. Edited by Joseph Jacobs. Vol. 1. London: David Nutt, 1890.

Paré, Ambroise. *The Workes of that famous Chirurgion Ambrose Parey translated out of Latine and compared with the French. by Th: Johnson*. Translated by Thomas Johnson. London: Th: Cotes and R. Young, 1634.

Parker, Henry. *Dives et Pauper*. Westmonstre: Wynkyn de Worde, 1496.

Parker, Matthew, et al., eds. *The holie Bible, conteynyng the Olde Testament and the newe*. London: Richard Jugge, 1568.

Patterson, Gordon M. *The Essentials of Medieval History: 500 to 1450 C.E., The Middle Ages*. Piscataway, NJ: Research & Education Association, 1993.

Perkins, William. *The Combat Betweene Christ and the Divell displayed*. London: Melchisedech Bradwood for E. E., 1606.

_____. *A Discourse of the Damned Art of Witchcraft*. Cambridge: Cantrel Legge, Printer to the Universitie of Cambridge, 1610.

_____. *A Godly and Learned Exposition of Christ's Sermon in the Mount*. Cambridge: Thomas Brooke and Cantrell Legge, 1608.

_____. *Satans Sophistrie Answered By Our Saviour Christ*. London: Richard Field for E. E., 1604.

Person, David. *Varieties: Or, A Surveigh of Rare and Excellent matters, necessary and delectable for all sorts of persons*. London: Richard Badger for Thomas Alchorn, 1635.

Phillips, Edward. *The New World of English Words, 1658*. Menston, England: Scolar Press, 1969.

Pilkington, James. *Aggeus and Abdias Prophetes*. London: Willyam Seres, 1562.

Pliny the Elder. *The Historie of the World: Commonly called, The Naturall Historie of C. Plinius Secundus*. Translated by Philemon Holland. London: Adam Islip, 1634.

_____. *A Summarie of the Antiquities, and wonders of the worlde*. Translated by John Alday. London: Henry Denham for Thomas Hacket, 1566.

Plutarch. *The Lives of the Noble Grecians and Romanes*. Translated by Thomas North.

London: Thomas Vautroullier and John Wight, 1579.

_____. *The Philosophie, commonlie called, The Morals Written By the learned Philosopher Plutarch of Chaeronea.* Translated by Philemon Holland. London: Arnold Hatfield, 1603.

Pollard, Alfred W. *Shakespeare Folios and Quartos.* New York: Cooper Square Publishers, 1909.

Pope, Alexander. "[Against Barbarity to Animals.]" In *The Guardian,* edited by John Calhoun Stephens, 233–237. Lexington, KY: University Press of Kentucky, 1982.

Preston, John. *The Saints Daily Exercise.* London: W. Jones, 1629.

_____. *A Sermon Preached at a Generall Fast before the Commons-House Of Parliament: The Second Of July, 1625.* London: Richard Badger for Nicholas Bourne, 1633.

Prynne, William. *The Aphorismes of the Kingdome.* London: Allen in Popes-head Alley, 1642.

_____. *Histrio-Mastix.* London: E.A. and W.J. for Michael Sparke, 1633.

Radford, Edwin, and Mona Augusta Radford. *The Encyclopedia of Superstitions.* Edited by Christina Hole. New York: Barnes and Noble, 1996.

Raleigh, Walter. *The History of the World.* London: Walter Burre, 1614.

Ray, John. *A Collection of English Words not Generally Used.* London: H. Bruges for Tho. Burrell, 1674.

_____. *The Correspondence of John Ray.* Edited by Edwin Lankester. London: For The Ray Society, 1848.

Reed, Isaac, ed. *Old Plays.* Vol. 9. London: Septimus Prowett, 1825.

Renaudot, Théophraste. *A General Collection of Discourses of the Virtuosi of France.* Translated by George Havers. London: Thomas Dring and John Starkey, 1664.

Ridley, Nicholas. *A brief declaracion of the Lordes Supper.* Emden: E. van der Erve, 1555.

Rivers, George. *The Heroinae.* London: R. Bishop for John Colby, 1639.

The Riverside Dictionary of Biography. Boston: Houghton Mifflin, 2005.

Rogers, Richard. *A Commentary upon the*

Whole Booke of Judges. London: Felix Kyngston for Thomas Man, 1615.

Ross, Alexander. *Mystagogus Poeticus, Or The Muses Interpreter.* London: For Richard Whitaker, 1647.

Rowlands, Samuel. *The Famous History, of Guy Earle of Warwicke.* London: Elizabeth All-de, 1607.

Rowley, William. *A New Wonder, A Woman Never Vext.* London: George Purslowe for Francis Constable, 1632.

_____. *William Rowley, His All's Lost by Lust, and a Shoe-Maker, a Gentleman.* Edited by Charles Wharton Stork. Philadelphia: University of Pennsylvania Press, 1910.

R.T. *The Opinion of Witchcraft Vindicated.* London: E. O. for Francis Haley, 1670.

Sabie, Francis. *Adams Complaint.* London: Richard Johnes, 1596.

Saker, Austin. *Narbonus.* London: Richard Jones, 1580.

Sawyer, Edmund. *Memorials of Affairs of State in the Reigns of Q. Elizabeth and K. James I.* London: W.B. for T. Ward, 1725.

Shakespeare, William. *The Elizabethan Shakespere: The Tragedie of Macbeth.* Edited by Mark Harvey Liddell. New York: Doubleday, Page & Co., 1903.

_____. *An excellent conceited Tragedie of Romeo and Juliet.* London: John Danter, 1597.

_____. *Loves Labour's Lost.* Edited by Horace Howard Furness. Philadelphia: J.B. Lippincott Co., 1904.

_____. *Macbeth.* Edited by Henry Morley. London: Cassell and Co., 1910.

_____. *Macbeth.* Edited by Horace Howard Furness. Philadelphia: J.B. Lippincott Company, 1873.

_____. *The most excellent and lamentable Tragedie, of Romeo and Juliet.* London: Thomas Creede for Cuthbert Burby, 1599.

_____. *A Most pleasaunt and excellent conceited Comedie, of Syr John Falstaffe, and the merrie Wives of Windsor.* London: T. C. for Arthur Johnson, 1602.

_____. *The Plays and Poems of William Shakespeare.* Edited by Edmond Malone. Vol. 11. London: For F.C. and J. Rivington (etc.), 1821.

____. *The Plays of William Shakespeare.* Edited by Samuel Johnson and George Stevens. 2nd ed. Vol. 1. London: For C. Bathurst (etc.), 1778.

____. *The Rape of Lucrece.* London: Richard Field for John Harrison, 1594.

____. *Shake-Speares Sonnets.* London: G. Eld for T. T., 1609.

____. *Shakespeare's Tragedy of Macbeth.* Edited by William J. Rolfe. New York: American Book Company, 1903.

____. *Shakspere's Macbeth.* Edited by John Matthews Manly. New York: Longmans, Green, and Co. 1898.

____. *The Tragedie of Anthonie, and Cleopatra.* Edited by Horace Howard Furness. Philadelphia: J.B. Lippincott Co., 1907.

____. *The Tragicall Historie of Hamlet, Prince of Denmarke.* London: James Roberts for Nicholas Ling, 1605.

____. *The Tragicall historie of Hamlet Prince of Denmarke by William Shakespeare.* London: For NL and John Trundell, 1603.

____. *The Works of William Shakespeare.* Edited by Alexander Dyce. 6 vols. London: Edward Moxon, 1857.

Sharp, Jane. *The Midwives Book, Or the Whole Art of Midwifry Discovered.* Edited by Elaine Hobby. New York: Oxford University Press, 1999.

Shirley, James. *The Dramatic Works and Poems of James Shirley.* Edited by William Gifford. Vol. 1. London: John Murray, 1833.

Sill, Gertrude Grace. *A Handbook of Symbols in Christian Art.* New York: Touchstone, 1996.

Simpson, Percy. *Shakespearian Punctuation.* Oxford: Clarendon Press, 1911.

Skeat, Walter W. *A Concise Etymological Dictionary of the English Language.* Oxford: Clarendon Press, 1901.

Smith, Charles G. *Shakespeare's Proverb Lore: His Use of the Sententiae of Leonard Culman and Publilius Sysrus.* Cambridge, MA: Harvard University Press, 1968.

Smith, D. Nichol, ed. *Eighteenth Century Essays on Shakespeare.* Glasgow: Maclehose and Sons, 1903.

Spencer, John. *Kaina Kai Palaia. Things New and Old.* London: W. Wilson and J. Streater for John Spencer, 1658.

Spenser, Edmund. *The Works of Edmund Spenser.* Edited by Richard Morris. London: Macmillan and Co., 1893.

Stone, Lawrence. *The Family, Sex and Marriage in England 1500–1800.* New York: Harper and Row, 1977.

Stubbes, Phillip. *Anatomie of Abuses.* London: Richard Jones, 1583.

Swan, John. *Speculum Mundi.* Cambridge: The Printers to the Universitie of Cambridge, 1635.

Swetnam, Joseph. *The Araignment of Lewd, Idle, Froward, and unconstant women.* London: George Purslowe for Thomas Archer, 1615.

Tate, William Edward. *The Parish Chest: A Study of the Records of Parochial Administration in England.* 3rd ed. Cambridge: Cambridge University Press, 1969.

Taylor, John. *Early Prose and Poetical Works of John Taylor The Water Poet (1580–1653).* London: Hamilton, Adams & Co., 1888.

Topsell, Edward. *The Historie of Foure-Footed Beastes.* London: William Jaggard, 1607.

____. *The Historie of Serpents; or, the Second Book of Living Creatures.* London: William Jaggard, 1608.

____. *The Reward of Religion.* London: John Windet, 1596.

A Treatise of Equivocation. Edited by David Jardine. London: Longman, Brown, Green, and Longmans, 1851.

Tucker, Patrick. *Secrets of Acting Shakespeare: The Original Approach.* New York: Routledge, 2002.

Tyndale, William. *The Christen rule or state of all the worlde from the hyghest to the lowest: and how every man shulde lyve to please God in hys callynge.* London[?]: T Raynalde and William Hill, 1548[?].

Valbuena, Olga L. *Subjects to the King's Divorce: Equivocation, Infidelity, and Resistance in Early Modern England.* Bloomington, IN: Indiana University Press, 2003.

van Helmont, Jean Baptiste. *Van Helmont's Works: Containing his most Excellent Philosophy, Chirurgery Physick, Anatomy.* Translated by John Chandler. London: For Lodowick Lloyd, 1664.

Varner, Gary R. *Menhirs, Dolmen and Circles of Stone: The Folklore and Magic of Sacred Stone.* New York: Algora Publishing, 2004.

Virgil. *Translation of The first Four Books of the Æneis of P. Virgilius Maro: with other poetical Devices thereto annexed. [June] 1582.* Translated by Richard Stanyhurst. Edited by Edward Arber. London: Edward Arber, 1880.

von Nettesheim, Heinrich Cornelius Agrippa. *Fourth Book of Occult Philosophy.* Whitefish, MT: Kessinger Publishing, 1992.

_____. *Henrie Cornelius Agrippa, of the vanitie and uncertaintie of artes and sciences, Englished by Ja. San. Gent.* Translated by James Sandford. London: Henry Wykes, 1569.

Watkins, Ronald. *On Producing Shakespeare.* London: Michael Joseph, 1950.

Watson, Richard. *Akolouthos.* Hagh: Samuel Broun, 1651.

Weingust, Don. *Acting from Shakespeare's First Folio: Theory, Text, and Performance.* New York: Routledge, 2006.

Wheatley, Henry Benjamin. *Shakespeare's Editors 1623 to the Twentieth Century.* London: Blades, East, and Blades, 1919.

Wilkins, George. *The Painfull Adventures of Pericles Prince of Tyre.* London: T. Purfoot for Nathanial Butter, 1608.

Willet, Andrew. *Hexapla in Genesin & Exodum.* London: John Haviland, 1633.

Williams, Ann, Alfred P. Smyth, and David P. Kirby. *A Biographical Dictionary of Dark Age Britain: England, Scotland and Wales, c.500–c.1050.* London: B.A. Seaby, 1991.

Williams, Robert Folkestone, ed. *The Court and Times of James the First.* Vol. 1. London: Henry Colburn, 1848.

Williams, Tennessee. *Cat on a Hot Tin Roof.* New York: Signet, 1955.

Wilmot, John, Earl of Rochester. *The Works of John Wilmot Earl of Rochester.* Edited by Harold Love. New York: Oxford University Press, 1999.

Wilson, Christopher R., and Michela Calore. *Music in Shakespeare: A Dictionary.* London: Theommes Continuum: 2005.

Wilson, James, and Oliver Ames Goold. *Complete Dictionary of Astrology.* Whitefish, MT: Kessinger Publishing, 2003.

Wilson, Robert. *The Three Lords and Three Ladies of London, By R.W., 1590.* Edited by John S. Farmer. London: For Subscribers of The Tudor Facsimile Texts, 1912.

Wilson, Thomas. *A Discourse uppon usurye.* London: Richard Tottel, 1572.

Wimberly, Lowry Charles. *Folklore in the English and Scottish Ballads.* Whitefish, MT: Kessinger Publishing, 2006.

Wither, George. *The Psalms of David Translated into Lyrick-Verse.* Manchester: For The Spenser Society, 1881.

Wroth, Mary. *The Countesse of Mountgomeries Urania.* London: John Marriott and John Grismand, 1621.

Wycliffe Bible: Complete Text. Cranbrook, BC, Canada: Praotes Publishing, 2009.